7th Workshop on Challenges and Applications of Automated Extraction of Socio-political Events from Text (CASE 2024)

St. Julian's, Malta
22 March 2024

ISBN: 978-1-7138-9449-0

Printed from e-media with permission by:

Curran Associates, Inc.
57 Morehouse Lane
Red Hook, NY 12571

Some format issues inherent in the e-media version may also appear in this print version.

Printed with permission by Curran Associates, Inc. (2025)

Association for Computational Linguistics
209 N. Eighth Street
Stroudsburg, Pennsylvania 18360

Phone: 1-570-476-8006
Fax: 1-570-476-0860

acl@aclweb.org

Additional copies of this publication are available from:

Curran Associates, Inc.
57 Morehouse Lane
Red Hook, NY 12571 USA
Phone: 845-758-0400
Fax: 845-758-2633
Email: curran@proceedings.com
Web: www.proceedings.com

CASE 2024

7th Workshop on Challenges and Applications of Automated Extraction of Socio-political Events from Text (CASE 2024)

Proceedings of the Workshop

March 22, 2024

Association for Computational Linguistics (ACL)
209 N. Eighth Street
Stroudsburg, PA 18360
USA
Tel: +1-570-476-8006
Fax: +1-570-476-0860
acl@aclweb.org

Preface

The 7th edition of the CASE series of workshops aims to explore the advancements and issues in the automated extraction of socio-political events from textual data, offering a platform for discussing the latest research findings, innovative methodologies, and the future of automated text analysis in capturing and interpreting complex social phenomena.

The workshop encompasses a range of activities, including presentations of accepted papers and shared tasks that challenge participants to design and test innovative solutions for various aspects of event detection and related areas like hate speech analysis and stance detection.

This year the presented approaches and models address a wide range of advanced topics, including multimodal data analysis, fine-tuning large language models, as well as advanced ML for hate speech detection and extraction of event timelines. This variety and complexity of approaches and applications underscores the potential of automated text analysis in the socio-political field.

In this line of reasoning, the 7th edition of the CASE workshop series emphasises on addressing real-world issues, such as understanding discourse related to climate change, online hate speech, misinformation, as well as policy making.

This year the submitted works and shared task system descriptions reflect the growing commitment within the community to leverage natural language processing for social good. In the coming years, the workshop will continue to advance the intersection of natural language processing and socio-political topics, promoting cutting-edge research and interdisciplinary collaboration.

We do hope that our workshop lays the foundation of the research in the challenging and complex area of socio-political event extraction and provides insights into the state of the art, fostering collaboration among researchers and practitioners.

Organizing Committee

Organizing Committee

Ali Hürriyetoğlu, University of Wageningen
Erdem Yörük, Koç University
Hristo Tanev, European Commission, Joint Research Centre
Surendrabikram Thapa, Virginia Tech
Andrew Halterman, Michigan State University
Giuseppe Tirone, European Commission, Joint Research Centre
Osman Mutlu, Koç University
Fiona Anting Tan, University of Singapore
Tadashi Nomoto, National Institute of Japanese Literature
Onur Uca, Mersin University
Vanni Zavarella, University of Cagliari, Italy
Peratham Wiriyathammabhum, –
Marijn Schraagen, Utrecht University
Gaurav Singh, S&P Global
Alexandra DeLucia, Johns Hopkins University
Kumari Neha, Indraprastha, Institute of Information Technology Delhi
Maria Eskevich, Huygens Institute
Guanqun Yang, Stevens Institute of Technology
Cagri Toraman, Aselsan, Turkey
Debanjana Kar, IBM
Man Luo, Arizona State University
Nelleke Oostdijk, Radboud University
Hansi Hettiarachchi, Birmingham City University
Guneet Singh Kohli, Thapar University, India

Program Committee

Program Committee

Idris Abdulmumin, Ahmadu Bello University, Zaria
Diego Alves, Saarland University
Inanc Arin, Sabanci University
Angelo Basile, Symanto Research GmbH
Himanshu Beniwal, Indian Institute of Technology Gandhinagar
Paul Benner, University of Notre Dame
Isabelle Carvalho, University of São Paulo
Somaiyeh Dehghan, Sabanci University
Alexandra Delucia, Johns Hopkins University
Ambica Ghai, S.P. Jain Institute of Management and Research
Samuel Guimarães, UFMG
Hansi Hettiarachchi, Birmingham City University
Farhan Jafri, Electronics and Communication Engineering, Jamia Millia Islamia
Sandesh Jain, PhD Student
Raghav Jain, NLP Researcher
Myung Hee Kim, Defence Science Technology Group
Mrithula Kl, SSN College of Engineering
Guneet Singh Kohli, Thapar University
Vivek Kumar, University of Federal Armed Forces
Neha Kumari, IIIT Delhi
Maarten Marx, University of Amsterdam
Sneha Mehta, Bytedance
Arka Mitra, ETH Zurich
Shamsuddeen Hassan Muhammad, Bayero University, Kano
Osman Mutlu, Koc University
Usman Naseem, University of Sydney
Quynh Anh Nguyen, ETHZ
Tadashi Nomoto, National Institute of Japanese Literature
Rajat Patel, Chime Financial
Lidia Pivovarova, University of Helsinki
Kritesh Rauniyar, B. Tech in Computer Engineering, Delhi Technological University
Marijn Schraagen, Utrecht University
Siddhant Bikram Shah, Delhi Technological University
Shuvam Shiwakoti, DelhiTechnologicalUniversity
Mirnalinee Thankanadar, Sri Siva SubramaniayaNadar College of Engineering
Giuseppe Tirone, Fincons Group S.p.A. - European Commission – Joint Research Centre
Samia Touileb, University of Bergen
Onur Uca, Department of Sociology, Mersin University
Francielle Vargas, University of São Paulo
Hariram Veeramani, UCLA
Peratham Wiriyathammabhum, Self
Berrin Yanikoglu, Sabanci University
Kalliopi Zervanou, Eindhoven University of Technology
Yongjun Zhang, Stony Brook University
Arzucan Özgür, Bogazici University

Table of Contents

Program

Friday, March 22, 2024

09:00 - 09:10	*Opening Remarks*
09:10 - 10:10	*Event Extraction, Approaches and Resources*
10:10 - 10:30	*Large Language Models for Event Extraction, Part I*
10:30 - 11:00	*Coffee Break*
11:00 - 12:00	*Large Language Models for Event Extraction, Part II*
12:00 - 12:40	*Cllimate Activism Hate and Stance Event Detection Shared Task*
12:40 - 14:00	*Lunch Break*
14:00 - 14:45	*Hate Speech in Turkish and Arabic Tweets (HSD-2LANG)*
14:45 - 15:30	*Multimodal Hate Speech Event Detection*
15:30 - 16:00	*Coffee Break*
16:00 - 17:00	*Poster session*
17:00 - 17:20	*Closing remarks*

The Future of Web Data Mining: Insights from Multimodal and Code-based Extraction Methods

Evan Fellman*
Carnegie Mellon Univeristy
efellman@cs.cmu.edu

Jacob Tyo*
DEVCOM Army Research Laboratory
Carnegie Mellon Univeristy
jacob.p.tyo.civ@army.mil

Zachary C. Lipton
Carnegie Mellon Univeristy

Abstract

The extraction of structured data from websites is critical for numerous Artificial Intelligence applications, but modern web design increasingly stores information visually in images rather than in text. This shift calls into question the optimal technique, as language-only models fail without textual cues while new multimodal models like GPT-4 promise image understanding abilities. We conduct the first rigorous comparison between text-based and vision-based models for extracting event metadata harvested from comic convention websites. Surprisingly, our results between GPT-4 Vision and GPT-4 Text uncover a significant accuracy advantage for vision-based methods in an apples-to-apples setting, indicating that vision models may be outpacing language-alone techniques in the task of information extraction from websites. We release our dataset and provide a qualitative analysis to guide further research in multimodal models for web information extraction.

1 Introduction

The extraction of structured information from websites represents a critical challenge in the field of Artificial Intelligence (AI), especially in the context of rapidly evolving web technologies. As the virtual world becomes increasingly central to diverse aspects of society, the ability to efficiently and accurately mine web data is of high importance. This task, commonly known as web scraping, entails navigating the complexities of varied website architectures to extract useful information. The ubiquity of dynamic, visually-rich, and interactive content in modern web design further complicates this landscape, presenting a formidable challenge for automated data extraction technologies.

Historically, web scraping has been dominated by rule-based systems (Gulhane et al., 2011) (Lockard et al., 2018), meticulously designed to accommodate the specific structures of individual websites. The inherent diversity in web design necessitates a tailored approach for each site, significantly limiting the scalability of these systems. Moreover, the dynamic nature of web content, where a single page may present different types of data based on user interaction or other factors such as location or time, adds another layer of complexity. Because of the bespoke nature, rule-based systems often struggle to adapt to dynamic elements, often requiring manual intervention for maintenance and updates.

In the realm of machine learning (ML), the application to web scraping presents unique challenges. The vast differences between websites render the tuning of existing ML systems a daunting task. In most cases, ML-based scraping methods must operate in a zero-shot or few-shot setting, where the model has little to no prior exposure to the specific website from which data is to be extracted. This scenario places a heavy reliance on the innate capabilities of the model to generalize across highly varied environments, a task that has traditionally proven to be challenging for ML systems. As a result, these methods have often been less effective than their rule-based counterparts.

The advent of advanced multimodal AI models has signaled a potential paradigm shift in web scraping methodologies. Pioneering models such as GPT-4 (OpenAI, 2023) and LLaVA (Liu et al., 2023) have demonstrated remarkable capabilities in dealing with complex, multimodal data. These models are equipped to understand and interpret information that spans across text, images, and other web elements, offering a more holistic approach to data extraction. Their prowess in zero-shot performance, where the model can generate useful responses without prior specific training on a task, suggests a significant potential for application in web scraping.

Despite these advancements, the field lacks a

Proceedings of the 7th Workshop on Challenges and Applications of Automated Extraction of Socio-political Events from Text (CASE 2024), pages 1–5
March 22, 2024 ©2024 Association for Computational Linguistics

comprehensive and rigorous analysis of such multi-model AI models in the context of extracting practical web data. This gap in research motivates our current study, where we aim to critically evaluate and compare the effectiveness of these cutting-edge techniques in web scraping. Our contributions are as follows:

- A dataset, FanConInfo, of comic convention websites complete with cleaned HTML, a rendered screenshot, and human-annotated labels.
- A rigorous analysis of GPT-4 Vision, GPT-4 Text, and GPT3.5 in extracting information from FanConInfo. We find that leveraging information from a screen capture of a website boosts the accuracy of information extraction by over 20%.
- An error analysis of the methods guiding future work. We find that the vision model predictions align most with human preferences.

2 Related Works

Information extraction from websites has traditionally relied on processing raw HTML code and other text-based structures. Hao et al. (2011) presents a dataset of HTML code with well-defined tasks. For example, on a webpage that describes a book, the dataset asks a system to retrieve the title, author, ISBN-13, publisher, and publish-date using the HTML. Both Hao et al. (2011) and DOM-LM (Deng et al., 2022; Zhou et al., 2021) aim to simplify the DOM tree and feed simplified text embeddings to dense models, achieving state-of-the-art results on benchmarks. More recently, Large Language Models (LLMs) have been used to either directly extract information from website HTML, or to generate a Python program to extract the information from the HTML (Arora et al., 2023). They found this method, (Arora et al., 2023), outpaces methods directly using RoBERTa (Liu et al., 2019) to answer questions, a zero-shot relation extraction method (Lockard et al., 2020) and DOM-LM (Deng et al., 2022). However, these language-only approaches are intrinsically limited when data is stored visually.

Research on pairing vision and language capabilities together in a single model has made rapid progress in interpreting images with text, with models like GPT-4 demonstrating excellent text extraction capabilities from structured documents (OpenAI, 2023), even establishing a new state-of-the-art on the Text Visual Question Answering (TextVQA) dataset (Singh et al., 2019), a dataset designed to challenge model's ability to reason with images. Research is rapid and prolific in multimodal modeling, including the recent work of the multilingual PaLI (Chen et al., 2023) and the modular system of mPLUG-2 (Xu et al., 2023) for multimodal Question Answering (QA).

The dataset by Varlamov et al. (2022) features hand-labeled news articles in raw HTML format, focusing on identifying critical article components like titles and publication dates. Similarly, the Klarna Product Page Dataset (Hotti et al., 2022) contains 51,701 annotated product sale pages for locating key web elements such as buy buttons and prices. Additionally, the Boilerplate Detection using Shallow Text Features dataset (Kohlschütter et al., 2010) includes HTML files labeled to distinguish main content from extraneous elements like advertisements, thus aiding in refining web scraping accuracy. None of the aforementioned datasets provide the ability to compare purely text based and multimodal models on event information extraction.

3 Methodology

3.1 FanConInfo

To enable a fair comparison between visual and textual extraction techniques, we curate a novel dataset, FanConInfo, of comic convention websites which constitute a diverse corpus spanning a range of designs, conventions, and web architectures.

We first extract an initial list of upcoming comic conventions across North America from the aggregator site `FanCons.com`, encompassing fan gatherings to major comic expos. For each convention link, we collect a 3456 x 1878 screen capture and the corresponding HTML content with Selenium (SeleniumHQ, 2023). We remove all CSS styling and `<script>`s from the HTML. Following this, we manually annotate each event with the following attributes: name, start date, end date, and location.

We manually confirmed that when GPT-4 Turbo using the HTML of a webpage and GPT-4 Vision using the screenshot of a webpage agree on the convention name, the name is always correct for the entirety of the dataset. Thus, when the two models agree perfectly, we consider the response as the gold answer. When the models disagree, which occurs 41% of the time across all rows and columns, a human determines the gold response. We only evaluate performance of methods on items that have a label. It is conceivable that some webpages do not list their date nor location, demonstrated in Figure 1, in the above-the-fold portion. In total, our curated dataset contains 86 comic convention websites and is available here.

3.2 Models

For our vision-based model, we leverage the recently released GPT-4 Vision model from OpenAI, `gpt-4-vision-preview` - referred to as GPT-4V. We prompt the model as follows:

> <screen capture placed here>
>
> Get the following information from the given image as a JSON object of strings. Only write the JSON in your response. If any bit is unknown then write N/A instead:
>
> Conference Name: <Name of Conference>,
>
> Start Date: <YYYY-MM-DD>,
>
> End Date: <YYYY-MM-DD>,
>
> Location: <Address or other location>

For our code-based method, we employ the GPT-4 (`gpt-4-1106-preview` - referred to as GPT-4T) and GPT-3.5 (`gpt-3.5-turbo-1106`) models from OpenAI. Rarely when GPT-3.5's sequence length is insufficient to accommodate the entire HTML content, the HTML was truncated. These models were prompted as follows:

> <HTML placed here>
>
> Get the following information from the above HTML as a JSON object of strings. Only write the JSON in your response. If any bit is unknown then write N/A instead:
>
> Conference Name: <Name of Conference>,
>
> Start Date: <YYYY-MM-DD>,
>
> End Date: <YYYY-MM-DD>,
>
> Location: <Address or other location>

3.3 Evaluation

We assess extraction accuracy for 4 key metadata fields: name, start date, end date, and location. We combine the start date and end date into one category. Since the models never deviated from the requested format despite variations on the event pages, a prediction for date is only considered accurate if both are an exact match. To address minor errors, we evaluate predictions for event names and locations using case-insensitive Exact Match (EM) accuracy. Fuzzy matching employs the FuzzyWuzzy Python package (Inc, 2014), measuring:

- Event names: Partial ratio to capture semantic changes with word order (e.g., "ComicCon" vs. "Comic Convention").
- Locations: Partial token sort ratio to allow coherent reordering (e.g., "X Hall, Y Ave., City" vs. "Y Ave., City, X Hall").

This approach balances exact and fuzzy matching for a comprehensive assessment.

GPT	Name	Date	Location	Avg
3.5	0.58(0.05)	0.73(0.06)	0.46(0.06)	0.59
4T	0.62(0.05)	0.74(0.05)	0.56(0.06)	0.64
4V	**0.82 (0.04)**	**0.88 (0.04)**	**0.86 (0.04)**	**0.85**

Table 1: Exact Match accuracy for on the FanConInfo Dataset. The Avg column represents the average accuracy for each model.

GPT	Fuzzy Name Score	Fuzzy Name Accuracy	Fuzzy Location Score	Fuzzy Location Accuracy
3.5	0.88 (0.03)	0.78 (0.05)	0.77 (0.04)	0.62 (0.06)
4T	0.91 (0.02)	0.82 (0.04)	0.83 (0.04)	0.75 (0.06)
4V	**0.95 (0.02)**	**0.92 (0.03)**	**0.95 (0.02)**	**0.94 (0.03)**

Table 2: Partial ratio (name) and partial token sort ratio scores (location) on the FanConInfo Dataset. The score is the average ratio and the accuracy is calculated based on a score threshold of 0.85.

4 Results & Discussion

GPT	Name	Date	Location	Avg
3.5	0.58(0.05)	0.91(0.05)	0.53(0.07)	0.67
4T	0.63(0.05)	**1.00 (0.00)**	0.64(0.07)	0.76
4V	**0.83 (0.04)**	**1.00 (0.00)**	**0.87 (0.05)**	**0.90**

Table 3: Exact Match accuracy for on the FanConInfo Dataset, after removing instances where any of the models predicted that the information is not available. The Avg column represents the average accuracy for each model.

Table 1 shows the visual methodology achieves an average exact match score of 85% while the top text-based methodology achieves an average exact match score of 64%. When relaxing exact match criteria using fuzzy matching, we see the visual methodology achieves an average fuzzy score of 95% when retrieving the convention name while the top code-based method achieves an average fuzzy score of 91% for the same task, as shown in Table 2. When tasked to retrieve the convention

GPT	Fuzzy Name Score	Fuzzy Name Accuracy	Fuzzy Location Score	Fuzzy Location Accuracy
3.5	0.89(0.02)	0.79(0.05)	0.86(0.03)	0.71(0.06)
4T	0.92(0.02)	0.83(0.04)	0.94(0.02)	0.86(0.05)
4V	**0.96 (0.02)**	**0.92 (0.03)**	**0.98 (0.01)**	**0.96 (0.03)**

Table 4: Partial ratio (name) and partial token sort ratio scores (location) on the FanConInfo Dataset, after removing instances where any of the models predicted that the information is not available. The score is the average ratio and the accuracy is calculated based on a score threshold of 0.85.

location, the visual methodology achieves an average fuzzy score of 95% while the top code-based method achieves an average fuzzy score of 83%.

Interestingly, GPT-4 Vision was the highest-performing method across all categories and metrics. Because GPT-4 Vision and Text are the same model, we conclude there exists an advantage when rendering web information as a screen capture in human-readable format versus the traditional HTML machine code.

We also see that it may not always be necessary to use the biggest and most expensive model. GPT-3.5 reaches nearly the same performance as GPT-4 Text, especially when the name is the attribute of interest. This reinforces the advantage of representing web information in human-readable format, as increasing the model capability from GPT-3.5 to GPT-4 had little effect when presenting the model with the HTML representation.

We conducted a comparison between the results of vision-based and code-based methods when both indicate the presence of an answer within the provided mode. The findings are summarized in Tables 3 and 4. Remarkably, even when models express the existence of an answer, the vision-based method consistently delivers more human responses.

4.1 Error Analysis

GPT-4 Vision's errors predominantly come from reading an alternate name prominently displayed, demonstrated in Figure 1. Occasionally interpreting slogans or other emphasized information rather than main headers with event details. However, we do see that the model adapts well to unconventional designs and heavy visual styling, demonstrated in Figure 2. When given only the HTML, the errors tend to primarily originate from missing content, and in some cases, critical information may be exclusively conveyed through images, resulting in issues for models relying solely on the HTML.

Figure 1: Clandestine Comics. GPT-4 Vision read the wrong part as the event name; it predicted "Maryland's Longest-Running Comic Show."

Figure 2: Epic Animation Comic Game Fest. Despite the difficult to read font, GPT-4 Vision was capable of capturing the name. Meanwhile, the date only appears within an image.

Interestingly, we find that when both GPT-4 Text and GPT-4 Vision find a date for an event, Table 3, both methods are correct 100% of the time. The consistent format of dates enables models to achieve high precision in EM.

5 Conclusion and Future Work

In this work, we carry out the first rigorous comparison on practical website data showing strengths of emerging visual approaches versus enduring precision of code for harvesting event details. Our evaluations reveal superior performance in visual-based methods with unparalleled adaptability on designs with heavy imagery. As visual richness accelerates across the web, combining modalities will likely further outpace language-only methods and overcome the shortcomings from unimodal methodologies by blending state-of-the-art coding reasoning with cross-format graphical resilience. Furthermore, we release our dataset to facilitate additional development in event information extraction.

More broadly, our findings posit the understanding of complex webpage images as an important frontier with tangible value for structured data mining from online resources. GPT-4 Vision proves supreme through an average exact match of 85% and fuzzy matching rates of 95% and 95% for name and location data, respectively. We provide strong evidence that rather than competing, effectively integrating textual and visual cues can pave the way for next-generation techniques to achieve new levels of reliability in real-world information extraction across the full diversity of modern web experiences - establishing multimodal web comprehension as a critical area for cross-disciplinary AI development moving forward. Our future work includes expanding this analysis to a wide range of other datasets, including SWDE and the Klarna Product Pages.

References

Simran Arora, Brandon Yang, Sabri Eyuboglu, Avanika Narayan, Andrew Hojel, Immanuel Trummer, and Christopher Ré. 2023. Language models enable simple systems for generating structured views of heterogeneous data lakes.

Xi Chen, Xiao Wang, Soravit Changpinyo, AJ Piergiovanni, Piotr Padlewski, Daniel Salz, Sebastian Goodman, Adam Grycner, Basil Mustafa, Lucas Beyer, Alexander Kolesnikov, Joan Puigcerver, Nan Ding, Keran Rong, Hassan Akbari, Gaurav Mishra, Linting Xue, Ashish Thapliyal, James Bradbury, Weicheng Kuo, Mojtaba Seyedhosseini, Chao Jia, Burcu Karagol Ayan, Carlos Riquelme, Andreas Steiner, Anelia Angelova, Xiaohua Zhai, Neil Houlsby, and Radu Soricut. 2023. Pali: A jointly-scaled multilingual language-image model.

Xiang Deng, Prashant Shiralkar, Colin Lockard, Binxuan Huang, and Huan Sun. 2022. Dom-lm: Learning generalizable representations for html documents.

Pankaj Gulhane, Amit Madaan, Rupesh Mehta, Jeyashankher Ramamirtham, Rajeev Rastogi, Sandeep Satpal, Srinivasan H Sengamedu, Ashwin Tengli, and Charu Tiwari. 2011. Web-scale information extraction with vertex. In *2011 IEEE 27th International Conference on Data Engineering*, pages 1209–1220.

Qiang Hao, Rui Cai, Yanwei Pang, and Lei Zhang. 2011. From one tree to a forest: A unified solution for structured web data extraction. In *Proceedings of the 34th International ACM SIGIR Conference on Research and Development in Information Retrieval*, SIGIR '11, page 775–784, New York, NY, USA. Association for Computing Machinery.

Alexandra Hotti, Riccardo Sven Risuleo, Stefan Magureanu, Aref Moradi, and Jens Lagergren. 2022. Graph neural networks for nomination and representation learning of web elements.

SeatGeek Inc. 2014. *fuzzywuzzy: Fuzzy String Matching in Python*.

Christian Kohlschütter, Peter Fankhauser, and Wolfgang Nejdl. 2010. Boilerplate detection using shallow text features. In *Proceedings of the Third ACM International Conference on Web Search and Data Mining*, WSDM '10, page 441–450, New York, NY, USA. Association for Computing Machinery.

Haotian Liu, Chunyuan Li, Qingyang Wu, and Yong Jae Lee. 2023. Visual instruction tuning. *arXiv preprint arXiv:2304.08485*.

Yinhan Liu, Myle Ott, Naman Goyal, Jingfei Du, Mandar Joshi, Danqi Chen, Omer Levy, Mike Lewis, Luke Zettlemoyer, and Veselin Stoyanov. 2019. Roberta: A robustly optimized bert pretraining approach. *arXiv preprint arXiv:1907.11692*.

Colin Lockard, Xin Luna Dong, Arash Einolghozati, and Prashant Shiralkar. 2018. Ceres: Distantly supervised relation extraction from the semi-structured web.

Colin Lockard, Prashant Shiralkar, Xin Luna Dong, and Hannaneh Hajishirzi. 2020. Zeroshotceres: Zero-shot relation extraction from semi-structured webpages.

OpenAI. 2023. Gpt-4 technical report.

SeleniumHQ. 2023. Selenium. `https://selenium.dev`. Python language bindings for Selenium WebDriver.

Amanpreet Singh, Vivek Natarajan, Meet Shah, Yu Jiang, Xinlei Chen, Dhruv Batra, Devi Parikh, and Marcus Rohrbach. 2019. Towards vqa models that can read.

Maksim Varlamov, Denis Galanin, Pavel Bedrin, Sergey Duda, Vladimir Lazarev, and Alexander Yatskov. 2022. A dataset for information extraction from news web pages. In *2022 Ivannikov Ispras Open Conference (ISPRAS)*, pages 100–106.

Haiyang Xu, Qinghao Ye, Ming Yan, Yaya Shi, Jiabo Ye, Yuanhong Xu, Chenliang Li, Bin Bi, Qi Qian, Wei Wang, et al. 2023. mplug-2: A modularized multi-modal foundation model across text, image and video. *arXiv preprint arXiv:2302.00402*.

Yichao Zhou, Ying Sheng, Nguyen Vo, Nick Edmonds, and Sandeep Tata. 2021. Simplified dom trees for transferable attribute extraction from the web.

Fine-Tuning Language Models on Dutch Protest Event Tweets

Meagan B. Loerakker
Chalmers University of Technology
Netherlands Police
meagan@chalmers.se

Laurens H.F. Müter
Utrecht University
Netherlands Police
l.h.f.muter@uu.nl

Marijn P. Schraagen
Utrecht University
m.p.schraagen@uu.nl

Abstract

Being able to obtain timely information about an event, like a protest, becomes increasingly more relevant with the rise of affective polarisation and social unrest over the world. Nowadays, large-scale protests tend to be organised and broadcast through social media. Analysing social media platforms like X has proven to be an effective method to follow events during a protest. Thus, we trained several language models on Dutch tweets to analyse their ability to classify if a tweet expresses discontent, considering these tweets may contain practical information about a protest. Our results show that models pre-trained on Twitter data, including Bernice and TwHIN-BERT, outperform models that are not. Additionally, the results showed that Sentence Transformers is a promising model. The added value of oversampling is greater for models that were not trained on Twitter data. In line with previous work, preprocessing the data did not help a transformer language model to make better predictions.

1 Introduction

The number of protests across the globe has grown in the last decade (e.g. (Haig et al., 2020)).[1] Public safety can be threatened at these protests when riots can break out. For example, Trump supporters attacked the United States Capitol in Washington, D.C. on January 6, 2021 (Dave et al., 2021). State property was destroyed (repairs exceeding $1.5 million (United States Attorney's Office, 2021)) and several law enforcement officers lost their lives during the riots that followed (United States Senate Committee on Homeland Security & Governmental Affairs, 2021). While these examples of extreme social unrest are generally uncommon, they express a need to forecast these types of events. In the Netherlands, a possibility of large-scale protests exists. An example is the Curfew protests (Dutch: Avondklokrellen) held in 2020 and 2021 across several cities during the Covid-19 pandemic (Moors et al., 2022; COT, 2021). Internationally, an emergence of Covid-related protests at the end of 2020 was observed (van der Zwet et al., 2022). Additionally, people experience more confidence in influencing politics during a protest, compared to voting (Harding et al., 1986; Oliver, 2001), where Kleiner (2018) argues that extremists are likely to voice their opinions through protests.

Previous protests and stricter Covid rules might lead to a divided population over time due to decreased social mobility (Moors et al., 2022). This lack of social mobility is argued to be the source of growing discontent and polarisation in the country (Sandel, 2020). It is reported that these higher levels of affective polarisation have increased in the Netherlands (Harteveld and Wagner, 2023). Since polarisation might lead to more social unrest, the Dutch police are interested in gaining knowledge about the emergence of protests.

Nowadays, it is possible to follow incidents in real time as people increasingly use social media to broadcast live events (e.g. (Shamma et al., 2010)). As a result, X (formerly Twitter) is increasingly being studied as a news reporting platform more than anything else (Weng and Lee, 2011; Petrovic et al., 2013; Phuvipadawat and Murata, 2010). It is observed that disaster-related events are also being reported on X (Imran et al., 2015; Shamma et al., 2010; Thelwall et al., 2011; Williams and Burnap, 2015; Burnap et al., 2014). As an example, Starbird and Palen (2012) describe the Arab Spring protests in 2011 as uprisings of a political nature, where social media was pointed out as having gained a more important role in these types of protests. Subsequently, actors such as governments and policing agencies "aim to understand how events are reported using social media and how millions of online posts can be reduced to accurate but meaningful information that can support

[1] See also http://visionofhumanity.org/reports

Proceedings of the 7th Workshop on Challenges and Applications of Automated Extraction of Socio-political Events from Text (CASE 2024), pages 6–23
March 22, 2024 ©2024 Association for Computational Linguistics

decision making and lead to productive action" (Alsaedi et al., 2017, p. 2). Scholars studying social movements have argued that social networks–as established through social media–are fundamental to protest participation (e.g. (Snow et al., 1980; Boulianne et al., 2020)). Alsaedi et al. (2017) used an event detection framework in combination with temporal, spatial and textual content features from X to detect different kinds of events, including disruptive ones and those on smaller scale. Furthermore, they found that their method performs at least as well as using other terrestrial sources. In line with this, social media has been used as a way to warn people of unsafe areas and to spread awareness for disaster relief fundraising (Lindsay, 2011). This power that social media possesses has also been demonstrated during the Haiti earthquake in January 2010, where the awareness raising resulted in 8 million U.S. dollar donations to the Red Cross (Gao et al., 2011). This suggests that understanding the dynamics of social media messaging, especially during high-impact events like protests, are key to timely decision-making.

An advantage to social media analysis is that information about events can be extracted faster than official news reports publicise (Osborne and Dredze, 2014). However, one of the main research challenges in studying civil unrest, is the actual identification of such information in the fasts amount of data (Sech et al., 2020). We propose an analysis approach to recognising such information: classifying messages based on expressions of discontent.

2 Expression of Discontent

A link between discontent and collective protests is described by Somma (2017), where discontent is a negative feeling towards certain aspects of the world, which includes distrust in political authorities, rules, or decisions. Since X is a popular way to motivate people to protest (Doğu, 2019), we aim to detect expressions of discontent in tweets (see Section 5.1.2 for a precise definition). We hypothesise that people expressing discontent are more likely to start protesting.

This paper compares several BERTje, mBERT, Bernice, TwHIN-BERT and Sentence Transformers models fine-tuned to newly annotated datasets of Dutch tweets. We include experiments with the SetFit framework and compare to a logistic regression baseline.

We aim to understand how these models can identify expressions of discontent, and how well they perform on Dutch protest event tweets.

3 Social Media Analysis Challenges

OSINT utilises social media analysis to gain insights into events taking place in the country. However, current social media analysis practices pose several challenges related to privacy and the availability of suitable tools.

3.1 Privacy

In the context of the Dutch police, the OSINT unit aims to predict when and where police forces are needed in case a protest is organised. OSINT must take the GDPR (General Data Protection Regulation) into consideration when predicting these riots (Schermer et al., 2018). For example, the GDPR does not allow for the creation of profiles or monitoring of individuals' anticipation of potential crime or involvement in a riot.

As part of protest prediction, OSINT evaluates tweets according to their sentiment. If a tweet contains expressions of discontent, it is typically deemed as more relevant for analysis. Using machine learning models can result in more objective predictions of discontent. At the same time, OSINT requires models that respect individuals' privacy, as well as obtain insightful predictions. Individual privacy can be respected with models that focus on topics, communities, and sentiments of communities, rather than focusing on individuals. Moreover, the creation of these types of models can aid in the transfer of tacit knowledge within organisations. For example, the creation of manually tailored queries require experience from former protests, hence involving tacit knowledge that is difficult to express due to its non-codified disembodied nature (Howells, 1996; Ribeiro, 2013). Besides, a machine learning model's quality is assessed on its generalisability by evaluating their performance on previously unseen data (Roelofs, 2019; Raschka, 2018), whereas queries remain difficult to generalise due to their usage of specific keywords. Therefore, developing a machine learning model on a given task results in a more efficient prediction process.

3.2 Non-English Data

Despite the availability of numerous efficient and well-designed algorithms, models produced using these algorithms are often trained on the English language. This poses a challenge for organisations situated in countries where English is not the native language. Baden et al. (2022) discussed three research gaps in the field of Computational Text Analysis Methods (CTAM). One of these research gaps is the focus on the English language, which results in a lack of tools to study other languages. Entities situated in the Netherlands have to deal with Dutch text and information, primarily, for example when analysing social media posts. Hence, there is a need to evaluate how well language models perform on Dutch text, as well as evaluating to what extent fine-tuning a model may influence its performance. Unsurprisingly, the Dutch police and thereby OSINT have to deal with Dutch text and information, primarily. Hence, this calls for a need to evaluate how well language models perform on Dutch text, as well as evaluate to what extent fine-tuning existing models influences performance.

4 Models & Frameworks

De Vries et al. (2019) created BERTje for Dutch text, which outperforms a multilingual BERT model with Dutch training data on word-level tasks. However, De Vries et al. note that it remains unclear how well it performs with tasks on sentence-level, which relates to a model's deeper understanding of different types of information. In general, transformer models like BERT are restricted in their input length. Pascual et al. (2021, p. 2) note that a transformer's complexity 'scales quadratically with the length of their input.'

Bernice is a multilingual RoBERTa language model specifically trained on tweets through a custom tokenizer, which is described as the first BERT model to have been trained on this type of data (DeLucia et al., 2022). Another multilingual model trained on a large Twitter corpus has been released recently: TwHIN-BERT (Zhang et al., 2023). Both models were developed in 2022. The creators of both the Bernice and the TwHIN-BERT models found that they outperform or matches other models' performance on social media data. Therefore, we aim to evaluate how Bernice and TwHIN-BERT perform against other models on a specific task like discontent detection.

SetFit stands for 'Sentence Transformer Fine-Tuning' (Reimers and Gurevych, 2019). Sentence Transformer frameworks use Siamese and triplet network structures to modify pre-trained transformer models (Tunstall et al., 2022) to efficiently derive contextual embeddings for larger units of text such as sentences. SetFit has been used for social media data (Bates and Gurevych, 2023). A characteristic is its relatedness to few- and zero-shot approaches (Tunstall et al., 2022). These approaches have gained traction in the research community as they may prove helpful in domains lacking resources. Few-shot learning (FSL) refers to the principle of learning a task with a limited number of labelled inputs, the 'shots' (Liu et al., 2022). The training data is smaller than normally used to train models. Thus, FSL is relatively data-efficient. SetFit can achieve a high accuracy with few-shot fine-tuning, with a performance comparable to fine-tuned RoBERTa models.[2]

Although Sentence Transformers (ST) models using SetFit show promising results for languages such as German, Japanese and more on classification tasks[2], to our knowledge it has not been tested on Dutch yet. In this work, we test ST models both using regular fine-tuning and using FSL through the SetFit framework.

5 Method

The collected tweets are labelled according to the classes 'No discontent' and 'Expression of discontent'. Then, *mBERT*, *BERTje*, *Bernice*, *TwHIN-BERT*, and multilingual *Sentence Transformer* models are fine-tuned using the labelled datasets from the previous step. A Logistic Regression model is trained to determine baseline performance. We mainly focused on training a Sentence Transformers model without the SetFit framework due to time and resource constraints, as the SetFit framework took substantially longer to train.

The models are evaluated on several metrics. The anonymised data and used code for the models are publicly available at `https://github.com/Meaganium/Detecting-Discontent-in-Dutch-Events`. In summary, we evaluate whether or not there is a difference in models' performance in how well they predict a tweet's expression of discontent.

Table 2 provides an overview of the used models.

5.1 Data Collection

The data consists of Dutch tweets related to protests that took place in the years 2020–2022. Collecting the data for each protest was done in a reactive manner where tweets are downloaded a few days

[2] https://huggingface.co/blog/setfit

Protest	Date of collection	Filter keywords	Discontent / Total
Fireworks ban protest (RO)	November 20, 2022	protest †, rotterdam, protesters *, hooligans ‡	600 / 4214
Curfew riots (EI)	January 24, 2021	protest †, curfew §, eindhoven, riots ^	383 / 3892
Black Pete (MA)	November 14, 2020	protest †, piet, maastricht	1440 / 10395
Black Lives Matter (AM)	June 1, 2020	protest †, black lives matter, amsterdam	2064 / 6329

Table 1: Datasets related to Dutch protests used in this study. Each dataset is defined by specific keywords used to retrieve relevant tweets. Original Dutch keywords: † demonstratie, * betogers, ‡ relschoppers, ^ rellen, § avondklok.

after the incident. Since the X API allows downloading historic tweets not older than two weeks, the available data spans between two to three days before and after the incident. On the days of the protests themselves, we extracted the majority of the tweets. The tweets were collected via the X API. A filter was applied to select Dutch tweets only related to protests. Table 1 provides an overview of the specific filters and result set size per protest. Retweets are excluded and since a free version of the API is used, only a subset of the tweets is available.

5.1.1 Preparing the Data

Solely the tweets' contents were used. Any meta information such as geolocation, number of likes, number of retweets, and comments were ignored, as this type of meta information is mostly relevant for the creation of networks rather than determining sentiment. Elements such as hashtags, emojis and punctuation are included in the analysis. From the tweet texts, any personal information was replaced by a placeholder. Username mentions in the tweet were not masked. During the labelling process, off-topic tweets (see Appendix C), tweets containing personal information, duplicates, and auto-generated tweets were removed from the datasets.

5.1.2 Data Labelling

The tweets were labelled according to whether the tweet contained an 'Expression of discontent' (**EOD**). If the tweet included an indication that the corresponding user disagreed with the government's actions, the rioters' actions, or provided a potential reasoning for protesting, the tweet was labelled as EOD. For this labelling process, weekly meetings were held to discuss tweets that were more difficult to label, e.g., due to nuance, sarcasm and jokes. This labelling process was performed by the first and second author with eight other annotators, including university students and police employees. Each dataset was annotated by a different composition of the annotator team. The average inter-annotator agreement across all datasets was around 70%, which is considered respectable, especially for linguistic annotations (Artstein, 2017). The labelling was done in a self-made tool named Tweeti, available at `https://github.com/LMuter/Tweeti`. The labelling process was conducted over a period of 18 months. Table 7 (Appendix B) provides some example annotations.

5.1.3 Test and Training Data

The data is divided into two sets: training (80%) and testing (20%). The training data is used to train model weights and the test set is used to test the models' performance. We used fixed hyperparameter settings for all models. Due to the small size of the training set and spelling variations in tweets, words might not overlap between training and test, impeding direct keyword mapping. This prompts the model to focus on the context of the keyword occurrences instead of the words themselves, which can make the model more flexible. The datasets were imbalanced (Table 1), as they contained substantially more tweets in the 'No discontent' class than the EOD class. Due to this imbalance, we took into consideration four other evaluation metrics (precision (P), recall (R), F1 and Area Under the Curve (AUC)) besides accuracy (ACC), as accuracy will be influenced by how well the majority class can be predicted (Abd Elrahman and Abraham, 2013). In this paper, we report the macro averages of ACC and AUC, and the micro averages of P, R and F1. The micro averages allowed us to gain more insight into, i.e., the distribution of the number of true positives and false positives across the two classes. The metrics were measured per class, as macro-averages are heavily influenced by imbalance.

5.2 Training Phase

We consider several models for our study. As a baseline, a bag-of-words based Logistic Regression (LR) model is trained. Furthermore, pre-trained mBERT, Bernice, TwHIN-BERT, BERTje and Sentence Transformer (ST) models are fine-tuned. Ini-

Model	Hugging Face URI
BERT	bert-base-uncased
mBERT	nlptown/bert-base-multilingual-uncased-sentiment
BERTje	GroNLP/bert-base-dutch-cased
Sentence Transformers (ST)	sentence-transformers/paraphrase-multilingual-mpnet-base-v2
Bernice	jhu-clsp/bernice
TwHIN-BERT-base	Twitter/twhin-bert-base
TwHIN-BERT-large	Twitter/twhin-bert-large

Table 2: Overview of the models used from the Hugging Face platform.

tial experiments were performed using the SetFit framework with an ST model.

5.2.1 Pre-Training Phase

For the implementation of the models, we used the 'text-classification' task in the pipeline in order to be able to assign the EOD label to a tweet. See Table 6 in Appendix A for a more extensive overview of the used Python libraries and functions. in order to make their produced results more comparable with one another, as this task allows for the tokenization of sequences of text, rather than one individual word. These (sub)words are the result of the separated text sequences, representing the tokens.[3] Note that these subword tokenizers partially solve the issue of error mistakes. By declaring this task for BERTje, they perform the same tokenization process, hence making their results comparable.

The Hugging Face tokenizers are used in the pre-training phase. The tokenization process consists of three steps. Firstly, indicators are added to demarcate the start and end of the tweet, signified by the special tokens [CLS] and [SEP], respectively. Secondly, uniformity in the tweet length is ensured by adding [PAD] to short tweets and truncating long tweets. Finally, the converted tokens are assigned IDs, and an attention mask is created.

5.2.2 Pre-Processing the Data for LR

We trained various additional models on a pre-processed version of the datasets in order to evaluate the difference in performance, considering it can provide better results for bag-of-words techniques (Angiani et al., 2016). Pre-processing the data involved lowercasing and lemmatization, and removing all URLs, Dutch stopwords, username mentions, accents on letters and punctuation from the tweet text. Furthermore, only content words like verbs, nouns, adjectives, adverbs and proper nouns were typically included after pre-processing.

[3]https://huggingface.co/docs/transformers/v4.28.1/en/task_summary#sequence-classification

6 Results

To evaluate the results for the EOD prediction, we focused mainly on the results for the EOD label, as this was the minority class for all individual datasets. See Tables 3 and 4 for the prediction results. First, we ran all the models with all four dataset combined, see Table 1. In this round, the models were run with the oversampling technique with the assumption that oversampling the minority class would compensate for the data imbalance. We further investigated the outcomes on the datasets separately by training the best models from the previous round on all the datasets combined with oversampling to identify differences in performance per dataset. After some test runs without oversampling (see Table 12, Appendix D), we observed that oversampling may not produce substantially different results. As such, we ran the models without oversampling the minority class to evaluate the models' sensitivity to data imbalance. Lastly, we did some extra experimentation with the multilingual model mBERT.

6.1 Logistic Regression

First, we evaluated the baseline performance with the Logistic Regression (LR) model. While pre-processing is not always beneficial for deep learning methods (Camacho-Collados and Pilehvar, 2018), for bag-of-words models it is commonly used, hence its inclusion. LR did not perform better than the other models, which is highlighted by the fact that LR has no bold numbers in Table 3.

To evaluate LR's potential further, we experimented with all possible combinations of pre-processing steps as given in Section 5.2.2. See Appendix D, Table 8. The best combination of pre-processing steps was a combination of lowercasing and removal of URLs, username mentions, diacritics and punctuation. This pre-processing combination resulted in similar results (F1: .418) compared to no pre-processing (F1: .422).

Model	Measure	ACC	AUC	Expression of discontent P	R	F1	No discontent P	R	F1
Bernice	AVG	.870	**.784**	.652	.646	**.649**	**.919**	.921	.920
BERTje	AVG	.867	.745	**.685**	.548	.609	.899	.941	.919
TwHIN-BERT-base	AVG	.859	.782	.631	**.657**	.643	.917	.908	.912
TwHIN-BERT-large	AVG	.828	.609	.600	.261	.248	.856	**.957**	.900
Sentence Transformers	AVG	**.871**	.766	.682	.597	.636	.908	.935	**.921**
Logistic Regression	AVG	.808	.708	.530	.539	.534	.881	.877	.879
Bernice	STD	.004	.009	.018	.024	.012	.005	.008	.003
BERTje	STD	.008	.014	.021	.029	.022	.006	.007	.005
TwHIN-BERT-base	STD	.004	.010	.015	.028	.008	.006	.009	.003
TwHIN-BERT-large	STD	.021	.028	.071	.110	.012	.056	.054	.011
Sentence Transformers	STD	.004	.004	.020	.006	.009	.006	.004	.003
Logistic Regression	STD	.009	.006	.016	.011	.006	.007	.009	.006
Bernice	MIN	**.865**	.772	.623	.619	.632	**.914**	.907	**.917**
BERTje	MIN	.859	.721	**.670**	.497	.609	.890	**.934**	.914
TwHIN-BERT-base	MIN	.853	**.776**	.611	**.639**	**.635**	**.914**	.894	.908
TwHIN-BERT-large	MIN	.810	None	None	None	None	.810	.854	.889
Sentence Transformers	MIN	.864	.761	.656	.589	.625	.899	.931	.916
Logistic Regression	MIN	.797	.704	.516	.523	.528	.875	.871	.870
Bernice	MAX	.875	.793	.667	.679	**.663**	.926	.926	.923
BERTje	MAX	**.877**	.756	**.720**	.570	.629	.905	**.950**	**.926**
TwHIN-BERT-base	MAX	.864	**.800**	.647	.707	.656	**.928**	.918	.916
TwHIN-BERT-large	MAX	.864	.792	.650	**.731**	.628	**.928**	None	.917
Sentence Transformers	MAX	.874	.771	.704	.605	.644	.912	.940	.924
Logistic Regression	MAX	.820	.718	.558	.552	.542	.892	.889	.888
SetFit		.869	.758	.689	.577	.628	.904	.939	.921

Table 3: Comparison between the models for EOD prediction in combination with oversampling of the minority class. The models were run five times, except for SetFit. The averages, standard deviations, minima and maxima values of those rounds are provided. The numbers are rounded, and the best scores for the averages, minima and maxima per metric are in bold. Table 9 in Appendix D provides the results of all the runs.

6.2 Averages, Standard Deviations, Minima and Maxima

We ran the Bernice, BERTje, TwHIN-BERT-base, TwHIN-BERT-large, ST and Logistic Regression models five times to get insight into the range of possible scores they provide. The results of all five runs are provided in Appendix D, Table 9. Of the five runs, we mainly focus on discussing the minima, maxima and averages.

For the minima scores, we observe that the TwHIN-BERT-base overall produces the best scores on EOD (AUC: .776, F1: .635), though Bernice had the highest accuracy (.865).

Similarly for the maxima scores on EOD, TwHIN-BERT-base (AUC: .800) and Bernice (F1: .663) score the best overall. BERTje scored best on accuracy and precision. For both the minima and maxima scores, neither ST nor LR scored highest on a particular metric.

In line with the minima and maxima, we observe that Bernice scores the best on average for the minority class (AUC: .784, F1: .649). Notably, ST scored highest on accuracy for EOD (.871). Universally, we observe that Bernice and TwHIN-BERT-base provide better results compared to TwHIN-BERT-large, BERTje, ST and LR.

6.3 Separate Datasets

In this section, we describe the results for the individual AM, EI, MA and RO datasets. Note that the RO dataset is divided in two, wherein each version ('22 and '23) was labelled by other annotators. The subsets of the RO dataset overlapped to some degree, but not fully. The annotators of the '23 version were the same annotators for AM.

6.3.1 With Oversampling

From the former round, we identified that Bernice and TwHIN-BERT-base outperformed the other models with oversampling. Arguably, Bernice performs slightly better than TwHIN-BERT-base due to its average AUC and F1 scores.

As shown in Table 4, when running Bernice and TwHIN-BERT-base on the separate datasets, we observe that the models perform worst on the EI dataset on EOD. The MA dataset was the second worst performing dataset.

Bernice produced the highest scores for the ACC (.893) and P (.754) metrics on the RO dataset. Though, the AM dataset was observable the best performing dataset, with TwHIN-BERT-base producing the highest scores for AUC (.791), R (.732) and F1 (.712) on this dataset.

6.3.2 Without Oversampling

In Table 10 are the results provided by running BERTje, Bernice, TwHIN-BERT-base and TwHIN-BERT-large on all separate datasets without oversampling the minority class.

The EI dataset performs substantially worse compared to the other datasets. The AM dataset also again outperforms the other datasets, with BERTje producing the highest P (.765), and Bernice producing the best AUC (.806), R (.760) and F1 (.731) on the EOD class.

The poor results on the EI dataset can be partially attributed by the labelling process. Whereas the AM dataset was solely labelled with the EOD class, the EI and MA datasets were labelled with substantially more classes, with only tweets labelled as EOD or 'No discontent' retained and all other tweets removed from the data. The usage of more labels poses greater opportunity for disagreements among annotators, hence affecting the quality of the labels. Moreover, the proportion of EOD tweets is substantially lower for these two datasets.

6.3.3 Oversampling vs Non-Oversampling

Besides the observations previously mentioned, it is noteworthy that the oversampling technique does not always guarantee better results for some models. For some models, oversampling has more added value compared to others.

For example, oversampling on the EI dataset did not help for the Bernice model on some metrics, including AUC, P, R and F1.

Furthermore, we observed that the oversampling was ineffective for the TwHIN-BERT-base model on the ACC and P metrics. This was the case for all datasets RO23 on ACC. Although this finding may suggest that oversampling provides less added value for the models trained on Twitter data due to their higher performance in general, this observation warrants further investigation.

6.4 Notable Results

In this section, we describe some noteworthy additional results we found.

6.4.1 TwHIN-BERT-large

The TwHIN-BERT-large model was unable to converge in some runs on the data. This is likely due to the small size of the datasets, whereby the model is unable to fine-tune all its parameters due to its large size. When TwHIN-BERT-large was able to configure all its parameters, it produced good results. As shown in Table 9, run 1 provided the best R score (.731) across all runs and models. Run 5 also configured correctly, with some notable results being the ACC and P.

6.4.2 BERTje

To investigate if the pre-trained data influences the results, we trained a BERTje model based on a Dutch text corpus with a variety of settings. The extra results for BERTje can be found in Appendix D, Tables 8 and 11.

For BERTje, we experimented with preprocessing to evaluate whether our results are in line with previous work (e.g. (Camacho-Collados and Pilehvar, 2018; Kurniasih and Manik, 2022; Alzahrani and Jololian, 2021)). For each metric, except recall in the 'No discontent' class, preprocessing lowered BERTje's performance. Especially the recall (.091) and F1 (.153) scores were particularly poor in the minority class. This is explained by BERT's use of contextual information, like punctuation, morphology and sentence structure.

To find out if there is a difference in performance between annotators for the same dataset, we trained BERTje on the two RO dataset versions. We found a noticeable difference for all metrics.

Using all datasets provided the best score compared to using the datasets separately for EOD on precision (.863), though recall was poor (.328). This shows that providing BERTje with more data, despite the imbalance, will result in the model classifying a large number of items with the minority class correctly whilst still missing quite a large portion of tweets to label as 'discontent'. This shows that BERTje can identify strong markers in the tweets that suggest discontent, as long as it is given a sufficient amount of data. At the same time, the low recall score would suggest that identifying discontent is still a nuanced task, meaning that these nuances make it difficult to define all concrete markers of discontent. Generally, it is questionable if it is possible to capture this complex notion with a language model using short social media messages.

6.4.3 SetFit

We ran SetFit once, and it did not produce better results over Bernice and TwHIN-BERT-base (see Table 3). SetFit also takes substantially longer to

Model	Data	ACC	AUC	Expression of discontent P	R	F1	No discontent P	R	F1
Bernice	AM	.826	.781	.745	.664	.702	.857	.898	.877
Bernice	EI	.888	.574	.368	.182	.243	.915	**.966**	**.940**
Bernice	MA	.866	.639	.508	.328	.399	.901	.950	.925
Bernice	RO22	**.893**	.768	.622	.595	.608	.935	.941	.938
Bernice	RO23	.884	.765	**.754**	.573	.652	.906	.957	.931
TwHIN-BERT-base	AM	.813	**.791**	.694	**.732**	**.712**	.873	.851	.862
TwHIN-BERT-base	EI	.886	.653	.412	.364	.386	.931	.943	.937
TwHIN-BERT-base	MA	.868	.665	.514	.386	.441	.908	.943	.925
TwHIN-BERT-base	RO22	.864	.769	.510	.638	.567	**.939**	.901	.920
TwHIN-BERT-base	RO23	.866	.749	.677	.560	.613	.901	.938	.919

Table 4: Comparison between the models Bernice and TwHIN-BERT-base for EOD prediction across all four datasets with oversampling of the minority class. The numbers are rounded.

train than the other models. Due to these constraints, we did not experiment with SetFit further. However, the underlying ST model did produce reasonable results when oversampling the minority class for both the AM and MA datasets. Therefore, future work with less restrictions regarding time and resources could explore SetFit's potential further.

6.4.4 Multilingual BERT: mBERT

Since multilingual models are known to perform well on monolingual tasks (Rust et al., 2021), we experimented shortly with the multilingual version of the BERT model: mBERT (see Appendix D for extra results). Oversampling the minority class in the AM dataset produced reasonable scores for AUC (.758), recall (.646) and F1 (.677). However, this introduces a performance reduction for the 'No discontent' class of around .08. Notably, mBERT scored particularly well on precision (.833) for a pre-processed dataset, while ACC, R and F1 came out relatively low.

The mBERT results are not in line with previous work where monolingual models outperform multilingual models (e.g. (De Vries et al., 2019; Rust et al., 2021)), but they are not totally unexpected given the substantial amount of English words and phrases used in Dutch social media. Similar to other models, combining oversampling and including emojis did not improve the results compared to solely applying oversampling. However, we suggest future work to take this multilingual nature of social media messaging into consideration through analyses based on the principle of code-switching (e.g. (Das and Gambäck, 2014)), like Language Identification (see (Aguilar et al., 2020; Barman et al., 2014; Khanuja et al., 2020; Molina et al., 2019; Solorio et al., 2014)).

6.5 T-test Results

To gain insight into how different the models perform compared to one another, we conducted two-way t-tests on the average F1 of five runs. Table 5 provides a full overview of the t-test results. However, note that the t-test results for comparison between TwHIN-BERT-large and other models were influenced by the fact that TwHIN-BERT-large could not compute several runs. Naturally, runs that were not completed successfully were excluded from the tests.

From the t-tests, we find that Bernice's, TwHIN-BERT-base's, and the ST's F1 scores are significantly different from logistic regression ($p < .001$). Furthermore, we found that BERTje's F1 score was significantly difference compared to TwHIN-BERT-base's and logistic regression with $p < .01$.

These results support our previous findings that the models trained on Twitter data (Bernice and TwHIN-BERT) report better prediction of EOD, as Bernice and TwHIN-BERT-base perform significantly different from the baseline (logistic regression). Notably, BERTje and ST also perform significantly different from the baseline, suggesting that these models also have the potential to provide reasonable results on the data.

7 Discussion

In this paper, we aimed to identify how future NLP models can be improved in order to provide better predictions for social media text. Our work provides an overview of several language models' performances on Dutch tweets for the prediction of *Expression of Discontent*.

Whether someone expresses discontent is dependent on human interpretation, thus complicating the identification process of parameters that determine tweet sentiment. Moreover, human annotators may

	Bernice	BERTje	TwHIN-BERT-base	TwHIN-BERT-large	Sentence Transformers
BERTje	.022*				
TwHIN-BERT-base	.250	.006**			
TwHIN-BERT-large	.030*	.038*	.030*		
Sentence Transformers	.029*	.028*	.170	.032*	
Logistic Regression	7.4E-06***	.002**	5.4E-06***	.068	2.8E-05***

Table 5: Overview of the t-test results between the F1 scores of the models' predictions on all of the four datasets combined. Asterisks denote p-values: * $p < .05$, ** $p < .01$, *** $p < .001$.

consider other kinds of information subconsciously when labelling a tweet for discontent. This claim is supported by results we found when training models on subsets of the RO dataset labelled by two different annotator teams.

The results showed that the models trained on Twitter data, namely TwHIN-BERT and Bernice, performed best. Pre-processing did not improve the results for any model. This highlights the importance of using models that have been pre-trained on similar types of data for event prediction, which is in line with a review conducted by Zimbra et al. (2018). They found that the average accuracy for sentiment analysis on Twitter data was 61%, and that state-of-the-art approaches performed similarly, with accuracies routinely below the 70%. However, they did find that domain-specific approaches performed better by 11%, which is an average increase in performance we did not achieve. For all datasets combined, Bernice and TwHIN-BERT-base achieved average scores ranging from .63 to .65 for precision, recall and F1 on the EOD class, though for both classes (EOD and 'No discontent') the average accuracy and AUC scores were substantially higher, ranging from .78 to .87.

Surprisingly, we found that the Sentence Transformers models perform on par with Bernice and TwHIN-BERT, despite not being a pre-trained model on Twitter data. Additional results showed that mBERT, a multilingual model, performed better than BERTje. This may be because social media users tend to lend words from other languages, including English. Furthermore, mBERT is trained on a larger corpus of text compared to BERTje. This indicates that the selection of a specific dataset to pre-train a language model is one of the main indicators to acquire a greater return on prediction performance.

Lastly, we found that oversampling provides substantial benefits for smaller datasets, like EI and MA in our work, whereas the benefit is limited for larger ones, like AM in our work. Furthermore, when combining all datasets together, the benefit of oversampling was also limited. However, the issue of highly imbalanced datasets cannot be fully solved with oversampling, which was observed in the results. In line with this, some models gain more benefit from oversampling than others. In particular, oversampling had the least added value for the models trained on Twitter data, potentially due to their relatively high base performance.

All in all, the results indicate that the identification of discontent in social media text is a feasible approach to filtering relevant to irrelevant messaging, given that the appropriate language models are chosen. The ability to accurately filter the data provides opportunities for more efficient extraction of a variety of information relevant to entities like the police and OSINT, including locations, dates and time stamps.

7.1 Limitations

First, in all of the used datasets, the number of 'No discontent' tweets outnumbers the number of discontent tweets with a ratio of around one to five. In order try to make up for this limitation, we used the widely used oversampling technique named Synthetic Minority Oversampling TEchnique (SMOTE) (Chawla et al., 2002) for the discontent tweets. However, SMOTE has limitations, including misclassification of the majority class, resulting in negative effects for the model's overall balance (Puntumapon and Waiyamai, 2012).

Second, some publicly available tweets may have been removed by the corresponding users since the tweets have been extracted via the X API, which may reduce the reproducibility of the study. Besides that, it is possible that some of the results were unsatisfactory partially due to the switch-ups in the annotator teams. The compositions in the annotator teams may have resulted in some inconsistencies in the labelling process.

Third, we did not conduct an error analysis in this work. Therefore, future work that aims to build upon this paper should consider aiming to gain more insights into, i.e., whether the degree of false positives for a specific dataset correlates with the (perceived) difficulty of the annotation task. However, to support such an error analysis, we propose follow-up studies to report more details on the inter-annotator agreement.

Fourth, being able to predict a protest's location, date, time or size is also of interest to OSINT and the Dutch police, especially in times of higher affective polarisation and social unrest. In this work, we did not explore the extraction of such information from the tweets, presenting an opportunity for future work.

Lastly, the practice of combining all four datasets may be flawed. Some protests may have been more extreme in terms of the events that took place, hence (indirectly) influencing how the annotators interpret discontent per protest. Therefore, some datasets may capture a limited, or even a different, meaning of expression of discontent, given that the datasets were labelled for different protests and/or with more labels, affecting classification performance.

8 Ethics Statement

Ethical approval to conduct this study, including approval for the collection and annotation of the datasets, was acquired from the appropriate local institutional review boards and ethics committees. To minimise potential privacy issues, we excluded direct and indirect personal identifiers from the data, including names and locations. In line with the GDPR guidelines, the data has been anonymised by hashing usernames and mentions.

Besides the focus on Dutch text, it is desirable for high-impact applications, like those used in medical practice and law enforcement, to work with models and algorithms that have low false negative rates, due to potential societal and ethical complications that arise with false positives. For example, it is unethical and socially undesirable to inaccurately label a person's social media message along the lines of 'high-risk' or 'negative'. Therefore, in this work, we focused on the optimisation of the precision metric, as this indicates lower false positives. We encourage future work to put low false positive rates at the forefront in the evaluation of models' performance.

Furthermore, we followed the European Data Protection Board (EDPB) guidelines to assess the risks and potential impacts of the data.[4] These guidelines were followed in order to minimise potential risks for individuals' freedoms, and to use the data in a lawful and transparent manner.

For future work, we provide several suggestions on how to use social media data in an ethical manner. First, ethical data assessment methodologies should be used before the analysis is conducted in order to evaluate potential conflicts with (public) values and to minimise social disruption. We recommend using approaches like 'De Ethische Data Assistent' (DEDA, 'The Ethical Data Assistent') from Schäfer et al. (2022). Second, when conducting social media analysis, the focus should be on groups rather than individuals, so that privacy is ensured and the results remain 'superficial' in nature. As previously mentioned, the GDPR emphasises that *monitoring* and *profiling* is not allowed, even in the context of anticipating crimes and riots. Therefore, social media analyses for research purposes should emphasise the recognition of general trends, sentiments and events instead, as presented in this paper.

Acknowledgements

This work was supported by the Swedish Research Council, award number 2022-03196.

References

Shaza Abd Elrahman and Ajith Abraham. 2013. A review of class imbalance problem. *Journal of Network and Innovative Computing*, 1:332–340.

Gustavo Aguilar, Sudipta Kar, and Thamar Solorio. 2020. LinCE: A centralized benchmark for linguistic code-switching evaluation. *Proceedings of the Twelfth Language Resources and Evaluation Conference*, page 1803–1813.

Nasser Alsaedi, Pete Burnap, and Omer Rana. 2017. Can we predict a riot? Disruptive event detection using Twitter. *ACM Transactions on Internet Technology (TOIT)*, 17(2):1–26.

Esam Alzahrani and Leon Jololian. 2021. How different text-preprocessing techniques using the BERT model affect the gender profiling of authors. *3rd International Conference on Machine Learning & Applications (CMLA 2021)*, pages 1–8.

Giulio Angiani, Laura Ferrari, Tomaso Fontanini, Paolo Fornacciari, Eleonora Iotti, Federico Magliani, and Stefano Manicardi. 2016. A comparison between

[4]https://edpb.europa.eu/sites/default/files/consultation/edpb_guidelines_202008_onthetargetingofsocialmediausers_en.pdf

preprocessing techniques for sentiment analysis in Twitter. In *Proceedings of KDWeb 2016*.

Ron Artstein. 2017. Inter-annotator agreement. *Handbook of Linguistic Annotation*, pages 297–313.

Christian Baden, Christian Pipal, Martijn Schoonvelde, and Mariken van der Velden. 2022. Three gaps in computational text analysis methods for social sciences: A research agenda. *Communication Methods and Measures*, 16(1):1–18.

Utsab Barman, Amitava Das, Joachim Wagner, and Jennifer Foster. 2014. Code mixing: A challenge for language identification in the language of social media. In *Proceedings of the First Workshop on Computational Approaches to Code Switching*, pages 13–23. Association for Computational Linguistics, Doha, Qatar.

Luke Bates and Iryna Gurevych. 2023. Like a good nearest neighbor: Practical content moderation with Sentence Transformers. *arXiv preprint 2302.08957*.

Shelley Boulianne, Karolina Koc-Michalska, and Bruce Bimber. 2020. Mobilizing media: Comparing tv and social media effects on protest mobilization. *Information, Communication & Society*, 23(5):642–664.

Pete Burnap, Matthew Williams, Luke Sloan, Omer Rana, William Housley, Adam Edwards, Vincent Knight, Rob Procter, and Alex Voss. 2014. Tweeting the terror: Modelling the social media reaction to the Woolwich terrorist attack. *Social Network Analysis and Mining*, 4:1–14.

Jose Camacho-Collados and Mohammad Taher Pilehvar. 2018. On the role of text preprocessing in neural network architectures: An evaluation study on text categorization and sentiment analysis. In *Proceedings of the 2018 EMNLP Workshop BlackboxNLP: Analyzing and Interpreting Neural Networks for NLP*, pages 40–46. Association for Computational Linguistics.

Nitesh Chawla, Kevin Bowyer, Lawrence Hall, and W. Philip Kegelmeyer. 2002. SMOTE: Synthetic Minority Over-sampling Technique. *Journal of Artificial Intelligence Research*, 16:321–357.

COT. 2021. Een machteloos gevoel: Leerevaluatie naar aanleiding van de ongeregeldheden in Den Bosch op 25 januari 2021. *AON*, pages 1–27.

Amitava Das and Björn Gambäck. 2014. Identifying languages at the word level in code-mixed Indian social media text. *Proceedings of the 11th International Conference on Natural Language Processing*, page 378–387.

Dhaval Dave, Drew McNichols, and Joseph Sabia. 2021. Political violence, risk aversion, and non-localized disease spread: Evidence from the US capitol riot. Technical report, National Bureau of Economic Research.

Wietse De Vries, Andreas van Cranenburgh, Arianna Bisazza, Tommaso Caselli, Gertjan van Noord, and Malvina Nissim. 2019. BERTje: A Dutch BERT model. *arXiv preprint 1912.09582*.

Alexandra DeLucia, Shijie Wu, Aaron Mueller, Carlos Aguirre, Philip Resnik, and Mark Dredze. 2022. Bernice: A multilingual pre-trained encoder for Twitter. In *Proceedings of the 2022 Conference on Empirical Methods in Natural Language Processing*, pages 6191–6205. Association for Computational Linguistics.

Burak Doğu. 2019. Environment as politics: Framing the Cerattepe protest in Twitter. *Environmental Communication*, 13(5):617–632.

Huiji Gao, Geoffrey Barbier, and Rebecca Goolsby. 2011. Harnessing the crowdsourcing power of social media for disaster relief. *IEEE Intelligent Systems*, 26(3):10–14.

Christian S Haig, Katherine Schmidt, and Samuel Brannen. 2020. The age of mass protests: Understanding an escalating global trend. `https://www.csis.org/analysis/age-mass-protests-understanding-escalating-global-trend` (accessed: 2 February, 2024).

Stephen Harding, David Phillips, and Michael Patrick Fogarty. 1986. *Contrasting values in Western Europe: Unity, diversity and change*. Macmillan Publishing Company.

Eelco Harteveld and Markus Wagner. 2023. Does affective polarisation increase turnout? Evidence from Germany, The Netherlands and Spain. *West European Politics*, 46(4):732–759.

Jeremy Howells. 1996. Tacit knowledge. *Technology Analysis & Strategic Management*, 8(2):91–106.

Muhammad Imran, Carlos Castillo, Fernando Diaz, and Sarah Vieweg. 2015. Processing social media messages in mass emergency: A survey. *ACM Computing Surveys (CSUR)*, 47(4):1–38.

Simran Khanuja, Sandipan Dandapat, Anirudh Srinivasan, Sunayana Sitaram, and Monojit Choudhury. 2020. GLUECoS: An evaluation benchmark for code-switched NLP. *Proceedings of the 58th Annual Meeting of the Association for Computational Linguistics*, page 3575–3585.

Tuuli-Marja Kleiner. 2018. Public opinion polarisation and protest behaviour. *European Journal of Political Research*, 57(4):941–962.

Aliyah Kurniasih and Lindung Parningotan Manik. 2022. On the role of text preprocessing in BERT embedding-based DNNs for classifying informal texts. *International Journal of Advanced Computer Science and Applications (IJACSA)*, 13(6):927–934.

Bruce Lindsay. 2011. Social media and disasters: Current uses, future options, and policy considerations. Technical report, Congressional Research Service Washington, DC.

Haokun Liu, Derek Tam, Mohammed Muqeeth, Jay Mohta, Tenghao Huang, Mohit Bansal, and Colin Raffel. 2022. Few-shot parameter-efficient fine-tuning is better and cheaper than in-context learning. *36th Conference on Neural Information Processing Systems (NeurIPS 2022)*, 35:1950–1965.

Giovanni Molina, Fahad AlGhamdi, Mahmoud Ghoneim, Abdelati Hawwari, Nicolas Rey-Villamizar, Mona Diab, and Thamar Solorio. 2019. Overview for the second shared task on language identification in code-switched data. *Proceedings of the Second Workshop on Computational Approaches to Code Switching*, page 40–49.

Hans Moors, Lea Klarenbeek, Emily Berger, Michel Dückers, Menno van Duin, Gijs Kist, Marte Luesink, Tess Schrijvenaars, and Mary van der Wijngaart. 2022. 'Avondklokrellen': Lokale dynamiek in een mondiale crisis: Analyse van de voedingsbodem van de ordeverstoringen in vier Noord-Brabantse steden. *Technology Analysis & Strategic Management*.

J Eric Oliver. 2001. *Democracy in suburbia*. Princeton University Press.

Miles Osborne and Mark Dredze. 2014. Facebook, Twitter and Google Plus for breaking news: Is there a winner? In *Proceedings of the International AAAI Conference on Web and Social Media*, volume 8, pages 611–614.

Damian Pascual, Sandro Luck, and Roger Wattenhofer. 2021. Towards BERT-based automatic ICD coding: Limitations and opportunities. *Proceedings of the BioNLP 2021 workshop*, pages 54–63.

Sasa Petrovic, Miles Osborne, Richard McCreadie, Craig Macdonald, Iadh Ounis, and Luke Shrimpton. 2013. Can Twitter replace Newswire for breaking news? In *Proceedings of the 7th International AAAI Conference on Web and Social Media*, volume 7 of *ICWSM 2013*, pages 713–716.

Swit Phuvipadawat and Tsuyoshi Murata. 2010. Breaking news detection and tracking in Twitter. In *2010 IEEE/WIC/ACM International Conference on Web Intelligence and Intelligent Agent Technology*, volume 3, pages 120–123. IEEE.

Kamthorn Puntumapon and Kitsana Waiyamai. 2012. A pruning-based approach for searching precise and generalized region for synthetic minority over-sampling. In *Advances in Knowledge Discovery and Data Mining: 16th Pacific-Asia Conference, PAKDD 2012, Part II 16*, pages 371–382. Springer.

Sebastian Raschka. 2018. Model evaluation, model selection, and algorithm selection in machine learning. *arXiv preprint 1811.12808*.

Nils Reimers and Iryna Gurevych. 2019. Sentence-BERT: Sentence embeddings using siamese BERT-networks. *Proceedings of the 2019 Conference on Empirical Methods in Natural Language Processing and the 9th International Joint Conference on Natural Language Processing (EMNLP-IJCNLP)*, page 3982–3992.

Rodrigo Ribeiro. 2013. Tacit knowledge management. *Phenomenology and the Cognitive Sciences*, 12:337–366.

Rebecca Roelofs. 2019. *Measuring generalization and overfitting in machine learning*. Ph.D. thesis, University of California, Berkeley.

Phillip Rust, Jonas Pfeiffer, Ivan Vulić, Sebastian Ruder, and Iryna Gurevych. 2021. How good is your tokenizer? On the monolingual performance of multilingual language models. In *Proceedings of the 59th Annual Meeting of the Association for Computational Linguistics and the 11th International Joint Conference on Natural Language Processing (Volume 1: Long Papers)*, pages 3118–3135. Association for Computational Linguistics.

Michael Sandel. 2020. *The tyranny of merit: What's become of the common good?* Penguin Books: UK.

Mirko Tobias Schäfer, Aline Franzke, Danique van der Hoek, Marjolein Krijgsman, Iris Muis, Julia Straatman, Redmar Fransen, and Sammy Hemerik. 2022. De ethische data assistent handleiding: Inventarisatie van ethische kwesties rond data projecten bij overheden. *Utrecht Data School, Utrecht University*, pages 1–42.

Bart Schermer, Dominique Hagenauw, and Nathalie Falot. 2018. Handleiding Algemene verordening gegevensbescherming en Uitvoeringswet Algemene verordening gegevensbescherming. `https://www.rijksoverheid.nl/onderwerpen/privacy-en-persoonsgegevens/documenten/rapporten/2018/01/22/handleiding-algemene-verordening-gegevensbescherming` (accessed: 2 February, 2024).

Justin Sech, Alexandra DeLucia, Anna Buczak, and Mark Dredze. 2020. Civil unrest on Twitter (CUT): A dataset of tweets to support research on civil unrest. In *Proceedings of the Sixth Workshop on Noisy User-generated Text (W-NUT 2020)*, pages 215–221. Association for Computational Linguistics.

David Shamma, Lyndon Kennedy, and Elizabeth F Churchill. 2010. Tweetgeist: Can the Twitter timeline reveal the structure of broadcast events? *CSCW Horizons*, 26.

David Snow, Louis Zurcher Jr, and Sheldon Ekland-Olson. 1980. Social networks and social movements: A microstructural approach to differential recruitment. *American Sociological Review*, 45:787–801.

Thamar Solorio, Elizabeth Blair, Suraj Maharjan, Steven Bethard, Mona Diab, Mahmoud Ghoneim, Abdelati Hawwari, Fahad AlGhamdi, Julia Hirschberg, Alison Chang, and Pascale Fung. 2014. Overview for the first shared task on language identification in code-switched data. In *Proceedings of the First Workshop on Computational Approaches to Code Switching*, pages 62–72. Association for Computational Linguistics, Doha, Qatar.

Nicolás Somma. 2017. Discontent, collective protest, and social movements in Chile. *Malaise in Representation in Latin American Countries: Chile, Argentina, and Uruguay*, pages 47–68.

Kate Starbird and Leysia Palen. 2012. (How) will the revolution be retweeted? Information diffusion and the 2011 Egyptian uprising. In *Proceedings of the ACM 2012 Conference on Computer Supported Cooperative Work*, CSCW '12, pages 7–16. Association for Computing Machinery.

Mike Thelwall, Kevan Buckley, and Georgios Paltoglou. 2011. Sentiment in Twitter events. *Journal of the American Society for Information Science and Technology*, 62(2):406–418.

Lewis Tunstall, Nils Reimers, Unso Eun Seo Jo, Luke Bates, Daniel Korat, Moshe Wasserblat, and Oren Pereg. 2022. Efficient few-shot learning without prompts. *36th Conference on Neural Information Processing Systems (NeurIPS 2022)*, pages 1–14.

United States Attorney's Office. 2021. One year since the Jan. 6 attack on the Capitol. https://www.justice.gov/usao-dc/one-year-jan-6-attack-capitol.

United States Senate Committee on Homeland Security & Governmental Affairs. 2021. Examining the U.S. Capitol attack: A review of the security, planning, and response failures on January 6. https://www.hsdl.org/?view&did=854959.

Jianshu Weng and Bu-Sung Lee. 2011. Event detection in Twitter. In *Proceedings of the 5th International AAAI Conference on Web and Social Media*, volume 5, pages 401–408.

Matthew Williams and Pete Burnap. 2015. Cyberhate on social media in the aftermath of Woolwich: A case study in computational criminology and big data. *British Journal of Criminology*, 56(2):211–238.

Xinyang Zhang, Yury Malkov, Omar Florez, Serim Park, Brian McWilliams, Jiawei Han, and Ahmed El-Kishky. 2023. TwHIN-BERT: A socially-enriched pre-trained language model for multilingual tweet representations. In *Proceedings of the 29th ACM SIGKDD Conference on Knowledge Discovery and Data Mining*, KDD '23, page 5597–5607. Association for Computing Machinery.

David Zimbra, Ahmed Abbasi, Daniel Zeng, and Hsinchun Chen. 2018. The state-of-the-art in Twitter sentiment analysis: A review and benchmark evaluation. *ACM Transactions on Management Information Systems (TMIS)*, 9(2):1–29.

Koen van der Zwet, Ana Barros, Tom van Engers, and Peter Sloot. 2022. Emergence of protests during the COVID-19 pandemic: Quantitative models to explore the contributions of societal conditions. *Humanities and Social Sciences Communications*, 9(68):1–11.

A List of Used Python Libraries

Processing Step	Libraries
Pre-processing	re
	string
	pandas
	sklearn (TfidfVectorizer)
	nltk (word_tokenize, stopwords)
	spacy (nsubj, VERB)
	WordCloud
	datasets (Dataset, DatasetDict)
Training BERT models	codecs
	tqdm
	datasets (concatenate_datasets, load_dataset, Dataset, DatasetDict)
	pandas
	numpy
	sklearn (f1_score, roc_auc_score, accuracy_score, train_test_split)
	torch
	transformers (BertTokenizerFast, AutoTokenizer, AutoModelForSequenceClassification, TrainingArguments, Trainer, EvalPrediction, pipeline)
Training SetFit frameworks	sentence_transformers (CosineSimilarityLoss)
	setfit (SetFitModel, SetFitTrainer)
EOD Prediction	pycm
	emoji
	matplotlib
Additional testing	random

Table 6: Overview of the Python libraries used to train the models.

B Example Tweets and their Corresponding Label

Translated tweet from Dutch to English	Label	Annotators' reasoning for the given label
Half of the hooligans in #Rotterdam were underage!!!! Where are the parents????	EOD	* Usage of the word 'hooligans'. * Usage of 4 exclamation marks. * Indirect expression of discontent towards the parents of the hooligans, implying that they did not raise their kids correctly.
Only 3 wounded in Rotterdam from last night's riots? It is time for the police to take some shooting lessons...	EOD	* The 'Only 3 wounded [...]' subsentence has a sarcastic tone. * Suggesting that police officers should take shooting lessons, implies that the user wants the police to shoot at rioters and succeed.
The Austrian Baudet could not accompany the anti-vaccin protest. He was so ill from the corona-virus that he is staying at the hospital.	No discontent	* Without additional contextual information, it is unclear from the tweet itself who is meant with 'The Austrian Baudet'. * The tweet is too descriptive in order to determine the user's intent with certainty.
Has someone already called themselves in for the torn off finger ? #Rotterdam	No discontent	* A potential expression of discontent towards people who light fireworks. * Too unclear what is meant with a torn off finger.

Table 7: Overview of some example tweets with their corresponding label, including the reasoning used by the annotators to assign the 'Expression of Discontent' (EOD) or the 'No discontent' class. Although tweet examples 1 and 3 were relatively easy to label, tweet examples 2 and 4 were more difficult, causing annotators to have differing opinions on how to interpret the nuances in the text.

C Annotation Rules

A tweet was considered relevant or 'on-topic' for the EOD classification if:

1. The tweet refers to the protest for which it was scraped;
2. The tweet contains expressions of indignation towards the corresponding protest;
3. The tweet contains first-person observations of a protest and includes explicit disdain for the situation;
4. The tweet uses slurs, slang, and other inflammatory words to describe the opinions and actions of others (e.g. protesters, government);
5. The tweet uses expressive symbols like capital letters and punctuation (e.g. exclamation marks) to express their disdain towards the situation at hand;
6. The tweet shows support for the incitement of violence (towards any person or groups of people).

A tweet was considered irrelevant for the EOD classification, hence given 'No discontent', if:

1. The tweet contains solely observations regarding the situation at hand or the general public;
2. The tweet contains the person's own opinion, but the person highlights the perspectives from both sides, e.g., the protesters and the government;
3. The tweet contains expressions of confusion, e.g., towards what and why the protests are happening;
4. The tweet seems to contain sarcasm but it could be interpreted in multiple ways;
5. The tweet includes discussions about the topic at hand whereby the protest is used to support one's non-inflammatory opinions.

A tweet was excluded from the dataset, hence considered 'off-topic', if:

1. The tweet refers to a different protest for which it was scraped;
2. The tweet is a response to another tweet potentially related to the protest, but the content of the considered tweet does not refer to the protest;
3. The tweet contains signs of discontent towards parties relevant in protests (e.g. police, protesters), but it is not explicitly concerning the protest for which it was scraped.

D Extra Results

						Expression of discontent			No discontent		
Model	**Data**	**FT**	**PP**	**ACC**	**AUC**	**P**	**R**	**F1**	**P**	**R**	**F1**
LR	ALL	N	Y	.867	.629	.577	.293	.389	.890	.964	.925
LR Best PP Step †	MA	N	Y	.872	.642	.611	.318	.418	.893	.966	.928
LR	MA	N	N	.867	.646	.570	.335	.422	.895	.957	.925
BERT	MA	Y	N	.861	.541	.647	.091	.159	.866	**.992**	.924
BERTje	MA	Y	Y	.855	.537	.489	.091	.153	.865	.984	.921
BERTje	MA	Y	N	.882	.672	.664	.376	.480	.902	.968	.934
BERTje	ALL	Y	N	.862	.658	**.863**	.328	.475	.862	.988	.920
BERTje Emojis	MA	Y	N	.885	.672	.687	.372	.483	.901	.971	.935
BERTje Overs & Emojis ‡	MA	Y	N	.886	.686	.681	.405	.508	.906	.968	.936
BERTje Oversampling	AM	Y	N	.791	.755	.691	**.653**	.672	.835	.858	.846
BERTje Oversampling	EI	Y	N	**.902**	.553	.391	.127	.191	.918	.980	**.948**
BERTje Oversampling	MA*	Y	N	.899	.752	.667	.549	.602	**.929**	.956	.942
BERTje Oversampling	MA	Y	N	.876	.706	.592	.467	.522	.913	.945	.929
BERTje '22 Oversampling	RO	Y	N	.861	.633	.667	.294	.408	.876	.971	.921
BERTje '23 Oversampling	RO	Y	N	.816	.660	.571	.395	.467	.856	.924	.889
mBERT	MA	Y	N	.877	.698	.603	.446	.513	.910	.950	.930
mBERT	AM	Y	N	.799	.720	.777	.506	.613	.804	.933	.864
mBERT	AM	Y	Y	.779	.684	.833	.407	.547	.769	.960	.854
mBERT Oversampling	AM	Y	N	.798	**.759**	.711	.646	**.677**	.835	.872	.853
mBERT Overs & Emojis	AM	Y	N	.803	.752	.746	.606	.668	.823	.899	.859
ST EN	MA	Y	N	.855	None	None	None	None	.855	None	.922
ST EN	MA	N	N	.812	.526	.227	.124	.160	.862	.929	.894
ST EN Oversampling	AM	Y	N	.745	.708	.598	.605	.602	.815	.810	.812
ST EN Oversampling	MA	Y	N	.836	.725	.447	.570	.501	.924	.881	.902

Table 8: Comparison between the models from fine-tuning (FT) or not (Y and N, respectively), pre-processing (PP) the data or not (Y and N, respectively) for the prediction type *Expression of Discontent* (EOD). Some models were given a particular focus, e.g. emojis and oversampling the minority class. Highest scores on accuracy, precision, recall, F1 and AUC are in bold. The numbers are rounded. Abbreviations 'AM', 'EI', 'MA', 'RO' and 'ALL' stand for the Black Lives Matter (Amsterdam), curfew riots (Eindhoven), Black Pete (Maastricht), fireworks ban protest (Rotterdam) and all four datasets, respectively. Notes: † LR was run with the combination of pre-processing steps that provided the best results, and ‡ BERTje was run by combining the focus on emojis with oversampling. By default, MA refers to a subset of the MA dataset, though MA* refers to the full dataset. When a model is marked with 'emojis', we run the model on a subset of the MA dataset solely containing tweets with at least one emoji. This subset was around 12% of the original dataset's size.

Model	Run	ACC	AUC	Expression of discontent			No discontent		
				P	**R**	**F1**	**P**	**R**	**F1**
Bernice	1	.875	.792	.667	.659	**.663**	.922	.925	.923
Bernice	2	.870	.772	.646	.619	.632	.917	.925	.921
Bernice	3	.865	.793	.623	.679	.649	.926	.907	.917
Bernice	4	.869	.776	.662	.625	.643	.914	.926	.920
Bernice	5	.868	.785	.660	.649	.654	.917	.920	.919
BERTje	1	.860	.721	.674	.497	.572	.890	.944	.916
BERTje	2	.859	.745	.673	.555	.609	.895	.934	.914
BERTje	3	.872	.756	.689	.570	.624	.905	.941	.923
BERTje	4	**.877**	.754	**.720**	.558	.629	.904	**.950**	**.926**
BERTje	5	.864	.749	.670	.561	.611	.900	.935	.917
TwHIN-BERT-base	1	.853	.777	.620	.651	.635	.914	.903	.908
TwHIN-BERT-base	2	.861	.781	.637	.650	.643	.916	.911	.914
TwHIN-BERT-base	3	.858	**.800**	.611	.707	.656	**.928**	.894	.911
TwHIN-BERT-base	4	.864	.778	.647	.639	.643	.915	.918	.916
TwHIN-BERT-base	5	.860	.776	.637	.639	.638	.914	.913	.913
TwHIN-BERT-large	1	.820	None	None	None	None	.820	None	.901
TwHIN-BERT-large	2	.830	.792	.551	**.731**	.628	**.928**	.854	.890
TwHIN-BERT-large	3	.810	None	None	None	None	.810	None	.895
TwHIN-BERT-large	4	.815	None	None	None	None	.815	None	.898
TwHIN-BERT-large	5	.864	.753	.650	.576	.611	.906	.929	.917
ST	1	.864	.761	.694	.589	.637	.899	.934	.916
ST	2	.870	.764	.656	.596	.625	.912	.931	.921
ST	3	.871	.766	.665	.601	.631	.912	.932	.922
ST	4	.874	.771	.690	.605	.644	.911	.937	.924
ST	5	.873	.767	.704	.594	.644	.906	.940	.923
LR	1	.820	.718	.532	.552	.542	.892	.884	.888
LR	2	.797	.704	.522	.542	.532	.875	.866	.870
LR	3	.812	.706	.558	.523	.540	.875	.889	.882
LR	4	.804	.706	.516	.541	.528	.882	.871	.877
LR	5	.805	.704	.523	.534	.529	.879	.875	.877

Table 9: Comparison between the models for EOD prediction with oversampling of the minority class. The models are run five times in order to get insight into the range of the possible scores. The numbers are rounded, and the best scores per metric are in bold.

Model	Data	ACC	AUC	Expression of discontent			No discontent		
				P	**R**	**F1**	**P**	**R**	**F1**
BERTje	AM	.808	.755	**.765**	.600	.673	.822	.910	.864
Bernice	AM	.823	**.806**	.703	**.760**	**.731**	.885	.852	.868
TwHIN-BERT-large	AM	.637	None	None	None	None	.637	None	.778
TwHIN-BERT-base	AM	.817	.782	.721	.687	.704	.858	.877	.868
BERTje	EI	.901	None	None	None	None	.901	None	.948
Bernice	EI	.902	.616	.513	.260	.345	.923	.973	.947
TwHIN-BERT-large	EI	.901	None	None	None	None	.901	None	.948
TwHIN-BERT-base	EI	**.909**	.591	.625	.195	.297	.918	**.987**	**.951**
BERTje	MA	.867	.595	.519	.222	.311	.888	.968	.926
Bernice	MA	.872	.723	.527	.519	.523	**.925**	.927	.926
TwHIN-BERT-large	MA	.865	None	None	None	None	.865	None	.928
TwHIN-BERT-base	MA	.874	.644	.559	.328	.413	.901	.960	.930
BERTje	RO22	.885	.680	.639	.397	.489	.908	.964	.935
BERTje	RO23	.869	.761	.677	.587	.629	.907	.935	.920
Bernice	RO22	.882	.718	.594	.491	.538	.920	.946	.933
Bernice	RO23	.877	.760	.717	.573	.637	.905	.947	.926
TwHIN-BERT-large	RO22	.894	.725	.663	.491	.564	.921	.960	.940
TwHIN-BERT-large	RO23	.811	None	None	None	None	.811	None	.896
TwHIN-BERT-base	RO22	.875	.675	.575	.397	.469	.907	.953	.929
TwHIN-BERT-base	RO23	.866	.728	.704	.507	.589	.892	.950	.920

Table 10: Comparison between the models Bernice, BERTje, TwHIN-BERT-base and TwHIN-BERT-large for the EOD prediction across all four datasets without oversampling the minority class. The numbers are rounded, and the best scores per metric are in bold.

Model	Run	ACC	AUC	Expression of discontent P	R	F1	No discontent P	R	F1
Bernice	1	**.878**	**.788**	.668	.647	**.657**	**.923**	.929	**.926**
TwHIN-BERT-base	1	.858	.778	.630	**.648**	.639	.915	.909	.912
BERTje	1	.865	.728	.715	.504	.591	.889	.952	.919
BERTje	2	.868	.744	.699	.544	.612	.898	.945	.921
BERTje	3	.875	.776	.681	.619	.649	.914	.933	.924
BERTje	4	.869	.717	.757	.469	.579	.884	.964	.923
BERTje	5	.872	.718	**.776**	.469	.585	.885	**.968**	.925
BERTje	AVG	.870	.737	.726	.521	.603	.894	.952	.922

Table 11: Comparison between the models Bernice, BERTje and TwHIN-BERT-base for EOD prediction without oversampling. For BERTje, five runs were completed in order to get insight into the range of the possible scores. The numbers are rounded, and the best scores are in bold.

Model	Data	ACC	AUC	Expression of discontent P	R	F1	No discontent P	R	F1
BERTje	AM	.814	.770	.762	.639	.695	.834	.901	.866
BERTje	EI	.901	None	None	None	None	.901	None	.948
BERTje	MA	.868	.678	.568	.410	.476	.904	.947	.925

Table 12: Test runs with BERTje for EOD prediction without oversampling on three separate datasets, namely AM, EI and MA. The numbers are rounded.

Timeline Extraction from Decision Letters Using ChatGPT

Femke Bakker
University of Amsterdam
The Netherlands
femke.bakker2@student.uva.nl

Ruben van Heusden
University of Amsterdam
The Netherlands
r.j.vanheusden@uva.nl

Maarten Marx
University of Amsterdam
The Netherlands
maartenmarx@uva.nl

Abstract

Freedom of Information Act (FOIA) legislation grants citizens the right to request information from various levels of the government, and aims to promote the transparency of governmental agencies. However, the processing of these requests is often met with delays, due to the inherent complexity of gathering the required documents. To obtain accurate estimates of the processing times of requests, and to identify bottlenecks in the process, this research proposes a pipeline to automatically extract these timelines from decision letters of Dutch FOIA requests. These decision letters are responses to requests, and contain an overview of the process, including when the request was received, and possible communication between the requester and the relevant agency. The proposed pipeline can extract dates with an accuracy of .94, extract event phrases with a mean ROUGE-L F1 score of .80 and can classify events with a macro F1 score of .79.

Out of the 50 decision letters used for testing (each letter containing one timeline), the model correctly classified 10 of the timelines completely correct, with an average of 3.1 mistakes per decision letter.

1 Introduction

Timeline extraction is the process of extracting dated events and ordering them along a timeline (Cornegruta and Vlachos, 2016). The task can be seen as a variant of event extraction, where the date is the operand of the event, and a type is associated with each date-event pair.

Our goal is to retrieve all triples of the form (date, event, event class) from a given document using a pipeline consisting of SpaCy and ChatGPT. After the triples have been extracted, we place them along a timeline to create an overview of the decision process, an example of which can be seen in Figure 1. Note that each event is grounded in the document, and can be hyperlinked to the exact position in the document, allowing for quick verification. These constructed timelines can have several purposes, such as the graphical summarization of content (Hoeve et al., 2022), as well as being a part of process mining, where the event classification helps to gain insights in the different parts and their durations in a process. Furthermore, timeline extraction over a (dynamic) corpus is a valuable tool in automatic process monitoring. Our timelines are machine interpretable overviews of processes, making it easier to control and check them in real-time. Thus, timeline extraction also creates valuable metadata about temporal relations and intervals of events and event sequencing (Allen, 1983).

This study focuses on extracting timelines from decision letters produced by the Dutch government in response to a request made under the Dutch FOIA legislation. We used SpaCy to detect and extract dates from sentences, and ChatGPT to extract the event phrases and their classes. Out of the 524 triples in the test set, roughly 76% of them were classified correctly, and out of the 50 decision letters, the timelines of 10 of them were extracted perfectly.

2 Related Work

The field of timeline extraction has seen quite some interest in recent years, and it was featured as part of the SemEval 2010 TempEval and SemEval 2015 TimeLine challenges (Pustejovsky and Verhagen, 2009; Minard et al., 2015), where several aspects, such as the grounding of dates with events as well as the creation of cross-document timelines for entities were addressed. Traditionally, the systems used for timeline extraction have consisted of pipeline approaches, with a system containing a Part-of-Speech tagger, Named Entity Recognition (NER) and coreference resolution modules

Proceedings of the 7th Workshop on Challenges and Applications of Automated Extraction of Socio-political Events from Text (CASE 2024), pages 24–31
March 22, 2024 ©2024 Association for Computational Linguistics

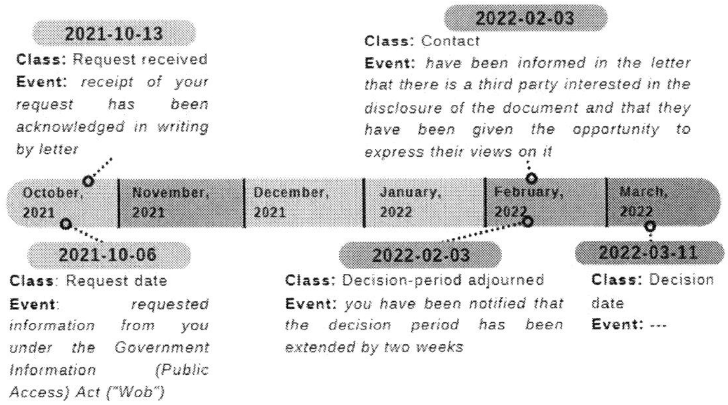

Figure 1: A timeline with five dated and classified events

in succession to extract event phrases (Aone and Ramos-Santacruz, 2000; Ahn, 2006; Minard et al., 2015), and systems such as HeidelTime (Strötgen and Gertz, 2010) to extract temporal phrases. As the annotation of these timelines can be quite expensive, some works focused on automatically constructing additional data, such as work done by Cornegruta and Vlachos (2016), who use distant supervision to create timelines for entities and use this additional data to train their pipeline model. A major downside of these pipeline approaches, as discussed by Du and Cardie (2020), is the propagation of errors from individual components in these systems, harming overall performance. The authors propose a method that does not use a pipeline, but instead uses a BERT model to extract events by posing the problem as a Question Answering task and querying the model, which is in some regards similar to our approach using ChatGPT. Another approach that replaces part of the pipeline with a neural component is work from Leeuwenberg and Moens (2018), which relies on entity annotations being present, and uses an LSTM network to predict the temporal durations of these entities, relative to each other.

With the advent of pre-trained Large Language Models (LLMs) such as ChatGPT and Llama (Touvron et al., 2023), new event extraction methods have been developed using these models (Xu et al., 2023). These methods are similar to the ones using BERT, but instead prompt these large language models to extract (actor, event, event type) triples directly from the input text. Although some of the models can be fine-tuned, a pre-trained LLM can usually perform quite well on new tasks, especially when using few-show prompting or in-context-learning. This involves providing several examples of the task that has to be performed to the model in the same prompt, helping the model in performing the task. Several techniques and best-practices for in-context learning exist, as surveyed by Dong et al. (2022). In our paper we experiment with the selection of the in-context examples, and use BM25 to select the top-k most similar datapoints from the trainingset, an approach similar to that used by Liu et al. (2021).

3 Method

3.1 Creation of the dataset

The dataset used in this research consists of 100 decision letters, written in Dutch, originating from Dutch ministries, all published in 2022. These decision letters were released as part of the WOOGLE project [1], and the documents are available as part of a curated dataset on the Dutch Scientific Data Repository (DANS)[2].

SpaCy[3] was used to extract sentences containing dates for annotation, which were subsequently filtered using regular expressions to remove false positives, resulting in a total of 812 sentences for annotation. The annotation process also included converting dates to ISO-format, such as *first of June 2021* to *01-06-2021*. The annotation was done by two annotators using an encoding scheme introduced by Schumann and QasemiZadeh (2015) for the annotation of terms and phrases in specialized domains. Events can be classified into eight possible classes, which were created through manual inspection of the decision letters, and by consulting

[1] https://woogle.wooverheid.nl/
[2] https://doi.org/10.17026/dans-zau-e3rk
[3] https://spacy.io

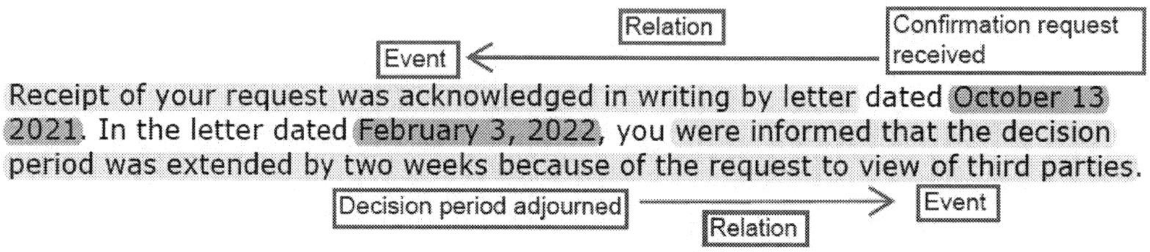

Figure 2: Example of an annotated segment of a decision letter (translated to English) with two dates each linked to one event

Task	κ	N
Date	1.0	26
Event Phrase	0.68	26
Event Class	0.91	26
Relation	0.62	26

Table 1: Inter-annotator agreement for a subset of the sentences calculated using Cohen's Kappa (N=26)

experts familiar with the Dutch FOIA legislation process.

To verify the agreement between the annotators, Cohen's Kappa was calculated for the dates, the event phrases, the event classes and the relations between dates and events (whether or not an event was linked to the correct date). The scores for these four different tasks are shown in Table 1. For the inter-annotator agreement of the event phrases, exact matching was used for the comparison, resulting in a relatively low score. However, the ROUGE-L F1 score, which measures the longest common subsequence between phrases, yields a score of 0.86, indicating a close alignment between the phrases extracted by both annotators. The Relation class also shows a relatively low score, something that is partially caused by the fact that event phrases consisting of multiple parts are rare, therefore having a large influence on the final agreement score. All event phrases consisting of a single phrase were correctly linked for both annotators. An example of an annotated text is shown in Figure 2, where two dates are linked to one event each.

The dataset was splitted equally into a training and a test set, where the two sets were split so that they each contained complete documents. The main statistics of both sets are presented in Table 2, and the distribution of the number of sentences in each document and the number of dates per sentence is shown in Figure 3. Of the 812 sentences in the dataset, 14 percent of the sentences contained more than one date.

3.2 Model

We used the *gpt-3.5-turbo-1106* checkpoint of ChatGPT, the latest iteration at the time of writing (December 2023), with the prompts written in Dutch, but translated to English for presentation in the paper. To facilitate the reproducibility of the results, the ChatGPT model was run with a temperature setting of 0.0, limiting the randomness in the output of the model. The code and dataset are publicly available on GitHub. [4]

3.3 Our timeline extraction approach

Our timeline extraction pipeline operates directly on the text extracted from a decision letter, obtained using either text extraction tools for PDF, or through optical character recognition software. Below is a brief outline of the approach, also illustrated in Figure 4.

- **Sentence Splitting** The text extracted from a PDF file is split into individual sentences with a sentence tokenizer for Dutch from NLTK.
- **Date Extraction** Sentences containing dates are extracted using SpaCy, and several rules are applied to filter out non-dates.
- **Event Phrase Extraction** Given a sentence and a list of dates, ChatGPT is prompted to return the event phrase associated with each date.
- **Event Phrase Classification** Given a list of event phrases, ChatGPT is prompted to classify the event phrase into seven possible classes.
- **Decision Date Classification** Extract the *Decision date* using regular expressions, as these dates are usually not linked to an event in text.

[4] https://github.com/irlabamsterdam/TimeLineExtractionDecisionLettersCASE

Portion	Number of Documents	Number of Sentences	Number of dates
Train	50	376	414
Test	50	445	524
Total	100	812	938

Table 2: Overview of the number of documents, number of sentences and the number of dates for both the train and test partitions

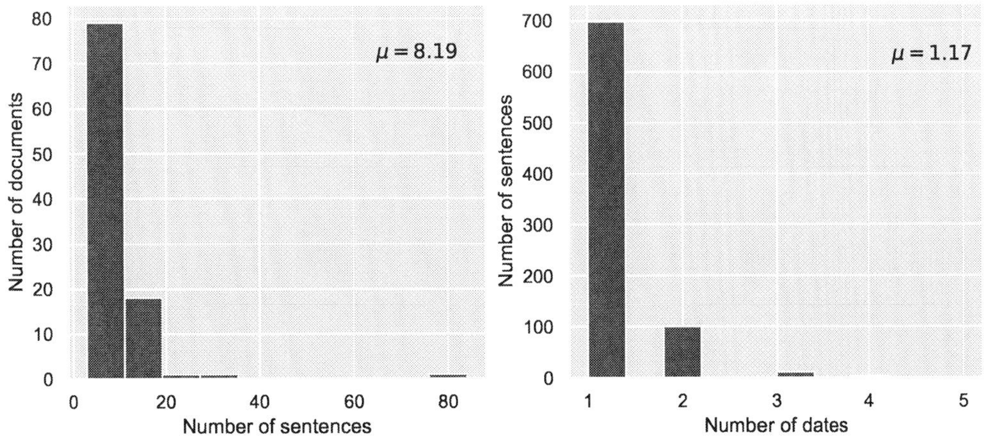

Figure 3: Number of sentences in each document for the complete dataset (N=100) and the number of dates in each sentence for all sentences in the dataset (N=812)

The individual steps of the algorithm are explained in more detail below.

Step 1: Sentence Splitting The first step in the pipeline is the splitting of the text of a document into separate sentences, which is done by using a sentence tokenizer for Dutch from NLTK. By splitting the text into sentences, sentences without dates can easily be discarded in the next step.

Step 2: Extract sentences containing dates with SpaCy In the second step, SpaCy is run to identify sentences that contain dates. This produces quite a lot of false positives, which are filtered by discarding dates that do not contain a month, as most false positives had that form.

Step 3: Extract event phrases and classes using ChatGPT The extraction and classification of the events associated with the dates from Step 2 is done by prompting the model two times. In the first step, a list of dates and a sentence containing these dates is fed to ChatGPT, and the model has to return the event phrase associated with each date, or return 'no event' if no event was detected.

Prompt: *You are given a list of dates and a sentence containing these dates. It is your task to extract the descriptions of the events happening on these dates, or to return 'No event' if no event took place on that date.*

Return your output as a list of tuples with each tuple consisting of a date and the event associated with it.

Example input: Concerning the decision on your WOO-request, October 1st, 2022

Example output: [('2020-10-01', 'Decision on your WOO-request')]

After these events were extracted, the model was prompted a second time, now with the list of event phrases, and was asked to classify them into the seven possible classes. If no event was detected in the first step then the event was automatically labelled with 'no event'.

Prompt: *You are given a list of event descriptions and it is your task to classify each of these descriptions into one of the following classes.*
1. Decision period adjourned: The decision on the WOO request has been adjourned
2. Contact: Communication took place between

the person filing the request and the relevant organization
3. WOO legislation in effect: The woo legislation came into effect, on the first of May 2020
4. Confirmation request received: The confirmation of receiving the WOO request
5. Request date: On this date a WOO request has been filed, requesting information trough the WOO legislation
6. Requested received: The WOO requested has been received by the relevant organization
7. Other: Any description that does not fall under any of the previous classes

Example input: ['you have been informed of the latest status update at the departments of ILT and RWS']

Example output: ['contact']

For both steps, the examples provided to ChatGPT were selected using an approach mentioned by Liu et al. (2021). BM25 is used to select the top examples for both the event extraction and event classification prompts. In the case of event phrase extraction, the examples were selected from the training set by retrieving the 5 most similar sentences together with their ground truth event phrases. For the classification of the event, 2 examples of similar event phrases were retrieved from the training set for each event phrase in the sentence.

Step 3: Classifying decision dates As the decision dates are usually not linked to an event in the text, but often appear at the top of a letter in a set format, these were not extracted using ChatGPT, but by using regular expressions to capture patterns such as *Datum: 2023-11-01*.

3.4 Evaluation

The evaluation of the date extraction is done by using accuracy, comparing the predicted an ground truth dates. For the evaluation of the event phrase extraction the ROUGE-L metric (Lin, 2004) is used, which computes the Longest Common Subsequence (LCS) between the tokenized representations of the ground truth and predicted texts. This metric is well-suited for the evaluation of the event extraction component, as the extracted events should be literal extracts from the letter.

To determine whether or not an extracted event phrase is correct, we follow work done by Kuhn et al. (2023) and classify an extracted event as correct only if it has a ROUGE-L F1 score of 0.5 or higher.

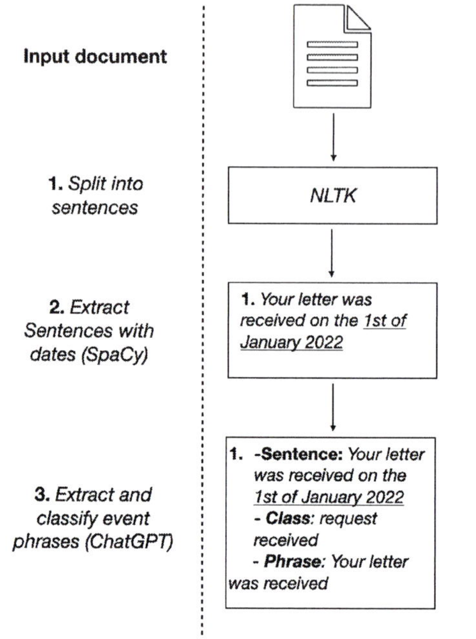

Figure 4: High level overview of the timeline extraction pipeline for an input document.

We evaluate the total accuracy of the model both in the percentage of triples that are classified correctly, as well as how many documents the pipeline classifies completely correct. For the evaluation of the event extraction and classification parts, only the triples of dates that were returned by ChatGPT were considered, as in several instances extra triples that were not in the ground truth were returned by ChatGPT. For the event classification task, the inputs to the model were the ground truth event phrases, to judge its classification performance without being influenced by the previous steps.

4 Results

4.1 Date Extraction

The date extraction part of the pipeline achieves an accuracy of .94 on all the dates in the test set. When the model is incorrect, it was usually because of ambiguity in the date, such as *In the month of June*, where the model might pick a random date belonging to that month.

4.2 Event Extraction

For the event phrase extraction, the model achieves an average ROUGE-L F1 score of .80 on the event

Table 3: Evaluation scores for event classification using ChatGPT (N=218)

	Precision	Recall	F1-score	Support
Decision period adjourned	0.93	0.93	0.93	29
Contact	0.89	0.79	0.84	42
WOO legislation in effect	1.00	1.00	1.00	16
Confirmation request received	1.00	0.98	0.99	44
Other	0.73	0.67	0.70	24
Request date	0.98	0.98	0.98	48
Request received	0.75	1.00	0.86	15

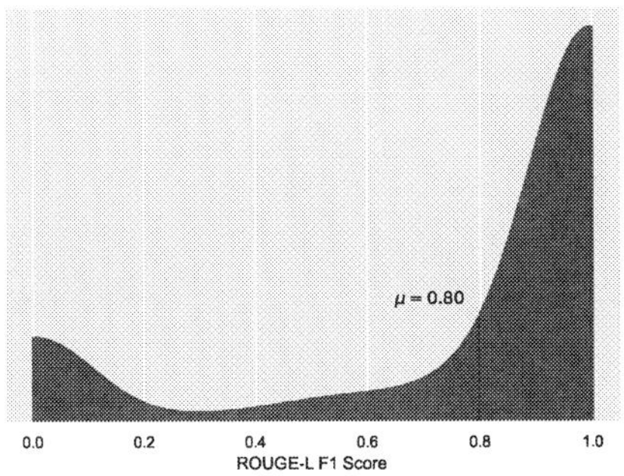

Figure 5: Distribution of the ROUGE-L F1 scores for the event phrases extracted by ChatGPT.

phrases, with a precision of .83 and a recall of .78. When thresholded at 0.5, 82% of the extracted event phrases were correct. The distribution of the ROUGE-L scores is shown in Figure 5. Although most scores are quite close to one, there is a significant number of event phrases that received a score of zero. Upon further examination it was found that these were exclusively cases where the date was not associated with an event in the ground truth, but the model still retrieved an event phrase.

4.3 Event Classification

Table 3 shows the results of the event classification with ChatGPT, with an overall macro F1 score of .79. The 'WOO legislation in effect' class achieves an almost perfect score, which is explained by the fact that this event is almost always described using the exact same phrase, simply specifying the date on which the law became effective. The model performs worst on the *other* class, which is unsurprising given the fact that this class contains all the events that could not be classified into the other classes and thus there is no clear description for what fits in this class. In these cases, the provided examples will most likely not help much either.

One of the reasons that the model performs very well on the event classification task is that most of the event phrases follow similar patterns and use similar vocabulary across different documents, and thus supplying the model with similar sentences in the prompt helps in classifying the event correctly.

4.4 Decision Date Classification

The decision dates that were extracted using regular expressions achieved an accuracy of .96, where two mistakes were made out of the total of 48 triples that contained a decision date.

4.5 Timeline Construction

Out of the 524 the triples in the test set, roughly 76% of them were completely correct, where a majority of the mistakes can be attributed to ChatGPT failing to return a prediction for the date (for examples four dates being given as input put only three event phrases being returned).

Finally, we look at the correctness of the constructed timelines, where each decision letter contains exactly one timeline. In 20% of the letters, the complete timeline was extracted correctly, with the mode of the number of mistakes in a timeline being 1 and the average being 3.2. This relatively low amount of completely correct documents can be explained by the fact that documents contain on average roughly 8 dates, and thus classifying all of them correctly is quite a strict way of evaluating the performance. Although the amount of completely correct timeline is relatively low, the fact that a majority of the triples is correct and the mode of the number of mistakes is quite low, means that the graphical summarization can still be considered useful in getting a rough idea on the timelines, and mistakes can be easily spotted. Moreover, as there is a clear chronological order in the events (a request has to be received before a confirmation can be sent for example), this logic can be used to filter out obvious mistakes in event classification, and will most likely result in even less errors.

5 Discussion

Although the proposed pipeline achieves good performance on the task of event extraction and classification for decision letters, the fact that it relies on ChatGPT, a commercial and closed-source product has certain downsides. Although we have tried to mitigate the inherent randomness in the ChatGPT model, it is possible that there are minor inconsistencies in performance between runs. A possible direction for future work is the usage of open-source LLMs such as Llama-2 to facilitate the usage of this work in practice, and to alleviate some of the aforementioned problems. The goal of this work was to evaluate a pipeline consisting of SpaCy and ChatGPT, with as little components as possible, to prevent the propagation of errors. Although several components could have been implemented by using different models, such as a parsing-based approach for the event extraction, or by using another neural model such as BERT, the fact that ChatGPT is pre-trained meant that there was very little need for training data, and a small dataset could be used for evaluating the proposed approach.

6 Conclusion

We have shown that a quite accurate timeline extractor for a specific domain can be constructed using a promptable LLM like ChatGPT, with a very limited number of training examples, in a relatively low-resource language such as Dutch, using few-shot prompting and selecting similar examples using BM25. For future work, we could look into fine-tuning an open-source LLM such as Llama for this specific task, or maybe consider generating training samples for the task using an LLM and using these to train another system.

Acknowledgements

This research was supported in part by the Netherlands Organization for Scientific Research (NWO) through the ACCESS project grant CISC.CC.016.

References

David Ahn. 2006. The Stages of Event Extraction. In *Proceedings of the Workshop on Annotating and Reasoning about Time and Events*, pages 1–8.

James F Allen. 1983. Maintaining Knowledge About Temporal Intervals. *Communications of the ACM*, 26(11):832–843.

Chinatsu Aone and Mila Ramos-Santacruz. 2000. REES: A Large-Scale Relation and Event Extraction System. In *Sixth Applied Natural Language Processing Conference (ANLP)*, pages 76–83, Seattle, Washington, USA. Association for Computational Linguistics.

Savelie Cornegruta and Andreas Vlachos. 2016. Timeline Extraction using Distant Supervision and Joint Inference. In *Proceedings of the 2016 Conference on Empirical Methods in Natural Language Processing (EMNLP)*, pages 1936–1942.

Qingxiu Dong, Lei Li, Damai Dai, Ce Zheng, Zhiyong Wu, Baobao Chang, Xu Sun, Jingjing Xu, and Zhifang Sui. 2022. A Survey for In-Context Learning. *arXiv preprint arXiv:2301.00234*.

Xinya Du and Claire Cardie. 2020. Event Extraction by Answering (Almost) Natural Questions. In *Proceedings of the 2020 Conference on Empirical Methods in Natural Language Processing (EMNLP)*, pages 671–683. Association for Computational Linguistics.

Maartje ter Hoeve, Julia Kiseleva, and Maarten de Rijke. 2022. Summarization with Graphical Elements. *arXiv preprint arXiv:2302.13971*.

Lorenz Kuhn, Yarin Gal, and Sebastian Farquhar. 2023. Semantic uncertainty: Linguistic invariances for uncertainty estimation in natural language generation. *arXiv preprint arXiv:2302.09664*.

Artuur Leeuwenberg and Marie-Francine Moens. 2018. Temporal Information Extraction by Predicting Relative Time-lines. In *Proceedings of the 2018 Conference on Empirical Methods in Natural Language Processing (EMNLP)*, pages 1237–1246, Brussels, Belgium. Association for Computational Linguistics.

Chin-Yew Lin. 2004. ROUGE: A Package for Automatic Evaluation of Summaries. In *Text Summarization Branches Out*, pages 74–81, Barcelona, Spain. Association for Computational Linguistics.

Jiachang Liu, Dinghan Shen, Yizhe Zhang, Bill Dolan, Lawrence Carin, and Weizhu Chen. 2021. What Makes Good In-Context Examples for GPT-3? *arXiv preprint arXiv:2101.06804*.

Anne-Lyse Myriam Minard, Manuela Speranza, Eneko Agirre, Itziar Aldabe, Marieke Van Erp, Bernardo Magnini, German Rigau, and Ruben Urizar. 2015. Semeval-2015 Task 4: Timeline: Cross-Document Event Ordering. In *proceedings of the 9th International Workshop on Semantic Evaluation (SemEval 2015)*, pages 778–786.

James Pustejovsky and Marc Verhagen. 2009. SemEval-2010 Task 13: Evaluating Events, Time Expressions, and Temporal Relations (TempEval-2). In

Proceedings of the Workshop on Semantic Evaluations: Recent Achievements and Future Directions (SEW-2009), pages 112–116.

Anne-Kathrin Schumann and Behrang QasemiZadeh. 2015. The ACL RD-TEC Annotation Guideline: A Reference Dataset for the Evaluation of Automatic Term Recognition and Classification.

Jannik Strötgen and Michael Gertz. 2010. HeidelTime: High Quality Rule-Based Extraction and Normalization of Temporal Expressions. In *Proceedings of the 5th International Workshop on Semantic Evaluation (SemEval)*, pages 321–324.

Hugo Touvron, Thibaut Lavril, Gautier Izacard, Xavier Martinet, Marie-Anne Lachaux, Timothée Lacroix, Baptiste Rozière, Naman Goyal, Eric Hambro, Faisal Azhar, et al. 2023. Llama: Open and Efficient Foundation Language Models. *arXiv preprint arXiv:2302.13971*.

Xin Xu, Yuqi Zhu, Xiaohan Wang, and Ningyu Zhang. 2023. How to Unleash the Power of Large Language Models for Few-shot Relation Extraction? In *Proceedings of The Fourth Workshop on Simple and Efficient Natural Language Processing (SustaiNLP)*, pages 190–200, Toronto, Canada (Hybrid). Association for Computational Linguistics.

Leveraging Approximate Pattern Matching with BERT for Event Detection

Hristo Tanev
European Commission, Joint Research Centre,
via Enrico Fermi 2749,
Ispra 21020, Italy
hristo.tanev@ec.europa.eu

Abstract

We describe a new weakly supervised method for sentence-level event detection, based exclusively on linear prototype patterns. We propose a BERT based algorithm for approximate pattern matching to identify event phrases, semantically similar to these prototypes. To the best of our knowledge, this is the first time a similar approach is used in the context of event detection. We experimented with two event corpora in the area of disease outbreaks and terrorism and we achieved promising results in sentence level event identification, 0.78 F1 score for new disease cases and 0.68 F1 for terrorist attacks. Results were in line with two state-of-the art systems, based on supervised ML and sophisticated linguistic rules.

1 Introduction

Early event extraction systems predominantly rely on pattern matching and linguistic rules (Xiang and Wang, 2019). This approach remains particularly effective in well-defined domains, such as disease outbreaks, biomedical papers, disasters, security, and socio-political developments, where language is clearly structured Tanev et al. (2008); Valenzuela-Escárcega et al. (2015); Nitschke et al. (2022).

In specific contexts, linguistic rules can offer competitive precision and enhanced transparency compared to machine learning (ML) models (Chiticariu et al., 2013). Linguistic rules can also be used for automatic corpus annotation, when new domains of event extraction are being considered and no training data is available (Wang et al., 2019). The transparency inherent in linguistic rules is particularly vital in real-world event extraction applications. End users can provide feedback on the performance of specific keywords and phrases, thereby improving the accuracy and breadth of the rule set.

In this work we argue that the combination of manually crafted linear patterns and Large Language Models (LLM) is a promising avenue for combining the strengths of the knowledge based approaches and the LLM in the domain of event detection. We experimented in the domains of security and health, but we think that the approach is applicable across a wide range of domains and event classes. LLM like BERT (Devlin et al., 2018) offer the capability to create utterance abstractions, using the contextualized word embeddings, which can be received from the embedding layer of the BERT neural network, see Figure 1. In the context of event detection, this allows for creating simple linear patterns as prototypes, e.g. "people have got a disease", and using the BERT contextualized embeddings of both prototypes and analysed text to find the semantic relation between the patterns and their lexical variations in the text, e.g. "children have got influenza".

More concretely, we propose the following approach, starting with prototype patterns (here we consider the event types *new disease cases* and *terrorist attacks*) like "disease outbreak", "number people were infected" or "bomb exploded", to discovers in the test set sentences containing text fragments, containing words with similar BERT embedding vectors - "influenza outbreak", "COVID was discovered in 2 foreign nationals", or "blast killed", etc. These phrases are supposed to be semantically similar to the prototypes, because of their similarity in the BERT encoding. Our experiments demonstrated that BERT-based pattern matching is able to infer event mentions which have significant lexical and syntactic differences with respect to the prototype patterns.

We tested our approach on the task of detecting sentences containing events of a predefined event type. Two event classes were considered in our experiments: *new disease cases* and *terrorist attacks*. For both of them we achieved performance much higher than the baseline. Moreover, for the event type *new disease cases*, the achieved performance was in line with other systems, based on supervised

Proceedings of the 7th Workshop on Challenges and Applications of Automated Extraction of Socio-political Events from Text (CASE 2024), pages 32–39
March 22, 2024

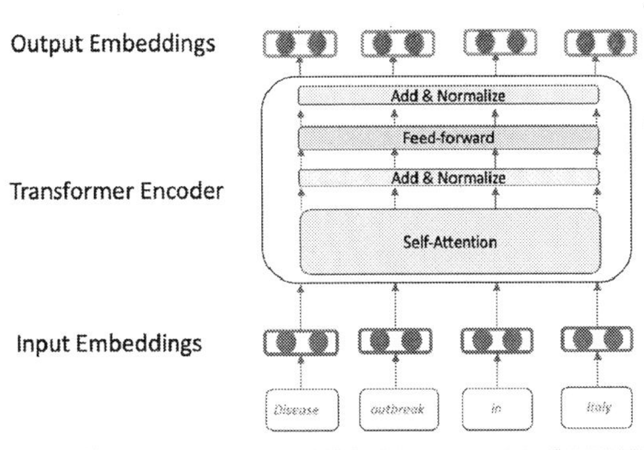

Figure 1: BERT contextualized embeddings

ML.

2 Related work

Event detection at various levels: token, sentence and document level has been largely addressed in previous work. The CASE shared task on protest detection and the participating systems (Hürriyetoğlu et al., 2021) tackle event detection at all the three levels. Various methods for sentence-level event detection are studied in Naughton et al. (2010).

A survey of the existing event detection and extraction approaches were presented in (Hogenboom et al., 2011) and (Xiang and Wang, 2019)

Pattern matching is a well established method for extracting event triggers and arguments. Earlier event extraction systems massively exploited lexico-syntactic patterns (Xiang and Wang, 2019). Most of these systems used domain specific grammars and ontologies in complex linguistic patterns. It is noteworthy that some of the state-of-the-art systems in the domain of security use linear patterns and linguistic rules Tanev et al. (2008); Atkinson et al. (2013); Nitschke et al. (2022). Similarly, rule-based event extraction is used in the biomedical domain Bui et al. (2013); Valenzuela-Escárcega et al. (2015).

Related to the prototype pattern matching we propose here, is another BERT based entity matching approach (Paganelli et al., 2022). BERT pattern matching is also used in Question Answering to find similar questions (Wang et al., 2020). Supervised learning, considering event triggers, is described in several works: (Liao et al., 2021), (Hao et al., 2023), (Lai et al., 2021), and (Tuo et al., 2023).

3 The approach

The approximate pattern matching approach is designed to identify in a test corpus the sentences containing event descriptions. At the same time, the algorithm identifies an n-gram in each of these sentences, matching best one of the prototypes.

In our experiments we considered two event types - *new disease cases* and *terrorist attacks*, however we think that the method is applicable across various domains and event classes.

3.1 User-Generated Pattern Set

The foundation of our method rests on an input set of prototypes, which are linear event detection patterns. The prototypes are phrases describing event triggers together with the most important event arguments, such as actors or victims. In this experiment, we used as triggers and arguments generic concepts, such as "disease", "people", "sick", etc. A sentence containing a phrase semantically similar to one of the prototype patterns should indicate the presence of the targeted event. In the context of disease outbreak detection, relevant patterns include "people got disease," "people are sick," "new cases of disease," and "disease outbreak," encapsulating generic concepts such as "people" and "disease."

To perform approximate pattern matching, we leverage BERT context embeddings (Figure 1), comparing the token embeddings of each pattern with the token embeddings of the test sentence. The vector sequence matching is described in the following subsection. The matching process enables the identification of texts containing more

Corpus	Event type	All sent.	Positive sent.	Patterns
Disease outbreaks	New disease cases	212	62	40
Political violence and disasters	Terrorist attack	994	97	21

Table 1: Test data and evaluation settings

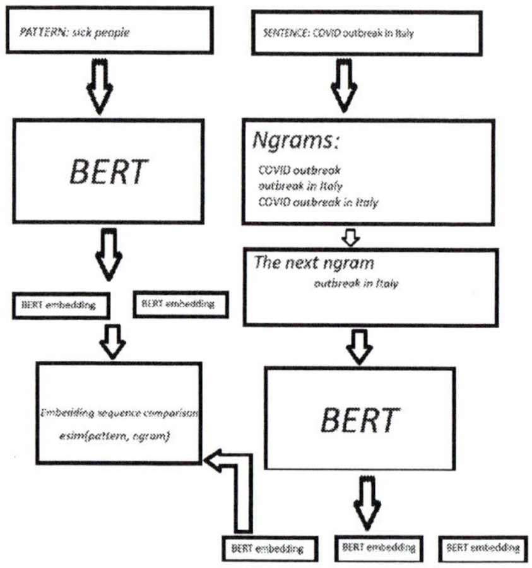

Figure 2: Comparing pattern and a sentence

concrete concepts or synonyms instantiating the generic ones from the prototypes, illustrated by event phrases like "students got influenza," "men are ill," "new cases of COVID," and "zika outbreak."

In our experimental configuration, we opted for the use of generic concepts, such as "people" in the input set of patterns, driven by the simplicity in pattern creation. Nevertheless, we have to acknowledge that the incorporation of concrete concepts, such as in "children got flu," is also a viable prototyping approach.

3.2 Calculating sentence eventness via approximate pattern matching

Given a set of event detection patterns

$Patterns = p_1, p_2, \ldots, p_n$ and a sentence s,

the approximate pattern recognition is used to calculate the *sentence eventness* of s, a non probability function in the interval $[0, 1]$, which shows how well the best pattern from the sequence matches the text.

Since patterns should be created in such a way that they describe unambiguously an event, the $eventness$ score should also be indicative about the likelihood of s containing an event of the specified class. Clearly, various discourse phenomena like questioning, conditional statements, negation, semantic ambiguity and others can play a role in preventing pattern matching from estimating correctly the sentence eventness.

Below, we outline the procedure for calculating the "eventness" of a sentence s. Steps 1 to 5 of this algorithm are also shown on Figure 2.

1. Each pattern $p_i = w_1 w_2 ... w_{in}$, where w_k is a word, generates a sequence of BERT embedding vectors, one for each word w_k. The sequence is denoted as $es(p_i)$.

2. From s, all word ngrams with size between 2 and 20 words are generated, denoted as $ngrams(s)$.

   For example, for the sentence s ="The crowd in Damascus shouted slogans.", $ngrams(s)$ ={"crowd in Damascus", "crowd in Damascus shouted", crowd in Damascus shouted slogans", "Damascus shouted", "Damascus shouted slogans", "shouted slogans"}

3. The sentence s is transformed into a sequence of word embedding vectors $es(s)$, in the same way $es(p_i)$ was obtained in step 1.

4. For each ngram $ng \in ngrams(s)$, its subsequence of corresponding embedding vectors is taken from $es(s)$. For example, for the ngram

Event type	$\alpha = 0.6$	$\alpha = 0.65$	$\alpha = 0.7$	Baseline
New disease cases	0.75	**0.78**	0.65	0.32
Terrorist attack	0.61	0.68	0.68	0.09
Macro average	0.68	0.73	0.67	0.21

Table 2: F1 score for various thresholds and baseline "exact pattern matching"

"crowd in Damascus", we will take the second, third and fourth embedding vector from $es(s)$. We denote the subsequence of embedding vectors for ng as $ses(ng, s)$.

5. Finally, we propose a similarity function $esim$ for comparing sequences of embedding vectors and calculating the eventness of s, $ev(s)$, via the following formula:
   $ev(s) = \max_{p,ng} esim(es(p), ses(ng, s))$, where $p \in Patterns, ng \in ngrams(s)$.

6. If $ev(s) > \alpha$, then s is considered a sentence containing an event. The threshold α is being set empirically.

We describe in details the eventness calculation in Appendix A and in Figure 3.

4 Experiments

To assess the efficacy and adaptability of our event detection methodology, we collected a test set of two distinct event corpora, each derived from a disparate domain: disease outbreaks (Piskorski et al., 2023) and politically motivated violence and disasters (Atkinson et al., 2017a). A unique targeted event type was specified for each corpus. Table 1 shows the parameters of the corpora and the targeted event types.

Our approach involves the systematic crafting of a set of carefully tailored linear patterns for the specific event types. The formulation of patterns drew upon insights derived from a development set, encompassing 300 sentences extracted from each respective corpus. This was done in the following steps:

1. We have created an initial set of patterns using our knowledge of the domain, getting additional insights from the development set.

2. Then, we matched these patterns on the sentences from the development corpus, using our approximate pattern matching algorithm.

3. We analyzed in random a subset of the false positives and false negatives.

4. We deleted patterns generating many false positives and created new patterns to detect the false negatives

5. This pattern development cycle was repeated several times (3-7) for each event type.

Generally, the creation of linguistic patterns is a intricate process, usually encompassing a combination of machine learning techniques and expert assessment (Tanev et al., 2009). However, in this study, our approach involved crafting patterns primarily based on linguistic expertise, with the development set used to assess their coverage and precision. The pattern development process was not the central focus of our work. Instead, we followed a pragmatic approach akin to what an average pattern developer might undertake, aiming for optimal results without substantial time investment.

In order to test the accuracy of the prototypes, we randomly selected a test subset from each corpus, non overlapping with the development set. Table 1 provides a comprehensive overview of the parameters defining each test set. These encompass the corpus name, targeted event type, total sentence count, and the frequency of positive instances (the sentences featuring the targeted event type), along with the number of developed linear patterns.

Before we run the algorithm, we had to set the α eventness threshold. Our observation on the development set was that the threshold delivers meaningful results in the interval 0.6 to 0.7. Therefore, we have run the evaluation with three different values for α: 0.6, 0.65, and 0.7.

We applied our approximate pattern matching detection of sentences on each corpus for each of the three α threshold values. Table 2 reports the obtained F1 score for each of the three thresholds.

We have also defined a baseline - *exact pattern matching*: if even one pattern is contained as a substring in a sentence, then the sentence is considered to contain an event. In Table 2 we report the F1 measure of this baseline.

Experiments showed that our method outpaced by a considerable margin the baseline. At the same

Matching n-gram with surroundings	Pattern
...the **number of confirmed** COVID-19 cases...	number of infected
The **number of Zika virus cases** has crossed 100 ...	number of infected
...raising the **death toll due to the disease** to 11 ...	death toll from the outbreak
...the situation where the **observed number of cases** exceeds...	number of infected
...the number of people **testing positive for the infection** rose...	testing positive for virus
...321 new domestically **transmitted coronavirus cases**...	confirmed disease cases
...**proportion of those testing** positive to the total tests...	number of infected
...**New clusters of coronavirus infections are igniting** concerns...	new infection cases
...new **confirmed coronavirus infections** have hit a record...	confirmed disease cases

Table 3: Patterns and their **matching n-grams** with the surrounding sentence fragment

time, the performance of the event class *new disease cases* achieved quite promising $F1$ score. Although conducted on different test sets, it is worth mentioning that this $F1$ score is in line with the accuracy achieved by some supervised systems in the outbreak detection domain. (Conway et al., 2009; Khatua et al., 2019).

Approximate pattern matching showed lower accuracy on the terrorist attacks with respect to the disease cases detection, still the $F1$ score stayed close to the performance of another early event extraction system in the area of security (Tanev et al., 2008; Atkinson et al., 2017b). It's important to emphasize that these evaluations were conducted on different corpora, providing only a general and imprecise basis for comparison.

Analysing the errors for the terrorist attack event type, we saw that there are text fragments matched against the patterns, where terrorists were victims, rather than attackers. Some sentences describing assassinations and kidnappings, especially in the Middle East were also erroneously labeled as terrorist attacks. For example, the phrase "victim of an assassination attempt" erroneously matched the pattern "victim of a terrorist attack". Also "air raid killed civilians" erroneously matched the pattern "market bomb targeted civilians". These and other pattern matching errors clearly show that in some cases the BERT pattern matching may be misled by particular phrases in certain contexts.

5 Conclusions

Results from Table 2 indicate that our approach attains satisfactory accuracy; nonetheless, its performance may vary across event classes. The performance, achieved in the detection of *new disease cases*, was a notable outcome considering the absence of supervision and the comparable accuracy observed in other supervised systems for detection of disease reports, (Conway et al., 2009), (Khatua et al., 2019). In Table 3 we show some of the prototypes for new disease cases and their matching n-grams in context. It is evident that approximate pattern matching can capture various syntactic and lexical variations.

Moreover, some of the detected n-grams are relevant as event detecting phrases and they themselves can constitute prototypes. Following this line of thinking, the approximate pattern matching algorithm can also be used for learning of new patterns.

As a conclusion, our experiments show that BERT-based pattern matching is an efficient weakly supervised event classifier. This method combines the simplicity and transparency of the pattern-based approaches and the implicit semantic knowledge, encoded in large language models like BERT.

References

Martin Atkinson, Mian Du, Jakub Piskorski, Hristo Tanev, Roman Yangarber, and Vanni Zavarella. 2013. Techniques for multilingual security-related event extraction from online news. *Computational Linguistics: Applications*, pages 163–186.

Martin Atkinson, Jakub Piskorski, Hristo Tanev, and Vanni Zavarella. 2017a. On the creation of a security-related event corpus. In *Proceedings of the Events and Stories in the News Workshop*, pages 59–65.

Martin Atkinson, Jakub Piskorski, Hristo Tanev, and Vanni Zavarella. 2017b. On the creation of a security-related event corpus. In *Proceedings of the Events and Stories in the News Workshop*, pages 59–65, Vancouver, Canada. Association for Computational Linguistics.

Quoc-Chinh Bui, David Campos, Erik van Mulligen, and Jan Kors. 2013. A fast rule-based approach for biomedical event extraction. In *proceedings of the BioNLP shared task 2013 workshop*, pages 104–108.

Laura Chiticariu, Yunyao Li, and Frederick Reiss. 2013. Rule-based information extraction is dead! long live rule-based information extraction systems! In *Proceedings of the 2013 conference on empirical methods in natural language processing*, pages 827–832.

Mike Conway, Son Doan, Ai Kawazoe, and Nigel Collier. 2009. Classifying disease outbreak reports using n-grams and semantic features. *International journal of medical informatics*, 78(12):e47–e58.

Jacob Devlin, Ming-Wei Chang, Kenton Lee, and Kristina Toutanova. 2018. BERT: Pre-training of deep bidirectional transformers for language understanding. *arXiv preprint arXiv:1810.04805*.

Anran Hao, Anh Tuan Luu, Siu Cheung Hui, and Jian Su. 2023. A contrastive learning framework for event detection via semantic type prototype representation modelling. *Neurocomputing*, 556:126613.

Frederik Hogenboom, Flavius Frasincar, Uzay Kaymak, and Franciska De Jong. 2011. An overview of event extraction from text. *DeRiVE@ ISWC*, pages 48–57.

Ali Hürriyetoğlu, Hristo Tanev, Vanni Zavarella, Jakub Piskorski, Reyyan Yeniterzi, and Erdem Yörük. 2021. Challenges and applications of automated extraction of socio-political events from text (CASE 2021): Workshop and shared task report. *arXiv preprint arXiv:2108.07865*.

Aparup Khatua, Apalak Khatua, and Erik Cambria. 2019. A tale of two epidemics: Contextual word2vec for classifying twitter streams during outbreaks. *Information Processing & Management*, 56(1):247–257.

Viet Lai, Franck Dernoncourt, and Thien Huu Nguyen. 2021. Learning prototype representations across few-shot tasks for event detection. In *Proceedings of the 2021 Conference on Empirical Methods in Natural Language Processing (EMNLP 2021)*.

Jinzhi Liao, Xiang Zhao, Xinyi Li, Lingling Zhang, and Jiuyang Tang. 2021. Learning discriminative neural representations for event detection. In *Proceedings of the 44th International ACM SIGIR Conference on Research and Development in Information Retrieval*, pages 644–653.

Martina Naughton, Nicola Stokes, and Joe Carthy. 2010. Sentence-level event classification in unstructured texts. *Information retrieval*, 13:132–156.

Remo Nitschke, Yuwei Wang, Chen Chen, Adarsh Pyarelal, and Rebecca Sharp. 2022. Rule based event extraction for artificial social intelligence. In *Proceedings of the First Workshop on Pattern-based Approaches to NLP in the Age of Deep Learning*, pages 71–84, Gyeongju, Republic of Korea. International Conference on Computational Linguistics.

Matteo Paganelli, Francesco Del Buono, Andrea Baraldi, Francesco Guerra, et al. 2022. Analyzing how BERT performs entity matching. *Proceedings of the VLDB Endowment*, 15(8):1726–1738.

Jakub Piskorski, Nicolas Stefanovitch, Brian Doherty, Jens P Linge, Sopho Kharazi, Jas Mantero, Guillaume Jacquet, Alessio Spadaro, and Giulia Teodori. 2023. Multi-label infectious disease news event corpus. In *Proceedings of the Text2Story'23 Workshop*.

Hristo Tanev, Jakub Piskorski, and Martin Atkinson. 2008. Real-time news event extraction for global crisis monitoring. In *Natural Language and Information Systems: 13th International Conference on Applications of Natural Language to Information Systems, NLDB 2008 London, UK, June 24-27, 2008 Proceedings 13*, pages 207–218. Springer.

Hristo Tanev, Vanni Zavarella, Jens Linge, Mijail Kabadjov, Jakub Piskorski, Martin Atkinson, and Ralf Steinberger. 2009. Exploiting machine learning techniques to build an event extraction system for portuguese and spanish. *Linguamática*, 1(2):55–66.

Aboubacar Tuo, Romaric Besançon, Olivier Ferret, and Julien Tourille. 2023. Trigger or not trigger: Dynamic thresholding for few shot event detection. In *European Conference on Information Retrieval*, pages 637–645. Springer.

Marco A Valenzuela-Escárcega, Gus Hahn-Powell, Mihai Surdeanu, and Thomas Hicks. 2015. A domain-independent rule-based framework for event extraction. In *Proceedings of ACL-IJCNLP 2015 system demonstrations*, pages 127–132.

Xiaozhi Wang, Xu Han, Zhiyuan Liu, Maosong Sun, and Peng Li. 2019. Adversarial training for weakly supervised event detection. In *Proceedings of the 2019 Conference of the North American Chapter of the Association for Computational Linguistics: Human Language Technologies, Volume 1 (Long and Short Papers)*, pages 998–1008, Minneapolis, Minnesota. Association for Computational Linguistics.

Zizhen Wang, Yixing Fan, Jiafeng Guo, Liu Yang, Ruqing Zhang, Yanyan Lan, Xueqi Cheng, Hui Jiang, and Xiaozhao Wang. 2020. Match^2: A matching over matching model for similar question identification. In *Proceedings of the 43rd international ACM SIGIR conference on research and development in information retrieval*, pages 559–568.

Wei Xiang and Bang Wang. 2019. A survey of event extraction from text. *IEEE Access*, 7:173111–173137.

A Approximate pattern matching and eventness calculation algorithm

Given a set of event detection patterns
$Patterns = p_1, p_2, \ldots, p_n$
and a sentence s, the approximate pattern recognition calculates how likely it is that s contains an event, which we call *sentence eventness*. The approximate matching and the related *eventness* calculation happen in the following steps:

1. Encode each pattern p_i via a sequence of contextualized embedding vectors, using BERT: For each token from the pattern we take the contextualized word embedding vector from the *last layer of the encoder network*. Thus, we have a *sequence of context embedding vectors* with the length of the number of tokens in p_i. If, for example, the pattern is "protesters demand", the sequence will consist of two embedding vectors, one for each word. Lets call this *context embedding sequence* $es(p_i)$. Similarly, we obtain a sequence of embedding vectors for the sentence s, $es(s)$.

2. From the target sentence s, generate all the 2 to 20-grams which start and finish with a non-stop word, lets denote these n-grams with $ngrams(s)$. As an example, consider the sentence $s =$"The crowd in Damascus shouted slogans.", the $ngrams(s)$ will consists of the following ngrams: "crowd in Damascus", "crowd in Damascus shouted", crowd in Damascus shouted slogans", "Damascus shouted", "Damascus shouted slogans", and "shouted slogans".

3. For each n-gram $ng \in ngrams(s)$ we obtain the contextualized BERT embeddings $ses(ng, s)$: Note, we do not pass the ng to BERT for calculating the contextualized embedding vectors, but rather we take the corresponding embedding vectors from the embedding vector sequence of the whole sentence $es(s)$, ensuring better contextualization.

   In the example above, the vector sequence obtained from "crowd in Damascus" will be obtained as a subsequence (namely, the second, third and fourth vector) of the embedding vector sequence $es(s)$ of the full sentence "The crowd in Damascus shouted slogans".

4. Finally, we find the similarity of the embedding vector sequence of each pattern $es(p)$ with the embedding vector sequence of each n-gram, $ses(ng, s), ng \in ngrams(s)$. Then, we take as sentence eventness the maximal similarity between a pattern and an n-gram embedding sequence.

   We denote as $esim(es(p), ses(ng, s)$ the similarity of the embedding sequences $es(p)$ and $ses(ng, s)$. The eventness of the sentence, $ev(s)$, is calculated with the following formula:

   $ev(s) = \max_{p,ng} esim(p, ng)$, where $p \in Patterns, ng \in Ngrams(s)$.

5. If $ev(s) > \alpha$, then s is considered a sentence containing an event. The threshold α is being set empirically.

A.1 Calculating $esim$, similarity of a pattern and an n-gram embedding vector sequences

1. In order to compare how similar a pattern like $p =$"protesters demand" is similar to a n-gram like $ng =$"crowd in Damascus shouted slogans", our model first builds two sequences of embeddings corresponding to the two phrases: $es(p)$ and $ses(ng, s)$.

2. Then, the algorithm finds for each word in the pattern p the most similar word from ng, using the cosine similarity between the corresponding embedding vectors. In our example, the most similar word from ng for the word "protesters" is "crowd" and the most similar to "demand" is "slogans".

   We call these pairs of matching words *matching-pairs*: In the example above, they form the following set: $\{(protesters, crowd), (demand, slogans)\}$.

3. Then, we calculate the similarity between each pair of matching words and find their normalized sum, as it is shown in the formula on Figure 3: It is based on the sum of the similarities of the matching words, the inverse document frequency of the pattern words, and the difference of the positions of the matching words. In case of perfect similarity, equal pattern and event phrase, similarity function returns the value of 1.

$$esim(es(p), ses(ng,s)) = \frac{\sum_{(wp,wn)\in matching-pairs} cos(CE(wp), CE(wn)).idf(wp).\sqrt{\frac{1}{1+\delta(wp,wn)}}}{\sum_{(wp,-)\in matching-pairs} idf(wp)}$$

$matching - pairs$ - the set of pairs of words - first from the pattern p, the second from the n-gram ng, such that each word from p is paired with its most similar from ng, considering the cosine between their embedding vectors
$CE(w)$ - contextualised embedding vector of a word w
$idf(w)$ - inverse document frequency
$\delta(wp, wn)$ - the difference in the positions of the matching words

Figure 3: Similarity between pattern p and an ngram ng

Socio-political Events of Conflict and Unrest: A Survey of Available Datasets

Helene Bøsei Olsen* and **Étienne Simon*** and **Erik Velldal** and **Lilja Øvrelid**
University of Oslo, Language Technology Group

Abstract

There is a large and growing body of literature on datasets created to facilitate the study of socio-political events of conflict and unrest. However, the datasets, and the approaches taken to create them, vary a lot depending on the type of research they are intended to support. For example, while scholars from natural language processing (NLP) tend to focus on annotating specific spans of text indicating various components of an event, scholars from the disciplines of political science and conflict studies tend to focus on creating databases that code an abstract but structured representation of the event, less tied to a specific source text. The survey presented in this paper aims to map out the current landscape of available event datasets within the domain of social and political conflict and unrest – both from the NLP and political science communities – offering a unified view of the work done across different disciplines.

1 Introduction and background

Like in most social sciences, political scientists started to rely more and more on quantitative data to empirically test their hypotheses during the course of the 20th century. Hutter (1972) observes a rapid increase in the use of quantitative data, from 11.6% of political science articles in 1946–1948 to 58.5% in 1968–1970. To satisfy this demand for numerical data, researchers started manually collecting large databases of politically significant events from news journals (McClelland, 1978; Azar, 1980). These databases contain structured abstract descriptions of real-world events, enabling researchers to perform large-scale analysis. From an NLP perspective, these sorts of databases can be viewed as the desired output of the event extraction task. Event extraction models are trained on natural language texts, such as news or Wikipedia articles, annotated with event information at the token-level. Yet, while information extraction was originally motivated by practical endeavours (Sundheim and Chinchor, 1993; Grishman and Sundheim, 1996), modern event extraction is more closely associated with linguistic formalisations of sentential semantics and natural language understanding (Doddington et al., 2004).

When we look at both modern socio-political event databases and annotated NLP datasets, we observe several discrepancies that make annotated datasets less suited for the evaluation of socio-political event extraction systems. A first discrepancy pertains to the *link precision between text and events*. While the events encoded by database approaches commonly reflect information scattered in entire documents (typically one or multiple new articles), NLP events tend to be defined by word or phrase-level annotations tied to specific spans of text in a given document. A second and closely related discrepancy is what we refer to as the *abstraction gap*. For political science, the text of news articles is but a clue to what happened. Socio-political databases purpose to contain information about what actually happened in the real-world, which can only be elucidated through a combination of sources and expert knowledge. Moreover, the recorded events are typically defined within the context of the phenomena, theories, or research goals that are explored. In NLP, events are often defined based on linguistic motivations, meaning they are defined and specified within the text based on linguistic structures, patterns, or features present. The events defined in the text annotations of NLP datasets are usually more atomic and granular compared to the more aggregated and high-level events typically found in database resources. A third discrepancy has to do with *source text availability*, which is in turn closely tied to the underlying *purpose* of the data resource. While the main point of socio-political event databases is simply the set of

*These authors contributed equally to this work.

Proceedings of the 7th Workshop on Challenges and Applications of Automated Extraction of Socio-political Events from Text (CASE 2024), pages 40–53
March 22, 2024

events themselves, i.e. the actual information that is recorded, the text annotations found within NLP, in contrast, are meant to enable training and/or testing of event extraction systems, i.e. systems that can map text into structured representations like those of the annotations. In NLP, therefore, it is generally seen as vital to make the annotated texts freely available, whereas it is significantly less common that the text sources used to build socio-political databases are shared. This has the unfortunate consequence of making many event databases not as directly applicable for NLP research as they might have been. A fourth discrepancy is related to the account of *temporal dynamics*. Socio-political event databases describe an evolving world, while annotated event extraction datasets are typically comprised of independent and identically distributed samples.

Several surveys in NLP describe annotated event datasets together with methodologies and techniques approaching the task of event extraction (Li et al., 2022; Yu et al., 2020; Xiang and Wang, 2019). Similarly, multiple articles describe socio-political databases, often with a focused comparison within the same domain, such as protest events (Hutter, 2014; Ward et al., 2013) or violent events (Hammond and Weidmann, 2014; Gleditsch et al., 2014). However, comprehensive studies linking the two fields together are notably lacking.

Considering the extensive data sources available, our survey does not aim to be exhaustive. Our primary focus is on central databases used in the social sciences and prominent annotated datasets in NLP concerning conflict and unrest. In structuring this survey, we classify datasets according to their purported goal. We start in Section 2 with datasets created for the main purpose of studying the recorded events themselves. We refer to these as *socio-political event databases*. The section will start by introducing manually annotated databases before we introduce databases created using automated methods. This naturally leads to Section 3 on *annotated event datasets* from the field of NLP covering socio-political events. The key characteristic of the datasets in this section is that they contain text-span annotations with the purpose of training and evaluating machine learning models for the event extraction task. We then describe and analyse the gap between the two types of event data and discuss works that can be seen as early attempts to bridge this gap in Section 4. Finally, we give special attention to our Ethics Section, as biases in the selection and description of datasets are critical when political analyses are derived from them.

As a note on terminology, while writing this survey, we opted to use the vocabulary of NLP, but also to make the parallel between the practices found between the two fields clearer. Instead of speaking of *annotation*, political scientists prefer the term of *coding*, which usually refers to manual annotation performed by human experts, but can also include *machine coding*, which refers to the automatic annotation of text by algorithms. Socio-political events usually involve one or more *actors*, those are entities, often states, armed groups, or other politically relevant organisations. Finally, the process of extracting political events from text is described in a *codebook*, which can be seen as similar in purpose to an annotation guideline.

2 Socio-political event databases

Early on, McClelland (1961) noted the necessity of building databases of politically relevant events to better our understanding of international politics. In contrast to annotated datasets geared towards training and evaluating systems for information extraction, these types of databases are built solely for the knowledge they encode, without much importance given to an underlying source text. The source texts are typically only included in the form of a reference for checking the validity of the event or indicating its provenance. However, most events recorded in such databases could, in principle, be automatically extracted from published texts.[1] Following this observation, there was an attempt to automatically extract these databases from news feeds in the late 1980s. These efforts resulted in the Kansas Event Data System (KEDS; Schrodt et al., 1994), extracting events from Reuters. This initiated the advance of machine-coded databases, which parallels the development of event extraction systems on the NLP side.

In this section, we describe important databases of socio-political conflict and unrest. While the focus of this survey is on data rather than modelling, we do briefly touch on methodology when we discuss the automatically extracted databases, where modelling and data are inherently intertwined. The main manually annotated databases included in this

[1] For recent conflicts, some databases such as UCDP GED use other sources of information in addition to text sources, such as images or videos posted on social media, but this is still an uncommon practice.

section are listed in Table 1.

2.1 Manually annotated databases

The first two widely used databases for socio-political events are manually annotated by humans and include the World Events Interaction Survey (WEIS; McClelland, 1978) and the Conflict and Peace Data Bank (COPDAB; Azar, 1980). While both focus on inter-state political events, they diverge in their selection of news sources to extract the events, consequently resulting in distinct geographical focus (Howell, 1983).

Even though the WEIS and COPDAB projects cover a broad range of politically relevant events, one of the main limitations is that these events only cover a limited set of actors. Attempting to code every potentially relevant political event is time-consuming, resource-intensive, and costly, and might be beyond human capacity.

Consequently, more recently manually annotated databases tend to have a very restricted focus, particularly oriented towards addressing a specific research question. For example, Turchin (2012) attempts to find a temporally repeating pattern in the occurrence of violence in the United States. To do so, they compile a list of what they consider political violent acts over the last two centuries. Such highly specialised databases may have little to offer with respect to other types of research questions. On the other hand, some databases are used in the analysis of a wide variety of research questions. One of the most widely used comes from the Correlates of War Project (COW; Sarkees and Wayman, 2010), which lists all wars with more than a 1 000 battle-related deaths since 1816 and is a popular database for research on inter-state conflicts.

A particularity of these databases is that the coded information is not necessarily reliant on a specific underlying news article. As described in Section 1, the extracted events in databases are typically not designed to facilitate mapping from text to a structured event representation but rather focus on being faithful recordings of actual events in the world. This places them at a higher level of abstraction compared to the annotations commonly encountered in NLP. Moreover, it is common that multiple sources such as news articles,[2] and reports from non-governmental organisations are used by expert annotators in deducing information about the recorded event in the database.

The Uppsala Conflict Data Program Georeferenced Event Dataset (UCDP GED; Sundberg and Melander, 2013) is one such database. It focuses on a single event type: fatalities from armed conflict involving at least one organised actor. The UCDP GED events go back decades and are continuously updated with the same coding process: every month, region-specialised human experts read news articles about violent events and transcribe them into the database following the UCDP GED codebook (Högbladh, 2023). The data is widely used in peace and conflict studies and for research projects such as conflict escalation prediction (Hegre et al., 2022).

A similar program is the Armed Conflict Location & Event Data project (ACLED; Raleigh et al., 2010). Although it covers violent deaths to a lesser extent compared to UCDP GED, ACLED includes a larger number of event types such as protests, territory changes, and troop movements. The database provides researchers with an alternative trade-off between domain coverage and data quality compared to UCDP GED. Similarly, the Social Conflict Analysis Database (SCAD; Salehyan et al., 2012) has an analogous purpose to ACLED. It contains 10 event types and is designed to supplement the UCDP GED specifically in the African, Latin American, and Caribbean regions. While having a more narrow event domain compared to ACLED, SCAD has the advantage of being easy to merge with the high-quality UCDP GED armed conflict events.

The NAVCO database (Nonviolent and Violent Campaigns and Outcomes; Chenoweth et al., 2019) is designed to answer the following research question: *do nonviolent campaigns have better or worse odds of success compared to violent ones?* (Chenoweth and Stephan, 2011). The criteria for nonviolent campaigns within this database are more restrictive compared to SCAD because they require comparability with violent ones. Consequently, only nonviolent campaigns with a *maximalist* goal are included, i.e. protests and strikes that in other contexts could be violent.

Rather than focusing on a specific research question, some databases concentrate on a set of events with high political significance. An example of this approach is the Iraq Body Count database (IBC; Hicks et al., 2011). This database records civilian casualties resulting from violence following the

[2] Many socio-political event databases still rely on specific news articles, typically sourced from news aggregators like Factiva and LexisNexis, which provide access to thousands of news sources.

Database	Domain	Sources	# Events ×1000	ML Filter	Reference
COW	wars	news	1	no	Sarkees and Wayman (2010)
USPVD	violence	other databases...	2	no	Turchin (2012)
UCDP GED	fatal organised violence	news, social media...	316	no	Sundberg and Melander (2013)
ACLED	conflict & protest	news, social media...	1 967	no	Raleigh et al. (2010)
SCAD	protest	news	23	no	Salehyan et al. (2012)
NAVCO	non-violent & violent	news	112	no	Chenoweth et al. (2019)
IBC	civilian deaths	news, NGO...	52	no	Hicks et al. (2011)
MMAD	protest	news	31	yes	Weidmann and Rød (2019)
GTD	terrorism	news...	200	yes	START (2022)
SPEED	protest	news	62	yes+	Nardulli et al. (2015)

Table 1: Manually annotated socio-political event databases described in Section 2.1. Note that some of these databases are still being actively updated, the number of events is given at the time of writing. The "ML Filter" columns indicate whether news articles are selected using a simple keyword system or a machine learning system. SPEED is going one step further by pre-extracting named entities and is thus labelled "yes+".

2003 invasion of Iraq. Until 2007, it only recorded fatalities reported in at least two different news sources, and from 2017 onward, it only reported aggregated death counts. One specificity of this database is that it targets personal information, such as names or demographic details about the victims whenever available. The Bosnian book of dead (BBD; Ball et al., 2007) is a similar endeavour for the 1992–1995 war in Bosnia and Herzegovina.

All of these news-sourced databases use a set of search terms to pre-filter articles from news aggregators (Yörük et al., 2022). For instance, the search string used by the UCDP GED contains terms such as "kill", "die" or "massacre". Additionally, these databases indirectly rely on automatic tagging by filtering out news articles based on topic tags automatically assigned by the news aggregators (e.g. to remove sport-related articles that may use similar terms metaphorically).

Furthermore, some databases take an extra step by employing their own machine learning models to filter news aggregators. Nevertheless, they continue to involve human experts in extracting the specifics of the events. An illustration of this is the Mass Mobilisation in Autocracies Database (MMAD; Weidmann and Rød, 2019). This database approaches the filtering as a binary classification task where articles are categorised based on their inclusion of an MMAD event. For the filtering process, they train an ensemble of Support Vector Machines (SVMs) and naive Bayes classifiers on a set of 250 000 manually annotated articles (Croicu and Weidmann, 2015). They report that their system reduces the workload for human coders by half while discarding 10% of relevant articles.

In the same vein, the Global Terrorism Database (GTD; START, 2022) compiles terrorist incidents. Initially, the news articles are filtered by an unspecified machine learning algorithm before the events are extracted by a human expert. The implementation of this filtration method began in 2012, with the sole mention of a deduplication algorithm using cosine similarity on n-grams at that time. This uncertainty about the underlying model is prevalent with numerous databases within political sciences; there is often a lack of comprehensive publication detailing the filtering mechanisms used.

An example of the next step towards automation is the Social, Political and Economic Event Database project (SPEED; Nardulli et al., 2015). In addition to the filtering of relevant news articles, they use statistical models to extract potentially relevant entities such as locations and actors. These entities are then reviewed and combined by a human expert to form events.

2.2 Automatically extracted databases

Automatically extracted databases allow for potentially broader coverage by reducing the costs of human expert annotation. However, this advantage is counterbalanced by reduced accuracy. Consequently, when political scientists select a database to address their research questions, they are faced with a trade-off between quantity and quality. In practice, hand-annotated databases are favoured if they cover the specific research question, while machine-coded ones are preferred otherwise.

Similar to how the schema of manually annotated databases is described by a codebook (annotation guidelines), automatically extracted databases follow an *event ontology* or *event coding scheme*. These ontologies define the set of event types with the meaning of the various arguments within the event. Usually, the set of possible arguments remains constant for all event types and includes at least a source and a target actor.

In contrast to manually annotated databases for which there is a one-to-one relationship between codebook and databases, automatic event ontologies are often used and reused to define several databases. Initially though, ontologies and databases were jointly developed relying on preexisting codebooks.

The extensively used WEIS ontology, derived from the manually annotated WEIS database detailed in Section 2.1, serves as a foundational ontology for several efforts aiming to automate event databases. These efforts often build upon the WEIS ontology, either augmenting or expanding it to align with specific research questions or targeted domains. The Kansas Event Data System (KEDS; Schrodt et al., 1994) adapted WEIS for developing a database on inter-state interactions, but WEIS was also extended in a KEDS-model-compatible way within the PANDA project (Bond et al., 1994) with a focus on nonviolent direct action.

The KEDS model uses symbolic rules for matching words to classify events and identify named entities. It focuses on the first sentence of news articles, using the structure to complete event details. This method involves a simple form of parsing, by examining how entities and action words are related without analysing the entire sentence structure. These KEDS ideas were later incorporated into a new model named Textual Analysis by Augmented Replacement Instructions (TABARI; Schrodt, 2001). This evolution was followed by formalisations of coding schemes specific to automatic event extraction.

Currently one of the most popular event ontologies for machine-coded databases concerned with inter-state events is the CAMEO event ontology (Conflict and Mediation Event Observations; Gerner et al., 2002). It is specifically designed for rule-based extraction models, such as TABARI, describing more than 20 event types with over 200 subtypes. Additionally, the CAMEO codebook details a hierarchical coding scheme for events and entities, distinguishing CAMEO as a genuine ontology rather than merely an event catalogue.

Another widely used ontology is IDEA (Integrated Data for Events Analysis; King and Lowe, 2003), an earlier alternative to CAMEO. It is a direct successor of the previously mentioned PANDA project, concentrating on intra-state conflict and citizen direct actions. The popularity of these ontologies comes mostly from the fact that they provided a list of patterns to be used with TABARI-like models, both for actors and verbs associated with the events. In practice, these patterns resemble simplified regular expressions, indeed some "verbs" given by CAMEO are not conventional grammatical verbs, similar to how nouns can be event triggers in NLP.

A given machine-coded event database can be defined as a combination of a model, an ontology, and the utilised news sources. For example, a popular machine-extracted database is ICEWS (Integrated Crisis Early Warning System; O'brien, 2010), created at the initiative of DARPA for conflict forecasting. ICEWS is a database extracted from several international and regional sources (AP, UPI, BBC Monitor, India Today, etc) using the TABARI model with classification into the CAMEO ontology. Similarly, GDELT (Global Database of Events, Language, and Tone; Leetaru and Schrodt, 2013) is an academic initiative, a database containing CAMEO-events extracted by TABARI from the LexisNexis news aggregator. GDELT is one order of magnitude larger than ICEWS, with a tendency to be less conservative in its inclusion of events (Ward et al., 2013).

In 2014, the TABARI model was phased out in favour of new models named PETRARCH (Python Engine for Text Resolution And Related Coding

Hierarchy; Norris et al., 2017). These models are still rule-based, however, the rules are designed on parse trees extracted by Standford CoreNLP (Manning et al., 2014) instead of using basic string templates. The PETRARCH-2 model is used by the TERRIER database (Temporally Extended, Regular, Reproducible International Event Records; Grant et al., 2019) to extract CAMEO events from newspapers from 1979 to 2016. The PHOENIX database (Salam et al., 2020) is also using a PETRARCH model (UD-PETRARCH) to extract CAMEO events from more than 250 news sources, including Spanish language sources.

Recently, Halterman et al. (2023a) introduced the PLOVER ontology (Political Language Ontology for Verifiable Event Records) together with the POLECAT dataset (Political Event Classification, Attributes, and Types) as a replacement for the CAMEO ontology and ICEWS dataset. The dataset is extracted using the NGEC model (Halterman et al., 2023b), which is composed of SVM, distilBERT and RoBERTa.

3 Text annotation for event extraction

On the NLP side, annotated datasets are created for the purpose of training models, shaping their design and annotation to align with the event extraction task's approach. Event extraction has been a central task in NLP, dating back to the Message Understanding Conferences (MUC) series in the 1990s. Initially, annotating event participants was formulated to fit a template-filling task, where information from a document is to be structured into a predefined set of fields such as finding the victims, time and location from a terrorist attack report. Following these early attempts, the highly influential Automatic Content Extraction (ACE) program released manual event annotations for text spans at the sentence level, performed jointly with annotation of rich information about entities, temporal expressions, and relations between entities. Below we describe these in more detail and also compare them with more recent annotation efforts. The NLP datasets covered in this survey are summarised in Table 2.

While looking at the 1990s MUC datasets, it is striking how closely they resonate with current socio-political event databases compared to modern NLP annotated datasets. The evolution of template filling into event extraction is not clearly defined, and similar models are used for the two tasks (Du et al., 2021). Indeed, both of them capture a semantic relationship between entities, as described by the template or event schema. Two other closely related tasks are relation extraction – which usually focuses on binary templates, often in the context of knowledge bases – and semantic role labelling – which usually focuses on the argument relations conveyed by specific predicates. Even though all of these tasks can be relevant to socio-political event databases, in this section, we only focus on annotated datasets for event extraction and template-filling, describing them in chronological order.

The Message Understanding Conferences (MUC; Grishman and Sundheim, 1996), held from 1987 to 1997 and funded by DARPA, are regarded as pioneering efforts in generating annotated datasets for information extraction. The conferences operated as shared tasks, where each MUC is associated with a designated dataset covering the corresponding information to be extracted and prepared by human annotators for training purposes along with a task definition. Although MUC maintains mainly a military theme, the various datasets focus on different types of events.

The first two conferences centred on military messages from the tactical Navy domain. In MUC-1 the participants were provided with merely 10 paragraphs as data without any formal evaluation. Building on MUC-1, MUC-2 introduced a dataset with 130 messages and 10 elements to be extracted, such as event type, agent, time, place, and the effect of the event (Sundheim and Chinchor, 1993).

Following the initial conferences, MUC-3 and MUC-4 introduced annotated datasets focused on terrorist events in Central and South America, reported by the Foreign Broadcast Information Service. These iterations of MUC marked a shift by increasing the complexity of the task, both by including several event and argument types, but also by moving from extraction of information from simple and short military messages to longer texts with more complex language. MUC-4 includes 4 event types `Arson`, `Attack`, `Bombing`, `Kidnapping`, with the 4 arguments roles Perpetrator, Instrument, Target, and Victim, which are shared across event types. Additionally, the datasets increased in size, with respectively 1 400 and 1 700 news articles for MUC-3 and MUC-4.

The last two instalments, MUC-6 and MUC-7, shift the focus towards domain-independent annotations, targeting named entity recognition, coref-

Dataset	Domain	Source	Annotation scope	# Doc	# Event Types
MUC-4	terrorist attack	news	document	1 700	4
ACE2005	general	news, conversation	sentence	599	33
Light ERE	general	news, discussion forum	sentence	902	33
Rich ERE	general	news, discussion forum	sentence	288	38
MAVEN	general	Wikipedia	sentence	4 480	168
WIKIEVENTS	general	Wikipedia, news articles	document	246	67
DocEE	historical & news	Wikipedia, news articles	document	27 485	59
MEE	general	Wikipedia	5 sentences	31 226†	16

Table 2: Overview of annotated text datasets in the field of NLP for event extraction. †: In the case of MEE, the "# Doc" column reports the number of 5 sentences spans in the dataset, not the number of documents.

erence resolution, and relation identification. This transition also includes an expansion to more languages. Interestingly, this shift was accompanied by a return to smaller training datasets, comprising only 100 documents. MUC-6 consists of events involving high-level officers joining or departing from companies, while MUC-7 targets satellite launch events, with event arguments such as Date, Country of Launch, and Payload Information.

These were followed by the automatic content extraction (ACE) program. The event annotation in the ACE tradition has become a de facto standard for the evaluation of event extraction systems in the field of NLP. The ACE dataset-2005 (Doddington et al., 2004) provides manual annotation for entities, relations, and events for joint evaluation of multiple IE tasks and in multiple languages (ACE05 in English, Chinese, and Arabic). The annotations distinguish specific text spans indicating the event trigger and associated arguments of an event at the sentence level. An event trigger is typically the word(s) in the text that most clearly describes an event, such as "bomb", which evokes an `Attack` event in the example sentence "U.S. forces continued to bomb Fallujah" where "U.S. forces" is the associated Attacker argument. ACE annotates 8 general event types, e.g. `Life`, `Conflict`, `Transaction` with 33 subtypes (e.g. `Conflict.Attack`) and 22 argument roles, e.g. Attacker, Agent and Recipient. Of particular relevance in the current setting are the `Conflict` event type (with subtypes `Attack` and `Demonstration`) as well as the `Life.Die` and `Life.Injure` event types.

More recently, the Entities, Relations and Events (ERE) annotation effort (Song et al., 2015) has contributed both data and annotation guidelines for event extraction purposes. From the Light ERE to Rich ERE datasets, the ERE effort has evolved from lightweight annotation automating the ACE guidelines to more complex treatment of entities and events aimed at paving the way for event coreference at the document-level. The Rich ERE annotation scheme extends on that of ACE, annotating 38 event subtypes under 9 main event types, including more fine-grained event subtypes in the `Movement`, `Contact`, and `Transaction` event types. In Light ERE, an event trigger can be associated with only one event. Still, in Rich ERE, an event trigger can be annotated for more than one event due to correlations of different event types. For instance, an `Attack` event and an `Injure` event can share the same event trigger; it is natural that when a person is attacked, the person is also injured. In Light ERE, only asserted events are annotated; in Rich ERE, apart from assorted events, events that did not actually occur are also annotated, hence annotating event modality.

The MAssive eVENt detection dataset (MAVEN; Wang et al., 2020) is introduced to provide a large-scale annotated event dataset in the general domain, covering 168 event types. MAVEN follows the ACE terminology, targeting events at the sentence-level, and consists of event-related articles from English Wikipedia. FrameNet frames (Baker et al., 1998) are used to derive event types, with the lexical units serving as the corresponding triggers. Automatic POS-tagging and heuristic methods are used to narrow down trigger candidates and the corresponding event type candidates to aid human annotators. In MAVEN, the event types follow a hierarchical schema resembling a tree structure, prioritising the most detailed event types. If no fine-grained event type aligns with the event, the annotators resort to more general event types. For example, the most coarse-grained event type `Action` includes the event subtype `Violence`, which again contains subsubtypes such as `Killing`, `Attack`, `Terrorism`, and `Military Operation`. In the context of social and political conflict and unrest, the event types `Terrorism`, `Kidnapping`, `Violence`, `Use firearm`, `Military operation`, and `Attack` are especially relevant event types.

Li et al. (2021) presents WIKIEVENTS, a document-level annotated dataset based on Wikipedia articles and their referenced news articles. The annotations resemble ACE, but expand the number of sub-events from 33 to 67 following the KAIROS ontology. Additionally, it incorporates a more fine-grained event-type hierarchy. For instance, whereas ACE identifies the event type and subtype such as `Conflict.Attack`, WIKIEVENTS introduces event types at three levels, such as `Conflict.Attack.DetonateExplode`. Furthermore, Li et al. (2021) expand their annotations to include events that extend beyond the sentence boundary, capturing event arguments occurring in sentences lacking an explicit event trigger. Apart from the `Conflict.Attack` events, the dataset includes event types such as `Life.Die` and `Conflict.Demonstrate`, each with subtypes that are relevant in the socio-political domain context. Human annotators label event types, event mentions (triggers and arguments), and event coreferences across sentences in the document.

The DocEE dataset (Tong et al., 2022) is the largest document-level annotated dataset containing 27 485 documents and covers a wide range of event types in the socio-political domain, including `Armed Conflicts`, `Riot` and `Protest`. It includes two types of events, historical events, defined as events with their own Wikipedia page, and timeline events, which are news events organised in chronological order on Wikipedia. The Wikipedia article is annotated for the historical events, while the corresponding news article is used for the timeline events. Each document is manually given an event type based on the title and then annotated with event arguments from the event type schema. For example, the event type `Protest` is annotated with arguments Date, Location, Protesters, Cause, Slogan, Method, Arrested, Government Reaction, Casualties and Losses, and Damaged Property.

The recently released MEE dataset (Pouran Ben Veyseh et al., 2022) provides event-annotated data for eight typologically diverse languages (English, Spanish, Portuguese, Polish, Turkish, Hindi, Korean and Japanese). The data is based on Wikipedia articles under the subcategory *Event* from a number of different domains (e.g. Economy, Politics, Crimes and Military). The annotation scheme is based on the ACE guidelines and its 8 event types, however, limit the set of annotated subtypes to 16. Unlike ACE, the articles are split into 5-sentence segments and argument relations may span across the full-text segment. For the most relevant category in the current context, the dataset only includes the `Conflict.Attack`, `Life.Die` and `Life.Injure` event types.

4 Bridging the gap

In this section, we start by highlighting the main obstacles to transferring event extraction NLP expertise to the automatic extraction of socio-political event databases. One obstacle currently being addressed in the field of NLP is the restriction of events to single sentences. As we show in Section 3, document-level event extraction datasets are now starting to reemerge. In the second part of this section, we describe datasets that establish bridges between political science databases and annotated datasets.

Token-level annotations To facilitate model training, NLP event extraction datasets include token-level annotations delineating which words correspond to specific event triggers or arguments. On the other hand, manually coded socio-political event databases do not usually include this information, with the exception of the NER-automated SPEED database. Therefore, training machine learning models from socio-political databases requires either token-level annotation efforts or weakly supervised learning techniques. Alternatively, and perhaps more interestingly, one could directly prioritise research on end-to-end learning of document-level event extraction.

Source availability Regardless of the learning strategy used, a prerequisite is having available source texts, preferably in a free and open manner. The news articles used to code socio-political event databases are usually unavailable, mostly due to copyright restrictions. This significantly limits the appeal of these datasets within the NLP community.

Abstraction gap Furthermore, all the annotated datasets described in Section 3 solely capture the mapping between text and structured information, while the socio-political databases described in Section 2.1 attempt to record whether the event actually occurred in the real world. In the first case, only linguistic knowledge is necessary, even when encoding event modality. In the second, socio-political event databases require expert knowledge to evaluate and corroborate what is conveyed in the text. This implies that future research on learning to automatically extract document-level events should also address how to incorporate domain knowledge.

Temporal dynamic The socio-political databases describe an ever-changing situation with new actors regularly appearing and engaging in new conflicts. On the other hand, annotated datasets tend to be more stationary, with little to no temporal variation in the distribution of events.

In a way, the efforts to automatically create socio-political event databases overlook these issues because they tend to rely on older, rule-based models that do not necessitate data supervision. They fall into the abstraction gap by overcounting events, extracting from all uncorroborated news. Moreover, as they are typically not disclosed to the NLP community, there is no requirement to publish their source data.[3] This comes at the cost of reliability.

Some previous work has made efforts to bridge this gap between socio-political event databases and annotated event datasets. The MUC datasets, detailed in Section 2, represent the initial strides in this effort. We will here describe some of the more recent approaches.

The Iraq body count corpus (IBC-C; Žukov-Gregorič et al., 2016) is introduced to automate the annotation process for the Iraq body count project (Hicks et al., 2011) discussed in Section 2.1. The corpus provides event annotations for whole documents, where each document contains references to one or multiple events. The annotations for the IBC-C are created through a form of distant supervision (Mintz et al., 2009), using different pattern matching and semantic functions to create named entity labels corresponding to ten argument roles, such as Fatality Numbers, Named Individuals, and Location. IBC-C provides token-level annotations, somewhat addresses the abstraction gap and can capture the temporal dynamic of the evolving war. Unfortunately, the complete dataset is no longer available due to copyright restrictions (and potential privacy concerns).

The Global Contentious Politics database (GLOCON; Duruşan et al., 2022; Hürriyetoğlu et al., 2021b; Yörük et al., 2022) is a partly automated protest event database. Part of the data used to train the event extraction model is referred to as GLOCON GOLD and is freely available upon request.[4] It includes manually annotated datasets for three sub-tasks: document classification, sentence classification, and event extraction. It encodes five specific event sub-types: `Demonstrations`, `Industrial actions`, `Group clashes`, `Armed militancy`, and `Electoral mobilisation`. Regarding the concerns we identified, the dataset includes token-level annotations, is associated with source texts, and preserves the temporal dynamic of the political system. However, although future or hypothetical events are not annotated, these types of events can be recognised from linguistic cues alone, leading to continued susceptibility to the abstraction gap. Subsequently, the GLOCON GOLD dataset was extended to define the CASE 2021 and 2022 shared task 1 on protest news detection (Hürriyetoğlu et al., 2021a, 2022). Compared to GLOCON, the shared task datasets include more source articles and define an additional subtask: event sentence coreference identification. Finally, shared task 2 in 2021 (Haneczok et al., 2021) and 2023 (Tanev et al., 2023) attempt to bridge the gap more directly as they use data annotated following the ACLED codebook for evaluation. The 2023 task 2 tackles the prediction of battle events from social media messages in the Russo–Ukrainian war. On the prediction of whether a PRIO-grid cell contained a battle event, the two systems submitted for the task reached F_1 scores of 0.04 and 0.152, demonstrating the considerable amount of work that lies ahead.

5 Limitations

Due to space constraints, we needed to limit the number of datasets discussed. We strive to high-

[3]One exception is that ontologies underlying automatically extracted databases provide some short examples in their codebook. For example, the PLOVER ontology comes with a small (323 samples) hand-annotated dataset from the CAMEO codebook.

[4]`https://github.com/emerging-welfare/glocongold`

light datasets that are both central and relevant to the domain of political conflicts and unrest and showcase the evolution of practices in their respective fields. However, most of the datasets we selected are based on English-language news, even when used to analyse the political situation in non-English-speaking countries.

Some notable mentions that could not be included for relevancy or duplication concerns are POLDEM (Kriesi et al., 2020), MAR (Gurr, 2000), ICBe (Douglass et al., 2022), UCDP VPP (Svensson et al., 2022), PITF's WAD (Schrodt and Ulfelder, 2016), RAMS (Ebner et al., 2020), etc. Additionally, there has been a rise in annotated datasets made from user-generated text not encompassed in this survey, such as the Twitter-based datasets on civil unrest CUT (Sech et al., 2020) and G-CUT (Chinta et al., 2021).

6 Ethics

Working on event data concerning sensitive topics such as armed conflict, protest data, or other socio-political events necessitates a high degree of ethical consideration and responsibility.

The fact that the main source for several of the socio-political event databases is news articles, one should raise awareness of the inherent bias when reporting on these topics in the news. In the context of creating databases for conflict events based on media reporting, Chojnacki et al. (2012) highlights the importance of awareness towards both description bias, meaning errors in how conflicts are reported, and selection bias, meaning which conflicts are reported, and more importantly, those that remain unreported. Regarding selection bias, Chojnacki et al. (2012) suggests that researchers can solely make assumptions about the representativeness of the reported news, while for description bias, efforts should be made to mitigate and reduce potential bias in the extracted events. While similar biases can be present in manually annotated databases (McClelland, 1983), both description and selection biases from media sources can be partly mitigated using human experts to assess the validity of the reported events and or seek out sources to confirm the information. However, these types of biases do not seem to be addressed for annotated datasets in NLP.

Another concern is that this paper describes a dataset (IBC-C) that has been retracted due to copyright restrictions and is no longer accessible because of the mishandling of sensitive personal data. Other datasets are still accessible but do not clarify the handling of personal data and/or licences for redistributing data. Access to data while upholding copyright and privacy considerations is crucial to ethical research practice. Including these datasets in this work does not represent endorsement but is necessary to discuss different approaches and challenges associated with socio-political event data.

An important consideration when dealing with annotated datasets and databases involves the annotators' exposure to distressing or harmful content. Constantly engaging with descriptions of conflict and violence can lead to desensitisation, emotional numbness, and potential emotional and psychological distress. Recently, more attention has been directed toward the impact of secondary or vicarious trauma and the psychological well-being of annotators, content moderators, and others handling harmful content (Das et al., 2020; Steiger et al., 2021; Kirk et al., 2022). However, strategies and specific actions to alleviate potential risks for annotators, such as providing psychological support, remain limited or inadequately addressed in the datasets described in this paper. We strongly advocate for a more focused approach on supporting annotators to mitigate the effects of exposure and encourage leveraging existing datasets in research on automatic event extraction instead of creating new event datasets in order to minimise exposure.

We now address the concern of misuse and misinterpretations of socio-political event data. For instance, the GLOCON dataset strives to use neutral terms to describe different actors, e.g. using *militant*, instead of *terrorist*. Other datasets vary in their approaches when dealing with language that might be insulting, marginalising, or criminalising. The extent of this handling often depends on factors such as the use of standardised actor lists and whether the datasets are manually annotated by experts. Notably, in annotated datasets used for NLP, with a one-to-one mapping between text-span and label, this issue remains unaddressed. The vocabulary used to describe individuals and groups, particularly those from minority communities, holds the dual power to shape our perceptions of said groups and might impact the reliability of extracted events and subsequent analyses derived from event databases.

Finally, some datasets described in this work may contain fine-grained details about individuals, organisations, or groups, which can be used maliciously. Some datasets, such as GLOCON enforce responsible data use and seek to mitigate unethical usage by assessing the declared research intentions before granting access to the dataset (Yörük et al., 2022).

Acknowledgments

We would like to thank the anonymous reviewers as well as Mert Can Yilmaz for their valuable comments. We are also grateful to the Peace Science Infrastructure project collaborators from PRIO and UCDP for insightful discussions on the peace science perspective.

References

Edward E Azar. 1980. The conflict and peace data bank (COPDAB) project. *Journal of Conflict Resolution*, 24(1):143–152.

Collin F. Baker, Charles J. Fillmore, and John B. Lowe. 1998. The Berkeley FrameNet project. In *36th Annual Meeting of the Association for Computational Linguistics and 17th International Conference on Computational Linguistics, Volume 1*, pages 86–90, Montreal, Quebec, Canada. Association for Computational Linguistics.

Patrick Ball, Ewa Tabeau, and Philip Verwimp. 2007. The bosnian book of dead: assessment of the database (full report). Technical report, Households in Conflict Network.

Doug Bond, Brad Bennett, and William Vogele. 1994. Data development and interaction events analysis using KEDS/PANDA: an interim report. *International Studies Association, Washington*.

Erica Chenoweth, Jonathan Pinckney, and Orion A. Lewis. 2019. NAVCO 3.0 Dataset.

Erica Chenoweth and Maria J Stephan. 2011. *Why civil resistance works: The strategic logic of nonviolent conflict*. Columbia University Press.

Abhinav Chinta, Jingyu Zhang, Alexandra DeLucia, Mark Dredze, and Anna L. Buczak. 2021. Study of manifestation of civil unrest on Twitter. In *Proceedings of the Seventh Workshop on Noisy User-generated Text (W-NUT 2021)*, pages 396–409, Online. Association for Computational Linguistics.

Sven Chojnacki, Christian Ickler, Michael Spies, and John Wiesel. 2012. Event data on armed conflict and security: New perspectives, old challenges, and some solutions. *International Interactions*, 38(4):382–401.

Mihai Croicu and Nils B Weidmann. 2015. Improving the selection of news reports for event coding using ensemble classification. *Research & Politics*, 2(4):2053168015615596.

Anubrata Das, Brandon Dang, and Matthew Lease. 2020. Fast, accurate, and healthier: Interactive blurring helps moderators reduce exposure to harmful content. In *AAAI Conference on Human Computation & Crowdsourcing*.

George R Doddington, Alexis Mitchell, Mark A Przybocki, Lance A Ramshaw, Stephanie M Strassel, and Ralph M Weischedel. 2004. The automatic content extraction (ace) program-tasks, data, and evaluation. In *International Conference on Language Resources and Evaluation*, volume 2, pages 837–840. Lisbon.

Rex W. Douglass, Thomas Leo Scherer, J. Andrés Gannon, Erik Gartzke, Jon Lindsay, Shannon Carcelli, Jonathan Wilkenfeld, David M. Quinn, Catherine Aiken, Jose Miguel Cabezas Navarro, Neil Lund, Egle Murauskaite, and Diana Partridge. 2022. Introducing the icbe dataset: Very high recall and precision event extraction from narratives about international crises.

Xinya Du, Alexander Rush, and Claire Cardie. 2021. Template filling with generative transformers. In *Proceedings of the 2021 Conference of the North American Chapter of the Association for Computational Linguistics: Human Language Technologies*, pages 909–914, Online. Association for Computational Linguistics.

Fırat Duruşan, Ali Hürriyetoğlu, Erdem Yörük, Osman Mutlu, Çağrı Yoltar, Burak Gürel, and Alvaro Comin. 2022. Global contentious politics database (GLOCON) annotation manuals.

Seth Ebner, Patrick Xia, Ryan Culkin, Kyle Rawlins, and Benjamin Van Durme. 2020. Multi-sentence argument linking. In *Proceedings of the 58th Annual Meeting of the Association for Computational Linguistics*, page 8057–8077, Online. Association for Computational Linguistics.

Deborah J Gerner, Philip A Schrodt, Omür Yilmaz, and Rajaa Abu-Jabr. 2002. Conflict and mediation event observations (CAMEO): A new event data framework for the analysis of foreign policy interactions. *International Studies Association, New Orleans*.

Kristian Skrede Gleditsch, Nils W Metternich, and Andrea Ruggeri. 2014. Data and progress in peace and conflict research. *Journal of Peace Research*, 51(2):301–314.

Christan Grant, Andrew Halterman, Jill Irvine, Yan Liang, and Khaled Jabr. 2019. OU event data project.

Ralph Grishman and Beth Sundheim. 1996. Message Understanding Conference- 6: A brief history. In *COLING 1996 Volume 1: The 16th International Conference on Computational Linguistics*.

Ted Robert Gurr. 2000. *Peoples versus states: Minorities at risk in the new century*. US Institute of Peace Press.

Andrew Halterman, Benjamin Bagozzi, Andreas Beger, Phil Schrodt, and Grace Scraborough. 2023a. PLOVER and POLECAT: A new political event ontology and dataset.

Andrew Halterman, Philip A. Schrodt, Andreas Beger, Benjamin E. Bagozzi, and Grace I. Scarborough. 2023b. Creating custom event data without dictionaries: A bag-of-tricks. *arXiv preprint arXiv:2304.01331*.

Jesse Hammond and Nils B Weidmann. 2014. Using machine-coded event data for the micro-level study of political violence. *Research & Politics*, 1(2).

Jacek Haneczok, Guillaume Jacquet, Jakub Piskorski, and Nicolas Stefanovitch. 2021. Fine-grained event classification in news-like text snippets - shared task 2, CASE 2021. In *Proceedings of the 4th Workshop on Challenges and Applications of Automated Extraction of Socio-political Events from Text (CASE 2021)*, pages 179–192, Online. Association for Computational Linguistics.

Håvard Hegre, Paola Vesco, and Michael Colaresi. 2022. Lessons from an escalation prediction competition. *International Interactions*, 48(4):521–554.

Madelyn Hsiao-Rei Hicks, Hamit Dardagan, Gabriela Guerrero Serdán, Peter M. Bagnall, John A. Sloboda, and Michael Spagat. 2011. Violent deaths of iraqi civilians, 2003–2008: Analysis by perpetrator, weapon, time, and location. *PLOS Medicine*, 8(2):1–15.

Llewellyn D Howell. 1983. A comparative study of the WEIS and COPDAB data sets. *International Studies Quarterly*, 27(2):149–159.

Ali Hürriyetoğlu, Osman Mutlu, Fırat Duruşan, Onur Uca, Alaeddin Gürel, Benjamin J. Radford, Yaoyao Dai, Hansi Hettiarachchi, Niklas Stoehr, Tadashi Nomoto, Milena Slavcheva, Francielle Vargas, Aaqib Javid, Fatih Beyhan, and Erdem Yörük. 2022. Extended multilingual protest news detection - shared task 1, CASE 2021 and 2022. In *Proceedings of the 5th Workshop on Challenges and Applications of Automated Extraction of Socio-political Events from Text (CASE)*, pages 223–228, Abu Dhabi, United Arab Emirates (Hybrid). Association for Computational Linguistics.

Ali Hürriyetoğlu, Osman Mutlu, Erdem Yörük, Farhana Ferdousi Liza, Ritesh Kumar, and Shyam Ratan. 2021a. Multilingual protest news detection - shared task 1, CASE 2021. In *Proceedings of the 4th Workshop on Challenges and Applications of Automated Extraction of Socio-political Events from Text (CASE 2021)*, pages 79–91, Online. Association for Computational Linguistics.

Ali Hürriyetoğlu, Erdem Yörük, Osman Mutlu, Fırat Duruşan, Çağrı Yoltar, Deniz Yüret, and Burak Gürel. 2021b. Cross-context news corpus for protest event-related knowledge base construction. *Data Intelligence*, 3(2):308–335.

James L. Hutter. 1972. Statistics and political science. *Journal of the American Statistical Association*, 67(340):735–742.

Swen Hutter. 2014. Protest event analysis and its offspring. In *Methodological Practices in Social Movement Research*. Oxford University Press.

Stina Högbladh. 2023. UCDP georeferenced event dataset codebook version 23.1. *Department of Peace and Conflict Research*.

Gary King and Will Lowe. 2003. An automated information extraction tool for international conflict data with performance as good as human coders: A rare events evaluation design. *International Organization*, 57(3):617–642.

Hannah Kirk, Abeba Birhane, Bertie Vidgen, and Leon Derczynski. 2022. Handling and presenting harmful text in NLP research. In *Findings of the Association for Computational Linguistics: EMNLP 2022*, pages 497–510, Abu Dhabi, United Arab Emirates. Association for Computational Linguistics.

Hanspeter Kriesi, Bruno Wüest, Jasmine Lorenzini, Peter Makarov, Matthias Enggist, Klaus Rothenhäusler, Thomas Kurer, Silja Häusermann, Patrice Wangen, Argyrios Altiparmakis, et al. 2020. Poldem-protest dataset 30 european countries.

Kalev Leetaru and Philip A Schrodt. 2013. GDELT: Global data on events, location, and tone, 1979–2012. In *ISA annual convention*, volume 2, pages 1–49. Citeseer.

Qian Li, Jianxin Li, Jiawei Sheng, Shiyao Cui, Jia Wu, Yiming Hei, Hao Peng, Shu Guo, Lihong Wang, Amin Beheshti, and Philip S. Yu. 2022. A survey on deep learning event extraction: Approaches and applications. *IEEE Transactions on Neural Networks and Learning Systems*, pages 1–21.

Sha Li, Heng Ji, and Jiawei Han. 2021. Document-level event argument extraction by conditional generation. In *Proceedings of the 2021 Conference of the North American Chapter of the Association for Computational Linguistics: Human Language Technologies*, pages 894–908, Online. Association for Computational Linguistics.

Christopher Manning, Mihai Surdeanu, John Bauer, Jenny Finkel, Steven Bethard, and David McClosky. 2014. The Stanford CoreNLP natural language processing toolkit. In *Proceedings of 52nd Annual Meeting of the Association for Computational Linguistics: System Demonstrations*, pages 55–60, Baltimore, Maryland. Association for Computational Linguistics.

Charles McClelland. 1978. World event/interaction survey, 1966-1978. *WEIS Codebook ICPSR*, 5211(640):49.

Charles A McClelland. 1961. The acute international crisis. *World Politics*, 14(1):182–204.

Charles A McClelland. 1983. Let the user beware. *International Studies Quarterly*, 27(2):169–177.

Mike Mintz, Steven Bills, Rion Snow, and Daniel Jurafsky. 2009. Distant supervision for relation extraction without labeled data. In *Proceedings of the Joint Conference of the 47th Annual Meeting of the* ACL *and the 4th International Joint Conference on Natural Language Processing of the* AFNLP, pages 1003–1011, Suntec, Singapore. Association for Computational Linguistics.

Peter F. Nardulli, Scott L. Althaus, and Matthew Hayes. 2015. A progressive supervised-learning approach to generating rich civil strife data. *Sociological Methodology*, 45(1):148–183.

Clayton Norris, Philip A Schrodt, and John Beieler. 2017. PETRARCH2: Another event coding program. *J. Open Source Softw.*, 2(9):133.

Sean P O'brien. 2010. Crisis early warning and decision support: Contemporary approaches and thoughts on future research. *International studies review*, 12(1):87–104.

Amir Pouran Ben Veyseh, Javid Ebrahimi, Franck Dernoncourt, and Thien Nguyen. 2022. MEE: A novel multilingual event extraction dataset. In *Proceedings of the 2022 Conference on Empirical Methods in Natural Language Processing*, pages 9603–9613, Abu Dhabi, United Arab Emirates. Association for Computational Linguistics.

Clionadh Raleigh, Andrew Linke, Havard Hegre, and Joakim Karlsen. 2010. Introducing acled: An armed conflict location and event dataset. *Journal of Peace Research*, 47(5):651–660.

Sayeed Salam, Patrick Brandt, Vito D'Orazio, Jennifer Holmes, Javiar Osorio, and Latifur Khan. 2020. An online structured political event dataset based on CAMEO ontology.

Idean Salehyan, Cullen S Hendrix, Jesse Hamner, Christina Case, Christopher Linebarger, Emily Stull, and Jennifer Williams. 2012. Social conflict in africa: A new database. *International Interactions*, 38(4):503–511.

Meredith Sarkees and Frank Wayman. 2010. *Resort to War, 1816-2007*. CQ Press.

Philip A Schrodt. 2001. Automated coding of international event data using sparse parsing techniques. In *annual meeting of the International Studies Association, Chicago*. Citeseer.

Philip A. Schrodt, Shannon G. Davis, and Judith L. Weddle. 1994. Political science: KEDS—a program for the machine coding of event data. *Social Science Computer Review*, 12(4):561–587.

Philip A Schrodt and Jay Ulfelder. 2016. Political instability task force atrocities event data collection codebook. *Parus Analytics*.

Justin Sech, Alexandra DeLucia, Anna L. Buczak, and Mark Dredze. 2020. Civil unrest on Twitter (CUT): A dataset of tweets to support research on civil unrest. In *Proceedings of the Sixth Workshop on Noisy User-generated Text (W-NUT 2020)*, pages 215–221, Online. Association for Computational Linguistics.

Zhiyi Song, Ann Bies, Stephanie Strassel, Tom Riese, Justin Mott, Joe Ellis, Jonathan Wright, Seth Kulick, Neville Ryant, and Xiaoyi Ma. 2015. From light to rich ERE: annotation of entities, relations, and events. In *Proceedings of the the 3rd Workshop on EVENTS: Definition, Detection, Coreference, and Representation*, pages 89–98.

START. 2022. Global terrorism database 1970–2020.

Miriah Steiger, Timir J. Bharucha, Sukrit Venkatagiri, Martin Johannes Riedl, and Matthew Lease. 2021. The psychological well-being of content moderators: The emotional labor of commercial moderation and avenues for improving support. *Proceedings of the 2021 CHI Conference on Human Factors in Computing Systems*.

Ralph Sundberg and Erik Melander. 2013. Introducing the UCDP georeferenced event dataset. *Journal of Peace Research*, 50(4):523–532.

Beth M. Sundheim and Nancy A. Chinchor. 1993. Survey of the Message Understanding Conferences. In *Human Language Technology: Proceedings of a Workshop Held at Plainsboro, New Jersey, March 21-24, 1993*.

Isak Svensson, Susanne Schaftenaar, and Marie Allansson. 2022. Violent political protest: Introducing a new uppsala conflict data program data set on organized violence, 1989-2019. *Journal of Conflict Resolution*.

Hristo Tanev, Nicolas Stefanovitch, Andrew Halterman, Onur Uca, Vanni Zavarella, Ali Hurriyetoglu, Bertrand De Longueville, and Leonida Della Rocca. 2023. Detecting and geocoding battle events from social media messages on the russo-Ukrainian war: Shared task 2, CASE 2023. In *Proceedings of the 6th Workshop on Challenges and Applications of Automated Extraction of Socio-political Events from Text*, pages 160–166, Varna, Bulgaria. INCOMA Ltd., Shoumen, Bulgaria.

MeiHan Tong, Bin Xu, Shuai Wang, Meihuan Han, Yixin Cao, Jiangqi Zhu, Siyu Chen, Lei Hou, and Juanzi Li. 2022. DocEE: A large-scale and fine-grained benchmark for document-level event extraction. In *Proceedings of the 2022 Conference of the North American Chapter of the Association for Computational Linguistics: Human Language Technologies*, pages 3970–3982, Seattle, United States. Association for Computational Linguistics.

Peter Turchin. 2012. Dynamics of political instability in the united states, 1780–2010. *Journal of Peace Research*, 49(4):577–591.

Xiaozhi Wang, Ziqi Wang, Xu Han, Wangyi Jiang, Rong Han, Zhiyuan Liu, Juanzi Li, Peng Li, Yankai Lin, and Jie Zhou. 2020. MAVEN: A Massive General Domain Event Detection Dataset. In *Proceedings of the 2020 Conference on Empirical Methods in Natural Language Processing (EMNLP)*, pages 1652–1671, Online. Association for Computational Linguistics.

Michael D Ward, Andreas Beger, Josh Cutler, Matthew Dickenson, Cassy Dorff, and Ben Radford. 2013. Comparing GDELT and ICEWS event data. *Analysis*, 21(1):267–297.

Nils B Weidmann and Espen Geelmuyden Rød. 2019. *The Internet and political protest in autocracies*, chapter 4. Oxford Studies in Digital Poli.

Wei Xiang and Bang Wang. 2019. A survey of event extraction from text. *IEEE Access*, 7:173111–173137.

Erdem Yörük, Ali Hürriyetoğlu, Fırat Duruşan, and Çağrı Yoltar. 2022. Random sampling in corpus design: Cross-context generalizability in automated multicountry protest event collection. *American Behavioral Scientist*, 66(5):578–602.

Manzhu Yu, Myra Bambacus, Guido Cervone, Keith Clarke, Daniel Duffy, Qunying Huang, Jing Li, Wenwen Li, Zhenlong Li, Qian Liu, et al. 2020. Spatiotemporal event detection: A review. *International Journal of Digital Earth*, 13(12):1339–1365.

Andrej Žukov-Gregorič, Zhiyuan Luo, and Bartal Veyhe. 2016. IBC-C: A dataset for armed conflict analysis. In *Proceedings of the 54th Annual Meeting of the Association for Computational Linguistics (Volume 2: Short Papers)*, pages 374–379.

Evaluating ChatGPT's Ability to Detect Hate Speech in Turkish Tweets

Somaiyeh Dehghan[1,2] and **Berrin Yanikoglu**[1,2]
[1]Faculty of Engineering and Natural Sciences, Sabanci University, Istanbul, Turkey 34956
[2]Center of Excellence in Data Analytics (VERIM), Sabanci University, Istanbul, Turkey 34956
{somaiyeh.dehghan, berrin}@sabanciuniv.edu

Abstract

ChatGPT, developed by OpenAI, has made a significant impact on the world, mainly on how people interact with technology. In this study, we evaluate ChatGPT's ability to detect hate speech in Turkish tweets and measure its strength using zero- and few-shot paradigms and compare the results to the supervised fine-tuning BERT model. On evaluations with the SIU2023-NST dataset, ChatGPT achieved 65.81% accuracy in detecting hate speech for the few-shot setting, while BERT with supervised fine-tuning achieved 82.22% accuracy. This results supports previous findings that show that, despite its much smaller size, BERT is more suitable for natural language classifications tasks such as hate speech detection.

1 Introduction

ChatGPT, developed by OpenAI (OpenAI.), has revolutionized the way people interact with technology. As a state-of-the-art language model, ChatGPT leverages the power of deep learning to understand and generate human-like text, enabling natural and coherent conversations. Its applications range from question answering in various domains, to generating creative content like writing, poetry, and more. Thanks to its tremendous success as a large language model, there has been interest to test its abilities in various natural language understanding problems, such as sentiment analysis and hate speech detection.

Hate speech refers to any form of communication, in speech, writing, or behavior, that offends, threatens, or insults individuals or groups based on attributes such as race, ethnicity, religion, sexual orientation, disability, or gender (Beyhan et al., 2022). Hate speech detection, followed by potential measures such as blocking or counter-speech, is aimed to create safer digital spaces. Detecting hate speech is a challenging problem, since hate speech is subjective, context-dependent, and the language of tweets show high variability with the use of contractions, emojis, and typos.

The performances of hate speech detection systems show a lot of variation in the literature, as researchers often report results on proprietary or different datasets. However, state-of-art methods often use transformer based models, such as BERT (Devlin et al., 2019) or ChatGPT (Brown and et al., 2020).

BERT (Devlin et al., 2019), a pre-trained contextual language model, is widely used to detect hate speech. BERT is a transformer-based model designed for various natural language processing tasks, such as sentiment analysis, named entity recognition, and hate speech detection. It was trained in an unsupervised manner by predicting masked words in a sentence.

ChatGPT (Brown and et al., 2020), on the other hand is also based on the transformer architecture, but is specifically designed for generating coherent and contextually relevant text given an input prompt. It is trained using a language modeling objective, where it learns to predict the next word in a sentence given the context of preceding words.

Related to the problem at hand, BERT uses a bidirectional context, which helps capture complex relationships and dependencies within the text. It is also free, open-source and much smaller (110 million parameters) compared to ChatGPT which has 175 billion parameters. Nonetheless, ChatGPT was selected in this work due to the interest it receives and relatively low cost[1].

In this study, we contribute to the body of work assessing ChatGPT's ability to detect implicit or explicit hate speech in Turkish tweets, as well as its estimation of the strength of hate speech. Its performance is compared to that of fine-tuned BERTurk classifier and regressor models.

[1]Its online use is free and API is cheaper than that of GPT-4s

Proceedings of the 7th Workshop on Challenges and Applications of Automated Extraction of Socio-political Events from Text (CASE 2024), pages 54–59
March 22, 2024

The rest of the paper is organized as follows: in Section 2, we provide a summary about related works; in Section 3, the dataset used to train and test our models is defined; in Section 4, the methodology is presented. Experiments are provided in Section 5. Finally, conclusions and future work are presented in Section 6.

2 Related Work

Many studies have been conducted to evaluate ChatGPT in detection of hate speech in English, each of which used different dataset, but similar studies are rare for the Turkish language. Studies show the importance of the prompts when using ChatGPT.

Among the recent works, Chiu et al. (2022) used ChatGPT to classify English text as sexist or racist. They used zero-, one-, and few-shot learning paradigms. For zero- and one-shot learning, they achieved an average accuracy between 55% and 67% depending on the category of text and type of learning. For few-shot learning, they used a different example set in prompt and they found that with few-shot learning, the model's accuracy could be as high as 85%.

Han and Tang (2022) used ChatGPT to detect hate speech and investigated designing effective prompts for better performance. They demonstrated that numbers of training examples in the prompt matters. Additionally, they discovered that giving the model clear instructions works better than other approaches for incorporating our past knowledge into the model and enhancing its functionality. They achieved accuracy of 86% and macro-F1 of 85% for English comments from YouTube and Reddit.

Huang et al. (2023) examined whether ChatGPT can be used for providing natural language explanations (NLEs) for implicit hateful speech detection. They reported that ChatGPT correctly identifies 80% of the implicit hateful tweets in their experiment setting. Additionally, they discovered that ChatGPT-generated NLEs tend to be interpreted as clearer than NLEs created by humans and can reinforce human perception. This does, however, underline the need for more caution when utilizing ChatGPT as a tool to aid in data annotation because, in the event that it makes a mistake, it may mislead lay people

Li et al. (2023) aimed to use the potential power of ChatGPT to detect harmful content in English.They evaluated ChatGPT in comprehending hateful, offensive, and toxic concepts. They showed that ChatGPT can achieve an accuracy of approximately 80% when compared to Amazon MTurker[2] annotations.

Das et al. (2023) evaluated ChatGPT's performance for multilingual and emoji-based hate speech detection for 11 languages. They achieved highest macro-F1 score (89.2%) for English language and lowest macro-F1 score for Hindi language (67.3%).

Similar to our study, Çam and Ozgur (2023) compared ChatGPT to BERT on a Turkish dataset containing 1,000 tweets against ethnic groups, with three labels (None, Aggressor, Hate). They conducted three different experiments: aggressor tweets was counted as hate, aggressor tweets was removed, and multi classification with these three labels. They also used different pretrained versions of Turkish BERT (BERTurk-base and BERTurk-offensive). In all three experiments, BERTurk-offensive (previously fine tuned with 31,277 Turkish twitter data) showed better performance than ChatGPT. They achieved highest F1 score of 66.6% for ChatGPT in their first experiment (aggressor tweets was counted as hate).

3 Dataset Overview

We use the extended version of the publicly available SIU2023-NST dataset[3] towards immigrants and refugees (İnanç Arın et al., 2023). This dataset is labelled in two ways: binary classification (based on presence or absence of hate speech) and multiclass classification, ranging from insult to threat of harm, assumed to correspond to the strength of hate speech. Tables 1 and 2 show the statistics for the train- and test-split of this dataset.

Table 1: Statistics for the train-split of the Refugee dataset.

Strength	Size	Category	Size
0: Not hate speech	4,477	0: No hate speech	4,477
1: Insult	864	1: Hate speech	1,447
2: Exclusion	410		
3: Wishing harm	137		
4: Threatening harm	36		
Total	5,924	-	5,924

[2]https://www.mturk.com/

[3]https://github.com/verimsu/hate-speech-detection-dataset

<table>
<tr><td>Zero-shot prompt</td><td>You are an AI language model trained to analyze and detect hate speech.

Given a tweet, decide whether the post contains implicitly or explicitly hate speech and also measure the strength of hate speech on a scale of [0-4].
Give your prediction as a yes or no in lowercase for using the following JSON format:
{"prediction": prediction, "strength": strength}

Tweet: benim cebime bu ay 50 lira az giricekse 10 milyon suriyeli ve afgan ölebilir. tayyip çıkıp 40 milyar dolar harcadık bi 40 daha harcarız diyor. lan benim paramı harcıyon?</td></tr>
<tr><td>ChatGPT Response</td><td>prediction: yes, strength: 3</td></tr>
</table>

Figure 1: Our zero-shot prompt and ChatGPT response for an hate speech post towards refugees

<table>
<tr><td>Few-shot prompt</td><td>You are an AI language model trained to analyze and detect hate speech.

Given a tweet, decide whether the post contains implicitly or explicitly hate speech and also measure the strength of hate speech on a scale of [0-4].
For example:

Tweet: 'Depremden hemen sonra asker sahaya insin, milletin canını malını korusun dedim.. Yağmacılar çoğalıyor bunun sonu iyi değil..'
label: no, strength: 0
;
Tweet: 'Yağmacılar ile yağmacı olmayanlar birbirine karıştı, ceza keseceğim diye toplanan gruplar, söylem,duyum ile hareket ediyorlar,daha kötüye doğru gidiyoruz. yağmacılar'
label: no, strength: 0
;
Tweet: 'ne kadar sığınmacı varsa istisnasız sınır dışı edilmeli ve ülkemiz bunlardan temizlenmelidir. ne tedirginlikler ne göç politikası hakkında bilinçlendirilmeye ihtiyacımız yok, biz her şeyin farkındayız.'
label: no, strength: 0
;
Tweet: 'gerçekler ağır gelir suri tarih kitapları sizi isyancı terörist olarak yazacak gelecek nesillerdeki suriyeli çocuklar sizi böyle anacak, devlete kim ihanet ederse teröristtir bunun lamı cimi yoktur .'
label: yes, strength: 1
;
Tweet: 'Tırları yağmalayanları tokat manyağı yapan bir abimiz... Analar aslan doğurmuş helal olsun hırsızlara mallarımızı çaldırmayın ,! suriyeliler Deprem Yağmacılar'
label: yes, strength: 2
;
Tweet: 'suriyeli çetelerin evlilik vaadiyle kandırıp binlerce tl dolandırılan cahillere zerre kadar üzülmüyorum ...türkiye'de kadın kalmadı de mi? beter olun... 15 ocak çarşamba'
label: yes, strength: 3
;
Tweet: 'yagmacilar deprem HalukLevent şimdi bunların yagmacidan ne farkı kaldı vatan hainleri hırsızlar bunlar gibiler olduğu sürece daha başımıza çok işler gelir bizim Allah'ım sen kurunun yanında yasida yakma ama bunları cehennemin en dibine....'
label: yes, strength: 4
;
Give your prediction as a yes or no in lowercase for using the following JSON format:
{"prediction": label, "strength": strength}
;
Tweet: Hocam bu yağmacılar gitsin artık ülkemdemülteciistemiyorum ültecilersınırdışıedilsin suriyelileriistemiyoruz SuriyelilerSehirlerdenCıkartın SuriyeliYağmacılar suriyelikatiller</td></tr>
<tr><td>ChatGPT Response</td><td>prediction: yes, strength: 4</td></tr>
</table>

Figure 2: Our few-shot prompt and ChatGPT response for an hate speech post towards refugees

Table 2: Statistics for the test-split of the Refugee dataset.

Strength	Size	Category	Size
0: Not hate speech	1,119	0: No hate speech	1,119
1: Insult	216		
2: Exclusion	103	1: Hate speech	361
3: Wishing harm	34		
4: Threatening harm	8		
Total	1,480	-	1,480

4 Methodology

We evaluate two approaches , namely BERT and ChatGPT, to detect hate speech and measure the strength of hate speech. The two problems are formulated as a binary-classification problem and a regression problem respectively.

In the first approach, we fine-tune the BERTurk model in the Huggingface Transformer package[4], using a classification or regression head that consists of a linear layer on top of the pooled output. The input to both models are preprocessed to remove usernames, URLs and the # signs, while keeping the text of the hashtags.

For the classification problem, we use cross-entropy (CE) loss to fine-tune BERT:

$$L_{CE} = -\sum_{i=1}^{N} y_i log(\hat{y}_i) \quad (1)$$

where y_i is the target value for the ith input and $\hat{y}_i$ is the prediction.

For the regression problem, we used mean squared error (MSE) loss to fine-tune BERT:

$$L_{MSE} = \frac{1}{n}\sum_{i=1}^{n}(y_i - \hat{y}_i)^2 \quad (2)$$

where y_i and $\hat{y}_i$ are desired and predicted values, respectively.

For the second approach, we use the ChatGPT with zero- and few-shot learning paradigms. For zero- and few-shot learning, we design two prompts to interact with ChatGPT as shown in Figure 1 and 2. Our few-shot prompt contains seven examples from train-split of the Refugee dataset, three of which are examples with non-hate label and four examples with hate labels ranging strength from 1 to 4.

[4]https://huggingface.co/docs/transformers

5 Experiments

We conduct two experiments: Experiment-1: binary classification problem (hateful and non-hateful); Experiment-2: regression problem for predicting strength of hate speech.

Using the transfer learning approach, we fine-tune BERTurk[5] model. We use the cross-entropy loss and mean-squared error (MSE) loss for the classification and regression problems respectively, using stratified 10-fold cross validation.

For zero- and few-shot learning, we use "ChatGPT-text-davinci-003" model as it is one of the most powerful versions of the GPT language model developed by OpenAI. It is trained on a larger and more diverse dataset and designed to generate high-quality natural language responses to a wide range of tasks, including language translation, summarization, question-answering, and more.

Tables 3 and 4 show the results for Experiment-1 and Experiment-2, respectively. Moreover, confusion matrices for these three models are show in Figure 3.

Classification Results: As show in Table 3, supervised BERTurk-CE achieved better performance (82.22% accuracy) compared to ChatGPT (70.81% with zero-shot and 65.81% with few-shot learning) in accuracy, macro-F1, precision, and recall values.

In the case of ChatGPT (zero-shot) and ChatGPT (few-shot), we see that although the accuracy of ChatGPT (zero-shot) is higher, ChatGPT (few-shot) has higher macro-F1, precision and recall values compared to it.

While we give accuracy along with the macro-F1 scores so that our results are comparable to those in the literature, we pay importance to macro-F1 score for ranking the systems since our data is imbalanced. Indeed, the confusion matrices shown in Figure 3 show that ChatGPT (few-shot) is able to correctly identify more positives (higher recall) and avoid more false positives (higher precision) compared to ChatGPT (zero-shot).

Regression Results: The mean squared errors are shown in Table 4. We observe that the BERTurk-MSE regressor has significantly lower MSE (0.46) compared to ChatGPT, with either paradigm (zero- or few-shot). In fact, we can say that without any dedicated training, ChatGPT is not able to predict the strength of hate speech, as its mean-squared

[5]https://huggingface.co/dbmdz/bert-base-turkish-uncased

Table 3: Classification results on Refugee dataset in Experiment-1 for detecting hate speech

	Refugee Dataset			
	Accuracy	Macro-F1	Precision	Recall
BERTurk-CE (supervised transfer learning)	**82.22**	**74.86**	**76.12**	**73.89**
ChatGPT-text-davinci-003 (zero-shot learning)	70.81	58.50	59.04	58.17
ChatGPT-text-davinci-003 (few-shot learning)	65.81	60.19	60.27	63.12

BERTurk-CE (supervised)

Predicted Label \ True Label	0	1
0	1009	110
1	153	208

ChatGPT (zero-shot)

Predicted Label \ True Label	0	1
0	927	192
1	240	121

ChatGPT (few-shot)

Predicted Label \ True Label	0	1
0	765	354
1	152	209

Figure 3: Confusion matrix for BERTurk-CE (supervised), ChatGPT (zero-shot), and ChatGPT (few-shot) models for binary classification in Experiment-1

Table 4: Regression results on Refugee dataset in Experiment-2 for estimating strength of hate speech

	Refugee Dataset
	Mean squared error
BERTurk-MSE (supervised transfer learning)	0.46
ChatGPT-text-davinci-003 (zero-shot learning)	2.49
ChatGPT-text-davinci-003 (few-shot learning)	3.10

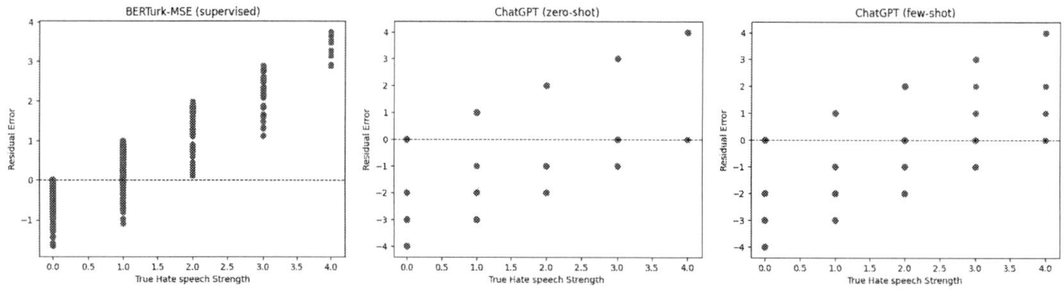

Figure 4: Residual error value for BERTurk-MSE (supervised), ChatGPT (zero-shot), ChatGPT (few-shot)

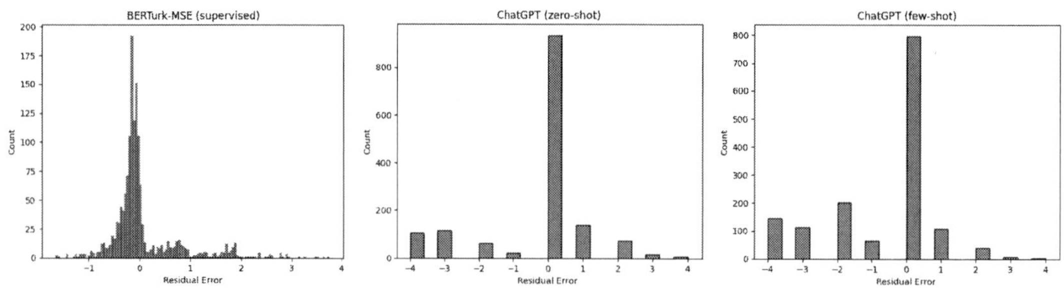

Figure 5: Residual value's histogram for BERTurk-MSE (supervised), ChatGPT (zero-shot), ChatGPT (few-shot)

error is 2.49 for zero-shot and 3.10 for few-shot cases.

The histogram of the residual errors of these approaches are shown in Figure 4 and Figure 5, respectively. Here, we see that the zero-shot paradigm outperforms the few shot with a slight margin.

6 Conclusions and Future Work

In this paper, we evaluate ChatGPT's ability for hate speech detection and measuring strength of hate speech in Turkish tweets. Our experimental results on the extended SIU2023-NST dataset show that fine-tuning the pre-trained BERTurk performs quite well for the challenging problem of hate speech detection. It achieves an accuracy of 82.22% and macro-F1 score of 74.86 in detecting hate speech and a mean square error of 0.46 in estimating the strength of the hate speech. These results are also significantly better than those obtained with ChatGPT, whether in zero- or few-shot paradigm.

Our experience with ChatGPT parallels previous results in the literature, showing that the performance depends strongly on the prompt. Possibly related to this, the relative results of ChatGPT with the zero- or few-shot paradigms are mixed: Zero-shot is better in terms of accuracy and MSE, while the few-shot is better in terms of precision, recall and macro-F1. On the other hand, the performance of the few-shot increased by increasing samples (from 3 to 7), as expected.

As a result, we suggest that ChatGPT may be used as an auxiliary tool in big data annotation. However, care must be taken in the design of prompt that the instructions are simple and clear and the number of samples is appropriate.

As future work direction, we aim to evaluate the explaining ability of ChatGPT in detecting hate speech.

7 Acknowledgements

This work was supported by the EU project "Combating Hate Speech and Discrimination Using Digital Technologies" (EuropeAid/170389/DD/ACT/Multi), carried out by the Hrant Dink Foundation.

References

Fatih Beyhan, Buse Çarık, İnanç Arın, Ayşecan Terzioğlu, Berrin Yanikoglu, and Reyyan Yeniterzi. 2022. A Turkish hate speech dataset and detection system. In *Proceedings of the 13th Conference on Language Resources and Evaluation (LREC 2022)*, pages 4177–4185.

Tom B. Brown and et al. 2020. Language models are few-shot learners. *ArXiv:2005.14165*.

Ke-Li Chiu, Annie Collins, and Rohan Alexander. 2022. Detecting hate speech with GPT-3. *arXiv:2103.12407*.

Mithun Das, Saurabh Kumar Pandey, and Animesh Mukherje. 2023. Evaluating ChatGPT's performance for multilingual and emoji-based hate speech detection. *arXiv:2305.13276*.

Jacob Devlin, Ming-Wei Chang, Kenton Lee, and Kristina Toutanova. 2019. BERT: Pre-training of deep bidirectional transformers for language understanding. In *proceedings of the 2019 Conference of the North American Chapter of the Association for Computational Linguistics: Human Language Technologies*, volume 1, pages 4171–4186.

Lawrence Han and Hao Tang. 2022. Designing of prompts for hate speech recognition with in-context learning. In *2022 International Conference on Computational Science and Computational Intelligence (CSCI)*.

Fan Huang, Haewoon Kwak, and Jisun An. 2023. Is ChatGPT better than human annotators? potential and limitations of ChatGPT in explaining implicit hate speech. *arXiv:2302.07736*.

Lingyao Li, Lizhou Fan, Shubham Atreja, and Libby Hemphill. 2023. "HOT" ChatGPT: The promise of ChatGPT in detecting and discriminating hateful, offensive, and toxic comments on social media. *arXiv:2304.10619*.

OpenAI. *ChatGPT: Optimizing Language Model for Dialogue*.

Nur Bengisu Çam and Arzucan Ozgur. 2023. Evaluation of ChatGPT and BERT-based models for Turkish hate speech detection. In *Proceedings of the International Conference on Computer Science and Engineering (UBMK)*.

İnanç Arın, Zeynep Işık, Seçilay Kutal, Somaiyeh Dehghan, Arzucan Özgür, and Berrin Yanikoğlu. 2023. SIU2023-NST - hate speech detection contest. In *Proceedings of the 31. IEEE Conference on Signal Processing and Communications Applications, Istanbul*.

YYama @ Multimodal Hate Speech Event Detection 2024: Simpler Prompts, Better Results - Enhancing Zero-shot Detection with a Large Multimodal Model

Yosuke Yamagishi
Graduate School of Medicine, The University of Tokyo, Japan
yamagishi-yosuke0115@g.ecc.u-tokyo.ac.jp

Abstract

This paper introduces a zero-shot hate detection experiment using a multimodal large model. Although the implemented model comprises an unsupervised method, results demonstrate that its performance is comparable to previous supervised methods. Furthemore, this study proposed experiments with various prompts and demonstrated that simpler prompts, as opposed to the commonly used detailed prompts in large language models, led to better performance for multimodal hate speech event detection tasks. While supervised methods offer high performance, they require significant computational resources for training, and the approach proposed here can mitigate this issue.

The code is publicly available at https://github.com/yamagishi0824/zeroshot-hate-detect.

1 Introduction

In the contemporary era marked by extensive use of social media, the forms of hate speech have diversified significantly. Hate speech embedded in images on social media, in particular, has become prevalent, rendering its detection crucial (Thapa et al., 2022; Bhandari et al., 2023). The Multimodal Hate Speech Event Detection 2024 shared task at The 7th Workshop on Challenges and Applications of Automated Extraction of Socio-political Events from Text (CASE @ EACL 2024) was a unique task focusing on detecting hateful content in text-embedded images posted on social media concerning the Russia-Ukraine conflict (Thapa et al., 2024). This task is an expanded version of the one conducted in the previous year (Thapa et al., 2023).

Prompt engineering is a method to improve the inference accuracy of a pre-trained model by adding task-specific information to the prompts that serve as inputs to the model. This approach has been extensively researched, particularly with large language models. Various studies have also been conducted on multimodal large models (Gu et al., 2023), proposing different techniques such as task instruction prompting (Efrat and Levy, 2020) and in-context learning (Brown et al., 2020).

In this multimodal hate speech event detection task, it was particularly important to acknowledge that the image was uploaded against the backdrop of the Russia-Ukraine conflict, and that the definition of hate speech was crucial for labeling. Therefore, this study examined the change in performance by using prompts that, in addition to being simple, also included contextual information explaining the task.

The main contributions of this research are as follows:

- The proposed method employs a widely accessible large multimodal model, enhancing its accessibility.
- The method operates under zero-shot conditions, eliminating the need for further model training and facilitating execution in computationally constrained environments, as long as inference is possible.
- This paper have engaged in prompt engineering to achieve improved performance under zero-shot conditions. While prompt engineering is extensively practiced for large language models, it remains limited for multimodal large models. By employing effective prompts, the performance will be improved.

2 Related Works

2.1 Multimodal Large Model

Using multimodal models enables the combination of multiple data types, including images, text, and audio, for input (Wu et al., 2023). While large language models were limited to only text data input, the ability to handle data from multiple modalities

Proceedings of the 7th Workshop on Challenges and Applications of Automated Extraction of Socio-political Events from Text (CASE 2024), pages 60–66
March 22, 2024

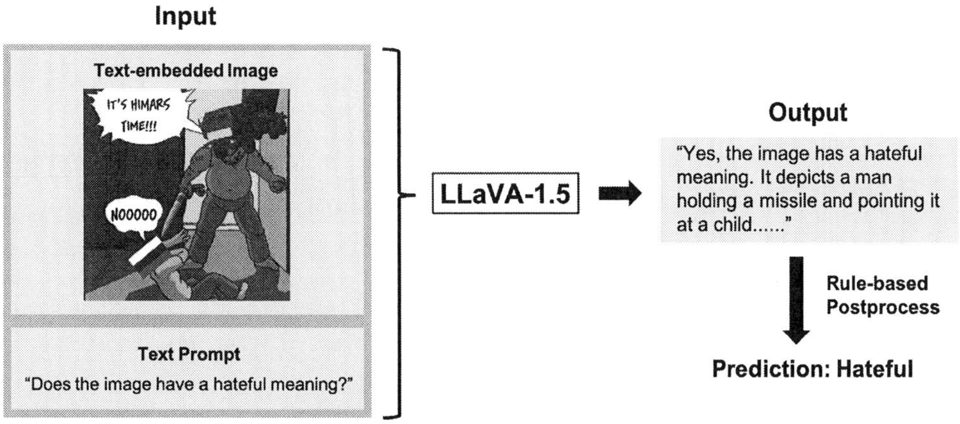

Figure 1: Flowchart of zero-shot hate detection.

expands the potential applications, making it a technology of growing interest. GPT-4 (Achiam et al., 2023) is a notable example of a large multimodal model, but its architecture details are confidential and not freely accessible. In contrast, LLaVA (Liu et al., 2023b) is an openly available model, and its updated version, LLaVA-1.5 (Liu et al., 2023a), has achieved top performance in various benchmarks and is also being used for zero-shot image classification (Islam et al., 2023).

2.2 Hate Speech Detection using Multimodal Large Model

The detection of hate speech in text-embedded images using multimodal models has been implemented for the dataset utilized in this study (Bhandari et al., 2023). In this method, multimodal models such as CLIP (Radford et al., 2021) and GroupViT (Xu et al., 2022) have been employed and fine-tuned, demonstrating superior results compared to unimodal models that use either text or images alone. Furthermore, as a method for detecting hate speech from internet memes, approaches using multimodal models with zero-shot prompting have also been experimented with (Van and Wu, 2023). In this study, by employing the LLaVA, there are cases where it surpasses the performance of past fine-tuned multimodal models. We aim to further leverage the potential of LLaVA by conducting a more detailed comparison of prompt performance.

3 Dataset & Task

3.1 Dataset

This study was conducted in line with the Multimodal Hate Speech Event Detection 2024 shared task at CASE @ EACL 2024. The dataset used was CrisisHateMM, consisting of 4,723 images collected from social media platforms such as Twitter, Facebook, and Reddit (Bhandari et al., 2023). These images are embedded with text and labeled to indicate whether they contain hateful content or not. Additionally, labels are provided to denote whether the subject is an individual, community, or organization.

3.2 Task

The shared task comprises two sub-tasks (Sub-task A & B), of which we participated solely in sub-task A.

Sub-task A is focused on hate speech detection where the objective is to examine images containing text to detect any instances of hate speech (Bhandari et al., 2023; Thapa et al., 2024). This process will utilize a dataset which has already been annotated in advance to assess the frequency of such content. For the sub-task, the dataset comprises 4,723 text-embedded images categorized into two classes: 'Hate' and 'No Hate'. Of these, 2,665 images (56.43%) are labeled as 'Hate', and 2,058 (43.57%) are labeled as 'No Hate'. Additionally, 443 of these images are designated as test data, but the breakdown of labels within the test subset is not provided.

4 Methodology

Using a pre-trained multimodal large model, we input images and text prompts, prompting the model to generate text. Then, by applying rule-based post-processing to the generated texts, we obtained predicted values of whether the content is hateful or non-hateful. The example of flowchart is Figure 1.

4.1 Multimodal Large Model

We adopted the state-of-the-art Large Language-and-Vision Assistant model, LLaVA-1.5, as a multimodal large model (Liu et al., 2023a). LLaVA-1.5 is available to anyone under the LLAMA 2 Community License (Touvron et al., 2023). Out of the available 7 billion and 13 billion parameter versions, we chose the 13 billion parameter model for its robust capabilities. It outputs generated text when given image and text prompts as inputs. We devised multiple prompts and performed inference using images from the dataset as inputs.

4.2 Prompts

We devised various prompts and compared their performance by combining them. We prepared multiple simple prompts. One of these was selected as the base prompt, to which we added contextual information, thereby creating several variations of the prompt. The contextual information included the fact that 'the images were uploaded to social media in the context of the Russia-Ukraine conflict,' definitions of 'hateful,' and 'non-hateful.' The descriptions of these informations were cited from the expressions in the dataset paper (Bhandari et al., 2023).

Specifically, the following prompts were used as input for the model (All detailed prompts are listed in the appendixA). The abbreviations within the parentheses are used in Table 1:

- Simple Base Prompt (**Simple Base**):
  - *"Does this image have a hateful meaning?"*

    This prompt was repeatedly used as a baseline prompt, along with contextual information.

- Other Simple Prompts:

  These prompts were used to evaluate the performance of simple prompts with slight variations, such as replacing words. The detailed prompts in Tabel 2.

- Prompt with Background Information on the Russia-Ukraine Conflict (**Conflict**):
  - *"Note: the image is about the war between Russia and Ukraine that occurred in 2022, posted on social media."*

    This incorporated background information about the image being uploaded on social media related to the conflict between Russia and Ukraine.

- Prompt with Definition of 'hateful' (**Hate**):
  - *"Note: A text-embedded image is classified as hateful if it contains visual or textual hateful content such as threats, personal attacks, slander, or abuse."*

    The definition of 'hateful' was cited from the dataset paper.

- Prompt with Definition of 'non-hateful' (**Non-hate**):
  - *"Note: A text-embedded image is considered non-hateful if it reports events or objectively reports others' opinions in a non-hateful manner."*

    The definition of 'non-hateful' was cited from the dataset paper.

- Prompt with Both 'hate' and 'non-hate' Definitions (**Hate + Non-hate**):

  This prompt incorporated both the definitions of 'hateful' and 'non-hateful'.

- Prompt with All Contextual Information (**Conflict + Hate + Non-hate**):

  This prompt included all background information about the image, as well as both 'hateful' and 'non-hateful' definitions.

4.3 Postprocess

The outputs from LLaVA-1.5 were received as text, which necessitated their conversion into a binary categorization of either 'hate' or 'non-hate.' We confirmed that by inputting closed questions as prompts, without the need for detailed adjustments, the output would begin with 'Yes' if it contained hate speech. Consequently, a simple post-processing step was implemented. Outputs containing "Yes" were classified as 'hate,' and those without it were classified as 'non-hate'.

5 Results

5.1 Performance of Simple Prompts

The comparison of performance using simple prompts is shown in Table1. Although there are some variations, the main evaluation metric used in this shared task, the F1 score, only varied from

Prompt	Recall	Precision	F1	Accuracy
Does this image have a hateful meaning? (**Simple Base**)	0.761	0.759	0.758	0.758
Does this picture have a hateful meaning?	0.748	0.747	0.743	0.743
Does this image have hateful content?	0.757	0.804	0.759	0.774
Does this image convey any hateful messages?	0.755	0.756	0.747	0.747
Is this image hateful?	0.757	0.755	0.755	0.756

Table 1: Comparison of different simple prompts for hate detection.

Prompt	Recall	Precision	F1 Score	Accuracy
Simple Base	**0.761**	**0.759**	**0.758**	**0.758**
Conflict	0.735	0.742	0.737	0.743
Hate	0.715	0.731	0.697	0.700
Non-hate	0.641	0.694	0.595	0.614
Hate + Non-hate	0.716	0.749	0.689	0.695
Conflict + Hate + Non-hate	0.720	0.736	0.702	0.704

Table 2: Comparison of prompts with contextual information.

0.743 to 0.759, a maximum difference of 0.016. It is reasonable to conclude that minor variations in the wording of prompts do not result in significant performance differences.

5.2 Performance of Prompts with Contextual Information

Table2 shows the results. When the contextual information was added to the simple prompts, performance decreased in all cases, with the simple baseline prompt performing the best.

The decrease in performance was particularly notable when the definition of 'Non-hate' was added, with a reduction of 0.120 in the F1 score. In the case of the simple prompts, the number predicted as 'hateful' was 220 (49.7%), whereas with the 'Non-hate' prompt, it dropped to 105 (23.7%), less than half.

In prompts with added contextual information, the 'Conflict' prompt performed the best. However, even then, there was a decrease in performance in terms of precision, recall, and F1 score compared to any of the other simple baselines. The performance was also the lowest in terms of accuracy, matching the lowest score among them.

5.3 Comparison with Previous Baselines

Compare with the baseline performance shown in the dataset paper (Bhandari et al., 2023). In the baselines, fine-tuning and prediction were performed for models with only text, only image, and multimodal of text and image. Table3 displays the performance of each along with the F1 score and accuracy by our simple base prompt. Our proposed method demonstrated superior performance compared to the image model, yet it showed inferior results when compared to the text and multimodal models. The difference in the F1 score relative to the text model was 0.011.

Method	F1	Accuracy
Textual	0.769	0.779
Visual	0.739	0.741
Multimodal	0.786	0.798
Ours	0.758	0.758

Table 3: Comparison with previous baselines.

5.4 Output Characteristics for Development Data

The labels for the test data have not been published, therefore, we conducted error analysis using the development data using the simple base prompt.

The performance on the development data was a recall of 0.794, a precision of 0.794, an F1 score of 0.772, and an accuracy of 0.774.

Of the outputs generated by LLaVA 1.5, the initial sentences included phrases like *"Yes, the image has a hateful meaning"* or *"Yes, the image contains a hateful meaning,"* comprising 243 instances (54.9%). There were 186 instances (42.0%) that clearly predicted no-hate, containing either *"No, the image does not have a hateful meaning"* or *"The image does not have a hateful meaning."* The remaining 14 instances (3.2%) were either merely descriptions of the image content or avoided explicitly stating whether the content was hate or no-hate.

5.5 Qualitative Error Analysis

LLaVA-1.5 not only predicts but also outputs the reasoning behind its predictions. This was utilized for a qualitative error analysis.

The figure 2 represents an example where the label is 'no hate', but it was predicted as 'hate'. This image depicts the Lithuanian independence revolution, during which Ukraine supported Lithuania, and now Lithuania is supporting Ukraine, making it a 'no hate' content.

The model interpreted it completely oppositely as *"It shows a protest sign with a message that is anti-Ukrainian, which is offensive and promotes discrimination"*, although no OCR results of the sign or text were provided (the full output is in the appendixA).

It is presumed that an understanding of historical context and accurate OCR are necessary for prediction, but these seem to have failed in this case.

Figure 2: An example where it was predicted as hate despite being labeled as no hate.

6 Discussion

In this study, we found that prompts containing background information performed worse than the base simple prompts. While it is generally expected that performance improves with the use of instruction prompting, it is intriguing that performance declined when task-specific information, such as the definition of hate speech, was provided. Particularly, adding the definition of no-hate to the prompt seemed to decrease performance. This can be attributed to the bias introduced in the inference due to the information included in the prompt, resulting in an increased prediction of no-hate.

On the other hand, simply providing simple prompts surpassed the performance of past fine-tuned image models and closely matched text models. This result demonstrates the potential of pre-trained multimodal large models to be utilized for hate speech detection even under zero-shot conditions.

This study was exclusively focused on using LLaVA-1.5, and exploring other large multimodal models might produce different results. Given that LLaVA-1.5 is a top-performing, freely available model, the emergence of new models may necessitate additional validation. The research was specifically aimed at detecting hate speech in images containing text on social media, a critical but narrowly focused task. Applying more complex prompts in varied tasks could enhance performance. The significance of identifying hate speech in such images is heightened by the extensive use of social media today. As datasets grow, continued research in this field will be increasingly valuable.

Due to the emergence of large language and multimodal models, zero-shot detection is expected to be increasingly used for sensitive tasks. It's essential to balance the freedom of social media posting with avoiding excessive censorship. Hence, enhanced performance and proper management in zero-shot hate detection are imperative as future tasks.

7 Acknowledgements

We would like to express my sincere gratitude to the hosts of the shared task for providing us with the opportunity to conduct our research. We state that this research was carried out independently without any financial support.

References

Josh Achiam, Steven Adler, Sandhini Agarwal, Lama Ahmad, Ilge Akkaya, Florencia Leoni Aleman, Diogo Almeida, Janko Altenschmidt, Sam Altman, Shyamal Anadkat, et al. 2023. Gpt-4 technical report. *arXiv preprint arXiv:2303.08774*.

Aashish Bhandari, Siddhant Bikram Shah, Surendrabikram Thapa, Usman Naseem, and Mehwish Nasim. 2023. Crisishatemm: Multimodal analysis of directed and undirected hate speech in text-embedded images from russia-ukraine conflict. In *Proceedings of the IEEE/CVF Conference on Computer Vision and Pattern Recognition*.

Tom Brown, Benjamin Mann, Nick Ryder, Melanie Subbiah, Jared D Kaplan, Prafulla Dhariwal, Arvind Neelakantan, Pranav Shyam, Girish Sastry, Amanda Askell, et al. 2020. Language models are few-shot learners. *Advances in neural information processing systems*, 33:1877–1901.

Avia Efrat and Omer Levy. 2020. The turking test: Can language models understand instructions? *arXiv preprint arXiv:2010.11982*.

Jindong Gu, Zhen Han, Shuo Chen, Ahmad Beirami, Bailan He, Gengyuan Zhang, Ruotong Liao, Yao Qin, Volker Tresp, and Philip Torr. 2023. A systematic survey of prompt engineering on vision-language foundation models. *arXiv preprint arXiv:2307.12980*.

Ashhadul Islam, Md Rafiul Biswas, Wajdi Zaghouani, Samir Brahim Belhaouari, and Zubair Shah. 2023. Pushing boundaries: Exploring zero shot object classification with large multimodal models. In *2023 Tenth International Conference on Social Networks Analysis, Management and Security (SNAMS)*, pages 1–5. IEEE.

Haotian Liu, Chunyuan Li, Yuheng Li, and Yong Jae Lee. 2023a. Improved baselines with visual instruction tuning. *arXiv preprint arXiv:2310.03744*.

Haotian Liu, Chunyuan Li, Qingyang Wu, and Yong Jae Lee. 2023b. Visual instruction tuning. *arXiv preprint arXiv:2304.08485*.

Alec Radford, Jong Wook Kim, Chris Hallacy, Aditya Ramesh, Gabriel Goh, Sandhini Agarwal, Girish Sastry, Amanda Askell, Pamela Mishkin, Jack Clark, et al. 2021. Learning transferable visual models from natural language supervision. In *International conference on machine learning*, pages 8748–8763. PMLR.

Surendrabikram Thapa, Farhan Jafri, Ali Hürriyetoğlu, Francielle Vargas, Roy Ka-Wei Lee, and Usman Naseem. 2023. Multimodal hate speech event detection - shared task 4, CASE 2023. In *Proceedings of the 6th Workshop on Challenges and Applications of Automated Extraction of Socio-political Events from Text*, pages 151–159, Varna, Bulgaria. INCOMA Ltd., Shoumen, Bulgaria.

Surendrabikram Thapa, Kritesh Rauniyar, Farhan Ahmad Jafri, Hari Veeramani, Raghav Jain, Sandesh Jain, Francielle Vargas, Ali Hürriyetoğlu, and Usman Naseem. 2024. Extended multimodal hate speech event detection during russia-ukraine crisis - shared task at case 2024. In *Proceedings of the 7th Workshop on Challenges and Applications of Automated Extraction of Socio-political Events from Text (CASE)*.

Surendrabikram Thapa, Aditya Shah, Farhan Jafri, Usman Naseem, and Imran Razzak. 2022. A multimodal dataset for hate speech detection on social media: Case-study of russia-Ukraine conflict. In *Proceedings of the 5th Workshop on Challenges and Applications of Automated Extraction of Socio-political Events from Text (CASE)*, pages 1–6, Abu Dhabi, United Arab Emirates (Hybrid). Association for Computational Linguistics.

Hugo Touvron, Louis Martin, Kevin Stone, Peter Albert, Amjad Almahairi, Yasmine Babaei, Nikolay Bashlykov, Soumya Batra, Prajjwal Bhargava, Shruti Bhosale, et al. 2023. Llama 2: Open foundation and fine-tuned chat models. *arXiv preprint arXiv:2307.09288*.

Minh-Hao Van and Xintao Wu. 2023. Detecting and correcting hate speech in multimodal memes with large visual language model. *arXiv preprint arXiv:2311.06737*.

Jiayang Wu, Wensheng Gan, Zefeng Chen, Shicheng Wan, and Philip S. Yu. 2023. Multimodal large language models: A survey. In *2023 IEEE International Conference on Big Data (BigData)*, pages 2247–2256.

Jiarui Xu, Shalini De Mello, Sifei Liu, Wonmin Byeon, Thomas Breuel, Jan Kautz, and Xiaolong Wang. 2022. Groupvit: Semantic segmentation emerges from text supervision. In *Proceedings of the IEEE/CVF Conference on Computer Vision and Pattern Recognition*, pages 18134–18144.

A Appendix

A.1 Prompts

These are the entire texts of the input prompts:

- Simple Base Prompt
  - *"Does this image have a hateful meaning?"*
- Other Simple Prompts:
  - *"Does this picture have a hateful meaning?"*
  - *"Does this image have hateful content?"*
  - *"Does this image convey any hateful messages?"*
  - *"Is this image hateful?"*
- Prompt with Background Information on the Russia-Ukraine Conflict:
  - *"Does this image have a hateful meaning?\nNote: the image is about the war between Russia and Ukraine that occurred in 2022, posted on social media."*

- Prompt with Definition of 'hateful':
  - *"Does this image have a hateful meaning?\nNote: A text-embedded image is classified as hateful if it contains visual or textual hateful content such as threats, personal attacks, slander, or abuse."*
- Prompt with Definition of 'non-hateful':
  - *"Does this image have a hateful meaning?\nNote: A text-embedded image is considered non-hateful if it reports events or objectively reports others' opinions in a non-hateful manner."*
- Prompt with Both 'hate' and 'non-hate' Definitions:
  - *"Does this image have a hateful meaning?\nNote: A text-embedded image is classified as hateful if it contains visual or textual hateful content such as threats, personal attacks, slander, or abuse. A text-embedded image is considered non-hateful if it reports events or objectively reports others' opinions in a non-hateful manner."*
- Prompt with All Background Information:
  - *"Does this image have a hateful meaning?\nNote: the image is about the war between Russia and Ukraine that occurred in 2022, posted on social media. A text-embedded image is classified as hateful if it contains visual or textual hateful content such as threats, personal attacks, slander, or abuse. A text-embedded image is considered non-hateful if it reports events or objectively reports others' opinions in a non-hateful manner."*

A.2 Incorrect Output

This is the entire output that contains incorrect predictions for Figure 2.

"Yes, the image has a hateful meaning. It shows a protest sign with a message that is anti-Ukrainian, which is offensive and promotes discrimination. The sign is being held by a crowd of people, indicating that the message is being supported by others. Such messages should not be tolerated, as they can lead to further division and harm among people. It is essential to promote respect, understanding, and inclusivity in society."

RACAI at ClimateActivism 2024: Improving Detection of Hate Speech by Extending LLM Predictions with Handcrafted Features

Vasile Păiș
Research Institute for Artificial Intelligence "Mihai Drăgănescu", Romanian Academy
Bucharest, Romania
vasile@racai.ro

Abstract

This paper describes the system that participated in the Climate Activism Stance and Hate Event Detection shared task organized at The 7th Workshop on Challenges and Applications of Automated Extraction of Socio-political Events from Text (CASE 2024). The system tackles the important task of hate speech detection by combining large language model predictions with manually designed features, while trying to explain where the LLM approach fails to predict the correct results.

1 Introduction

Hate speech identification is an important task when analyzing climate change activism events. The shared task (Thapa et al., 2024) organized at the CASE 2024 workshop provided a place to test different approaches for detecting hate speech in short messages specific to social media platforms, such as X (previously known as Twitter). Hate speech can be defined as any message that denigrates individuals or groups based on some characteristic such as race, color, ethnicity, gender, sexual orientation, nationality, or religion (Nockleby, 1994). Messages of interest for the task are exchanged during or related to climate change activism events.

Since many recent works focus on the application of Large Language Models (LLMs) for classifying messages as hateful or not, this work investigated the possibility of improving LLM predictions using handcrafted features. A decision tree was trained in the hope that the resulting decisions could explain the failure of LLM predictions in certain cases.

The rest of this paper is organized as follows: Section 2 provides related work, Section 3 briefly introduces the task and describes the dataset, Section 4 gives an overview of the participating system, including pre-processing and architecture, Section 5 presents the results, and Section 6 gives conclusions and future work.

2 Related work

The survey of Schmidt and Wiegand (2017) presents a number of methods and features useful for hate speech classification, including simple surface features, word generalization, sentiment analysis, lexical resources, linguistic features, knowledge-based features, and meta-information. Further analysis is provided by Parihar et al. (2021). Poletto et al. (2021) provides a review of existing resources and benchmark corpora for hate speech detection. The survey of Jahan and Oussalah (2023) presents different methods employing word embedding representations (both static and contextualized) for hate speech detection.

The recent HaSpeeDe3 shared task (Lai et al., 2023) provided another place for evaluating hate speech detection systems. The system of Grotti and Quick (2021) employed two pre-trained cased BERT-based (Devlin et al., 2019) LLMs, with initial pre-processing by turning hashtags into words to reduce noise. The system of Di Bonaventura et al. (2023) made use of ALBERTo (Polignano et al., 2019) LLM, combined with the Ontology of Dangerous Speech (Stranisci et al., 2022).

Apart from general hate speech detection, specific lexical phenomena have been studied. Dinu et al. (2021) studied the usage of pejorative language in social media. Davidson et al. (2017) acknowledges the distinctions between hate speech and offensive language, which makes the task of hate speech detection more challenging.

3 Dataset and task

The goal of the hate speech detection task is to identify for a given message if it contains hate speech or not. This is a binary label associated with each provided message in the dataset. Dataset files (with

Proceedings of the 7th Workshop on Challenges and Applications of Automated Extraction of Socio-political Events from Text (CASE 2024), pages 67–72
March 22, 2024

splits for training, validation and testing) were provided in CSV format, containing three columns: *index* is a numeric value identifying the message; *tweet* is the actual message; *label* is a numeric value, 1 if the message contains hate speech and 0 otherwise. The dataset is described in detail by Shiwakoti et al. (2024).

The training file contains 7,284 messages of various sizes. The shortest message has only 29 characters, while the largest has 985 characters. The validation file has 1,561 messages with sizes from 29 characters to 940 characters. The test file has 1,562 messages with sizes from 1 character to 960 characters. The size distribution is given in Figure 1. Overall there are 10,407 messages in the entire dataset, 1,277 marked as containing hate speech (12.27%).

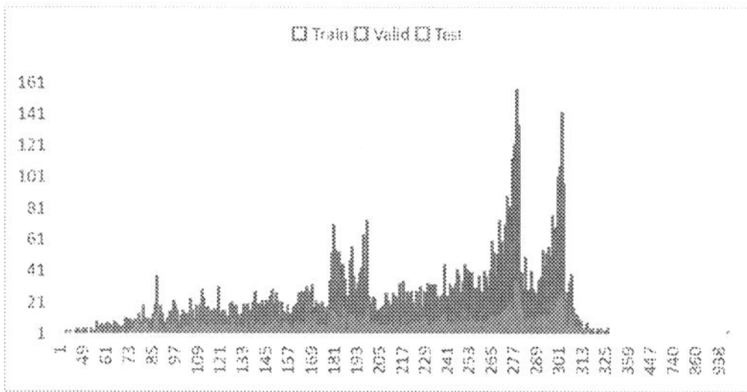

Figure 1: Raw message size distribution.

The messages are included as they were collected from the Internet, without any pre-processing. Therefore, they contain elements such as hashtags, emojis, user references, new lines, spelling errors, inconsistent casing (including all uppercase letters for the entire message or message parts), new lines, URLs.

Some messages contain a large number of hashtags (the maximum number in the training set is 26 in a single message), URLs (maximum 6) or user mentions (maximum 50 in a single message). This is sometimes used to make a message easily discoverable by people looking for a certain hashtag. However, hashtags (sometimes comprised of multiple words, such as "#stopfakegreen") are used to convey a message, which could be hateful. An example message is: *This is why UK politicians are so reluctant to divest from fossil fuels: 1/7 GOVUK #Corruption #ToryCorruption #ExtinctionRebelliom #XR #KeepItInTheGround #ClimateJustice #FridaysForFuture #GreenNewDeal #UKPolitics #TalkingClimate Lets_Discuss_CC*. In this message, simply ignoring the hashtags provide no clues as to why it was marked as hate speech. However, considering the hashtags (especially "#Corruption" and "#ToryCorruption") clarifies the labeling.

URLs present in the dataset are shortened, always starting with "https://t.co" and followed by a code. Therefore URL itself does not add information useful for hate speech detection.

Shiwakoti et al. (2024) mention that rigorous measures were taken to anonymize all usernames and identifiable user information within the dataset. Therefore, the text associated with the user references was not considered relevant for this work.

4 Methodology

4.1 Pre-Processing

The pre-processing operation aimed to transform the raw messages into regular text. All blank characters, including new lines, tabs and other UTF-8 characters, were transformed to regular spaces. Multiple space characters were replaced with a single space. Different UTF-8 characters representing quotation marks were removed. URLs and user mentions were removed as well. Hashtags were split into words when possible, using an algorithm similar to the one described by Micu et al. (2022).

Special characters, including emojis, were removed from text. Even though the use of emojis was shown to improve the results on certain tasks, such as sentiment polarity classification (Gupta et al., 2023), for this work emojis were not considered, primarily because they were not properly handled by the LLMs used.

Due to the inconsistent use of casing in messages, the text was transformed to all lowercase characters.

The resulting pre-processed message size distribution is given in Figure 2. The distribution is more even compared to the original distribution. A large number of messages now have 36 characters, the smallest message having 0 characters (initially had 1 character) and the largest message has 266 characters. Given the relative shortness of the messages, no special considerations are needed when tokenizing and encoding using a LLM.

User mentions are sometimes used as a forwarding mechanism (also known as "retweet") where a user repeats a message to make specific users aware of its content. By using the pre-processing steps above, a number of 1,249 messages were identified as duplicates, thus from the total of 7,284 training examples, only 6,035 were unique.

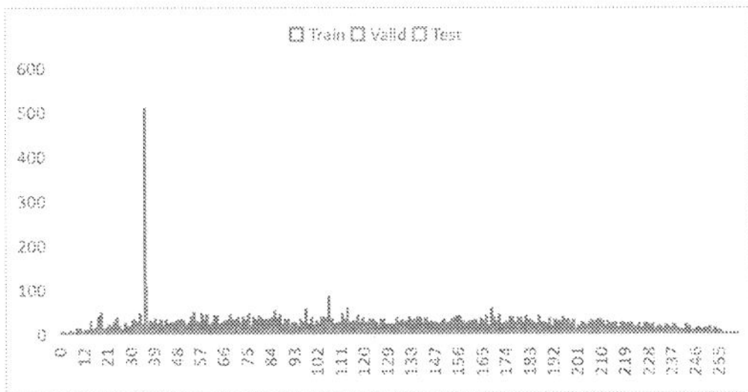

Figure 2: Raw message size distribution.

4.2 System architecture

The system is developed around a text classifier employing a BERT LLM. It has two additional linear layers, with 2,048 and 1,024 cells respectively, employing ReLU and tanh activation functions respectively. These are followed by a final class prediction head.

In order to potentially improve on the LLM predictions and to explore the cases where the LLM gets the result wrong, a set of handcrafted features were produced. The initial set of features that were considered comprises: number of raw hashtags, remaining hashtags after pre-processing, hashtags that were split during pre-processing, user mentions, URLs, raw size, pre-processed size, size difference, TF-IDF prediction. Out of these the raw size, pre-processed size, size difference and raw hashtags were removed from the final system, their influence being limited. Initial experiments showed they had no contribution towards increasing the decision tree accuracy. Furthermore, their usage as leafs on the tree may lead to the model overfitting on potentially less relevant features. On the other hand, there is a difference between the average number of hashtags per message (4.9 for non-hate vs 6.89 for hate speech), the average number of user mentions per message (1.06 for non-hate vs 0.59 for hate), and the average number of URLs per message (0.83 for non-hate vs 0.26 for hate). The numbers were computed on the training set.

For TF-IDF predictions only, the text was further lemmatized using the WordNet (Fellbaum, 1998) lemmatizer available in the NLTK library[1]. Common English words were removed using the stop words set provided by the same NLTK library.

The final stage of the system is represented by a decision tree which combines the LLM predictions with the features. The overall system architecture is presented in Figure 3. At this stage, the different features were written as numerical columns in a CSV file, each row representing a message. Predictions from BERT and TF-IDF were added as two new columns. Only the actual predicted label (0 or 1) was added, without any probabilities. Finally, the resulting file was fed into a decision tree classifier.

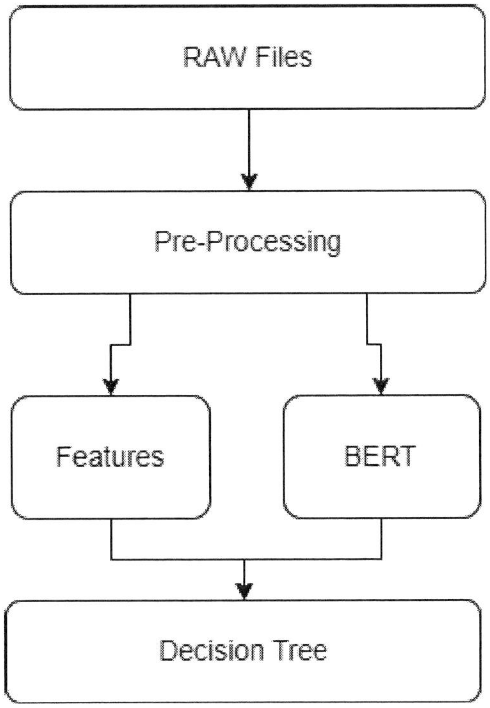

Figure 3: System architecture.

5 Results and discussion

The LLM used for training the system was BERT-large-uncased. The choice of an uncased model version is justified by the pre-processing step that removes capitalization and transforms the text into lowercase characters. The model was trained for at least 5 epochs and a maximum of 20 epochs, with early stopping, when there was no improvement for 3 epochs. During the first 3 epochs, the LLM was frozen and only the last linear layers were actually trained. A batch size of 128 was used. The learning rates for the LLM and the other layers were kept separated. The best hyper-parameters were determined by performing a grid search, with the encoder learning rate possible values of 1e-05, 2e-05, 3e-05, 5e-05, 9e-06, and the learning rate for the linear layers with values of 5e-05, 4e-05, 3e-05, 2e-05, 8e-05. The choice for these specific values is justified by previous experience as well

[1] https://www.nltk.org/

System	P	R	F1	Acc
BERT	89.07	**82.79**	**85.55**	94.37
TF-IDF	**96.79**	78.69	84.93	**94.81**
DT	91.17	81.53	85.48	94.56
Baseline	-	-	70.80	90.10

Table 1: Results on the test dataset.

as the time constraints associated with the shared task, further exploration was not possible within the allocated time.

During training, a 10-fold cross validation approach was used. For each hyper-parameter values 10 experiments were performed and the best values were selected. This resulted in the final system using 3e-05 for the encoder learning rate and 2e-05 as the learning rate for the linear layers. The final model training lasted 11 epochs.

Results are given in Table 1. "Baseline" represents the results reported in the dataset description paper (Shiwakoti et al., 2024), based on a BERT model. "BERT" is the system trained in this paper, using bert-large-uncased with the classification head and parameters described above. "TF-IDF" is the application of a TF-IDF algorithm, as implemented by the Sci-Kit[2] learn library, on the preprocessed text. "DT" is the application of a decision tree based on the results of "BERT", "TF-IDF" and the rest of the features described in Section 4.2. Results were computed using the official evaluation script, available in the shared task's CodaLab environment.

Interestingly, all three systems, including the basic TF-IDF were able to surpass the F1 and Accuracy scores reported by Shiwakoti et al. (2024), using a BERT model. This is probably due to the pre-processing described in Section 4.1. Each system has its strong points, "TF-IDF" provides the best precision and accuracy, "BERT" provides the best recall and F1, while the combination of the two systems, as well as additional features, using the decision tree "DT" provides good values for all metrics. However, since the shared task evaluation was conducted based on F1 score only, the results of the fine-tuned BERT model were submitted for the final evaluation.

Analyzing the decision tree diagram, shows that apart from the TF-IDF and BERT predictions (these are the top-level decision nodes in the tree), the most important features are the number of hashtags that were split during pre-processing, the number of remaining hashtags (without being split) and the number of URLs. Analyzing the message numbers, an average of 0.57 hashtags were split on non-hate messages, compared to an average of 0.11 in hate messages. This seem to indicate that the presence of a large number of these elements makes the text harder to classify by both BERT and TF-IDF. However, the results of the decision tree classifier indicate that relying solely on these numbers to adjust the predictions is not possible. Instead, research is needed into properly handling messages with a large number of hashtags and URLs. Furthermore, research is needed into handling difficult hashtags, containing multiple words or names that are harder to split using automated methods.

6 Conclusion

Results, as discussed above, indicate that simpler algorithms, such as TF-IDF, may provide good enough results for certain tasks within a reduced amount of time compared to deep neural networks. However, the result is clearly influenced by proper pre-processing operations, since TF-IDF when applied on pre-processed text provides improved results compared to the baseline BERT approach applied on raw text.

Explainable AI approaches try to improve our understanding of black-box neural models by explaining their predictions and thus contributing to our trust in such models (Dwivedi et al., 2023; Nauta et al., 2023; Xu et al., 2019). In this paper, by using a decision tree to combine LLM results with TF-IDF and other features, the final model tries to explain and improve upon failures of the LLM approach. This highlighted a need for further research into handling social media messages with a large number of hashtags, URLs, or complex hashtags that may not be easily split into words.

During the pre-processing operations, special characters, including emojis were discarded. However, the inclusion of emoji representations, such as Emoji2Vec (Eisner et al., 2016), may improve the system's results. Furthermore, the current work focused only on BERT-like LLM. Exploration of other model architectures for hate speech detection is needed. Inclusion of additional features, such as the usage of pejorative words, could better the explanation of when the LLM fails to provide correct results.

The dataset provided for this task provided

[2]https://scikit-learn.org/stable/

boolean indications of messages containing or not hate speech. Other tasks offered additional classification, such as the targets of hate speech (individual, organization, and community targets). For the purposes of this work only the task-specific dataset was considered, with no additional resources. However, further investigation may involve combining other datasets in order to better understand if a certain type of hate speech is less likely to be identified by the proposed system. Even more, other authors explore the intensity associated with hate speech (Geleta et al., 2023) or other classifications (Paz et al., 2020). Extending the dataset with additional indicators may allow future work to better explore a model's failures and provide clues that may aid in improving the model's performance.

In accordance with open science principles, the source code of the participating system is made open source in our GitHub repository[3]. A rendered diagram of the decision tree is available in the same place[4], while the image size prevents its inclusion directly in the paper.

Limitations

The current system implementation, models and resources are limited to the English language. The system architecture does not take into account long messages that surpass the direct capability of the LLMs used.

Ethics Statement

We do not foresee ethical concerns with the research presented in this paper. However, it is important to acknowledge that unintended bias might be present in the dataset, even considering the high level of agreement between annotators, and this could be reflected in the resulting models.

References

Thomas Davidson, Dana Warmsley, Michael Macy, and Ingmar Weber. 2017. Automated hate speech detection and the problem of offensive language. *Proceedings of the International AAAI Conference on Web and Social Media*, 11(1):512–515.

Jacob Devlin, Ming-Wei Chang, Kenton Lee, and Kristina Toutanova. 2019. BERT: Pre-training of deep bidirectional transformers for language understanding. In *Proceedings of the 2019 Conference of the North American Chapter of the Association for Computational Linguistics: Human Language Technologies, Volume 1 (Long and Short Papers)*, pages 4171–4186, Minneapolis, Minnesota. Association for Computational Linguistics.

Chiara Di Bonaventura, Arianna Muti, Marco Antonio Stranisci, B McGillivray, and A Meroño-Peñuela. 2023. O-dang at hodi and haspeede3: A knowledge-enhanced approach to homotransphobia and hate speech detection in italian. *Proceedings of the Eighth Evaluation Campaign of Natural Language Processing and Speech Tools for Italian (EVALITA 2023)*, 3473.

Liviu P. Dinu, Ioan-Bogdan Iordache, Ana Sabina Uban, and Marcos Zampieri. 2021. A computational exploration of pejorative language in social media. In *Findings of the Association for Computational Linguistics: EMNLP 2021*, pages 3493–3498, Punta Cana, Dominican Republic. Association for Computational Linguistics.

Rudresh Dwivedi, Devam Dave, Het Naik, Smiti Singhal, Rana Omer, Pankesh Patel, Bin Qian, Zhenyu Wen, Tejal Shah, Graham Morgan, and Rajiv Ranjan. 2023. Explainable ai (xai): Core ideas, techniques, and solutions. *ACM Comput. Surv.*, 55(9).

Ben Eisner, Tim Rocktäschel, Isabelle Augenstein, Matko Bošnjak, and Sebastian Riedel. 2016. emoji2vec: Learning emoji representations from their description. In *Proceedings of the Fourth International Workshop on Natural Language Processing for Social Media*, pages 48–54, Austin, TX, USA. Association for Computational Linguistics.

Christiane Fellbaum. 1998. *WordNet: An electronic lexical database*. MIT press.

Raisa Romanov Geleta, Klaus Eckelt, Emilia Parada-Cabaleiro, and Markus Schedl. 2023. Exploring intensities of hate speech on social media: A case study on explaining multilingual models with XAI. In *Proceedings of the 4th Conference on Language, Data and Knowledge*, pages 532–537, Vienna, Austria. NOVA CLUNL, Portugal.

Leonardo Grotti and Patrick Quick. 2021. Berticelli at haspeede 3: Fine-tuning and cross-validating large language models for hate speech detection. *world*, 2(3):4.

Shelley Gupta, Archana Singh, and Vivek Kumar. 2023. Emoji, text, and sentiment polarity detection using natural language processing. *Information*, 14(4).

Md Saroar Jahan and Mourad Oussalah. 2023. A systematic review of hate speech automatic detection using natural language processing. *Neurocomputing*, 546:126232.

[3] https://github.com/racai-ai/CASE2024_HateSpeech/

[4] https://github.com/racai-ai/CASE2024_HateSpeech/blob/master/tree.png

Mirko Lai, Fabio Celli, Alan Ramponi, Sara Tonelli, Cristina Bosco, and Viviana Patti. 2023. Haspeede3 at evalita 2023: Overview of the political and religious hate speech detection task. In *Proceedings of the Eighth Evaluation Campaign of Natural Language Processing and Speech Tools for Italian. Final Workshop (EVALITA 2023), CEUR. org, Parma, Italy*, pages 1–8.

Roxana Micu, Carol Luca Gasan, and Vasile Păiș. 2022. Splitting hashtags in romanian micro-blogging texts. In *Proceedings of the 17th Edition of the International Conference on Linguistic Resources and Tools for Natural Language Processing (CONSILR 2022)*, Chișinău, Moldova.

Meike Nauta, Jan Trienes, Shreyasi Pathak, Elisa Nguyen, Michelle Peters, Yasmin Schmitt, Jörg Schlötterer, Maurice van Keulen, and Christin Seifert. 2023. From anecdotal evidence to quantitative evaluation methods: A systematic review on evaluating explainable ai. *ACM Comput. Surv.*, 55(13s).

John T Nockleby. 1994. Hate speech in context: The case of verbal threats. *Buff. L. Rev.*, 42:653.

Anil Singh Parihar, Surendrabikram Thapa, and Sushruti Mishra. 2021. Hate speech detection using natural language processing: Applications and challenges. In *2021 5th International Conference on Trends in Electronics and Informatics (ICOEI)*, pages 1302–1308.

María Antonia Paz, Julio Montero-Díaz, and Alicia Moreno-Delgado. 2020. Hate speech: A systematized review. *SAGE Open*, 10(4):2158244020973022.

Fabio Poletto, Valerio Basile, Manuela Sanguinetti, Cristina Bosco, and Viviana Patti. 2021. Resources and benchmark corpora for hate speech detection: a systematic review. *Language Resources and Evaluation*, 55(2):477–523.

Marco Polignano, Pierpaolo Basile, Marco De Gemmis, Giovanni Semeraro, Valerio Basile, et al. 2019. Alberto: Italian bert language understanding model for nlp challenging tasks based on tweets. In *CEUR Workshop Proceedings*, volume 2481, pages 1–6. CEUR.

Anna Schmidt and Michael Wiegand. 2017. A survey on hate speech detection using natural language processing. In *Proceedings of the Fifth International Workshop on Natural Language Processing for Social Media*, pages 1–10, Valencia, Spain. Association for Computational Linguistics.

Shuvam Shiwakoti, Surendrabikram Thapa, Kritesh Rauniyar, Akshyat Shah, Aashish Bhandari, and Usman Naseem. 2024. Analyzing the dynamics of climate change discourse on twitter: A new annotated corpus and multi-aspect classification. *Preprint*.

Marco Antonio Stranisci, Simona Frenda, Mirko Lai, Oscar Araque, Alessandra Teresa Cignarella, Valerio Basile, Cristina Bosco, and Viviana Patti. 2022. O-dang! the ontology of dangerous speech messages. In *Proceedings of the 2nd Workshop on Sentiment Analysis and Linguistic Linked Data*, pages 2–8, Marseille, France. European Language Resources Association.

Surendrabikram Thapa, Kritesh Rauniyar, Farhan Ahmad Jafri, Shuvam Shiwakoti, Hari Veeramani, Raghav Jain, Guneet Singh Kohli, Ali Hürriyetoğlu, and Usman Naseem. 2024. Stance and hate event detection in tweets related to climate activism - shared task at case 2024. In *Proceedings of the 7th Workshop on Challenges and Applications of Automated Extraction of Socio-political Events from Text (CASE)*.

Feiyu Xu, Hans Uszkoreit, Yangzhou Du, Wei Fan, Dongyan Zhao, and Jun Zhu. 2019. Explainable ai: A brief survey on history, research areas, approaches and challenges. In *Natural Language Processing and Chinese Computing: 8th CCF International Conference, NLPCC 2019, Dunhuang, China, October 9–14, 2019, Proceedings, Part II 8*, pages 563–574. Springer.

CLTL@Multimodal Hate Speech Event Detection 2024: The Winning Approach to Detecting Multimodal Hate Speech and Its Targets

Yeshan Wang
CLTL, Vrije Universiteit Amsterdam
Amsterdam, The Netherlands
yestin-wang@outlook.com

Ilia Markov
CLTL, Vrije Universiteit Amsterdam
Amsterdam, The Netherlands
i.markov@vu.nl

Abstract

In the context of the proliferation of multimodal hate speech related to the Russia-Ukraine conflict, we introduce a unified multimodal fusion system for detecting hate speech and its targets in text-embedded images. Our approach leverages the Twitter-based RoBERTa and Swin Transformer V2 models to encode textual and visual modalities, and employs the Multilayer Perceptron (MLP) fusion mechanism for classification. Our system achieved macro F1 scores of 87.27% for hate speech detection and 80.05% for hate speech target detection in the Multimodal Hate Speech Event Detection Challenge 2024, securing the 1st rank in both subtasks. We open-source the trained models at https://huggingface.co/Yestin-Wang

1 Introduction

In the ever-evolving digital age, social media platforms have emerged as pivotal arenas for information exchange and social interaction. This surge in online engagement, while fostering connectivity and the exchange of ideas, has also led to a rise in online abuse, including the spread of hate speech. Hate speech, commonly defined as communication that disparages a person or a group on the basis of some characteristic such as race, color, ethnicity, gender, sexual orientation, nationality, religion, or other characteristics (Nockleby, 2000), has emerged as a significant societal issue. The complexity of identifying hate speech is further amplified by the multimodal nature of online content, often in the form of text-embedded images. These images, which combine visual and textual elements, are a prevalent mode of expression on social media platforms (Shang et al., 2021). The challenge of detecting hate speech in text-embedded images arises from the multimodal nature of the content, where textual cues are intertwined with visual content. Traditional unimodal models, which focus solely on text or image classification, fall short in effectively interpreting the nuanced and often context-dependent nature of hate speech in these multimodal scenarios (Kiela et al., 2020). Therefore, there is a critical need for advanced multimodal models that can effectively integrate and analyze both textual and visual information to accurately identify hate speech in text-embedded images.

In light of this need, the Multimodal Hate Speech Event Detection Challenge[1] at CASE 2024 (Thapa et al., 2024) provides a platform for developing and evaluating models capable of detecting hate speech in text-embedded images, concerning politically controversial topics related to the Russia-Ukraine War. This task builds on the 2023 iteration of this shared task (Thapa et al., 2023), which includes subtasks aimed at not only determining the presence of hate speech in such images but also identifying the targets of hateful content, whether they are individuals, organizations, or communities. Most of the participating teams from previous year had employed supervised approaches based on unimodal transformer models (e.g., BERT, XLM-Roberta, etc.) (Armenta-Segura et al., 2023; Singh et al., 2023) or methods based on feature engineering (e.g., lexical features, named entities, amongst others) and ensemble learning strategies (Sahin et al., 2023). However, these approaches often required complex feature engineering and specialized model structure for specific subtasks, which makes it challenging to generalize across different subtasks, such as detecting hate speech and its targets (Thapa et al., 2023).

We introduce an unified multimodal architecture for both hate speech and target detection tasks. Our approach employs Twitter-based RoBERTa (Loureiro et al., 2023) and Swin Transformer V2 models (Liu et al., 2022) to extract features for

[1] `https://codalab.lisn.upsaclay.fr/competitions/16203`

Proceedings of the 7th Workshop on Challenges and Applications of Automated Extraction of Socio-political Events from Text (CASE 2024), pages 73–78
March 22, 2024

encoding textual and visual content and concatenates them via the Multilayer Perceptron (MLP) fusion technique. Without the need for feature engineering, our system achieved first place in both subtasks, outperforming the previous year's top team by 1.62% F1 score in subtask A and 3.71% F1 score in subtask B, respectively.

2 Related Work

In the intersection of natural language processing and computer vision, the detection of hate speech in multimodal content, especially in text-embedded images, has increasingly attracted scholarly attention. This trend is driven by both the development of innovative multimodal methodologies and the creation of extensive datasets (Bhandari et al., 2023; Fersini et al., 2022; Pramanick et al., 2021; Suryawanshi et al., 2020). A pivotal advancement was the Hateful Memes Challenge at NeurIPS 2020 (Kiela et al., 2020), which provided an open-source dataset comprising 10,000 meme examples, fostering a competitive environment for developing state-of-the-art methods. The winning approach by Zhu (2020) combined VL-BERT (Su et al., 2020), UNITER (Chen et al., 2020), VILLA (Gan et al., 2020) and ERNIE-ViL (Yu et al., 2021) through ensemble learning, demonstrating enhanced capability in multimodal hate speech detection.

Research on multimodal hate speech detection has predominantly focused on multimodal fusion approaches, essential for handling the dual-modality of text-embedded images. These methodologies are typically divided into early fusion, which combines text and visual features at the initial stages using deep fusion encoders with cross-modal attention (Atrey et al., 2010), and late fusion, which employs separate processing of image and text modalities before merging them at a decisive alignment stage (Li et al., 2022). Recent studies employed novel feature extraction techniques to improve classification efficacy. For instance, Zhou et al. (2021) proposed an image captioning-based feature extraction method, generating descriptive texts from multimodal memes. Blaier et al. (2021) showed that incorporating caption features during model fine-tuning improves the performance of various multimodal models for hateful meme detection.

The scope of multimodal hate speech detection is continually widening to cover a wide range of hate speech triggering events, such as presidential elections (Suryawanshi et al., 2020), the COVID-19 pandemic (Pramanick et al., 2021), and geopolitical conflicts like the Russia-Ukraine War (Thapa et al., 2022). Initiatives to label and detect harmful text-embedded images in these specific contexts contribute to a deeper understanding of how multimodal hate speech manifests itself during various significant events.

3 Dataset & Task Description

3.1 Dataset Description

The dataset used for the shared task is CrisisHateMM (Bhandari et al., 2023). It comprises 4,723 text-embedded images, reflecting diverse social media discourses related to the Russia-Ukraine conflict. The dataset is meticulously compiled from popular social media platforms such as Twitter, Reddit, and Facebook. Each item in the dataset comprises an original image file alongside its extracted textual content, obtained via OCR technology using the Google Vision API[2].

Subtask	Classes	Train	Eval	Test
Subtask A	Hate	1,942	243	243
	No Hate	1,658	200	200
Subtask B	Individual	823	102	102
	Community	335	40	42
	Organization	784	102	98

Table 1: Dataset statistics: number of instances across different subtasks.

For both subtasks, the dataset is split into training, evaluation, and test sets. Table 1 provides the number of instances in each set. Notably, the test set labels remain undisclosed during the challenge phase to ensure an unbiased performance evaluation.

3.2 Subtask A: Hate Speech Detection

Subtask A focuses on identifying whether a given text-embedded image contains hate speech or not, corresponding to the binary classification problem. There are 2,428 text-embedded images labeled as containing hate speech, and 2,058 non-hate speech examples in the dataset, which is divided into 3,600 training, 443 evaluation, and 443 testing instances. This division ensures that there is the same number of instances per class in the evaluation and test sets.

[2]https://cloud.google.com/vision/docs/ocr

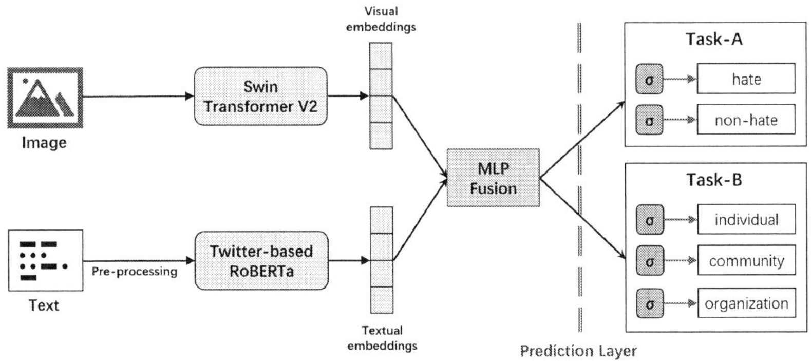

Figure 1: An overview of the CLTL's system.

3.3 Subtask B: Target Detection

Subtask B aims to identify the targets of hate speech within 2,428 text-embedded hateful images. Each text-embedded image in this subtask is annotated for targeting specific groups or entities: "community", "individual" or "organization", which is viewed as a multi-class, single-label classification problem.

4 Methodology

Our approach is based on a multimodal architecture that integrates large-scale pre-trained models, Twitter-based RoBERTa (Loureiro et al., 2023) and Swin Transformer V2 (Liu et al., 2022), to extract contextualized embeddings from textual and visual inputs, respectively. These embeddings are then concatenated using the Multilayer Perceptron (MLP) fusion module (Shi et al., 2021) for classifying each instance into one of the predefined categories. Our model is universally applicable to both subtasks A and B, differing only in the output layer, as depicted in Figure 1.

4.1 Text Preprocessing

The provided dataset comes with the textual data extracted from text-embedded images via Google OCR Vision API. We applied simple preprocessing steps, which involve removing URLs, username mentions (i.e., @username), and emojis using regular expressions, followed by setting the text truncation length to 512 tokens. These preprocessing steps are commonly applied when dealing with social media data (Gupta and Joshi, 2017).

4.2 Transformers Models

4.2.1 Twitter-based RoBERTa

The Twitter-based RoBERTa model (Loureiro et al., 2023) is a RoBERTa-large model (Liu et al., 2019) trained on a large corpus of 154M tweets covering the periods between 2018-01 and 2022-12, possibly covering tweets related to the Russia-Ukraine conflict as well. Considering that the properties of tweets are to some extent similar to the properties of texts embedded in images in our data: both are short texts, containing informal language, abbreviations and slang specific to social media, a domain-specific large language model is expected to be more suitable for encoding textual input. The Twitter-based RoBERTa model is publicly available via the Hugging Face Transformer API[3].

4.2.2 Swin Transformer V2

Swin Transformer V2 (Liu et al., 2022) is an improved version of the Swin Transformer (Liu et al., 2021), which employs a window-based attention mechanism for efficient image processing across various scales and resolutions by partitioning the image into non-overlapping patches and processing these sequentially at each stage. This approach mitigates the computational and memory burden issues of large-scale image processing in traditional transformer architectures that apply global self-attention mechanisms across the entire image. In our experiments, we use the TIMM framework implementation of the Swin Transformer V2 model[4]. The model was pretrained on the ImageNet-1k dataset, containing a collection of 1.2 million labeled images with one thousand object categories (Russakovsky et al., 2015).

4.3 MLP Fusion & Prediction

Our fusion strategy entails the concatenation of text and image embeddings through the Multilayer

[3]https://huggingface.co/cardiffnlp/twitter-roberta-large-2022-154m

[4]https://huggingface.co/timm/swinv2_base_window8_256.ms_in1k

Team	Recall	Precision	F1-score	Rank
Ours (CLTL)	87.37	87.20	87.27	1st (2024)
ARC-NLP	85.67	85.63	85.65	1st (2023)
AAST-NLP	85.46	85.40	85.43	2nd (2024)
bayesiano98	85.61	85.28	85.28	2nd (2023)
Baseline (CLIP)	-	-	78.60	-

Table 2: Performance comparison for the baseline approach (Bhandari et al., 2023) and top-performing teams in 2023/24 multimodal hate speech detection task (Thapa et al., 2023, 2024).

Perceptron (MLP) fusion module (Shi et al., 2021), where the top vector representations from different models are pooled (concatenated) into a single vector. A prediction layer is added at the end to perform classification: for subtask A, the sigmoid outputs a single value to yield a probability of hate speech presence. For subtask B, each target category (individual, community, and organization) has a separate sigmoid function that outputs the corresponding probability.

5 Experimentals and Evaluation Results

5.1 Experimental Settings

Our multimodal classification system was developed using the PyTorch framework and AutoGluon library (Shi et al., 2021) for a robust and flexible implementation. We fine-tuned Twitter-based RoBERTa and Swin Transformer V2 models on the training data with the following hyperparameters: a base learning rate of 1e-4, decay rate of 0.9 using cosine decay scheduling, batch size of 8, and a manual seed of 0 for reproducibility. The models were optimized using the AdamW optimizer for up to 10 epochs, or until an early stopping criterion was met to prevent overfitting. After fine-tuning, the models were assessed on the evaluation set. All experiments were conducted on the Google Colaboratory platform with a NVIDIA A100 GPU, taking approximately 25 minutes for subtask A and 20 minutes for subtask B.

5.2 Results & Discussion

The official evaluation metric to score participating systems was macro-averaged F1 score as the test set is imbalanced. Table 2 and 3 showcase the comparative performance of the CLTL team's system in addressing the challenging tasks of multimodal hate speech detection (subtask A) and target detection (subtask B), reflect the superior performance of our system in comparison to the baseline approach (Bhandari et al., 2023) and other top-ranked participating systems (Thapa et al., 2023, 2024).

In subtask A, our system obtained an F1 score of 87.27%, achieving the top rank on the leaderboard. This performance represents a substantial improvement over the previous year's winning entry (Sahin et al., 2023), with an increase of 1.62% in F1 score. Notably, our system excelled across all classification metrics within the test results, and outperformed the CLIP model baseline approach by 8.67% in terms of F1 score, highlighting the robustness of our approach for multimodal hate speech detection.

In subtask B, our system again led the rankings, achieving an F1 score of 80.05%. This is a notable advancement of 18.55% over the F1 score of the baseline approach, which validates the effectiveness of our system in identifying the specific targets of multimodal hate speech.

The success of our system across both subtasks could be potentially attributed to several factors. The extensive pre-training on large volumes of textual and visual content has been instrumental, partially due to the Twitter-based RoBERTa's domain-specific knowledge of social media discourse, and the Swin Transformer V2's proficiency in visual understanding. The subsequent fine-tuning on the CrisisHateMM training set has further enhanced the system's capacity for classifying multimodal hateful content. Moreover, the concatenation of text and image modalities via the MLP fusion module, has proven effective in capturing the complex interplay between textual and visual cues inherent in multimodal hate speech and its targets.

6 Conclusion

In this work, we introduced the multimodal architecture designed by CLTL team for the Multimodal Hate Speech Event Detection Challenge 2024. Leveraging the Twitter-based RoBERTa and Swin Transformer V2 for feature extraction and

Team	Recall	Precision	F1-score	Rank
Ours (CLTL)	79.07	81.48	80.05	1st (2024)
AAST-NLP	74.65	82.40	76.71	2nd (2024)
ARC-NLP	76.36	76.37	76.34	1st (2023)
bayesiano98	75.54	73.30	74.10	2nd (2023)
Baseline (CLIP)	-	-	61.50	-

Table 3: Performance comparison for the baseline approach (Bhandari et al., 2023) and top-performing teams in 2023/24 multimodal hate speech target detection task (Thapa et al., 2023, 2024).

employing the MLP fusion mechanism, our system achieved the top rank with the highest macro F1 score on both subtasks, which sets a new state-of-the-art in detecting hate speech and its targets on the CrisisHateMM dataset. In future work, we aim to refine our approach by experimenting with advanced fine-tuning strategies such as parameter-efficient fine-tuning (PEFT), using larger multimodal datasets to improve the generalization capabilities of our approach across diverse social media domains.

References

Jesus Armenta-Segura, César Jesús Núñez-Prado, Grigori Olegovich Sidorov, Alexander Gelbukh, and Rodrigo Francisco Román-Godínez. 2023. Ometeotl@multimodal hate speech event detection 2023: Hate speech and text-image correlation detection in real life memes using pre-trained BERT models over text. In *Proceedings of the 6th Workshop on Challenges and Applications of Automated Extraction of Socio-political Events from Text*, pages 53–59, Varna, Bulgaria. INCOMA Ltd., Shoumen, Bulgaria.

Pradeep K. Atrey, M. Anwar Hossain, Abdulmotaleb El Saddik, and Mohan S. Kankanhalli. 2010. Multimodal fusion for multimedia analysis: A survey. *Multimedia Syst.*, 16(6):345–379.

Aashish Bhandari, Siddhant B. Shah, Surendrabikram Thapa, Usman Naseem, and Mehwish Nasim. 2023. CrisisHateMM: Multimodal analysis of directed and undirected hate speech in text-embedded images from Russia-Ukraine conflict. In *2023 IEEE/CVF Conference on Computer Vision and Pattern Recognition Workshops (CVPRW)*, pages 1994–2003.

Efrat Blaier, Itzik Malkiel, and Lior Wolf. 2021. Caption enriched samples for improving hateful memes detection. In *Proceedings of the 2021 Conference on Empirical Methods in Natural Language Processing*, pages 9350–9358, Online and Punta Cana, Dominican Republic. Association for Computational Linguistics.

Yen-Chun Chen, Linjie Li, Licheng Yu, Ahmed El Kholy, Faisal Ahmed, Zhe Gan, Yu Cheng, and Jingjing Liu. 2020. UNITER: Universal image-text representation learning. In *Computer Vision–ECCV 2020: 16th European Conference, Glasgow, UK, August 23–28, 2020, Proceedings, Part XXX*, pages 104–120. Springer.

Elisabetta Fersini, Francesca Gasparini, Giulia Rizzi, Aurora Saibene, Berta Chulvi, Paolo Rosso, Alyssa Lees, and Jeffrey Sorensen. 2022. SemEval-2022 task 5: Multimedia automatic misogyny identification. In *Proceedings of the 16th International Workshop on Semantic Evaluation (SemEval-2022)*, pages 533–549, Seattle, United States. Association for Computational Linguistics.

Zhe Gan, Yen-Chun Chen, Linjie Li, Chen Zhu, Yu Cheng, and Jingjing Liu. 2020. Large-scale adversarial training for vision-and-language representation learning. In *Advances in Neural Information Processing Systems*, volume 33, pages 6616–6628. Curran Associates, Inc.

Itisha Gupta and Nisheeth Joshi. 2017. Tweet normalization: A knowledge based approach. In *2017 International Conference on Infocom Technologies and Unmanned Systems (Trends and Future Directions) (ICTUS)*, pages 157–162.

Douwe Kiela, Hamed Firooz, Aravind Mohan, Vedanuj Goswami, Amanpreet Singh, Pratik Ringshia, and Davide Testuggine. 2020. The Hateful Memes Challenge: Detecting hate speech in multimodal memes. In *Advances in Neural Information Processing Systems*, volume 33, pages 2611–2624. Curran Associates, Inc.

Liunian Harold Li, Pengchuan Zhang, Haotian Zhang, Jianwei Yang, Chunyuan Li, Yiwu Zhong, Lijuan Wang, Lu Yuan, Lei Zhang, Jenq-Neng Hwang, Kai-Wei Chang, and Jianfeng Gao. 2022. Grounded language-image pre-training. In *2022 IEEE/CVF Conference on Computer Vision and Pattern Recognition (CVPR)*, pages 10955–10965.

Yinhan Liu, Myle Ott, Naman Goyal, Jingfei Du, Mandar Joshi, Danqi Chen, Omer Levy, Mike Lewis, Luke Zettlemoyer, and Veselin Stoyanov. 2019. RoBERTa: A robustly optimized BERT pretraining approach. *arXiv/1907.11692*.

Ze Liu, Han Hu, Yutong Lin, Zhuliang Yao, Zhenda Xie, Yixuan Wei, Jia Ning, Yue Cao, Zheng Zhang, Li Dong, Furu Wei, and Baining Guo. 2022. Swin

Transformer V2: Scaling up capacity and resolution. In *2022 IEEE/CVF Conference on Computer Vision and Pattern Recognition (CVPR)*, pages 11999–12009.

Ze Liu, Yutong Lin, Yue Cao, Han Hu, Yixuan Wei, Zheng Zhang, Stephen Lin, and Baining Guo. 2021. Swin Transformer: Hierarchical vision transformer using shifted windows. In *Proceedings of the IEEE/CVF International Conference on Computer Vision (ICCV)*, pages 10012–10022.

Daniel Loureiro, Kiamehr Rezaee, Talayeh Riahi, Francesco Barbieri, Leonardo Neves, Luis Espinosa Anke, and José Camacho-Collados. 2023. Tweet insights: A visualization platform to extract temporal insights from twitter. *arXiv/2308.02142*.

John T Nockleby. 2000. Hate speech. *Encyclopedia of the American constitution*, 3(2):1277–1279.

Shraman Pramanick, Dimitar Dimitrov, Rituparna Mukherjee, Shivam Sharma, Md. Shad Akhtar, Preslav Nakov, and Tanmoy Chakraborty. 2021. Detecting harmful memes and their targets. In *Findings of the Association for Computational Linguistics: ACL-IJCNLP 2021*, pages 2783–2796, Online. Association for Computational Linguistics.

Olga Russakovsky, Jia Deng, Hao Su, Jonathan Krause, Sanjeev Satheesh, Sean Ma, Zhiheng Huang, Andrej Karpathy, Aditya Khosla, Michael Bernstein, Alexander C. Berg, and Li Fei-Fei. 2015. ImageNet Large Scale Visual Recognition Challenge. *International Journal of Computer Vision (IJCV)*, 115(3):211–252.

Umitcan Sahin, Izzet Emre Kucukkaya, Oguzhan Ozcelik, and Cagri Toraman. 2023. ARC-NLP at multimodal hate speech event detection 2023: Multimodal methods boosted by ensemble learning, syntactical and entity features. In *Proceedings of the 6th Workshop on Challenges and Applications of Automated Extraction of Socio-political Events from Text*, pages 71–78, Varna, Bulgaria. INCOMA Ltd., Shoumen, Bulgaria.

Lanyu Shang, Yang Zhang, Yuheng Zha, Yingxi Chen, Christina Youn, and Dong Wang. 2021. AOMD: An analogy-aware approach to offensive meme detection on social media. *Information Processing Management*, 58(5):102664.

Xingjian Shi, Jonas Mueller, Nick Erickson, Mu Li, and Alex Smola. 2021. Multimodal AutoML on structured tables with text fields. In *8th ICML Workshop on Automated Machine Learning (AutoML)*.

Karanpreet Singh, Vajratiya Vajrobol, and Nitisha Aggarwal. 2023. IIC_Team@multimodal hate speech event detection 2023: Detection of hate speech and targets using xlm-roberta-base. In *Proceedings of the 6th Workshop on Challenges and Applications of Automated Extraction of Socio-political Events from Text*, pages 136–143, Varna, Bulgaria. INCOMA Ltd., Shoumen, Bulgaria.

Weijie Su, Xizhou Zhu, Yue Cao, Bin Li, Lewei Lu, Furu Wei, and Jifeng Dai. 2020. VL-BERT: Pretraining of generic visual-linguistic representations. In *International Conference on Learning Representations*.

Shardul Suryawanshi, Bharathi Raja Chakravarthi, Mihael Arcan, and Paul Buitelaar. 2020. Multimodal meme dataset (MultiOFF) for identifying offensive content in image and text. In *Proceedings of the Second Workshop on Trolling, Aggression and Cyberbullying*, pages 32–41, Marseille, France. European Language Resources Association (ELRA).

Surendrabikram Thapa, Farhan Jafri, Ali Hürriyetoğlu, Francielle Vargas, Roy Ka-Wei Lee, and Usman Naseem. 2023. Multimodal hate speech event detection - shared task 4, CASE 2023. In *Proceedings of the 6th Workshop on Challenges and Applications of Automated Extraction of Socio-political Events from Text*, pages 151–159, Varna, Bulgaria. INCOMA Ltd., Shoumen, Bulgaria.

Surendrabikram Thapa, Kritesh Rauniyar, Farhan Ahmad Jafri, Hari Veeramani, Raghav Jain, Sandesh Jain, Francielle Vargas, Ali Hürriyetoğlu, and Usman Naseem. 2024. Extended multimodal hate speech event detection during Russia-Ukraine crisis - shared task at CASE 2024. In *Proceedings of the 7th Workshop on Challenges and Applications of Automated Extraction of Socio-political Events from Text (CASE)*.

Surendrabikram Thapa, Aditya Shah, Farhan Jafri, Usman Naseem, and Imran Razzak. 2022. A multimodal dataset for hate speech detection on social media: Case-study of Russia-Ukraine conflict. In *Proceedings of the 5th Workshop on Challenges and Applications of Automated Extraction of Socio-political Events from Text (CASE)*, pages 1–6, Abu Dhabi, United Arab Emirates (Hybrid). Association for Computational Linguistics.

Fei Yu, Jiji Tang, Weichong Yin, Yu Sun, Hao Tian, Hua Wu, and Haifeng Wang. 2021. ERNIE-ViL: Knowledge enhanced vision-language representations through scene graphs. *Proceedings of the AAAI Conference on Artificial Intelligence*, 35(4):3208–3216.

Yi Zhou, Zhenhao Chen, and Huiyuan Yang. 2021. Multimodal learning for hateful memes detection. In *2021 IEEE International Conference on Multimedia Expo Workshops (ICMEW)*, pages 1–6.

Ron Zhu. 2020. Enhance multimodal transformer with external label and in-domain pretrain: Hateful meme challenge winning solution. *arXiv/2012.08290*.

HAMiSoN-Generative at ClimateActivism 2024: Stance Detection using generative large language models

Jesús M. Fraile-Hernández and **Anselmo Peñas**
NLP & IR Group at UNED
jfraile@lsi.uned.es and anselmo@lsi.uned.es

Abstract

CASE in EACL 2024 proposes the shared task on Hate Speech and Stance Detection during Climate Activism. In our participation in the stance detection task, we have tested different approaches using LLMs for this classification task. We have tested a generative model using the classical seq2seq structure. Subsequently, we have considerably improved the results by replacing the last layer of these LLMs with a classifier layer. We have also studied how the performance is affected by the amount of data used in training. For this purpose, a partition of the dataset has been used and external data from posture detection tasks has been added.

1 Introduction

CASE in EACL 2024 is a shared task focusing on Climate Activism (Thapa et al., 2024). This task consists of three subtasks, the first two are focused on Hate Speech detection, a task that is important for peace and harmony in society (Parihar et al., 2021). The last subtask consists of the posture detection of tweets on this topic.

Stance detection seeks to determine the author's point of view - usually in favour, against or neutral - on certain topics, using textual analysis (AlDayel and Magdy, 2020; Küçük and Can, 2020). Due to the large amount of information that is processed daily on social networks, stance detection has become an important task that facilitates the understanding of social and political changes (Darwish et al., 2017).

Due to the large amount of information that large Language Models (LLMs) receive during their training and their good results in many benchmarks, they are being used for tasks such as posture detection in text (Cruickshank and Ng, 2023; Mets et al., 2023). In which models such as ChatGPT, GPT-NeoX (Black et al., 2022), Falcon 7B and 40B (Almazrouei et al., 2023) and Llama 2 7B and 13B (Touvron et al., 2023) were used. All of them were used as Sequence-to-Sequence models.

In this paper we will compare the performance of different LLama 2 model structures for stance detection tasks. It also seeks to study how the performance is affected by the amount of data used in training. For this purpose, a partition of the dataset will be used and external data from stance detection tasks will be added.

The rest of this paper is structured as follows: Section 2 describes the datasets to be used along with the task to be solved. Section 3 describes the methodology followed including the models, the data processing, the model inputs and the training dataset. Section 4 presents the results, which will be discussed in Section 5. Finally, conclusions and future work are given in Section 6.

2 Dataset and task

The dataset on climate activism (Shiwakoti et al., 2024) has been used, focusing on the subtask of stance detection. This dataset has a collection of tweets labeled according to their stance about climate activism. Henceforth, we will refer to it as CASE.

Additionally, the dataset from (Mohammad et al., 2016) has been employed, which is related to the stance detection task too. This dataset was used in the International Workshop on Semantic Evaluation (SemEval-2016). It includes tweets labeled with stances about various targets such as climate change, atheism, feminism, etc.

3 Methodology

This document aims to make a comparison between different Llama 2 model approaches, in addition to studying how the performance is affected by the amount of data

Proceedings of the 7th Workshop on Challenges and Applications of Automated Extraction of Socio-political Events from Text (CASE 2024), pages 79–84
March 22, 2024

3.1 Models

Four different approaches have been used, always based on the auto-regressive language model, Llama 2 7B.

- Llama 2 7B Chat (**7B Chat - seq2seq**). This model is specially trained to be used as a chatbot, for this reason the prompts that will be the inputs to the model will follow the guide proposed in (Touvron et al., 2023). These prompts will be described in section 3.3. In our case we are looking for a response with a word that indicates the stance of the entered text.

- Llama 2 7B Chat with a final classification layer and using prompts formatted (**7B Chat - clf prompt**). In this model we start from the Llama 2 7B Chat model and eliminate the last linear layer to add another linear layer that has as input the last hidden state of the model and as output 3 neurons, one for each stance label. With this model, text formatted following the prompt guide mentioned above has been used as input.

- Llama 2 7B Chat with a final classification layer and using raw prompts (**7B Chat - clf no Prompt**). It is a model with the same architecture as the previous one, however the text without formatting has been used as input.

- Llama 2 7B with a final classification layer (**7B - clf**). In this model we start from the Llama 2 7B model and carry out the same process as the two previous models. The non-chat model has not been trained to be used as a chatbot so the text used as input will not have any specific format.

3.2 Dataset preparation

Each approach use the text of the tweet in the input. However, a pre-processing of the text has been performed, consisting of the following steps:

- Remove all urls from tweets.

- Remove all users in the form @user.

- Separate hashtags into individual words. For this we have used the wordninja library, which uses a probabilistic division of concatenated words using NLP based on the frequencies of unigrams from the English Wikipedia.

Four experiments have been performed varying the dataset used for training. Two of them are using only the CASE dataset and the other two are using the whole SemEval dataset together with the CASE data. Regarding the CASE dataset. One of the experiments uses a stratified partition for each label of the training set with a size of 70% for training and 30% for validation (hereafter referred to as part or partition) and another experiment uses the training set for training and the development set for validation (hereafter referred to as full).

3.3 Model inputs

Since models that have not been trained to have conversations are being used, a particular input format has been used for each model. For the **7B Chat - clf no Prompt** and **7B Chat - clf** models the input is the processed text as shown in 3.2.

For the models **7B Chat - seq2seq** and **7B Chat - clf prompt** the prompt guide proposed by Meta has been used together with a description of the task as shown below.

> <s>[INST]«SYS»
> Classify the stance of the following text. If the stance is in favour of ***stance-target***, write FAVOR, if it is against of ***stance-target*** write AGAINST and if it is ambiguous, write NONE. The answer only has to be one of these three words: FAVOR, AGAINST or NONE.«/SYS»
> ***Processed Text*** [/INST]

Where ***stance-target*** is the target that the tweet is talking about. In the case of the CASE dataset this would be Climate Activism. In the case of the SemEval dataset tweets have targets such as climate change, atheism, feminism, etc.

3.4 Training phase

To train each of the proposed models, a Fine Tuning has been performed using the LoRA technique: Low-Rank Adaptation of Large Language Models (Hu et al., 2021) together with a 4-bit Quantization (Dettmers et al., 2023). As hyperparameters for training we have selected a range $r = 64$, an $\alpha = 16$, and a dropout of 0.1.

With this configuration, it is possible to train around 350M parameters, which is a 95.5% reduction of the total number of parameters of the original models.

4 Results

This section presents the results, evaluated on the test set, of all the experiments that have been carried out.

Table 1 shows the F1 macro value of the 8 different runs. The results are split into part if the 70-30 partition was used or full if the whole dataset was used for training, as explained in section 3.2. Models marked with * indicate that they have been trained with the CASE and SemEval dataset. In addition, the results of the Baseline model used in (Shiwakoti et al., 2024) are included. This Baseline model, named ClimateBERT (Webersinke et al., 2022), is an adaptation of a BERT model, a language model trained on a corpus sourced from climate-related news, abstracts, and reports.

Hereafter, model (1) is the 7B Chat - clf prompt model trained with the partition of the data and model (2) is the 7B Chat - clf non prompt model trained with the total data.

Approach	part	full
Baseline	0.545	
Best model leaderboard	0.7483	
7B Chat - seq2seq	0.7043	0.7062
7B Chat - seq2seq *	0.6986	0.6845
7B Chat - clf prompt (1)	**0.7246**	0.6958
7B Chat - clf prompt *	0.7102	0.7009
7B Chat - clf no prompt (2)	0.7068	**0.7366**
7B Chat - clf no prompt *	0.7231	0.7300
7B - clf	0.7245	0.7189
7B - clf *	0.7190	0.7160

Table 1: Results for the test set (trained on the 70-30 % CASE partition or the full CASE train set). Models marked as * indicate that they have been trained with the CASE and SemEval dataset.

Table 2 shows the percentage of misclassified and well-classified instances for each number of systems. For example, the first value of 7.9 % in the second row indicates that 7.9 % of the instances have been misclassified by two systems and the other 6 systems have classified them correctly.

Some metrics for the best performing models using the partition (1) and with the total data (2) will be shown below.

Figure 1 shows the normalised confusion matrix over the rows for model (1). Similarly, Figure 2 shows the normalised confusion matrix over the rows for model (2).

Number of systems	part Wrong	part Right	full Wrong	full Right
1	13.3 %	5.4 %	16.5 %	6.2 %
2	7.9 %	5.1 %	9.9 %	5.3 %
3	6.3 %	4.2 %	6.9 %	4.9 %
4	5.3 %	5.3 %	6.6 %	6.6 %
5	4.2 %	6.3 %	4.9 %	6.9 %
6	5.1 %	7.9 %	5.3 %	9.9 %
7	5.4 %	13.3 %	6.2 %	16.5 %
8	9.9 %	42.6 %	8.1 %	35.9 %

Table 2: Percentage of misclassified instances per number of systems (trained on the 70-30 % CASE partition or the full CASE train set).

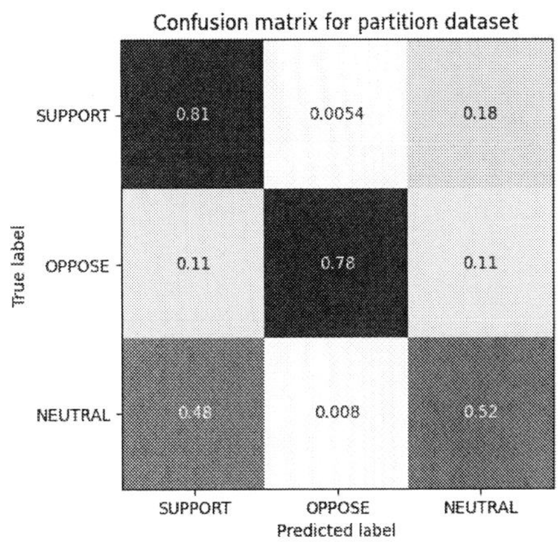

Figure 1: Confusion matrix for (1) model.

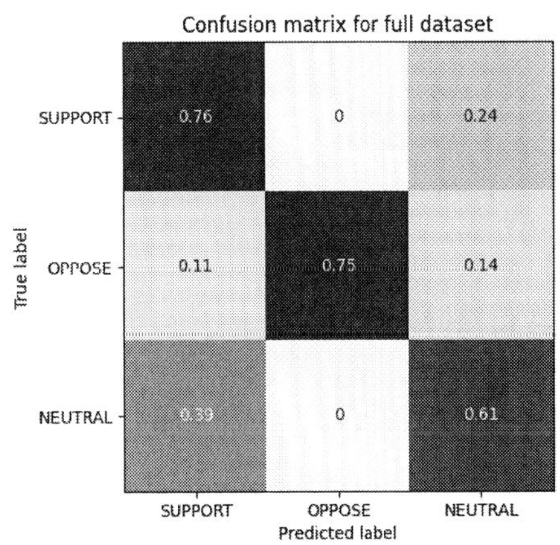

Figure 2: Confusion matrix for (2) model.

Furthermore, if we limit ourselves to studying only the misclassified instances, Table 3 shows the percentage of misclassified instances for each class for model (1). For example, the value of

37.53 % in the first row means that 37.53 % of the misclassified instances were Support and have been classified as Neutral. In the same way, Table 4 shows the percentage of misclassified instances for each class for model (2).

True label		Predicted label		
		Support	Oppose	Neutral
	Support	-	1.12 %	37.53%
	Oppose	3.60 %	-	3.37 %
	Neutral	53.48 %	0.90 %	-

Table 3: Percentage of instances misclassified by model (1) per class, over the set of misclassified labels.

True label		Predicted label		
		Support	Oppose	Neutral
	Support	-	0 %	48.66 %
	Oppose	3.35 %	-	4.46 %
	Neutral	43.53 %	0 %	-

Table 4: Percentage of instances misclassified by model (2) per class, over the set of misclassified labels.

5 Discussion

From the results shown in Table 1 it can be seen that all models outperform the Baseline model by quite some distance. This could be expected since the Baseline model has far fewer parameters than the Llama 2 7B model. Moreover, our best model obtains the 7th position in the leaderboard, only 0.0117 behind the leading model for this task.

As for using the CASE partition or the total data we see that although using all the data is how the best result is obtained, only 3 of the 8 models improve. In particular the Chat models improve with a classification layer at the end and without using the prompts system. However, the difference in performance is quite small.

Regarding the addition of SemEval data, if we look model by model, we see that the performance is only improved in 2 of them. The difference between adding the data at most worsens 0.0217 and at most improves 0.0163. This could be because the SemEval dataset contains about 3k examples of various topics compared to 7k in CASE. Of the SemEval dataset, only 13.5% of the data was related to climate activism and 86.5% was related to another topic. This data distribution may add noise to the training. This is why the models do not specialise in stance detection on Climate Activism as much as using only Climate Activism data. However, when adding the data, there is a considerable increase in training times.

As for the 4 different approaches to the Llama 2 model that have been used. As the seq2seq results are the lowest, we can conclude that it is better to remove the layer that allows to obtain a text sequence and replace it by a classifier layer. In addition, although the 7B Chat classifier models were the best performers, model 7B shows results with less variation when more data is added.

Looking at the results in Table 2 we can see that in the partition 9.9 % of the instances are incorrect for all models compared to 8.1 % if all data is used. However, when using partitioning we see that 42.6 % of the instances are classified well by all models, compared to 35.9 % if all data is used. All systems as a whole classify better if partitioning is used than if all data is used. This is consistent with the previous discussion as only 3 of the 8 models improve when using all data.

Comparing the confusion matrices in Figure 1 and Figure 2 we can see that for the Support and Oppose instances the model trained with the partition classifies better than the model trained with all. However, the latter classifies better the Neutral instances, thus obtaining the F1 difference between both.

Regarding the percentages of misclassified instances per class collected in Table 3 and Table 4 both models have little tendency to misclassify end-to-end (real label Support and predicted label Oppose or vice versa). Almost all misclassified instances are due to the Neutral label.

6 Post-competition analysis

Since this is a generative model, we could use a zero-shot approach. However, using this approach Llama 2 7B Chat model obtained an F1 result of 0.5685. This result is somewhat higher than the Baseline model proposed by the organisers, but significantly lower than the Fine-Tuned models.

In addition, adding the SemEval collection to the models caused a decrease in the performance of the models. One of the reasons could be due to the use of data not related to climate change. For this reason, the best architecture (7B Chat - clf no prompt) was re-trained by adding only the SemEval climate change related data. This model obtained an F1 of 0.7346, only 0.002 below the model that not use additional data. Looking more closely at these two models we could see that there was only a difference of two misclassified instances. By carefully studying the structure of the SemEval-2016 dataset and the CASE dataset, we realise that there is a temporal difference between the instances of both datasets. The CASE dataset contains terms such as Greta Thunberg or the Ukrainian-Russian war that SemEval does not. In addition, there are hashtags such as #FridaysForFuture or #ClimateStrike which are movements started in 2018. Therefore both datasets contain different lexical fields.

7 Conclusions and Future Work

In this paper, we have reported our participation in CASE in the framework of EACL 2024 in the stance detection subtask. For this task we have compared the performance of several variants of Llama 2 models and studied the effect of adding more data to the models.

Our results are significantly better than the proposed Baseline model and we have found that for this classification task it is better to dispense with the seq2seq structure of Llama 2 and use a classifier layer. We have also seen that adding more data tends to make the models behave worse.

As lines of future work it would be interesting to make an ensemble of all the models and analyse the performance of the models by training with different percentages of the CASE dataset. As the smaller Llama 2 model has been used, it would also be interesting to test these architectures with the larger Llama 2 models, 13B and 70B. In addition, to be able to use several related collections. If they are spaced in time, more robust semantic dimensions could be studied or datasets close in time could be used.

Limitations

The models described have been trained using only English text. For this reason, if a different language is used, good results may not be obtained. Additionally, the number of GPUs, the time required for training and inference, and the energy needed are resources that not everyone may have access to.

Acknowledgements

This work was supported by the HAMiSoN project grant CHIST-ERA-21-OSNEM-002, AEI PCI2022-135026-2 (MCIN/AEI/10.13039/501100011033 and EU "NextGenerationEU"/PRTR).

References

Abeer AlDayel and Walid Magdy. 2020. Stance detection on social media: State of the art and trends. *CoRR*, abs/2006.03644.

Ebtesam Almazrouei, Hamza Alobeidli, Abdulaziz Alshamsi, Alessandro Cappelli, Ruxandra Cojocaru, Mérouane Debbah, Étienne Goffinet, Daniel Hesslow, Julien Launay, Quentin Malartic, Daniele Mazzotta, Badreddine Noune, Baptiste Pannier, and Guilherme Penedo. 2023. The falcon series of open language models.

Sid Black, Stella Biderman, Eric Hallahan, Quentin Anthony, Leo Gao, Laurence Golding, Horace He, Connor Leahy, Kyle McDonell, Jason Phang, Michael Pieler, USVSN Sai Prashanth, Shivanshu Purohit, Laria Reynolds, Jonathan Tow, Ben Wang, and Samuel Weinbach. 2022. Gpt-neox-20b: An open-source autoregressive language model.

Iain J Cruickshank and Lynnette Hui Xian Ng. 2023. Use of large language models for stance classification. *arXiv preprint arXiv:2309.13734*.

Kareem Darwish, Walid Magdy, and Tahar Zanouda. 2017. Trump vs. hillary: What went viral during the 2016 US presidential election. *CoRR*, abs/1707.03375.

Tim Dettmers, Artidoro Pagnoni, Ari Holtzman, and Luke Zettlemoyer. 2023. Qlora: Efficient finetuning of quantized llms.

Edward J. Hu, Yelong Shen, Phillip Wallis, Zeyuan Allen-Zhu, Yuanzhi Li, Shean Wang, Lu Wang, and Weizhu Chen. 2021. Lora: Low-rank adaptation of large language models.

Dilek Küçük and Fazli Can. 2020. Stance detection: A survey. *ACM Computing Surveys (CSUR)*, 53(1):1–37.

Mark Mets, Andres Karjus, Indrek Ibrus, and Maximilian Schich. 2023. Automated stance detection in complex topics and small languages: the challenging case of immigration in polarizing news media. *arXiv preprint arXiv:2305.13047*.

Saif Mohammad, Svetlana Kiritchenko, Parinaz Sobhani, Xiaodan Zhu, and Colin Cherry. 2016. A dataset for detecting stance in tweets. In *Proceedings of the Tenth International Conference on Language Resources and Evaluation (LREC'16)*, pages 3945–3952.

Anil Singh Parihar, Surendrabikram Thapa, and Sushruti Mishra. 2021. Hate speech detection using natural language processing: Applications and challenges. In *2021 5th International Conference on Trends in Electronics and Informatics (ICOEI)*, pages 1302–1308.

Shuvam Shiwakoti, Surendrabikram Thapa, Kritesh Rauniyar, Akshyat Shah, Aashish Bhandari, and Usman Naseem. 2024. Analyzing the dynamics of climate change discourse on twitter: A new annotated corpus and multi-aspect classification. *Preprint.*

Surendrabikram Thapa, Kritesh Rauniyar, Farhan Ahmad Jafri, Shuvam Shiwakoti, Hariram Veeramani, Raghav Jain, Guneet Singh Kohli, Ali Hürriyetoğlu, and Usman Naseem. 2024. Stance and hate event detection in tweets related to climate activism - shared task at case 2024. In *Proceedings of the 7th Workshop on Challenges and Applications of Automated Extraction of Socio-political Events from Text (CASE).*

Hugo Touvron, Louis Martin, Kevin Stone, Peter Albert, Amjad Almahairi, Yasmine Babaei, Nikolay Bashlykov, Soumya Batra, Prajjwal Bhargava, Shruti Bhosale, et al. 2023. Llama 2: Open foundation and fine-tuned chat models, 2023.

Nicolas Webersinke, Mathias Kraus, Julia Anna Bingler, and Markus Leippold. 2022. Climatebert: A pretrained language model for climate-related text.

JRC at ClimateActivism 2024: Lexicon-based Detection of Hate Speech

Hristo Tanev
European Commission, Joint Research Centre,
via Enrico Fermi 2749,
Ispra 21020, Italy
hristo.tanev@ec.europa.eu

Abstract

In this paper we describe the participation of the JRC team in the Sub-task A: "Hate Speech Detection" in the Shared task *Stance and Hate Event Detection in Tweets Related to Climate Activism* at the CASE 2024 workshop. Our system is purely lexicon (keyword) based and does not use any statistical classifier. The system ranked 18 out of 22 participants with F1 of 0.83, only one point below a system, based on LLM. Our system also obtained one of the highest achieved precision scores among all participating algorithms.

1 Introduction

In this paper we report on the participation of the Joint Research Centre team at Subtask A: *Hate speech detection* in the shared task *Stance and Hate Event Detection in Tweets Related to Climate Activism* at CASE 2024 (Thapa et al., 2024) using a simple lexicon - based hate speech detection approach.

Over the past few years, the convergence of NLP and sociopolitical discourse has led to the development of diverse technologies such as hate speech detection, sentiment analysis, and other opinion detection technologies. At the same time, climate activism has taken a momentum on the social Web and has captured the attention of NLP researcher community working in these areas (Shiwakoti et al., 2024). As the public discussions in this topic proliferated, the escalation of hate speech started to raise concerns among users.

Within the climate change discourse, hate speech manifests as a concerning trend, often taking aim at specific entities such as climate activists, influential environmental and political organizations like Greenpeace, and even entire governmental bodies responsible for environmental policies. The targeting extends beyond institutions to include environmental initiatives like FridaysForFuture (Niininen and Baumeister, 2022), amplifying the scope of the issue.

Adding another layer to this complex scenario, there is a noteworthy phenomenon involving individuals who pretend allegiance to the climate activist cause. These people employ hate speech in a troll like manner as a weapon in defending their version of climate advocacy.

This dual nature of hate speech within the climate change discourse unveils the intricate interplay between genuine concerns, political discontent, and the broader socio-political landscape. This highlights the need for nuanced approaches in addressing hate speech, considering its diverse sources and motivations within the context of environmental activism.

In this picture, automatic hate speech detection is becoming important, keeping "clean" the space of the social platforms and preventing online users from exposure to extreme content and disinformation. On the other hand, hate speech shows also increase of the discontent and frustration towards certain topics and public personalities. It serves as an indicator of the significance of these issues and people and their public perception; it also plays a crucial role as a marker for a negative bias in the social discourse. In fact, in USA certain hate speech acts are given constitutional protection (Rosenfeld, 2002) under the laws defending the freedom of speech.

The purpose of our experiment was to put in comparison a keyword based system with the other shared task participants, which were expected to predominantly exploit machine learning methods. As the simplicity of our method suggests, our system achieved score only little above the average system performance, and ranked 18th out of 22 systems, with F1 score of 0.83. Our score was 0.03 lower than the system in the middle of the ranking; our method scored F1 lower by 0.07 from the top ranked system. The experiment proved that

Proceedings of the 7th Workshop on Challenges and Applications of Automated Extraction of Socio-political Events from Text (CASE 2024), pages 85–88
March 22, 2024 ©2024 Association for Computational Linguistics

Why are powerful men so scared of Greta Thunberg? The FridaysForFuture movement and the idea that we'd all have the gall to conduct a ClimateStrike every Friday frightens and infuriates plutocrats.
How Billionaires with Greta Thunberg uproot the system, important thread 2 read:
Mitigate or die! Adaptation, even successful, to today's accelerating climate crisis is a deadly delusion for complacent inaction. Possible survival = immediate emissions decline!
the struggle continues greed capitalism and stupidity r the main reasons the planet is dying
For some third-rate TV presenters, attacking Greta Thunberg is the only way to get back into conversation again. In 50 years, no one will know who Brendan O'Neill was, but Greta Thunberg will still be known.
First we destroy nature The rich keep getting richer The poor are increasing in numbers Measly check in the mail When there's still hell to pay Bills and pills Then we destroy ourselves Push back Despite all this

Table 1: Example of hate speech detected by our system

lexicon based detection is less accurate than statistical methods, still not very far behind: we have obtained a score only 0.01 lower than the preceding in the ranking system, which used a large language model; moreover, our precision was the among the highest ones.

2 Related work

Hate speech is a topic of debate among lawmakers (Rosenfeld, 2002) and NLP experts (Jahan and Oussalah, 2023), (Parihar et al., 2021). Automatic hate speech detection has been predominantly approached as a binary text classification, using machine learning (Fortuna and Nunes, 2018); multilingual dimension has also been explored in previous works and shared tasks (Siino et al., 2021)

Lexicon-based hate speech analysis has also been addressed in previous works (MacAvaney et al., 2019), (Gitari et al., 2015). According to (MacAvaney et al., 2019), keyword-based approaches offer elevated precision but suffer from insufficient recall due to challenges in resolving word sense ambiguity and handling figurative language. Essentially, systems relying on keywords may overlook hateful content that doesn't employ explicit hate terms. In contrast, (Gitari et al., 2015) presents a lexicon-based approach that contradicts this assertion by demonstrating reasonably high levels of both precision and recall.

Hate speech detection is also strongly related to sentiment analysis and opinion mining, where lexicon-based approaches are still used: a comprehensive study of these techniques is presented in (Bonta et al., 2019).

3 Dataset and Task

The purpose of the Shared task on Detecting Hate Speech During Climate Activism was identification of tweets discussing the climate change topic and containing hate speech. The tweets have been retrieved by a team of researchers from Delhi Tech University, Virginia Tech, and James Cook University, Australia. The retrieval and annotation are described in (Shiwakoti et al., 2024). The data collection process aimed at tweets posted between January 1, 2022, and December 30, 2022. The selection criteria involved hashtags such as #climatecrisis, #climatechange, #ClimateEmergency, #ClimateTalk, #globalwarming, as well as activist-oriented hashtags like #fridaysforfuture, #actonclimate, #climatestrike, #extinctionrebellion, #ClimateAlliance, #climatejustice, #climateaction, etc. Only tweets composed in the English language have been considered by the data collection team. In this way above 15,000 tweets have been collected, which were subsequently annotated for presence of hate speech, relevance to the climate change discourse, stance, the direction of hate speech, targets of hate speech, and humor. For our shared task, only three aspects were considered from this annotation: hate speech, target of the hate speech (who or what is targeted) and stance (does the tweet support, oppose or is neutral). Given we participated in subtask A: Hate speech detection, only the hate speech annotation (1 - presence of hate speech, 0 - absence) was considered.

4 Methodology

In our approach we have used the Liu and Hu Lexicon (Ding et al., 2008), which is ranked as a high performing sentiment analysis lexicon by several studies: It was evaluated on Twitter data with information about people and other entities (Al-Shabi, 2020), as well as on product reviews (Khoo and Johnkhan, 2018). In both cases this lexicon has delivered very competitive results, with respect to other repositories of sentiment keywords. Considering our shared task on climate activism, the above mentioned Twitter based evaluation showed that the lexicon was relevant for the task.

The Hu and Liu lexicon has been created by two researchers from the Department of Computer Science of the University of Illinois at Chicago, Minqing Hu and Bing Liu. It is composed of two lists of words: 2006 positive keywords and 4783 negative ones.

Since the task targets hate speech, we have used only the list of negative words. Experimenting on the training set, we have identified the minimal optimal number of keywords to appear in a tweet, so that it is considered to contain hate speech. Our experiment showed that this minimal number is 4: Every tweet with four or more negative words were labeled as containing hate speech.

After manually inspecting the training set, we have also identified few entities which were strongly associated with hate speech inside the training and evaluation corpora (one of them "Greta Thunberg") and added them to the lexicon.

5 Results and discussion

We have participated in Sub task A, whose goal was to detect from the test set the tweets, containing hate speech. Our system ranked 18 out of 22 participating systems, with F1 score of 0.83. (F1 was the official ranking criteria of this shared task). Our score was 0.03 lower than the system in the middle of the ranking. We have obtained a score only 0.01 lower than the preceding in the ranking system, which used a large language model; moreover, our precision was among the highest ones.

Considering our accuracy, we ranked 13, which is caused by the high precision of the rule based approach and the prevalence of instances, belonging to the negative category (no hate speech). Our accuracy was also higher than the accuracy of the established baselines for this task, reported in (Shiwakoti et al., 2024).

Table 1 displays examples of hate speech tweets identified by our system. Notably, the detection of a substantial number of hate speech tweets was facilitated by the presence of the named entity "Greta Thunberg", which we had identified as a hate speech indicator in the training set. However, it's important to note that this observation reflects a specificity of the shared task data rather than a broader trend on Twitter.

Moreover, refining the focus on tweets containing a high number of negative keywords proved to be an effective strategy for achieving high precision in hate speech detection.

6 Conclusions

We introduced a lexicon-based system designed to identify hate speech in tweets related to climate change. Despite its simplicity and orientation towards high precision, our system achieved accuracy above the baseline and F1 score comparable to some machine learning approaches. Our lexicon-based method achieved one of the highest precision scores of 0.92.

However, it ranked in the low part of the leaderboard, primarily attributed to its notably low recall of 0.777. This was due to the simplicity of our approach with respect to other lexicon based works. We invested relatively little time in its development, which did not allow us to exploit the full potential of this class of methods.

References

MA Al-Shabi. 2020. Evaluating the performance of the most important lexicons used to sentiment analysis and opinions mining. *IJCSNS*, 20(1):1.

Venkateswarlu Bonta, Nandhini Kumaresh, and N Janardhan. 2019. A comprehensive study on lexicon based approaches for sentiment analysis. *Asian Journal of Computer Science and Technology*, 8(S2):1–6.

Xiaowen Ding, Bing Liu, and Philip S Yu. 2008. A holistic lexicon-based approach to opinion mining. In *Proceedings of the 2008 international conference on web search and data mining*, pages 231–240.

Paula Fortuna and Sérgio Nunes. 2018. A survey on automatic detection of hate speech in text. *ACM Computing Surveys (CSUR)*, 51(4):1–30.

Njagi Dennis Gitari, Zhang Zuping, Hanyurwimfura Damien, and Jun Long. 2015. A lexicon-based approach for hate speech detection. *International Journal of Multimedia and Ubiquitous Engineering*, 10(4):215–230.

Md Saroar Jahan and Mourad Oussalah. 2023. A systematic review of hate speech automatic detection using natural language processing. *Neurocomputing*, page 126232.

Christopher SG Khoo and Sathik Basha Johnkhan. 2018. Lexicon-based sentiment analysis: Comparative evaluation of six sentiment lexicons. *Journal of Information Science*, 44(4):491–511.

Sean MacAvaney, Hao-Ren Yao, Eugene Yang, Katina Russell, Nazli Goharian, and Ophir Frieder. 2019. Hate speech detection: Challenges and solutions. *PloS one*, 14(8):e0221152.

Outi Niininen and Stefan Baumeister. 2022. 12 fridays for future wants to save the world—but what do people think about the movement? *Social Media for Progressive Public Relations*, page 66.

Anil Singh Parihar, Surendrabikram Thapa, and Sushruti Mishra. 2021. Hate speech detection using natural language processing: Applications and challenges. In *2021 5th International Conference on Trends in Electronics and Informatics (ICOEI)*, pages 1302–1308.

Michel Rosenfeld. 2002. Hate speech in constitutional jurisprudence: a comparative analysis. *Cardozo L. Rev.*, 24:1523.

Shuvam Shiwakoti, Surendrabikram Thapa, Kritesh Rauniyar, Akshyat Shah, Aashish Bhandari, and Usman Naseem. 2024. Analyzing the dynamics of climate change discourse on twitter: A new annotated corpus and multi-aspect classification. *Preprint*.

Marco Siino, Elisa Di Nuovo, Ilenia Tinnirello, Marco La Cascia, et al. 2021. Detection of hate speech spreaders using convolutional neural networks. In *CLEF (Working Notes)*, pages 2126–2136.

Surendrabikram Thapa, Kritesh Rauniyar, Farhan Ahmad Jafri, Shuvam Shiwakoti, Hariram Veeramani, Raghav Jain, Guneet Singh Kohli, Ali Hürriyetoğlu, and Usman Naseem. 2024. Stance and hate event detection in tweets related to climate activism - shared task at case 2024. In *Proceedings of the 7th Workshop on Challenges and Applications of Automated Extraction of Socio-political Events from Text (CASE)*.

HAMiSoN-MTL at ClimateActivism 2024: Detection of Hate Speech, Targets, and Stance using Multi-task Learning

Raquel Rodriguez-Garcia
NLP & IR Group
UNED, Spain
rrodriguez@lsi.uned.es

Roberto Centeno
NLP & IR Group
UNED, Spain
rcenteno@lsi.uned.es

Abstract

The automatic identification of hate speech constitutes an important task, playing a relevant role towards inclusivity. In these terms, the shared task on Climate Activism Stance and Hate Event Detection at CASE 2024 proposes the analysis of Twitter messages related to climate change activism for three subtasks. Subtasks A and C aim at detecting hate speech and establishing the stance of the tweet, respectively, while subtask B seeks to determine the target of the hate speech. In this paper, we describe our approach to the given subtasks. Our systems leverage transformer-based multi-task learning. Additionally, since the dataset contains a low number of tweets, we have studied the effect of adding external data to increase the learning of the model. With our approach we achieve the fourth position on subtask C on the final leaderboard, with minimal difference from the first position, showcasing the strength of multi-task learning.

1 Introduction

The shared task on Climate Activism Stance and Hate Event Detection at CASE 2024 (Thapa et al., 2024) focuses on climate change discussions on Twitter. As of late, climate change is experiencing an increase in political polarization (Falkenberg et al., 2022), and these trends have revealed connections to a higher power controlling the public's discourse (Farrell, 2016). This situation highlights the importance of an in-depth study of the issue and the many challenges it still poses, from the data collection to the added difficulty of multilingual approaches (Parihar et al., 2021). This task, which studies the content of tweets in relation to hate speech and other essential characteristics, such as the target of the message, can serve to provide more insights regarding how these messages are transmitted and their common features.

Recent competitions have been held for the detection of hate speech or offensive language (Lai et al., 2023) as well as the target of the message (Bhandari et al., 2023; Zampieri et al., 2019b), focusing on issues such as multilingual Twitter data or multimodal content. State-of-the-art results are obtained through the use of transformer-based approaches, that are capable of employing the entire context of the data. Additional contextual knowledge, such as social information or newspaper articles, has also shown its effectiveness to improve a system's performance (Nagar et al., 2023; Pérez et al., 2023). Similarly, stance detection has been a traditional research topic for shared tasks (Cignarella et al., 2020; Davydova and Tutubalina, 2022), where transformer-based approaches, along with data augmentation, tend to outperform other methods.

In our approach to this task, we leverage the potential of multi-task learning (MTL) with a pre-trained transformer model for the subtasks. MTL, as originally presented by Caruana (1993), is able to extract information from one task to boost the performance of another, without the necessity of transferring the knowledge attained and the complications it poses with the differences in tasks or annotations. It also reduces the risk of overfitting (Baxter, 1997) due to the shared representation it generates for all the tasks.

In our systems, we experiment with added datasets, to fully exploit the capabilities of MTL. We explore the effects of additional data for each of the tasks, with different levels of relatedness. To fully study that effect, we also fine-tune our systems without external data, other than the three subtasks. We aim to discover what works best in this situation, where we have three highly related subtasks, but there is a lack of data, especially for subtask B.

The paper is structured as follows: in section 2 we briefly discuss the characteristics of the shared task, as well as the dataset provided. In section 3 we describe our approach by leveraging MTL and

Proceedings of the 7th Workshop on Challenges and Applications of Automated Extraction of Socio-political Events from Text (CASE 2024), pages 89–95
March 22, 2024 ©2024 Association for Computational Linguistics

Subtask	Class	train	dev	test
A	Non Hate Speech	6385	1371	1374
	Hate Speech	899	190	188
B	Individual	563	120	121
	Organization	105	23	23
	Community	31	7	6
C	Support	4328	897	921
	Oppose	2256	153	141
	Neutral	700	511	500

Table 1: Annotation statistics of the dataset for each subtask and set: train, dev and test.

external data sources. In section 4 we include the results of our systems and discuss the approaches. Finally, we highlight the conclusions in section 5.

2 Dataset & Task

The dataset for the shared task on Climate Activism Stance and Hate Event Detection, introduced in Shiwakoti et al. (2024), contains a total of 10,407 tweets, only including the textual content. These instances were collected using hashtags linked to climate change and related activism and only selecting English tweets. Finally, they were manually annotated for different tasks. We describe below each of the subtasks that are part of the shared task. The tweet distribution for each subtask is shown in Table 1.

2.1 Subtask A: Hate Speech Detection

Subtask A is aimed at determining whether a tweet is considered hate speech or not. The tweets are annotated for this binary classification task with two labels: *Hate Speech* and *No Hate Speech*.

2.2 Subtask B: Target Detection

The objective of this subtask is to establish the target of the hate speech. The annotation for this multi-class classification task is given by three classes: *Individual*, *Organization* or *Community*. In these tweets there is hate speech, therefore, only a part of the tweets in the full dataset are annotated with the target.

2.3 Subtask C: Stance Detection

The goal of this last subtask is to establish the stance of each tweet. This is also a multi-class classification task with three possible classes: *Support*, *Oppose* or *Neutral*. These are the same tweets used for subtask A.

3 Methodology

For our experiments, we use the same pre-trained transformer model throughout the different combinations for comparability purposes. The selection of the model is influenced by two main factors: generalization and robustness. Models trained on domain-specific data or from select data sources, such as Twitter, would not be ideal for our study, since we incorporate other corpus not Twitter nor climate related. Additionally, we want to ensure the selected model provides robustness in terms of textual classification tasks. These considerations justified our selection of the RoBERTa (Liu et al., 2019) pretrained model we used.

The architecture of the MTL system corresponds with a hard parameter sharing approach: for each task we make use of one classification head and a RoBERTa shared encoder for all of them. Since the data sources are different in most cases, each input instance only corresponds with one classification task. The model uses size-proportional sampling, in regard to each of the datasets for the classification tasks, when selecting the next instance during training, with a fixed batch size of 32.

As we previously introduced, we are using external data for the task. We briefly describe them below.

- Offensive Language Identification Dataset (OLID) (Zampieri et al., 2019a). This dataset, composed of Twitter data, was used in the SemEval 2019 Task 6, OffensEval (Zampieri et al., 2019b). It has three tasks: offensive language identification (*Offensive* or *Not Offensive*), categorization of offense types (*Targeted* or *Untargeted*) and offense target identification (*Individual*, *Group* or *Others*). Due to the similarity between the offense and target identification tasks to subtask A and B, we select these OLID tasks for our training. We combine the train and test partitions into one dataset for the training of our system, generating a total of 14,100 and 4,089 tweets for the offense and target tasks, respectively.
- The stance dataset presented in Mohammad et al. (2016a), which was used in SemEval-2016 Task 6 (Mohammad et al., 2016b). For easier reference throughout the paper, we will refer to it as StancEval. This dataset is divided into different sections depending on the topic of the tweet. These include abortion, Hillary Clinton, atheism,

climate and feminism, for a total of 4,163 tweets. The classification of the tweets considers three classes: *Against*, *Favor* or *None*. The train and test data are combined for our training.

- COP27 data. This source of data is composed of unannotated tweets gathered during COP27, using related hashtags. Given that the tweets had no relevant annotation, we decided to assign a simple label for the ease of use as a classification task. We created a binary task to determine the presence or absence of a retweet. Although the task is unrelated and the annotation might be irrelevant, the tweets are related, and it might provide additional context to the system. To establish if unannotated data could be useful, we select a total of 45,000 random tweets. We aim to determine if having more available data can compensate for the weak annotation or lower relatedness to the task.
- The Multi-Genre Natural Language Inference (MultiNLI) corpus (Williams et al., 2018). This dataset consists of a textual premise and a hypothesis, and the class indicates if there is *Entailment*, *Contradiction* or a *Neutral* relationship between them. Contrary to previous datasets, this one is unrelated to the task. To make it comparable, we select a class-balanced sample of 12,000 instances.

These datasets are combined into the models displayed in Table 2. Below, we explain each of them.

- **BASE**. For this run, we only consider the base data for this CASE task, with one model for the three subtasks.
- **BASE StancEval climate**. Since StancEval contains information not related to climate change, we only select the climate topic, in addition to the base subtasks.
- **BASE StancEval full**. For this run, we include the whole StancEval dataset with the base subtasks.
- **BASE OLID**. This run includes the offense and target identification subtasks from OLID.
- **BASE OLID, StancEval**. For this run, we use the full OLID and StancEval datasets and the three subtasks.
- **BASE MultiNLI**. For this model, we use the three subtasks and the MultiNLI task.
- **BASE COP27**. This run adds the unrelated annotation from the COP tweets to the three subtasks.
- Only one base task and the closest task from another dataset. For this run, we select only one of the individual subtasks from the task and run an MTL model with another similar task. For subtask A (**Hate Only**) and B (**Target Only**), we use the OLID offense and the target identification, respectively. For subtask C (**Stance Only**) we use the full StancEval dataset.
- Best model configuration retrained on all data (**Best model**). The best model obtained during the evaluation, without accounting for the final test results, is run with the full training data.

Regarding the preprocessing of the textual input, only the Twitter data is altered. Since it includes hashtags and user mentions that the transformer might not be able to represent, we need to consider a previous step for normalization. All the mentions and URLs have been removed from the text. For the hashtags, we have followed a different approach by splitting the text into words using wordninja (Keredson, 2019), since hashtags are usually a concatenation of words that might provide additional insight into the user's opinion. In the case of the MultiNLI dataset, the premise and the hypothesis are combined into an input with a separator in-between the texts for the model.

For our experiments, we explore the combinations of an initial set of parameters shown in Table 3. Although more combinations were initially tested, we discarded them due to low results. For the final submissions, we select the parameter combination with the highest F1 on our evaluation data, for each subtask, and submit the results for all the combinations outlined above. We aim to use a comparable configuration to better analyze the results of the different combinations described.

Since the dev labels were not available when we first trained our systems, we created our class balanced partition of 70-30 for the training and evaluation of the subtasks (except for subtask B, which had fewer instances, so we decided on 80-20). After they were made public, we also uploaded our systems using the dev partition for evaluation and the train set for training. We report all the results in the next section for a more in-depth analysis. Additionally, for the best model retrained, in our first partition we use all the training data, while in the second we use the training and dev data combined.

Run	CASE			StancEval		OLID		MultiNLI	COP27
	A	B	C	climate topic	all topics	offense	target		
BASE	✓	✓	✓						
BASE StancEval climate	✓	✓	✓	✓					
BASE StancEval full	✓	✓	✓		✓				
BASE OLID	✓	✓	✓			✓	✓		
BASE OLID, StancEval	✓	✓	✓		✓	✓	✓		
BASE MultiNLI	✓	✓	✓					✓	
BASE COP27	✓	✓	✓						✓
Hate Only	✓					✓			
Target Only		✓					✓		
Stance Only			✓		✓				

Table 2: Different models tested and their data sources.

Parameter	Values
Epochs	3 and 4
Learning rate (LR)	2e-5 to 5e-5, step 1e-5
Weight decay	1e-3
Epochs	3 and 4
Learning rate (LR)	3e-5 and 4e-5
Weight decay	1e-2 and 1e-4

Table 3: Ranges of parameters used for training.

Task	Partition	LR	Epochs	Weight decay
A	70-30	3e-5	4	0.001
	train-dev	4e-5	4	0.0001
B	80-20	3e-5	4	0.0001
	train-dev	3e-5	3	0.0001
C	70-30	2e-5	3	0.001
	train-dev	4e-5	4	0.001

Table 4: Final parameter configuration for the submitted runs, for each task and partition.

4 Results & Discussion

The F1 results for the final configuration of the parameters uploaded for each subtask and partition is detailed in Table 4, based on the results of the evaluation (the 30% partition or the dev set), which are gathered in Table 5. For the A and C subtasks, regardless of the partition, values are very similar for most runs. There are slight differences between the partitions, which could be caused by differences between the tweets in the sets. Additional data does not appear to have a pronounced effect, although it achieves the best results. In subtask C for the dev partition, the COP27 run seems ineffective, which might indicate the difference in the data. In subtask B there is a higher variance between results. We can better appreciate the improvement of external datasets, especially with the most related ones, maybe due to the low amount of data. In this case, unrelated data does not have a positive effect.

The results for the F1 metric on the test set for each of the runs described above, based on the partitions, are gathered in the Table 6. The baselines included are the ones reported in Shiwakoti et al. (2024) and we can observe how our systems significantly outperform them. For subtask A, most of the results are similar, which might indicate the models are already reaching their plateau. We can also appreciate that less relevant data (MultiNLI or COP27) achieves relatively good results, which might indicate additional data is not necessary, or it hinders performance, especially considering that our best result is achieved with only the original data, attaining the sixth position in the leaderboard.

In subtask B there is a much higher difference between the results. The low amount of data, particularly compared to the other tasks the model was trained with, might have caused an imbalance when the model was learning for this task. Adjusting the size of the datasets, or augmenting the data, may have a positive impact. It is also interesting to note that the best result is achieved when training with 80% of the training set and the most similar task. Seemingly, adding highly related data has the best impact, securing the eighth position in the ranking.

In subtask C we notice that most results are similar, although COP achieves the lowest in one run. We can observe again that additional data does not have a very high impact, but it achieves the highest result with the fourth position in the leaderboard and minimal difference to the best system.

In terms of error analysis for the subtasks, we have noticed some tendencies. For subtask A, in over half of the runs, *Hate Speech* is correctly detected for a total of 98% of the class instances. Meanwhile, all runs predict the wrong class for *Non Hate Speech* in 10% of the instances for that class. Even though *Non Hate Speech* is the majority class, the system struggles to differentiate it. For subtask B we observe a similar effect, with over half of the runs being able to detect the *Individual* and *Organization* for over 90% of those instances.

Approach	Task A		Task B		Task C	
	part	**dev**	**part**	**dev**	**part**	**dev**
BASE	0.8666	0.8609	0.5227	0.6742	0.7080	0.6908
BASE StancEval climate	0.8682	0.8643	0.6665	0.5365	0.7187	0.6989
BASE StancEval full	0.8597	0.8483	0.6908	0.5326	0.7100	0.6824
BASE OLID	**0.8781**	**0.8738**	**0.8711**	0.8304	0.7083	**0.7137**
BASE OLID, StancEval	0.8739	0.8637	0.7197	0.8136	0.7073	0.6973
BASE MultiNLI	0.8566	0.8587	0.5882	0.5458	0.7162	0.6983
BASE COP27	0.8485	0.8202	0.5315	0.5327	0.7130	0.5102
Hate Only	0.8572	0.8675				
Target Only			0.7189	**0.8699**		
Stance Only					**0.7213**	0.6986

Table 5: Results for the subtasks, for the evaluation set (the 20-30% partition or the dev set).

Approach	Task A		Task B		Task C	
	part	**full**	**part**	**full**	**part**	**full**
Baseline	0.708		0.554		0.545	
Best Systems	0.9144		0.7858		0.7483	
BASE	0.8713	**0.8840**	0.5505	0.6668	0.7220	0.7274
BASE StancEval climate	0.8638	0.8788	0.6052	0.5752	0.7263	0.7212
BASE StancEval full	0.8757	0.8706	0.6280	0.5565	**0.7351**	0.7322
BASE OLID	0.8757	0.8731	0.7124	0.7046	0.7218	**0.7402**
BASE OLID, StancEval	0.8725	0.8806	0.6828	**0.7206**	0.7156	0.7324
BASE MultiNLI	0.8632	0.8656	0.5431	0.5345	0.7319	0.7263
BASE COP27	0.8672	0.8461	0.6259	0.5496	0.7298	0.5394
Hate Only	0.8609	0.8574				
Target Only			**0.7329**	0.6640		
Stance Only					0.7309	0.7214
Best model	**0.8794**	0.8774	0.7111	0.6375	0.7240	0.7320

Table 6: Results for the subtasks, for the test set (training on the 80-70% partition or the train set). The best model retrained refers to the model from Table 5 with the highest score.

In this case, we notice the system errs while identifying the *Community*, although that could be due to being the minority class. Finally, over half the runs for subtask C tend to coincide for the *Support* and *Oppose* classes with 88% and 75% of accuracy respectively, although it decreases to 50% for *Neutral*. Our runs tend to predict *Support* when the class is *Neutral*, which could be due to noisy data or some level of ambiguity in the texts.

In summary, it appears that external data has achieved the best result in subtasks B and C. Even when the dataset was not as related to the subtask, it still appeared to add some additional knowledge. There is a high difference between the evaluation and the test results for subtask B, which could indicate some problems already mentioned for the data or a low sampling for the MTL models. Regarding subtask A, since most of the results were very similar, the differences between the runs might be more related to randomness rather than the ineffectiveness of the additional data.

5 Conclusion

Hate speech is a growing cause of concern on social media, and it is still on the rise, spreading polarization to seemingly uncontroversial new topics, such as climate change. With our approach to this task, we propose to leverage other existing datasets through transformer-based MTL. Our models present a robust approach to address data scarcity, especially for the target detection subtask, without the need to adapt annotations or merge unrelated data, while creating models with a higher capacity to generalize. Our findings reveal that external data that is highly related to the task has an overall positive effect, while the lower the relatedness, the worse results we achieve.

As a result from our experiments, our models have shown that the most promising performances are achieved when external data is used to improve one of the tasks. As future work, we plan on having a more balanced dataset for target identification, as well as experimenting with other pre-trained or already fine-tuned models for specific tasks that might provide additional context, such as sentiment analysis. Additionally, we want to study the effect that each external dataset had on the models' predictions and their contributions to the results, which might provide insights into how to further improve this approach.

Limitations

The high variance in results from validation to test in subtask B indicates the presence of overfitting, possibly reducing the ability of the model to generalize in that task. Adjusting the sizes of the datasets, through augmentation or oversampling, or tuning the sample sizes would be necessary to address this issue.

Since the goal was to optimize each of the subtasks for the shared task, models were not evaluated for each of the auxiliary tasks and datasets included. Additional testing would be necessary to create a more robust approach and to determine if the MTL system improves other tasks' performances, although that might impact the effectiveness of the models for this shared task, therefore, the tradeoff should be considered.

Acknowledgements

This work was supported by the HAMiSoN project grant CHIST-ERA-21-OSNEM-002, AEI PCI2022-135026-2 (MCIN/AEI/10.13039/501100011033 and EU "NextGenerationEU"/PRTR).

References

Jonathan Baxter. 1997. A Bayesian/Information Theoretic Model of Learning to Learn via Multiple Task Sampling. *Machine learning*, 28:7–39.

Aashish Bhandari, Siddhant B. Shah, Surendrabikram Thapa, Usman Naseem, and Mehwish Nasim. 2023. CrisisHateMM: Multimodal Analysis of Directed and Undirected Hate Speech in Text-Embedded Images from Russia-Ukraine Conflict. In *2023 IEEE/CVF Conference on Computer Vision and Pattern Recognition Workshops (CVPRW)*, pages 1994–2003.

Richard A. Caruana. 1993. Multitask Learning: A Knowledge-Based Source of Inductive Bias. In *Machine Learning Proceedings 1993*, pages 41–48.

Alessandra Teresa Cignarella, Mirko Lai, Cristina Bosco, Viviana Patti, Rosso Paolo, et al. 2020. SardiStance@ EVALITA2020: Overview of the Task on Stance Detection in Italian Tweets. In *EVALITA Evaluation of NLP and Speech Tools for Italian - December 17th, 2020*, page 177–186. Accademia University Press.

Vera Davydova and Elena Tutubalina. 2022. SMM4H 2022 task 2: Dataset for stance and premise detection in tweets about health mandates related to COVID-19. In *Proceedings of The Seventh Workshop on Social Media Mining for Health Applications, Workshop & Shared Task*, pages 216–220, Gyeongju, Republic of Korea. Association for Computational Linguistics.

Max Falkenberg, Alessandro Galeazzi, Maddalena Torricelli, Niccolò Di Marco, Francesca Larosa, Madalina Sas, Amin Mekacher, Warren Pearce, Fabiana Zollo, Walter Quattrociocchi, and Andrea Baronchelli. 2022. Growing polarization around climate change on social media. *Nature Climate Change*, 12(12):1114–1121.

Justin Farrell. 2016. Corporate funding and ideological polarization about climate change. *Proceedings of the National Academy of Sciences*, 113(1):92–97.

Keredson. 2019. Wordninja Python Package.

Mirko Lai, Fabio Celli, Alan Ramponi, Sara Tonelli, Cristina Bosco, and Viviana Patti. 2023. HaSpeeDe3 at EVALITA 2023: Overview of the Political and Religious Hate Speech Detection task. In *Proceedings of the Eighth Evaluation Campaign of Natural Language Processing and Speech Tools for Italian. Final Workshop (EVALITA 2023), CEUR, Parma, Italy*, volume 3473.

Yinhan Liu, Myle Ott, Naman Goyal, Jingfei Du, Mandar Joshi, Danqi Chen, Omer Levy, Mike Lewis, Luke Zettlemoyer, and Veselin Stoyanov. 2019. RoBERTa: A Robustly Optimized BERT Pretraining Approach. *ArXiv*, arXiv:1907.11692.

Saif Mohammad, Svetlana Kiritchenko, Parinaz Sobhani, Xiaodan Zhu, and Colin Cherry. 2016a. A Dataset for Detecting Stance in Tweets. In *Proceedings of the Tenth International Conference on Language Resources and Evaluation (LREC'16)*, pages 3945–3952, Portorož, Slovenia. European Language Resources Association (ELRA).

Saif Mohammad, Svetlana Kiritchenko, Parinaz Sobhani, Xiaodan Zhu, and Colin Cherry. 2016b. SemEval-2016 Task 6: Detecting Stance in Tweets. In *Proceedings of the 10th International Workshop on Semantic Evaluation (SemEval-2016)*, pages 31–41, San Diego, California. Association for Computational Linguistics.

Seema Nagar, Ferdous Ahmed Barbhuiya, and Kuntal Dey. 2023. Towards more robust hate speech detection: using social context and user data. *Social Network Analysis and Mining*, 13(1):47.

Anil Singh Parihar, Surendrabikram Thapa, and Sushruti Mishra. 2021. Hate speech detection using natural language processing: Applications and challenges. In *2021 5th International Conference on Trends in Electronics and Informatics (ICOEI)*, pages 1302–1308.

Juan Manuel Pérez, Franco M. Luque, Demian Zayat, Martín Kondratzky, Agustín Moro, Pablo Santiago Serrati, Joaquín Zajac, Paula Miguel, Natalia Debandi, Agustín Gravano, and Viviana Cotik. 2023. Assessing the Impact of Contextual Information in Hate Speech Detection. *IEEE Access*, 11:30575–30590.

Shuvam Shiwakoti, Surendrabikram Thapa, Kritesh Rauniyar, Akshyat Shah, Aashish Bhandari, and Usman Naseem. 2024. Analyzing the Dynamics of Climate Change Discourse on Twitter: A New Annotated Corpus and Multi-Aspect Classification. *Preprint*.

Surendrabikram Thapa, Kritesh Rauniyar, Farhan Ahmad Jafri, Shuvam Shiwakoti, Hari Veeramani, Raghav Jain, Guneet Singh Kohli, Ali Hürriyetoğlu, and Usman Naseem. 2024. Stance and Hate Event Detection in Tweets Related to Climate Activism - Shared Task at CASE 2024. In *Proceedings of the 7th Workshop on Challenges and Applications of Automated Extraction of Socio-political Events from Text (CASE)*.

Adina Williams, Nikita Nangia, and Samuel Bowman. 2018. A Broad-Coverage Challenge Corpus for Sentence Understanding through Inference. In *Proceedings of the 2018 Conference of the North American Chapter of the Association for Computational Linguistics: Human Language Technologies, Volume 1 (Long Papers)*, pages 1112–1122. Association for Computational Linguistics.

Marcos Zampieri, Shervin Malmasi, Preslav Nakov, Sara Rosenthal, Noura Farra, and Ritesh Kumar. 2019a. Predicting the Type and Target of Offensive Posts in Social Media. In *Proceedings of the 2019 Conference of the North American Chapter of the Association for Computational Linguistics: Human Language Technologies, Volume 1 (Long and Short Papers)*, pages 1415–1420, Minneapolis, Minnesota. Association for Computational Linguistics.

Marcos Zampieri, Shervin Malmasi, Preslav Nakov, Sara Rosenthal, Noura Farra, and Ritesh Kumar. 2019b. SemEval-2019 Task 6: Identifying and Categorizing Offensive Language in Social Media (OffensEval). In *Proceedings of the 13th International Workshop on Semantic Evaluation*, pages 75–86, Minneapolis, Minnesota, USA. Association for Computational Linguistics.

NLPDame at ClimateActivism 2024: Mistral Sequence Classification with PEFT for Hate Speech, Targets and Stance Event Detection

Christina Christodoulou
Institute of Informatics & Telecommunications,
National Centre for Scientific Research, "Demokritos"
Athens, Greece
ch.christodoulou@iit.demokritos.gr

Abstract

The paper presents the approach developed for the *Climate Activism Stance and Hate Event Detection* Shared Task at CASE 2024, comprising three sub-tasks. The Shared Task aimed to create a system capable of detecting hate speech, identifying the targets of hate speech, and determining the stance regarding climate change activism events in English tweets. The approach involved data cleaning and pre-processing, addressing data imbalance, and fine-tuning the *mistralai/Mistral-7B-v0.1* LLM for sequence classification using PEFT (Parameter-Efficient Fine-Tuning). The LLM was fine-tuned using two PEFT methods, namely LoRA and prompt tuning, for each sub-task, resulting in the development of six Mistral-7B fine-tuned models in total. Although both methods surpassed the baseline model scores of the task organizers, the prompt tuning method yielded the highest results. Specifically, the prompt tuning method achieved a Macro-F1 score of 0.8649, 0.6106 and 0.6930 in the test data of sub-tasks A, B and C, respectively.

1 Introduction

Climate change is an ever-growing concern that has garnered significant attention worldwide. As the severity of its impacts becomes increasingly undeniable, it has also become an issue that has sparked diverse reactions and discussions on social media platforms. Within these discussions, the prevalence of hate speech, the identification of its targets, and the detection of various stances towards climate change and activist movements have become vital areas of interest. Understanding the dynamics of hate speech, targets of hate speech, and different stances within climate change discourse is crucial for fostering informed discussions, addressing concerns, and promoting positive change. Hate speech, defined as harmful or offensive language directed towards individuals or groups, has the potential to exacerbate division, hinder productive conversations, and impede constructive collaboration. Identifying hate speech in climate change discourse provides a deeper understanding of the negative impact it can have on the overall conversation. Additionally, recognizing the targets of hate speech helps shed light on the specific groups or entities facing hostility, enabling targeted interventions and support. Examining the different stances towards climate change and activist movements also unveils the diversity of perspectives within these discussions. Stance detection allows for the identification of supporters, skeptics, and deniers, providing a nuanced understanding of the range of viewpoints on this pressing issue. By capturing shifts in opinions, trends can be identified, informing future discussions and policy-making.

Natural Language Processing (NLP) models have proven to be valuable assets in detecting hate speech, determining its targets, and classifying stances within various domains. However, when it comes to climate change discourse, there is a need for well-annotated datasets that specifically address the unique challenges present in this field. The scarcity of such datasets poses a significant obstacle to harnessing NLP models effectively. To address this gap, Thapa et al. (2024) created the *Climate Activism Stance and Hate Event Detection* Shared Task at CASE 2024 which challenged participants to develop binary and multi-class text classification systems that are able to detect hate speech, targets of hate speech as well as stance detection concerning climate change, events and movements. The Shared Task leveraged several aspects of the annotated English Twitter dataset regarding climate discourse made by Shiwakoti et al. (2024). This paper presents the system developed for this Task, with the code available on the provided GitHub link.[1]

[1]https://github.com/christinacdl/Climate_Activism_Stance_and_Hate_Event_Detection_CASE_

Proceedings of the 7th Workshop on Challenges and Applications of Automated Extraction of Socio-political Events from Text (CASE 2024), pages 96–104
March 22, 2024

The structure of this paper is as follows: Firstly, Section 2 presents a discussion of the previous related work followed by the presentation of the task and data analysis in Section 3, and an overview of the developed methodology in Section 4. Section 5 presents the results and error analysis. Finally, the paper concludes with Section 6, which discusses future work, as well as the limitations during participating in the Task.

2 Related Work

As social media usage continues to grow and user-generated content becomes more prevalent, numerous studies have focused on identifying and categorizing insulting messages that target individuals or groups across different platforms. To accomplish this, researchers have utilized NLP in conjunction with machine learning. While initial studies focused solely on the English language, the need to address this issue in a multi-lingual context has emerged in recent years. Many studies and shared tasks have been conducted, utilizing various terms such as abuse, aggression, cyberbullying, hate speech, and toxic or offensive language to classify these messages. SemEval's 6th shared task, OffensEval: *Identifying and Categorizing Offensive Language in Social Media*, introduced the detection of offensive language on social media. The task consisted of three sub-tasks that aimed to implement binary or multi-class text classification. Sub-task A sought to differentiate between offensive and non-offensive English tweets, while sub-task B aimed to identify the type of offensive tweets and whether they were targeted or not. Sub-task C aimed to identify the target of the offensive posts. Participants were provided with a dataset containing 13,240 English tweets and a test set of 860 tweets, called the *Offensive Language Identification Dataset* (OLID), which were annotated according to the three sub-tasks (Zampieri et al., 2019). This task was extended the following year as the 12th task of SemEval 2020 named as *Multilingual Offensive Language Identification in Social Media* to encourage offensive language detection in other languages, such as Arabic, Danish, Greek and Turkish, based on the sub-tasks of the previous SemEval (Zampieri et al., 2020). Moreover, SemEval's 5th task in 2019 addressed the issue of hate speech directed towards immigrants and women on Twitter, in both English and Spanish. The two sub-tasks required binary classification - indicating whether a post was hateful or not - and determining whether the target was a generic group or an individual (Basile et al., 2019). In addition, Gautam et al. (2019) analyzed 9,973 tweets related to the *MeToo* movement. They identified five dimensions: stance, relevance, hate speech, dialogue acts, and sarcasm. This analysis provided valuable insights into how people use language to discuss sensitive social issues like *MeToo* on social media platforms. Nevertheless, Parihar et al. (2021) released a paper that discussed the challenges in hate speech detection, including the subjective nature of annotations and the lack of language models for regional languages. Despite the great endeavour in mitigating hate speech and dealing with various social issues, there remains a significant gap in the study of climate change discourse, particularly in the analysis of climate discourse on social media platforms from multiple perspectives. In their efforts to advance this field, Webersinke et al. (2021) introduced *ClimateBERT*, a domain-specific LM that was trained on a staggering 2,046,523 climate-related paragraphs. Additionally, Stammbach et al. (2023) curated a dataset of 3,000 binary datasets focused on environmental claims, often made by businesses in the finance sector. As per their experiments, transformer models have outperformed non-neural models.

2024.git

3 Task & Dataset

3.1 Task

The identification of hate speech and stance detection are critical components in recognizing events that occur during climate change activism. In order to detect hate speech, it is essential to identify the occurrence of hate speech as the event, the entity as the target of the hate speech, and the relationship between the two. The identification of targets is a crucial task in hate speech event detection. Furthermore, stance event detection is a vital part of comprehending whether activist movements and protests related to climate change are being supported or opposed. The Shared Task at CASE 2024 aimed to address these issues and was divided into three sub-tasks: detection of hate speech (sub-task A), targets of hate speech (sub-task B), and stance (sub-task C). More particularly, sub-task A, Hate Speech Detection, involved identifying whether a given text contains hate speech or not. The text dataset for this sub-task consisted of binary annotations for the prevalence of hate speech. Sub-task B, Targets of Hate Speech Detection, involved identifying the targets of hate speech in a given hateful text. The text was annotated for *individual*, *organization*, and *community* targets. Finally, sub-task C, Stance Detection, involved identifying the stance in a given text. The text was annotated for three different stances: *support*, *oppose*, and *neutral*. Hence, sub-task A required binary text classification, while sub-task B and C required multi-class text classification (Thapa et al., 2024).

3.2 Dataset

The provided dataset was created by Shiwakoti et al. (2024) who collated 15,309 English tweets related to climate change, events, and activist movements posted during the year 2022 using the Twitter API. They employed relevant hashtags, including #climatecrisis, #climatechange, #ClimateEmergency, #ClimateTalk, #globalwarming, #fridaysforfuture, #actonclimate, #climatestrike, #extinctionrebellion, #ClimateAlliance, #climatejustice, and #climateaction to retrieve the tweets. The tweets were then annotated for various aspects, such as relevance, stance, humor, hate speech as well as direction and targets of hate speech.

The training data for sub-tasks A and C consisted of 7,284 tweets. In comparison, the validation data included 1,561 tweets. The test data comprised 1,562 tweets. For sub-task B, the training data amounted to 699 tweets, while the validation and test data had 150 tweets each. While cleaning the data, it was discovered that all data sets contained duplicate tweets. The training data had 365 duplicate tweets, while the validation and test data had 33 and 47 duplicate tweets, respectively, for sub-tasks A and C. For sub-task B, the training data had 237 duplicate tweets, while the validation and test data had 18 and 31 duplicate tweets, respectively. To ensure data uniformity, only the first occurrence of each tweet was retained in the training and validation datasets. However, no duplicates were removed from the test data to ensure the final evaluation of the system was not affected. The training data was used only for training, no data splitting was applied for evaluation. The class distribution of the three training sets before and after data cleaning as well as the categorical labels, along with their respective numerical labels provided by the organizers, are presented in Table 1. From the training data, it became evident that several classes, namely *HATE*, *COMMUNITY*, and *OPPOSE* in sub-task A, B and C, respectively, were under-represented and formed the minority of the classes. For this reason, different weights were assigned to the loss function for each class providing higher weight to the minority classes and lower weight to the majority classes. Although the labels of all the validation and test sets were provided after the end of the evaluation and testing phases, it became evident that their class distribution was consistent with the class distribution of the training set.

Class Label	Before Data Cleaning	After Data Cleaning
Sub-task A		
NON-HATE (0)	6,385	6,262
HATE (1)	899	657
Sub-task B		
INDIVIDUAL (1)	563	326
ORGANIZATION (2)	105	105
COMMUNITY (3)	31	31
Sub-task C		
SUPPORT (1)	4,328	4,246
OPPOSE (2)	700	458
NEUTRAL (3)	2,256	2,215

Table 1: Categorical & Numerical Labels with Class Distribution in Training Sets.

4 Methodology

4.1 Mistral LLM & PEFT Methods

Mistral is a 7-billion-parameter language model that has been designed to deliver high performance and efficiency in text generation (Jiang et al., 2023). It utilizes grouped-query attention (GQA) to ensure faster inference and sliding window attention (SWA) to handle long sequences effectively. The model has been evaluated and outperforms the Llama 2 13B model across all benchmarks. It also outperforms the Llama 1 34B model in reasoning, mathematics, and code generation. The model's architecture is based on a transformer with specific parameters such as a window size of 4096 and a context length of 81,922. It is available on Hugging Face under the name *mistralai/Mistral-7B-v0.1* for easy deployment and fine-tuning across various tasks.[2] There are also

[2]https://huggingface.co/mistralai/Mistral-7B-v0.1

two instruct versions of Mistral (*mistralai/Mistral-7B-Instruct-v0.1* and *mistralai/Mistral-7B-Instruct-v0.2*) which were fine-tuned using a variety of publicly available conversation datasets. To leverage for fine-tuning, they require surrounding the prompt with the *[INST]* and *[/INST]* tokens. After careful consideration, it was decided that the Mistral base model architecture would be the sole focus of the presented approach, even though there was the possibility of using more LLMs for experimentation and comparison. The decision was based on the understanding that the Mistral base model offered a solid foundation for evaluating text generation performance, and it would be interesting to assess its text classification performance as well. Additionally, assessing multiple models could detract from the accuracy and clarity of the results. Therefore, it was determined that a focused approach would be more effective in achieving the research objectives.

The PEFT library, which is integrated with Hugging Face's Transformers, includes methods that are designed for the efficient adaptation of large pre-trained models to various downstream applications. These methods enable fine-tuning a small subset of additional model parameters, which helps in reducing the computational and storage demands.[3]

LoRA (Low-Rank Adaptation) is one of the PEFT methods which adapts LLMs to specific tasks while reducing the number of trainable parameters (Hu et al., 2021). This method freezes pre-trained model weights and injects trainable rank decomposition matrices into each layer of the Transformer architecture. This significantly reduces the number of parameters that need to be trained, making it more efficient in terms of memory and storage usage. With LoRA, LLMs allow efficient task switching while reducing hardware requirements for training. Moreover, LoRA introduces no additional inference latency compared to fully fine-tuned models. Empirical investigations have shown that LoRA performs on par or better than fine-tuning on various models like RoBERTa and DeBERTa, suggesting that it amplifies important features for specific downstream tasks that were learned but not emphasized during general pre-training. To fine-tune a model using LoRa, the task type, the dimension of the low-rank matrices (LoRA r), the scaling factor for the weight matrices (LoRA alpha), and the dropout probability of the LoRA layers (LoRA dropout) as well as the LoRA bias to train all bias parameters needed to be defined. For the present approach, the selected task type was *SEQ_CLS* and the default LoRA dropout was used. The same number was set for r and alpha as a starting point as was suggested because it is very easy to reduce the impact of LORA data after the training, in case it appears to be too dominant and overtakes the entire model.[4]

Prompt tuning is a technique used to adapt large pre-trained language models for specific downstream tasks by learning *soft prompts* that are added to the input text (Lester et al., 2021). These soft prompts are learned by backpropagation and can incorporate signals from labelled examples. This is different from the discrete text prompts used by models. The main advantage of prompt tuning is that it allows for the reuse of a single frozen model across multiple tasks, which is more efficient in terms of storage and computational resources compared to traditional model tuning where all model parameters are adjusted. The effectiveness of prompt tuning is demonstrated by its ability to outperform few-shot learning approaches like GPT-3's prompt design and to match the strong performance of model tuning as the size of the language model increases. It also shows improved robustness to domain shifts, suggesting that it can help avoid overfitting to specific domains. After creating multiple prompts, Table 2 displays the final versions of the prompts that were created using this method for each sub-task. During experimentation, it was revealed that Mistral performs better when the *[INST]* and *[/INST]* tokens are added at the beginning and end of the prompt. Thus, it appears that the Mistral base model closely resembles its instruction models during prompt construction.

4.2 Environment Setup

The presented methodology was implemented in three separate Python files, one dedicated to each sub-task. The experiments were mainly conducted using the *Transformers*, *PEFT* and *Hugging Face* libraries and 1 NVIDIA RTX, 24210.125MB. The model was loaded in 4-bit Quantization using the *BitsAndBytesConfig* library which is integrated with Hugging Face. Quantization was used to reduce memory usage and speed up model execution while maintaining accuracy.

[3] https://huggingface.co/docs/peft/index

[4] https://medium.com/@fartypantsham/what-rank-r-and-alpha-to-use-in-lora-in-llm-1b4f025fd133

Text Prompt
Sub-task A
[INST]Your task is to classify if the text contains hate speech or not, and return the answer as the corresponding label '0' or '1'[/INST]
Sub-task B
[INST]Your task is to classify the target of hate speech as individual, organization or community, and return the answer as the corresponding label '0' or '1' or '2'[/INST]
Sub-task C
[INST]Your task is to classify the stance of hate speech as support, oppose or neutral, and return the answer as the corresponding label '0' or '1' or '2'[/INST]

Table 2: Text Prompts created for prompt tuning with Mistral-7B in each sub-task.

4.3 Pre-processing & Hyperparameters

Several pre-processing steps were applied to the tweets of all training, validation, and test sets using a function that included regular expressions and other functions. Firstly, all emojis were converted to their textual representations (Taehoon et al., 2022).[5] The *&* and *&* were replaced with *and*. The ASCII encoding apostrophe was replaced with the UTF-8 encoding apostrophe. Consecutive non-ASCII characters were replaced with whitespace, and all extra whitespace was removed. Then, the python *wordsegment*[6] library as well as the *Ekphrasis* library were leveraged for hashtag segmentation (Baziotis et al., 2017).[7] The *Ekphrasis* library was also employed for normalizing the usernames, links and emails by converting them into the special tokens *<user>*, *<url>* and *<email>*, respectively. They were selected to be anonymized for data privacy. They were not removed completely, instead, they were replaced by the aforementioned special tokens to avoid any loss of context. Removing the usernames, especially in sub-task B whose aim is to detect the hate speech target, would result in great loss of performance. Finally, the case and punctuation were maintained as they contribute to the context of the text.

Following the pre-processing steps, the training, validation and test data were converted from dataframes into JSON datasets. The datasets were passed to the LLM's tokenizer, which tokenized and returned the tweets into input IDs and attention masks. The train, validation and test datasets were concatenated for each sub-task to get the overall maximum sequence length of the input IDs, which was employed in each sub-task and is shown in Table 7 of Appendix A along with all hyperparameters. Identical hyperparameters were employed for both LoRA and Prompt Tuning models in each sub-task to ensure consistency and easy model comparison. Only one specific random seed (42) was selected during fine-tuning across all experiments of sub-tasks to ensure reproducibility.

To address the data imbalance, the weight of each class was calculated based on the ratio of the total number of training samples to the number of training samples in that class. These weights were then passed into the *CrossEntropy Loss* function. This approach ensured that classes with fewer samples had a higher weight, whereas classes with more samples, which were over-represented in the dataset, had a lower weight during fine-tuning. At this point, it is important to note that the labels in sub-tasks B and C were converted from 1,2,3 to the corresponding integers 0,1,2 for fine-tuning the LLM. The correct labels were assigned during the creation of the submission files. In Table 6 of Appendix A, the calculated weights for each class in each sub-task are presented.

The system's efficiency and final ranking were primarily evaluated based on the Macro-F1 score of the test set predictions. Thapa et al. (2024), the task organizers, had released their fine-tuned models as baselines along with their Macro-F1 and accuracy scores for each task, which were employed for comparison with the approach presented in this paper in Table 4. Finally, the Macro-F1 score for each class and Confusion Matrices were calculated for error analysis.

5 Results & Discussion

Table 3 shows that Mistral with the prompt tuning method achieved the highest Macro-F1 score in both validation and test sets across all sub-tasks, hence, revealing the potential of a causal language model like Mistral to perform sequence classification with the appropriate prompt. For this reason, the predicted test set labels of the prompt tuning Mistral models were selected as the final submissions and received a rank based on their results.

[5] https://pypi.org/project/emoji/

[6] https://pypi.org/project/wordsegment/

[7] https://github.com/cbaziotis/ekphrasis

Validation Set	
Sub-task A	
Model	**Macro-F1**
Mistral LoRA	0.7942
Mistral Prompt Tuning	0.8385
Model	**Macro-F1**
Sub-task B	
Model	**Macro-F1**
Mistral LoRA	0.5829
Mistral Prompt Tuning	0.6071
Sub-task C	
Model	**Macro-F1**
Mistral LoRA	0.5854
Mistral Prompt Tuning	0.6446
Test Set	
Sub-task A	
Model	**Macro-F1**
Mistral LoRA	0.7990
Mistral Prompt Tuning	0.8649
Sub-task B	
Model	**Macro-F1**
Mistral LoRA	0.5713
Mistral Prompt Tuning	0.6106
Sub-task C	
Model	**Macro-F1**
Mistral LoRA	0.6160
Mistral Prompt Tuning	0.6930

Table 3: Results of all models on test and validation sets based on Macro-F1 score.

Specifically, in sub-task A, the Mistral prompt tuning method achieved the 10th place out of 22 submissions with a Macro-F1 score of 0.8649. In subtask B, it achieved the 11th place out of 18 submissions with a Macro-F1 score of 0.6106. Lastly, in sub-task C, it achieved the 13th place out of 19 submissions with a Macro-F1 score of 0.6930. According to Table 4, it is revealed that the submitted Mistral prompt tuning models managed to beat the baseline accuracy and Macro-F1 scores of the models developed by the dataset creators across all sub-tasks (Shiwakoti et al., 2024). The dataset creators have experimented with Transformer models like BERT (Devlin et al., 2019), DistilBERT (Sanh et al., 2020), RoBERTa (Liu et al., 2019) and ClimateBERT (Webersinke et al., 2021) using a batch size of 16 for 3 epochs with a learning rate of 1e-5 for DistilBERT and 1e-3 for the rest of the models. By taking into account the Macro-F1 score of each class on the validation and test sets in Table 5, it is demonstrated that the models are not able to identify the *COMMUNITY* minority class and, surprisingly, the *NEUTRAL* majority class, since they achieved the lowest scores. On the other hand, the *NON-HATE* and *INDIVIDUAL* majority classes yielded the highest scores. In subtask A, both models can identify non-hateful content more accurately than hateful content. However, the Mistral Prompt Tuning model outperforms the Mistral LoRA model in detecting hateful tweets. In subtask B, the models successfully detect individuals as targets of hate speech, but fail to identify organizations and communities. Both models in sub-task C perform better at identifying stances that show support or opposition rather than neutral stances. The Mistral Prompt Tuning model exhibited better performance in the support and oppose classes compared to the Mistral LoRA model. The Mistral LoRA model's performance was higher in identifying the *OPPOSE* stance on the test set than on the validation set, the same applied to the *NEUTRAL* stance as well. Finally, the Mistral Prompt Tuning model achieved a higher score for the *OPPOSE* stance on the test set than on the validation set.

Sub-task A		
Model	**Macro-F1**	**Accuracy**
BERT	0.708	0.901
DistilBERT	0.664	0.896
RoBERTa	0.662	0.842
ClimateBERT	0.704	0.884
Mistral Prompt Tuning	**0.864**	**0.946**
Sub-task B		
Model	**Macro-F1**	**Accuracy**
BERT	0.554	0.641
DistilBERT	0.550	0.603
RoBERTa	0.501	0.716
ClimateBERT	0.549	0.604
Mistral Prompt Tuning	**0.610**	**0.840**
Sub-task C		
Model	**Macro-F1**	**Accuracy**
BERT	0.466	0.586
DistilBERT	0.527	0.610
RoBERTa	0.542	0.648
ClimateBERT	0.545	0.651
Mistral Prompt Tuning	**0.693**	**0.665**

Table 4: Comparison of submitted fine-tuned models with baseline models on test set based on Macro-F1 score and accuracy.

Class Label	Macro-F1 Validation	Macro-F1 Test
Sub-task A		
Mistral LoRA		
NON-HATE	0.9514	0.9478
HATE	0.6371	0.6502
Mistral Prompt Tuning		
NON-HATE	0.9664	0.9697
HATE	0.7107	0.7600
Sub-task B		
Mistral LoRA		
INDIVIDUAL	0.9101	0.9487
ORGANIZATION	0.5660	0.5652
COMMUNITY	0.2727	0.2000
Mistral Prompt Tuning		
INDIVIDUAL	0.9167	0.9487
ORGANIZATION	0.5714	0.5128
COMMUNITY	0.3333	0.3704
Sub-task C		
Mistral LoRA		
SUPPORT	0.6737	0.6835
OPPOSE	0.6169	0.6838
NEUTRAL	0.4657	0.4806
Mistral Prompt Tuning		
SUPPORT	0.7038	0.7195
OPPOSE	0.7250	0.8244
NEUTRAL	0.5052	0.5351

Table 5: Macro-F1 scores in each class on test and validation sets.

5.1 Error Analysis

The confusion matrices were generated after the release of the test set labels. The purpose was to reveal the errors and strengths of the submitted Mistral Prompt Tuning models. Figure 1 displays the performance of the Prompt Tuning models on the test set of sub-tasks A, B and C respectively, through the confusion matrices. Firstly, it is evident from the confusion matrix of sub-task A that the model performed better in identifying tweets that do not contain hate speech. This could be attributed to the limited data available in the *HATE* class. The model placed greater emphasis on boosting the *NON-HATE* class, which further skewed the models' ability to accurately detect hate speech tweets. Moreover, from the confusion matrix of sub-task B, it is evident that the model managed to detect tweets that target individuals with greater confidence and success because it was the majority class. The *COMMUNITY* class contained the least examples in the training set, hence the model was able to classify fewer examples than expected into this category and more examples into the other categories. The model also seemed to have gotten a bit confused when it came to identifying between the *ORGANIZATION* and *COMMUNITY* classes, as texts that belonged to the *COMMUNITY* class were assigned to the *ORGANIZATION* class. Finally, it has been proven that the model found it difficult to distinguish between tweets that belonged to the *SUPPORT* and *NEUTRAL* stance classes in sub-task C, since many texts were falsely classified as expressing support or neutral stance, respectively.

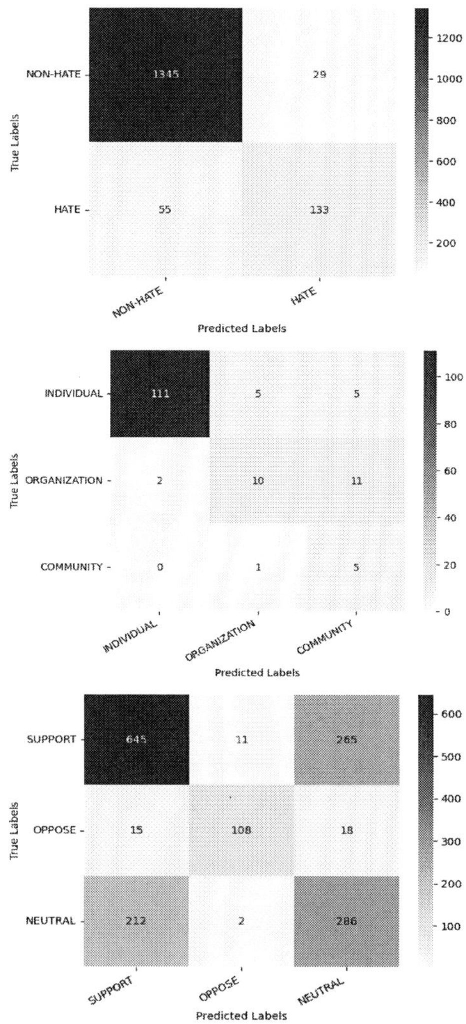

Figure 1: Test Set Confusion Matrices of Mistral Prompt Tuning models.

6 Conclusion

The Climate Activism Stance and Hate Event Detection Shared Task at CASE 2024 involved fine-tuning the LLM Mistral-7B with two PEFT methods (LoRA and prompt tuning) for binary and multi-class text classification. This resulted in the creation of six models that can detect hate speech, targets of hate speech, and stance regarding climate change and activist events. The approach also included adding weights to deal with class imbalance, as well as data cleaning and pre-processing. Comparing the two PEFT methods showed that the prompt tuning method yielded the best performance by crafting the most appropriate and precise prompt for each task. Both methods, particularly the prompt tuning method that was submitted, outperformed all Transformer language models that were fine-tuned by the task organizers and whose scores were presented as baselines. To further improve the models' performance, future efforts should concentrate on adding more tweets in the sub-tasks, especially hate speech and targets of hate speech. Although the Mistral model was originally designed for text generation, it demonstrated its potential to perform sequence classification effectively as well.

7 Limitations

The experimentation process across all sub-tasks revealed a major issue of class imbalance. Despite assigning higher weights to the minority classes, it became clear that detecting hate speech, targets of hate speech, and stances concerning climate change and events was indeed very challenging. The primary reason for this is the scarcity of data available for these categories. The lack of sufficient data causes the trained models to be biased towards the majority classes, which results in poor performance on the minority classes. Unfortunately, there was no other relevant climate activism dataset to leverage for this task. As possible solutions, more data related to climate activism stances and hate events as well as further model experimentation are necessary. More data will certainly help balance the classes and train the models to be less biased and more successful in detecting hate speech, targets of hate speech and stances concerning climate change and events.

References

Valerio Basile, Cristina Bosco, Elisabetta Fersini, Debora Nozza, Viviana Patti, Francisco Manuel Rangel Pardo, Paolo Rosso, and Manuela Sanguinetti. 2019. SemEval-2019 task 5: Multilingual detection of hate speech against immigrants and women in Twitter. In *Proceedings of the 13th International Workshop on Semantic Evaluation*, pages 54–63, Minneapolis, Minnesota, USA. Association for Computational Linguistics.

Christos Baziotis, Nikos Pelekis, and Christos Doulkeridis. 2017. Datastories at semeval-2017 task 4: Deep lstm with attention for message-level and topic-based sentiment analysis. In *Proceedings of the 11th International Workshop on Semantic Evaluation (SemEval-2017)*, pages 747–754, Vancouver, Canada. Association for Computational Linguistics.

Jacob Devlin, Ming-Wei Chang, Kenton Lee, and Kristina Toutanova. 2019. Bert: Pre-training of deep bidirectional transformers for language understanding.

Akash Gautam, Puneet Mathur, Rakesh Gosangi, Debanjan Mahata, Ramit Sawhney, and Rajiv Ratn Shah. 2019. metooma: Multi-aspect annotations of tweets related to the metoo movement.

Edward J. Hu, Yelong Shen, Phillip Wallis, Zeyuan Allen-Zhu, Yuanzhi Li, Shean Wang, Lu Wang, and Weizhu Chen. 2021. Lora: Low-rank adaptation of large language models.

Albert Q. Jiang, Alexandre Sablayrolles, Arthur Mensch, Chris Bamford, Devendra Singh Chaplot, Diego de las Casas, Florian Bressand, Gianna Lengyel, Guillaume Lample, Lucile Saulnier, Lélio Renard Lavaud, Marie-Anne Lachaux, Pierre Stock, Teven Le Scao, Thibaut Lavril, Thomas Wang, Timothée Lacroix, and William El Sayed. 2023. Mistral 7b.

Brian Lester, Rami Al-Rfou, and Noah Constant. 2021. The power of scale for parameter-efficient prompt tuning.

Yinhan Liu, Myle Ott, Naman Goyal, Jingfei Du, Mandar Joshi, Danqi Chen, Omer Levy, Mike Lewis, Luke Zettlemoyer, and Veselin Stoyanov. 2019. Roberta: A robustly optimized bert pretraining approach.

Anil Singh Parihar, Surendrabikram Thapa, and Sushruti Mishra. 2021. Hate speech detection using natural language processing: Applications and challenges. In *2021 5th International Conference on Trends in Electronics and Informatics (ICOEI)*, pages 1302–1308.

Victor Sanh, Lysandre Debut, Julien Chaumond, and Thomas Wolf. 2020. Distilbert, a distilled version of bert: smaller, faster, cheaper and lighter.

Shuvam Shiwakoti, Surendrabikram Thapa, Kritesh Rauniyar, Akshyat Shah, Aashish Bhandari, and Usman Naseem. 2024. Analyzing the dynamics of climate change discourse on twitter: A new annotated corpus and multi-aspect classification. *Preprint*.

Dominik Stammbach, Nicolas Webersinke, Julia Anna Bingler, Mathias Kraus, and Markus Leippold. 2023. Environmental claim detection.

Kim Taehoon, Tahir Kevin, Wurster, and Jalilov. 2022. Emoji.

Surendrabikram Thapa, Kritesh Rauniyar, Farhan Ahmad Jafri, Shuvam Shiwakoti, Hariram Veeramani, Raghav Jain, Guneet Singh Kohli, Ali Hürriyetoğlu, and Usman Naseem. 2024. Stance and hate event detection in tweets related to climate activism - shared task at case 2024. In *Proceedings of the 7th Workshop on Challenges and Applications of Automated Extraction of Socio-political Events from Text (CASE)*.

Nicolas Webersinke, Mathias Kraus, Julia Anna Bingler, and Markus Leippold. 2021. Climatebert: A pretrained language model for climate-related text. *CoRR*, abs/2110.12010.

Marcos Zampieri, Shervin Malmasi, Preslav Nakov, Sara Rosenthal, Noura Farra, and Ritesh Kumar. 2019. SemEval-2019 task 6: Identifying and categorizing offensive language in social media (OffensEval). In *Proceedings of the 13th International Workshop on Semantic Evaluation*, pages 75–86, Minneapolis, Minnesota, USA. Association for Computational Linguistics.

Marcos Zampieri, Preslav Nakov, Sara Rosenthal, Pepa Atanasova, Georgi Karadzhov, Hamdy Mubarak, Leon Derczynski, Zeses Pitenis, and Çağrı Çöltekin. 2020. SemEval-2020 task 12: Multilingual offensive language identification in social media (OffensEval 2020). In *Proceedings of the Fourteenth Workshop on Semantic Evaluation*, pages 1425–1447, Barcelona (online). International Committee for Computational Linguistics.

A Appendix

Class Label	**Weight**
Sub-task A	
NON-HATE (0)	1.1049185563717663
HATE (1)	10.531202435312025
Sub-task B	
INDIVIDUAL (0)	1.4171779141104295
ORGANIZATION (1)	4.4
COMMUNITY (2)	14.903225806451612
Sub-task C	
SUPPORT (0)	1.6295336787564767
OPPOSE (1)	15.106986899563319
NEUTRAL (2)	3.1237020316027087

Table 6: Calculated Weights Based on Class Distribution in Training Sets.

Hyperparams	**Sub-task A**	**Sub-task B**	**Sub-task C**
Classes	2	3	3
Epochs	10	10	10
Seq. Length	195	193	195
Batch Size	16	16	16
Learning Rate	1e-4	1e-4	1e-4
Weight Decay	0.0001	0.0001	0.0001
M. G. Norm	0.3	0.3	0.3
Warm-up R.	0.1	0.1	0.1
AdamW E.	1e-8	1e-8	1e-8
G. A. Steps	2	2	2
Early Stop.	5	5	5
Seed	42	42	42
Virtual Tokens	37	11	15
LoRA r	16	16	16
LoRA alpha	16	16	16
LoRA dropout	0.05	0.05	0.05
LoRA bias	none	none	none

Table 7: Model Hyperparameters in Each Sub-task.

AAST-NLP at ClimateActivism 2024: Ensemble-Based Climate Activism Stance and Hate Speech Detection : Leveraging Pretrained Language Models

Ahmed El-Sayed and **Omar Nasr**
Arab Academy for Science and Technology
{ahmedelsayedhabashy,omarnasr5206}@gmail.com

Abstract

Climate activism has emerged as a powerful force in addressing the urgent challenges posed by climate change. Individuals and organizations passionate about environmental issues use platforms like Twitter to mobilize support, share information, and advocate for policy changes. Unfortunately, amidst the passionate discussions, there has been an unfortunate rise in the prevalence of hate speech on the platform. Some users resort to personal attacks and divisive language, undermining the constructive efforts of climate activists. In this paper, we describe our approaches for three subtasks of ClimateActivism at CASE 2024. For all the three subtasks, we utilize pretrained language models enhanced by ensemble learning. Regarding the second subtask, dedicated to target detection, we experimented with incorporating Named Entity Recognition in the pipeline. Additionally, our models secure the second, third and fifth ranks in the three subtasks respectively.

1 Introduction

Climate activism has emerged as a formidable force in contemporary society, reflecting a collective global consciousness towards environmental stewardship. The advocates of climate activism ardently emphasize the urgency of addressing climate change as a paramount global challenge. Through various channels, such as organized protests, advocacy campaigns, and international collaborations, climate activists strive to raise awareness about the detrimental impact of human activities on the planet's ecosystems (Fisher and Nasrin, 2020). Social media has played a pivotal role in amplifying the voices of climate activists, providing a powerful platform for the dissemination of information and the mobilization of global communities. Platforms like Twitter, Instagram, and Facebook have facilitated the rapid spread of awareness campaigns, enabling activists to reach diverse audiences and garner widespread support for climate action.(Arnot et al., 2024; Gómez-Casillas and Márquez, 2023) However, the same social media channels have also been susceptible to the spread of misinformation and targeted attacks against climate activists (Levantesi). Instances of hate speech and online harassment have, unfortunately, been prevalent, underscoring the double-edged nature of social media in the context of climate activism. The Climate Activism 2024 shared task (Thapa et al., 2024) delves into this significant subject by providing a dataset that encourages collaboration among researchers to address this crucial issue. The paper is organized into several key sections: related work, dataset and task description, methodology, results, and a discussion leading to a conclusion.

2 Related Work

In the realm of social media, the challenge of hate speech detection arises as a pressing concern (Jahan and Oussalah, 2023b). A number of researcher have proposed models to tackle this issue. Language models, in particular, have been a major driving force or this recent succes. Roberta, for instance, was used in detecting hate speech from social media data (Alonso et al., 2020). Some BERT based models were trained specifically for hate speech detection and achieved incredible results (Caselli et al., 2021). Language models were also adapted to multiple languages and were noticed to perform high results (Mujahid et al., 2023; Plaza-Del-Arco et al., 2021). A number of papers provide a comprehensive overview over the latest challenges and trend in hate speech detection, some of which serve as a starting point for any researcher working on this topic (Parihar et al., 2021; Jahan and Oussalah, 2023a). Hate speech manifests in various forms, and scholars have focused on creating systems to tackle issues like Cyber Bullying (Akhter et al., 2023; Hsien et al., 2022), racism (Schütz et al., 2021), and sexism (Plaza et al., 2023).

Proceedings of the 7th Workshop on Challenges and Applications of Automated Extraction of Socio-political Events from Text (CASE 2024), pages 105–110
March 22, 2024 ©2024 Association for Computational Linguistics

Despite the ongoing and comprehensive endeavors of researchers, as far as we are aware, there has not been a unified research initiative to monitor hate speech specifically directed at climate activists, a significant and alarming occurrence.

3 Dataset & Task

The shared task on Climate Activism Stance and Hate Event Detection at CASE 2024[1]consists of three main subtasks.Each subtask will be discussed in details in the following subsections. The provided dataset primarily comprises tweets expressing either support or opposition towards climate activists in various contexts (Shiwakoti et al., 2024). The subsequent subsections will present an overview of the distribution for each dataset, emphasizing the challenges posed by imbalances, particularly instances where certain classes were underrepresented.

3.1 Subtask A: Hate Speech Detection

The first subtask is a binary classification problem where tweets given are classified into two distinct classes: "Hate Speech" and "No Hate Speech". Table 1 illustrates the data distribution for the different classes within the dataset.

	Training	Validation	Testing
No Hate	6385	1371	1374
Hate	899	190	188
Overall	7284	1561	1562

Table 1: Subtask A's Dataset Distribution.

3.2 Subtask B: Targets of Hate Speech Identification

The second subtask is a multiclass classification problem where tweets given are classified into three distinct classes: "Individual", "Organization", and "Community". Table 2 illustrates the data distribution for the different classes within the dataset.

	Training	Validation	Testing
Individual	563	120	121
Organization	105	23	23
Community	31	7	6
Overall	699	150	150

Table 2: Subtask B's Dataset Distribution.

3.3 Subtask C: Stance Detection

The third subtask is a multiclass classification problem where tweets given are classified into three distinct classes: "Support", "Oppose", and "Neutral". Table 3 illustrates the data distribution for the different classes within the dataset.

	Training	Validation	Testing
Support	4328	897	921
Oppose	2256	153	141
Neutral	700	511	500
Overall	7284	1561	1562

Table 3: Subtask C's Dataset Distribution.

3.4 Data Preprocessing

Prior to being fed into the model, the text undergoes a rigorous preprocessing stage aimed at addressing various challenges related to the nature of social media data, where texts contain relatively high noise. This noise, if not properly handled, has the potential to adversely impact our classifier's performance. Therefore, the preprocessing stage is crucial in mitigating such adverse effects and ensuring the robustness of the model against the inherent noise in social media texts.

- Removal of punctuation as many tweets contained .
- Applying PySpellChecker[2] to check for misspelled words and correct them.
- Removal of hyperlinks and emojis as they did not meaning needed for our classification process.
- Removal of hashtags and tags as most of the text contained relatively similar hashtags like #ClimateChange and #ClimateStrike.

4 Methodology

In the following subsections, we will expand on the proposed models for each subtask. We will also expand on the main ideas we experimented on to tackle the class imbalance issue we encountered.

4.1 Proposed Model

4.1.1 Language Models

Several language models were experimented with through the process of fine-tuning, driven by their

[1]https://codalab.lisn.upsaclay.fr/competitions/16206

[2]https://pypi.org/project/pyspellchecker/

remarkable performance in the context of our specific topic, We finetuned RoBERTa(Liu et al., 2019), XLM-RoBERTa (Conneau et al., 2020) and HateBERT (Caselli et al., 2021) on all of the datasets. Roberta showed superior performacne in terms of f1-score on all of the subtasks as will be shown in the results section5. However, XLM-RoBERTa and HateBERT where shown to shine in different aspects either achieving higher recall or precision, something that encouraged us to use our ensemble-based approach.

4.1.2 NER Based Classifier

For Subtask B, we experimented with 2 Named Entity Recognition modules, SpaCy[3] and a BERT based NER[4], to extract important landmarks. The BERT based NER showed superior performance in extracting names whilst SpaCy was used to extract ORG and NoORG landmarks. This approach was inspired by (Sahin et al., 2023) work on multimodal hate speech detection. The extracted features would then be classified using a classifier or simply through checking which token appeared the most and assigning the class accordingly. To further illustrate how the NER works, consider the following dataset sample after it went through preprocessing "You ve been fooled by Greta Thunberg" the NER would report the following tokens illustrated in Table 4.

Class	Person	ORG	NoORG
Token Count	1	0	0

Table 4: NER Tokens extracted.

4.2 Ensembling

Ensembling machine learning models involves combining diverse models to improve robustness, generalization, and predictive performance. Our strategy employs hard voting, where individual models within the ensemble make predictions on a dataset, and the final prediction is determined by majority voting. We conducted experiments involving the ensemble of top-k learners for each subtask, culminating in the derivation of our predictions.

4.3 Tackling Class Imbalance

4.3.1 Resampling

Resampling involves modifying the distribution of training datasets to elevate the significance of minority classes (Kraiem et al., 2021), Random under-sampling (RUS) entails randomly removing data points from the majority class, while random oversampling (ROS) involves duplicating instances from the minority class. Both ROS and RUS were employed to address the imbalance in the dataset, yet ROS was the one incorporated in the final submission as it was found to increase the f1-score.

4.3.2 Loss Functions

Several loss functions were experimented with, and initially, Weighted Cross-Entropy loss was employed for our subtasks. The weights were calculated using the scikit[5] class weight function, resulting in a slight improvement. Focal Loss was also used yet it provided us with minimal improvements. Ultimately, an experiment was conducted using Dice Loss, a customized loss function tailored to NLP tasks based on the Sørensen–Dice coefficient (Li et al., 2019).

4.4 Experiment Settings

The training procedure was conducted using the Google Colab [6] platform for training our pipeline, which has 12.68 GB of RAM, a 14.75 GB NVIDIA Tesla T4 GPU, and Python language.We employed the autofit functionality from ktrain (Maiya, 2022), incorporating a triangular learning rate policy (Smith, 2017). The specific parameters chosen for our experiment are outlined in the table below.

Hyperparameter	Value
Epochs	30
Learning Rate	2e-5
Batch Size	16
Max length	40
Optimizer	Adam
Early Stopping Patience	5
Reduce On Plateau	2
Loss Function	Dice Loss

Table 5: Training Hyperparameters.

5 Results

This section elaborates on the results obtained from using the mentioned systems. It's crucial to note that RoBERTa, XLM-RoBERTa, and HateBERT underwent multiple training sessions with varying

[3]https://spacy.io/

[4]https://huggingface.co/dslim/bert-base-NER

[5]https://scikit-learn.org/stable/

[6]https://colab.google/

dataset distributions through resampling. Additionally, both base and large versions were experimented with for RoBERTa and XLM-RoBERTa. The Top-k Ensemble method selected the highest k submissions for ensembling.

5.1 Subtask A

Table 6 provides a visual representation of how the mentioned models performed on the test set. It is evident that certain models outperformed others in specific metrics. Notably, Roberta achieved the highest precision among all models, while HateBERT exhibited the highest recall among the reported models. These findings prompted us to adapt our ensemble approach, aiming to leverage the strengths of various models.

Model	**Precision**	**Recall**	**F1-Score**
RoBERTa	**0.8688**	0.8775	0.8731
XLM-RoBERTa	0.8544	0.9174	0.8824
HateBERT	0.7994	**0.9611**	0.8579
Top-3 Ensemble	0.8544	0.9174	0.8824
Top-5 Ensemble	0.8654	0.9231	**0.8914**

Table 6: Results For Subtask A.

5.2 Subtask B

Table 7 illustrates the performance of the previously mentioned models on the test set. Roberta significantly surpasses the performance of all other models, with XLM-RoBERTa also demonstrating relatively strong performance.The NER-based classifier exhibited solid performance, even outperforming HateBERT. Employing a hard voting scheme to ensemble predictions, with greater emphasis on RoBERTa, resulted in consistently high outcomes.

Model	**Precision**	**Recall**	**F1-Score**
RoBERTa	0.7416	0.7501	0.7434
XLM-RoBERTa	0.7271	0.7191	0.7232
HateBERT	0.7071	0.6788	0.6919
NER Based	0.7123	0.7185	0.7063
Top-3 Ensemble	0.7561	0.7629	0.7570
Top-5 Ensemble	**0.7706**	**0.7689**	**0.7665**

Table 7: Results For Subtask B.

5.3 Subtask C

Table 8 illustrates the performance of the previously mentioned models on the test set. Roberta slightly surpassed the other two models in performance. However, upon ensembling the three models, we observed only a slight improvement in performance. This raises a pertinent question about whether the marginal increase, in our specific case, justifies the computational costs associated with real-time implementation for this subtask.

Model	**Precision**	**Recall**	**F1-Score**
RoBERTa	**0.7169**	0.7664	0.7356
XLM-RoBERTa	0.7022	0.7154	0.7070
HateBERT	0.7001	0.7869	0.7319
Top-3 Ensemble	0.7078	**0.7931**	**0.7398**

Table 8: Results For Subtask C.

5.4 Leaderboard Results

During the evaluation phase of the shared task, we submitted our models for assessment on the test sets of both Subtask A, Subtask B and Subtask C. The outcomes of the tests are presented in Table 6, Table 7 and Table 8, respectively. Our ensemble based approach, which combines multiple BERT-based models, achieved the second place among the 23 participating teams in Subtask A. Similarly, the same model secured the second position among the 18 participating teams in Subtask B. Whilst in subtask C, our model achieves the fifth place.

6 Discussion & Future Work

The results obtained show that leveraging pre-trained models for the classification of hate tweets could provide very promising results, even when faced with unbalanced data. These results form a great basis for further research, including but not limited to incorporating more language models into the ensemble, such as the FALCON series of models (Almazrouei et al., 2023) or Mistral (Jiang et al., 2023). Creating synthetic data with the aim of enhancing model robustness or improving performance on underrepresented classes or ones the model faces difficulties in identifying is also an intriguing strategy. Attempting different hyperparameter configurations is also worthy of further investigation. Overall, with further refinement, this approach could definitely have a real impact on reducing the hate experienced by climate activists all around the world.

7 Conclusion

This study centers on analyzing tweets that convey opinions and emotions, but regrettably, these tweets are also employed as channels for disseminating hate speech, propaganda, and extremist ideologies. Particularly, amidst the recent surge in climate activism, social media emerged as a primary platform not just for raising awareness but unfortunately for spreading negativity as well. The increasing prevalence of offensive content on social media presents challenges in efficiently identifying and moderating such material. To tackle this alarming issue, we present our solution based on ensembling top-k performing models. Language models remain the crucial tool for addressing contemporary Natural Language Processing (NLP) challenges, consistently attaining top positions across various subtasks. Our research findings paves the way for upcoming enhancements to address and mitigate this highly concerning issue in the near future.

References

Arnisha Akhter, Uzzal Kumar Acharjee, Md. Alamin Talukder, Md. Manowarul Islam, and Md. Ashraf Uddin. 2023. A robust hybrid machine learning model for Bengali cyber bullying detection in social media. *Natural Language Processing Journal*, 4:100027.

Ebtesam Almazrouei, Hamza Alobeidli, Abdulaziz Alshamsi, Alessandro Cappelli, Ruxandra Cojocaru, Mérouane Debbah, Étienne Goffinet, Daniel Hesslow, Julien Launay, Quentin Malartic, Daniele Mazzotta, Badreddine Noune, Baptiste Pannier, and Guilherme Penedo. 2023. The falcon series of open language models.

Pedro Alonso, Rajkumar Saini, and György Kovacs. 2020. TheNorth at SemEval-2020 task 12: Hate speech detection using RoBERTa. In *Proceedings of the Fourteenth Workshop on Semantic Evaluation*, pages 2197–2202, Barcelona (online). International Committee for Computational Linguistics.

Grace Arnot, Hannah Pitt, Simone McCarthy, Chloe Cordedda, Sarah Marko, and Samantha L. Thomas. 2024. Australian youth perspectives on the role of social media in climate action. *Australian and New Zealand Journal of Public Health*, 48(1):100111.

Tommaso Caselli, Valerio Basile, Jelena Mitrović, and Michael Granitzer. 2021. Hatebert: Retraining bert for abusive language detection in english.

Alexis Conneau, Kartikay Khandelwal, Naman Goyal, Vishrav Chaudhary, Guillaume Wenzek, Francisco Guzmán, Edouard Grave, Myle Ott, Luke Zettlemoyer, and Veselin Stoyanov. 2020. Unsupervised cross-lingual representation learning at scale.

Dana R. Fisher and Sohana Nasrin. 2020. Climate activism and its effects. *WIREs Climate Change*, 12(1).

Amalia Gómez-Casillas and Victoria Gómez Márquez. 2023. The effect of social network sites usage in climate change awareness in Latin America. *Population and Environment*, 45(2).

Yeo Khang Hsien, Zailan Arabee Abdul Salam, and Vinothini Kasinathan. 2022. Cyber Bullying Detection using Natural Language Processing (NLP) and Text Analytics. *2022 IEEE International Conference on Distributed Computing and Electrical Circuits and Electronics (ICDCECE)*.

Md Saroar Jahan and Mourad Oussalah. 2023a. A systematic review of hate speech automatic detection using natural language processing. *Neurocomputing*, 546:126232.

Saroar Jahan and Mourad Oussalah. 2023b. A systematic review of hate speech automatic detection using natural language processing. *Neurocomputing*, 546:126232.

Albert Q. Jiang, Alexandre Sablayrolles, Arthur Mensch, Chris Bamford, Devendra Singh Chaplot, Diego de las Casas, Florian Bressand, Gianna Lengyel, Guillaume Lample, Lucile Saulnier, Lélio Renard Lavaud, Marie-Anne Lachaux, Pierre Stock, Teven Le Scao, Thibaut Lavril, Thomas Wang, Timothée Lacroix, and William El Sayed. 2023. Mistral 7b.

Mohamed S. Kraiem, F. Sánchez, and María N. Moreno García. 2021. Selecting the suitable resampling strategy for imbalanced data classification regarding dataset properties. an approach based on association models. *Applied sciences*, 11(18):8546.

Stella Levantesi. "Enemies of Society": How the media portray climate activists.

Xiaoya Li, Xiaofei Sun, Yuxian Meng, Junjun Liang, Fei Wu, and Jiwei Li. 2019. Dice loss for data-imbalanced NLP tasks. *arXiv (Cornell University)*.

Yinhan Liu, Myle Ott, Naman Goyal, Jingfei Du, Mandar Joshi, Danqi Chen, Omer Levy, Mike Lewis, Luke Zettlemoyer, and Veselin Stoyanov. 2019. Roberta: A robustly optimized bert pretraining approach.

Arun S. Maiya. 2022. ktrain: A low-code library for augmented machine learning.

Muhammad Mujahid, Khadija Kanwal, Furqan Rustam, Wajdi Aljadani, and Imran Ashraf. 2023. Arabic ChatGPT tweets classification using ROBERTA and BERT ensemble model. *ACM Transactions on Asian and Low-Resource Language Information Processing*, 22(8):1–23.

Anil Singh Parihar, Surendrabikram Thapa, and Sushruti Mishra. 2021. Hate speech detection using natural language processing: Applications and challenges. In *2021 5th International Conference on Trends in Electronics and Informatics (ICOEI)*, pages 1302–1308.

Laura Plaza, Jorge Carrillo-De-Albornoz, Roser Morante, Enrique Amigó, Julio A. Gonzalo, Damiano Spina, and Paolo Rosso. 2023. 68 *Overview of EXIST 2023: SEXism Identification in Social NETWorks.*

Flor Miriam Plaza-Del-Arco, M. Dolores Molina-González, L. Alfonso Ureña-López, and María Teresa Martín–Valdivia. 2021. Comparing pre-trained language models for Spanish hate speech detection. *Expert Systems with Applications*, 166:114120.

Umitcan Sahin, Izzet Emre Kucukkaya, Oguzhan Ozcelik, and Cagri Toraman. 2023. ARC-NLP at multimodal hate speech event detection 2023: Multimodal methods boosted by ensemble learning, syntactical and entity features. In *Proceedings of the 6th Workshop on Challenges and Applications of Automated Extraction of Socio-political Events from Text*, pages 71–78, Varna, Bulgaria. INCOMA Ltd., Shoumen, Bulgaria.

Mina Schütz, Jaqueline Boeck, Daria Liakhovets, Djordje Slijepčević, Armin Kirchknopf, Manuel Hecht, Johannes Bogensperger, Sven Schlarb, Alexander Strobel, and Matthias Zeppelzauer. 2021. Automatic Sexism Detection with Multilingual Transformer Models. *arXiv (Cornell University).*

Shuvam Shiwakoti, Surendrabikram Thapa, Kritesh Rauniyar, Akshyat Shah, Aashish Bhandari, and Usman Naseem. 2024. Analyzing the dynamics of climate change discourse on twitter: A new annotated corpus and multi-aspect classification. *Preprint.*

Leslie N. Smith. 2017. Cyclical learning rates for training neural networks.

Surendrabikram Thapa, Kritesh Rauniyar, Farhan Ahmad Jafri, Shuvam Shiwakoti, Hariram Veeramani, Raghav Jain, Guneet Singh Kohli, Ali Hürriyetoğlu, and Usman Naseem. 2024. Stance and hate event detection in tweets related to climate activism - shared task at case 2024. In *Proceedings of the 7th Workshop on Challenges and Applications of Automated Extraction of Socio-political Events from Text (CASE).*

ARC-NLP at ClimateActivism 2024: Stance and Hate Speech Detection by Generative and Encoder Models Optimized with Tweet-Specific Elements

Ahmet Kagan Kaya and **Oguzhan Ozcelik** and **Cagri Toraman**
ASELSAN, Ankara, Turkey
kagankaya, ogozcelik, ctoraman@aselsan.com.tr

Abstract

Social media users often express hate speech towards specific targets and may either support or refuse activist movements. The automated detection of hate speech, which involves identifying both targets and stances, plays a critical role in event identification to mitigate its negative effects. In this paper, we present our methods for three subtasks of the Climate Activism Stance and Hate Event Detection Shared Task at CASE 2024. For each subtask (i) hate speech identification (ii) targets of hate speech identification (iii) stance detection, we experiment with optimized Transformer-based architectures that focus on tweet-specific features such as hashtags, URLs, and emojis. Furthermore, we investigate generative large language models, such as Llama2, using specific prompts for the first two subtasks. Our experiments demonstrate better performance of our models compared to baseline models in each subtask. Our solutions also achieve third, fourth, and first places respectively in the subtasks.

Bias Statement: This paper discusses harmful content and hate speech stereotypes. The authors do not support the use of harmful language, nor any of the harmful representations quoted below.

1 Introduction

There is a growing challenge of detecting hate speech within the context of digital communication, particularly in climate change activism, by means of natural language processing (Parihar et al., 2021). The shared task on Hate Speech and Stance Detection during Climate Activism organized in the workshop on Challenges and Applications of Automated Extraction of Socio-political Events from Text (CASE) (Thapa et al., 2024) aims to provide an opportunity to study important components in identifying events during climate change activism. The task includes three subtasks for detecting (a) hate speech, (b) its target, and (c) stance being supported or opposed.

Our proposed approach in the shared task is to employ large encoder models, such as BERTweet (Nguyen et al., 2020), enhanced with Optuna (Akiba et al., 2019) to improve model performance by optimizing deep learning hyperparameters and also tweet-specific elements, such as hashtags, URLs, and emojis. Additionally, we leverage the capabilities of generative large language models, such as Llama2 (Touvron et al., 2023). Lastly, we propose hybrid solutions that benefit from both encoder and generative models. Generative models serve as a decision support mechanism, particularly in instances where the encoder model's predictions are ambiguous or uncertain.

The performances of our models are measured on the ClimaConvo dataset (Shiwakoti et al., 2024). In this study, we report the details of our solutions, which obtain 3rd place in Subtask A, 4th place in Subtask B, and 1st place in Subtask C.

2 Subtasks and Datasets

2.1 Subtasks

Subtask A: Hate Speech Detection In Subtask A, our primary objective is to develop and implement a robust hate speech detection system. In this subtask, we aim to automatically identify whether a given text contains hate speech or not, providing binary labels of "hate" and "non-hate".

Subtask B: Target Detection Subtask B aims to identify the targets of hate speech within a given hateful tweet. The dataset provided for this subtask includes labels categorizing the hate speech targets into "individual", "organization" and "community".

Subtask C: Stance Detection Subtask C aims to identify the stance in a given tweet text. The dataset provided for this subtask includes labels categorizing the stance targets into "support", "oppose", and "neutral".

Proceedings of the 7th Workshop on Challenges and Applications of Automated Extraction of Socio-political Events from Text (CASE 2024), pages 111–117
March 22, 2024 ©2024 Association for Computational Linguistics

Table 1: The distribution of the classes in train, validation, and test splits for each subtask.

Task	Class	Train	Validation	Test
A	Hate	899	190	188
	Non-Hate	6,385	1,371	1,374
B	Individual	563	120	121
	Organization	105	23	23
	Community	31	7	6
C	Support	4,328	897	921
	Oppose	700	153	141
	Neutral	2,256	511	500

Table 2: Statistics for tweet-specific elements (hashtag, URL, and emoji).

Task	Data	Avg. Htag per Tweet	Avg. URL per Tweet	Avg. Emoji per Tweet
A	Train	5.13	0.76	0.78
	Val	5.15	0.78	0.91
	Test	5.19	0.76	0.92
B	Train	7.65	0.16	0.15
	Val	7.41	0.22	0.05
	Test	7.83	0.19	0.06
C	Train	5.13	0.76	0.78
	Val	5.15	0.78	0.91
	Test	5.19	0.76	0.92

2.2 Datasets

The dataset (Shiwakoti et al., 2024) is split into train, validation, and test subsets. Table 1 gives the distribution of classes in the datasets for each subtask. The presence of hashtags, URLs, and emojis in the tweets within these datasets adds an extra layer of complexity. Table 2 presents average counts of hashtags, URLs, and emojis per tweet for each subtask. We observe that the substantial presence of hashtags, URLs, and emojis in tweets significantly impacts the predictivity of our models. These elements can be important to convey context, emotion, and additional information.

3 Main Approach

Our approach includes three solutions. First, we employ encoder models for text classification with a specific focus on tweet-specific elements such as hashtags, URLs, and emojis. Second, we employ generative large language models. Lastly, we provide hybrid solutions that benefit from both encoder and generative models. We use PyTorch (Paszke et al., 2017) and Hugging Face (Wolf et al., 2019) for model implementations.

3.1 Encoder Models

We experiment with Transformer-based architectures (Vaswani et al., 2017). The descriptions of employed models are listed below with the reasons why we select them for this task:

Megatron (Shoeybi et al., 2019): Megatron is known to perform well in hate speech detection (Toraman et al., 2022). We optimize the Megatron model in terms of the tweet features and hyperparameters using the validation dataset. The optimization process is discussed in detail in Section 3.4.

BERTweet (Nguyen et al., 2020): BERTweet has a special tokenizer that handles noisy tweet texts properly. We conduct the same optimization procedure for this model as in the Megatron model.

DeBERTa (He et al., 2021): DeBERTa shows challenging performance for text classification problems, even for noisy tweet texts (Sahin et al., 2022). We conduct the same optimization procedure for this model as in the Megatron model.

3.2 Generative Models

We employ the following open-source generative large language models. Text generation configuration has greedy decoding with a temperature setting of 1e-8 and an output length of 512 tokens.

Llama2 (Touvron et al., 2023): Llama2 is a state-of-the-art generative large language model that is specifically designed to analyze and interpret complex language patterns. This model is characterized by its large number of parameters, enabling it to process and generate highly detailed and contextually relevant text responses. We employ `Llama-2-7b-chat-hf`[1].

Mistral (Jiang et al., 2023): Mistral is an efficient model for text generation with a significantly reduced number of parameters. Its architecture not only improves computational efficiency but also detects hate speech content. We employ `Mistral-7B-Instruct-v0.1`[2] and `Mistral-7B-Instruct-v0.2`[3].

Prompts We examine existing prompts (Bach et al., 2022) to observe the performance in our preliminary experiments. We decide to use the following zero-shot prompt for Subtask A: *"Does*

[1]https://huggingface.co/meta-llama/Llama-2-7b-chat-hf

[2]https://huggingface.co/mistralai/Mistral-7B-Instruct-v0.1

[3]https://huggingface.co/mistralai/Mistral-7B-Instruct-v0.2

Table 3: Optimized parameters of the experimented models for each subtask.

Task	Model	Hashtag Removed	URL Removed	Emoji Removed	Learning Rate	Weight Decay	Training Epoch	Training Batch	Sequence Length
A	BERTweet	✗	✗	✓	1.6e-5	0.070	3	16	128
	DeBERTa	✗	✗	✓	1.1e-5	0.027	6	16	128
	Megatron	✓	✓	✓	1.0e-5	0.010	3	16	128
B	BERTweet	✗	✗	✗	7.1e-5	0.084	9	8	128
	DeBERTa	✓	✓	✓	5.3e-5	0.049	12	8	128
C	BERTweet	✗	✗	✗	1.0e-5	0.000	3	16	96
	DeBERTa	✗	✓	✓	1.0e-5	0.000	3	16	160
	Megatron	✗	✗	✗	1.2e-5	0.035	3	8	160

this tweet convey the author's hatred towards something or someone?".

For Subtask B, we could not find existing prompts. Instead, we curate a new prompt based on our preliminary experiments: *"The goal of this subtask is to identify the targets of tweets. Give one of the labels (individual, organization, or community) for the given tweet text."*

Different from Subtask A, we observe that zero-shot prompting does not provide sufficient instruction to the model. We therefore follow few-shot prompting to provide three training examples, one for each class, in the prompt.

For Subtask C, we could not run generative models due to limited hardware and time constraints.

3.3 Hybrid Models

In Subtask A, we implement a hybrid approach that combines encoder and generative models (BERTweet+Llama2). Also, in Subtask B, we use a hybrid approach that combines encoder models and named entity recognition (BERTweet+NER).

BERTweet+Llama2 In our preliminary experiments for Subtask A, we observe that our optimized BERTweet (Nguyen et al., 2020) outperforms other encoder models. Despite its success, we observe instances where BERTweet exhibits a lack of confidence in its predictions, particularly with certain tweets that present ambiguous or subtle indications of hate speech. To address this, we incorporate Llama2 as a secondary layer of analysis. In cases where BERTweet's output logits have low confidence, i.e., lower than 0.6, we employ Llama2 to reassess the prediction label.

BERTweet+NER Following the winning model (Sahin et al., 2023) of the previous shared task (Thapa et al., 2023), we integrate named entities with the prediction output of the Transformer-based model. Named entity recognition can extract individual, organization, and community-related entities from unstructured text (Ozcelik and Toraman, 2022). We obtain entities through the spaCy library (Honnibal and Montani, 2017), employing the English Transformer pipeline model[4]. We then combine the counts of each entity with the output logits of our optimized BERTweet model. Finally, these six features are fed to a random forest model.

3.4 Optimization

We obtain our best models by optimizing the learning phase using the validation dataset. For this purpose, we employ Optuna (Akiba et al., 2019) with the following tweet-specific elements and deep learning hyperparameters:

- Hashtag: A binary feature that determines whether all hashtags are removed.
- URL: A binary feature that determines whether all URLs are removed.
- Emoji: A binary feature that determines whether all emojis are removed.
- Learning rate: Uniform range bw. 1e-5 and 1e-4.
- Weight decay: Uniform range bw. 1e-3 and 1e-1.
- Epochs: Discrete range from 3 to 10.
- Train batch size: 8, 16, or 32.
- Sequence length: 64, 96, 128, and 160

3.5 Baseline Models

We report baseline scores of four Transformer-based models provided by the organizers (Shiwakoti et al., 2024): BERT (Devlin et al., 2018), DistillBERT (Sanh et al., 2019), RoBERTa (Liu et al., 2019), and ClimateBERT (Webersinke et al., 2021).

4 Leaderboard Results

In this section, we report the results of all submitted models on the test data. The optimized parameters of our submitted models are reported in Table 3. Our final submitted models are listed as follows.

[4]en_core_web_trf

Table 4: **Subtask A: Hate Speech Detection.** Test results in terms of precision, recall, F1 score, and accuracy. The model which achieves the highest test scores on the final leaderboard is indicated with a bold font. Baseline scores are obtained from Shiwakoti et al. (2024).

	Model	Pre	Rec	F1	Acc
Baseline	BERT	-	-	0.7080	0.9010
	DistilBERT	-	-	0.6640	0.8960
	RoBERTa	-	-	0.6620	0.8420
	ClimateBERT	-	-	0.7040	0.8840
Ours	Megatron	0.8003	0.9415	0.8532	0.9475
	BERTweet	0.8687	0.8923	0.8800	0.9507
	DeBERTa	0.8623	0.8836	0.8725	0.9475
	Llama2	0.5248	0.3894	0.4471	0.8827
	Mistralv0.1	0.5416	0.1368	0.2184	0.8808
	Mistralv0.2	0.3571	0.3947	0.3750	0.8398
	BERTweet+Llama2	0.8973	0.8833	**0.8901**	0.9526

Table 5: **Subtask B: Target Detection.** Notations are the same as Table 4.

	Model	Pre	Rec	F1	Acc
Baseline	BERT	-	-	0.5540	0.6410
	DistilBERT	-	-	0.5500	0.6030
	RoBERTa	-	-	0.5010	0.7160
	ClimateBERT	-	-	0.5490	0.6040
Ours	BERTweet	0.7728	0.7588	**0.7638**	0.9133
	DeBERTa	0.7149	0.7005	0.6997	0.9000
	BERTweet+NER	0.7421	0.7588	0.7500	0.9133
	DeBERTa+NER	0.7149	0.7005	0.6997	0.9000
	Llama2	0.5775	0.5152	0.4439	0.8067

Table 6: **Subtask C: Stance Detection.** Notations are the same as Table 4.

	Model	Pre	Rec	F1	Acc
Baseline	BERT	-	-	0.4660	0.5860
	DistilBERT	-	-	0.5270	0.6100
	RoBERTa	-	-	0.5420	0.6480
	ClimateBERT	-	-	0.5450	0.6510
Ours	Megatron	0.7509	0.7200	0.7342	0.7298
	BERTweet	0.7848	0.7226	**0.7483**	0.7490
	DeBERTa	0.7555	0.7242	0.7385	0.7356

Subtask A Our hybrid model (BERTweet+ Llama2) gets the 3rd place among 22 participants.

Subtask B Our optimized encoder (BERTweet) gets the 4th place among 18 participants.

Subtask C Our optimized encoder (BERTweet) gets the 1st place among 19 participants.

In Table 4, we present evaluation results for Subtask A, highlighting the better performance of our optimized BERTweet model, particularly over DeBERTa. This might show that the special tweet tokenizer can handle noisy tweet text. Generative models, Llama2 and Mistral, misinterpret some tweets (e.g., the tweets having many hashtags). We obtain better performance when they are used as a support tool for BERTWeet in uncertain cases.

In Table 5, we report that the optimized BERTweet model outperforms others in Subtask B, while the inclusion of named entities does not enhance performance for identifying individual, organization, and community targets. This ineffectiveness can be attributed to the prevalence of "individual" entities such as Greta Thunberg surpassing other entities. Moreover, Llama2 performs poorly using few-shot prompts. Unlike Subtask A, we do not integrate Llama2 with BERTweet, since output logits are mostly above the confidence threshold.

In Table 6, we report the evaluation results for Subtask C. We obtain our highest score by using an optimized version of BERTweet. It has a short length of input tokenization (96 tokens) with special tokens for tweet-specific elements. We could not implement generative models for Subtask C due to limited hardware and time constraints. Nevertheless, we obtain the highest score among other participants in this subtask.

5 Discussion

Encoder Models and Tweet-specific Elements We observe that the removal of hashtags and URLs is insignificant for the BERTweet model. This is because the it demonstrates proficient tokenization even when hashtags and URLs are retained. However, in Subtask A, the removal of emojis is an important hyperparameter since we observe that emojis can be misleading in detecting hate speech.

Generative Models and Error Analysis We provide sample outputs generated by Llama2 with zero-shot prompts for Subtask A in Table 7. We find that there are many near-duplicate tweets that have many hashtags but similar content regarding Greta Thunberg (e.g. False Negative in the table). Most of them are predicted as not hateful by the generative model, however the ground truth is labeled as hate. We suspect that the high number of such false negatives profoundly could impact its overall accuracy. On the other hand, the generative model gives a reasonable response such that the tweet content is critical of Greta Thunberg, instead of hate speech. The degree of offensiveness in this tweet is indeed controversial. This may show that the knowledge of generative models does not necessarily align with human annotation for hate speech detection.

Table 7: Error analysis of Llama2 with zero-shot prompts for Subtask A Hate Speech Detection. TP: True Positive, FN: False Negative, FP: False Positive, TN: True Negative.

	Tweet	Ground Truth	Response
TP	#India least bothered over #ClimateCrisis. Majority argues they are preoccupied with their own devised Hindu-Muslim issues. Irony, #policymakers hiding the fact: #climate disaster will wipe everyone out along with progeny, or the threat is ignored? #FridaysForFuture byadavbjp https://t.co/2LAESz7s9Y	Hate	Yes. The author of the tweet is expressing frustration and disappointment towards the people of India for being more concerned about their own religious differences (Hindu-Muslim issues) than taking action to address the climate crisis, which they believe will have severe consequences for everyone, including their own progeny
FN	#ExtinctionRebellion #ClimateCrisis #ClimateAction #GlobalWarming #FridaysForFuture #ClimateChange #Greenwashing #Renewables #ClimateStrike You've been fooled by Greta Thunberg:,	Hate	No, the tweet does not convey the author's hatred towards Greta Thunberg or anyone else. The tweet is critical of Greta Thunberg and the movement she is leading, but it does not express hatred towards her.
FP	•Week 19• The Time Is Ticking,And We Have No Chance For Saying, "We'll Do This/That Tomorrow,For The Environment,ACT NOW!" #ActNow #FridaysForFuture #ClimateActionNow @Fridays4future @FFFMAPA @Riseupmovt @UNEP @spicewarriors https://t.co/IWs0cIYTpn,	Non-Hate	Yes. The tweet conveys a sense of urgency and frustration towards the lack of action being taken to address the climate crisis, with the use of phrases like "We have no chance" and "ACT NOW!"
TN	Let us celebrate the PLANET and take care of EARTH #Climatechange #ClimateStrike #ClimateAction #ClimateCrisis #savetheearth #savetheplanet #FridaysForFuture #Bangladesh https://t.co/xrwYnQuDJw,	Non-Hate	No, the tweet does not convey the author's hatred towards something or someone. The tweet is focused on celebrating the planet and taking care of the Earth, using hashtags related to climate change and environmental activism. There is no indication of hatred or negative sentiment towards any particular entity.

We provide another sample for a False Positive prediction. The model response is non-trivial such that it gives some examples of frustration in the tweet. However, human annotation is not hateful for this tweet. This is also another example of an alignment problem between the knowledge of generative models and human annotations for climate activism and hate speech detection.

In Table 7, we also provide a sample case where our hybrid solution, BERTweet+Llama2, is useful in this task. The True Positive (TP) sample in the table is predicted as non-hate by BERTweet with a confidence score of 0.6. However, Llama2 evaluates this tweet as hate with an insightful explanation.

6 Conclusion

We conclude that the optimized BERTweet model outperforms other encoder models in all subtasks, indicating the importance of tweet-specific elements (hashtag, URL, and emoji) in hate event detection. Overall, generative models perform poorly in this task. More investigation is needed to understand their capabilities for hate speech detection. A possible reason for poor performance could be our prompts or generation config. Nevertheless, the support of Llama2 increases the performance in Subtask A.

In future work, state-of-the-art generative models like GPT3.5[5] or GPT4[6] can be employed in addition to Llama2 and Mistral. Moreover, prompt tuning can improve the performance of generative models and extend the work for generalizing model understanding capacity.

7 Limitations

The dataset has only English text in this study. More experiments in different languages can be conducted to generalize the results to other languages. Also, the optimized hyperparameters for encoder models are limited to the dataset used in this study. Generative models may in some instances produce inaccurate, biased, or other objectionable responses to user prompts.

8 Ethics Statement

The authors do not support the use of harmful language or any of the harmful representations featured in this paper. Furthermore, our proposed models are trained on an annotated dataset; therefore, they may have certain bias towards specific subjects, individuals, organizations, and communities. We acknowledge the necessity of bias mitigation for future research. Lastly, for reproducibility, we share details such as hyperparameters, libraries, and tools in Section 3, and the datasets are published by Shiwakoti et al. (2024).

[5]https://platform.openai.com/docs/models/gpt-3-5
[6]https://openai.com/gpt-4

References

Takuya Akiba, Shotaro Sano, Toshihiko Yanase, Takeru Ohta, and Masanori Koyama. 2019. Optuna: A next-generation hyperparameter optimization framework. In *Proceedings of the 25th ACM SIGKDD international conference on knowledge discovery & data mining*, pages 2623–2631.

Stephen H. Bach, Victor Sanh, Zheng-Xin Yong, Albert Webson, Colin Raffel, Nihal V. Nayak, Abheesht Sharma, Taewoon Kim, M Saiful Bari, Thibault Fevry, Zaid Alyafeai, Manan Dey, Andrea Santilli, Zhiqing Sun, Srulik Ben-David, Canwen Xu, Gunjan Chhablani, Han Wang, Jason Alan Fries, Maged S. Al-shaibani, Shanya Sharma, Urmish Thakker, Khalid Almubarak, Xiangru Tang, Xiangru Tang, Mike Tian-Jian Jiang, and Alexander M. Rush. 2022. Promptsource: An integrated development environment and repository for natural language prompts.

Jacob Devlin, Ming-Wei Chang, Kenton Lee, and Kristina Toutanova. 2018. Bert: Pre-training of deep bidirectional transformers for language understanding. *arXiv preprint arXiv:1810.04805*.

Pengcheng He, Jianfeng Gao, and Weizhu Chen. 2021. Debertav3: Improving deberta using electra-style pre-training with gradient-disentangled embedding sharing. *arXiv preprint arXiv:2111.09543*.

Matthew Honnibal and Ines Montani. 2017. spacy 2: Natural language understanding with bloom embeddings, convolutional neural networks and incremental parsing.

Albert Q Jiang, Alexandre Sablayrolles, Arthur Mensch, Chris Bamford, Devendra Singh Chaplot, Diego de las Casas, Florian Bressand, Gianna Lengyel, Guillaume Lample, Lucile Saulnier, et al. 2023. Mistral 7b. *arXiv preprint arXiv:2310.06825*.

Yinhan Liu, Myle Ott, Naman Goyal, Jingfei Du, Mandar Joshi, Danqi Chen, Omer Levy, Mike Lewis, Luke Zettlemoyer, and Veselin Stoyanov. 2019. Roberta: A robustly optimized bert pretraining approach. *arXiv preprint arXiv:1907.11692*.

Dat Quoc Nguyen, Thanh Vu, and Anh Tuan Nguyen. 2020. BERTweet: A pre-trained language model for English tweets. In *Proceedings of the 2020 Conference on Empirical Methods in Natural Language Processing: System Demonstrations*, pages 9–14, Online. Association for Computational Linguistics.

Oguzhan Ozcelik and Cagri Toraman. 2022. Named entity recognition in Turkish: A comparative study with detailed error analysis. *Information Processing & Management*, 59(6):103065.

Anil Singh Parihar, Surendrabikram Thapa, and Sushruti Mishra. 2021. Hate speech detection using natural language processing: Applications and challenges. In *2021 5th International Conference on Trends in Electronics and Informatics (ICOEI)*, pages 1302–1308.

Adam Paszke, Sam Gross, Soumith Chintala, Gregory Chanan, Edward Yang, Zachary DeVito, Zeming Lin, Alban Desmaison, Luca Antiga, and Adam Lerer. 2017. Automatic differentiation in pytorch.

Umitcan Sahin, Izzet Emre Kucukkaya, Oguzhan Ozcelik, and Cagri Toraman. 2023. ARC-NLP at multimodal hate speech event detection 2023: Multimodal methods boosted by ensemble learning, syntactical and entity features. In *Proceedings of the 6th Workshop on Challenges and Applications of Automated Extraction of Socio-political Events from Text*, pages 71–78, Varna, Bulgaria. INCOMA Ltd., Shoumen, Bulgaria.

Umitcan Sahin, Oguzhan Ozcelik, Izzet Emre Kucukkaya, and Cagri Toraman. 2022. ARC-NLP at CASE 2022 task 1: Ensemble learning for multilingual protest event detection. In *Proceedings of the 5th Workshop on Challenges and Applications of Automated Extraction of Socio-political Events from Text (CASE)*, pages 175–183, Abu Dhabi, United Arab Emirates (Hybrid). Association for Computational Linguistics.

Victor Sanh, Lysandre Debut, Julien Chaumond, and Thomas Wolf. 2019. Distilbert, a distilled version of bert: smaller, faster, cheaper and lighter. *arXiv preprint arXiv:1910.01108*.

Shuvam Shiwakoti, Surendrabikram Thapa, Kritesh Rauniyar, Akshyat Shah, Aashish Bhandari, and Usman Naseem. 2024. Analyzing the dynamics of climate change discourse on twitter: A new annotated corpus and multi-aspect classification. *Preprint*.

Mohammad Shoeybi, Mostofa Patwary, Raul Puri, Patrick LeGresley, Jared Casper, and Bryan Catanzaro. 2019. Megatron-lm: Training multi-billion parameter language models using model parallelism. *arXiv preprint arXiv:1909.08053*.

Surendrabikram Thapa, Farhan Ahmad Jafri, Ali Hürriyetoğlu, Francielle Vargas, Roy Ka-Wei Lee, and Usman Naseem. 2023. Multimodal hate speech event detection - shared task 4, case 2023. In *Proceedings of the 6th Workshop on Challenges and Applications of Automated Extraction of Socio-political Events from Text (CASE)*.

Surendrabikram Thapa, Kritesh Rauniyar, Farhan Ahmad Jafri, Shuvam Shiwakoti, Hariram Veeramani, Raghav Jain, Guneet Singh Kohli, Ali Hürriyetoğlu, and Usman Naseem. 2024. Stance and hate event detection in tweets related to climate activism - shared task at case 2024. In *Proceedings of the 7th Workshop on Challenges and Applications of Automated Extraction of Socio-political Events from Text (CASE)*.

Cagri Toraman, Furkan Şahinuç, and Eyup Yilmaz. 2022. Large-scale hate speech detection with cross-domain transfer. In *Proceedings of the Thirteenth Language Resources and Evaluation Conference*, pages 2215–2225.

Hugo Touvron, Louis Martin, Kevin Stone, Peter Albert, Amjad Almahairi, Yasmine Babaei, Nikolay Bashlykov, Soumya Batra, Prajjwal Bhargava, Shruti Bhosale, et al. 2023. Llama 2: Open foundation and fine-tuned chat models. *arXiv preprint arXiv:2307.09288.*

Ashish Vaswani, Noam Shazeer, Niki Parmar, Jakob Uszkoreit, Llion Jones, Aidan N Gomez, Łukasz Kaiser, and Illia Polosukhin. 2017. Attention is all you need. *Advances in neural information processing systems*, 30.

Nicolas Webersinke, Mathias Kraus, Julia Anna Bingler, and Markus Leippold. 2021. Climatebert: A pretrained language model for climate-related text. *arXiv preprint arXiv:2110.12010.*

Thomas Wolf, Lysandre Debut, Victor Sanh, Julien Chaumond, Clement Delangue, Anthony Moi, Pierric Cistac, Tim Rault, Rémi Louf, Morgan Funtowicz, et al. 2019. Huggingface's transformers: State-of-the-art natural language processing. *arXiv preprint arXiv:1910.03771.*

HAMiSoN-Ensemble at ClimateActivism 2024: Ensemble of RoBERTa, Llama 2, and Multi-task for Stance Detection

Raquel Rodriguez-Garcia and **Julio Reyes-Montesinos** and
Jesús M. Fraile-Hernandez and **Anselmo Peñas**
NLP & IR Group
UNED, Spain
{rrodriguez, jreyes, jfraile, anselmo}@lsi.uned.es

Abstract

CASE @ EACL 2024 proposes a shared task on Stance and Hate Event Detection for Climate Activism discourse. For our participation in the stance detection task, we propose an ensemble of different approaches: a transformer-based model (RoBERTa), a generative Large Language Model (Llama 2), and a Multi-Task Learning model. Our main goal is twofold: to study the effect of augmenting the training data with external datasets, and to examine the contribution of several, diverse models through a voting ensemble. The results show that if we take the best configuration during training for each of the three models (RoBERTa, Llama 2 and MTL), the ensemble would have ranked first with the highest F_1 on the leaderboard for the stance detection subtask.

1 Introduction

Social media is a popular tool and has adopted an essential role in this day and age. With its massive spread and usage, a global discourse arises regarding numerous topics. Climate change has become a most prominent topic, as well as a very polarized one (Tyagi et al., 2020; Chen et al., 2023). As debates develop, the emergence of hate speech becomes a concern that must not be left unattended.

Although the case for freedom of speech has been voiced, it cannot be confused with a complete lack of regulations. Touting that rhetoric has brought harmful effects (Hickey et al., 2023). It delves into the paradox of tolerance, where unlimited freedom of speech can cause the corrosion of our society. Rampant hate speech can create a breeding ground for intolerance and discrimination. All of these circumstances justify the necessity to study controversial public discourse, to promote online safety and inclusion.

For the reasons argued above, the Climate Activism Stance and Hate Event Detection task at CASE 2024 (Thapa et al., 2024) has significant relevance. This task focuses on climate activism discourse, and it consists of three distinct subtasks: hate speech detection, target identification and stance detection. It can provide valuable knowledge on the diffusion of hate speech and the polarization of users' stances, addressing some current open challenges (Parihar et al., 2021).

As described in this paper, our proposal leverages an ensemble voting system with two different voting strategies for the stance detection subtask. Ensemble voting has been used in other stance detection shared tasks (Cignarella et al., 2020), achieving the best results. These systems provide some additional advantages, such as model regularization and an increase of diversity (Polikar, 2006), as they consider different approaches simultaneously. For our ensemble, we exploit three different systems: a transformer-based baseline model, a Large Language Model and Multi-Task Learning.

Beyond exploring a set of diverse systems for the proposed task, our approach has the goal of studying the effect of external data on the stance detection subtask. We aim to determine the effect that external training data has on our proposed models, and to evaluate the suitability of these external datasets towards improving a model's performance in the context of climate activism. To this end, we propose two datasets related to hate speech and stance detection that we detail below.

This paper is organized as follows. In section 2 we introduce the dataset for the task. In section 3 we present the strategy for the ensemble models, as well as the additional data that were used. In section 4 we introduce our results, we discuss them in section 5, and we perform a post-competition analysis in section 6. Finally, in section 7, we exhibit our conclusions and future work.

2 Dataset and Task

This shared task, Climate Activism Stance and Hate Event Detection, uses the ClimaConvo dataset in-

Proceedings of the 7th Workshop on Challenges and Applications of Automated Extraction of Socio-political Events from Text (CASE 2024), pages 118–124
March 22, 2024

troduced in Shiwakoti et al. (2024). It consists of tweets containing hashtags from a curated list linked to climate change and climate activism, collected over a one-year period. Non-English tweets were filtered out. The final dataset only reflects the textual content of the tweets and was manually annotated in six dimensions. The shared task at hand is based on a subset of ClimaConvo and contains 10,407 instances. Below, we describe the three subtasks proposed over this dataset.

2.1 Subtask A

The goal of subtask A is to establish whether a tweet contains hate speech or not. This is a binary classification task with HATE SPEECH and NO HATE SPEECH as the annotated labels.

2.2 Subtask B

Subtask B aims to discover the target of the hate speech, with a multiclass classification task with the INDIVIDUAL, ORGANIZATION, or COMMUNITY labels. Subtask B is based on a smaller subset of 999 instances, corresponding to tweets where hate speech is present and labeled as DIRECTED in ClimaConvo (Shiwakoti et al., 2024).

2.3 Subtask C

Finally, the objective of subtask C is to determine the stance of the tweets. The data used for this task is the same as subtask A. Similarly to subtask B, this is a multi-class classification task with three labels: SUPPORT, OPPOSE and NEUTRAL.

3 Methodology

Different models have been employed for the ensemble described in this paper. In this section we review the external datasets used by the models, the pre-processing step applied to all the data sources, the descriptions of each model and the characteristics of the ensemble classifier. We aim at determining whether an ensemble makes a robust model, and whether the additional context of other datasets provides an advantage to this task.

3.1 External Data

We experiment with two main data sources: an offensive language and target dataset, and a stance dataset. Although we have only participated in subtask C with this ensemble, additional related data, as well as the hate speech and target subtasks, have been included in some of these models.

One of the considered data sources has been the Offensive Language Identification Dataset (OLID) (Zampieri et al., 2019a), which was used in the SemEval 2019 Task 6 (Zampieri et al., 2019b). It is composed of Twitter data with each tweet being annotated for three subtasks: offensive language identification (whether a tweet is offensive or not), characterization of offense types (whether it is targeted or not) and offense target identification (the target of the offense: INDIVIDUAL, GROUP or OTHERS). The train and test sets have been combined for training, generating a total of 14,100 annotated samples for the offensive language identification and 4,089 for the target task.

In addition to the OLID dataset, the stance dataset by Mohammad et al. (2016a), used in the SemEval 2016 Task 6 (Mohammad et al., 2016b), has been included. This Twitter dataset is comprised of different sections, determined by the topics of the tweets. There is a total of 4,163 tweets organized by the topics of abortion, climate, Hillary Clinton, feminism and atheism. This is a multi-class classification task, which considers three classes: AGAINST, FAVOR or NONE. Using the same approach as with the previous dataset, the train and test sets have been combined.

3.2 Dataset Preparation

All our models use the text of the tweet as input. We pre-processed this text with a pipeline consisting of the following steps:

- Removal of URLs from tweets.
- Replacement of username mentions by the generic token `@USER`.
- Splitting of hashtags into individual words. To accomplish this endeavor we have utilized the Word Ninja[1] library, which uses a probabilistic division of concatenated words, based on the frequencies of unigrams from the English Wikipedia.

3.3 Model Description

For this ensemble, we leveraged three different approaches that participated individually in the shared task. Below, we discuss the characteristics of the models, as well as a description of each of the runs:

3.3.1 RoBERTa

We established baseline systems based on RoBERTa-base (Liu et al., 2019) transformers with

[1] https://github.com/keredson/wordninja

a classification head. We fine-tuned a RoBERTa-base model for each of the subtasks using only the data proposed in the shared task, and a second set of RoBERTa-base models on both the data proposed in the shared task and the additional data proposed for each subtask. With this, we aim at providing a baseline comparison of the impact of using additional training data in each subtask that subsequent models can elaborate on. A more in-detail description of our fine-tuning methodology for RoBERTa can be found in Reyes-Montesinos and Rodrigo (2024).

3.3.2 Llama 2

Next, we fine-tuned a Llama 2 7B Chat model with a final classification layer, using raw prompts. In this model, we start from the Llama 2 7B Chat model proposed by Meta in Touvron et al. (2023). Then, we removed the last linear layer to add another linear layer that has as input the last hidden state of the model and as output 3 neurons, one for each stance label. As model input, we use the tweets pre-processed as explained in 3.2, therefore not following the officially suggested tag format. Moreover, as it is a generative model, we have tested the zero-shot approach, but our low initial results led us to use the classification layer. The full description of the model and the zero-shot approach can be found in Fraile-Hernandez and Peñas (2024).

3.3.3 Multi-Task Learning

This approach leverages the potential of transformer-based Multi-Task Learning (MTL) for this subtask, and it is detailed at length in Rodriguez-Garcia and Centeno (2024). In our system, we implement a hard parameter sharing Multi-Task model, as was originally described by Caruana (1993). The model is composed of a shared RoBERTa encoder and one classification head for each different task the model is training for. Considering the capabilities of this approach to extract context from related information, some of our MTL models have been trained with the three subtasks: hate speech, target, and stance.

3.4 Ensemble Description

Two different approaches have been explored for the ensemble process, a majority voting strategy and a conservative strategy. In the majority voting, the predicted stance will be the majority of the votes of the three base models, and a tie is resolved by returning the NEUTRAL label, given that no consensus was reached between SUPPORT and OPPOSE.

In the conservative strategy, the predicted stance will be the label that is obtained by unanimity of the votes of the three base models. In the case of no unanimity for a label, this strategy would return the value NEUTRAL. This strategy was motivated due to the error analysis during validation. We observed that the models had problems correctly classifying the NEUTRAL label, and they tended to classify these instances as SUPPORT.

4 Results

In total, we performed 10 experiments: 4 ensembles and 6 individual component systems. Half of the runs were performed using only the CASE dataset and the other half using data additional to the CASE stance dataset. Specific hyperparameters and training details are reflected in the individual papers for each system.

For the CASE only runs, we fine-tune RoBERTa and Llama 2 models on only Subtask C data. The Multi-task Learning (MTL) system was fined tuned on subtask A, B and C data to fully extract the knowledge from the task.

Regarding the runs with additional external data, the RoBERTa systems use the climate only topic from the SemEval stance dataset, while the Llama 2 models make use of all the topics from that dataset. Finally, the Multitask Learning model adds only the offensive language identification and the target tasks from the OLID dataset.

Table 1 shows the F_1 macro value of the 4 different runs. The results are divided into **CASE** if only the CASE dataset has been used in the training, or **Added** if the models have been trained with the CASE dataset and the additional data. The results of the individual models used for the ensemble are also included, in addition the results of the Baseline model used in Shiwakoti et al. (2024). This model, named ClimateBERT (Webersinke et al., 2022), is an adaptation of a BERT model, a language model trained on a corpus sourced from climate-related news, abstracts, and reports. Furthermore, we compute an oracle to establish the upper limit of the ensemble. The ideal version of our systems predicts the correct class if any of the three components managed to predict it on its own.

	Approach	CASE	CASE + external
	Baseline	0.5450	
	Best model leaderboard	0.7483	
Indiv.	RoBERTa	**0.7495**	**0.7406**
	Llama 2	0.7366	0.7300
	MTL (submitted)	0.7295	0.7320
Ensemble	Conservative	0.7265	0.7287
	Majority vote	0.7479	0.7397
	Oracle (upper bound)	0.8332	0.8259

Table 1: Comparison of F_1-scores for the best submitted individual models and the ensembles constructed from them, both trained on only task data and task and external data.

5 Discussion

As noted in Table 1, the performance of our proposed models greatly surpasses the baseline proposed by the organizers. Our best ensemble model – using the majority voting strategy – comes up second on the leaderboard by F_1 score for Subtask C. Regarding the use of additional data, we see that performance only improves in MTL and worsens for both RoBERTa and LLama 2. In the case of Llama 2, it could be due to the fact that the external dataset we used covers several topics – only 13.5% of the instances were related to climate activism. This distribution of data can add noise to training. As for RoBERTa, we only used the additional data of the same topic. We conclude that the strategy of augmenting training data with these particular external datasets did not improve the performance. We note that further analysis of the relation between external and task data is needed to establish whether training data augmentation in general is a suitable strategy for this task.

Figure 1 shows the confusion matrices of the best performing ensemble models, both with the majority strategy, using the CASE dataset and using aggregated data.

A study of the errors of the different runs shows that the four sets were wrong simultaneously in 17.47% of the total number of test instances, three of them were wrong in 7.3% of the instances, two of them in 5.63% and only one of them in 8.32%. Grouping by label, we observe that 11.62% of the instances labelled as SUPPORT are misclassified by all models, 24.11% for those labelled as OPPOSE and 26.4% for NEUTRAL. Grouping by ensemble strategy, we notice that for the majority one, 22.02% of instances are misclassified by the two models, while it is 24.2% for the conservative one. For the majority voting, the error for SUPPORT is 11.62% of all instances labelled as SUPPORT, 24.11% for OPPOSE and 40.6% for NEUTRAL. In the case of the conservative strategy, SUPPORT is 23.02%, OPPOSE 24.11% and NEUTRAL 26.4%.

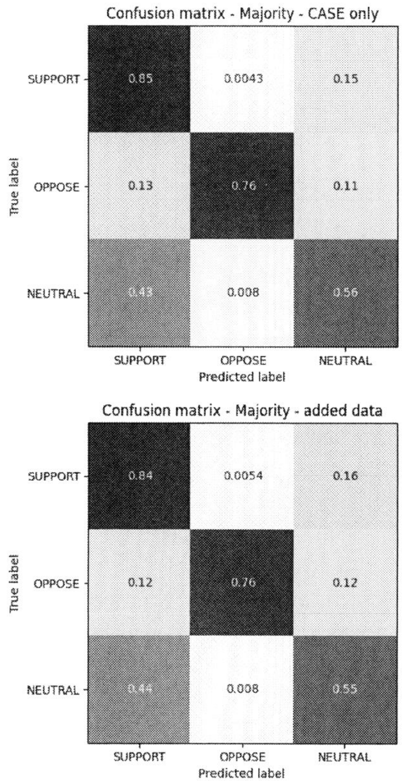

Figure 1: Confusion matrix for the best performing ensemble models using CASE and using added data.

Based on the errors per label, it can be seen that the conservative strategy, where predictions more often skew towards NEUTRAL, afforded a worse performance. Conservative ensembles were better at classifying NEUTRAL instances, but this was at the expense of the SUPPORT label. Since NEUTRAL instances are limited in the dataset, the use of the conservative strategy did not offer an advantage, whereas the majority more faithfully reproduced the expected distribution of labels in the dataset.

However, our RoBERTa baseline performed better than any of the ensemble strategies we submitted to the competition. In that light, we decided to conduct a post-competition examination with fewer restrictions to construct the ensemble system.

	Approach	F_1	Acc.
	Baseline	0.5450	0.6510
	Best model leaderboard	0.7495	0.7458
Indiv.	RoBERTa	0.7495	0.7458
	Llama 2	0.7366	0.7132
	MTL (best in training)	0.7402	0.7433
Ensemble	Conservative	0.7300	0.7004
	Mayority vote	**0.7529**	**0.7510**
	Oracle (upper bound)	0.8481	0.8451

Table 2: Comparison of F_1-scores and Accuracies for the best individual models (regardless of train data regime) and the ensembles of best models.

6 Post-competition Analysis

Our ensemble is based on the idea of combining the diversity given by a Transformer-based system (RoBERTa), a generative model (Llama 2) and a Multitask Learning (MTL) approach. Therefore, we just selected one configuration for each of the three approaches. Furthermore, we constrained ourselves to two options: whether all the systems use external datasets or none of them do.

After submission, we relaxed this constraint and performed a post-competition run selecting our best RoBERTa, Llama 2 and MTL models from the training stage, regardless of whether they use external data. In this case, as shown in Table 2, the majority vote ensemble achieves the best F_1 result, surpassing our RoBERTa based system that would have attained the highest position on the leaderboard for the stance detection subtask. If we look at accuracy, our majority vote ensemble surpasses the best model on the leaderboard.

The difference between both ensembles is due only to the use of a different configuration of the MTL model. This shows that the diversity introduced by the best in training MTL model is valuable to the ensemble.

7 Conclusions and Future Work

Our contribution focused on studying the influence of external data in the context of climate activism. We have done this through three different systems, whose combination into the proposed ensemble we present in this paper. The impact of external data on this particular subtask has been limited, only being effective in the case of the MTL system, which we theorize might be due to the different classification heads for each dataset, allowing them to keep the task-specific information of each task and maintaining the encoder with the general shared knowledge. In spite of this situation, we have gained some insight regarding our ensembles. Although our submitted runs do not improve the best individual result of the RoBERTa baseline, the post competition analysis reveals that an ensemble with our best models, regardless of the training set, would have achieved the first position in the competition.

As future work, a thorough study of the best combination of models, to find a higher divergence, is crucial. We have also determined that three systems might be insufficient for classification tasks with 3 classes, generating uncertainty in the test. To reduce this uncertainty, we plan on studying the effects of an ensemble with several models per approach, and of different voting strategies, such as a weighted voting schema, which could add a higher confidence level to the models and correct potential biases.

A central goal of our contribution, analyzing the effect of training with external data on this dataset, remains inconclusive. The proposed additional datasets did not always improve the results. We hypothesize that an analysis of the lexical and semantic distance between task data and external data could help to determine the suitability of the chosen collections. This analysis should potentially be extended over alternative external datasets in order to make an informed choice. A similar analysis of the particular instances of ClimaConvo in which each of the different models of the ensemble were successful – or failed – could contribute to better determine each model's strengths and clarify an optimal ensemble strategy.

As for individual models, another avenue to explore is studying the effect of other dimensions, such as pre-processing of the input data, as well as altering the threshold to assign a label to the instances. Although the conservative strategy did not have a high performance, the NEUTRAL tag still proves problematic. Optimizing the value for this threshold may improve the detection of this tag, thus enhancing the models. Additionally, an in-depth study of the effect of external data, and how each model performs for those tasks, would be necessary to determine why it is not as effective in the case of RoBERTa and Llama-2 and how we can improve it.

Limitations

An important drawback is the lack of regularization regarding external data usage in the constituent models of the ensemble presented in this paper. This situation limits the scope of the paper when addressing the value of additional data and requires a comprehensive analysis to determine its added value.

Another limitation relates to the high GPU requirements of some of our models. It is also relevant to note that some of the individual approaches achieve comparable results without such shortcomings. An additional study to determine if the usage of highly complex models for classification tasks may prove necessary.

Acknowledgements

This work was supported by the HAMiSoN project grant CHIST-ERA-21-OSNEM-002, AEI PCI2022-135026-2 (MCIN/AEI/10.13039/501100011033 and EU "NextGenerationEU"/PRTR).

References

Richard A. Caruana. 1993. Multitask Learning: A Knowledge-Based Source of Inductive Bias. In *Proceedings of the Tenth International Conference on Machine Learning*, pages 41–48.

Kaiping Chen, Amanda L. Molder, Zening Duan, Shelley Boulianne, Christopher Eckart, Prince Mallari, and Diyi Yang. 2023. How climate movement actors and news media frame climate change and strike: Evidence from analyzing twitter and news media discourse from 2018 to 2021. *The International Journal of Press/Politics*, 28(2):384–413.

Alessandra Teresa Cignarella, Mirko Lai, Cristina Bosco, Viviana Patti, Rosso Paolo, et al. 2020. SardiStance@ EVALITA2020: Overview of the Task on Stance Detection in Italian Tweets. In *Proceedings of the Seventh Evaluation Campaign of Natural Language Processing and Speech Tools for Italian. Final Workshop (EVALITA 2020)*, pages 1–10. CEUR.

Jesus M. Fraile-Hernandez and Anselmo Peñas. 2024. HAMiSoN-Generative at ClimateActivism 2024: Stance Detection using generative large language models. *Preprint*.

Daniel Hickey, Matheus Schmitz, Daniel Fessler, Paul E. Smaldino, Goran Muric, and Keith Burghardt. 2023. Auditing elon musk's impact on hate speech and bots. *Proceedings of the International AAAI Conference on Web and Social Media*, 17(1):1133–1137.

Yinhan Liu, Myle Ott, Naman Goyal, Jingfei Du, Mandar Joshi, Danqi Chen, Omer Levy, Mike Lewis, Luke Zettlemoyer, and Veselin Stoyanov. 2019. Roberta: A robustly optimized BERT pretraining approach. *CoRR*, abs/1907.11692.

Saif Mohammad, Svetlana Kiritchenko, Parinaz Sobhani, Xiaodan Zhu, and Colin Cherry. 2016a. A Dataset for Detecting Stance in Tweets. In *Proceedings of the Tenth International Conference on Language Resources and Evaluation (LREC'16)*, pages 3945–3952, Portorož, Slovenia. European Language Resources Association (ELRA).

Saif Mohammad, Svetlana Kiritchenko, Parinaz Sobhani, Xiaodan Zhu, and Colin Cherry. 2016b. SemEval-2016 Task 6: Detecting Stance in Tweets. In *Proceedings of the 10th International Workshop on Semantic Evaluation (SemEval-2016)*, pages 31–41, San Diego, California. Association for Computational Linguistics.

Anil Singh Parihar, Surendrabikram Thapa, and Sushruti Mishra. 2021. Hate speech detection using natural language processing: Applications and challenges. In *2021 5th International Conference on Trends in Electronics and Informatics (ICOEI)*, pages 1302–1308.

R. Polikar. 2006. Ensemble based systems in decision making. *IEEE Circuits and Systems Magazine*, 6(3):21–45.

Julio Reyes-Montesinos and Alvaro Rodrigo. 2024. HAMiSoN-baselines at ClimateActivism 2024: A Study on the Use of External Data for Hate Speech and Stance Detection. *Preprint*.

Raquel Rodriguez-Garcia and Roberto Centeno. 2024. HAMiSoN-MTL at ClimateActivism 2024: Detection of Hate Speech, Targets, and Stance using Multitask Learning. *Preprint*.

Shuvam Shiwakoti, Surendrabikram Thapa, Kritesh Rauniyar, Akshyat Shah, Aashish Bhandari, and Usman Naseem. 2024. Analyzing the dynamics of climate change discourse on twitter: A new annotated corpus and multi-aspect classification. *Preprint*.

Surendrabikram Thapa, Kritesh Rauniyar, Farhan Ahmad Jafri, Shuvam Shiwakoti, Hariram Veeramani, Raghav Jain, Guneet Singh Kohli, Ali Hürriyetoğlu, and Usman Naseem. 2024. Stance and hate event detection in tweets related to climate activism - shared task at case 2024. In *Proceedings of the 7th Workshop on Challenges and Applications of Automated Extraction of Socio-political Events from Text (CASE)*.

Hugo Touvron, Louis Martin, Kevin Stone, Peter Albert, Amjad Almahairi, Yasmine Babaei, Nikolay Bashlykov, Soumya Batra, Prajjwal Bhargava, Shruti Bhosale, et al. 2023. Llama 2: Open foundation and fine-tuned chat models, 2023. *ArXiv*.

Aman Tyagi, Joshua Uyheng, and Kathleen M. Carley. 2020. Affective polarization in online climate change discourse on twitter. In *2020 IEEE/ACM International Conference on Advances in Social Networks Analysis and Mining (ASONAM)*, pages 443–447.

Nicolas Webersinke, Mathias Kraus, Julia Anna Bingler, and Markus Leippold. 2022. Climatebert: A pretrained language model for climate-related text.

Marcos Zampieri, Shervin Malmasi, Preslav Nakov, Sara Rosenthal, Noura Farra, and Ritesh Kumar. 2019a. Predicting the Type and Target of Offensive Posts in Social Media. In *Proceedings of the 2019 Conference of the North American Chapter of the Association for Computational Linguistics: Human Language Technologies, Volume 1 (Long and Short Papers)*, pages 1415–1420, Minneapolis, Minnesota. Association for Computational Linguistics.

Marcos Zampieri, Shervin Malmasi, Preslav Nakov, Sara Rosenthal, Noura Farra, and Ritesh Kumar. 2019b. SemEval-2019 Task 6: Identifying and Categorizing Offensive Language in Social Media (OffensEval). In *Proceedings of the 13th International Workshop on Semantic Evaluation*, pages 75–86, Minneapolis, Minnesota, USA. Association for Computational Linguistics.

MasonPerplexity at Multimodal Hate Speech Event Detection 2024: Hate Speech and Target Detection Using Transformer Ensembles

Amrita Ganguly*, **Al Nahian Bin Emran***, **Sadiya Sayara Chowdhury Puspo**
Md Nishat Raihan, Dhiman Goswami, Marcos Zampieri
George Mason University, USA
{agangul, abinemra}@gmu.edu

Abstract

The automatic identification of offensive language such as hate speech is important to keep discussions civil in online communities. Identifying hate speech in multimodal content is a particularly challenging task because offensiveness can be manifested in either words or images or a juxtaposition of the two. This paper presents the *MasonPerplexity* submission for the Shared Task on Multimodal Hate Speech Event Detection at CASE 2024 at EACL 2024. The task is divided into two sub-tasks: subtask A focuses on the identification of hate speech and sub-task B focuses on the identification of targets in text-embedded images during political events. We use an XLM-roBERTa-large model for sub-task A and an ensemble approach combining XLM-roBERTa-base, BERTweet-large, and BERT-base for sub-task B. Our approach obtained 0.8347 F1-score in sub-task A and 0.6741 F1-score in sub-task B ranking 3rd on both sub-tasks.

1 Introduction

In the context of polarized political discussions, when feelings and perspectives are strong, identifying offensive content is essential to moderation efforts in online communities. The challenge is increased by the use of text-embedded images in which negative emotions can be expressed both verbally and visually. Besides, in the current era of vlogging and reels, people are inclined to utilize memes and emojis or opt for text-embedded images to express their sentiments and comment on online content. As a result, the task of detecting hate speech is expanding to encompass images, posing a new challenge beyond the realm of textual content and across diverse languages.

The Shared Task on Multimodal Hate Event Detection at CASE 2024 (Thapa et al., 2024) deals with the identification of hate speech and its targets in text-embedded images during political events. The main objective is to automatically determine if an image that includes text contains hate speech (sub-task A) and, if so, to identify its targets categorized as community, individual, and organization (sub-task B). Identifying the target of offensive messages is vital to understanding their potential harm as demonstrated by annotation taxonomies such as OLID (Zampieri et al., 2019) and TBO (Zampieri et al., 2023).

In this paper, we discuss transformer-based approaches to hate speech detection in political events using the Multimodal Hate Speech Event Detection dataset (Bhandari et al., 2023). The paper sheds light on the challenges of handling multimodal content, particularly text-embedded images. For sub-task A (hate speech detection), we employ the XLM-roBERTa-large (Conneau et al., 2020) model. For sub-task B (target detection), we adopt an ensemble approach combining XLM-roBERTa-base, BERTweet-large (Ushio and Camacho-Collados, 2021), and BERT-base (Devlin et al., 2019). These models are selected to effectively address the unique challenges posed by diverse multimodal content. We report that our approach obtained a 0.8347 F1-score in sub-task A and a 0.6741 F1-score in sub-task B, ranking 3rd on both sub-tasks.

2 Related Work

Offensive Content and Hate Speech Offensive content is pervasive in social media motivating the development of systems capable of recognizing it automatically. While definitions may vary, hate speech is arguably the most widely explored type of offensive content (Schmidt and Wiegand, 2017; Fortuna and Nunes, 2018). Several studies have proposed new datasets and models to label hateful posts on social media (Davidson et al., 2017; Zia et al., 2022). More recently, studies have focused on recognizing the specific parts of an instance that

*** denotes equal contribution.**
This paper contains offensive examples.

Proceedings of the 7th Workshop on Challenges and Applications of Automated Extraction of Socio-political Events from Text (CASE 2024), pages 125–131
March 22, 2024 ©2024 Association for Computational Linguistics

may be considered offensive or hateful, as in the case of HateXplain (Mathew et al., 2021), TSD (Pavlopoulos et al., 2021), and MUDES (Ranasinghe and Zampieri, 2021). The vast majority of work on text-based hate speech detection is on English but several papers have created resources and models for languages such as Bengali (Raihan et al., 2023b), French (Chiril et al., 2019), Greek (Pitenis et al., 2020), Marathi (Gaikwad et al., 2021), and Turkish (Çöltekin, 2020).

Multimodal Hate Speech While the aforementioned studies have focused on the identification of hateful content in texts, there has been growing interest in identifying hateful content in text and images simultaneously. Hermida and Santos (2023), Ji et al. (2023), and Yang et al. (2022) highlight the significance of multimodal analysis offering a comprehensive overview of various methodologies employed to detect hate speech in images and memes. Various datasets have been introduced for multimodal hate speech detection (Grimminger and Klinger, 2021; Bhandari et al., 2023; Thapa et al., 2022) The study by Grimminger and Klinger (2021) presents a Twitter corpus with content related to the US elections of 2020. The study by Boishakhi et al. (2021) explores the combination of various modalities for hate speech detection such as text, video, and audio. While the clear majority of studies deal with English, research on different languages (Karim et al., 2022; Rajput et al., 2022; Perifanos and Goutsos, 2021).

Related Shared Tasks Thapa et al. (2023) organizes CASE 2023, a series of shared tasks identifying Multimodal Hate Speech Event Detection. There are two sub-tasks to identify hate speech and targets in the different sub-tasks. Participants present the utilization of transformer models like BERT, RoBERTa, and XLNet, as well as effective approaches such as vision transformers and CLIP which contributed to the outstanding outcomes. Similarly, different shared tasks have been organized to identify offensive language from texts i.e. (Aragón et al., 2019), (Modha et al., 2021). All of this research highlights how important it is to combine several data modalities in order to improve hate speech or offensive language detection.

3 Datasets

In sub-task A, the training dataset provided by the organizers contains 3,600 images. Additionally, a development set and a testing set were provided by the organizers each including 443 instances. Instances in the sub-task A dataset (Bhandari et al., 2023) are annotated using two labels: NO-HATE (labeled as 0) and HATE (labeled as 1). We present an example of the training data of sub-task A in Figure 1.

Figure 1: Training data example (Left: NO-HATE, Right: HATE)

The label distribution, presented in Table 1, is skewed in the dataset, with a slightly higher percentage of instances labeled as HATE in the training, testing, and evaluation sets.

	sub-task A		
Label	**Train**	**Eval**	**Test**
HATE	53.95	54.85	54.85
NO-HATE	46.05	45.15	45.15

Table 1: Distribution of labels in the training, evaluation, and test sets of the sub-task A dataset in terms of percentage.

In sub-task B, the training, evaluation, and test sets include 1,942, 244, and 242 images respectively. Instances in the sub-task B dataset (Thapa et al., 2022) are labeled into three categories: Individual (labeled as 0), Community (labeled as 1), and Organization (labeled as 2). Examples of training data for sub-task B are shown in Figure 2.

Figure 2: Training data example (Left: Organization, Top-right: Individual, Bottom-right: Community)

There is an imbalance among the three labels and the distribution is shown in Table 2. The class INDIVIDUAL is the most prevalent. The imbalance can impact the model's ability to generalize across different classes, potentially leading to biased results. Addressing this imbalance through techniques like data augmentation or re-balancing strategies may be crucial for developing robust models that perform well across all label categories.

sub-task B			
Label	**Train**	**Eval**	**Test**
INDIVIDUAL	42.38	41.80	42.15
COMMUNITY	17.25	16.40	17.35
ORGANIZATION	40.37	41.80	40.50

Table 2: label wise data percentage of sub-task B

We have used Google Vision API[1] to retrieve text from the images of all the phases of both the subtasks. Although the OCR can detect text in a variety of languages, the accuracy may change depending on the language. It's possible that some languages are more accurate and supported than others. The input image quality has an impact on OCR accuracy. In certain situations, the original formatting may not be preserved by the API.

4 Experiments

In sub-task A, we use BERTweet-large (Ushio and Camacho-Collados, 2021) (Ushio et al., 2022), BERT-base (Devlin et al., 2019), and XLM-R (Conneau et al., 2020) models. Notably, XLM-R shows the best F1 score. We also use GPT-3.5[2] zero-shot and few-shot prompting with test F1 score 0.73, 0.77. For sub-task B, we also start with BERTweet-large, BERT-base, and XLM-R using the same learning rate and epochs as in sub-task A. Later, we apply a weighted ensemble approach to these models, resulting in the 0.65 F1 score for the task. To tackle class imbalance in sub-task B, we employed back translation, converting the training data through Xosha to Twi to English and Lao to Pashto to Yoruba to English. This significantly improves overall model performance from 0.65 to 0.67.

The ensemble method with majority voting is proven helpful in this type of case where a single model may not be able to label the data correctly due to class imbalance (Goswami et al., 2023). Moreover, we follow the approach of back translation of (Raihan et al., 2023a). We follow the approach of back translation of (Raihan et al., 2023a). For this, we select languages that demonstrate limited or no cultural overlap with the original language featured in the dataset. Xosha, Twi, Lao, Pashto, and Yoruba are languages that are very diverse culturally and geographically. This diversity underscores the significance of considering a wide range of cultural and geographical influences when working with these languages. By intentionally selecting these languages without cultural overlap, we introduce a purposeful aspect of diversity, mitigating potential biases, and enhancing the dataset with a broader spectrum of linguistic expressions. Moreover, the Ensemble method with majority voting is also proven helpful in this type of case where a single model may not label the data correctly due to class imbalance (Goswami et al., 2023). For instance, when two out of three models predict a sentence as a hate event, the sentence is subsequently labeled as a hate event through the application of majority voting. We also use GPT-3.5 zero-shot and few-shot prompting with test F1 scores of 0.53, and 0.57. The prompt provided to GPT3.5 is available in Figure 3.

> **Role:** You are a helpful AI assistant. You are given the task of *<sub-task_name>*.

> **Definition:** *<sub-task_definition>*. You will be given a text to label either *<label1>* or *<label2>* or *<label3>*.

> **Task:** Generate the label for this **text** in the following format: *<label>* *Your_Predicted_Label* *<\label>*. Thanks.

Figure 3: Sample GPT-3.5 prompt.

We also utilize GPT-3.5 through the OpenAI API for two primary sub-tasks: Hate Speech Detection (sub-task A) and Hate Speech Target Detection (sub-task B). We fine-tune GPT-3.5 using specifically curated training and evaluation datasets, conducting the process over four epochs. It is worth noting that, no other hyper parameter can be set other than epochs while fine-tuning GPT3.5 through the API. Notably, the OpenAI API does not provide conventional metrics such as training loss, validation loss, precision, or recall. Upon

[1]`https://cloud.google.com/vision/`

[2]`https://platform.openai.com/docs/models/gpt-3-5-turbo`

completion of the fine-tuning, the API assigns a unique ID to our model. We use this ID to process the test dataset for both sub-tasks. For labeling and predictions, the API returns results based on the test dataset. In sub-task A, which focuses on detecting hate speech, our model achieves an F1 score of 0.82, indicating a high level of accuracy. Conversely, in sub-task B, where the objective is to identify the targets of hate speech, the model attains a lower F1 score of 0.63, reflecting the inherent challenges in this particular aspect of hate speech analysis.

Hyperparameters of all the models used excluding GPT3.5 in the experiments are available in Figure 3.

Parameter	Value
Learning Rate	$1e-5$
Train Batch Size	8
Test Batch Size	8
Epochs	5

Table 3: Training Configuration Parameters

5 Results

The detailed experimental results of the models in sub-task A and sub-task B are available in Tables 4, and 5, respectively. In sub-task A, we evaluate a BERT-base, BERTweet-large, and XLM-R model. XLM-R delivers the best performance with a 0.83 F1-score. In sub-task B, our ensemble approach was provides the best F1-score of 0.67.

Model	Eval F1	Test F1
GPT3.5 (Zero Shot)	–	0.73
GPT3.5 (Few Shot)	–	0.77
GPT3.5 (FineTuned)	0.86	0.82
BERT-base	0.81	0.75
BERTweet-large	0.89	0.81
XLM-R	0.95	**0.83**

Table 4: Results of sub-task A.

6 Error Analysis

In sub-task A, our aim is to detect non-hate (labeled as 0) and hate (labeled as 1) speeches. Therefore, the task of our model is to categorize text into two categories: non-hate or hate. The confusion matrix, presented in Figure 4, illustrates both the true labels and predicted labels, indicating that our model

Model	Eval F1	Test F1
GPT3.5 (Zero Shot)	–	0.53
GPT3.5 (Few Shot)	–	0.57
GPT3.5 (FineTuned)	0.65	0.63
BERT-base	0.61	0.60
XLM-R	0.63	0.61
BERTweet-large	0.68	0.64
Ensemble	0.69	0.65
BERT-base (Aug.)	0.63	0.61
XLM-R (Aug.)	0.65	0.64
BERTweet-large (Aug.)	0.70	0.66
Ensemble (Aug.)	0.71	**0.67**

Table 5: Results of sub-task B (before and after data augmentation).

excels in recognizing hate speech than the non-hate ones. The observed bias towards recognizing hate speech in the model may stem from the prevalence of HATE-labeled texts in both training and evaluation datasets. As both the training and evaluation datasets are used to train the model, the model may develop a bias, impacting its accuracy when dealing with non-hate speeches.

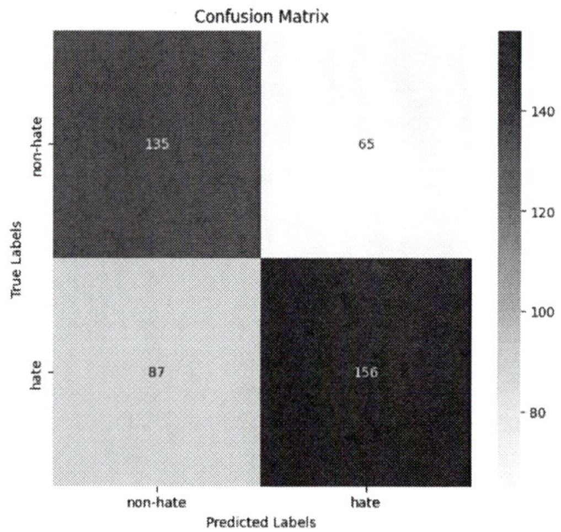

Figure 4: Confusion matrix of sub-task A evaluation set.

In sub-task B, our ensemble model is assigned the challenge of categorizing targets from text-embedded images into three labels: individual (labeled as 0), community (labeled as 1), and organization (labeled as 2). Analysis of the Confusion Matrix shown in Figure 5, indicates that our model shows difficulties in identifying community categories, compared to labeling organizations and individuals. However, the model excels in accu-

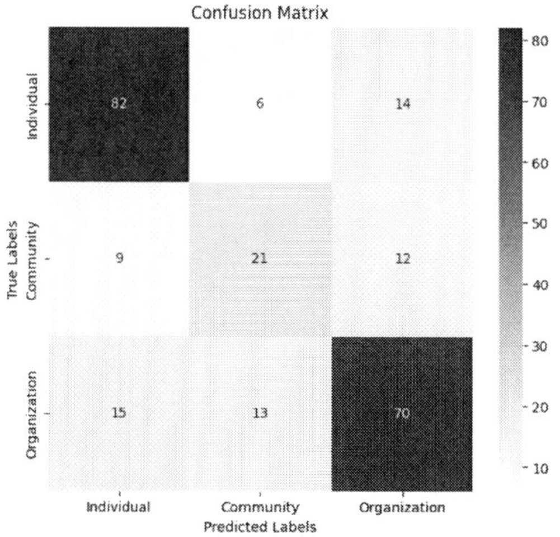

Figure 5: Confusion matrix of sub-task B evaluation set.

rately categorizing individuals. This underscores the significance of having a balanced dataset. The observed challenges in the model's performance, particularly in identifying the community category, can be attributed to an imbalance in the training and evaluation datasets.

According to our initial analysis, there are some challenges that can affect our results. Firstly, there is an imbalance in label distribution within our dataset, where certain data classes contain more Instances than others. This makes it difficult for the model to learn properties of classes that contain fewer examples. Secondly, we observed that some labels in the dataset are correctly attributed. This is the case of many offensive and hate speech datasets due to the intrinsic subjectivity of the task, as noted by Weerasooriya et al. (2023). Incorrect labels can confuse our model, making it harder for it to learn properly and leading to mistakes in the evaluation state. It may also explain why GPT3.5 underperformed, even after finetuning. Also, as this is primarily a text classification task - models like XLM-R do better than GPT3.5.

Finally, another limitation lies in the impact of external factors on the reliability of our Multimodal Hate Event Detection Model over time. The dynamic nature of online discourse and political shifts may affect its efficacy. Even though our models achieve good results, recognizing and dealing with these challenges is important when developing high-performing models that work well in the ever-changing world of online conversations and political events.

7 Conclusion and Future Work

This paper evaluated various approaches to Multimodal Hate Event Detection. We tested multiple models such as GPT, XLM-R, and BERT on subtask a and sub-task b of the competition and we addressed the difficulties associated with handling multimodal content. Our XLM-R model performed well in subtask A ranking third, achieving an F1 score of 0.83. In the same way, for subtask B, our ensemble method, which combined BERT base, BERTweet large, and XLM-R, also ranked third, achieving an F1 score of 0.67.

Despite encountering label distribution imbalances in the training and evaluation sets, our approaches successfully navigated these challenges. Future studies will focus on exploring potential biases in our models and further refining strategies for handling class imbalance as in Akhbardeh et al. (2021). Moreover, as online communication continues to increase multimodality, developing robust hate speech detection systems requires fusing information from different modalities. Future work should focus on faceted annotation schemes and semi-supervised approaches to improve generalization. Evaluating model biases, and exploring the impacts of label imbalance are also important areas needing attention. We hope our experiments provide a valuable starting point for further research towards safer online spaces.

Acknowledgment

We thank the shared task organizers for providing us with this interesting dataset. We further thank the anonymous reviewers for their insightful feedback.

Ethics Statement

This study adheres to the ACL Ethics Policy and seeks to make a contribution to the realm of online safety. The dataset is supplied to us by the organizers and has undergone anonymization to secure the privacy of the users. The technology in question possesses the potential to serve as a beneficial instrument for the moderation of online content, thereby facilitating the creation of safer digital environments. However, it is imperative to exercise caution to prevent its potential misuse for purposes such as monitoring or censorship.

References

Farhad Akhbardeh, Cecilia Ovesdotter Alm, Marcos Zampieri, and Travis Desell. 2021. Handling extreme class imbalance in technical logbook datasets. In *Proceedings of ACL*.

Mario Ezra Aragón, Miguel Angel Alvarez Carmona, Manuel Montes-y Gómez, Hugo Jair Escalante, Luis Villasenor Pineda, and Daniela Moctezuma. 2019. Overview of mex-a3t at iberlef 2019: Authorship and aggressiveness analysis in mexican spanish tweets. In *Proceedings of IberLEF*.

Aashish Bhandari, Siddhant B Shah, Surendrabikram Thapa, Usman Naseem, and Mehwish Nasim. 2023. Crisishatemm: Multimodal analysis of directed and undirected hate speech in text-embedded images from russia-ukraine conflict. In *Proceedings of IEEE CVF*.

Fariha Tahosin Boishakhi, Ponkoj Chandra Shill, and Md. Golam Rabiul Alam. 2021. Multi-modal hate speech detection using machine learning. In *Proceedings of IEEE Big Data*.

Patricia Chiril, Farah Benamara Zitoune, Véronique Moriceau, Marlène Coulomb-Gully, and Abhishek Kumar. 2019. Multilingual and multitarget hate speech detection in tweets. In *Proceedings of TALN*.

Çağrı Çöltekin. 2020. A corpus of Turkish offensive language on social media. In *Proceedings of LREC*.

Alexis Conneau, Kartikay Khandelwal, Naman Goyal, Vishrav Chaudhary, Guillaume Wenzek, Francisco Guzmán, Edouard Grave, Myle Ott, Luke Zettlemoyer, and Veselin Stoyanov. 2020. Unsupervised cross-lingual representation learning at scale. In *Proceedings of ACL*.

Thomas Davidson, Dana Warmsley, Michael W. Macy, and Ingmar Weber. 2017. Automated hate speech detection and the problem of offensive language. In *Proceedings of ICWSM*.

Jacob Devlin, Ming-Wei Chang, Kenton Lee, and Kristina Toutanova. 2019. BERT: Pre-training of deep bidirectional transformers for language understanding. In *Proceedings NAACL*.

Paula Fortuna and Sérgio Nunes. 2018. A survey on automatic detection of hate speech in text. *ACM Computing Surveys (CSUR)*, 51(4):1–30.

Saurabh Sampatrao Gaikwad, Tharindu Ranasinghe, Marcos Zampieri, and Christopher Homan. 2021. Cross-lingual offensive language identification for low resource languages: The case of Marathi. In *Proceedings of RANLP*.

Dhiman Goswami, Md Nishat Raihan, Sadiya Sayara Chowdhury Puspo, and Marcos Zampieri. 2023. nlpBDpatriots at BLP-2023 task 2: A transfer learning approach towards Bangla sentiment analysis. In *Proceedings of BLP*.

Lara Grimminger and Roman Klinger. 2021. Hate towards the political opponent: A twitter corpus study of the 2020 us elections on the basis of offensive speech and stance detection. In *Proceedings of WASSA*.

Paulo Cezar de Q Hermida and Eulanda M dos Santos. 2023. Detecting hate speech in memes: a review. *Artificial Intelligence Review*, pages 1–19.

Junhui Ji, Wei Ren, and Usman Naseem. 2023. Identifying creative harmful memes via prompt based approach. In *Proceedings of WWW*.

Md Rezaul Karim, Sumon Kanti Dey, Tanhim Islam, Md Shajalal, and Bharathi Raja Chakravarthi. 2022. Multimodal hate speech detection from bengali memes and texts. In *Proceedings of SPELL*.

Binny Mathew, Punyajoy Saha, Seid Muhie Yimam, Chris Biemann, Pawan Goyal, and Animesh Mukherjee. 2021. Hatexplain: A benchmark dataset for explainable hate speech detection. *Proceedings of AAAI*.

Sandip Modha, Thomas Mandl, Gautam Kishore Shahi, Hiren Madhu, Shrey Satapara, Tharindu Ranasinghe, and Marcos Zampieri. 2021. Overview of the hasoc subtrack at fire 2021: Hate speech and offensive content identification in english and indo-aryan languages and conversational hate speech. In *Proceedings of FIRE*.

John Pavlopoulos, Jeffrey Sorensen, Léo Laugier, and Ion Androutsopoulos. 2021. SemEval-2021 task 5: Toxic spans detection. In *Proceedings of SemEval*.

Konstantinos Perifanos and Dionysis Goutsos. 2021. Multimodal hate speech detection in greek social media. *Multimodal Technologies and Interaction*, 5(7):34.

Zesis Pitenis, Marcos Zampieri, and Tharindu Ranasinghe. 2020. Offensive language identification in Greek. In *Proceedings of LREC*.

Md Nishat Raihan, Dhiman Goswami, Sadiya Sayara Chowdhury Puspo, and Marcos Zampieri. 2023a. nlpBDpatriots at BLP-2023 task 1: Two-step classification for violence inciting text detection in Bangla - leveraging back-translation and multilinguality. In *Proceedings of BLP*.

Md Nishat Raihan, Umma Tanmoy, Anika Binte Islam, Kai North, Tharindu Ranasinghe, Antonios Anastasopoulos, and Marcos Zampieri. 2023b. Offensive language identification in transliterated and code-mixed bangla. In *Proceedings of BLP*.

Kshitij Rajput, Raghav Kapoor, Kaushal Rai, and Preeti Kaur. 2022. Hate me not: detecting hate inducing memes in code switched languages. In *Proceedings of AMCIS*.

Tharindu Ranasinghe and Marcos Zampieri. 2021. MUDES: Multilingual Detection of Offensive Spans. In *Proceedings of NAACL*.

Anna Schmidt and Michael Wiegand. 2017. A Survey on Hate Speech Detection Using Natural Language Processing. In *Proceedings of SocialNLP*.

Surendrabikram Thapa, Farhan Jafri, Ali Hürriyetoğlu, Francielle Vargas, Roy Ka-Wei Lee, and Usman Naseem. 2023. Multimodal hate speech event detection - shared task 4, CASE 2023. In *Proceedings of CASE*.

Surendrabikram Thapa, Kritesh Rauniyar, Farhan Ahmad Jafri, Hariram Veeramani, Raghav Jain, Sandesh Jain, Francielle Vargas, Ali Hürriyetoğlu, and Usman Naseem. 2024. Extended multimodal hate speech event detection during russia-ukraine crisis - shared task at case 2024. In *Proceedings of CASE*.

Surendrabikram Thapa, Aditya Shah, Farhan Jafri, Usman Naseem, and Imran Razzak. 2022. A multimodal dataset for hate speech detection on social media: Case-study of russia-Ukraine conflict. In *Proceedings of CASE*.

Asahi Ushio and Jose Camacho-Collados. 2021. T-NER: An all-round python library for transformer-based named entity recognition. In *Proceedings of EACL*.

Asahi Ushio, Leonardo Neves, Vitor Silva, Francesco. Barbieri, and Jose Camacho-Collados. 2022. Named Entity Recognition in Twitter: A Dataset and Analysis on Short-Term Temporal Shifts. In *Proceedings of AACL*.

Tharindu Weerasooriya, Sujan Dutta, Tharindu Ranasinghe, Marcos Zampieri, Christopher Homan, and Ashiqur Khudabukhsh. 2023. Vicarious offense and noise audit of offensive speech classifiers: unifying human and machine disagreement on what is offensive. In *Proceedings of EMNLP*.

Chuanpeng Yang, Fuqing Zhu, Guihua Liu, Jizhong Han, and Songlin Hu. 2022. Multimodal hate speech detection via cross-domain knowledge transfer. In *Proceedings of ACM MM*.

Marcos Zampieri, Shervin Malmasi, Preslav Nakov, Sara Rosenthal, Noura Farra, and Ritesh Kumar. 2019. Predicting the type and target of offensive posts in social media. In *Proceedings of NAACL*.

Marcos Zampieri, Skye Morgan, Kai North, Tharindu Ranasinghe, Austin Simmmons, Paridhi Khandelwal, Sara Rosenthal, and Preslav Nakov. 2023. Target-based offensive language identification. In *Proceedings of ACL*.

Haris Bin Zia, Ignacio Castro, Arkaitz Zubiaga, and Gareth Tyson. 2022. Improving zero-shot cross-lingual hate speech detection with pseudo-label fine-tuning of transformer language models. In *Proceedings of ICWSM*.

MasonPerplexity at ClimateActivism 2024: Integrating Advanced Ensemble Techniques and Data Augmentation for Climate Activism Stance and Hate Event Identification

Al Nahian Bin Emran*, **Amrita Ganguly***, **Sadiya Sayara Chowdhury Puspo**
Dhiman Goswami, Md Nishat Raihan
George Mason University, USA
{abinemra, agangul}@gmu.edu

Abstract

The task of identifying public opinions on social media, particularly regarding climate activism and the detection of hate events, has emerged as a critical area of research in our rapidly changing world. With a growing number of people voicing either to support or oppose to climate-related issues - understanding these diverse viewpoints has become increasingly vital. Our team, *MasonPerplexity*, participates in a significant research initiative focused on this subject. We extensively test various models and methods, discovering that our most effective results are achieved through ensemble modeling, enhanced by data augmentation techniques like back-translation. In the specific components of this research task, our team achieved notable positions, ranking 5th, 1st, and 6th in the respective sub-tasks, thereby illustrating the effectiveness of our approach in this important field of study.

1 Introduction

In the ever-evolving landscape of climate change activism, encouraging meaningful conversations and comprehending how things change throughout events depends critically on the ability to recognize hate speech and the understanding of attitude during these events. This paper presents our effort in the Shared Task on Hate Speech and Stance Detection during Climate Activism (Thapa et al., 2024), where our goal is to develop effective models for hate speech detection, target identification, and stance detection.

This task consists of three subtasks that work together to support an integrated approach to event identification. The goal of the first subtask is to identify whether the given text contains hate speech or not. The second subtask focuses on identifying if people, groups, or communities are targets of hate speech. Lastly, Stance Detection provides insight into the dynamics of climate activism protests by assessing the support, opposition, or neutrality indicated within texts.

Our paper serves as a comprehensive system description, outlining the approaches and models used to address these subtasks within the framework of activist events related to climate change. We present our ensemble method for identifying hate speech, which combines robust models like XLM-roBERTa-large (Conneau et al., 2019), BERTweet-large (Ushio and Camacho-Collados, 2021a), and fBERT (Sarkar et al., 2021). Notably, for Target Detection, the best-performing model is BERTweet-large (Ushio and Camacho-Collados, 2021b) while BERTweet-base (Nguyen et al., 2020) excels in Stance Detection.

We also discuss our fine-tuning strategies and dataset augmentation techniques, demonstrating our commitment to refining model performance. Our approach's effectiveness is demonstrated by our remarkable F1 scores of 0.8885, 0.7858, and 0.7373. Furthermore, our team named *MasonPerplexity* has secured 5th, 1st, and 6th ranks in the respective subtasks, underscoring the competence of our models in comparison to peers.

Through this paper, we aim to contribute to the advancement of hate speech and stance detection in the context of climate activism, fostering a safer and more informed space for dialogue and understanding during crucial events. We employ ensemble methods to better classify the texts - our approach increases the accuracy metrics for the first sub-task where we encounter a comparatively larger amount of data. We also use data augmentation methods, which further improve our results.

2 Related Works

The paper (Parihar et al., 2021) explores the rising concern of hate speech on the internet and its potential impact. It emphasizes machine learning and deep learning models in automatically identifying hate speech. In (Malmasi and Zampieri, 2017),

* **denotes Equal Contribution**

Proceedings of the 7th Workshop on Challenges and Applications of Automated Extraction of Socio-political Events from Text (CASE 2024), pages 132–138
March 22, 2024 ©2024 Association for Computational Linguistics

English tweets are subjected to supervised classification using n-gram features and a linear SVM classifier. Even at 78% accuracy, it is still difficult to discern offensive language from hate speech. By combining recurrent neural networks and user features, (Pitsilis et al., 2018) outperforms current systems and achieves a remarkable F-score of 0.9320 on a Twitter dataset. Additionally, Warner and Hirschberg (Warner and Hirschberg, 2012) define hate speech and despite limitations in capturing larger language patterns, SVM classification can detect anti-Semitic speech with 94% accuracy.

The literature on target detection in hate speech unveils valuable insights through various studies in the field. (Lemmens et al., 2021) focuses on Dutch Facebook comments, exploring hateful metaphors to enhance hate speech type and target detection. The study incorporates manual metaphor annotations as features for SVM and BERT models, observing improvements in F1 scores. Conversely, (Zampieri et al., 2019) proposes a hierarchical annotation scheme for offensive language in English tweets, creating the OLID dataset. The study employs SVM, CNN, and BiLSTM models, achieving notable results and providing a valuable resource for offensive language research.

Stance detection, a crucial aspect of NLP, involves determining a person's position towards a concept. (Küçük and Can, 2021) outlines the significance and challenges in this domain, emphasizing its relation to sentiment analysis, emotion detection, and other tasks. It highlights the evolution facilitated by shared tasks, varied approaches, including traditional SVMs and newer LSTM models, and the necessity of annotated datasets. Additionally, (Upadhyaya et al., 2023) introduces a multitasking approach, enhancing performance on multiple datasets, and showcasing the potential of incorporating auxiliary tasks. Furthermore, (Küçük and Can, 2018) contributes a valuable stance-annotated Turkish Twitter dataset, showcasing the diversity of research efforts in stance detection.

3 Datasets

From the tables for Subtask 1, Subtask 2, and Subtask 3, it is evident that the dataset (Shiwakoti et al., 2024) is imbalanced across different labels.

3.1 Hate Speech Detection

In subtask A, the distribution between NON-HATE and HATE is heavily skewed towards NON-HATE, with approximately 87.66% in the training set, 87.83% in the evaluation set, and 87.96% in the test set. This indicates a significant class imbalance, which may pose challenges for model training and evaluation.

3.2 Target Detection

In subtask B, there is an imbalance among the labels INDIVIDUAL, ORGANIZATION, and COMMUNITY. The majority of instances belong to the individual category, with around 80.54% in the training set, 80.00% in the evaluation set, and 80.67% in the test set.

3.3 Stance Detection

Subtask C exhibits an imbalance, between the SUPPORT, OPPOSE, and NEUTRAL labels. SUPPORT dominates the dataset, comprising 59.42% in the training set, 57.46% in the evaluation set, and 58.96% in the test set, where OPPOSE has respective percentages 9.61%, 9.80%, and 9.03%.

In summary, the dataset for all three subtasks is not well-balanced, and addressing this imbalance may be crucial for developing models that generalize well across different classes.

	Subtask A		
Label	**Train**	**Eval**	**Test**
NON-HATE	87.66	87.83	87.96
HATE	12.34	12.17	12.04

Table 1: label wise data percentage of subtask A

	Subtask B		
Label	**Train**	**Eval**	**Test**
INDIVIDUAL	80.54	80.00	80.67
ORGANIZATION	15.02	15.33	15.33
COMMUNITY	4.44	4.67	4.00

Table 2: label wise data percentage of subtask B

	Subtask C		
Label	**Train**	**Eval**	**Test**
SUPPORT	59.42	57.46	58.96
OPPOSE	9.61	9.80	9.03
NEUTRAL	30.97	32.74	32.01

Table 3: label wise data percentage of subtask C

4 Experiments

In subtask A, we initially employ GPT3.5 (OpenAI, 2023) zero shot and few shot prompting with Test F1 score 0.66 and 0.73. The prompt provided to GPT3.5 is available in Figure 1.

> **Role:** You are a helpful AI assistant. You are given the task of *<subtask_name>*.

> **Definition:** *<subtask_definition>*. You will be given a text to label either *<label1>* or *<label2>* or *<label3>*.

> **Task:** Generate the label for this **text** in the following format: *<label> Your_Predicted_Label* <\label>. Thanks.

Figure 1: Sample GPT-3.5 prompt.

Then we use BERTweet large (Ushio and Camacho-Collados, 2021a) (Ushio et al., 2022), XLM-R (Conneau et al., 2019), HATE-BERT (Caselli et al., 2021) and fBERT (Sarkar et al., 2021). Following this, we adopt a weighted ensemble approach (Ensemble 1) for the best three models (BERTweet, XLM-R, fBERT). Similarly, we perform another weighted ensemble approach (Ensemble 2) with the same models only replacing BERTweet with HATE-BERT, as these two models show the same F1 score on test data with the same setting. However, the former ensemble strategy yields the highest F1 score for this task.

To address class imbalance in subtask A, we implement back translation by converting the training data of those specific labels that have a smaller ratio with respect to the whole training set through various languages, including Xosha to Twi to English, Lao to Pashto to Yoruba to English, Yoruba to Somali to Kinyarwanda to English, and Zulu to Oromo to Shona to Tsonga to English. This approach significantly contributed to improving the overall F1 score of Ensemble 1 from 0.85 to 0.88 and Ensemble 2 from 0.86 to 0.89.

We follow the approach of back translation of (Raihan et al., 2023). For this, we select languages that demonstrate limited or no cultural overlap with the original language featured in the dataset. Xosha, Twi, Lao, Pashto, Yoruba, Somali, Kinyarwanda, Zulu, Oromo, Shona, and Tsonga are languages that are very diverse culturally and geographically. This diversity underscores the significance of considering a wide range of cultural and geographical influences when working with these languages. By intentionally selecting these languages without cultural overlap, we introduce a purposeful aspect of diversity, mitigating potential biases, and enhancing the dataset with a broader spectrum of linguistic expressions. Moreover, the Ensemble method with majority voting is also proven helpful in this type of case where a single model may not label the data correctly due to class imbalance (Goswami et al., 2023). For instance, when two out of three models predict a sentence as a hate event, the sentence is subsequently labeled as a hate event through the application of majority voting.

In subtask B, we utilize BERTweet-large (Ushio and Camacho-Collados, 2021a), BERT base (Devlin et al., 2018), and XLM-R (Conneau et al., 2019). Additionally, like subtask 1, we implement back translation using the same language sequences mentioned earlier to address class imbalance. Notably, BERTweet large (Ushio and Camacho-Collados, 2021a) demonstrates the highest F1- score among these models. We also use GPT3.5 zero shot and few shot prompting with 0.63 and 0.64 test F1 scores.

BERTweet-large (Ushio and Camacho-Collados, 2021a), BERT base (Devlin et al., 2018), and BERTweet base (Nguyen et al., 2020) models are applied in subtask C for stance detection. Among these models, the BERTweet base achieves the highest F1 score. F1 score for GPT3.5 zero shots and few shot prompting are 0.63 and 0.67.

Hyperparameters of all the models used excluding GPT3.5 in the experiments are available in Figure 4.

Parameter	Value
Learning Rate	$1e-5$
Train Batch Size	8
Test Batch Size	8
Epochs	5
Dropout	0.2

Table 4: Training Configuration Parameters

5 Results

The results in Tables 5, 6, and 7 provide a comprehensive evaluation of various NLP models across the three subtasks of the shared task.

In subtask A, our ensemble approach (Ensemble 2 with HATE-BERT, XLM-R and fBERT models) secures the fifth rank. For subtask B, BERTweet large secures the top position (Rank 1), while in subtask C, we achieve the sixth rank utilizing BERT-Base.

Model	Eval F1	Test F1
GPT3.5-(ZERO SHOT)	–	0.66
GPT3.5-(FEW SHOT)	–	0.73
HATE-BERT	0.88	0.83
BERTWEET-LARGE	0.89	0.84
XLM-R	0.89	0.85
F-BERT	0.90	0.85
*ENSEMBLE 1	0.90	0.85
**ENSEMBLE 2	0.91	0.86
HATE-BERT (AUG.)	0.91	0.87
BERTWEET-LARGE (AUG.)	0.92	0.87
XLM-R (AUG.)	0.91	0.88
F-BERT (AUG.)	0.93	0.88
*ENSEMBLE 1 (AUG.)	0.93	0.88
**ENSEMBLE 2 (AUG.)	0.94	**0.89**

Table 5: Results of subtask A (before and after data augmentation). *Ensemble 1 (BERTweet-large, XLM-R, fBERT), **Ensemble 2 (HATE-BERT, XLM-R, fBERT)

Model	Eval F1	Test F1
GPT3.5-(ZERO SHOT)	–	0.63
GPT3.5-(FEW SHOT)	–	0.64
XLM-R	0.75	0.60
BERT-BASE	0.86	0.69
BERTWEET-LARGE	0.97	**0.79**

Table 6: Results of subtask B.

Model	Eval F1	TEST F1
GPT3.5-(ZERO SHOT)	–	0.63
GPT3.5-(FEW SHOT)	–	0.67
BERT-BASE	0.71	0.69
BERTWEET-LARGE	0.71	0.70
BERTWEET-BASE	0.80	**0.74**

Table 7: Results of subtask C.

6 Error Analysis

Upon evaluating our models' performance across the three subtasks, we identify several key sources of errors that contributed to limiting our scores.

In subtask A on hate speech detection, our ensemble model struggles with longer text segments that express hate in subtle or nuanced ways. The models are not always able to pick up on the underlying mocking or criticism woven into complex rhetorical devices. Additionally, sarcasm and irony continue to pose challenges, as models interpret literally what is meant to convey the opposite meaning.

For subtask B on target identification, errors frequently occur in distinguishing between organizations and communities as categories. Our models have difficulty consistently applying the definitions and criteria that delineate these two groups as targets of hate speech. There are also inconsistencies in labeling individual people who are associated with or represent a broader community.

Regarding subtask C on stance detection, our models struggle to some extent with longer text segments, having more trouble identifying stances from among nuanced discussions. Shorter, more direct statements of opposition or support were simpler for the models to categorize accurately.

To visualize label-wise models' performance we can see the Figures 2, 3, and 4 of confusion matrices for all the subtasks.

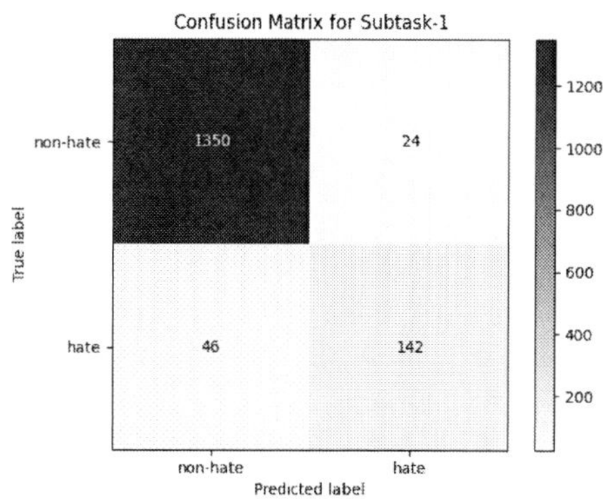

Figure 2: Confusion Matrix for Hate Speech Detection

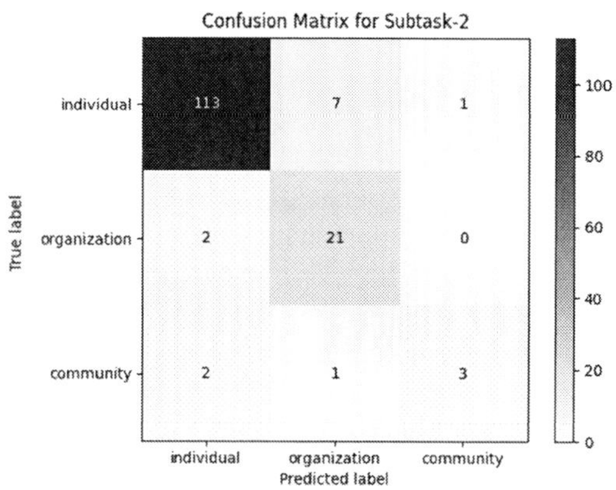

Figure 3: Confusion Matrix for Target Detection

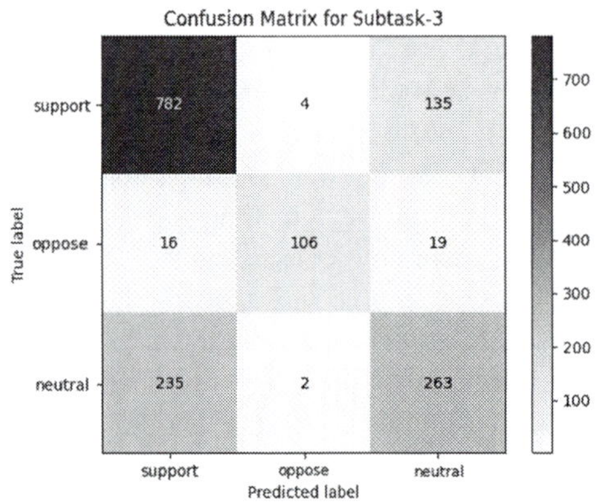

Figure 4: Confusion Matrix for Stance Detection

7 Conclusion

In conclusion, the *MasonPerplexity* team has made significant strides in the domain of detecting climate activism stances and hate events on social media. Through a comprehensive evaluation of various models, our research underscores the efficacy of ensemble modeling coupled with data augmentation techniques like back-translation. Our achievements in the shared task, marked by rankings of 5th, 1st, and 6th in the respective subtasks, reflect the potential of our methodologies in addressing the complexities of sentiment analysis in the context of climate activism.

There are several avenues for future research. Firstly, addressing the challenge of label imbalance in our dataset could enhance the accuracy and reliability of our models. Exploring advanced techniques in data sampling or synthetic data generation may provide viable solutions. Secondly, the refinement of label quality through more rigorous annotation processes or leveraging semi-supervised learning techniques could further improve model performance. Finally, the integration of Large Language Model (LLM) fine-tuning presents a promising direction. Fine-tuning pre-trained models specifically for the nuances of climate activism discourse and hate speech detection could yield more nuanced and contextually aware results. Additionally, expanding our research to include multilingual datasets would enhance the applicability and relevance of our findings in a global context, fostering a more comprehensive understanding of public sentiment on climate issues worldwide.

Limitations

This study encounters some limitations that affect its outcomes. The first issue is with the balance of labels in our dataset. We have more examples of some types of data than others, a problem known as label imbalance. This imbalance can lead our model to be better at recognizing the more common types and not as good with the rare ones, creating a bias in our results. The second limitation is the quality of the labels themselves. In our dataset, some labels are incorrect or not consistent with each other. This poor quality can confuse the model, making it harder for it to learn correctly and possibly leading to inaccurate results. Lastly, we did not fine-tune Large Language Models (LLMs) for our specific task. Fine-tuning is a process where a pre-trained model, like an LLM, is further trained on a specific type of data. Not doing this fine-tuning means we may not be taking full advantage of the LLM's capabilities, which can improve our model's understanding of complex patterns in climate activism and hate event data. However, due to a lack of computing resources, we are not fine-tuning.

Acknowledgment

We would like to thank the shared task organizers for providing us with the dataset used in our study. Moreover, we also want to express our gratitude to Dr. Marcos Zampieri for his effective guidelines throughout the span of the competition.

Ethics Statement

The present study, which centers on the identification of Climate Activism Stance and Hate Event, rigorously adheres to the ACL Ethics Policy and seeks to make a valuable contribution to the realm of online safety. The dataset is supplied to us by the organizers and has undergone anonymization to secure the privacy of the users. The technology in question possesses the potential to serve as a beneficial instrument for the moderation of online content, thereby facilitating the creation of safer digital environments. However, it is imperative to exercise caution and implement stringent regulations to prevent its potential misuse for purposes such as monitoring or censorship.

References

Tommaso Caselli, Valerio Basile, Jelena Mitrović, and Michael Granitzer. 2021. HateBERT: Retraining BERT for abusive language detection in English. In *Proceedings of the 5th Workshop on Online Abuse and Harms (WOAH 2021)*, pages 17–25, Online. Association for Computational Linguistics.

Alexis Conneau, Kartikay Khandelwal, Naman Goyal, Vishrav Chaudhary, Guillaume Wenzek, Francisco Guzmán, Edouard Grave, Myle Ott, Luke Zettlemoyer, and Veselin Stoyanov. 2019. Unsupervised cross-lingual representation learning at scale. *CoRR*, abs/1911.02116.

Jacob Devlin, Ming-Wei Chang, Kenton Lee, and Kristina Toutanova. 2018. BERT: pre-training of deep bidirectional transformers for language understanding. *CoRR*, abs/1810.04805.

Dhiman Goswami, Md Nishat Raihan, Sadiya Sayara Chowdhury Puspo, and Marcos Zampieri. 2023. nlpBDpatriots at BLP-2023 task 2: A transfer learning approach towards Bangla sentiment analysis. In *Proceedings of the First Workshop on Bangla Language Processing (BLP-2023)*, pages 286–292, Singapore. Association for Computational Linguistics.

Dilek Küçük and Fazli Can. 2021. Stance detection: Concepts, approaches, resources, and outstanding issues. In *Proceedings of the 44th International ACM SIGIR Conference on Research and Development in Information Retrieval*, SIGIR '21, page 2673–2676, New York, NY, USA. Association for Computing Machinery.

Dilek Küçük and Fazli Can. 2018. Stance detection on tweets: An svm-based approach. *CoRR*, abs/1803.08910.

Jens Lemmens, Ilia Markov, and Walter Daelemans. 2021. Improving hate speech type and target detection with hateful metaphor features. In *Proceedings of the Fourth Workshop on NLP for Internet Freedom: Censorship, Disinformation, and Propaganda*.

Shervin Malmasi and Marcos Zampieri. 2017. Detecting hate speech in social media. In *Proceedings of the International Conference Recent Advances in Natural Language Processing (RANLP)*, pages 467–472.

Dat Quoc Nguyen, Thanh Vu, and Anh Tuan Nguyen. 2020. BERTweet: A pre-trained language model for English Tweets. In *Proceedings of the 2020 Conference on Empirical Methods in Natural Language Processing: System Demonstrations*, pages 9–14.

OpenAI. 2023. Gpt-3.5 turbo fine-tuning and api updates. Accessed: 2023-08-28.

Anil Singh Parihar, Surendrabikram Thapa, and Sushruti Mishra. 2021. Hate speech detection using natural language processing: Applications and challenges. In *2021 5th International Conference on Trends in Electronics and Informatics (ICOEI)*, pages 1302–1308.

Georgios K. Pitsilis, Heri Ramampiaro, and Helge Langseth. 2018. Effective hate-speech detection in twitter data using recurrent neural networks. *Applied Intelligence*, 48:4730 – 4742.

Md Nishat Raihan, Dhiman Goswami, Sadiya Sayara Chowdhury Puspo, and Marcos Zampieri. 2023. nlpBDpatriots at BLP-2023 task 1: Two-step classification for violence inciting text detection in Bangla - leveraging back-translation and multilinguality. In *Proceedings of the First Workshop on Bangla Language Processing (BLP-2023)*, pages 179–184, Singapore. Association for Computational Linguistics.

Diptanu Sarkar, Marcos Zampieri, Tharindu Ranasinghe, and Alexander Ororbia. 2021. fbert: A neural transformer for identifying offensive content. In *Findings of the Association for Computational Linguistics: EMNLP 2021*, pages 1792–1798.

Shuvam Shiwakoti, Surendrabikram Thapa, Kritesh Rauniyar, Akshyat Shah, Aashish Bhandari, and Usman Naseem. 2024. Analyzing the dynamics of climate change discourse on twitter: A new annotated corpus and multi-aspect classification. *Preprint*.

Surendrabikram Thapa, Kritesh Rauniyar, Farhan Ahmad Jafri, Shuvam Shiwakoti, Hariram Veeramani, Raghav Jain, Guneet Singh Kohli, Ali Hürriyetoğlu, and Usman Naseem. 2024. Stance and hate event detection in tweets related to climate activism - shared task at case 2024. In *Proceedings of the 7th Workshop on Challenges and Applications of Automated Extraction of Socio-political Events from Text (CASE)*.

Apoorva Upadhyaya, Marco Fisichella, and Wolfgang Nejdl. 2023. Toxicity, morality, and speech act guided stance detection. In *Findings of the Association for Computational Linguistics: EMNLP 2023*, pages 4464–4478, Singapore. Association for Computational Linguistics.

Asahi Ushio and Jose Camacho-Collados. 2021a. T-NER: An all-round python library for transformer-based named entity recognition. In *Proceedings of the 16th Conference of the European Chapter of the Association for Computational Linguistics: System Demonstrations*, pages 53–62, Online. Association for Computational Linguistics.

Asahi Ushio and Jose Camacho-Collados. 2021b. T-NER: An all-round python library for transformer-based named entity recognition. In *Proceedings of the 16th Conference of the European Chapter of the Association for Computational Linguistics: System Demonstrations*, pages 53–62, Online. Association for Computational Linguistics.

Asahi Ushio, Leonardo Neves, Vitor Silva, Francesco. Barbieri, and Jose Camacho-Collados. 2022. Named Entity Recognition in Twitter: A Dataset and Analysis on Short-Term Temporal Shifts. In *The 2nd Conference of the Asia-Pacific Chapter of the Association for Computational Linguistics and the 12th*

International Joint Conference on Natural Language Processing, Online. Association for Computational Linguistics.

William Warner and Julia Hirschberg. 2012. Detecting hate speech on the world wide web. pages 19–26.

Marcos Zampieri, Shervin Malmasi, Preslav Nakov, Sara Rosenthal, Noura Farra, and Ritesh Kumar. 2019. Predicting the type and target of offensive posts in social media. In *Proceedings of the 2019 Conference of the North American Chapter of the Association for Computational Linguistics: Human Language Technologies, Volume 1 (Long and Short Papers)*.

AAST-NLP at Multimodal Hate Speech Event Detection 2024 : A Multimodal Approach for Classification of Text-Embedded Images Based on CLIP and BERT-Based Models.

Ahmed El-Sayed and **Omar Nasr**
Arab Academy For Science and Technology
{ahmedelsayedhabashy,omarnasr5206}@gmail.com

Abstract

With the rapid rise of social media platforms, communities have been able to share their passions and interests with the world much more conveniently. This, in turn, has led to individuals being able to spread hateful messages through the use of memes. The classification of such materials requires not only looking at the individual images but also considering the associated text in tandem. Looking at the images or the text separately does not provide the full context. In this paper, we describe our approach to hateful meme classification for the Multimodal Hate Speech Shared Task at CASE 2024. We utilized the same approach in the two subtasks, which involved a classification model based on text and image features obtained using Contrastive Language-Image Pre-training (CLIP) in addition to utilizing BERT-Based models. We then utilize predictions created by both models in an ensemble approach. This approach ranked second in both subtasks, respectively.

1 Introduction

Social media has become the biggest form of communication in recent years. However, with this rise comes an increase in the usage of hate speech to spread hostile and hateful messages. The effects of hate speech have been very apparent in recent years and have been demonstrated in multiple studies (Parihar et al., 2021). Some malicious entities have even been shown to use memes to create such hateful content. While these memes might seem humorous in nature, studies show that this use of humor to spread hateful messages creates hostile perceptions within the audience (Schmid, 2023). The use of machine learning and AI to combat this problem and classify these memes has been on the rise lately, with the collection of large amounts of data and the creation of datasets to support these tasks (Kiela et al., 2021). The use of such hateful attacks has been widespread and particularly evident in the Russia-Ukraine conflict, where both parties engaged in masquerading these attacks as memes. The Multimodal Hate Classification shared task at CASE 2024 (Thapa et al., 2024) focused on tackling this problem by providing a multimodal dataset primarily focused on this conflict (Bhandari et al., 2023). The rest of this paper is dedicated to our approach in the two subtasks provided in this shared task where we utilized CLIP (Radford et al., 2021) in conjunction with concatenation and a classification head to achieve second place on both subtasks. The following sections of the paper will include a related work section, a section describing the dataset, a section describing the system proposed, a discussion section and a conclusion.

2 Related Work

Research has extensively explored the application of AI in hate speech detection. However, fewer studies have delved into the use of multimodal data for classifying memes in these contexts. One notable study is (Pramanick et al., 2021), where they employed four different models for feature extraction, including CLIP, VGG-19 (Simonyan and Zisserman, 2015), and DistilBERT (Sanh et al., 2019), complemented by a CMAF fusion layer at the end. Another innovative approach was introduced by (Kumar and Nandakumar, 2022), presenting the HateClipper architecture. They utilized CLIP for feature extraction and implemented various fusion methods, such as alignment, concatenation, and cross fusion, resulting in promising outcomes. Additional methodologies were elucidated in (Cao et al., 2023), where researchers leveraged prompts and language models for classification. CASE 2023 featured a similar shared task (Thapa et al., 2023), with (Sahin et al., 2023) employing an ensemble of syntactical feature outputs passed into XGBOOST (Chen and Guestrin, 2016), coupled with encoder outputs, to achieve their noteworthy results.In recent times, researchers have presented datasets aimed at addressing this issue

Proceedings of the 7th Workshop on Challenges and Applications of Automated Extraction of Socio-political Events from Text (CASE 2024), pages 139–144
March 22, 2024

(Thapa et al., 2022; Bhandari et al., 2023). These datasets mark a significant advancement, providing researchers with valuable resources to more effectively confront the problem and explore various architectures. One Interesting approach is the one proposed by (Yang et al., 2022) which incorporated a multimodal backbone with three additional modules semantic adaptation module, definition adaptation module and domain adaptation module which boosted the performance significantly.

3 Dataset & Task

The Multimodal Hate Speech Event Detection challenge at CASE 2024 (Thapa et al., 2024)[1] encompasses two specific subtasks: Subtask A and B. The dataset makes use of the CrisisHateMM dataset (Bhandari et al., 2023) which is a collection of Text-Embedded Images of Directed and Undirected Hate Speech from Russia-Ukraine Conflict. The following subsections expand on each subtask highlighting the data distribution of each label. For the test labels, these labels remain undisclosed and are reserved for assessing the ultimate prediction performance, influencing the leaderboard rankings at the conclusion of the shared task.

3.1 Subtask A: Hate Speech Detection

The first subtask is a binary classification problem where tweets given are classified into two distinct classes: "Hate Speech" and "No Hate Speech". Table 1 illustrates the data distribution for the different classes within the dataset.

	Training	Validation
No Hate	1658	200
Hate	1942	243
Overall	3600	443

Table 1: Subtask A's Dataset Distribution.

3.2 Subtask B: Target Detection

The second subtask is a multiclass classification problem where tweets given are classified into three distinct classes: "Individual", "Organization", and "Community". Table 2 illustrates the data distribution for the different classes within the dataset.

[1]https://codalab.lisn.upsaclay.fr/competitions/16203

	Training	Validation
Individual	823	102
Organization	784	40
Community	335	102
Overall	1942	244

Table 2: Subtask B's Dataset Distribution.

3.3 Textual Data Extraction

The Google Vision API[2] was employed to extract textual information embedded in images. While the API demonstrates commendable accuracy and delivers high-quality results, its utilization is financially challenging for numerous researchers. This situation prompts the exploration of alternative tools such as various open-source Python packages or the creation of a comparable tool that maintains high quality but at a significantly lower cost.

3.4 Textual Data Preprocessing

Prior to being fed into the model, the text undergoes a rigorous preprocessing stage aimed at addressing various challenges related to the nature of social media data, where texts contain relatively high noise. This noise, if not properly handled, has the potential to adversely impact our classifier's performance. Therefore, the preprocessing stage is crucial in mitigating such adverse effects and ensuring the robustness of the model against the inherent noise in social media texts.

- Removal of punctuation as many tweets contained .
- Applying PySpellChecker[3] to check for misspelled words and correct them.
- Removal of hyperlinks as they did not meaning needed for our classification process.
- Removal of hashtags.

3.5 Visual Data Preprocessing

No preprocessing was applied to the images except for resizing them to dimensions of 224 x 224 pixels.

4 Methodology

In the following subsections, we will expand on the proposed models for each subtask, highlighting the reasoning behind each.

[2]https://cloud.google.com/vision
[3]https://pypi.org/project/pyspellchecker/

4.1 Language Models

Language Models were found to achieve state of the art performance on many tasks including ones related to hate speech detection. After examining existing literature on multimodal hate speech detection, we discovered that relying solely on textual features yielded commendable results, approaching those achieved by approaches incorporating multiple modalities (Singh et al., 2023; Aziz et al., 2023). Consequently, we opted to conduct experiments employing several pretrained language models, with a primary focus on HateBERT (Caselli et al., 2021), RoBERTa (Liu et al., 2019) and XLM-RoBERTa (Conneau et al., 2020).

4.2 Vision Models

After a thorough review of past literature, including research findings from last year's competition (Thapa et al., 2023) and various other sources, we have chosen not to investigate vision models on their own, as their performance on comparable tasks has been relatively subpar. Instead, our strategy entails conducting experiments with them as feature extractors within our multimodal framework. In the multimodal approach we adopted, we opted to employ ViT (Dosovitskiy et al., 2021) and Swin (Liu et al., 2021) as feature extractors.

4.3 Multimodal Approach

The multimodal approach comprises two main models that will be elucidated in the subsequent subsections.

4.3.1 Pairing Models

The initial approach aimed to harness the combined capabilities of vision and language models as this approach proved to beneficial in similar settings(Chen and Pan, 2022; Das et al., 2020). In the experiments, both language and vision models were employed as feature extractors without undergoing model finetuning. Subsequently, as part of the training procedure, both models were finetuned. The finetuned models yielded slightly higher results compared to the alternative. Throughout our exterminations, we experimented with pairing a number of models yet only 2 of them were used for submitting results through the official contest page as they mostly produced bad results. One important aspect to mention is the fact that our Swin + HateBERT model used the pretrained model weights without any further fintuning whilst the ViT + HateBERT model was fully fine tuned on the chosen dataset.

4.3.2 CLIP

State-of-the-art performances on numerous subtasks have been achieved by CLIP (Contrastive Language–Image Pre-training) (Radford et al., 2021). High results on comparable tasks were also observed (Kumar and Nandakumar, 2022). CLIP, functioning as both a textual and visual feature extractor, demonstrated extremely high performance on our task. We experimented with two types of fusion in case of of CLIP. Firstly, the concatenation of visual and textual features generated by CLIP was experimented with. Secondly, cross fusion for the same features was explored in which the extracted feature vectors had their outer product computed into a resulting matrix $R = p_t \otimes p_i$. Surprisingly, higher results were obtained by concatenating the features. A 3-layer classification head was implemented, utilizing RELU as its activation function.

4.4 Ensembling

Combining various models to enhance robustness, generalization, and predictive performance is a practice known as ensembling in machine learning. In our approach, hard voting is utilized, where predictions on a dataset are made by individual models within the ensemble, and the final prediction is determined through majority voting. Experiments were conducted involving the ensemble of top-k learners for each subtask, leading to the derivation of our predictions.

4.5 Experiment Settings

The training procedure was conducted using the Google Colab [4] platform for training our pipeline, which has 12.68 GB of RAM, a 14.75 GB NVIDIA Tesla T4 GPU, and Python language. Table 3 and Table 4 illustrate the hyperparameters used both in experimenting with CLIP and BERT-Based models.

5 Results

This section will expand on the result obtained through the usage of the aforementioned systems. For CLIP, HateBERT, Swin and ViT, we experimented with a variety of model sizes. Top-k Ensemble would then choose the highest k submissions to ensemble them.

[4]https://colab.google/

Hyperparameter	Value
Epochs	30
Learning Rate	2e-5
Batch Size	16
Max length	128
Optimizer	Adam
Early Stopping Patience	5
Reduce On Plateau	2
Loss Function	Dice Loss

Table 3: Training Hyperparameters for BERT-BASED.

Hyperparameter	Value
Epochs	10
Learning Rate	1e-5
Batch Size	16
Optimizer	Adam
Early Stopping Patience	5
Reduce On Plateau	2
Loss Function	Cross Entropy

Table 4: Training Hyperparameters for CLIP.

5.1 Subtask A

Table 5 illustrates the performance of the previously mentioned models on the test set. Text models demonstrated good outcomes, surpassing certain suggested multimodal models. Notably, CLIP outperforms all proposed models without requiring fine-tuning, presenting significant advantages in terms of training time. It is noteworthy that ensembling various models resulted in a marginal performance improvement, prompting inquiries about the effectiveness of an ensemble approach when compared to using only CLIP.

Model	Precision	Recall	F1-Score
RoBERTa	0.8243	0.8246	0.8245
HateBERT	0.8214	0.8186	0.8169
XLMRoBERTa	0.7676	0.7676	0.7676
Swin+HateBERT	0.7599	0.7576	0.7576
ViT+HateBERT	0.8161	0.8153	0.8157
CLIP (Cross)	0.8464	0.8448	0.8454
CLIP (Concat)	0.8546	**0.8540**	0.8543
Top-3 Ensemble	**0.8550**	0.8539	**0.8544**

Table 5: Results For Subtask A.

5.2 Subtask B

Table 6 illustrates the performance of the previously mentioned models on the test set, yet for this subtask out other multimodal approaches were not able to converge really well so unlike the first subtask they were not used for testing. Concatenating CLIP features outperformed all of its peers yet was beaten by ensembling top-3 performing models with a very small margin. This raises doubts about the effectiveness of the ensemble approach compared to utilizing only CLIP.

Model	Precision	Recall	F1-Score
RoBERTa	0.6832	0.7208	0.6960
HateBERT	0.6669	0.7479	0.6877
XLMRoBERTa	0.5866	0.5990	0.5910
CLIP (Cross)	0.7391	0.7372	0.7379
CLIP (Concat)	0.7465	0.8240	0.7671
Top-3 Ensemble	**0.7499**	**0.8273**	**0.7703**

Table 6: Results For Subtask B.

5.3 Leaderboard Results

During the evaluation phase of the shared task, we submitted our models for assessment on the test sets of both Subtask A and Subtask B. The outcomes of the tests are presented in Table 5 and Table 6, respectively. Our multimodal ensemble, which combines CLIP and BERT-based models, achieved the second place among the 7 participating teams in Subtask A. Similarly, the same model secured the second position among the 5 participating teams in Subtask B. One really intriguing direction is exploring explainable AI. In recent years, there has been a lot of approaches to explain the reasoning behind the model's predictions like Grad-Cam (Selvaraju et al., 2019), LIME(Ribeiro et al., 2016) and many others. (Chefer et al., 2021) proposed a technique for explaining transformer based models that could be adapted to our model, something that would further solidify our model's performance and open the door for many improvements as we may use such a technique for advanced error analysis.

6 Discussion & Future Work

The results obtained underscore the capability of CLIP in achieving promising outcomes for multimodal text-embedded image classification. These findings lay a robust groundwork for future research pursuits. One avenue worth investigating involves understanding the reasons behind the limited generalization of vision models on text-embedded images. In fact, an intriguing strategy is presented in (Pramanick et al., 2021), where image attributes are extracted instead of encoded features. Another compelling approach is to delve into language models with visual understanding, such as GPT-4.

7 Conclusion

This study outlines the endeavors of our team, "AAST-NLP," in addressing the pervasive issue of using text-embedded images for hate speech and propaganda. However, it is important to note that text-embedded images also have the potential to be utilized for positive purposes. Despite their potential for misuse, as observed during the Russia-Ukraine war, the identification and mitigation of such instances are crucial, particularly in times of prolonged conflict. Our solution makes use of ensembling via hard voting based on CLIP and BERT-Based models. Our model has the potential to be used in lots of aspects as a result of its relatively high performance on both subtasks.

References

Abdul Aziz, MD. Akram Hossain, and Abu Nowshed Chy. 2023. CSECU-DSG@multimodal hate speech event detection 2023: Transformer-based multimodal hierarchical fusion model for multimodal hate speech detection. In *Proceedings of the 6th Workshop on Challenges and Applications of Automated Extraction of Socio-political Events from Text*, pages 101–107, Varna, Bulgaria. INCOMA Ltd., Shoumen, Bulgaria.

Aashish Bhandari, Siddhant Bikram Shah, Surendrabikram Thapa, Usman Naseem, and Mehwish Nasim. 2023. Crisishatemm: Multimodal analysis of directed and undirected hate speech in text-embedded images from russia-ukraine conflict. In *Proceedings of the IEEE/CVF Conference on Computer Vision and Pattern Recognition*.

Rui Cao, Roy Ka-Wei Lee, Wen-Haw Chong, and Jing Jiang. 2023. Prompting for multimodal hateful meme classification.

Tommaso Caselli, Valerio Basile, Jelena Mitrović, and Michael Granitzer. 2021. Hatebert: Retraining bert for abusive language detection in english.

Hila Chefer, Shir Gur, and Lior Wolf. 2021. Generic attention-model explainability for interpreting bimodal and encoder-decoder transformers.

Tianqi Chen and Carlos Guestrin. 2016. Xgboost: A scalable tree boosting system. In *Proceedings of the 22nd ACM SIGKDD International Conference on Knowledge Discovery and Data Mining*, KDD '16. ACM.

Yuyang Chen and Feng Pan. 2022. Multimodal detection of hateful memes by applying a vision-language pre-training model. *PLOS ONE*, 17(9):e0274300.

Alexis Conneau, Kartikay Khandelwal, Naman Goyal, Vishrav Chaudhary, Guillaume Wenzek, Francisco Guzmán, Edouard Grave, Myle Ott, Luke Zettlemoyer, and Veselin Stoyanov. 2020. Unsupervised cross-lingual representation learning at scale.

Abhishek Das, Japsimar Singh Wahi, and Siyao Li. 2020. Detecting hate speech in multi-modal memes. *arXiv (Cornell University)*.

Alexey Dosovitskiy, Lucas Beyer, Alexander Kolesnikov, Dirk Weissenborn, Xiaohua Zhai, Thomas Unterthiner, Mostafa Dehghani, Matthias Minderer, Georg Heigold, Sylvain Gelly, Jakob Uszkoreit, and Neil Houlsby. 2021. An image is worth 16x16 words: Transformers for image recognition at scale.

Douwe Kiela, Hamed Firooz, Aravind Mohan, Vedanuj Goswami, Amanpreet Singh, Pratik Ringshia, and Davide Testuggine. 2021. The hateful memes challenge: Detecting hate speech in multimodal memes.

Gokul Karthik Kumar and Karthik Nandakumar. 2022. Hate-clipper: Multimodal hateful meme classification based on cross-modal interaction of clip features.

Yinhan Liu, Myle Ott, Naman Goyal, Jingfei Du, Mandar Joshi, Danqi Chen, Omer Levy, Mike Lewis, Luke Zettlemoyer, and Veselin Stoyanov. 2019. Roberta: A robustly optimized bert pretraining approach.

Ze Liu, Yutong Lin, Yue Cao, Han Hu, Yixuan Wei, Zheng Zhang, Stephen Lin, and Baining Guo. 2021. Swin transformer: Hierarchical vision transformer using shifted windows.

Anil Singh Parihar, Surendrabikram Thapa, and Sushruti Mishra. 2021. Hate speech detection using natural language processing: Applications and challenges. In *2021 5th International Conference on Trends in Electronics and Informatics (ICOEI)*, pages 1302–1308.

Shraman Pramanick, Shivam Sharma, Dimitar Dimitrov, Md Shad Akhtar, Preslav Nakov, and Tanmoy Chakraborty. 2021. Momenta: A multimodal framework for detecting harmful memes and their targets.

Alec Radford, Jong Wook Kim, Chris Hallacy, Aditya Ramesh, Gabriel Goh, Sandhini Agarwal, Girish Sastry, Amanda Askell, Pamela Mishkin, Jack Clark, Gretchen Krueger, and Ilya Sutskever. 2021. Learning transferable visual models from natural language supervision.

Marco Tulio Ribeiro, Sameer Singh, and Carlos Guestrin. 2016. "why should i trust you?": Explaining the predictions of any classifier.

Umitcan Sahin, Izzet Emre Kucukkaya, Oguzhan Ozcelik, and Cagri Toraman. 2023. Arc-nlp at multimodal hate speech event detection 2023: Multimodal methods boosted by ensemble learning, syntactical and entity features.

Victor Sanh, Lysandre Debut, Julien Chaumond, and Thomas Wolf. 2019. Distilbert, a distilled version of bert: smaller, faster, cheaper and lighter. *ArXiv*, abs/1910.01108.

Ursula Kristin Schmid. 2023. Humorous hate speech on social media: A mixed-methods investigation of users' perceptions and processing of hateful memes. *New Media Society*.

Ramprasaath R. Selvaraju, Michael Cogswell, Abhishek Das, Ramakrishna Vedantam, Devi Parikh, and Dhruv Batra. 2019. Grad-CAM: Visual Explanations from Deep Networks via Gradient-Based Localization. *International Journal of Computer Vision*, 128(2):336–359.

Karen Simonyan and Andrew Zisserman. 2015. Very deep convolutional networks for large-scale image recognition. In *International Conference on Learning Representations*.

Karanpreet Singh, Vajratiya Vajrobol, and Nitisha Aggarwal. 2023. IIC_Team@multimodal hate speech event detection 2023: Detection of hate speech and targets using xlm-roberta-base. In *Proceedings of the 6th Workshop on Challenges and Applications of Automated Extraction of Socio-political Events from Text*, pages 136–143, Varna, Bulgaria. INCOMA Ltd., Shoumen, Bulgaria.

Surendrabikram Thapa, Farhan Jafri, Ali Hürriyetoğlu, Francielle Vargas, Roy Ka-Wei Lee, and Usman Naseem. 2023. Multimodal hate speech event detection - shared task 4, CASE 2023. In *Proceedings of the 6th Workshop on Challenges and Applications of Automated Extraction of Socio-political Events from Text*, pages 151–159, Varna, Bulgaria. INCOMA Ltd., Shoumen, Bulgaria.

Surendrabikram Thapa, Kritesh Rauniyar, Farhan Ahmad Jafri, Hariram Veeramani, Raghav Jain, Sandesh Jain, Francielle Vargas, Ali Hürriyetoğlu, and Usman Naseem. 2024. Extended multimodal hate speech event detection during russia-ukraine crisis - shared task at case 2024. In *Proceedings of the 7th Workshop on Challenges and Applications of Automated Extraction of Socio-political Events from Text (CASE)*.

Surendrabikram Thapa, Aditya Shah, Farhan Jafri, Usman Naseem, and Imran Razzak. 2022. A multimodal dataset for hate speech detection on social media: Case-study of russia-Ukraine conflict. In *Proceedings of the 5th Workshop on Challenges and Applications of Automated Extraction of Socio-political Events from Text (CASE)*, pages 1–6, Abu Dhabi, United Arab Emirates (Hybrid). Association for Computational Linguistics.

Chuanpeng Yang, Fuqing Zhu, Guihua Liu, Jizhong Han, and Songiln Hu. 2022. Multimodal hate speech detection via Cross-Domain knowledge transfer. *Proceedings of the 30th ACM International Conference on Multimedia*.

CUET_Binary_Hackers at ClimateActivism 2024: A Comprehensive Evaluation and Superior Performance of Transformer-based Models in Hate Speech Event Detection and Stance Classification for Climate Activism

Salman Farsi, Asrarul Hoque Eusha and Mohammad Shamsul Arefin
Department of Computer Science and Engineering
Chittagong University of Engineering & Technology, Chattogram-4349, Bangladesh
{salman.cuet.cse, asrar2860}@gmail.com, sarefin@cuet.ac.bd

Abstract

The escalating impact of climate change on our environment and lives has spurred a global surge in climate change activism. However, the misuse of social media platforms like Twitter has opened the door to the spread of hatred against activism, targeting individuals, organizations, or entire communities. Also, the identification of the stance in a tweet holds paramount significance, especially in the context of understanding the success of activism. So, to address the challenge of detecting such hate tweets, identifying their targets, and classifying stances from tweets, this shared task introduced three sub-tasks, each aiming to address exactly one mentioned issue. We participated in all three sub-tasks and in this paper, we showed a comparative analysis between the different machine learning (ML), deep learning (DL), hybrid, and transformer-based models. Our approach involved proper hyper-parameter tuning of models and effectively handling class imbalance datasets through data oversampling. Notably, our fine-tuned m-BERT achieved a macro-average $f1$ score of 0.91 in sub-task A (Hate Speech Detection) and 0.74 in sub-task B (Target Identification). On the other hand, Climate-BERT achieved a $f1$ score of 0.67 in sub-task C. These scores positioned us at the forefront, securing 1st, 6th, and 15th ranks in the respective sub-tasks. The detailed implementation information for the tasks is available in the GitHub [1].

1 Introduction

Over the decades, climate change has evolved into a pressing issue for nature and all Earth's species, with alarming consequences. Reports from the Intergovernmental Panel on Climate Change (IPCC) confirm that climate change is resulting in more frequent and severe weather events, including heatwaves, droughts, and floods [2]. These events can lead to crop failures, food shortages, displacement of people, melting of glaciers and ice caps, rising sea levels, and increased coastal flooding.

Preserving a harmonious climate is vital for ensuring balanced ecosystems, optimal temperature conditions, and biodiversity (Weiskopf et al., 2020; Mikhaylov et al., 2020). This urgent issue has spurred people worldwide to voice their concerns and participate in a growing number of climate change activism events on a global scale (Damoah et al., 2023). These events aim to raise awareness about the impact of climate change and the urgent need for action. One such prominent movement is 'FridayForFuture' (FFF), initiated by Greta Thunberg, a Swedish schoolgirl, in August 2018, to exert pressure on policymakers to take necessary actions against climate change (Spaiser et al., 2022; Neas et al., 2022). Other notable climate activism movements, including 'Extinction Rebellion', 'Earth Strike', and 'Climate Justice Now', have further fueled the global movement against climate change (Gunningham, 2019; Schlosberg and Collins, 2014; Laux, 2021).

However, contemporary activism extends beyond street protests to online platforms, with social media users expressing their thoughts on climate movements through tweets and comments. But some people share hateful, aggressive, and humorous tweets targeting activism (Thapa et al., 2024). Hate speech not only undermines the objectives of activism but also poses a threat to the well-being of individuals, organizations, and communities involved in the movement (Arce-García et al., 2023). Whereas stance detection in text is also a vital component in assessing the dynamics of protests and activism. It helps understand whether activist movements and protests are being supported or opposed (Shiwakoti et al., 2024). Despite numerous studies conducted in recent years on identifying hate speech and its targets in social media text, this context in climate activism remains an under-explored

[1] https://github.com/Salman1804102/CASE-EACL-2024
[2] https://www.ipcc.ch/report/ar6/wg1/chapter/chapter-11/

Proceedings of the 7th Workshop on Challenges and Applications of Automated Extraction of Socio-political Events from Text (CASE 2024), pages 145–155
March 22, 2024 ©2024 Association for Computational Linguistics

domain (Parihar, Anil Singh and Thapa, Surendrabikram and Mishra, Sushruti, 2021; MacAvaney et al., 2019; Kovács et al., 2021). As these events serve as crucial platforms for promoting environmental awareness and policy changes, there is a need for a comprehensive understanding of the stance and mitigation strategy for hateful tweets. As contributors to this endeavor, our principal contributions are delineated below:

- We introduced and advocated for the utilization of BERT models by effectively handling the class imbalance data, leveraging their capabilities to classify textual content.
- By delving into diverse methodologies, we seek to provide valuable insights that can inform the development of more robust systems for addressing the intricacies of climate activism events on social media platforms.

The later part of the paper is organized as follows: Section 3 provides the task and dataset description, Section 4 outlines the methodology, Section 5 presents the result analysis, and Section 6 delves into error analysis for each task. Lastly, Section 7 encapsulates the conclusion.

2 Related Work

2.1 Hate Speech Detection

Over time, numerous research efforts have been dedicated to the detection and classification of hate speech, employing various methodologies. In an earlier study (Malmasi and Zampieri, 2017), a machine-learning approach was adopted, utilizing an SVM classifier with lexical features on a dataset comprising 14,509 English tweets. The results indicated a 78% accuracy using the 4-gram model. The exploration of machine learning methods continued in another study (Davidson et al., 2017), where Logistic Regression (LR) outperformed Naïve Bayes (NB), Decision Tree (DT), and Random Forest (RF) in identifying hate speech within a Twitter-based hate speech datasets.

As the popularity of deep learning algorithms grew, Zhang and Luo (2019) aimed to enhance the semantic understanding of hate speech. They introduced a CNN+(skipped-CNN) model, which showcased better performance compared to the CNN+GRU model across various publicly available Twitter datasets. Another deep learning-based study (Badjatiya et al., 2017) combined embeddings learned from LSTM with gradient-boosting decision trees, which achieved a higher $f1$ score of 93% in hate speech detection. The study also involved a comparative analysis utilizing various feature extraction methods such as character n-grams, word n-grams, fastText, GloVe, and Bag-of-words for LR, DT, and SVM. However, with the advent of transformer-based models like BERT, research trends shifted towards leveraging these models due to their capability to capture intricate semantic meanings in textual context. Mozafari et al. (2020) proposed BERT+LSTM, BERT+CNN, and BERT+Nonlinear-layers models for hate speech detection. Their BERT+CNN architecture demonstrated $f1$ scores of 88% and 92% for the Waseem (Waseem and Hovy, 2016) and Davidson (Davidson et al., 2019) hate datasets.

2.2 Hate Speech Target Identification

In the realm of hate speech target classification, researchers have extended their focus beyond merely detecting hate speech to the classification of hate speech targets. The study (Kurniawan and Budi, 2020) employed a labeled dataset of hate tweets in Indonesia, distinguishing between individual and group-targeted hate. Their work utilized word n-grams, Bag-of-words, and TF-IDF for machine learning models. Ultimately, the findings revealed that SVM surpassed NB and RF, achieving an impressive $f1$ score of 0.84772 with TF-IDF. In another work, (Shvets et al., 2021) entailed fine-tuning a semi-supervised concept extraction model by incorporating weight variables for hate target classification. Additionally, the author implemented a domain adaptation phase to detect targets and associated aspects in both the 'sexism' and 'racism' categories of the hate speech dataset.

2.3 Textual Stance Classification (TSC)

Various studies have delved into the classification of stance in text data across different domains, driven by the necessity to comprehend the dynamics within specific contexts, movements, and issues. The author (Upadhyaya et al., 2023) introduced MEMOCLiC, a multimodal multitasking framework for comprehensive stance detection in tweets. MEMOCLiC utilizes diverse embedding techniques and attention frameworks, incorporating learned emotional and offensive expressions. With a primary focus on stance detection, there were secondary tasks including emotion recognition and offensive language identification. The author's evaluation on climate change and benchmark datasets highlights a notable $f1$ score of 93.76%.

In this TSC scheme, another study (Vaid et al., 2022) focused on addressing climate change concerns through the development of a stance detection and fine-grained classification system for related social media text. The study delved into linguistic features using part-of-speech tagging and named entity recognition. Two English datasets, ClimateStance and ClimateEng, each containing 3,777 annotated tweets, were introduced. State-of-the-art models like BERT, RoBERTa, and Distil-BERT are utilized for benchmarking.

3 Task and Dataset Description

The shared task encompasses three distinct subtasks: sub-task A, focusing on hate speech detection; sub-task B, centered around target detection; and sub-task C, concentrating on stance detection (Thapa et al., 2024). The organizers introduced a dataset called ClimaConvo (Shiwakoti et al., 2024), comprising 15,309 tweets related to various climate movements. Sub-tasks A, B, and C utilized subsets of this dataset.

3.1 Sub-Task A: Hate Speech Detection

This problem involves binary classification with two annotated labels: 'hate' and 'non-hate'. The dataset comprises a total of 7,284 training samples, 1,561 validation samples, and 1,562 test samples. The labels were encoded to 1 ('non-hate') and 2 ('hate').

3.2 Sub-Task B: Target Detection

Sub-task B is specifically focused on identifying targets in hate speech. The dataset dedicated to this sub-task consists of 699 training samples, along with 150 samples each for validation and testing. There are three classes in this dataset, these are 'individual', 'organization', and 'community'. The labels were encoded to 1 ('individual'), 2 ('organization'), and 3 ('community').

3.3 Sub-Task C: Stance Detection

The last sub-task revolves around identifying the stance in a given text, classifying it as 'support', 'oppose', and 'neutral'. This is particularly valuable for discerning whether activism is being supported or opposed by individuals. The dataset for subtask C comprises of 7,284 training samples, 1,561 validation samples, and 1,562 test samples. The labels were encoded to 1 ('support'), 2 ('oppose'), and 3 ('neutral').

However, the dataset details are presented in Tables 1 and 2.

Tasks	Class	Initial	Duplicate Samples Removal	After sampling
Task A	1	6,385	5,899	5,899
	2	899	543	4,000
Task B	1	563	61	105
	2	105	105	105
	3	31	31	105
Task C	1	4,328	4,105	4,328
	2	700	190	2,000
	3	2,256	2,115	4,105

Table 1: Number of training samples per class after oversampling, considering the initial distribution and subsequent removal of duplicate entries.

4 Methodology

In this section, we delineate our methodology step by step. Figure 1 depicts a visual representation of the methodology.

4.1 Preprocessing of Data

Initially, we cleaned the provided dataset for all three sets—training, validation, and test. Employing a manually defined procedure using the Python regular expression library 're', we removed URLs, emojis, digits, and punctuation from the text. After that, we employed spaCy's [3] lemmatization by utilizing the English language model 'en_core_web_sm'. Considering that stopwords may not always be essential for classification and given the higher average length of the text, we removed stopwords using NLTK's [4] package 'stopwords' (Jefriyanto et al., 2023).

4.2 Duplicate Samples Removal from Dataset

To strengthen the instances of class 'hate' in subtask A, samples from sub-task B were combined with sub-task A, labeling them as 'hate'. It was possible to do so because all the samples in sub-task B correspond to hate tweets targeting a specific audience. Samples of 'hate' class increased to 1,898, while 'non-hate' class samples remained at 6,385 after concatenation. However, the sub-tasks A, B, and C contain 1,008, 49, and 874 duplicate samples, which were removed eventually.

[3]https://spacy.io/

[4]https://www.nltk.org/

Task	Class	Train				Dev				Test			
		SC	TW	UW	AL	SC	TW	UW	AL	SC	TW	UW	AL
Task A	1	5,899	10,343	12,521	155	1,371	23,820	5,178	17	1,374	23,603	5,278	17
	2	543	10,211	3,157		190	2,962	970		188	3,171	1,078	
Task B	1	61	1,213	738		120	1,595	261		121	1,573	200	
	2	105	2,166	1,142	169	23	472	330	15	23	500	367	15
	3	31	588	407		7	181	154		6	130	112	
Task C	1	4,105	74,452	10,513		897	16,365	4,226		921	16,364	4,238	
	2	190	3,530	1,657	156	153	2,177	587	18	141	2,005	538	17
	3	2,115	37,360	7,463		511	88,857	3,048		500	8,405	2,772	

Table 2: Overall statistics of the dataset after the removal of duplicate entries. Here, SC, TW, UW, and AL denote sample count, total words, unique words, and average length, respectively.

4.3 Data Oversampling

This section is crucial as all tasks face a class imbalance issue, requiring an effective class distribution handling strategy for an improved $f1$ score. In all the sub-tasks, random oversampling (Gosain and Sardana, 2017) was employed to address the imbalance and enhance the model's ability to learn minority class patterns. While doing oversampling, careful consideration was given to the class distribution scenario after duplicate samples removal. It ensured a balanced approach by not oversampling a particular class too much, especially one with a very low distribution, and avoided the potential loss of focus on the majority class. The number of training samples after oversampling is provided in Table 1.

4.4 Extraction of Features

We employed various feature extraction methods, namely TF-IDF and Word2Vec for machine learning, fastText and GloVe for deep learning models.

TF-IDF is a numerical statistic indicating the importance of a term within a document relative to its occurrence across the entire dataset. For TF-IDF, we employed the default character n-gram as the analyzer.

Word2Vec embeddings (Mikolov et al., 2013) were generated using the 'en_core_web_sm' model in spaCy. Word2Vec is a popular technique for mapping words to dense vectors in a continuous vector space.

fastText embeddings with 300 dimensions were used for training DL models. fastText, an extension of Word2Vec, represents words as bags of character n-grams, enabling it to capture subword information, especially effective for morphologically rich languages and handling out-of-vocabulary words (Bojanowski et al., 2017).

GloVe constructs word vectors based on global statistical information of word co-occurrences across the entire corpus, capturing comprehensive semantic relationships for word meanings (Pennington et al., 2014). 'Glove.twitter.27B.100d' model was utilized as GloVe embedding, leveraging 100-dimensional word embeddings.

4.5 Machine Learning Models

Our exploration into ML model selection commenced with the consideration of four prominent models: RF, LR, SVM, and Multinomial Naive Bayes (MNB) (Sarker, 2021). These models have demonstrated superior performance in text classification tasks, motivating our choice. However, identifying optimal hyperparameters is critical, given their substantial impact on model performance. To address this challenge, we conducted a systematic search to determine the most suitable parameters for each model.

Model	Hyper-parameters
RF	n_estimators = 1000, min_samples_split = 2 min_samples_leaf = 1
MNB	alpha = 0.1, fit_prior = true, class_prior = false
SVM	C = 1, kernel = 'linear'
LR	solver = 'liblinear', penalty = 'l2'

Table 3: ML model's hyperparameter setting.

4.6 Deep Learning Models

In the development of text classification models, diverse deep learning architectures were investigated to tackle the intricacies of the task.

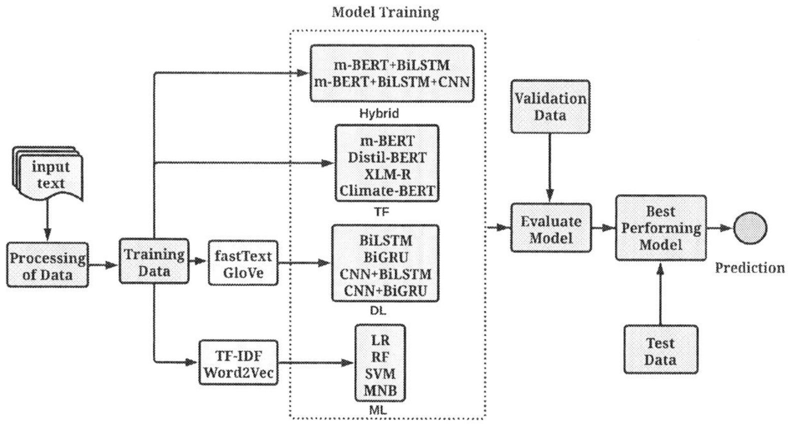

Figure 1: Visual representation of methodology.

BiLSTM: The initial model, employing a Bidirectional Long Short-Term Memory (**BiLSTM**) (Kalchbrenner et al., 2015) layer, served as the foundation. It featured a 100-dimensional embedding layer initialized with pre-trained word embeddings, a BiLSTM layer with 64 units for sequential data processing, followed by flattening and dense layers with dropout for regularization. This architecture laid the groundwork for subsequent models.

BiLSTM+CNN: The second model expanded on the BiLSTM design by integrating Convolutional Neural Network (CNN) components to make a hybrid BiLSTM+CNN model (Gehring et al., 2017). Additional Conv1D and MaxPooling1D layers were introduced to capture local features, enhancing the model's ability to discern patterns within the data.

CNN+GRU: The third model adopted another hybrid approach, combining CNN and Gated Recurrent Unit (GRU) layers to make CNN+GRU (Gehring et al., 2016). A Conv1D layer with 128 filters and a kernel size of 5 was followed by max-pooling, enhancing feature extraction. The bidirectional GRU (BiGRU) layer with 64 units provided a nuanced understanding of sequential dependencies. The model incorporated dense layers with dropout for regularization and concluded with an output layer.

BiGRU: The final model leveraged Bidirectional GRU (Cho et al., 2014) layers exclusively. It featured a 300-dimensional embedding layer, BiGRU with 256 units, and subsequent dense layers leading to an output layer. All the models underwent some common hyperparameters, which are shown in Table 4.

Parameters	Value
Learning Rate	$1e^{-3}$
Optimizer	Adam
Batch Size	32
AF(Hidden Layer)	Relu
AF(Output Layer)	Sigmoid (task A) Softmax (task B & C)
Dropout Rate	0.2

Table 4: DL model's hyperparameter setting, AF denotes the Activation Function.

4.7 Transformer-based Models

We conducted experiments using four pre-trained transformer-based models: m-BERT (Devlin et al., 2019), Distil-BERT (Sanh et al., 2019), XLM-R (Conneau et al., 2020), and Climate-BERT (Webersinke et al., 2021). To optimize training, we leveraged the 'fitonecycle' method from the ktrain library (Maiya, 2022). Prior to model training, we employed the 'find' method to visualize the learning rate curve, aiding in the identification of the optimal learning rate for each transformer-based model. Consequently, the learning rates and epochs varied among the models. Due to the substantial

Models	LR	Epochs	Batch Size	Max Length
m-BERT	$3e^{-5}$	10	16	256
Distil-BERT	$3e^{-5}$	12	16	
XLM-R	$2e^{-5}$	10	8	
Climate-BERT	$3e^{-5}$	10	16	

Table 5: Transformer-based model's hyperparameter setting. Here LR means Learning Rate.

volume of words and text size in tasks A and B, we adjusted the batch size accordingly, particularly for models such as XLM-R, ensuring efficient processing of the extensive textual data. We imported the transformer-based models from the 'Hugging Face' (Wolf et al., 2019). The detailed parameter settings are given in Table 5.

4.8 Hybrid Models

We experimented with BERT embedding by proposing two hybrid models. We considered m-BERT+BiLSTM (Jia, 2023) and m-BERT+BiLSTM+CNN (Mustavi Maheen et al., 2022) models. Figure 2 shows the overview of the hybrid models for both BiLSTM and BiLSTM+CNN utilizing BERT embedding.

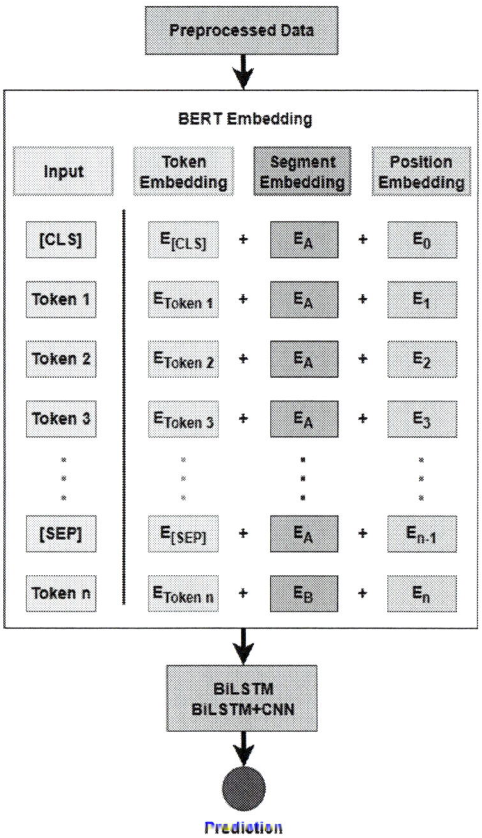

Figure 2: Overview of hybrid models.

m-BERT+BiLSTM: The first model integrates BERT embeddings, Bidirectional LSTM, and pooling layers for text classification. BERT embeddings are subject to dropout regularization and reshaped into a 3D tensor. A Bidirectional LSTM layer captures sequential context, while global pooling extracts key features. These pooled outputs are concatenated and processed through dense layers with ReLU activation and dropout. The final layer utilizes an activation function for ultimate prediction. This architecture leverages BERT's contextual embeddings and Bidirectional LSTM's sequential learning for enhanced text classification.

m-BERT+BiLSTM+CNN: The second model, combines BERT embeddings, Bidirectional LSTM, and a Convolutional Neural Network (CNN) to capture diverse contextual and sequential patterns in the input text. BERT embeddings undergo dropout regularization, followed by reshaping and processing through a bidirectional LSTM and a 1D CNN layer. Global average pooling, global max pooling, and flattened CNN outputs are concatenated. Two dense layers with dropout provide additional abstraction, leading to an output layer. This architecture aims to leverage the strengths of BERT embeddings, LSTM, and CNN to enhance the model's ability to discern patterns in sequential data for accurate classification. The parameter setting remains the same as the parameter settings for DL models (see Table 4).

5 Results and Analysis

In this section, we delve into a comprehensive comparative analysis of our proposed models across all three sub-tasks. Table 6 presents such a comprehensive evaluation.

5.1 Sub-Task A

In sub-task A, RF with Word2Vec demonstrated superior efficiency in achieving a higher $f1$ score compared to the TF-IDF counterpart. It outperformed all other ML models with a notable $f1$ score of 0.89. Even though several ML models performed almost nearly well, the MNB appeared to perform poorly on non-oversampled data. MNB struggled to handle class imbalance and due to the lack of minority class instances ('hate'), it is classifying all the samples into 'non-hate'. Among DL models, the hybrid CNN+BiGRU with GloVe embedding attained an impressive $f1$ score of 0.91 even before oversampling. As GloVe utilized global statistical information by offering improved representation of word meanings, the CNN+BiGRU model took benefit of this. It also performed better with fastText embedding as well. For transformer-based models, m-BERT excelled with a $f1$ score of 0.91, which was similar to CNN+BiGRU (GloVe). Its performance before

FET	Models	Without Oversampling						With Oversampling					
		Task A		Task B		Task C		Task A		Task B		Task C	
		$f1$	Acc	$f1$	Acc	$f1$	Acc	$f1$	Acc	$f1$	Acc	$f1$	Acc
TF-IDF	RF	0.81	0.91	0.56	0.88	**0.67**	0.69	0.80	0.92	**0.69**	0.89	0.28	0.68
	LR	0.83	0.91	**0.65**	0.91	0.65	0.91	0.85	0.93	0.59	0.87	**0.39**	0.64
	SVM	**0.86**	0.95	0.63	0.89	0.63	0.89	**0.88**	0.95	0.63	0.89	**0.39**	0.63
	MNB	0.47	0.88	0.56	0.88	0.56	0.88	0.83	0.91	0.66	0.89	0.34	0.62
Word2Vec	RF	**0.89**	0.95	0.54	0.87	0.54	0.87	**0.88**	0.94	0.67	0.86	0.53	0.64
	LR	0.73	0.83	0.70	0.89	**0.67**	0.88	0.72	0.83	0.70	0.89	0.55	0.57
	SVM	0.86	0.95	**0.71**	0.89	**0.67**	0.89	0.72	0.83	**0.71**	0.89	**0.56**	0.59
	MNB	0.47	0.87	0.54	0.87	0.55	0.87	0.71	0.84	**0.71**	0.89	0.27	0.60
GloVe	BiLSTM	0.87	0.95	**0.61**	0.87	0.65	0.65	0.47	0.88	**0.63**	0.86	0.66	0.67
	BiGRU	0.90	0.96	0.53	0.88	**0.66**	0.69	**0.80**	0.89	**0.63**	0.89	**0.67**	0.68
	BiLSTM+CNN	0.87	0.95	0.58	0.88	0.64	0.65	0.47	0.88	0.57	0.85	0.63	0.63
	CNN+BiGRU	**0.91**	0.96	**0.61**	0.87	0.59	0.67	0.47	0.88	0.51	0.82	0.66	0.68
fastText	BiLSTM	0.56	0.86	0.54	0.83	0.56	0.61	0.56	0.86	0.56	0.87	0.64	0.65
	BiGRU	0.70	0.81	0.57	0.85	0.60	0.61	0.70	0.81	0.59	0.87	0.64	0.64
	BiLSTM+CNN	0.85	0.92	**0.62**	0.88	0.63	0.65	0.84	0.92	**0.68**	0.87	**0.66**	0.66
	CNN+BiGRU	**0.90**	0.95	0.59	0.83	**0.64**	0.67	**0.90**	0.95	0.65	0.88	**0.66**	0.66
	m-BERT	**0.91**	0.96	0.64	0.86	0.63	0.62	**0.91**	0.96	**0.74**	0.89	0.66	0.65
	Distil-BERT	0.88	0.95	**0.65**	0.85	0.62	0.64	0.86	0.94	**0.74**	0.89	**0.67**	0.65
	XLM-R	0.82	0.93	0.63	0.85	0.60	0.62	0.88	0.88	0.70	0.88	0.65	0.69
	Climate-BERT	0.90	0.96	0.63	0.88	**0.67**	0.71	**0.91**	0.96	0.71	0.89	**0.67**	0.68
	m-BERT+BiLSTM	**0.83**	0.94	**0.54**	0.87	0.25	0.59	**0.73**	0.85	0.53	0.86	0.25	0.59
	m-BERT+BiLSTM+CNN	0.66	0.77	0.48	0.82	**0.31**	0.61	0.31	0.32	0.50	0.85	**0.62**	0.62

Table 6: Result comparison over test data. Here FET means feature extraction technique, $f1$ denotes macro-averaged $f1$ score and Acc means Accuracy.

and after oversampling remains the same. Finally, m-BERT and CNN+BiGRU (GloVe) embedding were identified as the best-performing models for this sub-task.

5.2 Sub-Task B

Turning to the sub-task B, m-BERT and Distil-BERT exhibited identical $f1$ scores of 0.74 in the oversampled dataset. Which suggests a very crucial improvement after increasing minority classes. Due to the increased number of samples, the BERT models were able to effectively identify the semantic and contextual meaning of the tweets rigorously. But interestingly the hybrid model with BERT embedding underperformed, even trailing behind some ML and DL models. The BERT's complex pre-trained architecture didn't provide substantial benefits compared to other embeddings like GloVe and fastText. ML models showed improved performance after oversampling. SVM and MNB achieved a $f1$ score of 0.71 in the oversampled dataset with Word2Vec embedding. DL models like BiLSTM and BiGRU with GloVe embedding performed better on oversampled data compared to non-oversampled counterparts. However, BiLSTM+CNN with fastText embedding appeared to be the best-performing DL model with a $f1$ score of 0.68. Consequently, m-BERT and Distil-BERT were identified as the best models for this sub-task. We submitted all the models for the shared task and finalized m-BERT for the final leaderboard standings.

5.3 Sub-Task C

In the case of ML models, it is seen that the performance of ML models on oversampled data degraded significantly. The reason is that the heavily imbalanced dataset along with the two most challenging and confusing classes 'support' and 'neutral' made classification difficult. The confusion of the classification was further fueled by oversampled data, resulting in poor performance with TF-IDF and Word2Vec. Nevertheless, transformer-based models surpassed the baseline score, indicating promise. Climate-BERT consistently performed best with a $f1$ score of 0.67, on both oversampled and non-oversampled data. As it is heavily trained on climate-related texts, therefore oversampling didn't affect its performance in this case. On the other hand, hybrid models that utilized BERT embedding performed better in oversampled data. Because of the capability to handle larger datasets, the BERT embedding appeared to perform better when dataset size increased by oversampling.

5.4 Performance Comparison

Table 7 shows that the performance of our team was promising as compared to other participating teams. In all of the sub-tasks, we were able to beat the baseline scores provided by the organizer on the ClimaConvo dataset.

Team Name	Sub-Task A				
	R	P	$f1$	Acc	Rank
CUET_Binary_Hackers	**0.9173**	**0.9116**	**0.9144**	**0.9635**	**1st**
AAST-NLP	0.8654	0.9231	0.8914	0.9571	2nd
MasonPerplexity	0.8689	0.9112	0.8885	0.9552	5th
Baseline Score	-	-	**0.708**	**0.901**	-
	Sub-task B				
MasonPerplexity	0.7823	0.8133	0.7858	0.9133	1st
AAST-NLP	0.7706	0.7689	0.7665	0.9133	3rd
CUET_Binary_Hackers	**0.7533**	**0.7431**	**0.7433**	**0.9000**	**6th**
Baseline Score	**-**	**-**	**0.716**	**0.901**	**-**
	Sub-Task C				
Hamison-Generative	0.7223	0.7827	0.7479	0.7478	1st
CUET_Binary_Hackers	**0.6691**	**0.6908**	**0.6794**	**0.6613**	**15th**
Z-AGI Labs	0.6294	0.7926	0.6372	0.6908	16th
Baseline Score	**-**	**-**	**0.651**	**0.545**	**-**

Table 7: Short rank list for all sub-tasks. P, R, $f1$, Acc denote precision, recall, macro $f1$ score, and accuracy respectively.

6 Error Analysis

The study investigated the performance of m-BERT (sub-task A and B) and Climate-BERT (sub-task C) models using quantitative and qualitative methods. Text samples were randomly chosen for all sub-tasks to facilitate quantitative analysis.

6.1 Sub-Task A

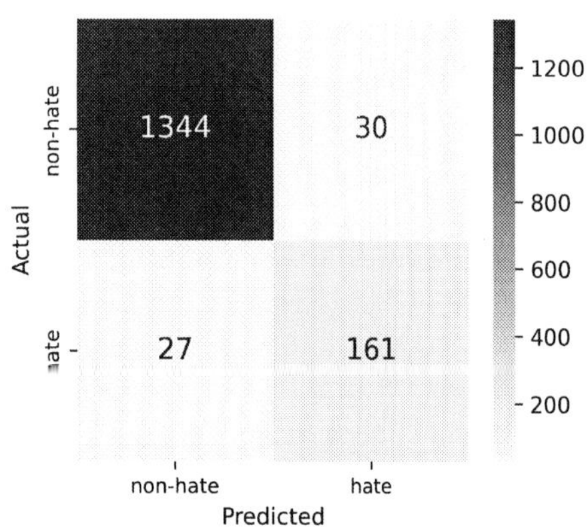

Figure 3: Confusion matrix for sub-task A by the m-BERT model.

Figure 3 indicates that out of 1,370 'non-hate' samples, 30 were misclassified, while 27 'hate' samples were misclassified as 'non-hate', despite oversampling achieving nearly 85% accuracy in 'hate' samples. The presence of common hashtags in most of the samples led to the misclassification of samples.

Table 8 describes the qualitative analysis of sub-task A, where samples 1, 2, and 3 were predicted the same as their actual label. However, samples 4, 5, and 6 resulted in misclassification by the m-BERT model.

Test Sample	Actual	Predicted
Sample 1: Love the artwork despite doubting its factual accuracy	non-hate	non-hate
Sample 2: Vladimir Putin is a global warming accelerationist. CdnNatSec FridaysForFuture	hate	hate
Sample 3: Happy EarthDay!	non-hate	non-hte
Sample 4: apparently now we have a "Planet Farm" nearby, guys!!climatechange ConsciousPlanet FridaysForFuture	non-hate	hate
Sample 5: Germany goes nuclear! Atomkraft NuclearPower FridaysForFuture Gruenen GruenerMist	non-hate	hate
Sample 6: Stop with the bullshit forecasts. @ExtinctionR ClimateStrike PeopleNotProfit FridaysForFuture 1BillionClimateVoices	hate	non-hate

Table 8: Some test samples for sub-task A, predicted by the m-BERT.

6.2 Sub-Task B

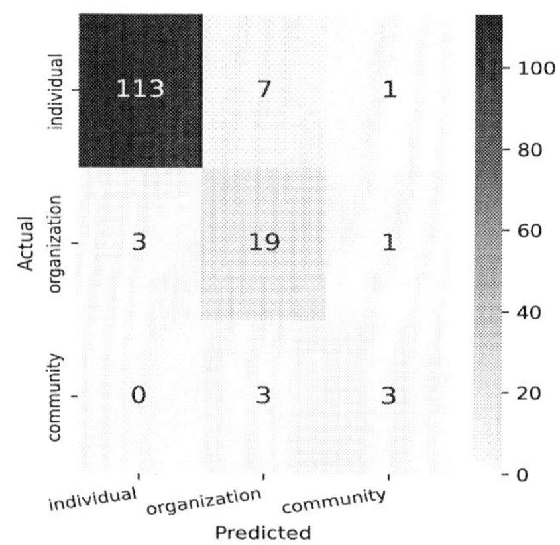

Figure 4: Confusion matrix for sub-task B by the m-BERT model.

Figure 4 reveals a higher misclassification rate in class 3 ('community') due to the lower number of training samples, resulting in a 50% misclassification rate. Classes 1 ('individual') and 2 ('organization') exhibited lower misclassification rates, with class 2 slightly higher due to class imbalance issues.

Qualitative analysis of sub-task B was presented in Table 9, where samples 1, 2, and 3 were misclassified by the m-BERT model. However, samples 4, 5, and 6 were predicted correctly, matching the actual labels of the samples.

Test Sample	Actual	Predicted
Sample 1: @Citi spent the last 5 years investing $285 billion into destroying our futures. FridaysForFuture Divest	individual	organization
Sample 2: Vladimir Putin is a global warming accelerationist. CdnNatSec FridaysForFuture	individual	organization
Sample 3: If any politicians you encounter tomorrow have been reluctant about ClimateActionNow and/or providing Reparations for LossAndDamage, PLEASE trap them in a WallPinOfLove (or, in this case, confrontation)!!! GlobalClimateStrike FridaysForFuture PeopleNotProfit @GretaThunberg	community	organization
Sample 4: Fuck Greta not the planet savetheplanet FridaysForFuture	individual	individual
Sample 5: Elections matter. Stop electing climate deniers and fossil fuels industry puppets.PeopleNotProfit ActOnClimate Australia auspol ClimateCrisis ExtinctionRebellion environment FFF FridaysForFuture	organization	organization
Sample 6: @dw_environment @Luisamneubauer @Fridays4future has remained influenced by strong left ideology/persons and denies the science using (existing) nuclear in climate/independence policies.	community	community

Table 9: Some test samples for sub-task B, predicted by the m-BERT.

6.3 Sub-Task C

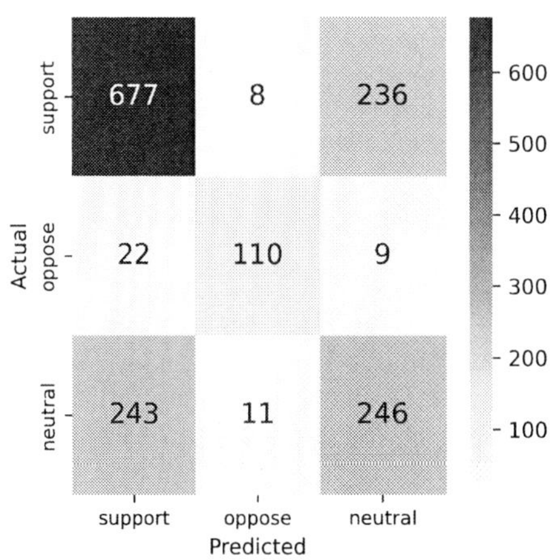

Figure 5: Confusion matrix for sub-task C by the Climate-BERT model.

Figure 5 illustrates misclassifications, particularly prominent between class 1 ('support') and class 3 ('neutral') in sub-task C. Among the predictions, 236 samples were classified as class 2 ('oppose'), while 243 were classified as class 3. The issue was exacerbated by class imbalance, resulting in 31 misclassified samples out of 141. The model struggled to differentiate between classes 1 and 3 due to their proximity.

Table 10 presents the output of several sample texts analyzed by the Climate-BERT model. Samples 1, 2, 3, and 4 were predicted dissimilar to their actual labels, whereas samples 5, 6, and 7 were predicted correctly, aligning with the actual labels.

Test Sample	Actual	Predicted
Sample 1: 4 year of FridaysForFuture	neutral	support
Sample 2: Gretas Gamlingar stockholm FridaysForFuture	neutral	oppose
Sample 3: Fuck Greta not the planet savetheplanet FridaysForFuture	oppose	support
Sample 4: Education is a human right! FridaysForFuture EducateGirlsForClimateJustice	support	neutral
Sample 5: Love and kindness are never wasted. KindnessMatters FridaysForFuture GlobalGoals	support	support
Sample 6: Germany goes nuclear! Atomkraft NuclearPower FridaysForFuture Gruenen GruenerMist	oppose	oppose
Sample 7: Is anything more dangerous than ClimateCrisis? FridaysForFuture	neutral	neutral

Table 10: Some test samples for sub-task C, predicted by the Climate-BERT model.

7 Conclusion

In this paper, we present a fine-tuned approach utilizing various models, specifically proposing fine-tuned m-BERT, Distil-BERT, Climate-BERT, and CNN+BiGRU. The results indicate that m-BERT achieved a higher $f1$ score for both sub-tasks A and B. The highest $f1$ score that we achieved for sub-task A is 0.91, for sub-task B it is 0.74, and for sub-task C it is 0.67. Several models like Climate-BERT, BiGRU, LR, and SVM performed equally well with the same $f1$ score for sub-task C. Our paper includes a detailed comparison among several models, both before and after addressing the class imbalance in the datasets. Notably, in most cases, the performance showed significant improvement. This paper also delved into effective preprocessing of data and data oversampling. These findings will create new opportunities for upcoming research work, drawing inspiration from this paper.

Limitations

Our system exhibits some key limitations:

- The significance and novelty of the research findings could be increased by introducing novel models or approaches.
- The efficiency of imbalance handling in detection models can be increased by including a wider range of data augmentation approaches.

References

Sergio Arce-García, Jesús Díaz-Campo, and Belén Cambronero-Saiz. 2023. Online hate speech and emotions on Twitter: a case study of Greta Thunberg at the UN Climate Change Conference COP25 in 2019. *Social Network Analysis and Mining*, 13(1):48.

Pinkesh Badjatiya, Shashank Gupta, Manish Gupta, and Vasudeva Varma. 2017. Deep learning for hate speech detection in tweets. In *Proceedings of the 26th international conference on World Wide Web companion*, pages 759–760.

Piotr Bojanowski, Edouard Grave, Armand Joulin, and Tomas Mikolov. 2017. Enriching word vectors with subword information. *Transactions of the association for computational linguistics*, 5:135–146.

Kyunghyun Cho, Bart Van Merriënboer, Caglar Gulcehre, Dzmitry Bahdanau, Fethi Bougares, Holger Schwenk, and Yoshua Bengio. 2014. Learning phrase representations using RNN encoder-decoder for statistical machine translation. *arXiv preprint arXiv:1406.1078*.

Alexis Conneau, Kartik Khandelwal, Naman Goyal, Vishrav Chaudhary, Guillaume Wenzek, Francisco Guzmán, Edouard Grave, Myle Ott, Luke Zettlemoyer, and Veselin Stoyanov. 2020. Unsupervised Cross-lingual Representation Learning at Scale. In *Proceedings of the 58th Annual Meeting of the Association for Computational Linguistics*. Association for Computational Linguistics.

Benjamin Damoah, Sagini Keengwe, Samuel Owusu, Clement Yeboah, and Francis Kekessie. 2023. The Global Climate and Environmental Protest: Student Environmental Activism a Transformative Defiance. *International Journal of Environmental, Sustainability, and Social Science*, 4(4):1180–1198.

Thomas Davidson, Debasmita Bhattacharya, and Ingmar Weber. 2019. Racial bias in hate speech and abusive language detection datasets. In *Proceedings of the Third Workshop on Abusive Language Online*, pages 25–35, Florence, Italy. Association for Computational Linguistics.

Thomas Davidson, Dana Warmsley, Michael W. Macy, and Ingmar Weber. 2017. Automated Hate Speech Detection and the Problem of Offensive Language. In *International Conference on Web and Social Media*.

Jacob Devlin, Ming-Wei Chang, Kenton Lee, and Kristina Toutanova. 2019. BERT: Pre-training of Deep Bidirectional Transformers for Language Understanding. In *Proceedings of the 2019 Conference of the North American Chapter of the Association for Computational Linguistics: Human Language Technologies, Volume 1 (Long and Short Papers)*. Association for Computational Linguistics.

Jonas Gehring, Michael Auli, David Grangier, and Yann N Dauphin. 2016. A convolutional encoder model for neural machine translation. *arXiv preprint arXiv:1611.02344*.

Jonas Gehring, Michael Auli, David Grangier, Denis Yarats, and Yann N Dauphin. 2017. Convolutional sequence to sequence learning. In *International conference on machine learning*, pages 1243–1252. PMLR.

Anjana Gosain and Saanchi Sardana. 2017. Handling class imbalance problem using oversampling techniques: A review. In *2017 international conference on advances in computing, communications and informatics (ICACCI)*, pages 79–85. IEEE.

Neil Gunningham. 2019. Averting climate catastrophe: environmental activism, extinction rebellion and coalitions of influence. *King's Law Journal*, 30(2):194–202.

Jefriyanto Jefriyanto, Nur Ainun, and Muchamad Arif Al Ardha. 2023. Application of Naïve Bayes Classification to Analyze Performance Using Stopwords. *Journal of Information System, Technology and Engineering*, 1(2):49–53.

Tao Jia. 2023. A Named Entity Recognition Method Based on Pre trained Models MBERT and BiLSTM. In *Proceedings of the 2023 6th International Conference on Information Science and Systems*, pages 30–35.

Nal Kalchbrenner, Ivo Danihelka, and Alex Graves. 2015. Grid long short-term memory. *arXiv preprint arXiv:1507.01526*.

György Kovács, Pedro Alonso, and Rajkumar Saini. 2021. Challenges of hate speech detection in social media: Data scarcity, and leveraging external resources. *SN Computer Science*, 2:1–15.

Sandy Kurniawan and Indra Budi. 2020. Indonesian tweets hate speech target classification using machine learning. In *2020 Fifth International Conference on Informatics and Computing (ICIC)*, pages 1–5. IEEE.

Thomas Laux. 2021. What makes a global movement? Analyzing the conditions for strong participation in the climate strike. *Social Science Information*, 60(3):413–435.

Sean MacAvaney, Hao-Ren Yao, Eugene Yang, Katina Russell, Nazli Goharian, and Ophir Frieder. 2019. Hate speech detection: Challenges and solutions. *PloS one*, 14(8):e0221152.

Arun S Maiya. 2022. ktrain: A low-code library for augmented machine learning. *The Journal of Machine Learning Research*, 23(1):7070–7075.

Shervin Malmasi and Marcos Zampieri. 2017. Detecting hate speech in social media. In *Proceedings of the International Conference Recent Advances in Natural Language Processing, RANLP 2017*, pages 467–472, Varna, Bulgaria. INCOMA Ltd.

Alexey Mikhaylov, Nikita Moiseev, Kirill Aleshin, and Thomas Burkhardt. 2020. Global climate change and greenhouse effect. *Entrepreneurship and Sustainability Issues*, 7(4):2897.

Tomas Mikolov, Ilya Sutskever, Kai Chen, Greg S Corrado, and Jeff Dean. 2013. Distributed representations of words and phrases and their compositionality. *Advances in neural information processing systems*, 26.

Marzieh Mozafari, Reza Farahbakhsh, and Noel Crespi. 2020. A BERT-based transfer learning approach for hate speech detection in online social media. In *Complex Networks and Their Applications VIII: Volume 1 Proceedings of the Eighth International Conference on Complex Networks and Their Applications COMPLEX NETWORKS 2019 8*, pages 928–940. Springer.

Syed Mustavi Maheen, Moshiur Rahman Faisal, Md. Rafakat Rahman, and Md. Shahriar Karim. 2022. Alternative non-BERT model choices for the textual classification in low-resource languages and environments. In *Proceedings of the Third Workshop on Deep Learning for Low-Resource Natural Language Processing*, pages 192–202, Hybrid. Association for Computational Linguistics.

Sally Neas, Ann Ward, and Benjamin Bowman. 2022. Young people's climate activism: A review of the literature. *Frontiers in Political Science*, 4:940876.

Parihar, Anil Singh and Thapa, Surendrabikram and Mishra, Sushruti. 2021. Hate speech detection using natural language processing: Applications and challenges. In *2021 5th International Conference on Trends in Electronics and Informatics (ICOEI)*, pages 1302–1308.

Jeffrey Pennington, Richard Socher, and Christopher D Manning. 2014. Glove: Global vectors for word representation. In *Proceedings of the 2014 conference on empirical methods in natural language processing (EMNLP)*, pages 1532–1543.

Victor Sanh, Lysandre Debut, Julien Chaumond, and Thomas Wolf. 2019. DistilBERT, a Distilled Version of BERT: Smaller, Faster, Cheaper and Lighter. In *Proceedings of the 2nd Workshop on Neural Machine Translation and Generation*. Association for Computational Linguistics.

Iqbal H Sarker. 2021. Machine learning: Algorithms, real-world applications and research directions. *SN computer science*, 2(3):160.

David Schlosberg and Lisette B Collins. 2014. From environmental to climate justice: climate change and the discourse of environmental justice. *Wiley Interdisciplinary Reviews: Climate Change*, 5(3):359–374.

Shuvam Shiwakoti, Surendrabikram Thapa, Kritesh Rauniyar, Akshyat Shah, Aashish Bhandari, and Usman Naseem. 2024. Analyzing the Dynamics of Climate Change Discourse on Twitter: A New Annotated Corpus and Multi-Aspect Classification. *Preprint*.

Alexander Shvets, Paula Fortuna, Juan Soler, and Leo Wanner. 2021. Targets and aspects in social media hate speech. In *Proceedings of the 5th Workshop on Online Abuse and Harms (WOAH 2021)*, pages 179–190, Online. Association for Computational Linguistics.

Viktoria Spaiser, Nicole Nisbett, and Cristina G Stefan. 2022. "How dare you?"—The normative challenge posed by Fridays for Future. *PLOS Climate*, 1(10):e0000053.

Surendrabikram Thapa, Kritesh Rauniyar, Farhan Ahmad Jafri, Shuvam Shiwakoti, Hariram Veeramani, Raghav Jain, Guneet Singh Kohli, Ali Hürriyetoğlu, and Usman Naseem. 2024. Stance and Hate Event Detection in Tweets Related to Climate Activism - Shared Task at CASE 2024. In *Proceedings of the 7th Workshop on Challenges and Applications of Automated Extraction of Socio-political Events from Text (CASE)*.

Apoorva Upadhyaya, Marco Fisichella, and Wolfgang Nejdl. 2023. A Multi-task Model for Emotion and Offensive Aided Stance Detection of Climate Change Tweets. In *Proceedings of the ACM Web Conference 2023*, pages 3948–3958.

Roopal Vaid, Kartikey Pant, and Manish Shrivastava. 2022. Towards fine-grained classification of climate change related social media text. In *Proceedings of the 60th Annual Meeting of the Association for Computational Linguistics: Student Research Workshop*, pages 434–443, Dublin, Ireland. Association for Computational Linguistics.

Zeerak Waseem and Dirk Hovy. 2016. Hateful symbols or hateful people? predictive features for hate speech detection on Twitter. In *Proceedings of the NAACL Student Research Workshop*, pages 88–93, San Diego, California. Association for Computational Linguistics.

Nicolas Webersinke, Mathias Kraus, Julia Anna Bingler, and Markus Leippold. 2021. Climatebert: A pretrained language model for climate-related text. *arXiv preprint arXiv:2110.12010*.

Sarah R Weiskopf, Madeleine A Rubenstein, Lisa G Crozier, Sarah Gaichas, Roger Griffis, Jessica E Halofsky, Kimberly JW Hyde, Toni Lyn Morelli, Jeffrey T Morisette, Roldan C Muñoz, et al. 2020. Climate change effects on biodiversity, ecosystems, ecosystem services, and natural resource management in the United States. *Science of the Total Environment*, 733:137782.

Thomas Wolf, Lysandre Debut, Victor Sanh, Julien Chaumond, Clement Delangue, Anthony Moi, Pierric Cistac, Tim Rault, Rémi Louf, Morgan Funtowicz, et al. 2019. Huggingface's transformers: State-of-the-art natural language processing. *arXiv preprint arXiv:1910.03771*.

Ziqi Zhang and Lei Luo. 2019. Hate speech detection: A solved problem? the challenging case of long tail on twitter. *Semantic Web*, 10(5):925–945.

HAMiSoN-baselines at ClimateActivism 2024: A Study on the Use of External Data for Hate Speech and Stance Detection

Julio Reyes-Montesinos and **Álvaro Rodrigo**
NLP & IR Group
UNED, Spain
{jreyes, alvarory}@lsi.uned.es

Abstract

The CASE@EACL2024 Shared Task addresses Climate Activism online through three subtasks that focus on hate speech detection (Subtask A), hate speech target classification (Subtask B), and stance detection (Subtask C) respectively. Our contribution examines the effect of fine-tuning on external data for each of these subtasks. For the two subtasks that focus on hate speech, we augment the training data with the OLID (Zampieri et al., 2019a) dataset, whereas for the stance subtask we harness the SemEval-2016 Stance dataset (Mohammad et al., 2016b). We fine-tune RoBERTa and DeBERTa models for each of the subtasks, with and without external training data. For the hate speech detection and stance detection subtasks, our RoBERTa models came up third and first on the leaderboard, respectively. While the use of external data was not relevant on those tasks, we found that it greatly improved the performance on the hate speech target categorization.

1 Introduction

In recent years, the escalating global awareness of the imminent climate crisis has not only prompted an upsurge in climate activism but has also given rise to a new wave of advocacy strategies, often marked by actions not devoid of controversy. While the urgency of addressing climate change has fostered a sense of shared responsibility in society, some of the actions of climate activists have also sparked debates regarding the boundaries of acceptable dissent. When translated to the online sphere, where climate activists looking to disseminate their messages and mobilize supporters encounter both climate deniers and corporate PR, these conversations become ever more heated, often precluding sensible debate. Our research aspires to contribute to a deeper understanding of the digital discourse surrounding climate activism and facilitate the creation of tools that can foster healthier online conversations while respecting the fundamental right to dissent in an age of environmental urgency.

This paper delves into the intricate landscape of online climate activism, with a focus on the automated detection of hate speech in this context. Specifically, our contribution looks at the effect of fine-tuning transformers on two external datasets selected for their relatedness to the tasks at hand, besides the data proposed by the task itself. For the subtasks focusing on hate speech detection and the categorization of its target, we augmented the training data with the OLID (Zampieri et al., 2019a) dataset. In turn, for the stance detection subtask we employed the section related to climate change of the SemEval-2016 Stance dataset (Mohammad et al., 2016b).

The rest of this paper describes the data provided by the task (section 2) as well as the external data (section 3) we chose to augment it. Next, we detail the system development process (section 4) and discuss the results (section 5. We finish with a brief Conclusion (section 6.

2 Dataset and Task

The ClimaConvo dataset Shiwakoti et al. (2024) exposes a cross-section of the public discourse around climate change on social media. It comprises 15,309 tweets collected around a series of hashtags related to climate activism over a one-year period. The dataset contains annotations in six layers: relevance, stance, the presence of hate speech; if present, whether it is directed; when directed, the type of target; and the presence of humor.

The shared task at hand, CASE@EACL2024 (Thapa et al., 2024), comprises three subtasks based on two subsets of ClimaConvo, corresponding to 10,407 tweets. These subsets have been split in train, validation and test sets by the authors. Table 1 describes the subsets, splits, and the balance of labels in them. Each of the tasks relates to one of the annotation layers in ClimaConvo, as follows:

Proceedings of the 7th Workshop on Challenges and Applications of Automated Extraction of Socio-political Events from Text (CASE 2024), pages 156–160
March 22, 2024 ©2024 Association for Computational Linguistics

2.1 Subtask A

The first subtask involved the detection of hate speech in tweets. It therefore contains all tweets labeled `RELEVANT` in ClimaConvo, which can in turn be labeled as containing `HATE SPEECH` or containing `NO HATE SPEECH`.

2.2 Subtask B

For this subtask, participants were asked to categorize the target of hate speech in tweets, resulting in a multi-class classification task with the labels `INDIVIDUAL`, `ORGANIZATION` and `COMMUNITY`. The subtask is based on the subset of tweets in ClimaConvo where hate speech is labeled as `RELEVANT`, that is, a smaller subset of the one introduced for the previous task, this time adding up to 999 tweets.

2.3 Subtask C

The stance subtask is based on the same subset of tweets as subtask A, i.e. `RELEVANT` tweets. The train, validation and test splits also remain constant. However, this subtasks asks participants to determine whether tweets `SUPPORT` or `OPPOSE` Climate Activism, or have `NEUTRAL` position towards it.

3 External Data

We sourced the additional training data for our experiments from two datasets external to the task: the OLID and the SemEval-2016 Task 6 datasets.

3.1 OLID

As external data related to hate speech, we consider the Offensive Language Identification Dataset (OLID) (Zampieri et al., 2019b) presented at SemEval-2019 (Zampieri et al., 2019c). OLID was Compiled with the goal of tackling the problem of offensive posts in social media as a whole, OLID consists of 14,100 tweets annotated in three layers: the presence of offensive language; if present, its categorization (as Targeted or Untargeted); and if targeted, the identification of this target (an `Individual`, a `Group` or `Other` type of entity). We manually compared a sample of tweets to match these labels to their `Individual`, `Organization` and `Community` counterparts in ClimaConvo.

For Subtask A, we use the full OLID dataset (since all tweets are annotated for presence of offensive speech). For Subtask B, we use the subset of 4,089 tweets identified as targeted, and therefore annotated for target type. Although the authors define train and test splits, we merge both splits as additional train data.

3.2 SemEval-2016 Task 6

For the stance detection subtask (Subtask B), we harness the Stance Dataset Mohammad et al. (2016a) presented at the SemEval-2016 Task 6 (Mohammad et al., 2016c). This dataset consists of a total of 4,870 tweets labeled with the stance they express about a certain target topic: abortion, climate, Hillary Clinton, feminism, atheism, and Donald Trump. For our purpose of training data augmentation, we use only the portion related to climate change, which totals 564 tweets. The labels (`Favor`, `Against` or `Neither`) are analogous to the ones in ClimaConvo.

4 Methodology

The present contribution has the goal of establishing state-of-the-art transformer baselines for the three subtasks, and then examine the influence of additional training data on each subtask. To this end, we developed systems based on the RoBERTa (Liu et al., 2019) and DeBERTa (He et al., 2020) transformers.

Both RoBERTa and DeBERTa improve upon BERT (Bidirectional Encoder Representations from Transformers) (Devlin et al., 2019) by introducing different training objectives: RoBERTa uses dynamic masking (where different tokens are masked every time the same sequence is fed to the model) and eliminates the next-sentence prediction training objective of BERT. DeBERTa adds a disentangled attention mechanism (where each word is represented using two vectors that encode its content and relative position) and enhanced masked decoding (where absolute word positions are added back). The version we use, DeBERTa-v3 (He et al., 2021), replaces the masked language model pre-training task with replace token detection task (RTD), further improving the models capacity to capture long-range dependencies over RoBERTa. On the other hand, it is key to note that RoBERTa has been pre-trained on double the amount of data.

Common to both of these transformer architectures is the notion that they can be fine-tuned at a low computational cost while still exceeding at a number of diverse Natural Language Understanding tasks. In the following subsections we provide technical details of how the proposed models were fine-tuned on the reference datasets:

subtask	A: hate speech		C: stance			
label	NO HATE SPEECH	HATE SPEECH	SUPPORT	OPPOSE	NEUTRAL	Total/split
train	6385	899	4328	2256	700	7284
validation	1371	190	897	511	153	1561
test	1374	188	921	500	141	1562
Total/label	9130	1277	6146	3267	994	10407

subtask	B: hate speech target			
label	INDIVIDUAL	ORGANIZATION	COMMUNITY	Total/split
train	563	105	31	699
validation	120	23	7	150
test	121	23	6	150
Total/label	804	151	44	999

Table 1: Per split label distribution in tweets assigned to each subtask.

4.1 Dataset pre-processing

Before feeding the data to the models, we followed a common text pre-processing pipeline for tweets, on both the task and the external data, consisting of the following actions:

- Replacement of URLs by the special tokens `[URL_TWITTER]` and `[URL_OTHER]`.
- Replacement of username mentions by the generic token `@USER`.
- Splitting of hashtags into individual words. To accomplish this endeavour we have utilized the Word Ninja[1] library, which uses a probabilistic division of concatenated words, based on the frequencies of unigrams in the English Wikipedia.

4.2 Fine-tuning configuration

We first fine-tuned off-the-shelf RoBERTa-base[2] and DeBERTa-v3-base[3] transformers with text classification heads for each of the subtasks using only the data proposed in the shared task. We then fine-tuned a second set of RoBERTa and DeBERTa models including the proposed additional training data for each subtask.

Some of the models' hyper-paramenters have been determined experimentally: All models have been fine-tuned for 3 epochs. Tweets are administered in a random order, and when using external data, these are lumped together with the subtask's original data. The batch size is 8 for RoBERTa, but 4 for DeBERTa due to memory constraints. The learning rates are 2×10^{-5} for RoBERTa and 1×10^{-5} for DeBERTa.

All learning rates are scheduled to first linearly increase from 0 to the aformentioned rates during an initial pediod of 100 training steps, and then decrease linearly for the rest of trainign steps. The chosen optimizer in all cases is AdamW.

During development, models were fine-tuned on the proposed train split only. The models submitted in the test phase, however, have been fine-tuned on both the train and the validation splits proposed by each subtask (as well as the proposed external data when applicable).

4.3 Submitted runs

Summing up, for each of the three subtasks we submitted four runs:

1. RoBERTa-base fine-tuned on subtask's data.
2. DeBERTa-v3-base on subtask's data.
3. RoBERTa-base on subtask's + additional data.
4. DeBERTa-v3-base fine-tuned on subtask's + additional data.

[1] https://github.com/keredson/wordninja
[2] https://huggingface.co/FacebookAI/roberta-base
[3] https://huggingface.co/microsoft/deberta-v3-base

5 Results and Discussion

Results on subtasks A (hate speech detection) and C (stance detection) follow a similar pattern: our best results are achieved by the RoBERTa models fine-tuned on subtask data only. As seen on table 2, models fine-tuned on external data perform worse that their counterparts trained on subtask data only, but more so the RoBERTa's. DeBERTa models perform similarly regardless of whether we fine-tuned them on additional data, while the divergence is bigger for RoBERTa's.

On these subtasks, our models come far above all of the baselines provided by the organizers. On subtask A, our models come close below the best in the leaderboard. On subtask C, our simple RoBERTa comes atop the leaderboard. We note that these results are also far superior to the RoBERTa baseline provided by the organizers — we attribute this difference to our more thorough pre-processing and the difference in hyper-parameters. We also note, however, that the organizer's baseline that is already fine-tuned on climate-related text (ClimateBERT) obtains better results than other baselines on these two subtasks.

The pattern of results on subtask B (hate speech target categorization) is different: here the impact of external data is notably positive in the results. The RoBERTa fine-tuned on additional data is our best model on this subtask, whereas the models trained on subtask data only do not improve on the organizer's baselines. We attribute this difference to the size of the subset of tweets designated for this task. The much larger size of the chosen additional dataset (4,089 vs. 999 tweets) is more attuned to what transformer models such as RoBERTa and DeBERTa expect.

Finally, we consider that RoBERTa models perform better than more advance DeBERTa models on this task due to contextual knowledge being more important than the ability to capture long-range dependencies when dealing with tweet data, whose instances are short in nature.

Model	F_1 score by subtask A	B	C
Best model on leaderboard	0.9144	0.7858	0.7483
Task's Baselines:			
BERT	**0.708**	**0.554**	0.466
DistillBERT	0.664	0.550	0.527
RoBERTa	0.662	0.501	0.542
ClimateBERT	0.704	0.549	**0.545**
RoBERTa	**0.8886**	0.5518	**0.7495**
DeBERTa	0.8751	0.5493	0.7408
RoBERTa ext.data	0.8682	**0.7017**	0.7406
DeBERTa ext.data	0.8713	0.6588	0.7392

Table 2: F_1 scores achieved by our submitted runs on each subtask compared to the baselines provided by the organizers and those achieved by the best participating systems. In bold, best baseline and best of our systems.

6 Conclusions and future work

This paper introduced carefully adjusted transformer baselines for the hate speech detection, hate speech target categorization, and stance detection in tweets subtasks proposed at CASE@EACL2024. Based on off-the-shelf models, we have conducted a study of the effects of related external train data, with mixed results. We consider that further analysis of the results is needed before discarding the use of external data for this task. In particular, we would like to study the lexical and semantic distance between the ClimaConvo dataset proposed by the task and the ones chosen as additional train data, aiming to extend this analysis to other potential external datasets.

This research contributes to the ongoing efforts to foster healthy online conversations surrounding climate change activism. As the field of natural language processing continues to advance, our systems serve as a foundation for future developments in hate speech and stance detection in the context of critical issues like climate change.

Acknowledgements

This work was supported by the HAMiSoN project grant CHIST-ERA-21-OSNEM-002, AEI PCI2022-135026-2 (MCIN/AEI/10.13039/501100011033 and EU "NextGenerationEU"/PRTR).

References

Jacob Devlin, Ming-Wei Chang, Kenton Lee, and Kristina Toutanova. 2019. BERT: Pre-training of deep bidirectional transformers for language understanding. In *Proceedings of the 2019 Conference of the North American Chapter of the Association for Computational Linguistics: Human Language Technologies, Volume 1 (Long and Short Papers)*, pages 4171–4186, Minneapolis, Minnesota. Association for Computational Linguistics.

Pengcheng He, Jianfeng Gao, and Weizhu Chen. 2021. Debertav3: Improving deberta using electra-style pre-training with gradient-disentangled embedding sharing. *CoRR*, abs/2111.09543.

Pengcheng He, Xiaodong Liu, Jianfeng Gao, and Weizhu Chen. 2020. Deberta: Decoding-enhanced BERT with disentangled attention. *CoRR*, abs/2006.03654.

Yinhan Liu, Myle Ott, Naman Goyal, Jingfei Du, Mandar Joshi, Danqi Chen, Omer Levy, Mike Lewis, Luke Zettlemoyer, and Veselin Stoyanov. 2019. Roberta: A robustly optimized BERT pretraining approach. *CoRR*, abs/1907.11692.

Saif Mohammad, Svetlana Kiritchenko, Parinaz Sobhani, Xiaodan Zhu, and Colin Cherry. 2016a. A dataset for detecting stance in tweets. In *Proceedings of the Tenth International Conference on Language Resources and Evaluation (LREC'16)*, pages 3945–3952, Portorož, Slovenia. European Language Resources Association (ELRA).

Saif Mohammad, Svetlana Kiritchenko, Parinaz Sobhani, Xiaodan Zhu, and Colin Cherry. 2016b. SemEval-2016 task 6: Detecting stance in tweets. In *Proceedings of the 10th International Workshop on Semantic Evaluation (SemEval-2016)*, pages 31–41, San Diego, California. Association for Computational Linguistics.

Saif Mohammad, Svetlana Kiritchenko, Parinaz Sobhani, Xiaodan Zhu, and Colin Cherry. 2016c. SemEval-2016 task 6: Detecting stance in tweets. In *Proceedings of the 10th International Workshop on Semantic Evaluation (SemEval-2016)*, pages 31–41, San Diego, California. Association for Computational Linguistics.

Shuvam Shiwakoti, Surendrabikram Thapa, Kritesh Rauniyar, Akshyat Shah, Aashish Bhandari, and Usman Naseem. 2024. Analyzing the dynamics of climate change discourse on twitter: A new annotated corpus and multi-aspect classification. *Preprint*.

Surendrabikram Thapa, Kritesh Rauniyar, Farhan Ahmad Jafri, Shuvam Shiwakoti, Hariram Veeramani, Raghav Jain, Guneet Singh Kohli, Ali Hürriyetoğlu, and Usman Naseem. 2024. Stance and hate event detection in tweets related to climate activism - shared task at case 2024. In *Proceedings of the 7th Workshop on Challenges and Applications of Automated Extraction of Socio-political Events from Text (CASE)*.

Marcos Zampieri, Shervin Malmasi, Preslav Nakov, Sara Rosenthal, Noura Farra, and Ritesh Kumar. 2019a. Predicting the type and target of offensive posts in social media. In *Proceedings of the 2019 Conference of the North American Chapter of the Association for Computational Linguistics: Human Language Technologies, Volume 1 (Long and Short Papers)*, pages 1415–1420, Minneapolis, Minnesota. Association for Computational Linguistics.

Marcos Zampieri, Shervin Malmasi, Preslav Nakov, Sara Rosenthal, Noura Farra, and Ritesh Kumar. 2019b. Predicting the type and target of offensive posts in social media. In *Proceedings of the 2019 Conference of the North American Chapter of the Association for Computational Linguistics: Human Language Technologies, Volume 1 (Long and Short Papers)*, pages 1415–1420, Minneapolis, Minnesota. Association for Computational Linguistics.

Marcos Zampieri, Shervin Malmasi, Preslav Nakov, Sara Rosenthal, Noura Farra, and Ritesh Kumar. 2019c. SemEval-2019 task 6: Identifying and categorizing offensive language in social media (OffensEval). In *Proceedings of the 13th International Workshop on Semantic Evaluation*, pages 75–86, Minneapolis, Minnesota, USA. Association for Computational Linguistics.

Z-AGI Labs at ClimateActivism 2024: Stance and Hate Event Detection on Social Media

Nikhil Narayan
Z-AGI Labs
nikhilnarayan73@gmail.com

Mrutyunjay Biswal
Z-AGI Labs
mrutyunjay.biswal.hmu@gmail.com

Abstract

In the digital realm, rich data serves as a crucial source of insights into the complexities of social, political, and economic landscapes. Addressing the growing need for high-quality information on events and the imperative to combat hate speech, this research led to the establishment of the Shared Task on Climate Activism Stance and Hate Event Detection at CASE 2024. Focused on climate activists contending with hate speech on social media, our study contributes to hate speech identification from tweets. Analyzing three sub-tasks - Hate Speech Detection (Sub-task A), Targets of Hate Speech Identification (Sub-task B), and Stance Detection (Sub-task C) - Team Z-AGI Labs evaluated various models, including LSTM, Xgboost, and LGBM based on Tf-Idf. Results unveiled intriguing variations, with Catboost excelling in Subtask-B (F1: 0.5604) and Subtask-C (F1: 0.7081), while LGBM emerged as the top-performing model for Subtask-A (F1: 0.8684). This research provides valuable insights into the suitability of classical machine learning models for climate hate speech and stance detection, aiding informed model selection for robust mechanisms.

1 Introduction

In the ever-evolving landscape of our digital era, an expansive tapestry of data unfolds, revealing profound insights into the intricate dynamics of social, political, and economic systems. The narratives of citizen responses to COVID policies (2020-2022) and the unfolding Russia-Ukraine conflict stand out as crucial chapters(Tanev et al., 2023), vividly demonstrating the indispensable role of event-centric data in unraveling the multifaceted tapestry of real-world scenarios. These narratives underscore the pressing need for sophisticated tools capable of discerning and addressing hate speech, ultimately leading to the inception of the Shared Task on Climate Activism Stance and Hate Event Detection at CASE 2024(Thapa et al., 2024).

Within the realms of social media platforms, where climate activists converge to share insights, mobilize support, and voice concerns, instances of hate speech can emerge, casting a shadow over the collaborative spirit of the movement. Sub-task A of our shared task(Shiwakoti et al., 2024), Hate Speech Detection, emerges from the very fabric of these real-world scenarios, challenging participants to meticulously scrutinize textual content for the presence of hate speech. Navigating the landscape of hate speech requires a profound understanding of its targets. Real-world examples abound, illustrating instances where individual activists, environmental organizations, and entire communities face the brunt of hateful rhetoric. Sub-task B, Targets of Hate Speech Identification, mirrors these authentic situations by urging participants to categorize hate speech targets into "individuals," "organisations," or "communities." In witnessing the unfolding narratives of climate activism, the importance of understanding stance dynamics becomes evident. Real-world scenarios often involve a spectrum of sentiments — from unwavering support to vehement opposition or maintaining a neutral stance. Sub-task C, Stance Detection, captures the essence of these dynamic narratives, prompting participants to decipher the sentiments expressed in textual content. By doing so, participants contribute to a deeper understanding of how the collective sentiment shapes the discourse surrounding climate change events.

The shared task thus emerges not as a detached academic exercise(Parihar et al., 2021) but as a direct response to the challenges faced in the trenches of climate activism. Through real-world instances and tangible connections, participants are invited to be catalysts for positive change, developing tools that align with the authentic dynamics of the digital discourse in climate change activism. In this endeavor, the shared task serves as a bridge between the virtual and the real, fostering a more resilient

Proceedings of the 7th Workshop on Challenges and Applications of Automated Extraction of Socio-political Events from Text (CASE 2024), pages 161–165
March 22, 2024

and empathetic space for those advocating for a sustainable and equitable future.

In this paper, we describe our approach to tackle the challenges. From here, the report continues in the following manner: In section 2, we give an overview of the dataset for each subtask and describe the challenge at hand. In section 3, we present our approach in detail, covering the intricacies of our experimental set-up, cross-validation strategy, models used, and intuition behind them. In section 4, we brief the results from the experiments section. Then, we conclude in section 5 with the final takeaways, our standings, and the scope of future work.

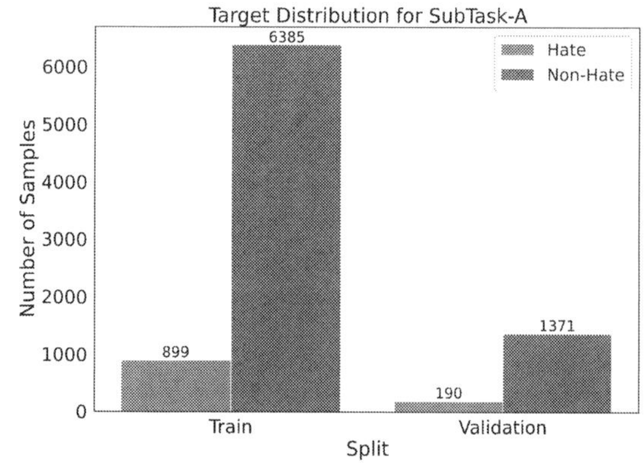

Figure 2: Target Distribution for Subtask-A.

2 Dataset Description

This section provides an overview of the dataset designed to facilitate the exploration and evaluation of these key aspects.

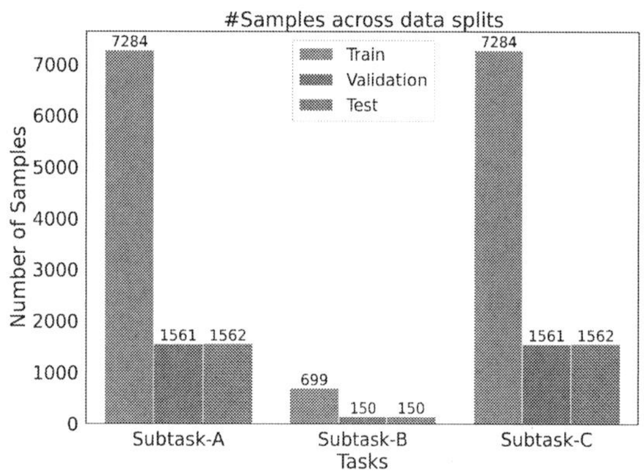

Figure 1: Train-Val-Test Split for different subtasks.

2.1 Hate Speech Detection (Sub-task A)

The primary objective of Sub-task A is to determine the presence or absence of hate speech within a given text. The text dataset for Sub-task A is enriched with binary annotations, explicitly indicating the prevalence of hate speech. Each instance is marked to signify whether it contains hate speech or remains devoid of such content. The Dataset provided for the task contains 7284 samples in the train set, 1561 samples in the Validation set and 1562 samples in the test set.

2.2 Targets of Hate Speech Detection (Sub-task B)

Sub-task B is dedicated to identifying the specific targets of hate speech within hateful texts. The dataset for Sub-task B is meticulously annotated to delineate the entities targeted by hate speech. Annotations classify the targets into three distinct categories: "individual," "organization," and "community." The Dataset provided for the task contains 699 samples in the train set, and 150 samples in both the Validation set and the test set.

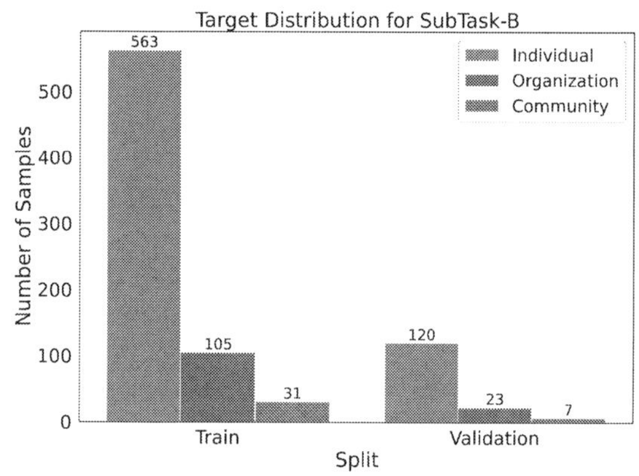

Figure 3: Target Distribution for Subtask-B.

2.3 Stance Detection (Sub-task C)

Sub-task C focuses on discerning the stance expressed in a given text within the context of climate change activism. The text dataset for Sub-task C is annotated to capture three distinct stances: "support," "oppose," and "neutral." The Dataset provided for the task contains 7284 samples in the train set, 1561 samples in the Validation set and 1562 samples in the test set.

3 Experimental Set-Up

In this section, we delve into our methodology and the specifics of the experimental setup. For

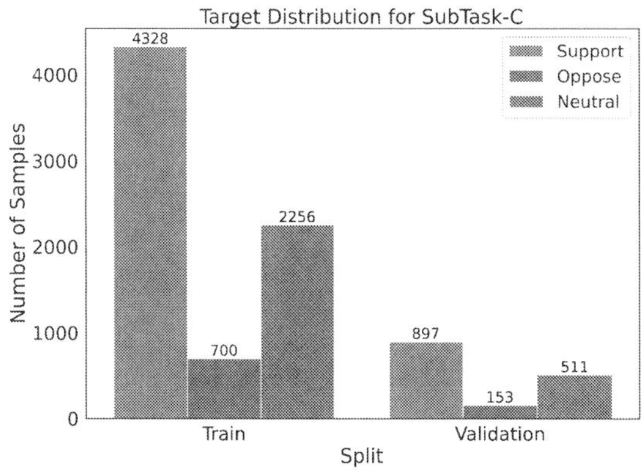

Figure 4: Target Distribution for Subtask-C.

each dataset, we first develop a validation technique. Since every dataset is not fairly balanced, we choose to use Stratified K-Fold cross-validation with 5 folds. Additionally, we used 42 as the random seed when generating the splits.

3.1 Preprocessing

The preprocessing phase plays a pivotal role in refining the content for subsequent feature extraction. Upon careful examination, it was noted that the majority of tweets exhibit a notable absence of emojis or redundant punctuation marks that necessitate attention. Although a substantial portion of the content is successfully cleansed, a distinctive characteristic emerged: the prevalence of extensive hashtags across all tweets. Furthermore, a noteworthy observation was made regarding tweets with similar textual content but distinct hashtags, resulting in disparate outcomes. To address these intricacies, the preprocessing pipeline involves the removal of URLs and hyperlinks associated with the content. Specifically, the focus is directed towards the hashtags, which undergo further processing using the Ekphrasis(Baziotis et al., 2017) tokenizer to segment them into semantically meaningful tokens. Notably, the decision was made to employ the Tokenizer Separator token to distinctively segregate normal text from hashtag texts. In the case of the former, tweet preprocessor was applied to facilitate the cleansing process.

3.2 Modeling

Our methodology commences with the establishment of baseline scores using Tf-Idf in conjunction with Naive Bayes for each of the three subtasks. This initial step allows us to gauge the performance of a rudimentary model before advancing to more sophisticated approaches. Moving beyond the baseline, we employ powerful classical machine learning models, namely Random Forest, Xgboost(Chen and Guestrin, 2016), CatBoost(Prokhorenkova et al., 2018), and LGBM(Ke et al., 2017), leveraging Tf-Idf as the feature extraction method. This ensemble of classical models provides a comprehensive understanding of the task's intricacies and sets a benchmark for further exploration. We also used hyperparameter tuning using optuna for models like Xgboost, CatBoost and LGBM.

To delve into the nuances of textual content and capture intricate dependencies, we introduce a deep learning approach. Our model architecture encompasses a bi-directional LSTM-based(Sundermeyer et al., 2014) framework with attention mechanisms(Vaswani et al., 2017). Specifically, two bi-directional LSTM layers precede an attention block, enhancing the model's capacity to grasp sequential patterns. The attention head is intricately connected through two dense layers, culminating in a sigmoid activation function in the final layer. The model is trained using the Adam optimizer(Kingma and Ba, 2014) and Binary Cross Entropy as the loss function. Crucial hyperparameters, including batch size, number of epochs, learning rate, vocabulary size, embedding dimension, and maximum length of the input sequence, undergo meticulous tuning on a case-to-case basis to optimize model performance.

We leverage the capabilities of Transformer-based language models to improve downstream job performance, taking into account the small sample size of the available datasets. These models use fine-tuning on the encoder layers while keeping the embedding layers frozen to maintain contextual knowledge that has already been learned. TFAutoModelForSequenceClassification is adopted as the Transformer-based model, with corresponding hyperparameters tailored for each subtask.

To ensure computational efficiency and scalability, all training and inference operations are carried out using the Kaggle runtime, Google Colab, and a MacBook Pro M1 with 16GB of unified memory.

4 Results

All the subtasks were evaluated using F1 Score, Precision, Recall, and Accuracy. It is evident from the results matrix 1 that the LSTM based model poses a strong competition in performance for all the subtasks nearing the best score for all the sub-

Models	Subtask-A	Subtask-B	Subtask-C
LSTM + Attention	0.8433	0.5370	0.5008
Tf-Idf + Logistic Regression	0.8516	0.5577	0.7075
Tf-Idf + LGBM	**0.8684**	0.5097	0.6055
Tf-Idf + CatBoost	0.8586	**0.5604**	**0.7081**
Tf-Idf + Xgboost	0.8228	0.5360	0.6994
Tf-Idf + Random Forest	0.8548	0.5496	0.6765
Tf-Idf + Naive Bayes	0.8516	0.5482	0.6065

Table 1: F1-Scores of different approaches

Team	Precision	F1-Score	Accuracy	Recall
mrutyunjay_research	**0.9686 (1)**	0.8539 (15)	0.9494 (6)	0.7922 (19)
refaat1731	0.9607 (2)	0.8556 (12)	0.9494 (6)	0.7968 (18)
kagankaya1	0.9415 (3)	0.8532 (16)	0.9475 (8)	0.8003 (17)
htanev	0.9246 (4)	0.8310 (18)	0.9405 (13)	0.7779 (20)
kojiro000	0.9226 (5)	**0.8699 (7)**	**0.9507 (5)**	**0.8319 (14)**

Table 2: Snippet of Leaderboard sorted by Recall for SubTask-1

Username	Recall	Precision	F1-Score	Accuracy
AhmedElSayed	0.7078 (8)	0.7931 (1)	0.7398 (6)	0.7439 (4)
mrutyunjay_research	0.6294 (16)	0.7926 (2)	0.6372 (16)	0.6908 (12)
gh_mhdi	0.7145 (5)	0.7863 (3)	0.7447 (4)	0.7311 (8)
kagankaya1	**0.7226 (3)**	0.7848 (4)	**0.7483 (2)**	**0.7490 (1)**
JesusFraile	0.7223 (4)	0.7827 (5)	0.7479 (3)	0.7478 (2)

Table 3: Snippet of Leaderboard sorted by Precision for SubTask-3

tasks.

In Subtask-A, the LGBM model on top of Tf-Idf performed the best for us with a F1-Score of 0.8684 while models like Naive Bayes, Logistic Regression, Random Forest and CatBoost on top of Tf-Idf were not too far away.

In Subtask-B, the CatBoost model on top of Tf-Idf performed the best with a score of 0.5604 while models like Naive Bayes, Logistic Regression and Random Forest were close with scores of 0.5482, 0.5577 and 0.5496 respectively.

In Subtask-C, the CatBoost model on top of Tf-Idf performed the best with a score of 0.7081, while models like Logistic Regression and Xgboost on top of Tf-Idf score 0.7075 and 0.6994 respectively and came very close.

We also performed fine-tuning using Transformers but the outcomes were inadequate, so we decided to use simpler models in order to achieve better performance.

We were eventually able to surpass the baseline F1 scores for Subtask-A: 0.708(BERT(Kenton and Toutanova, 2019)), Subtask-B: 0.554(BERT), and Subtask-C: 0.5495(Climate-BERT(Webersinke et al., 2021)) that were provided by the organizer.

Note that, all the scores mentioned are the performance on the hidden test set and directly taken from the system-run report provided on the competition website after finalized leaderboard 2, 3.

5 Conclusion

In summary, our research contributes crucial insights into hate speech and stance detection within climate activism. Employing classical machine learning models, such as LSTM, Xgboost, LGBM, and Catboost, revealed nuanced variations in performance. Notably, Catboost emerged as a strong performer, showcasing F1 scores of 0.5604 and 0.7081 for Subtask-B and Subtask-C. LGBM excelled in Subtask-A with an impressive F1 score of 0.8684. This study guides model selection for robust hate speech detection. As we conclude, our findings serve as a valuable resource for advancing tools aligned with the authentic dynamics of digital discourse in climate change activism.

References

Christos Baziotis, Nikos Pelekis, and Christos Doulkeridis. 2017. Datastories at semeval-2017 task 4: Deep lstm with attention for message-level and topic-based sentiment analysis. In *Proceedings of the 11th International Workshop on Semantic Evaluation (SemEval-2017)*, pages 747–754, Vancouver, Canada. Association for Computational Linguistics.

Tianqi Chen and Carlos Guestrin. 2016. Xgboost: A scalable tree boosting system. In *Proceedings of the 22nd ACM SIGKDD International Conference on Knowledge Discovery and Data Mining*. ACM.

Guolin Ke, Qi Meng, Thomas Finley, Taifeng Wang, Wei Chen, Weidong Ma, Qiwei Ye, and Tie-Yan Liu. 2017. Lightgbm: A highly efficient gradient boosting decision tree. In *Advances in Neural Information Processing Systems*, volume 30. Curran Associates, Inc.

Jacob Devlin Ming-Wei Chang Kenton and Lee Kristina Toutanova. 2019. Bert: Pre-training of deep bidirectional transformers for language understanding. In *Proceedings of naacL-HLT*, volume 1, page 2.

Diederik P Kingma and Jimmy Ba. 2014. Adam: A method for stochastic optimization. *arXiv preprint arXiv:1412.6980.*

Anil Singh Parihar, Surendrabikram Thapa, and Sushruti Mishra. 2021. Hate speech detection using natural language processing: Applications and challenges. In *2021 5th International Conference on Trends in Electronics and Informatics (ICOEI)*, pages 1302–1308.

Liudmila Prokhorenkova, Gleb Gusev, Aleksandr Vorobev, Anna Veronika Dorogush, and Andrey Gulin. 2018. Catboost: unbiased boosting with categorical features. In *Advances in Neural Information Processing Systems*, volume 31. Curran Associates, Inc.

Shuvam Shiwakoti, Surendrabikram Thapa, Kritesh Rauniyar, Akshyat Shah, Aashish Bhandari, and Usman Naseem. 2024. Analyzing the dynamics of climate change discourse on twitter: A new annotated corpus and multi-aspect classification. *Preprint.*

Martin Sundermeyer, Tamer Alkhouli, Joern Wuebker, and Hermann Ney. 2014. Translation modeling with bidirectional recurrent neural networks. In *Proceedings of the 2014 Conference on Empirical Methods in Natural Language Processing (EMNLP)*, pages 14–25, Doha, Qatar. Association for Computational Linguistics.

Hristo Tanev, Nicolas Stefanovitch, Andrew Halterman, Onur Uca, Vanni Zavarella, Ali Hurriyetoglu, Bertrand De Longueville, and Leonida Della Rocca. 2023. Detecting and geocoding battle events from social media messages on the russo-Ukrainian war: Shared task 2, CASE 2023. In *Proceedings of the 6th Workshop on Challenges and Applications of Automated Extraction of Socio-political Events from Text*, pages 160–166, Varna, Bulgaria. INCOMA Ltd., Shoumen, Bulgaria.

Surendrabikram Thapa, Kritesh Rauniyar, Farhan Ahmad Jafri, Shuvam Shiwakoti, Hariram Veeramani, Raghav Jain, Guneet Singh Kohli, Ali Hürriyetoğlu, and Usman Naseem. 2024. Stance and hate event detection in tweets related to climate activism - shared task at case 2024. In *Proceedings of the 7th Workshop on Challenges and Applications of Automated Extraction of Socio-political Events from Text (CASE).*

Ashish Vaswani, Noam Shazeer, Niki Parmar, Jakob Uszkoreit, Llion Jones, Aidan N Gomez, Ł ukasz Kaiser, and Illia Polosukhin. 2017. Attention is all you need. In *Advances in Neural Information Processing Systems*, volume 30. Curran Associates, Inc.

Nicolas Webersinke, Mathias Kraus, Julia Anna Bingler, and Markus Leippold. 2021. Climatebert: A pretrained language model for climate-related text. *arXiv preprint arXiv:2110.12010.*

Bryndza at ClimateActivism 2024: Stance, Target and Hate Event Detection via Retrieval-Augmented GPT-4 and LLaMA

Marek Šuppa[αβ] **Daniel Skala**[αγ] **Daniela Jašš**[α] **Samuel Sučík**[α] **Andrej Švec**[α] **Peter Hraška**[α]
[α]Cisco / Slido, [β]Comenius University in Bratislava, [γ]University of Groningen

Abstract

This study details our approach for the CASE 2024 Shared Task on Climate Activism Stance and Hate Event Detection, focusing on Hate Speech Detection, Hate Speech Target Identification, and Stance Detection as classification challenges. We explored the capability of Large Language Models (LLMs), particularly GPT-4, in zero- or few-shot settings enhanced by retrieval augmentation and re-ranking for Tweet classification. Our goal was to determine if LLMs could match or surpass traditional methods in this context.

We conducted an ablation study with LLaMA for comparison, and our results indicate that our models significantly outperformed the baselines, securing second place in the Target Detection task. The code for our submission is available at `https://github.com/NaiveNeuron/bryndza-case-2024`.

1 Introduction

The Climate Activism Stance and Hate Event Detection (Thapa et al., 2024) aims to extend the growing body of work on stance, target and hate event detection (Parihar et al., 2021) by exploring these tasks in the context of Climate Activism. It does so by utilizing a novel ClimaConvo dataset (Shiwakoti et al., 2024), which is one of the first multi-aspect datasets of its kind.

While traditional approaches to stance, target, and hate event detection rely on finetuned classifiers, our study takes a different route. We explore how a data scientist or analyst, with only API access to a Large Language Model (LLM) and without the option to finetune or alter the model, can still develop effective solutions. By creatively adjusting the prompts given to the LLM and using external tools like vector databases and pretrained ranking models for enhancement, we've found this simple method to be surprisingly competitive. Despite its simplicity, it secured the second-highest performance in the target detection subtask.

2 Related Work

For the past couple of years, the progress of Natural Language Processing has been driven largely by existence and availability of datasets and data resources. In the context of climate, some notable examples include Climatebert: A pretrained language model for climate-related text (Webersinke et al., 2021), a dataset for detecting real-world environmental claims (Stammbach et al., 2022) as well as the newly introduced ClimaConvo dataset (Shiwakoti et al., 2024), which forms the basis of the shared task on Stance and Hate Event Detection in Tweets Related to Climate Activism.

All of the subtasks of this shared task can be modeled as classification problems and as such there exists an extensive body of academic work on this topic. In particular, methods like SVM (Malmasi and Zampieri, 2017), LSTM (Del Vigna12 et al., 2017) as well as custom architectures such as DeepHate (Cao et al., 2020) have been proposed and evaluated. Inspired by outstanding generalizational ability of Large Language Models – including ChatGPT [1], GPT-4 (Achiam et al., 2023), LLaMA (Touvron et al., 2023) and others – and their performance in classification tasks, especially in zero- and few-shot settings, we investigate their adaptability and effectiveness for the tasks of stance, target and hate event detection. Although works whose aim would be similar do exist, such as for instance (Cruickshank and Ng, 2023) and (Guo et al., 2024), a shared task provides a unique opportunity for a thorough evaluation on many dimensions, which is lacking in the literature and uniquely distinguishes our work.

3 Dataset

To execute the described experiments we used the dataset introduced in (Shiwakoti et al., 2024) and described in Table 1. In line with the framework of

[1]`https://chat.openai.com`

Proceedings of the 7th Workshop on Challenges and Applications of Automated Extraction of Socio-political Events from Text (CASE 2024), pages 166–177
March 22, 2024 ©2024 Association for Computational Linguistics

shared tasks, during the "evaluation" stage of the shared task the organizers first shared the train split of the datasets, using the validation split for testing. When it came to the "testing" stage, the organizers released labels associated with the validation split, leaving the test part of the dataset for testing and final evaluation. Hence, the evaluated models had access to both the train and valid parts of the dataset.

Subtask	Classes	Train	Valid	Test
Subtask A	`Non-Hate`	6385	1371	1374
	`Hate`	899	190	188
Subtask B	`Individual`	563	120	121
	`Organization`	105	23	23
	`Community`	31	7	6
Subtask C	`Support`	4328	897	921
	`Oppose`	700	153	141
	`Neutral`	2256	511	500

Table 1: Statistics of the train, valid and test splits of the provided datset. Note that the datasets for Subtask A and Subtask B are exactly the same content-wise; it is just the labels that change.

As we can observe in Table 1, the splits of the datasets are generally evenly split across the three subtasks. It seems the only exception is the Subtask C (stance detection), in which both the train and valid sets were split in 59:31:10 and 57:33:10 rations respectively, whereas the test set was split in 59:32:9 ratio.

A cursory glance at the dataset has also revealed that a relatively significant proportion of its tweets (489 in total) contains the sentence "You've been fooled by Greta Thunberg". While an interesting tidbit, it is almost certainly an artefact of the data collection process and provides insight into the peculiarities of the task and the data it uses for evaluation – particularly since in an overwhelming number of cases the tweets that contain this substring are labelled as `Hate`, `Individual` and `Oppose` for Subtasks A, B and C, respectively.

4 System description

As outlined above, the primary component of our system is a Large Language Model, namely GPT-4, which was chosen for its strong zero-shot and few-shot capability. The model was accessed via the Azure OpenAI service and was not changed and/or finetuned as part of our experimentation – the only attribute of the system that changed from one configuration to the other is the prompt that is sent to the GPT-4 API. In our experiments we utilized the `2023-07-01-preview` version[2] and unless otherwise noted, the temperature has been set to 0 in order to make the experiments reproducible. We also utilize paralellism in order to decrease the time necessary for the whole pipeline to run. In the end, the evaluation of our models on Subtask A and Subtask C takes roughly 25 minutes, whereas it is possible to evaluate Subtask B within 2 minutes and 30 seconds.

4.1 Obtaining the prompt template

As we already established, the prompt is the crucial part of our system, as it is its only changing part. To arrive at a suitable prompt for each of the subtasks, we utilized GPT-4 itself. Let us illustrate this approach on Subtask A. To generate its prompt, a small sample of 30 `Non-Hate` and 30 Hate tweets has been selected and sent to GPT-4 along with the following prefix:

```
You will be given $n_examples
   tweets that were classified
    as hate speech. Your task
   is to find a common pattern
    these texts share and
   figure out why they were
   classified as hate speech.
   For a good comparison, I
   will also send you
   $n_examples non-hate speech
    tweets so you have
   something to compare it to.
     Since these are tweets,
   focus on hashtags (#).
```

Note further that the `$n_examples` in the prompt would be replaced with the actual number of examples provided after this "prompt prefix". The resulting response from GPT-4 would then be lightly edited by a human expert (typically done by one of the authors to ensure common formatting across all the prompts) such that the end result would be a prompt similar to that presented in Appendix A.

4.2 Retrieval-augmentation

As we can see in the prompts listed in Appendix A, Appendix B and Appendix C, each of the prompts (or prompt templates/prefixes) ends with a `##`

[2] `https://learn.microsoft.com/en-us/azure/ai-services/openai/reference`

Examples section. This section is optional and does not necessarily need to be populated, in which case GPT-4 would be used in so called zero-shot setup (model **GPT-4** in Table 2). If examples are to be used, however, there are multiple options for choosing them.

The first one is to choose a fixed number of examples (k) that will be part of the prompt template every time it is used and will not change with each example the model processes (the **GPT-4 few-shot** models in Table 2). An alternative approach would be to try to extend the prompt with examples from the training set similar to the input sample in the hopes of providing further context for the LLM to make the final classification decision. This is the core idea behind retrieval-augmented generation (RAG, introduced in (Lewis et al., 2020)) which we adapt for our classification problems.

In particular, we utilize the Chroma vector database [3] to create an index of embeddings generated by one of two pre-trained Sentence Transformer models [4]: all-MiniLM-L6-v2 which is the default embedding model the Chroma vector database makes use of and at the time of writing a Sentence Transformer with the best speed/performance ratio (resulting in the **GPT-4 RAG** model in Table 2) and all-mpnet-base-v2 which reports the best peformance on standardized benchmarks at the cost of being larger and slower (and results in the **GPT-4 RAG all** model in Table 2). At inference time the same model that was used for index creation will provide the embedding for the sample that is being evaluated and this representation will be used to query the database, which will return the k closest items from its index. These will then be lightly formatted[5] and provided as the final part of the prompt in the ### Examples section (please refer to Appendix A, Appendix B and Appendix C for more details).

Note that regardless of what process and model is being used the input tweets are used verbatim, without any pre-processing.

4.3 Re-ranking

Although the approach outlined in the section above is certain an improvement over a fixed list of examples, it can still potentially suffer from limitations of the underlying model(s). In particular, while they do leverage semantic information, they generally do not make use of contrastive information which in turn means that for instance the sentences "I love trees!" and "I hate trees!" will most probably have very high similarity score – an attribute that might not be desirable in tasks like Stance, Target and Hate Event detection.

A popular way of alleviating this issue is to make use of the concept of re-ranking in which a larger number of items (for instance $3 \times k$) is requested from the index and using a pre-trained model computes relevance scores for each and thus alters their order. The top k items can then be taken and processed further as described above.

In our case we use the flashrank library (Damodaran, 2023) which provides a finetuned rank-T5-flan model based on RankT5 (Zhuang et al., 2023). We also experiment with the RAGatouille library[6] but in our experiments its performance was at best comparable to that of flashrank, so we only report its scores in Table 2 (model **GPT-4 flashrank**).

4.4 Parsing the results

As can be seen in Appendix A, Appendix B and Appendix C, the prompts are designed to elicit chain-of-thought style reasoning in the model output (Wei et al., 2022). It is hence rather difficult to ensure the output matches a specific template which would imply one of the possible classes. To that end, we match a specific keyword (e.g. Prediction: 1) towards both the beginning as well as the end of the LLM output.

5 Results & Discussion

The results of our experiments can be found in Table 2. Nearly all of the models outperform the baselines introduced in (Shiwakoti et al., 2024) on F1 score, the primary metric chosen for this shared task. In Subtask B the baseline models report higher performance than the zero-shot evaluated GPT-4 but even a few hardcoded examples in the prompt changes the performance of the model rather dramatically (improvement of nearly 0.2 F1 points). In Subtask C we observe a similar situation, although simply adding hardcoded examples to prompt does not significantly help – curiously enough, it even leads to decreased performance.

[3]https://www.trychroma.com/

[4]https://www.sbert.net/docs/pretrained_models.html

[5]By "lightly formatted" we mean that a string denoting a beginning of the tweet would be added. There is no other pre- or post-processing done on the input data.

[6]https://github.com/bclavie/RAGatouille

Model	Subtask A					Subtask B					Subtask C				
	Acc	P	R	F1	rnk	Acc	P	R	F1	rnk	Acc	P	R	F1	rnk
Baseline	.901	-	-	.708	-	.716	-	-	.554		.651	-	-	.545	-
`GPT-4`	.935	.835	.880	.856	-	.900	.545	.656	.553	-	.693	.515	.513	.509	-
`GPT-4 few-shot` (k=6)	.932	.826	.895	.855	-	.927	**.809**	.723	.747	-	.693	.502	.507	.487	-
`GPT-4 few-shot` (k=8)	.916	.794	.886	.855	-	.927	**.809**	.723	.747	-	.702	.511	.512	.495	-
`GPT-4 RAG` (k=4)	.944	.859	.890	.874	-	.887	.641	.672	.654	-	.707	.517	.514	.498	-
`GPT-4 RAG` (k=6)	.941	.851	.889	.868	-	.927	.781	.776	.776	2/18	.690	.668	.681	.666	-
`GPT-4 RAG` (k=8)	.942	.855	.887	.870	-	.927	.733	.764	.769	-	.688	.666	.678	.661	-
`GPT-4 RAG all` (k=6)	.948	.866	.899	.881	7/22	.920	.776	.762	.767	-	.714	.692	.709	.692	-
`GPT-4 RAG all` (k=8)	.944	.864	.884	.874	-	.920	.715	.721	.716	-	.711	.687	.712	.693	12/19
`GPT-4 flashrank` (k=6)	.941	.853	.877	.864	-	**.940**	.635	.617	.625	-	.709	**.689**	.707	**.693**	-
`GPT-4 flashrank` (k=8)	.941	.851	.886	.868	-	.913	.733	.706	.713	-	.702	.683	.703	.688	-

Table 2: Model Performance Metrics for the respective subtasks. **Acc**, **P**, **R**, **F1** and **rnk** denote the Accuracy, Precision, Recall, the F1 score and the final rank in the Shared Task (measured by the F1 score), respectively. The final rank is reported as r/n where r denotes the position in the final results table for the respective subtask and n denotes the number of teams that participated in a specific subtask. The baseline results are from (Shiwakoti et al., 2024). Highest performance per each metric in each subtask is **bolded**. The performance of the model submitted to the final leaderboard is in green.

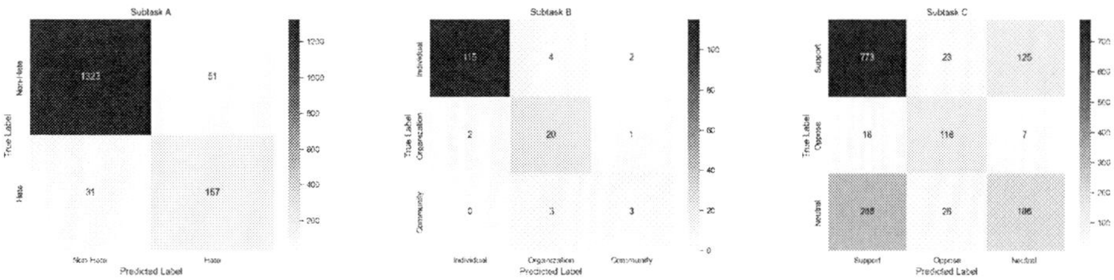

(a) Confusion matrix for Subtask A (b) Confusion matrix for Subtask B (c) Confusion matrix for Subtask C

Figure 1: Confusion matrices of for the best performing models on each of the subtasks.

In general, Table 2 suggest that adding retrieval agumentation generally helps, while the optimal number of examples and the optimal model in the prompt (k) varies per subtask. As we can see in the case of Subtask A and Subtask C, the `all-mpnet-base-v2` model has proven to be most effective, providing the final submission with $k = 6$ for Subtask A and obtaining the split best performance with **`GPT-4 flashrank`** ($k = 6$) in Subtask C (with $k = 8$). In Subtask B the retrieval-augmentation method based on `all-MiniLM-L6-v2` yielded the best results, although the difference between the top 3 models are very small, to the point of being attributable to noise more than model/method differences. The results also suggest that the re-ranking approach using `flashrank` did not bring significant benefit over retrieval-augmentation.

In Figure 1 we can see the confusion matrices for the best performing models (highlighted in green in Table 2) for each of the subtasks. As the figures suggest, in Subtask A and Subtask B the models made minimal mistakes whereas in Subtask C we can observe that the model often switched the Neutral stance to Support and vice versa. We explore this phenomenon further in the next section.

5.1 Error analysis

To better understand the error modes of the evaluated models, we take the incorrect predictions of the best performing models and classify them into three categories: "Error", when the model did indeed make an incorrect prediction; "Unclear", when it is not clear whether the model made a mistake or whether the provided label is wrong, and "Wrong-Label" in which our manual annotation disagreed with that obtained from the provided test set. The annotation was done by one of the authors, followed the guidelines outlined in (Shiwakoti et al., 2024) and its results can be seen in Table 3.

With regards to the Hate Event Detection subtask, the model did indeed make a mistake in 27 (33%) cases but in 36 (44%) cases we identified a wrong label, while 19 cases (23%) where unclear.

(a) SubTask A: Hate Event Detection

Prediction	Label	Error	Unclear	Wrong-Label
Non-Hate	Hate	1	5	25
Hate	Non-Hate	26	14	11

(b) SubTask B: Target Detection

Prediction	Label	Error	Unclear	Wrong-Label
Individual	Organization	0	1	1
Organization	Individual	1	0	3
Organization	Community	2	1	0
Community	Individual	1	0	1
Community	Organization	0	0	1

(c) SubTask C: Stance Detection

Prediction	Label	Error	Unclear	Wrong-Label
Support	Oppose	2	1	15
Support	Neutral	10	8	268
Oppose	Support	11	2	10
Oppose	Neutral	0	3	25
Neutral	Support	46	12	67
Neutral	Oppose	0	2	5

Table 3: Error type counts by Prediction and Label combinations across SubTasks. Prediction represents the model's prediction and Label the annotation obtained from the test set.

A closer look at the error cases reveals that the model seems to overtrigger on negative concepts such as "crimes against humanity" or "anger" and considers them a Hate event (see Table 5). We hypothesize that this might be an artefact of the retrieval-augmentation.

On the Target Detection subtask, the model only made 12 mistakes in total, some of which seem to stem from wrong labels (see Table 6).

In the Stance Detection task, a significant amount (80%) of tweets were mislabeled, especially from Support to Neutral direction (55%), highlighting difficulties in defining the Support class, like if a mention of a hashtag alone qualifies. A selection of the issues can be seen in Table 7.

Our analysis indicates that model performance evaluation could suffer due to issues with the underlying dataset, as it contains tweets such as marketing tweets irrelevant to climate activism [7] and single-character tweets ('0'). Had all Wrong-Label annotations been updated, the model perforamnce would be significantly higher. We recommend reannotating the at least the test sets and updating the annotation guide to address ambiguous cases. To assist with this effort, we are releasing our error annotations as part of our submission code.

[7] See the first example in Table 7.

6 Ablation study with LLaMA

To assess to what extent would a similar approach work with a model other than GPT-4 and to provide further insight into how much of the final performance is attributable to the base model versus the other additions (e.g. RAG and/or re-ranking) we conduct an ablation study in which we replace GPT-4 with LLaMA 2 70B (Touvron et al., 2023). We use Subtask B, in which we obtained the best results with GPT-4, as the benchmark task and due to limitations of the LLaMA's context window we further limit ourselves to $k = 6$ examples in the prompt. Other than that the evaluated models are identical to those described in Section 4.

Model	Subtask B				
	Acc	P	R	F1	rnk
Baseline	.716	-	-	.554	-
`LLaMA`	.813	.604	.348	.327	-
`LLaMA few-shot` (k=6)	.813	.477	.371	.372	-
`LLaMA RAG` (k=6)	.793	.386	.351	.343	-
`LLaMA RAG all` (k=6)	**.827**	**.811**	**.482**	**.539**	14/18
`LLaMA flashrank` (k=6)	**.827**	.656	.453	.492	-

Table 4: Model Performance Metrics for the LLaMA ablation study. The legend is identical to Table 2.

The results can be seen in Table 4 where we can observe a phenomenon similar to that presented in Table 2: adding examples to the prompt generally helps, retrieval-augmentation can further improve the performance while re-ranking does not yield substantial improvement. We note, however, that comparing the two tables show that the base model has substantial impact on the final performance. In case of LLaMA, none of the evaluated models was able beat the baseline F1 score, which would land it at the 14th place (out of 18 teams). This is in direct contrast with our best model based on GPT-4, which ended up ranking second.

7 Conclusion

In this work we evaluate GPT-4 extended with retrieval augmentation and re-ranking on the task of Stance, Target and Hate Event Detection. We investigate to what extent is it possible utilize GPT-4 as a black box and obtain solid performance by only changing its prompt and also compare it to the LLaMA model. Our results show that augmenting GPT-4 with retrieval mechanism can lead to it serving as a classification model with competitive performance, as evidenced by the fact that it ranked 2nd in Subtask B: Target Detection.

Limitations

The primary experiments presented in this work depend on access to a specific commercial Large Language Model which limits both the reproducibility and direct applicability of the obtained results. Similarly, the LLaMA model used in the ablation study requires a significant amount of computation resources, limiting its accessibility.

Acknowledgements

This work was partially supported by the grant APVV-21-0114.

References

Josh Achiam, Steven Adler, Sandhini Agarwal, Lama Ahmad, Ilge Akkaya, Florencia Leoni Aleman, Diogo Almeida, Janko Altenschmidt, Sam Altman, Shyamal Anadkat, et al. 2023. Gpt-4 technical report. *arXiv preprint arXiv:2303.08774*.

Rui Cao, Roy Ka-Wei Lee, and Tuan-Anh Hoang. 2020. Deephate: Hate speech detection via multi-faceted text representations. In *Proceedings of the 12th ACM Conference on Web Science*, pages 11–20.

Iain J. Cruickshank and Lynnette Hui Xian Ng. 2023. Use of large language models for stance classification.

Prithiviraj Damodaran. 2023. FlashRank, Lightest and Fastest 2nd Stage Reranker for search pipelines.

Fabio Del Vigna12, Andrea Cimino23, Felice Dell'Orletta, Marinella Petrocchi, and Maurizio Tesconi. 2017. Hate me, hate me not: Hate speech detection on facebook. In *Proceedings of the first Italian conference on cybersecurity (ITASEC17)*, pages 86–95.

Keyan Guo, Alexander Hu, Jaden Mu, Ziheng Shi, Ziming Zhao, Nishant Vishwamitra, and Hongxin Hu. 2024. An investigation of large language models for real-world hate speech detection.

Patrick Lewis, Ethan Perez, Aleksandra Piktus, Fabio Petroni, Vladimir Karpukhin, Naman Goyal, Heinrich Küttler, Mike Lewis, Wen-tau Yih, Tim Rocktäschel, et al. 2020. Retrieval-augmented generation for knowledge-intensive nlp tasks. *Advances in Neural Information Processing Systems*, 33:9459–9474.

Shervin Malmasi and Marcos Zampieri. 2017. Detecting hate speech in social media. *arXiv preprint arXiv:1712.06427*.

Anil Singh Parihar, Surendrabikram Thapa, and Sushruti Mishra. 2021. Hate speech detection using natural language processing: Applications and challenges. In *2021 5th International Conference on Trends in Electronics and Informatics (ICOEI)*, pages 1302–1308.

Shuvam Shiwakoti, Surendrabikram Thapa, Kritesh Rauniyar, Akshyat Shah, Aashish Bhandari, and Usman Naseem. 2024. Analyzing the dynamics of climate change discourse on twitter: A new annotated corpus and multi-aspect classification. *Preprint*.

Dominik Stammbach, Nicolas Webersinke, Julia Anna Bingler, Mathias Kraus, and Markus Leippold. 2022. A dataset for detecting real-world environmental claims. *Center for Law & Economics Working Paper Series*, 2022(07).

Surendrabikram Thapa, Kritesh Rauniyar, Farhan Ahmad Jafri, Shuvam Shiwakoti, Hariram Veeramani, Raghav Jain, Guneet Singh Kohli, Ali Hürriyetoğlu, and Usman Naseem. 2024. Stance and hate event detection in tweets related to climate activism - shared task at case 2024. In *Proceedings of the 7th Workshop on Challenges and Applications of Automated Extraction of Socio-political Events from Text (CASE)*.

Hugo Touvron, Louis Martin, Kevin Stone, Peter Albert, Amjad Almahairi, Yasmine Babaei, Nikolay Bashlykov, Soumya Batra, Prajjwal Bhargava, Shruti Bhosale, et al. 2023. Llama 2: Open foundation and fine-tuned chat models. *arXiv preprint arXiv:2307.09288*.

Nicolas Webersinke, Mathias Kraus, Julia Anna Bingler, and Markus Leippold. 2021. Climatebert: A pretrained language model for climate-related text. *arXiv preprint arXiv:2110.12010*.

Jason Wei, Xuezhi Wang, Dale Schuurmans, Maarten Bosma, Fei Xia, Ed Chi, Quoc V Le, Denny Zhou, et al. 2022. Chain-of-thought prompting elicits reasoning in large language models. *Advances in Neural Information Processing Systems*, 35:24824–24837.

Honglei Zhuang, Zhen Qin, Rolf Jagerman, Kai Hui, Ji Ma, Jing Lu, Jianmo Ni, Xuanhui Wang, and Michael Bendersky. 2023. Rankt5: Fine-tuning t5 for text ranking with ranking losses. In *Proceedings of the 46th International ACM SIGIR Conference on Research and Development in Information Retrieval*, pages 2308–2313.

A Prompt for Subtask A

```
Analyze the input tweet to
   determine if it is hate speech
    or not, based on the
   following criteria:

## Hate Speech Patterns

1. Presence of "You've been
   fooled by Greta Thunberg" or #
   FridaysForFuture in the tweet.
2. Embodies aggression or
   contempt towards specific
   groups or institutions,
   including dismissive attitudes
    towards climate activists,
   criticism of world leaders for
    climate inaction, or strong
   sentiments against companies
   investing in fossil fuels.
3. Frequent use of negative
   language, such as 'shame', '
   lie', 'greedy', 'fake', 'idiot
   ', to express dissatisfaction
   or attack others.
4. Highlights a strong
   ideological alignment or
   belief, often against fossil
   fuels and blaming capitalism
   for the climate crisis,
   indicating belief-driven
   intolerance.
5. The tone is accusatory,
   confrontational, and not
   oriented towards dialogue or
   understanding.

## \texttt{Non-Hate} Speech
   Patterns

1. Expresses concern about
   climate change and promotes
   action without aggression or
   contempt. Advocates for policy
    changes, shares environmental
    information, and encourages
   collective action rather than
   targeting individuals or
   groups.
2. Lacks negative language or
   personal attacks.
3. Presents a clear ideological
   stance on climate change in a
   constructive or informative
   manner, aiming to educate or
   raise awareness rather than
   cast blame.
4. The tone is conversational and
    informative, promoting
   understanding and engagement
   rather than confrontation.

## Evaluation

- If the tweet aligns more with
   the Hate Speech Patterns,
   output: 'Prediction: 1' (
   indicating it is hate speech).
- If the tweet aligns more with
   the \texttt{Non-Hate} Speech
   Patterns, output: 'Prediction:
    0' (indicating it is not hate
    speech).

## Examples
```

B Prompt for Subtask B

```
Analyze the following tweet and
   classify who the target of the
    hate speech is. Use the
   identified patterns and
   specific examples from the
   training data for
   classification. The categories
    are:

## Categories

1. Individual - Involves direct
   attacks on specific
   individuals. Common examples
   include derogatory remarks
   about individuals like "Trump"
    or "Greta Thunberg". Look for
    usage of individual names and
    personal attacks.

2. Organization - Involves
   criticisms targeted at larger
   entities such as governments,
   companies, or specific
   organizations. Key examples
```

include attacks on 'Government ', 'Big oil companies', ' Australia' (referring to its government), 'Wilderness Committee', and the 'EU'. Look for mentions of these entities and critiques of their policies or actions.

3. Community - Involves attacks on broader communities or societal groups. Typical terms used include 'White, middle class, educated, low earners', 'humans', 'adult society', and 'politicians'. This category shifts the focus from a single party to collective human behavior, demographic groups, or societal constructs .

Use chain of thought reasoning to explain your classification. After analyzing the tweet, classify it as "Prediction: 1" for an individual, " Prediction: 2" for an organization, or "Prediction: 3" for a community. Pick only one option and put it on a new line.

Examples

C Prompt for Subtask C

Analyze the following tweet and determine its stance towards the topic of Climate Activism. The stance categories are:

Stance Categories

1. Support - These tweets show explicit support for climate action. Look for advocacy phrases like "we are mobilizing", "#ClimateJustice ", "fight the #ClimateCrisis", and "Champion young people as 'drivers of change'". These often convey support through sharing news, events, or activities that promote environmental protection and sustainability.

2. Oppose - These tweets contain negative sentiments or skepticism about climate action initiatives. Phrases like "You've been fooled by Greta Thunberg", "Recycling is literally a scam!!", and rhetorical questions like " What are we saving?" are indicative of this stance. These tweets may criticize the activities of climate activists or question the credibility of climate change facts.

3. Neutral - Neutral tweets share information about climate-related activities or news without a clear stance. They use neutral language to describe events, initiatives, or outcomes, such as "At more than 750 locations worldwide - including Antarctica - youth organizers and allies united under the hashtag # PeopleNotProfit. # FridaysforFuture." These tweets do not show subjective bias or opinion towards climate action.

Keywords like 'support', ' solidarity', 'join us' suggest a supportive stance; 'fooled ', 'What are we saving?', ' Greenwashing' suggest opposition; and factual reports or informative language suggest a neutral stance. The context of word usage is key for correct categorization.

```
Use chain of thought reasoning to
    explain your classification.
   After analyzing the tweet,
   classify its stance as '
   Prediction: 1' for Support, '
   Prediction: 2' for Oppose, or
   'Prediction: 3' for Neutral.
   Pick only one option and put
   it on a new line. If the tweet
    is a factual statement,
   classify its target as
   described above.

## Examples
```

D Sample Errors

Prediction	Label	Tweet
Wrong-Label		
Non-Hate	Hate	Young people in Bangladesh took to the streets demanding a halt to the planned expansion of the #Matarbari coal-fired power plant. https://t.co/S5oo5Z3yCu #FridaysForFuture #ClimateActionNow
Hate	Non-Hate	FFF = 666. Greta Thunberg, WEF & build back better are fronts for satan. https://t.co/uRnK9nRKIq via @YouTube #FridaysForFuture #GretaThunberg #WEF #BuildBackBetter #Satanism
Unclear		
Hate	Non-Hate	With every lie they've told, it's our future that they've sold. Week 50!! #ClimateStrike #FridaysForFuture #PeopleNotProfit https://t.co/nATjq2ICKc
Non-Hate	Hate	This #FridaysForFuture on Zoom we will get boozy at 8pm CET (or drink soda if that's not your thing) and send some rage or wackiness to manufacturers of food items in our pantries about their packaging materials. Link information here: https://t.co/U3gdzYOcEC #peoplenotprofit
Error		
Hate	Non-Hate	This is huge. The top climate scientist in the world basically accuses Manchin of crimes against humanity. @s_guilbeault @JustinTrudeau @GeorgeHeyman #fridaysforfuture
Hate	Non-Hate	If you are unhappy about the lack of serious climate-positive actions, put pressure on politicians. Show your anger every #FridaysForFuture at 11 a.m. in front of Queen's Park and every other legislature and city hall in the world. Politicians are convinced that we don't care.

Table 5: Sample errors annotated as part of the Error Analysis for SubTask A: Hate Event Detection.

Wrong-Label		
Prediction	Label	Tweet
Organization	Individual	@Citi @Citi spent the last 5 years investing $285 billion into destroying our futures. #FridaysForFuture #Divest https://t.co/y28248UskW
Community	Individual	Wow. Blame young #FridaysForFuture climate activists for lack of protests on the specific days of the recent heatwave, after all the vilification they've had to endure for 'skipping school'? How about some #adultingnotadultification?
Unclear		
Community	Organization	Week 121. Finnish forestry is bad for the climate, biodiversity and people. What Finland has is a lot of plantations and hardly any natural and old-growth forests. Finland must stop harmful forestry practices and protect and restore more forests. #FridaysForFuture https://t.co/lLvdvlJGNh
Error		
Organization	Community	@dw_environment @Luisamneubauer @Fridays4future #FridaysForFuture has remained influenced by strong left ideology/persons and denies the science using (existing) nuclear in climate/independence policies.

Table 6: Sample errors annotated as part of the Error Analysis for SubTask B: Target Detection.

Prediction	Label	Tweet
Wrong-Label		
Neutral	Support	Saasland - MultiPurpose WordPress Theme for Saas Startup: https://t.co/qbEYbFIkFy Elementor WooCommerce WPML #WP #WebsiteBuilder #WebsiteDevelopment #100DaysOfCode #HTML #webdev #WordPress #ladningpage #FridaysForFuture #FridayMotivation https://t.co/4J0X5O2E3D
Support	Neutral	Humans are destroying the very air, land and water resources we need to survive. #ausvotes #ClimateAction #ClimateCrisis #environment #FridaysForFuture #nocoal #solarpower #StopAdani
Unclear		
Support	Neutral	Climate strike in Bergen, Norway. #FridaysForFuture #ClimateJustice #GreenFriday @fff_bergen https://t.co/zp4Jp6PmbP
Neutral	Support	#Fridaysforfuture, Dublin, Week 179. Supported by @tangfood @LoretoAbbey_ @Janemellett @mimsmo @AngelaDeegan1 @GretaThunberg https://t.co/dtxefh9e3Y
Error		
Oppose	Support	By no means do young people have the social & structural CAPACITIES to stand a chance against the threat that is runaway climate breakdown. Not to say that they actually did gang up and did ANYTHING in their power to deal with the problem. Look at @sunrisemvmt & #FridaysforFuture
Support	Neutral	Jim Cramer: Stay away from oil and gas stocks, I don't wan to touch it, stay away, no one wants oil https://t.co/Vs6DLZ1wcM , use better insulators in doors, #fridaysforfuture, look at @Dothegreenthing https://t.co/Apxwot66Wc

Table 7: Sample errors annotated as part of the Error Analysis for SubTask C: Stance Detection.

IUST at ClimateActivism 2024: Towards Optimal Stance Detection: A Systematic Study of Architectural Choices and Data Cleaning Techniques

Ghazaleh Mahmoudi and **Sauleh Eetemadi**
School of Computer Engineering, Iran University of Science and Technology, Iran
gh_mahmoodi@comp.iust.ac.ir, sauleh@iust.ac.ir

Abstract

This paper describes the IUST submission for sub-task C of the Climate Activism Shared Task at The 7th CASE workshop at EACL 2024. This work presents a systematic search of various model architecture configurations and data cleaning methods. The study evaluates the impact of data cleaning methods on the obtained results. Additionally, we demonstrate that a combination of CNN and Encoder-only models such as BERTweet outperforms FNNs. Moreover, by utilizing data augmentation, we are able to overcome the challenge of data imbalance. Our best system achieves 74.47% F1-Score on the unseen test set, outperforming the baseline by 19.97% and ranked 3th among 19 participants.

1 Introduction

Climate change stands as one of the most critical challenges of our time, impacting ecosystems, economies, and communities worldwide. At the same time, understanding the public stance towards this pivotal issue is increasingly vital. Leveraging NLP techniques to gauge public stance on climate change, especially from Twitter data, provides an innovative means to comprehend diverse perspectives and sentiments in real time. To advance research in this domain, the ClimateActivism 2024 Shared Task[1] proposes three sub-tasks focused on Stance and Hate Event Detection (Thapa et al., 2024).
Sub-Task C is about Stance detection (also known as stance classification) which is a problem related to social media analysis, and natural language processing, which aims to determine the position of a person from a piece of text they produce, towards a target (a concept, idea, event, etc.) either explicitly specified in the text or implied only (Küçük and Can, 2022).

Our work focuses on exploring various model architectures and data cleaning methods to improve the performance of stance detection models on Twitter data related to climate change. We also investigate the impact of data imbalance on model performance and propose a solution using data augmentation techniques.

Our best approach utilizes a combination of Convolutional Neural Networks (CNN) and BERTweet to capture both local and global context information in the input text with Weighted Cross Entropy as loss function. Our experiments show that a combination of CNN and BERTweet outperforms Feedforward Neural Networks (FNNs) in stance detection on climate change related tweets. We also demonstrate that data augmentation can address the challenge of data imbalance, resulting improvements in model performance. We also experiment with different data cleaning methods. Moreover, the best results in the data cleaning type are achieved by removing URLs and usernames, and all experiments of this method have yielded better results compared to other data cleaning methods. Code and results are publicly available on *https://github.com/ghazaleh-mahmoodi/Climate_Activism_Stance_Detection.*

2 Data

The Sub-Task C (Stance Detection) dataset is part of the Multi-Aspect Twitter Dataset (Shiwakoti et al., 2024). The data was collected from tweets posted between January 1, 2022, and December 30, 2022. The selection criteria involved hashtags such as #climatecrisis, #climatechange, #ClimateEmergency, #ClimateTalk, #globalwarming, as well as activist-oriented hashtags like #FridaysForFuture, #climatestrike, etc. The dataset distribution is illustrated in Table 1.

[1] https://emw.ku.edu.tr/case-2024/

Proceedings of the 7th Workshop on Challenges and Applications of Automated Extraction of Socio-political Events from Text (CASE 2024), pages 178–184
March 22, 2024

Split	%	Support	Neutral	Against
Train	70%	4328	2256	700
Dev	15%	897	511	153
Test	15%	921	500	141
All	100%	6146	3276	994

Table 1: Class distribution of stance detection dataset

2.1 Data Pre-processing

As the text data is sourced from Twitter, it is necessary to carry out pre-processing to enhance the extractable features and ensure the cleanliness of the text. When it comes to cleaning data, the principle is to not throw away any data. However, given that our data is limited and if we don't remove some noise, the model may be inaccurate (in limited data), so we need to perform a certain level of data cleaning. However, based on the assumptions we will explain below, we have examine a limited number of data cleaning methods. The defined methods will involve increasing levels of text input cleaning, from the least to the most aggressive.

I. **Original Tweet Text**: Without any changes in the text.

II. **Removing URL**: Considering that URLs are modified (e.g., ://t.co/rs1vhBp2ax), we assumed their presence in the data could cause errors.

III. **Removing username**: The existence of usernames without information about the person may create ambiguity.

IV. **Removing URL and username**: To determine the effect of removing the URL and username together.

V. **Removing URL and username and split hashtag**: For example `#FridaysForFuture` becomes `Fridays For Future`.

VI. **Removing URL and username, split hashtag, and convert all letters to lowercase**: Sometimes writing letters in capital form has a special meaning, which we want to observe its impact.

VII. **Complete cleaning**: Contains removing URL, username, stop words, punctuation, converting all letters to lowercase, and split hashtag.

2.2 Data Augmentation

One of the existing challenges is the imbalance of the dataset. In such conditions, the trained model tends to lean towards the class with more data. To address this issue, we generate additional data for minority class data. We use two different methods to generate data.

1. **Substitution**: We use synonym substitution as an augmentation method. We employ the method provided by python nlpaug library (Ma, 2019) based on RoBERTa (Liu et al., 2019a).

2. **Round-trip translation**: We translate the English texts to German and then back to generate extra data using python nlpaug library.

We generated 950 data points for the "oppose" class using the introduced data augmentation methods and added them to the training data . The class distribution of data before and after data augmentation can be observed in Figure 1.

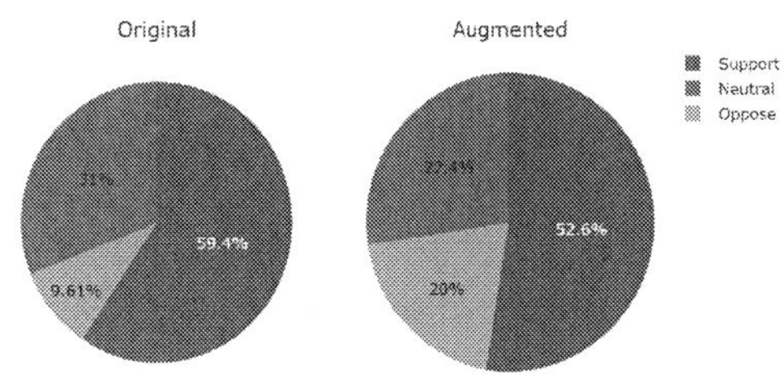

Figure 1: Train Set Class distribution

3 Methodology

We proposed a model comprising four modules, and to determine the most suitable parameters for each module, we conducted numerous experiments with various configurations, seeking the optimal values within the defined search space (Table 2). Using the Optuna library (Akiba et al., 2019), which employs a sampler using the TPE (Tree-structured Parzen Estimator) algorithm, we selected the optimal model configuration based on the Macro F1-score on the development set. In the following, we provide a brief explanation of the search space defined for each module.

1. **Embedding**: We are searching among several Encoder-only Language Models to determine which one to choose for extracting features from text. We chose Encoder-only models because they are more popular and efficient for text classification. The search space includes:
   - **BERT** (Devlin et al., 2019)
   - **RoBERTa**: Builds on BERT and modifies key hyperparameters, removing the

next-sentence pretraining objective and training with much larger mini-batches and learning rates.(Liu et al., 2019b).

- **BERTweet**: Trained based on the RoBERTa for English Tweets (Nguyen et al., 2020).
- **XLM-RoBERTa**: A multilingual pre-trained language model, trained on 2.5TB of filtered CommonCrawl data. (Ruder et al., 2019).
- **DEBERTA**: Improves the BERT and RoBERTa models using disentangled attention and enhanced mask decoder (He et al., 2021).

2. **Classifier**: There are two options.
   - **Fully Connected Neural Networks**. We use a three-layer network architecture with a linear layer, a ReLU activation function, and a dropout. Finally, we apply a softmax function to the output.
   - **Convolutional Neural Networks**. The architecture used is the same as the one introduced by Safaya et al. (2020), with the difference that instead of 4 last layers, we defined the search space and examined. In this architecture the embeddings are fed into parallel convolutional filters of five different sizes (768x1, 768x2, 768x3, 768x4, 768x5), with 32 filters for each size. Each Kernel utilizes the outputs from the preceding N last hidden layers[2] of Encoder-only (e.g., BERT) as separate channels and conducts a convolution operation. Following this, the resulting outputs undergo ReLU Activation and Global Max-Pooling processes. The pooled outputs are then concatenated, flattened, and fed through a dense layer and softmax function to obtain the final class.
3. **Optimizer**: The search space includes four well-known optimizers (Table 2) that have shown good performance.
4. **Loss Function**: Since we are dealing with the classification task and imbalanced data, we have chosen two loss functions that are suitable for our experiments.
   - **Focal Loss**: This loss addresses class imbalance by down-weighting easy well-classified examples during the training stage. It puts more emphasis on hard examples o improve overall performance (Lin et al., 2017).
   - **Weighted Cross Entropy**: This loss is a variant of the standard Cross-Entropy loss function that assigns different weights to individual class predictions. Class weight can be calculated for each class as the inverse of its proportion in the training data. This is commonly achieved by dividing the total number of samples by the number of samples in each class, thereby obtaining the weight to be assigned to that particular class.

Parameter	Search Space
Classifier	[FNN, CNN]
N_last_layer	[1, 2, 3, 4, 5]
Optimizer	[Adam, AdamW, RMSprop, SGD]
Loss	[Cross Entropy, Focal]

Table 2: Architecture search space

3.1 Hyperparameter Tuning

Hyper-parameters used in training stages are selected via tuning using the Optuna library. We choose the optimal hyperparameters by the Macro F1-score on the development set. The search space defined for hyper-parameters is present in the Table 4.

4 Experiments and Results

To evaluate the results, we used the Marco F1-score as the main metric and also reported Precision, Recall, and Accuracy. The hardware used in experiments is a GPU.1080Ti.xlarge with 31.3GB RAM. Each training epoch lasts 2–5 minutes on average.

In section 2.1, we introduced seven modes for data cleaning. Experiments are repeated for the mode without or with data augmentation. Therefore, we tested 14 configurations in total, including 7 modes for data cleaning and 2 modes for input data. For each configuration, we selected model

[2] This variable chooses in search space.

[3] CNN with last 5 layers of BERTTweet, Data Augmentation, Weight Cross Entropy as loss function and SGD as optimizer. Removing URL and username as data cleaning approach.

[4] CNN with last 3 layers of XLM-RoBERTa,Focal as loss function and SGD as optimizer. Removing URL and username as data cleaning approach.

Cleaning	Aug	Embedding	Classifier	Loss	Optimizer	F1-Score	Recall	Precision	Accuracy
C1	-	RoBERTa	CNN(N=1)	WCE	SGD	71.74	69.94	74.83	68.82
C2	-	XLM-RoBERTa	CNN(N=3)	WCE	AdamW	69.80	69.38	74.16	64.91
C2	-	BERT	CNN(N=2)	WCE	SGD	70.28	68.64	73.82	66.00
C2	✓	BERT	CNN(N=3)	WCE	SGD	68.75	66.27	75.26	70.16
C3	-	RoBERTa	FNN	WCE	SGD	71.89	68.89	79.55	73.81
C3	✓	XLM-RoBERTa	CNN(N=3)	F(g=4)	SGD	68.59	68.51	75.93	69.84
C4	-	XLM-RoBERTa	CNN (N=4)	WCE	RMSprop	71.82	69.56	74.80	69.52
C4	-	BERT	CNN(N=5)	WCE	SGD	72.82	69.56	74.80	72.85
C4	-	XLM-RoBERTa	CNN(N=3)	F(g=1)	SGD	**73.97**	**70.91**	**78.17**	**72.59**
C4	-	RoBERTa	FNN	WCE	RMSprop	71.52	68.31	78.17	70.06
C4	-	XLM-RoBERTa	CNN(N=4)	WCE	SGD	72.72	69.38	78.85	73.17
C4	✓	**BERTweet**	**CNN(N=5)**	**WCE**	**SGD**	**74.47**	**70.31**	**79.31**	**73.11**
C4	✓	BERT	CNN(N=4)	WCE	SGD	70.64	67.75	75.63	70.01
C5	-	DEBERTA	FNN	WCE	Adam	71.33	68.78	75.43	67.73
C5	-	XLM-RoBERTa	CNN(N=2)	WCE	SGD	72.70	69.63	77.18	72.15
C5	-	BERT	FNN	F(g=1)	SGD	72.01	68.62	77.44	71.75
C5	✓	DEBERTA	FNN	WCE	AdamW	71.20	68.51	77.68	72.72
C5	✓	BERT	CNN(N=3)	WCE	SGD	70.85	70.01	73.41	67.22
C6	-	BERT	FNN	F(g=2)	SGD	71.83	68.38	74.48	72.21
C6	-	BERT	FNN	WCE	RMSProp	70.13	67.18	74.85	69.65
C6	✓	XLM-RoBERTa	CNN(N=4)	WCE	SGD	72.70	69.43	78.56	72.85
C7	-	BERT	CNN(N=5)	F(g=1)	SGD	71.68	68.77	76.53	71.76
C7	✓	BERTweet	CNN(N=2)	F(g=4)	AdamW	69.36	66.56	74.09	69.06

Table 3: Experiment configuration and result on climate stance detection test data.
Data Cleaning Approuch(C1:Original Tweet Text, C2:Removing URL, C3:Removing username, C4:Removing URL and username, C5:Removing URL and username and split hashtag, C6:Removing URL and username, split hashtag, and convert all letters to lowercase, C7:Complete cleaning). **Classifier**(CNN: Convolutional Neural Networks, FNN: Fully Connected Neural Networks). **Loss Function**(WCE:Weighted Cross Entropy Loss, F:Focal Loss, g:Gamma parameter in focal loss).

Parameter	Search Space
Dropout	$[0.1 : 0.5]$
Learning Rate	$[1e^{-5} : 1e^{-2}]$
Batch Size	[4, 8]
Focal_gamma	[1, 2, 3, 4, 5]

Table 4: Hyperparameters search space

Model	ACC	F1
BERTTweet[3]	**73.11**	**74.47**
XLM-RoBERTa[4]	72.59	73.97
ClimateBERT (Baseline)*	65.1	54.5

Table 5: climate stance detection Accuracy and macro F1-Score result.* from Shiwakoti et al. (2024) report.

parameters and hyperparameters using Optuna and performed fine-tuning for 20 trials. In each trial, the parameters are selected using the sampling method TPE (Tree-structured Parzen Estimator), based on the defined search space. Additionally, a mechanism for pruning unsuccessful trials is also included by default in Optuna. Finally, the results with F1-Macro greater than 0.68 on the development set are present in Table 3 (Since we only included results F1 scores greater than 0.68, it is possible that the results for some cleaning methods may not be available for a specific classifier, such as FNN).

The experimental results indicate that the cleaning method, which removes URLs and usernames (C4), performs better compared to other methods. The complete cleaning and original text methods, on the other hand, yielded weaker results than other approaches. Additionally, it can be said that maintaining hashtags and not converting to lowercase is a better cleaning approach because sometimes writing all letters in capital letters indicates intensity of anger or opposition.

Furthermore, in general, BERT embeddings perform better in complete cleaning, while RoBERTa and XLM-RoBERTa models are more commonly used in other cleaning methods and yield better results and the best result is obtained with BERTweet.

Regarding the classifier type, usually a CNN with 4-5 last layers achieves better results. Evidence suggests that the defined CCN architecture, due to its use of different filters sizes and consideration of neighborhoods, has been able to achieve better results compared to FNN. Additionally, typically, RoBERTa and XLM-RoBERTa embeddings are used with CNN, while BERT is paired with FNN for better performance. Analyzing the experiments as a whole, it can be concluded that the best results were obtained by optimizing SGD and using Weighted Cross Entropy as loss function. Comparison of our results and the baseline illustrate in Table 5.

Parameter	Value
Epoch	8
Batch Size	4
Dropout	0.5
Learning Rate	0.007903
Learning schedule	Linear Schedule With Warmup
Embedding	BERTweet
Classifier	CNN
N_last_layer	5
Optimizer	SGD
Loss Function	Weighted Cross Entropy

Table 6: Best model configuration and hyperparameters.

To determine the impact of data cleaning on the results obtained, we repeated experiments with the best configuration (as shown in Table 6). In these experiments, hyperparameters and model architecture were kept identical, with the only variation being the method of cleaning data. For each cleaning technique, we repeated the experiments 10 times for 8 epochs. The results obtained are illustrated in the Table 7. The results indicate that C3(Removing username) and C4 (Removing URL and username) are significantly better than C1(Original Tweet Text) and C7(Complete cleaning). Thus, the influence of data cleaning methods on the final results is clearly evident.

Cleaning	F1-Score
C1	$73.98 \pm 0.0012^*$
C2	$73.92 \pm 0.0017^*$
C3	$74.35 \pm 0.0015^{*\dagger}$
C4	$74.11 \pm 0.0029^{*\dagger}$
C5	$73.76 \pm 0.0014^*$
C6	$73.72 \pm 0.0009^*$
C7	72.42 ± 0.0020

Table 7: Experiment with Best Model Configuration and hyperparameter. † indicates significance ($p < 0.005$) comparing to C1. $*$ indicates significance ($p < 0.005$) comparing to C7.

By repeating the experiment with the best configuration (Table 6), and only changed the classifier, it demonstrated the superiority of CNN over FNN. the results of which are illustrated in Table 8.

Classifier	Cleaning	F1-Score
CNN	C3	74.35 ± 0.0015
	C4	74.11 ± 0.0029
FNN	C3	73.73 ± 0.0058
	C4	73.91 ± 0.0045

Table 8: Classifier impact

5 Error Analysis

By analyzing the model errors, it can be concluded that as expected, the model struggles with detecting the oppose class. In addition to the low number of data points in this class, the presence of sarcasm and irony in the data makes it harder for the model to fully comprehend the situation and make accurate predictions. It is evident that in parts of the text where there is sarcasm, the probability of model error significantly increases. Consider the tweet `#FridaysForFuture #ClimateChange #ExtinctionRebellion #GlobalWarming What are we saving?`. Since some of the hashtags are used to collect data, they are present in all three classes.

6 Conclusion

This work involved a systematic exploration of model architecture and data cleaning methods. We find that the optimal configuration combining BERTweet and CNN with Weighted Cross Entropy and SGD, along with data augmentation, led to achieving an impressive Macro F1-Score of 0.7447.

7 Limitation

In our research, we encountered GPU limitations, which affected the scale and speed of our model training and experimentation. Despite our efforts to optimize code efficiency and parallel processing, these limitations restricted the size of our model architectures and the volume of data we could effectively process within a reasonable timeframe. Also, we confronted limitations stemming from insufficient labeled data and imbalanced class distributions. Despite employing data augmentation techniques to mitigate the imbalance, the inadequacy of labeled data impeded the depth and robustness of our model's learning, affecting its overall performance and generalization capabilities.

8 Acknowledgements

We'd like to thank the organizers for introducing this task. We are glad that we had the opportunity to engage more in the challenges.

References

Takuya Akiba, Shotaro Sano, Toshihiko Yanase, Takeru Ohta, and Masanori Koyama. 2019. Optuna: A next-generation hyperparameter optimization framework. In *Proceedings of the 25th ACM SIGKDD International Conference on Knowledge Discovery & Data Mining*, KDD '19, page 2623–2631, New York, NY, USA. Association for Computing Machinery.

Jacob Devlin, Ming-Wei Chang, Kenton Lee, and Kristina Toutanova. 2019. BERT: Pre-training of deep bidirectional transformers for language understanding. In *Proceedings of the 2019 Conference of the North American Chapter of the Association for Computational Linguistics: Human Language Technologies, Volume 1 (Long and Short Papers)*, pages 4171–4186, Minneapolis, Minnesota. Association for Computational Linguistics.

Pengcheng He, Xiaodong Liu, Jianfeng Gao, and Weizhu Chen. 2021. Deberta: Decoding-enhanced bert with disentangled attention. In *International Conference on Learning Representations*.

Dilek Küçük and Fazli Can. 2022. A tutorial on stance detection. In *Proceedings of the Fifteenth ACM International Conference on Web Search and Data Mining*, WSDM '22, page 1626–1628, New York, NY, USA. Association for Computing Machinery.

Tsung-Yi Lin, Priya Goyal, Ross Girshick, Kaiming He, and Piotr Dollar. 2017. Focal loss for dense object detection. In *Proceedings of the IEEE International Conference on Computer Vision (ICCV)*.

Yinhan Liu, Myle Ott, Naman Goyal, Jingfei Du, Mandar Joshi, Danqi Chen, Omer Levy, Mike Lewis, Luke Zettlemoyer, and Veselin Stoyanov. 2019a. Roberta: A robustly optimized BERT pretraining approach. *CoRR*, abs/1907.11692.

Yinhan Liu, Myle Ott, Naman Goyal, Jingfei Du, Mandar Joshi, Danqi Chen, Omer Levy, Mike Lewis, Luke Zettlemoyer, and Veselin Stoyanov. 2019b. Roberta: A robustly optimized bert pretraining approach. *arXiv preprint arXiv:1907.11692*.

Edward Ma. 2019. Nlp augmentation. https://github.com/makcedward/nlpaug.

Dat Quoc Nguyen, Thanh Vu, and Anh Tuan Nguyen. 2020. BERTweet: A pre-trained language model for English Tweets. In *Proceedings of the 2020 Conference on Empirical Methods in Natural Language Processing: System Demonstrations*, pages 9–14.

Sebastian Ruder, Anders Søgaard, and Ivan Vulić. 2019. Unsupervised cross-lingual representation learning. In *Proceedings of the 57th Annual Meeting of the Association for Computational Linguistics: Tutorial Abstracts*, pages 31–38, Florence, Italy. Association for Computational Linguistics.

Ali Safaya, Moutasem Abdullatif, and Deniz Yuret. 2020. KUISAIL at SemEval-2020 task 12: BERT-CNN for offensive speech identification in social media. In *Proceedings of the Fourteenth Workshop on Semantic Evaluation*, pages 2054–2059, Barcelona (online). International Committee for Computational Linguistics.

Shuvam Shiwakoti, Surendrabikram Thapa, Kritesh Rauniyar, Akshyat Shah, Aashish Bhandari, and Usman Naseem. 2024. Analyzing the dynamics of climate change discourse on twitter: A new annotated corpus and multi-aspect classification. *Preprint*.

Surendrabikram Thapa, Kritesh Rauniyar, Farhan Ahmad Jafri, Shuvam Shiwakoti, Hariram Veeramani, Raghav Jain, Guneet Singh Kohli, Ali Hürriyetoğlu, and Usman Naseem. 2024. Stance and hate event detection in tweets related to climate activism - shared task at case 2024. In *Proceedings of the 7th Workshop on Challenges and Applications of Automated Extraction of Socio-political Events from Text (CASE)*.

A Appendix

We explore the visualization of Parallel Coordinate (Figure 3) and FS-Importance (Figure 2) of our search space by functionalities offered by the Optuna package, providing a comprehensive understanding of the hyperparameter optimization process in our FNN model.

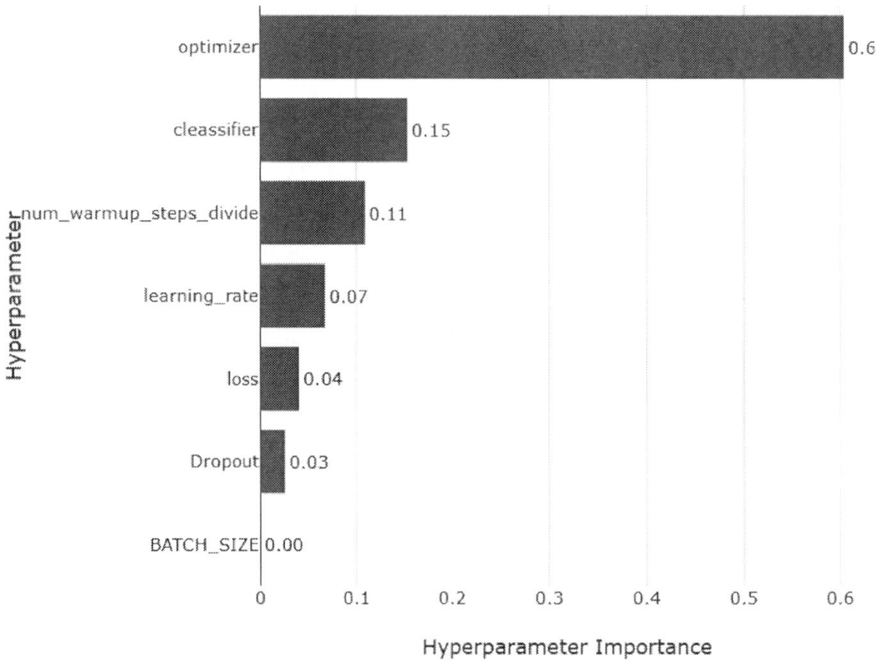

Figure 2: FS-Importanc

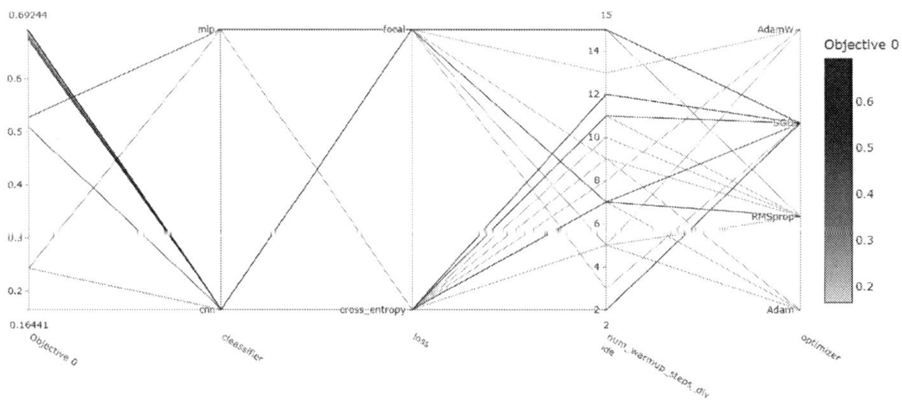

Figure 3: Parallel Coordinate

VRLLab at HSD-2Lang 2024: Turkish Hate Speech Detection Online with TurkishBERTweet

Ali Najafi[1], **Onur Varol**[1,2,*]
[1]Faculty of Engineering and Natural Sciences, Sabanci University
[2]Center of Excellence in Data Analytics, Sabanci University
[*]Corresponding author
{ali.najafi, onur.varol}@sabanciuniv.edu

Abstract

Social media platforms like Twitter - recently rebranded as X - produce nearly half a billion tweets daily and host a significant number of users that can be affected by content that is not properly moderated. In this work, we present an approach that ranked third at the `HSD-2Lang 2024` competition's subtask-A, along with additional methodology developed for this task and evaluation of different approaches. We utilize three different models, and the best-performing approach uses the publicly available TurkishBERTweet model with low-rank adaptation (LoRA) for fine-tuning. We also experiment with another publicly available model and a novel methodology to ensemble different hand-crafted features and outcomes of different models. Finally, we report the experimental results, competition scores, and discussion to improve this effort further.

1 Introduction

Despite the significant opportunities presented with the use of social media, these platforms are shifting towards more hostile environments, especially for marginalized groups. Social networks have been used to access information efficiently (Aral et al., 2009; Wang et al., 2022), participate important societal events (Bas et al., 2022; Ogan and Varol, 2017), and discuss political issues online (Varol et al., 2014; Tufekci, 2017; Jackson et al., 2020).

The increasing popularity of social networks and the opportunities presented to reach millions of individuals simultaneously made these platforms vulnerable to manipulation of discourse by bad actors who utilize automated accounts (Ferrara et al., 2016; Varol et al., 2017), spread disinformation (Mosleh and Rand, 2022; Keller et al., 2020), and coordinate targeted attacks (Shao et al., 2018; Varol and Uluturk, 2020). These targeted attacks can be coordinated or organic, and mostly, the target is minority and vulnerable groups. To prevent vulnerable groups and improve their experience in the online sphere, researchers develop systems to automatically identify these activities, and platforms build systems to moderate content and accounts.

Hate speech detection is a task to identify hateful content aimed towards groups such as refugees and individuals with certain beliefs or ethnicities (Waseem and Hovy, 2016; Zhang and Luo, 2019; MacAvaney et al., 2019). In this work, we demonstrate our approach as part of the `HSD-2Lang 2024` challenge to detect hate speech from textual information presented in social media posts.

2 Data

This challenge is organized in collaboration with the Hrant Dink Foundation for their ongoing project about "Media Watch on Hate Speech." Collaborative efforts of computational and social scientists defined hate speech on social media and carried out a detailed procedure to annotate posts around specific topics and keywords. The provided dataset in this competition contains 9,140 tweets in the context of Israel-Palestine and Turkish-Greek conflicts and content produced against refugees and immigration (Uludogan et al., 2024).

We preprocessed the dataset by removing samples with inconsistent ground truth information (exact text with different labels), and we applied deduplication, resulting in 8,805 tweets. Figure 1 shows word and character length distributions. When the ground-truth labels are considered, we measure that 30.5% of the dataset contains hate speech, suggesting an imbalance between the two classes. Since the dataset only contains the textual information presented in each tweet, we further processed them to take into account platform-specific features.

Removal of hyperlinks and mentions of other accounts in the tweets. This information could be valuable if we had a chance to process real-time data by scraping external web content or using profile information of accounts from Twitter's API since these fields are omitted in the dataset. Since

Proceedings of the 7th Workshop on Challenges and Applications of Automated Extraction of Socio-political Events from Text (CASE 2024), pages 185–189
March 22, 2024 ©2024 Association for Computational Linguistics

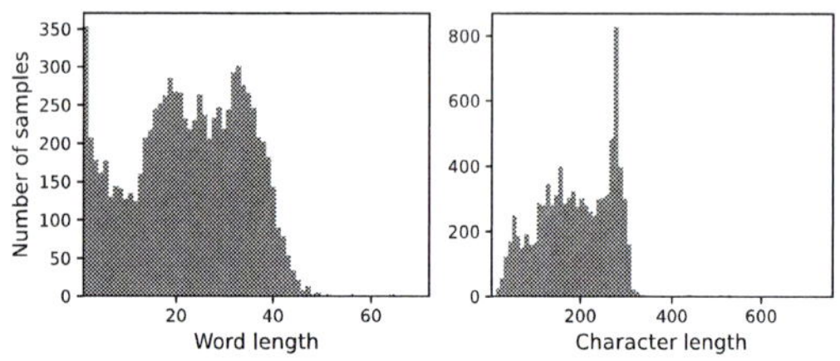

Figure 1: **Tweet statistics.** Distributions for word count (left) and character length (right) presented for the dataset. Character limits exhibit Twitter specific limitations while some tweets may contain fewer words possibly consist of hashtags.

we do not incorporate them into our analysis, we omit them from the dataset.

Preprocessing pipeline for TurkishBERTweet model. We consider different special tags for Twitter-specific entities and translated the Unicode characters of emojis to words describing the meaning using the preprocessor created for the TurkishBERTweet project (Najafi and Varol, 2023).

3 Methodologies

In this challenge, we built different approaches. We considered not only the textual data to fine-tune models but also incorporated additional signals obtained from text and blacklisted word dictionaries. Here, we present the language models used as the foundation and additional features we extracted to improve the model's performance. For the competition, we submitted the model with the best public leaderboard score; however, one of our approaches achieved an even higher score in the private evaluation. We presented all approaches and their respective performances in the results section.

TurkishBERTweet[1] is a new language model that was specifically trained on nearly 894M Turkish tweets and the model offers a special tokenizer that takes social media entities such as hashtags and emojis into account. This model utilized LoRA (Hu et al., 2021), which is a novel way of fine-tuning LLMs in an efficient way, and recent research reports state-of-the-art performance and generalizability capabilities (Najafi and Varol, 2023).

BERTurk[2] is a pre-trained model that utilizes large-scale corpus from various sources. It is a well-known model among the Turkish NLP community (Schweter, 2020).

[1] https://huggingface.co/VRLLab/TurkishBERTweet

[2] https://huggingface.co/dbmdz/bert-base-turkish-128k-uncased

Ensemble of models (EoM) approach combines outputs of aforementioned Hate Speech models along with custom features extracted for this task. These additional features consist of i) logits scores retrieved from an emotion classifier based on a bert-base model fine-tuned model for emotion analysis,[3] ii) logit scores of a sentiment classifier using TurkishBERTweet sentiment analysis model, iii) collection of Turkish blacked-list words[4] used for token level features such as binary exact match feature, Levenshtein distance, hashtag exact match, and hashtag Levenshtein distance. These features are concatenated, resulting in 16 features for the RandomForest classifier with 100 estimators trained to optimize gini-impurity. Since the outputs of ensemble models for imbalanced datasets can be biased, we calibrated the outputs of the model using Platt's scaling for interpreting output scores as probabilities (Niculescu-Mizil and Caruana, 2005).

4 Results

This section presents the experimental evaluation of approaches we tested within the dataset using stratified 5-fold cross-validation. We also report the performance of models we submitted to challenge for comparison. As Table 1 demonstrates, the `Ensemble of models` (EoM) gets the best performance compared to other approaches when all models are evaluated with 5-fold cross-validation. `TurkishBERTweet+Lora` model achieved the best private score, which led us to the third-best rank, although we observed a lower performance than the EoM model in cross-validated experiments. `BERTurk+Lora` model performed similarly to the TurkishBERTweet model using a 5-fold setting; however, it led to a lower private score. We suspect that the BERTurk model with standard or LoRA finetuning models was used by other teams, considering the popularity and availability of that model.

Considering the performance differences between public and private leaderboards, the EoM demonstrates less variability than the other two approaches. Even though it is not our best-performing model in both settings, we may consider it for our research projects since both cross-validated scores point to better performance, and the leaderboard score differences are negligible and can be due to

[3] https://huggingface.co/maymuni/bert-base-turkish-cased-emotion-analysis

[4] https://github.com/ooguz/turkce-kufur-karaliste

Table 1: **Model comparisons.** Weighted F1-score of the models in a 5-fold cross-validation setting. Best scores are presented in bold font, and more than one model is highlighted when the difference is not significant.

Model	F1-Weighted	Public Score	Private Score
TurkishBERTweet+LoRA	0.8137 ± 0.0059	**0.70697**	**0.66431**
BERTurk+LoRA	0.8132 ± 0.0054	**0.70476**	0.64944
Ensemble of Models	$\mathbf{0.8941 \pm 0.0073}$	0.68544	**0.66103**

noise in the test set of the competition.

We also conduct an error analysis to identify misclassifications that our model is making. This effort can reveal additional features we can implement and issues observed in the labeled dataset. Table 2 shows example tweets classified wrong. We first focus on false negatives since we can learn from these mistakes to improve our model. For instance, we could split hashtags into words to handle cases like #ülkemdemülteciistemiyorum (Turkish for #wedontwantrefugees) or handle popular hashtags differently. Regarding false positives, we noticed that our model correctly classifies tweets as hate speech based on our own judgment. We suspect the existence of mistakes in ground truth labels considering the examples we presented in Table 2. We highlight the words within the tweets that we suspect are mislabeling.

5 Discussion

In the provided dataset, we noticed tweets written in languages other than Turkish, such as Arabic and Hebrew. This could be an artifact of the data collection process, and one can consider i) language-level features, ii) filtering them, or iii) obtaining representation from LLMs. Furthermore, a study about the annotator's influence on the annotation quality for HateSpeech datasets shows that the expertise of annotators positively influences the data quality (Waseem, 2016). Considering the annotators' influence, applying impurity analysis by randomly or strategically changing the annotations and monitoring the Hate Speech system's performance could be a good practice.

Moreover, in this competition, we are only considering the text data to detect the existence of hate speech. Infusing the account information into these systems could help them be more accurate and reliable, such as the number of followers, number of followings, account creation date, etc.

Another approach for improving the performance of the systems is to expose pre-trained models with hateful content by further masked-language modeling on the hate speech dataset, like Caselli et al. (2020) presented in their recent work and improved the system's performance.

Multilingual models could also be utilized for this challenge since Turkish is a low-resource language, and the model can benefit from the other languages' hate speech datasets to infuse the broader knowledge of hate speech and then obtain a better performance (Röttger et al., 2022).

Recently, commercial models like ChatGPT have been used in various challenges. Huang et al. (2023) suggest that the ChatGPT demonstrates high accuracy and can be considered an alternative to human annotators in detecting implicit hate speech (Gilardi et al., 2023). Other work also investigated the performance of LLMs for hate-speech or offensive language detection tasks in English (Guo et al., 2024), Portuguese (Oliveira et al., 2023), and Turkish (Çam and Özgür, 2023). However, we want to raise a concern about the adversarial use of these models to attack vulnerable groups and bypass the detection systems. Additional information about accounts, network structure, and temporal activities should be incorporated into detection systems to address the mentioned risk.

6 Conclusion

In this challenge, the collective effort of research teams points to best practices and demonstrates the capabilities of the state-of-the-art models. Here, we demonstrated different approaches and their respective performances in detecting online hate speech toward three different groups. We obtained the third rank in the final leaderboard of the competition with the `TurkishBERT+Lora` model.

We hope language models like TurkishBERTweet will be used in different downstream tasks on Turkish social media. Research efforts especially need to assess the online participation of minority groups. There is a significant need for publicly available models since the quality of content moderation and use of automated accounts on platforms like X is questionable after the acquisition

Table 2: **Misclassification analysis.** We explored the errors of our model to improve further our approach (studying false negatives) and investigate issues with the ground-truth dataset (pointing to false positives). Here, we select instances where our model produces the correct outcome, but the annotation process suggests otherwise. We color the text in red that we believe suggests hate speech.

False positive Model predicts as HS Labeled no HS	• #Katilİsrail [URL] • Hükümet Cumhurbaşkanı Erdoğan Şerefsiz Suriyeliler Yağma Sizler şu an hem suç hem cinayet işliyorsunuz. İnsanlar Twitter ı kullanmak için VPN kullanıyor ve VPN mobil cihazların şarj süresini oldukça azaltıyor. Tarihe böyle geçeceksiniz. • onursuz ırkıcılar kökünüz kurusun lanet olsun size evet kürdüz türküz ermeniyiz afgan'ız arabız ırkcı itler geberin lan bu ülke hepimizin # #hepimizkürdüz • İnsanlık yapıp ülkeye alıyorsun hainlik,bu zor günde yağmacılık yapıyorlar.Bazı şeref yoksunu suriyeliler yüzünden masum olan insanlar arada kaynıyor.Açıkçası #ülkemdemülteciistemiyorum ! Allah herkesin yardımcısı olsun yardıma ihtiyacı olana koşulsun ama ülkemi terketsinler. [URL]
False negative Model predicts no HS Labeled as HS	• #UELKEMDEMUELTECİİSTEMİYORUM [URL] • Heryerde bilim uzmanı ve yer bilimci prof hocalar. Gerçeği açıklıyor. Sonra unutulup , açgözlü, rantçı,yağmacı yöneticiler soyguna devam eder. 3 yıllık bina yıkılmış, 3 yıl. #deprem #earthquake #Yağmacılar. • sayıları 8 milyon olan suriyeli, afgan, irak ne varsa çok acil ülkelerine geri gönderilmeli. *güvenlik tehdidi oluşturuyorlar. *işsizlik sorunu oluşturuyorlar. bill gates #billgates #sedatpeker10

of Twitter (Varol, 2023a; Hickey et al., 2023). Publicly available models will help researchers monitor these platforms more closely and even help them develop models to protect vulnerable groups.

Pre-trained models available online or developed through challenges can be easily adapted for other projects. Publicly available datasets like *#Secim2023* can be used to study political discourse (Pasquetto et al., 2020; Najafi et al., 2022; Varol, 2023b), and models can be utilized to study these datasets. The TurkishBERTweet that we used approach is publicly available on the HuggingFace platform along with the LoRA adapters for different tasks (Najafi and Varol, 2023).

Open source models: TurkishBERTweet model used in this challenge is available online at the HuggingFace platform. `https://huggingface.co/VRLLab/TurkishBERTweet`

Acknowledgements: We thank Hasan Kemik for discussing and supporting the challenge. We thank TUBITAK (121C220 and 222N311) for partially funding this project. The TurkishBERTweet model was trained and made publicly available thanks to the Google Cloud Research Credits program with the award GCP19980904.

References

Sinan Aral, Lev Muchnik, and Arun Sundararajan. 2009. Distinguishing influence-based contagion from homophily-driven diffusion in dynamic networks. *Proceedings of the National Academy of Sciences*, 106(51):21544–21549.

Ozen Bas, Christine L Ogan, and Onur Varol. 2022. The role of legacy media and social media in increasing public engagement about violence against women in Turkey. *Social Media+ Society*, 8(4):20563051221138939.

Nur Bengisu Çam and Arzucan Özgür. 2023. Evaluation of chatgpt and bert-based models for Turkish hate speech detection. In *Intl. Conf. on Computer Science and Engineering*, pages 229–233. IEEE.

Tommaso Caselli, Valerio Basile, Jelena Mitrović, and Michael Granitzer. 2020. Hatebert: Retraining bert for abusive language detection in english. *arXiv preprint arXiv:2010.12472*.

Emilio Ferrara, Onur Varol, Clayton Davis, Filippo Menczer, and Alessandro Flammini. 2016. The rise of social bots. *Communications of the ACM*, 59(7):96–104.

Fabrizio Gilardi, Meysam Alizadeh, and Maël Kubli. 2023. Chatgpt outperforms crowd-workers for text-annotation tasks. *arXiv preprint arXiv:2303.15056*.

Keyan Guo, Alexander Hu, Jaden Mu, Ziheng Shi, Ziming Zhao, Nishant Vishwamitra, and Hongxin Hu. 2024. An Investigation of Large Language Models for Real-World Hate Speech Detection. *arXiv preprint arXiv:2401.03346*.

Daniel Hickey, Matheus Schmitz, Daniel Fessler, Paul E Smaldino, Goran Muric, and Keith Burghardt. 2023. Auditing elon musk's impact on hate speech and bots. In *Proc. of the Intl. AAAI Conf. on Web and Social Media*, volume 17, pages 1133–1137.

Edward J Hu, Yelong Shen, Phillip Wallis, Zeyuan Allen-Zhu, Yuanzhi Li, Shean Wang, Lu Wang, and Weizhu Chen. 2021. Lora: Low-rank adaptation of large language models. *arXiv preprint arXiv:2106.09685*.

Fan Huang, Haewoon Kwak, and Jisun An. 2023. Is chatgpt better than human annotators? potential and limitations of chatgpt in explaining implicit hate speech. *arXiv preprint arXiv:2302.07736*.

Sarah J Jackson, Moya Bailey, and Brooke Foucault Welles. 2020. *# HashtagActivism: Networks of race and gender justice*. MIT Press.

Franziska B Keller, David Schoch, Sebastian Stier, and JungHwan Yang. 2020. Political astroturfing on twitter: How to coordinate a disinformation campaign. *Political Communication*, 37(2):256–280.

Sean MacAvaney, Hao-Ren Yao, Eugene Yang, Katina Russell, Nazli Goharian, and Ophir Frieder. 2019. Hate speech detection: Challenges and solutions. *PloS One*, 14(8):e0221152.

Mohsen Mosleh and David G Rand. 2022. Measuring exposure to misinformation from political elites on Twitter. *Nature Communications*, 13(1):7144.

Ali Najafi, Nihat Mugurtay, Ege Demirci, Serhat Demirkiran, Huseyin Alper Karadeniz, and Onur Varol. 2022. # Secim2023: First Public Dataset for Studying Turkish General Election. *arXiv preprint arXiv:2211.13121*.

Ali Najafi and Onur Varol. 2023. TurkishBERTweet: Fast and Reliable Large Language Model for Social Media Analysis. *arXiv preprint arXiv:2311.18063*.

Alexandru Niculescu-Mizil and Rich Caruana. 2005. Predicting good probabilities with supervised learning. In *Proc. of the Intl. Conf. on Machine Learning*, pages 625–632.

Christine Ogan and Onur Varol. 2017. What is gained and what is left to be done when content analysis is added to network analysis in the study of a social movement: Twitter use during Gezi Park. *Information, Communication & Society*, 20(8):1220–1238.

Amanda S Oliveira, Thiago C Cecote, Pedro HL Silva, Jadson C Gertrudes, Vander LS Freitas, and Eduardo JS Luz. 2023. How Good Is ChatGPT For Detecting Hate Speech In Portuguese? In *Anais do XIV Simpósio Brasileiro de Tecnologia da Informação e da Linguagem Humana*, pages 94–103. SBC.

Irene V Pasquetto, Briony Swire-Thompson, Michelle A Amazeen, Fabrício Benevenuto, Nadia M Brashier, Robert M Bond, Lia C Bozarth, Ceren Budak, Ullrich KH Ecker, Lisa K Fazio, et al. 2020. Tackling misinformation: What researchers could do with social media data. *The Harvard Kennedy School Misinformation Review*.

Paul Röttger, Haitham Seelawi, Debora Nozza, Zeerak Talat, and Bertie Vidgen. 2022. MULTILINGUAL HATECHECK: Functional Tests for Multilingual Hate Speech Detection Models. *arXiv preprint arXiv:2206.09917*.

Stefan Schweter. 2020. BERTurk - BERT models for Turkish.

Chengcheng Shao, Giovanni Luca Ciampaglia, Onur Varol, Kai-Cheng Yang, Alessandro Flammini, and Filippo Menczer. 2018. The spread of low-credibility content by social bots. *Nature Communications*, 9(1):1–9.

Zeynep Tufekci. 2017. *Twitter and tear gas: The power and fragility of networked protest*. Yale U. Press.

Gokce Uludogan, Somaiyeh Dehghan, Inanc Arin, Elif Erol, Berrin Yanıkoglu, and Arzucan Ozgur. 2024. Overview of the Hate Speech Detection in Turkish and Arabic Tweets (HSD-2Lang) Shared Task at CASE 2024. In *Proceedings of the 7th Workshop on Challenges and Applications of Automated Extraction of Socio-political Events from Text (CASE)*.

Onur Varol. 2023a. Should we agree to disagree about Twitter's bot problem? *Online Social Networks and Media*, 37:100263.

Onur Varol. 2023b. Who Follows Turkish Presidential Candidates in 2023 Elections? In *Signal Processing and Communications Applications Conference*, pages 1–4. IEEE.

Onur Varol, Emilio Ferrara, Clayton Davis, Filippo Menczer, and Alessandro Flammini. 2017. Online human-bot interactions: Detection, estimation, and characterization. In *Proc. of the Intl. AAAI Conf. on Web and Social Media*, volume 11, pages 280–289.

Onur Varol, Emilio Ferrara, Christine L Ogan, Filippo Menczer, and Alessandro Flammini. 2014. Evolution of online user behavior during a social upheaval. In *Proc. of the ACM Conf. on Web Science*, pages 81–90.

Onur Varol and Ismail Uluturk. 2020. Journalists on Twitter: self-branding, audiences, and involvement of bots. *Journal of Computational Social Science*, 3(1):83–101.

Xindi Wang, Onur Varol, and Tina Eliassi-Rad. 2022. Information access equality on generative models of complex networks. *Applied Network Science*, 7(1).

Zeerak Waseem. 2016. Are you a racist or am i seeing things? annotator influence on hate speech detection on twitter. In *Proc. of the first Workshop on NLP and Computational Social Science*, pages 138–142.

Zeerak Waseem and Dirk Hovy. 2016. Hateful symbols or hateful people? predictive features for hate speech detection on twitter. In *Proc. of the NAACL Student Research Workshop, pages=88–93*.

Ziqi Zhang and Lei Luo. 2019. Hate speech detection: A solved problem? the challenging case of long tail on twitter. *Semantic Web*, 10(5):925–945.

Transformers at HSD-2Lang 2024: Hate Speech Detection in Arabic and Turkish Tweets Using BERT Based Architectures

Kriti Singhal, Jatin Bedi
Computer Science and Engineering Department
Thapar Institute of Engineering and Technology
kritisinghal711@gmail.com, jatin.bedi@thapar.edu

Abstract

Over the past years, researchers across the globe have made significant efforts to develop systems capable of identifying the presence of hate speech in different languages. This paper describes the team Transformers' submission to the subtasks: Hate Speech Detection in Turkish across Various Contexts and Hate Speech Detection with Limited Data in Arabic, organized by HSD-2Lang in conjunction with CASE at EACL 2024. A BERT based architecture was employed in both the subtasks. We achieved an F1 score of 0.63258 using XLM RoBERTa and 0.48101 using mBERT, hence securing the 6th rank and the 5th rank in the first and the second subtask, respectively.

1 Introduction

Hate Speech is defined as the usage of expressions or phrases which are hostile, offensive, or threatening in nature. Hate Speech is usually targeted against an individual or a group of individuals, highlighting those unique characteristics that distinguish those individuals. Some people use online platforms, such as Twitter, to spread hateful content at the click of a button.

Access to the internet, along with social media platforms such as Twitter, Instagram, and Facebook, can enable anyone, anywhere in the world, to share their ideas with millions of people across the globe within a few milliseconds (Shanmugavadivel et al., 2022).

With the advancing technological age, it is getting easier to spread hateful content thousands of miles across the globe, even without revealing their identity, due to the increased anonymity offered by online platforms. Automated detection of hateful content has become crucial for enhancing content moderation to mitigate societal harm. Social media platforms encourage the users to report any hate speech content that violates the hateful conduct policy so that appropriate action can be taken. However, it is still visible to many users, which necessitates the use of an automated system to detect and curb such content (Abuzayed and Elsayed, 2020).

The task organized by HSD-2Lang[1] at CASE 2024 aimed at identifying the presence of hate speech in Turkish and Arabic languages (Gökçe Uludoğan, 2024). The task was divided into two subtasks, as listed below:

i. Subtask A: Hate Speech Detection in Turkish across Various Contexts

ii. Subtask B: Hate Speech Detection with Limited Data in Arabic

In the past few years, Natural Language Processing (NLP) has experienced major breakthroughs, especially in the Hate Speech identification domain. Some of which are Long Short Term Memory (Hochreiter and Schmidhuber, 1997) and the Gated Recurrent Units (Chung et al., 2014). But, there has been a paradigm shift with the introduction of transformers (Vaswani et al., 2017).

Arabic language is one of the six official languages of the United Nations. Arabic is also a critical and strategically useful language (Ryding, 2013). With 18.55 million users, Turkey had the 7th highest number of Twitter users in 2023 (Statista, 2022). Turkish is also one of the most widely spoken languages of the Turkic language family.

Both Arabic and Turkish are very different from the English language. The orthography of both languages significantly differs from English due to the right-to-left text orientation and the utilization of connecting letters. The presence of word elongation, common ligatures, zero-width diacritics, and allographic variants leads to further complications. The morphology is extremely intricate, showcasing a wealth of morphemes that are used as prefixes,

[1] https://github.com/boun-tabi/case-2024-hsd-2lang/

Proceedings of the 7th Workshop on Challenges and Applications of Automated Extraction of Socio-political Events from Text (CASE 2024), pages 190–194
March 22, 2024 ©2024 Association for Computational Linguistics

suffixes, or even circumfixes. These elements can denote various grammatical features such as case, number, gender, and definiteness, among others, resulting in a sophisticated morphotactic system (Malmasi and Dras, 2014; Budur et al., 2020).

2 Related Work

Researchers have made multiple efforts in the past to automatically detect the presence of hate speech in Arabic and Turkish, in the past. A variety of different approaches have been used in the past to address this problem.

Abuzayed and Elsayed (2020) compared 15 classical and neural network models to classify Arabic tweets based on the presence of hate speech. To solve the problem efficiently, a "quick and simple" approach was used. The experiments were conducted on a collection of 8,000 tweets, and it was found that neural learning models outperformed the classical ones. The best classifier was a joint architecture of a convolution and recurrent neural network. The classifier used data after pre-processing, in which the punctuation, foreign characters, numbers, repeated characters, and diacritics were removed from the text. The remaining Arabic text was then normalized.

In the approach adopted by Husain (2020), extensive pre-processing was performed. The pre-processing step involved seven different steps. The work showed the improvement that pre-processing the data makes by retaining only the important content and performing dimensionality reduction. The first step in pre-processing was the conversion of emojis and emoticons to a textual label to ensure that the meaning conveyed by them did not suffer due to their removal. Next, since the Arabic dialect exists in various different forms, the variations in the different forms were normalized. The words were then categorized and then letter normalization was performed. This was followed by hashtag segmentation, where the '#' symbol was removed and the text following it was left untouched. After this, the numbers, more than two consecutive spaces, and the occurrence of more than three repetitive characters was removed along with Arabic stop words. Lastly, to address the data imbalance, upsampling was performed.

Neural networks and discourse analysis techniques were used by Hüsünbeyi et al. (2022) to identify the presence of hate speech in Turkish text. A Hierarchical Attention Network and BERT based deep learning models were implemented to apprehend evolving verbal cues and comprehend the contextual nuances within the discourse. Additionally, linguistic features using critical discourse analysis techniques were designed and integrated with neural network models.

Table 1: Dataset Distribution for Subtask A

Dataset	Label	
	Hateful	Non-Hateful
Anti-Refugee sentiment	1447	4477
Israel-Palestine conflict	880	1360
Anti-Greek discourse	555	421

3 Dataset Description

3.1 Subtask A

The dataset provided by the organizers for subtask A comprised of three parts, broadly classified into three categories, namely, refugees, the Israel-Palestine conflict, and Anti-Greek discourse. The dataset contained a total of 9,140 tweets in Turkish language. The detailed data distribution has been shown in Table 1. The text also contained emojis, emoticons, special symbols, numbers, and hyperlinks.

3.2 Subtask B

The dataset provided for subtask B comprised of 1000 Arabic tweets. In this dataset provided by the organizers, 778 tweets did not contain hate speech, whereas the remaining 82 tweets contained hate speech. The text in some tweets had special symbols such as '#', '@', '', and '['. The text also contained links, and some words were written in English.

4 Methodology

In NLP, text classification in languages with limited resources and code-mixed nature, has been a prominent problem. It can be defined as assigning text labels depending upon the content, context and intention of it. Researchers have devised multiple models to tackle this problem. Many of these models followed a transformer based approach and have been pre-trained on large corpora of text and

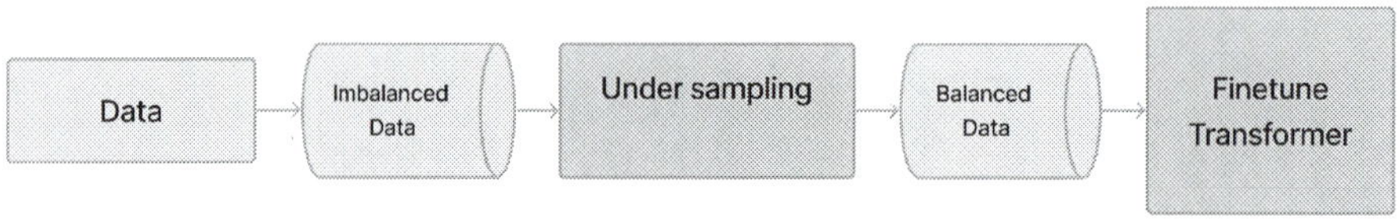

Figure 1: Proposed Methodology

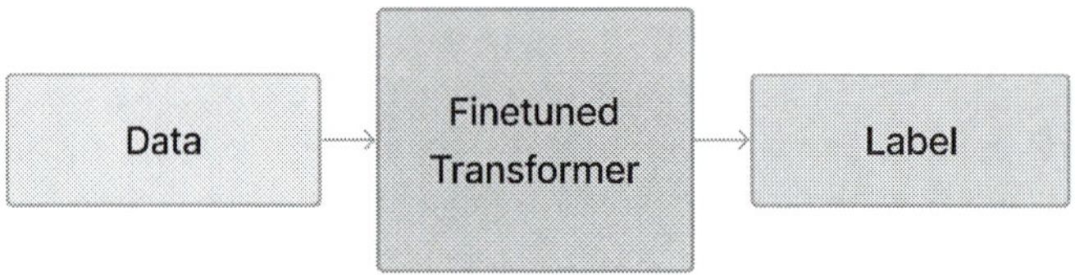

Figure 2: Label Generation for Unseen Data

have been made available for a multitude of solving problems like text classification. However, the corpora of text available to train such models is usually dominated by high-resourced languages like English. This problem is solved by the use of cross-lingual transfer learning.

4.1 Subtask A

The dataset provided for subtask A, as described in Section 3.1, comprised of three subsets. The data from all the three was first concatenated together to form one large dataset. The data also, had a huge data imbalance problem between the two classes of hateful and non-hateful tweets. The number of tweets for categorised as non-hateful were almost three times as many as the ones categorised as hateful. This issue was addressed by performing undersampling on the data, such that the number of tweets for both the classes became equal. The undersampling was performed randomly with no preference given to any particular type of data.

The data was then split such that 80% of the data was used for training and 20% was used for testing. The data was used to finetune the XLM RoBERTa Large (XLMR) model (Conneau et al., 2019). It was observed that the model performed the best when trained for 8 epochs using the weighted Adam optimizer and negative log likelihood loss.

The XLMR model is an unsupervised model trained on data of 100 different languages. This model is derived from the 2019 RoBERTa model launched by Facebook. XLMR is a large multilingual model which has been trained on 2.5TB of filtered data acquired from CommonCrawl. XLMR uses its own tokenizer, known as the XLMRoberta-Tokenizer.

4.2 Subtask B

In the dataset for subtask B, as elaborated in Section 3.2, there was a significant difference between the number of samples with and without hateful content. Hence, the data imbalance was addressed by performing undersampling on the data. After performing undersampling, both the classes had 82 tweets each. The undersampling was performed to randomly select 82 tweets from all the 778 tweets classified as non-hateful.

Next, 70% of the remaining data was used for training, and 30% of the data was used for testing, the multilingual BERT (mBERT) based architecture which was employed in this subtask. The model showed the best performance after training for 13 epochs and using the Adam optimizer and negative log likelihood loss.

The model, mBERT is a self-supervised transformer model pre-trained on a huge multilingual corpus. The corpus comprised of 104 languages, with the largest Wikipedia utilizing a masked language modeling objective. mBERT uses the Bert-Tokenizer to perform tokenization on the data.

5 Results and Discussion

Multilingual transformer models were used to detect the presence of hate speech in Arabic and Turkish tweets. The BERT based architectures were finetuned to improve their performance further.

The data imbalance present in the data of both the subtasks was addressed by performing random undersampling on the data to ensure that the number of tweets for both the classes are equal.

It was found that the model performed better when the unprocessed data was used to train the model. Hence, the text data was used without any pre-processing to train the model.

The methodology followed to finetune the transformers for both the subtasks has been summarized in Figure 1. The label generation for the testing data has been summarised in Figure 2 for both the subtasks.

The models achieved an F1 score of 0.63258 and 0.48101 in subtask A and subtask B, respectively. Overall, the highest F1 score achieved was 0.69644 and 0.68354 in subtask A and subtask B respectively by the teams ranked 1st in the shared task.

6 Conclusion and Future Work

Hate speech detection is the process of classifying text based on the presence or absence of hateful content. The aim of the shared task organized by HSD-2Lang in conjunction with CASE at EACL 2024 was to automatically detect whether the tweet was hateful or not in nature.

In this paper, we discussed our use of two multilingual BERT based transformers in the Hate Speech Detection in Turkish and Arabic Tweets shared task. We achieved an F1 score of 0.63258 in subtask A with XLMR and an F1 score of 0.48101 in subtask B with mBERT with the discussed approaches.

Transformers have shown great potential in the field of NLP and have consistently outperformed the classical models. Hence, combining different transformer models using ensembling techniques can help improve performance. Also, since limited resources are available for both Arabic and Turkish, the performance may be further enhanced by combining multiple datasets.

References

Abeer Abuzayed and Tamer Elsayed. 2020. "Quick and Simple Approach for Detecting Hate Speech in Arabic Tweets". In *Proceedings of the 4th Workshop on Open-Source Arabic Corpora and Processing Tools, with a Shared Task on Offensive Language Detection*, pages 109–114, Marseille, France. European Language Resource Association.

Emrah Budur, Rıza Özçelik, Tunga Gungor, and Christopher Potts. 2020. "Data and Representation for Turkish Natural Language Inference". In *Proceedings of the 2020 Conference on Empirical Methods in Natural Language Processing (EMNLP)*, pages 8253–8267, Online. Association for Computational Linguistics.

Junyoung Chung, Caglar Gulcehre, KyungHyun Cho, and Yoshua Bengio. 2014. Empirical evaluation of gated recurrent neural networks on sequence modeling. *arXiv preprint arXiv:1412.3555*.

Alexis Conneau, Kartikay Khandelwal, Naman Goyal, Vishrav Chaudhary, Guillaume Wenzek, Francisco Guzmán, Edouard Grave, Myle Ott, Luke Zettlemoyer, and Veselin Stoyanov. 2019. Unsupervised cross-lingual representation learning at scale. *arXiv preprint arXiv:1911.02116*.

İnanç Arın Elif Erol Berrin Yanikoglu Arzucan Özgür Gökçe Uludoğan, Somaiyeh Dehghan. 2024. Overview of the Hate Speech Detection in Turkish and Arabic Tweets (HSD-2Lang) Shared Task at CASE 2024. In *Proceedings of the 7th Workshop on Challenges and Applications of Automated Extraction of Socio-political Events from Text (CASE)*, Malta. Association for Computational Linguistics.

Sepp Hochreiter and Jürgen Schmidhuber. 1997. Long short-term memory. *Neural computation*, 9(8):1735–1780.

Fatemah Husain. 2020. "OSACT4 Shared Task on Offensive Language Detection: Intensive Preprocessing-Based Approach". In *Proceedings of the 4th Workshop on Open-Source Arabic Corpora and Processing Tools, with a Shared Task on Offensive Language Detection*, pages 53–60, Marseille, France. European Language Resource Association.

Zehra Melce Hüsünbeyi, Didar Akar, and Arzucan Özgür. 2022. "Identifying Hate Speech Using Neural Networks and Discourse Analysis Techniques". In *Proceedings of the First Workshop on Language Technology and Resources for a Fair, Inclusive, and Safe Society within the 13th Language Resources and Evaluation Conference*, pages 32–41, Marseille, France. European Language Resources Association.

Shervin Malmasi and Mark Dras. 2014. "Arabic Native Language Identification". In *Proceedings of the EMNLP 2014 Workshop on Arabic Natural Language Processing (ANLP)*, pages 180–186, Doha, Qatar. Association for Computational Linguistics.

Karin C. Ryding. 2013. Teaching Arabic in the United States. In Kassem M Wahba, Zeinab A Taha, and Liz England, editors, *Handbook for Arabic Language Teaching Professionals in the 21st Century*. Routledge.

Kogilavani Shanmugavadivel, Malliga Subramanian, Prasanna Kumar Kumaresan, Bharathi Raja Chakravarthi, B Bharathi, Subalalitha Chinnaudayar Navaneethakrishnan, Lavanya Sambath Kumar, Thomas Mandl, Rahul Ponnusamy, Vasanth Palanikumar, et al. 2022. Overview of the Shared Task on Sentiment Analysis and Homophobia Detection of YouTube Comments in Code-Mixed Dravidian Languages.

Statista. 2022. Number of active Twitter users in selected countries. Accessed: January 24, 2024.

Ashish Vaswani, Noam Shazeer, Niki Parmar, Jakob Uszkoreit, Llion Jones, Aidan N Gomez, Łukasz Kaiser, and Illia Polosukhin. 2017. Attention is all you need. *Advances in neural information processing systems*, 30.

ReBERT at HSD-2Lang 2024: Fine-Tuning BERT with AdamW for Hate Speech Detection in Arabic and Turkish

Utku Ugur Yagci
Middle East Technical University
utku.yagci@metu.edu.tr

Ahmet Emirhan Kolcak
Istanbul Technical University
kolcak20@itu.edu.tr

Egemen Iscan
King's Business School
egemen.iscan@kcl.ac.uk

Abstract

This research tackles the issue of detecting hate speech in Arabic and Turkish languages by utilizing pre-trained BERT models, namely TurkishBERTweet and Arabertv02-twitter. These models are enhanced through a comprehensive hyperparameter search to improve their performance. Our classifiers excelled in the HSD-2Lang 2024 contest, with the Turkish model placing second in Subtask A and the Arabic model first in Subtask B on the private leaderboard. Both models also ranked first on the public dataset. These results demonstrate the efficacy and adaptability of our approach in addressing the evolving challenges of hate speech detection in multilingual contexts.

1 Introduction

In this study, we have explored several fine-tuning strategies to establish BERT (Devlin et al., 2019) models and compared their performances on two separate datasets, one in Turkish and the other in Arabic. We aimed to outperform the competitor models in the HSD-2Lang Subtask A and Subtask B in detecting hate speech in tweets. The details of these subtasks are explained in the contest paper (Uludoğan et al., 2024).

BERT is a widely used and accepted approach in the field of natural language processing (NLP) due to its efficiency and high performance in detecting hate speech compared to most conventional model architectures. The original BERT paper proposed epoch numbers ranging from 2 to 4 and learning rates 5e-5, 3e-5, and 2e-5 with Adam optimizer for fine-tuning BERT (Devlin et al., 2019). However, during our experimentation, we extended the range of the proposed hyperparameters in the original study. By enlarging the range, we were able to try various combinations of hyperparameters to enhance our model's performance. Considering the competitive and limited nature of our task at hand, going beyond the suggested methods can be advantageous and provide a unique solution.

Our approach is insightful as it applies existing models and frameworks practically, and its competitive results offer valuable insights for future hate speech detection research in Arabic, Turkish, and other languages.

2 Related Work

The introduction of BERT (Bidirectional Encoder Representations from Transformers) by Devlin et al. (2019) has radically changed the field of detecting the nuances of languages contextually. The commonly adapted paradigm associated with BERT consists of a pre-training and a fine-tuning step (Xinxi, 2021). The fine-tuning step is intended for the model to specialize on a specific task. The fine-tuning of a pre-trained BERT model is proven to be significantly more robust compared to similar approaches offered in the past (Mosbach et al., 2020). In our case, this task was hate speech detection. Hence, we have chosen our pre-trained models accordingly. Mozafari et al. (2020) introduced a transfer learning approach where a pre-trained BERT model is used for detecting hate speech in social media. The body of past research has laid a solid foundation upon which our study is constructed, enabling us to train our models with novel insights and methodologies.

3 Methodology

We built and trained our models in Python using the PyTorch (Paszke et al., 2019) framework. We had access to Google Colab's A100 NVIDIA GPUs via subscription, which helped us experiment with several architectures efficiently. The performance of the GPU was crucial since we had time constraints for achieving both tasks. A powerful GPU creates a significant difference, especially when training with relatively high epoch numbers (e.g.,

Proceedings of the 7th Workshop on Challenges and Applications of Automated Extraction of Socio-political Events from Text (CASE 2024), pages 195–198
March 22, 2024 ©2024 Association for Computational Linguistics

100,1000). The training data consists of 9140 observations for Subtask A and 960 observations for Subtask B. No training or test data was used besides the datasets provided to us as a part of the competition. We initially tested the base performance of pre-trained models from Hugging Face [1] on each subtask's training data without applying fine-tuning or preprocessing. Respectively, the initial models we decided not to proceed with were "AraBert Hate Speech Detecter" [2] developed by WidadAwane and "Bert Base Turkish Uncased" [3] developed by Dbmdz. The used models are then selected according to their performance. Afterward, we conducted a more structured hyperparameter search for the selected pre-trained models for fine-tuning. While training, we detected a data imbalance issue between the number of negatively (non hate speech) and positively (hate speech) labeled observations: in Subtask A, the initial ratio was approximately 70/30, whereas in Subtask B, it was even more skewed at 90/10. The fact that the imbalance is more apparent in Subtask B is particularly significant due to the limited size of the data, which has the potential to make its effects more impactful. The reduced dataset size in Subtask B amplifies the risk of model overfitting to the over-represented class, thus increasing the challenges in achieving a balanced and robust model performance. This situation was preventing the expected performance increase through fine-tuning. Due to this observation, we only used 80 percent of the negatively labeled (non-toxic) training data for Subtask B. The excluded negatively labeled observations were chosen randomly. We opted not to remove too many rows because the data is already very limited, which necessitated a careful balancing to avoid excessively diminishing our dataset's size.

It is essential to mention that our initial goal was to have the best score in the competition rather than have a more general model that can detect hate speech on a wide variety of datasets. Our only performance benchmark during training was the unlabeled public test dataset. The public test data covers only 20 percent of the total test data. Therefore, we delve into finding a configuration for fine-tuning that performs better than the other competitors in the public dataset—assuming that the performance on the public dataset will carry over to the private test dataset (80 percent of the unlabeled test data).

4 Experimental Setup

For the preprocessing step, we didn't alter the grammatical attributes through processes such as lemmatization or stemmization. We therefore have not carried out any Part-of-Speech (POS) tagging, or similar analyses. This is due to the way that BERT and transformer (Vaswani et al., 2023) models function in general. From our literature review, we decided that it is best to keep the data as raw as possible, with the presence of punctuation as well as any expressions of tone, except only slight modifications to make it cleaner. We used the original preprocessing function by the TurkishBERTweet (Najafi and Varol, 2023) authors, which we then used as our main model for Subtask A. This preprocessing function only converts URL and emoticons into tags similar to HTML format, and doesn't apply any further modifications. For Subtask B, no preprocessing was applied.

We fine-tuned the submitted TurkishBERTweet model on NVIDIA A100 GPU and set the batch size equal to 32. After that, we set the max sequence length to 256, base learning rate to 5e-5, epsilon to 1e-8, and warm-up proportion to 10 percent of the total steps. We use the AdamW optimizer, introduced by Loshchilov and Hutter (2017), with the default parameters and set the scheduler to polynomial weight decay. Table 1 shows the results of the hyperparameter search conducted on the TurkishBERTweet model.

For the second Subtask, we used the pre-trained Arabertv02-twitter model (Antoun et al.). We fine-tuned the model on NVIDIA GTX 1070 and set the batch size equal to 8. We set the max sequence length to 250, base learning rate to 5e-4, epsilon to 1e-8, output attentions = False, output hidden states = False, and correct bias = False. Table 2 shows the results of the hyperparameter search conducted on the Arabertv02-twitter model.

5 Results and Discussion

Model configurations can be seen in Table 1 with corresponding F1 scores in public and private datasets. Best submitted model configurations are written in bold. The public scores for Subtask A and B were 0.89 and 0.74, respectively, placing our

[1] https://huggingface.co/

[2] https://huggingface.co/WidadAwane/AraBert_Hate_Speech_Detecter/

[3] https://huggingface.co/dbmdz/bert-base-turkish-uncased/

Subtask	Pre-trained Model	Optimizer	Learning Rate	Scheduler	Batch	Epoch	F1 Score	
							Public	Private
A	TurkishBERTweet	**AdamW**	**5e-5**	**Polynomial Decay with 10% Warmup**	**32**	**100**	**0.74**	**0.69**
		AdamW	5e-4	Linear Decay with No Warmup	32	100	0.74	0.69
		AdamW	5e-5	Linear Decay with 10% Warmup	32	100	0.73	0.69
		AdamW	5e-5	Linear Decay with No Warmup	32	1000	0.73	0.70
		AdamW	5e-5	Linear Decay with 10% Warmup	32	5	0.72	0.66
		Adafactor	-	Adafactor Schedule	128	15	0.70	0.66
B	Arabertv02-Twitter	**AdamW**	**5e-4**	**Linear Decay with No Warmup**	**8**	**8**	**0.89**	**0.74**
		AdamW	5e-5	Linear Decay with No Warmup	8	4	0.85	0.66
		AdamW	5e-5	Linear Decay with No Warmup	8	8	0.85	0.76
		AdamW	5e-5	Linear Decay with No Warmup	16	4	0.80	0.69

Table 1: Fine-Tuned model results for Private and Public datasets.

models at the top of the public leaderboard on both subtasks. With the release of the private leaderboard scores, our models ranked 1st in the Arabic Subtask with an F1 score of 0.74 and 2nd in the Turkish Subtask with an F1 score of 0.69.

During the hyperparameter search for Subtask A, we could only achieve minor performance differences up to -2 to +2 percent in terms of F1 score and accuracy by altering the base learning rate, epoch size, and batch size. One of the main findings for Subtask A is that we could enhance the performance only by implementing unconventional epoch lengths such as 100 and 1000. While the proposed range for epoch numbers is [2,4], we have achieved better-performing models up to 4 percent by using a relatively high number of epochs during the training phase. Furthermore, we also achieved better results by applying a 10 percent warmup during training. The best-performing score for Subtask A was achieved by implementing the polynomial weight decay scheduler with a 10 percent warmup. In addition to the hyperparameter search, we trained another model with a different optimizer named Adafactor (Shazeer and Stern, 2018). We used a batch size of 128 and an epoch number of 15. However, since the resulting F1 score was far below compared to the scores of models trained with the AdamW optimizer, we did not experiment any further.

Hyperparameter search for Subtask B involves different combinations of epoch numbers and batch sizes. Since the amount of training data for Subtask B is limited to 960, fine-tuning with limited data involves the risk of overfitting. With limited training data, there is a higher risk that the model will memorize the training examples rather than learn generalizable patterns. This situation can lead to poor performance on unseen data for hate speech detection. Furthermore, Arabertv02-twitter is pretrained on various tasks with more than 60 million tweets. Therefore, training on a small dataset may not effectively adapt the model's ability for hate speech detection. Taking this condition into account, we trained our models with a linear decay scheduler with no warmup. Our best-submitted model exceeded expectations performance-wise by scoring 0.89 in the public test set and 0.74 in the private test set.

When comparing our top-ranking models with each other, we observed that the fine-tuned TurkishBERTweet model performed worse than the fine-tuned Arabertv02-tweet model if our sole consideration as a benchmark was the F1 score. However, there may be other factors to discuss before reaching such a conclusion. One potential factor is the limited data in the Arabic Subtask. It is unclear whether the F1 score is a sufficient metric by itself to compare models when at least one of those models is trained or evaluated on limited data. We also noticed that our submissions had lower variation in F1 score for Subtask A, compared to Subtask B, which may also be due to the limited data constraint in Subtask B. Hence, it may be misleading and out of scope to compare these two types of models to each other.

6 Conclusion

In this paper, we conducted experiments to finetune pre-trained BERT models for the hate speech detection task. We explore various approaches to maximize the performance of each algorithm by adjusting the hyperparameters. This paper focuses on the three primary hyperparameters: learning rate, batch size, and epoch length. Our final leaderboard rankings in Arabic and Turkish Subtasks turned out to be 1 and 2, respectively. This is a demonstration of consistent success, indicating that finetuning BERT is a practical and effective approach for detecting hate speech in various aspects of a particular language. Several factors, such as the choice of a pre-trained model and hyperparameters used in fine-tuning, contribute to obtaining a satisfactory result. The selection of the pre-trained model should be done under consideration of the format of the data. Models pre-trained with data from Twitter can help achieve better results. Furthermore, the hate speech detection for this task requires a pre-trained model along with an effective tokenizer that is capable of tokenizing specific features for Twitter, such as hashtags, URLs, and emojis. Such particular features can enhance the performance of the classification task by expanding the perception of toxicity in our model.

7 Future Work

We plan to delve further into hate speech detection literature to improve the performance of our models. We believe that the performance of our models can be enhanced by implementing more advanced fine-tuning methods discussed by Sun et al. (2019). In addition, we aim to compare our findings with those from established machine learning algorithms, as well as more contemporary approaches such as GPT. This study will serve as a benchmark in our future studies of similar tasks.

Limitations

The use of specific GPU resources in this project might limit the reproducibility of our results for researchers with different setups. Our models are tailored for contest datasets. Hence, they may not perform well when applied to a wider variety of datasets for detecting hate speech. The hyperparameter optimization was constrained by the availability of only the public dataset for validation. This study does not prioritize the efficiency during training. Additionally, our reliance on pre-trained models restricts the adaptability of future research to modify initial model parameters.

References

Wissam Antoun, Fady Baly, and Hazem Hajj. AraBERT: Transformer-based Model for Arabic Language Understanding. In *LREC 2020 Workshop Language Resources and Evaluation Conference 11–16 May 2020*, page 9.

Jacob Devlin, Ming-Wei Chang, Kenton Lee, and Kristina Toutanova. 2019. Bert: Pre-training of deep bidirectional transformers for language understanding. *arXiv preprint arXiv:1810.04805*.

I. Loshchilov and F. Hutter. 2017. Fixing Weight Decay Regularization in Adam. *ArXiv*, abs/1711.05101.

Ilya Loshchilov and Frank Hutter. 2019. Decoupled weight decay regularization. *arXiv preprint arXiv:1711.05101*.

Marius Mosbach, Maksym Andriushchenko, and D. Klakow. 2020. On the Stability of Fine-tuning BERT: Misconceptions, Explanations, and Strong Baselines. *ArXiv*, abs/2006.04884.

Marzieh Mozafari, R. Farahbakhsh, and N. Crespi. 2020. Hate speech detection and racial bias mitigation in social media based on BERT model. *PLoS ONE*, 15.

Ali Najafi and Onur Varol. 2023. TurkishBERTweet: Fast and Reliable Large Language Model for Social Media Analysis. *arXiv preprint arXiv:2311.18063*.

Adam Paszke, Sam Gross, Francisco Massa, Adam Lerer, James Bradbury, Gregory Chanan, Trevor Killeen, Zeming Lin, Natalia Gimelshein, Luca Antiga, Alban Desmaison, Andreas Kopf, Edward Yang, Zachary DeVito, Martin Raison, Alykhan Tejani, Sasank Chilamkurthy, Benoit Steiner, Lu Fang, Junjie Bai, and Soumith Chintala. 2019. Pytorch: An imperative style, high-performance deep learning library. `https://pytorch.org/`.

Noam Shazeer and Mitchell Stern. 2018. Adafactor: Adaptive learning rates with sublinear memory cost. *arXiv preprint arXiv:1804.04235*.

Chi Sun, Xipeng Qiu, Yige Xu, and Xuanjing Huang. 2019. How to Fine-Tune BERT for Text Classification? pages 194–206.

Iulia Turc, Ming-Wei Chang, Kenton Lee, and Kristina Toutanova. 2019. Well-read students learn better: On the importance of pre-training compact models. *arXiv preprint arXiv:1908.08962*.

Gökçe Uludoğan, Somaiyeh Dehghan, İnanç Arın, Elif Erol, Berrin Yanikoglu, and Arzucan Özgür. 2024. Overview of the Hate Speech Detection in Turkish and Arabic Tweets (HSD-2Lang) Shared Task at CASE 2024. In *Proceedings of the 7th Workshop on Challenges and Applications of Automated Extraction of Socio-political Events from Text (CASE)*, Malta. Association for Computational Linguistics.

Ashish Vaswani, Noam Shazeer, Niki Parmar, Jakob Uszkoreit, Llion Jones, Aidan N. Gomez, Lukasz Kaiser, and Illia Polosukhin. 2023. Attention is all you need. *arXiv preprint arXiv:1706.03762*.

Z. Xinxi. 2021. Single task fine-tune BERT for text classification. 11911:119111Z – 119111Z–6.

DetectiveReDASers at HSD-2Lang 2024: A New Pooling Strategy with Cross-lingual Augmentation and Ensembling for Hate Speech Detection in Low-resource Languages

Fatima Zahra Qachfar*
fqachfar@uh.edu
University of Houston
Houston, TX, USA

Bryan E. Tuck*
betuck@uh.edu
University of Houston
Houston, TX, USA

Rakesh M. Verma
rmverma2@central.uh.edu
University of Houston
Houston, TX, USA

Abstract

This paper addresses hate speech detection in Turkish and Arabic tweets, contributing to the HSD-2Lang Shared Task. We propose a specialized pooling strategy within a soft-voting ensemble framework to improve classification in Turkish and Arabic language models. Our approach also includes expanding the training sets through cross-lingual translation, introducing a broader spectrum of hate speech examples. Our method attains F1-Macro scores of 0.6964 for Turkish (Subtask A) and 0.7123 for Arabic (Subtask B). While achieving these results, we also consider the computational overhead, striking a balance between the effectiveness of our unique pooling strategy, data augmentation, and soft-voting ensemble. This approach advances the practical application of language models in low-resource languages for hate speech detection.

1 Introduction

Hate speech and offensive language on social media pose significant challenges, affecting individuals and communities globally. These concerns are exacerbated by the anonymity afforded by online platforms, leading to more aggressive behaviors (Fortuna and Nunes, 2018).

Addressing hate speech is crucial for protecting vulnerable and marginalized populations from discrimination and racism. The issue is particularly profound in low-resource languages like Arabic and Turkish, where cultural and linguistic diversity adds additional complexity to detection.

Conventional approaches in hate speech detection, which often rely on standard tooling libraries, may opt to remove emojis due to the unavailability of specific language support. This shortcoming is especially pronounced in a social media text, characterized by its brevity and unconventional language, where special characters like emojis have an influential impact on performance. In response to these challenges, we implemented support for Arabic and Turkish in the Emoji package, a functionality previously absent.

Hate speech detection research has traditionally focused on English (Mansur et al., 2023), with a recent shift towards multilingual contexts, including hate speech against immigrants and women (Basile et al., 2019). Current efforts are increasingly addressing the challenges in low-resource languages like Arabic and Turkish through new frameworks, datasets, and shared tasks (Mubarak et al., 2020; Beyhan et al., 2022; Hasanain et al., 2023). However, data scarcity and class imbalance in these languages still present considerable challenges, necessitating ongoing research and development.

We make the following key contributions and improvements over previous work: (1) A new pooling strategy that significantly improves classification of hate speech in Turkish and Arabic, contributing to higher Macro F1 scores, (2) An evaluation of a cross-lingual data augmentation technique to broaden and enrich the training datasets, enhancing the model's ability to generalize by focusing on language-specific challenges in hate speech contrary to (Ranasinghe and Zampieri, 2021) that solely relies on transfer learning from resource-rich to less-resourced language models, and (3) An implementation of a soft-voting ensemble framework to further boost model performance, as evidenced by the achieved Macro F1 scores.

2 Task and Dataset Description

In the HSD-2Lang shared task (Uludoğan et al., 2024), we focused on two main tasks: Subtask A for Hate Speech Detection in Turkish Tweets and Subtask B for limited Arabic Tweets. Subtask A involves analyzing a dataset of 9,140 Turkish tweets, categorized across topics such as Anti-Refugee sentiment, the Israel-Palestine conflict, and Anti-Greek

*These authors contributed equally to this work.

Proceedings of the 7th Workshop on Challenges and Applications of Automated Extraction of Socio-political Events from Text (CASE 2024), pages 199–204
March 22, 2024 ©2024 Association for Computational Linguistics

discourse, with both hateful and non-hateful tweets. Subtask B presented the challenge of detecting hate speech in a smaller, imbalanced dataset with 82 "hateful" and 778 "not hateful" Arabic tweets, primarily centered on anti-refugee sentiment.

3 Proposed Framework

The key elements of our approach to hate speech detection for subtasks A and B include emoji conversion and bidirectional translation between Turkish and Arabic datasets. We selected `ConvBERTurk`[1] (Schweter, 2020) and `AraBERTv02-Twitter`[2] (Antoun et al., 2020) as our baseline models for Turkish and Arabic texts, respectively.

To tackle the limited and imbalanced data in Subtask B, we merged the translated Turkish dataset from Subtask A with Subtask B dataset. We applied a similar strategy for Subtask A, incorporating the translated Arabic tweets from Subtask B.

Our research introduces an innovative sequence representation technique, going beyond the conventional use of the `[CLS]` token. This method combines the mean and max values from the last hidden layer with the `[CLS]` token, each processed through separate linear layers with *tanh* activation and dropout. The outputs are then concatenated and fed into a final linear layer for classification as "hateful" or "not hateful".

Subtask A employed a soft-voting ensemble of five `ConvBERTurk` models in our application. In contrast, Subtask B utilized a single `AraBERTv02-Twitter` model. In the upcoming sections, we provide a comprehensive overview of the methodologies we employed in our project. These include a detailed description of how we preprocessed the data, consolidated the datasets, converted emojis, translated across Turkish and Arabic, pooled sequence representations, and finally, our training procedures.

3.1 Preprocessing and Dataset Consolidation

Data Preprocessing Our preprocessing approach rigorously standardizes text data, a vital step for reliable analysis. We use the ftfy[3] package to correct incorrectly encoded characters, resolving common encoding issues in text data. Next, we simplify whitespace by replacing excess newlines and tabs with a single space. Our method also uniquely addresses user mentions by substituting them with a standard term—"[مستخدم]" in Arabic and "[Kullanıcı]" in Turkish—to avoid skewing the language-specific processing. Likewise, we replace URLs and retweet indicators with consistent placeholders to minimize noise and point the focus on the textual content itself.

Emoji Conversion The emoji[4] package is updated as we implemented support for Arabic and Turkish languages. This update enables the conversion of emoji characters into their corresponding text descriptions in Arabic and Turkish. Emojis often carry significant emotional and contextual meanings (Hakami et al., 2022), and this conversion is vital for capturing these nuances.

Data Consolidation and Cross-Lingual Translation In our preprocessing workflow, we first address Subtask A by concatenating the three distinct datasets focusing on anti-refugee sentiment, the Israel-Palestine conflict, and anti-Greek discourse. Then, we split this unified dataset using an 80/20 train-test ratio. By adopting this unified approach, we can incorporate a broader range of data, thereby increasing the diversity of the dataset. Additionally, we translated Subtask B's Arabic dataset into Turkish using Google Translator[5] and merged this with Subtask A's training set. This step ensures linguistic consistency and enriches the training data's contextual scope.

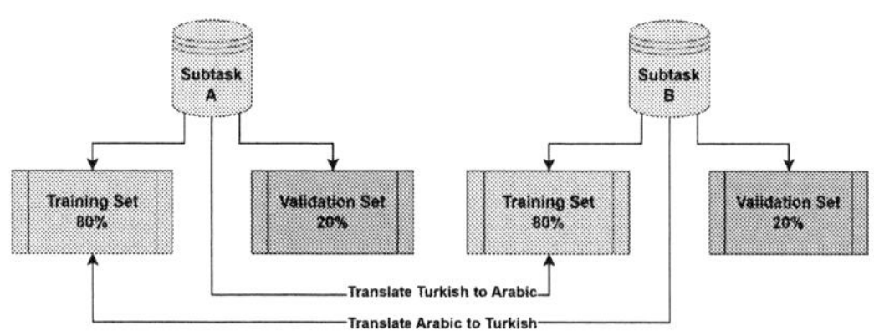

Figure 1: Data Augmentation Workflow

We tackle the challenges of limited and imbalanced data for Subtask B by leveraging thematic overlaps with Subtask A. We translate Subtask A's Turkish data into Arabic and integrate it into Subtask B's training set. This bidirectional translation strategy contributes to a more comprehensive and diverse training environment. We illustrate the similarity between subtasks in Appendix A.

[1] https://huggingface.co/dbmdz/convbert-base-turkish-cased
[2] https://huggingface.co/aubmindlab/bert-base-AraBERTv02-Twitter
[3] https://ftfy.readthedocs.io/
[4] https://github.com/carpedm20/emoji/
[5] https://deep-translator.readthedocs.io/

Throughout, we maintain a uniform preprocessing approach for both subtasks, adjusting slightly to accommodate the primary languages of Turkish for Subtask A and Arabic for Subtask B. This systematic data translation and consolidation approach is critical to our preprocessing strategy and aims to enhance our language models' overall quality and effectiveness.

3.2 Sequence Representation Pooling

We leverage a unique sequence representation technique for hate speech detection, termed "concat" pooling, which we apply in Bert-based models for both subtasks. Our method merges the `[CLS]` token with mean and max values from the last hidden layer's sequence dimension, aiming to enhance the comprehensiveness and diversity of sequence representation. This approach is in contrast to the Multi-CLS BERT method (Chang et al., 2023), which employs multiple `[CLS]` tokens in a singular BERT model, creating an ensemble-like effect without the substantial computational and memory costs typically associated with BERT ensembles.

In our implementation, we independently process the `[CLS]`, mean, and max outputs through separate linear layers, integrating *Tanh* activation and dropout before concatenation. This procedure ensures a robust and nuanced embedding, which we subsequently input into a final linear layer for classifying the inputs as "hateful" or "non-hateful". While inspired by Multi-CLS BERT's efficiency in managing multiple `[CLS]` embeddings, such an approach diverges by incorporating varied sequence elements to generate a more thorough representation for classification. Figure 2 illustrates our "concat" pooling architecture.

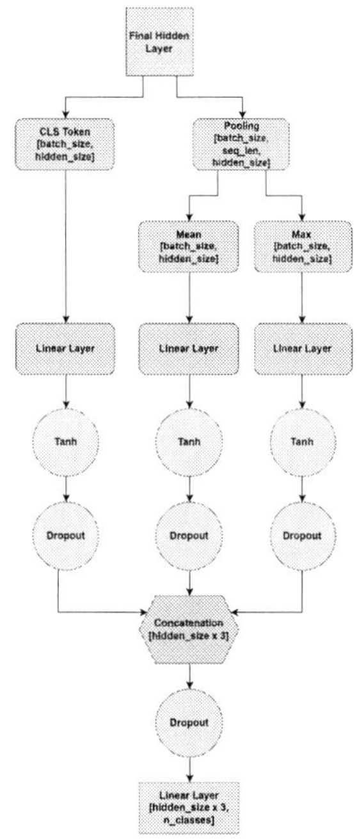

Figure 2: Concat Pooling Architecture

3.3 Soft-Voting Ensemble

Ensemble methods, rooted in collective decision-making, consistently demonstrate superior predictive accuracy and robustness over single-learner models (Jiang et al., 2023; Farooqi et al., 2021). For subtask A, we deploy a soft-voting ensemble consisting of five identical `ConvBERT-Turkish-Cased` models, differentiated only by their initializations. This strategy follows the methodology outlined by (Tuck et al., 2023) in Arabic deception detection, where we halt training at the two-epoch mark as soon as we reach the peak validation F1 Macro score. We use the TorchEnsemble[6] library, an open-source, community-driven project, to facilitate the implementation of this ensemble technique, offering streamlined support for various ensemble methods.

3.4 Training Procedure

Our approach consistently applied the same hyperparameters across all experiments for both subtasks to ensure reliability and consistency. We chose the *AdamW* optimizer (Loshchilov and Hutter, 2019) for its efficiency in fine-tuning large language models, paired with the *Cross-Entropy* loss function, which is well-suited for binary classification tasks. This combination was selected to balance efficient learning with accurate performance.

We limited our training to a maximum of twenty epochs, incorporating an early stopping mechanism with a patience setting of five epochs. This strategy enhances computational efficiency and prevents overfitting by stopping the training when validation F1 Macro scores no longer improve. Although initial trials included a linear learning rate scheduler, we did not use it in our final experiments. Our observations indicated that maintaining a constant learning rate, combined with our chosen optimizer and early stopping, was the most effective. The static hyperparameters we used are as follows: Max

[6] `https://github.com/TorchEnsemble-Community/Ensemble-Pytorch`

Pooling Type	Data Aug.	Ensemble		Single Model	
		Val.	Test	Val.	Test
		Subtask A			
concat	Included	**0.7336**	**0.6964**	0.7130	0.6705
concat	Not Included	0.7203	0.6814	0.7272	0.6608
cls	Included	0.6794	0.6832	0.7368	0.6674
cls	Not Included	0.7348	0.6508	0.6929	0.6781
		Subtask B			
concat	Included	0.7826	0.6027	**0.8333**	**0.6000**
concat	Not Included	0.8461	0.7123	0.8148	0.6582
cls	Included	0.6956	0.5915	0.7333	0.6373
cls	Not Included	0.8148	0.7179	0.8148	0.6052

Table 1: Performance of `ConvBERT-Turkish-Cased` (Subtask A) and `AraBERTv02-Twitter` (Subtask B) models, using Macro F1 scores. 'Pooling Type' distinguishes between `[CLS]` token and concatenated embeddings. 'Data Aug.' indicates if augmentation was used ('Included') or not ('Not Included'). Bold results denote official submissions for each subtask.

Length – 128, Dropout – 0.075, Batch Size – 16, Learning Rate – $2e-05$, Random Seed – 42.

4 Results and Discussion

Table 1 outlines the performance of our models in Subtasks A and B, with the official submissions in bold, achieving 1st place in Subtask A and 3rd place in Subtask B. We offer a systematic view, examining the effects of pooling strategies, comparing ensemble and single-model configurations, and augmenting training data.

For Subtask A, our ensemble model utilizing concatenated pooling—synthesizing the `[CLS]` token, mean, and max embeddings—demonstrated substantial dominance on the test set with a Macro F1 score of 0.6964. This superior performance is attributed to our novel sequence representation, which provides a holistic comprehension of the input data, as opposed to the `[CLS]` token-based approach that achieved a lower score of 0.6832 with data augmentation.

In Subtask B, the ensemble models exhibited a pronounced sensitivity to data augmentation. The ensemble with `[CLS]` token pooling and no data augmentation achieved the highest test score of 0.7179. Conversely, when data augmentation was introduced, the same ensemble approach reduced test performance to 0.5915. Similarly, the ensemble model with concatenated pooling reflected this trend, where the non-augmented approach yielded a robust score of 0.7123 on the test set, compared to a lower 0.6027 with data augmentation.

For single models in Subtask B, the concatenated pooling type with data augmentation resulted in a test score of 0.6000, indicating that the single models were less affected by augmentation. However, this score was still outperformed by the non-augmented ensemble model, highlighting the nuanced impact of augmentation strategies on model performance. The intricate dynamics of the impact of data augmentation are underscored in Subtask B, where its application does not enhance model effectiveness. This difference is particularly notable when comparing the performance of single models against ensemble configurations.

The test scores suggest that ensemble models, especially with non-augmented concatenated pooling, are robust across both subtasks. The discrepancy in performance between the concat and `[CLS]` methods within ensemble configurations highlights the effectiveness of our pooling strategy. These findings emphasize the need for careful consideration when applying data augmentation, as it may not always be beneficial and depends on the specific task and model architecture.

5 Conclusion

In conclusion, our paper introduces an innovative approach combining data augmentation, pooling strategy, and a soft-voting ensemble framework for effective hate speech detection in Turkish and Arabic, languages typically underrepresented in computational linguistics. We successfully enriched the training sets with a broader spectrum of examples by leveraging cross-lingual translation through Google Translator. This approach yielded impressive F1-Macro scores of 0.6964 and 0.7123 in Turkish and Arabic, respectively, demonstrating broad potential in diverse linguistic contexts. The effectiveness of our strategy in low-resource languages opens new avenues for future research, potentially addressing more nuanced aspects of hate speech detection and expanding to other underrepresented languages.

Acknowledgments.

Research partly supported by NSF grants 2210198 and 2244279, and ARO grants W911NF-20-1-0254 and W911NF-23-1-0191. Verma is the founder of Everest Cyber Security and Analytics, Inc.

References

Wissam Antoun, Fady Baly, and Hazem Hajj. 2020. AraBERT: Transformer-based model for Arabic language understanding. In *Proceedings of the 4th Workshop on Open-Source Arabic Corpora and Processing Tools, with a Shared Task on Offensive Language Detection*, pages 9–15, Marseille, France. European Language Resource Association.

Valerio Basile, Cristina Bosco, Elisabetta Fersini, Debora Nozza, Viviana Patti, Francisco Manuel Rangel Pardo, Paolo Rosso, and Manuela Sanguinetti. 2019. Semeval-2019 task 5: Multilingual detection of hate speech against immigrants and women in twitter. In *International Workshop on Semantic Evaluation*.

Fatih Beyhan, Buse Çarik, Inanç Arin, Aysecan Terzioglu, Berrin A. Yanikoglu, and Reyyan Yeniterzi. 2022. A turkish hate speech dataset and detection system. In *International Conference on Language Resources and Evaluation*.

Haw-Shiuan Chang, Ruei-Yao Sun, Kathryn Ricci, and Andrew McCallum. 2023. Multi-CLS BERT: An efficient alternative to traditional ensembling. In *Proceedings of the 61st Annual Meeting of the Association for Computational Linguistics (Volume 1: Long Papers)*, pages 821–854, Toronto, Canada. Association for Computational Linguistics.

Zaki Mustafa Farooqi, Sreyan Ghosh, and Rajiv Ratn Shah. 2021. Leveraging transformers for hate speech detection in conversational code-mixed tweets.

Paula Fortuna and Sérgio Nunes. 2018. A survey on automatic detection of hate speech in text. *ACM Comput. Surv.*, 51(4).

Shatha Ali A. Hakami, Robert Hendley, and Phillip Smith. 2022. Emoji sentiment roles for sentiment analysis: A case study in Arabic texts. In *Proceedings of the The Seventh Arabic Natural Language Processing Workshop (WANLP)*, pages 346–355, Abu Dhabi, United Arab Emirates (Hybrid). Association for Computational Linguistics.

Maram Hasanain, Firoj Alam, Hamdy Mubarak, Samir Abdaljalil, Wajdi Zaghouani, Preslav Nakov, Giovanni Da San Martino, and Abed Alhakim Freihat. 2023. Araieval shared task: Persuasion techniques and disinformation detection in arabic text. In *ARABICNLP*.

Dongfu Jiang, Xiang Ren, and Bill Yuchen Lin. 2023. Llm-blender: Ensembling large language models with pairwise ranking and generative fusion. *arXiv preprint arXiv:2306.02561*.

Ilya Loshchilov and Frank Hutter. 2019. Decoupled weight decay regularization.

Zainab Mansur, Nazlia Omar, and Sabrina Tiun. 2023. Twitter hate speech detection: A systematic review of methods, taxonomy analysis, challenges, and opportunities. *IEEE Access*, 11:16226–16249.

Hamdy Mubarak, Ammar Rashed, Kareem Darwish, Younes Samih, and Ahmed Abdelali. 2020. Arabic offensive language on twitter: Analysis and experiments. In *Workshop on Arabic Natural Language Processing*.

Tharindu Ranasinghe and Marcos Zampieri. 2021. Multilingual offensive language identification for low-resource languages. *Transactions on Asian and Low-Resource Language Information Processing*, 21:1 – 13.

Stefan Schweter. 2020. Berturk - bert models for turkish.

Bryan Tuck, Fatima Qachfar, Dainis Boumber, and Rakesh Verma. 2023. DetectiveRedasers at ArAIEval shared task: Leveraging transformer ensembles for Arabic deception detection. In *Proceedings of ArabicNLP 2023*, pages 494–501, Singapore (Hybrid). Association for Computational Linguistics.

Gökçe Uludoğan, Somaiyeh Dehghan, İnanç Arın, Elif Erol, Berrin Yanıkoğlu, and Arzucan Özgür. 2024. Overview of the hate speech detection in turkish and arabic tweets (hsd-2lang) shared task at case 2024. In *Proceedings of the 7th Workshop on Challenges and Applications of Automated Extraction of Socio-political Events from Text (CASE)*, Malta. Association for Computational Linguistics.

Laurens Van der Maaten and Geoffrey Hinton. 2008. Visualizing data using t-sne. *Journal of machine learning research*, 9(11).

A Appendix

Subtask Data Similarity

Figure 3 and Figure 4 represent the text embeddings of subtask A and B training sets from the models `ConvBERT-Turkish-Cased` and `AraBERTv02-Twitter` in the Turkish and Arabic embedding spaces respectively using the dimensionality reduction algorithm T-SNE (Van der Maaten and Hinton, 2008). The T-SNE algorithm draws the similarities between neighbors using the student t-distribution. As illustrated in Figure 3, we have plotted 10.000 samples consisting of 860 Arabic tweets translated to Turkish and 9.140 Turkish Original tweets from Subtask A training set.

According to Figure 3, the Arabic tweets that were translated into Turkish from Subtask B closely resemble the original Turkish tweets found in the training data for Subtask A. This observation is further supported by the findings presented in Table 1 Subtask A, which indicates that incorporating the additional translated data into the training process leads to an improvement in the F1-score.

In Figure 4, the Turkish-translated tweets are not as close to subtask B's original Arabic tweets and are in another cluster. This discrepancy has resulted in decreased performance in Subtask B when incorporated as additional translated training data, as shown in Table 1 Subtask B.

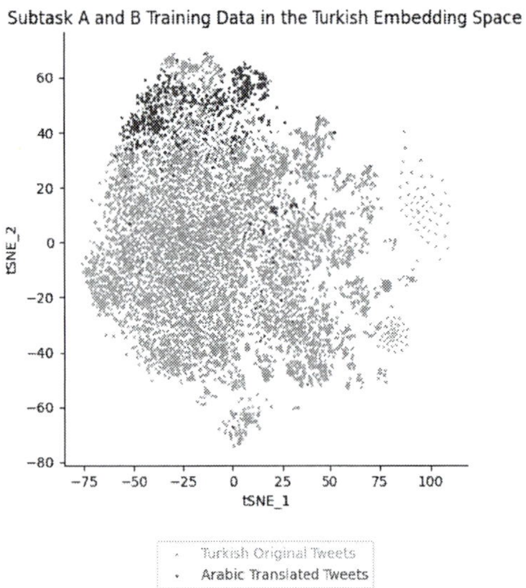

Figure 3: Training Data in Turkish Embedding Space using `ConvBERT-Turkish-Cased`

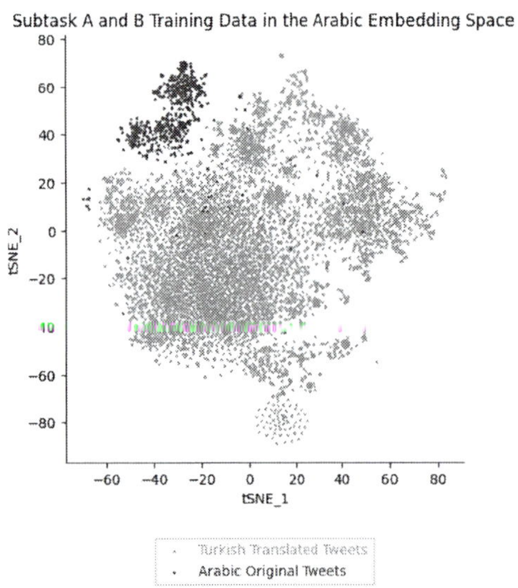

Figure 4: Training Data in Arabic Embedding Space using `AraBERTv02-Twitter`

Detecting Hate Speech in Turkish Print Media: A Corpus and A Hybrid Approach with Target-oriented Linguistic Knowledge

Gökçe Uludoğan[1] and **Atıf Emre Yüksel**[1] and **Ümit Can Tunçer**[2]
Burak Işık [2] and **Yasemin Korkmaz**[3] and **Didar Akar**[2] and **Arzucan Özgür**[1]
[1]Department of Computer Engineering, Bogazici University, Istanbul, Turkey 34342
[2]Department of Linguistics, Bogazici University, Istanbul, Turkey 34342
[3] Hrant Dink Foundatio, Istanbul, Turkey 34373
{gokce.uludogan,akar,arzucan.ozgur}@bogazici.edu.tr

Abstract

The use of hate speech targeting ethnicity, nationalities, religious identities, and specific groups has been on the rise in the news media. However, most existing automatic hate speech detection models focus on identifying hate speech, often neglecting the target group-specific language that is common in news articles. To address this problem, we first compile a hate speech dataset, TurkishHatePrintCorpus, derived from Turkish news articles and annotate it specifically for the language related to the targeted group. We then introduce the HateTargetBERT model, which integrates the target-centric linguistic features extracted in this study into the BERT model, and demonstrate its effectiveness in detecting hate speech while allowing the model's classification decision to be explained. We have made the dataset and source code publicly available at https://github.com/boun-tabi/HateTargetBERT-TR.

Warning: This paper contains hate speech and offensive terms directed towards specific groups.

1 Introduction

Hate speech, typically characterized by defamatory statements targeted at specific groups based on ethnicity, nationality, religion, color, gender, sexual orientation, among other characteristics (Schmidt and Wiegand, 2019), presents unique challenges in media discourse. Contrary to the expectation of objectivity in news and print media, hate speech is surprisingly prevalent(HDF Publications, 2019). This study explores this phenomenon, broadening the scope to include discriminatory speech, which, while not explicitly hateful, still fosters discrimination. Despite regulatory efforts, such speech persists in media, often masked by subtle linguistic tactics. For example, distortion involves making unfair generalizations, as seen in headlines like "Greeks deliberately target refugees on sinking boat." Similarly, symbolization uses identity traits to convey messages, evident in phrases like "Will a Muslim represent us at Eurovision?" These methods not only spread hate speech but also magnify its damaging effects, highlighting the need for vigilant monitoring and action.

With the significant advances in pre-trained large language models and the transformer architecture in natural language processing, researchers have developed various architectures based on BERT (Devlin et al., 2019) that have achieved successful results in the area of hate speech detection (Mozafari et al., 2019; Gupta et al., 2020; Mozafari et al., 2020; Caselli et al., 2021; Perifanos and Goutsos, 2021). Although lexical and linguistic features have been used in different model architectures (Nobata et al., 2016; Wiegand et al., 2018; Koufakou et al., 2020; Hüsünbeyi et al., 2022), the integration of target-oriented linguistic features into the BERT model has not yet been studied.

There are open data sets on certain aspects of hate speech in different languages and especially in social media (Zampieri et al., 2019; Basile et al., 2019; Sap et al., 2020; ElSherief et al., 2021). However, resources for languages like Turkish are scarce (Mayda et al., 2021). Recent studies have addressed this issue by compiling Turkish tweets from "hate domains" on specific topics like politics, religion, and vaccination where hate speech might emerge (Beyhan et al., 2022; Arın et al., 2023; İhtiyar et al., 2023). Concurrently, BERT-based models are being developed for hate speech detection (Toraman et al., 2022; Beyhan et al., 2022). Previous work has also focused on hate speech in Turkish news articles and proposed a hybrid model for hate speech detection by integrating linguistic features into BERT (Hüsünbeyi et al., 2022). However, the linguistic features used in this study rely on general morpho-syntactic properties of Turkish, neglecting the crucial aspect of the target groups of hate speech. In this study, we compile a dataset of hate speech derived from Turkish print news and

Proceedings of the 7th Workshop on Challenges and Applications of Automated Extraction of Socio-political Events from Text (CASE 2024), pages 205–214
March 22, 2024 ©2024 Association for Computational Linguistics

annotate it specifically for language related to the targeted group. We then introduce the HateTargetBERT model, which integrates the target-centric linguistic features extracted in this study into the BERT model, and demonstrate its effectiveness in detecting hate speech while allowing the model's classification decision to be explained.

The main contributions of this paper can be summarized as follows: (i) We develop HateTargetBERT, a model that couples BERT with hate speech target-oriented linguistic features extracted from hate speech content in the news articles and enables the generation of an explanation for the model's classification decision. (ii) We release `TurkishHatePrintCorpus`, a human-annotated hate speech dataset derived from Turkish print media and make the dataset, our model, and its source code publicly available[1].

2 Dataset

2.1 Collection

To compile a dataset of newspaper articles containing hate speech, we collected articles from various Turkish print media outlets. These articles were selected based on specific keywords associated with the target groups such as ethnicity, nationality, and religious identity. The keywords we used for querying were selected by the linguists in our team based on a combination of domain knowledge and an initial exploration of the print media. We aim to capture a wide range of hate speech instances in the Turkish print media context. The printed articles, initially in the form of scanned images, were obtained from PRNet, a company that provides a media archive and an OCR tool. We used this OCR tool to convert the scanned images into text format.

2.2 Filtering

Collecting articles from print media presents unique challenges. Many of these articles contain Optical Character Recognition (OCR) errors at both word and sentence levels. Instances have been observed where sentences are distorted as a result of the joining of two half-sentences from double-column printing. To enhance data quality, we adopted a filtering strategy that relies on scoring words and sentences using an n-gram language model. To achieve this, articles were segmented into sentences and tokenized using the Zemberek library[2]. Both the sentences and words were then scored employing a 5-gram model, which was trained with the KenLM library[3] on a recent dump of the Turkish Wikipedia using subword tokenization. The scoring process incorporated length-based normalization to facilitate fair comparisons. We calculated the mean and standard deviation of sentence scores for each article. A manual analysis was performed on both sentences and words to establish thresholds for anomalies. Next, we computed the ratio of anomalous words and sentences within an article. To refine the collected articles, we applied the following criteria:

- Articles shouldn't contain sentences that score less than -1.9 using a language model, indicating they are anomalous.
- The average proportion of anomalous tokens in a sentence should not exceed 20%.
- No sentence within the article should have an anomalous token ratio greater than 50%.
- On average, a sentence in an article should have 2 or fewer anomalous tokens.
- The mean score for the sentences in the article should be greater than -0.61.
- Sentence scores within an article should have a standard deviation below 0.2.

Additionally, we filtered content at the article level. During preprocessing, we removed URLs, emails, numbers, currency symbols, and non-Turkish words using the langdetect library[4].

2.3 Annotation

The annotation process involved both volunteers and a project team. These volunteers were predominantly university students from diverse fields, including media studies and sociology. Their selection was based on both their expressed interest in the topic and a review of their resumes. Before the annotation, we ensured that the volunteers underwent a comprehensive training session. In this session, they were introduced to our definition of hate speech: statements that marginalize, threaten, or insult groups based on their ethnicity, nationality, or religious identity. Notably, this definition

[1]https://github.com/boun-tabi/HateTargetBERT-TR

[2]https://github.com/loodos/zemberek-python

[3]https://github.com/kpu/kenlm

[4]https://github.com/Mimino666/langdetect

excludes comments directed at individual persons, institutions, or organizations.The analysis of articles that mention ethnic, national, or religious groups is guided by key questions: Following the clarification of various hate speech categories, the texts containing hate speech are discussed in relation to categories. To enhance their understanding, they were provided with representative examples from the print media. Several examples of hate speech expression in the news articles can be found in Table 1.

Each volunteer worked independently, identifying articles containing hate speech and marking those that were ambiguous. Once a day's articles were annotated, they were collectively reviewed with the project team. During this review process, any contradictory content within the articles sparked methodological and conceptual debates. Through collaborative discussions, the volunteers and project team achieved consensus on the article annotations. To validate the annotations, secondary annotators reviewed ten percent of the randomly selected articles, resulting in a Cohen's Kappa score of 0.675, indicating substantial agreement between annotators. Upon identifying newspaper articles containing hate speech, we selected one non-hateful newspaper article from the same day for each hateful newspaper article.

2.4 Statistics

Compiled from 859 distinct media sources, `TurkishHatePrintCorpus` provides an extensive scope for analyzing the linguistic characteristics and distinctions between hateful and nonhateful articles. The dataset displays the variety in the number of articles collected from each source. While we obtained only one article from 274 outlets, a significant portion of the corpus is supported by the prominent contributions of a few outlets. Notably, the top five outlets from which we gathered articles contributed 299, 205, 159, 155, and 143 articles, respectively.

The dataset comprises 3406 articles from local media sources along with 3275 articles from national ones. As for the hate speech categories, `TurkishHatePrintCorpus` contains 3678 nonhateful articles along with 3003 hateful ones.

Each article in the dataset, on average, comprises around 21 sentences. Articles in the dataset vary, with some being as brief as 2 sentences and others as lengthy as 263 sentences. Moreover, the average word count for an article stands at 350 words, with some articles having as few as 21 words and others boasting a word count as high as 3047.

Table 2 presents an overview of the general statistics for this annotated dataset, while Table 3 details the distribution of news articles with hate speech and the corresponding target groups.

The curated dataset was then divided into training, validation and test sets, ensuring that the ratio of hateful to non-hateful news articles remained consistent across all sets. The distribution of hateful and non-hateful newspaper articles across the splits is shown in Table 4.

3 Methodology

We develop HateTargetBERT, a model that couples BERT with target-oriented linguistic features specifically designed for hate speech detection. As illustrated in Figure 1, the model architecture consists of a BERT model followed by fully connected network (FCN) layers. These layers not only take the last hidden representation of the `[CLS]` token, which is typically used as a sentence embedding, but also incorporate the extracted linguistic features as input. To prevent overfitting, we incorporate dropout layers (Srivastava et al., 2014) between the FCN layers.

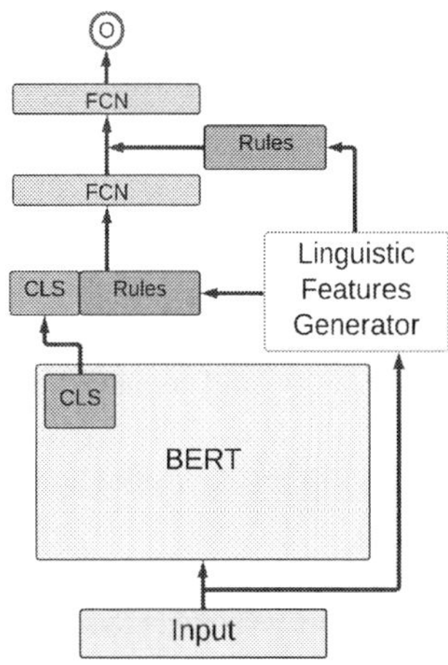

Figure 1: Overview of HateTargetBERT.

3.1 Linguistic Features

In HateTargetBERT, linguistic features serve as additional indicators for hate speech detection. These features focus on target groups, hateful words, ethnicity-specific rules, and unique pat-

Table 1: Examples of hate speech expression in the news articles

	Target	Type
...Bin mülteciye bakamayan Yunanlılar onları şiddet ve dayakla Türkiye'ye göndermeye devam ediyor... (...Greeks who cannot take care of a thousand refugees continue to send them to Turkey with violence and beatings...)	greek	hostility/war discourse
...Avrupalılar önce terörü üretti. Sonra güya kendileri mücadele ediyor... (...Europeans first produced terror. Then they are supposedly struggling themselves...)	european	exaggeration/attribution/distortion
...Böylesine zulmü gavur bile yapmadı... (...Even infidels did not commit such cruelty...)	infidel	symbolization

Table 2: Statistics of the human-annotated hate-speech print media dataset.

Statistics	Detail
Number of samples	6681
Number of sources	859
Articles from local sources / national sources	3406 / 3275
Time period	2014-2019
Average number of sentences per article	21
Average number of words per article	350

terns that identify hate speech for a specific target group. Linguists in our team derived these features by utilizing the trTenTen corpus [5] available on SketchEngine, using the names of target groups as keywords, to find patterns potentially indicative of hate speech.

The linguistic features are grouped into five categories (i.e., types), each with unique characteristics in terms of feature formulation, hate speech content search methodology, and semantic expression. A summary of these features is presented in Table 5. Each category, except the target agnostic type, is further divided into several subtypes based on the severity of hate speech, as determined by linguistic experts. The severity ranges from Degree 1 (least severe) to Degree 5 (most severe). Each feature is represented with one-hot encoding, except for those of target agnostic type, which accumulate the number of detected rules. Some feature types are searched in a range of window while others require strict matches.

Target-agnostic features aim to identify patterns common across all ethnicities and nationalities in news articles, using a variety of terms often found in hate speech. These patterns are searched within a 15-word range (see Table 6 for a list of patterns). These patterns were developed considering Turkish grammar, an agglutinative language with a Subject-Object-Verb structure where nouns take suffixes based on their role. For example, if a noun

Table 3: Number of occurrences of hate speech target groups in hateful and non-hateful articles within `TurkishHatePrintCorpus`.

Target	Hateful / Non-hateful	Target	Hateful / Non-hateful
Afghan	119 / 104	Immigrant	169 / 214
Alevi	25 / 82	Infidels	65 / 4
Arab	336 / 223	Iranian	20 / 24
Armenian	847 / 140	Iraqi	27 / 29
Assyrian	14 / 13	Italian	75 / 45
Atheist	36 / 4	Jewish	25 / 20
Buddhist	112 / 10	Kurdish	265 / 181
Bulgarian	61 / 46	Kyrgyz	12 / 11
Catholic	35 / 11	Lebanese	7 / 5
Chechen	12 / 4	Muslim	886 / 593
Chinese	17 / 17	Orthodox	32 / 11
Christian	372 / 128	Pakistani	65 / 68
Crusader	149 / 56	Refugee	265 / 374
Dutch	29 / 15	Russian	665 / 468
English	336 / 142	Saudi	118 / 80
European	117 / 65	Serbian	83 / 15
French	230 / 98	Syrian	646 / 555
German	348 / 307	Turbaned	3 / 1
Giaour	32 / 6	Turkmen	60 / 63
Greek (Rum)	799 / 728	Ukranian	1 / 8
Greek (Yunan)	541 / 379	Western	255 / 174
Gypsies	8 / 9	Yazidi	27 / 18
Hebrew	646 / 142	Yemeni	8 / 4
Hungarian	31 / 30		

[5]https://www.sketchengine.eu/trtenten-turkish-corpus

Table 4: Number of samples in each class across data splits.

Split	Hateful	Non-hateful
Training	2395	2949
Validation	305	363
Test	303	366

from a target group is near the active verb "öldür-" (to kill) and is in the nominative form (suffix-free in Turkish), it's likely the sentence's agent. Similarly, if "tarafından" (by) is near the passive verb "öldürül-" (to be killed), the preceding word is the agent. If this word is from the target group, it suggests that the target group is the agent. Patterns were created using fixed words and variables. Functional words like "tarafından" (by) and suffixes such as -A (dative), -(n)In (genitive) are fixed, while target group names, adjectives, verbs, and gerunds are variable. **Target-specific features**, on the other hand, aim to detect patterns that are generally associated with a particular group in news using the same approach (see Table 7 for details).

Pre-target and post-target features are designed to identify hateful patterns that are adjacent to particular targets. These features highlight the specific hate speech content that authors aim to promote in the news. The adjacent features are identified through direct pattern matching, without the use of a window parameter. These features are categorized based on their severity, as determined by linguistic experts. For instance, a pre-target pattern like "covert `[ETHN]`" is considered to be of Degree 1 severity, indicating a less severe form of hate speech. In this pattern, `[ETHN]` serves as a placeholder representing any ethnicity. On the other hand, a post-target pattern such as "`[ETHN]` treachery" is of Degree 5 severity, indicating a more severe form of hate speech. For a comprehensive list of pre-target and post-target features , please refer to Table 8 and 9, respectively.

Misleading nonhateful patterns are patterns that appear in newspaper articles about target groups but don't typically indicate hate speech. They are identified by detecting specific word sequences around the target keyword that are likely to come from a non-hateful context. For instance, "`[ETHN]` footballer" probably originates from a sports article. Moreover, some phrases with the target group are not considered hate speech. For example, "Kürt terör örgütü" (Kurdish terrorist organization) is seen as hate speech due to its ethnic emphasis, but "Kürtçü terör örgütü" (Kurdist terrorist organization) isn't, as it emphasizes the organization's ideology. Additionally, quotes from individuals, indicated with phrases like "dedi" (he/she said), are not evaluated for hate speech in this study. A comprehensive list of these patterns can be found in Table 10.

3.2 Baseline models

We compare our model with two other models: BERTurk (Schweter, 2020), which solely leverages BERT representations, and HateTargetNN, a basic two-layer fully-connected network that only uses the linguistic features extracted in this study.
BERTurk (Schweter, 2020) is a transformer based model pretrained on a compilation of Turkish OSCAR[6], Wikipedia dump, and various OPUS corpora[7]. It has been shown to be one of the state-of-the-art models for hate speech detection in Turkish text (Hüsünbeyi et al., 2022; Beyhan et al., 2022). To adapt it for hate speech detection, we fine-tuned the pretrained model on the curated hate speech dataset by adding a fully-connected layer that utilizes the `[CLS]` token representation.
HateTargetNN is another baseline model that we use to test the ability of the linguistic features alone in detecting hate speech. This model is a two-layer fully-connected neural network, which includes batch normalization and dropout layers.

3.3 Implementation Details

We adopt BERTurk (Schweter, 2020) as the initial checkpoint for our HateTargetBERT model. All hyperparameters are selected based on their performance on the validation set. We use the F1 score as the metric to evaluate the performance of the models on the validation set, with the validation performance assessed each epoch.

We trained BERTurk and HateTargetBERT for 3 epochs while HateTargetNN is trained for 10 epochs. For the BERT-based models, we used the AdamW optimizer (Loshchilov and Hutter, 2019) with a learning rate of 1e-5 and a weight decay of 1e-2. Conversely, for HateTargetNN, we retained the same settings but adjusted the learning rate to 1e-3. We also incorporated a scheduler for the learning rate, with a patience of 2 evaluation steps and a

[6]https://traces1.inria.fr/oscar/
[7]http://opus.nlpl.eu/

Table 5: Summary of the target-oriented linguistic features. These features are divided into six categories: target agnostic, target specific, pre-target, post-target, and misleading non-hateful features. Each type, except for the target agnostic type, is further divided into several subtypes based on the severity of hate speech, from Degree 1 (least severe) to Degree 5 (most severe). [ETHN] substitutes for any ethnicity.

Type	# Subtypes	# Patterns	Window	Example (in Turkish)	Translation
Target agnostic	-	14		[IRK]ın kuklası olan [IRK]	[ETHN] who are puppets of [OTHER ETHN]
Target specific	4	19		kripto ermeni	crypto armenian
Pre-Target	5	38		istilacı [IRK]	invading [ETHN]
Post-Target	5	60		[IRK] soykırımı	[ETHN] massacres
Misleading Nonhateful	4	30		[IRK] filozof	[ETHN] philosopher

Table 6: Target agnostic patterns that are frequently used in hate speech content. [ETHN] substitutes for any ethnicity to generate feature. Patterns are searched in determined window range. [ADJBEF] and [ADJAFTER] indicate that words from Tables 8 and 9 can be placed respectively.

ID	Pattern	EN Translation
1	[IRK]+lık yapmak	act like [ETHN]
2	[IRK]a bak sen	look at that [ETHN]
3	[IRK [IRK]+lığını yap(mak)	s/he does her/his [ETHN]
4	[IRK] kurşunlarıyla/bombalarıyla/parasıyla	with the bullets/bombs/money of [ETHN]
5	[IRK] paryası/skandalı/işgali/baskını	[ETHN] pariah/scandal/occupation/invasion
6	[IRK]+ın gerçekleştirdiği/yaptığı katliam/zulüm/soykırım	massacre/persecution/cruelty/oppressure of [ETHN]
7	[IRK]+ın uşağı/işbirlikçisi/piyonu/kuklası (olan) [IRK]	[ETHN] servant/pawn/collaborator/puppets of [OTHER ETHN]
8	[IRK] destekli [IRK] darbesi/saldırıları/katliamı/soykırımı	[ETHN] backed [OTHER ETHN] coup/genocide/massacre/attacks
9	[IRK] tarafından saldırıya/katliama/soykırıma maruz kalmak/uğramak	being attacked/subjected to genocide/massacred by the [ETHN]
10	[IRK] tarafından gerçekleştirilen/yapılan katliam/zulüm/soykırım	massacre/persecution/cruelty/oppressure done/carried out by [ETHN]
11	[IRK] ... öldürdü/katletti/etnik temizlik yaptı/kirletti/bastı/şehit etti	[ETHN] ... killed/massacred/did ethnic cleansing/disgloried/martyrized
12	[IRK] tarafından ... öldürüldü/katledildi/etnik temizlik yapıldı/basıldı/şehit edildi	killed/massacred/did ethnic cleansing/disgloried/martyrized ... by [ETHN]
13	[IRK] tarafından IRK+a yönelik saldırılar/katliam/zulüm/soykırım	genocide/massacre/persecution/cruelty/oppressure/attack of [ETHN] by [OTHER ETHN]
14	[IRK]+ın hain(ce)/vahşi(ce)/insanlık dışı/hunharca/kan donduran/şeytani/sinsi/[ADJBEF] teşebbüsleri/planları/oluşumları/[ADJAFTER]	sneaky/traitorous/wild/subhuman/bloodthirstily/terrifical/satanic/[ADJBEF] [ETHN]'s attempts/plans/organizations/[ADJAFTER]

Table 7: Target specific patterns. Higher degree points more serious hate speech content.

Degree 1	Degree 2	Degree 3	Degree 4
vahşi toplumlar (wild societies)	batıl batı (superstitious west)	yahudi ajanı (jewish agent)	yahudi çakallığı (jewish cowardice)
batı cehaleti (western ignorance)		yahudi uşağı (jewish servant)	katil rum (killer rum)
haçlı zihniyeti (crusader mentality)		kripto ermeni (crypto armenian)	haydut rumlar (rogue Greeks)
kriptolar (cryptos)		suriyeli işgali (syrian invasion)	rum zorbalığı (Greek bullying)
		afgan işgali (afghan invasion)	kafir alevi (infidel alevist)
		mülteci işgali (refugee invasion)	ateist alevi (atheist alevist)
		pakistanlı işgali (pakistani invasion)	
		arapların işgali (invasion of the arabs)	

Table 8: Pre-target features in hate speech content. A higher degree indicates a more serious hate speech content.

Degree 1	Degree 2	Degree 3	Degree 4	Degree 5
sapıtan (amok)	katleden (murderous)	kripto (crypto)	işgalci (invader)	hain (traitorous)
çakma (fake)	korkak (coward)	sinsi (sly)	gaspçı (grabber)	katleden (murderous)
facir (sinner)	yamyam (cannibal)	açgözlü (greedy)	lanetlenmiş (damned)	gavur (infidel)
gizli (covert)	başbelası (the very devil)	dönek (renegade)	Allah'ın lanetlediği (cursed by god)	kalleş (treacherous)
kışkırmış (spoiled)		iki yüzlü (two-faced)	zalim (cruel)	kan gölüne çeviren (vicious killer)
hırsız (thief)		azgın (ferocious)	şerefsiz (dishonourable)	insanlık suçu işleyen (perpetrator of crimes against humanity)
		edepsiz (shameless)	gaddar (grim)	bebek katili (baby murderer)
		yağmacı (predatory)	gasıp (usurper)	cani (villain)
		çapulcu (marauder)	canavarlaşmış (monstrous)	vahşi (wild)
				eli kanlı (bloody) hand

reduction factor of 0.5. The dropout probability of the additional layers in HateTargetBERT was set to 0.5. It is worth noting that the models underwent training on ten unique splits, each initialized with different seeds, and were subsequently evaluated on the test set.

4 Results

As shown in Table 11, HateTargetBERT, combining BERT with target-oriented features, demonstrated superior performance compared to the baseline HateTargetNN model, which solely relies on linguistic features. Additionally, HateTargetBERT performed at a comparable level to BERTurk. Al-

Table 9: Post-target features in hate speech content. A higher degree indicates a more serious hate speech content.

Degree 1	Degree 2	Degree 3	Degree 4	Degree 5
işbirlikçisi (collaborator)	yalanları (lies)	baskısı (pressure)	terörü (terror)	gaddarlığı (atrocity)
inadı (stubbornness)	iftiraları (slanders)	bozma (violation)	terör üssü (terror base)	imha (destruction)
doyumsuzluğu (dissatisfaction)	tehdidi (threat)	yalakalığı (fawning)	saldırıları (attacks)	zulmü (cruelty)
karısı (wife)	oyunu (games)	entrikaları (intrigues)	terörizmi (terrorism)	kırımı (politicide)
dolandırıcı (swindler)	yağmacılar (looters)	fesatları (mischief)	sapkınlığı (heresy)	vahşeti (brutality)
parmağı (hand)	çapulcusu (marauder)	sürüleri (herds)	köpekler (dogs)	zalimi (ferocity)
provokasyonu (provocation)	haydutlar (bandits)	kötülükleri (evil)	terör örgütü (terrorist organization)	hain (traitor)
artığı (reversion)		dönekliği (apostasy)	sırtlanlar (hyenas)	kalleşliği (treachery)
uşaklığı (servitude)		açgözlülüğü (greed)	soysuzlar (retrograde)	canilikleri (murderousness)
aşığı (lover)		sinsiliği (snakiness)	çakallar (coyotes)	kıyımları (massacres)
gaspçılar (usurpers)		yüzsüzlüğü (sassiness)	yamyamlar (cannibals)	piçleri (bastards)
kuklası (puppets)		iki yüzlülüğü (hypocrisy)	vandallar (vandals)	
piyonları (pawns)		baskını (raid)		
teröristi (terrorist)		tohumu (seed)		
virüsü (virus)		dölleri (spawn)		
sevici (lover)				

Table 10: Misleading hate speech content that are found mostly non hate speech news. [ETHN] substitutes for any ethnicity to generate a feature. A higher rating indicates less or no hate speech. "[ETHN]+ist" expresses ethnicity names and the suffix"-CU" in Turkish, which is derived nationalist names from it by attached them (e.g. Türkçü, Kürtçü).

Degree 1	Degree 2	Degree 3	Degree 4
[IRK] çeteleri ([ETHN] gangs)	haçlı seferi (crusade)	diye belirtti (s/he stated)	futbol (football)
[IRK] fanatiği ([ETHN] fanatics)	STK (non-governmental organizations)	dedi (said)	spor (sport)
[IRK]+cı terör örgütü ([ETHN]+ist terrorist organization)	tarihte bugün (today in history)	şeklinde açıkladı (expressed as)	maç (match)
[IRK] polisi ([ETHN] police)	takvimde bugün (today on the calendar)	şeklinde ifade etti (explained as)	antik yunan (ancient greek)
[IRK] yaygaracılığı ([ETHN] fuss)			yunan düşünür (greek thinker)
[IRK] askerleri ([ETHN] soldiers)			yunan filozof (greek philosopher)
[IRK] milisleri ([ETHN] militia)			
[IRK] militanları ([ETHN] militants)			
[IRK] yerleşimciler ([ETHN] settlers)			
[IRK] milliyetçiler ([ETHN] nationalists)			
[IRK] güçleri ([ETHN] forces)			
[IRK] isyanı ([ETHN] revolt)			
radikal [IRK] (radical [ETHN])			
ırkçı [IRK] (racist [ETHN])			
siyonistler (zionist jew)			
pontus rum (pontus empire)			

Table 11: Evaluation of the models on the test set .

Model	Accuracy (%)	Precision (%)	Recall (%)	F1-score (%)
HateTargetNN	66.38 $\pm$0.89	83.66 $\pm$4.45	31.39 $\pm$2.24	45.62 $\pm$2.75
BERTurk (Schweter, 2020)	90.60 $\pm$1.20	87.69 $\pm$2.49	92.02 $\pm$2.15	89.78 $\pm$1.53
HateTargetBERT	90.54 $\pm$0.84	88.47 $\pm$2.18	90.82 $\pm$2.07	89.60 $\pm$1.16

Table 12: Evaluation of the models on the test instances with at least one linguistic feature.

Model	Accuracy (%)	Precision (%)	Recall (%)	F1-score (%)
HateTargetNN	75.22 $\pm$2.10	83.70 $\pm$3.88	58.57 $\pm$4.47	68.79 $\pm$3.45
BERTurk (Schweter, 2020)	90.49 $\pm$1.92	88.39 $\pm$3.59	91.80 $\pm$1.90	90.03 $\pm$2.15
HateTargetBERT	90.75 $\pm$1.08	89.37 $\pm$2.75	91.19 $\pm$2.29	90.22 $\pm$1.24

though BERTurk exhibited slightly better scores across various metrics, except for precision, the differences were not statistically significant based on the two-tailed paired t-test conducted at a 95% confidence interval. It is important to note that while the linguistic features were applied to all instances, only a subset of test instances contained these features, limiting their coverage. Table 12 presents a comparison of model performances on these specific instances. Notably, the models utilizing target-oriented features achieved higher scores across metrics in this subset, suggesting the effectiveness of these features and emphasizing the need for a comprehensive feature set.

We also conducted a user study using the Qualtrics online survey tool[8] to demonstrate the effectiveness of the HateTargetBERT model. For this purpose, we randomly selected ten articles from the test set that were predicted to contain hateful content and asked participants to rank the linguistic features shown in the articles based on their helpfulness in understanding the model's prediction of hatefulness. Each article was rated on a 5-point Likert scale (Strongly agree = 5, Somewhat agree = 4, Neither agree nor disagree = 3, Somewhat disagree = 2, Strongly disagree = 1). Table 13 illustrates an excerpt from a sample article from the user study.

Table 13: Excerpt from the user study and its English translation where "rum sevici" (Greek-loving) is highlighted as a post-target feature of degree 1.

Article Excerpt
... bazı önemli milliyetçi şahsiyetler kişisel menfaatlerine hizmet edilmediği değerlendirmeleriyle gidip bir kez daha Akıncı veya benzeri teslimiyetçi ve rum sevici bir başka adaya, sırf inat olsun diye oy vererek göreve getirecekler ...
English Translation
... some significant nationalist figures, assessing that their personal interests are not served, will once again go and, just out of spite, vote for another candidate like Akıncı or a similar defeatist and Greek-loving , bringing them into office ...

The study involved 25 participants, all of whom hold at least a higher education degree. The responses, as shown in Figure 2, had an average score of 3.41 and a standard deviation of 1.24. The majority of these responses fell into the categories of "strongly agree" or "somewhat agree", suggesting that the linguistic features were helpful in understanding the model's choice.

5 Related Work

Automated detection of hate speech has been extensively studied over the years due to its positive impact on society. Many studies have proposed

[8]https://www.qualtrics.com

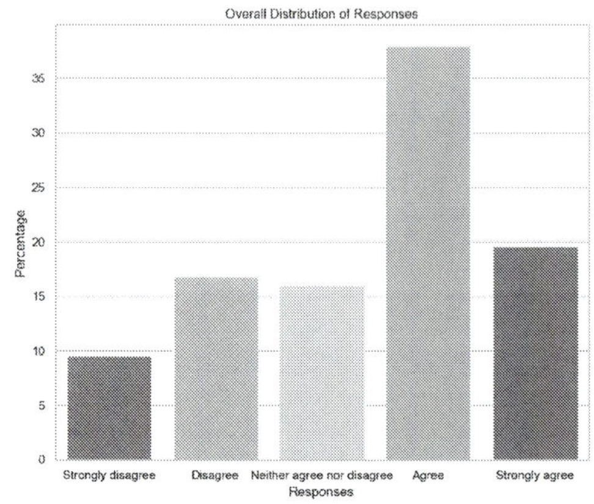

Figure 2: Distribution of participant's responses

methods to identify hateful content across different platforms in order to assist in content moderation. Previous work utilized traditional machine learning models and neural networks that leveraged features such as tf-idf, word vectors (Saha et al., 2018; de Andrade and Gonçalves, 2021), n-grams (Nobata et al., 2016; Waseem and Hovy, 2016), and lexical features (Warner and Hirschberg, 2012; Wiegand et al., 2018; Capozzi et al., 2019; Koufakou et al., 2020). However, more recent models have developed various architectures based on BERT, resulting in significant performance improvements (Mozafari et al., 2019; Gupta et al., 2020; Mozafari et al., 2020; Caselli et al., 2021; Perifanos and Goutsos, 2021).

Although hate speech is a topic that has attracted a lot of attention, there is a lack of resources for languages like Turkish (Mayda et al., 2021). Recently, several datasets have been compiled from Turkish tweets (Beyhan et al., 2022; Arın et al., 2023; İhtiyar et al., 2023). Concurrently, BERT-based models are being developed to detect hateful content in these tweets (Toraman et al., 2022; Beyhan et al., 2022). Previous work has focused on hate speech in Turkish news articles and proposed a hybrid model for hate speech detection by integrating linguistic features into BERT (Hüsünbeyi et al., 2022). However, the linguistic features used in this study rely on general morpho-syntactic properties of Turkish, neglecting the crucial aspect of the target groups of hate speech. In our work, we address this challenge by building a model that combines target-centric linguistic features with BERT. This approach achieves high performance while also providing explainability, which is particularly important when dealing with longer contexts such as news articles.

6 Conclusion

We introduced `TurkishHatePrintCorpus`, a manually annotated hate speech dataset, compiled from Turkish newspaper articles and categorized for target groups. In addition, we developed a model, HateTargetBERT, combining BERT with target-oriented linguistic features. The results demonstrate that integrating target-oriented linguistic knowledge into a transformer model is an effective strategy for hate speech detection and for the explanation of the model's classification decision.

Limitations

This study focuses on print media, excluding the less formal and more explicit language often found in social media. Therefore, the targeted linguistic feature set are derived from printed newspaper articles. Additionally, this work aims to detect hate speech against ethnicity, national and religious entities, and immigrants. As such, newspaper articles associated with other hate domains, such as gender, are not considered. It's also worth noting that some patterns in the targeted linguistic features might be unique to Turkish. Another limitation of this study is the model's inability to handle long context lengths, exceeding 512 tokens, a common occurrence in column articles.

Ethical Considerations

We acknowledge the potential risk associated with releasing our source code and the manually annotated hate speech dataset. However, we believe that the benefits of automatic hate speech detection outweigh the associated risks of releasing the code and the dataset.

Acknowledgments

This research was partially supported by the Swedish Consulate-General, İstanbul Turkey (Project number: UM2021/10687/ISTA).

References

İnanç Arın, Zeynep Işık, Seçilay Kutal, Somaiyeh Dehghan, Arzucan Özgür, and Berrin Yanikoğlu. 2023. SIU2023-NST- Hate speech detection contest. In *2023 31st Signal Processing and Communications Applications Conference (SIU)*, pages 1–4. IEEE.

Valerio Basile, Cristina Bosco, Elisabetta Fersini, Debora Nozza, Viviana Patti, Francisco Manuel Rangel Pardo, Paolo Rosso, and Manuela Sanguinetti. 2019. SemEval-2019 task 5: Multilingual detection of hate speech against immigrants and women in Twitter. In *Proceedings of the 13th International Workshop on Semantic Evaluation*, pages 54–63, Minneapolis, Minnesota, USA. Association for Computational Linguistics.

Fatih Beyhan, Buse Çarık, İnanç Arın, Ayşecan Terzioğlu, Berrin Yanikoglu, and Reyyan Yeniterzi. 2022. A Turkish hate speech dataset and detection system. In *Proceedings of the Thirteenth Language Resources and Evaluation Conference*, pages 4177–4185, Marseille, France. European Language Resources Association.

Arthur TE Capozzi, Mirko Lai, Valerio Basile, Fabio Poletto, Manuela Sanguinetti, Cristina Bosco, Viviana Patti, Giancarlo Ruffo, Cataldo Musto, Marco Polignano, et al. 2019. Computational linguistics against hate: Hate speech detection and visualization on social media in the" contro l'odio" project. In *CEUR Workshop Proceedings*, volume 2481, pages 1–6. CEUR-WS.

Tommaso Caselli, Valerio Basile, Jelena Mitrović, and Michael Granitzer. 2021. HateBERT: Retraining BERT for abusive language detection in English. In *Proceedings of the 5th Workshop on Online Abuse and Harms (WOAH 2021)*, pages 17–25, Online. Association for Computational Linguistics.

Claudio Moisés Valiense de Andrade and Marcos André Gonçalves. 2021. Profiling hate speech spreaders on twitter: Exploiting textual analysis of tweets and combinations of multiple textual representations. In *CEUR Workshop Proc*, volume 2936, pages 2186–2192.

Jacob Devlin, Ming-Wei Chang, Kenton Lee, and Kristina Toutanova. 2019. BERT: Pre-training of deep bidirectional transformers for language understanding. In *Proceedings of the 2019 Conference of the North American Chapter of the Association for Computational Linguistics: Human Language Technologies, Volume 1 (Long and Short Papers)*, pages 4171–4186, Minneapolis, Minnesota. Association for Computational Linguistics.

Mai ElSherief, Caleb Ziems, David Muchlinski, Vaishnavi Anupindi, Jordyn Seybolt, Munmun De Choudhury, and Diyi Yang. 2021. Latent hatred: A benchmark for understanding implicit hate speech. In *Proceedings of the 2021 Conference on Empirical Methods in Natural Language Processing*, pages 345–363, Online and Punta Cana, Dominican Republic. Association for Computational Linguistics.

Shailja Gupta, Sachin Lakra, and Manpreet Kaur. 2020. Study on BERT model for hate speech detection. In *2020 4th International Conference on Electronics, Communication and Aerospace Technology (ICECA)*, pages 1–8.

Hrant Dink Foundation HDF Publications. 2019. Hate speech and discriminatory discourse in media 2019.

Zehra Melce Hüsünbeyi, Didar Akar, and Arzucan Özgür. 2022. Identifying hate speech using neural networks and discourse analysis techniques. In *Proceedings of the First Workshop on Language Technology and Resources for a Fair, Inclusive, and Safe Society within the 13th Language Resources and Evaluation Conference*, pages 32–41, Marseille, France. European Language Resources Association.

Musa İhtiyar, Ömer Özdemir, Mustafa Erengül, and Arzucan Özgür. 2023. A dataset for investigating the impact of context for offensive language detection in tweets. In *Findings of the Association for Computational Linguistics: EMNLP 2023*, pages 1543–1549.

Anna Koufakou, Endang Wahyu Pamungkas, Valerio Basile, and Viviana Patti. 2020. HurtBERT: Incorporating lexical features with BERT for the detection of abusive language. In *Proceedings of the Fourth Workshop on Online Abuse and Harms*, pages 34–43, Online. Association for Computational Linguistics.

Ilya Loshchilov and Frank Hutter. 2019. Decoupled weight decay regularization. In *International Conference on Learning Representations*.

İslam Mayda, Yunus Emre Demir, Tuğba Dalyan, and Banu Diri. 2021. Hate speech dataset from Turkish tweets. In *2021 Innovations in Intelligent Systems and Applications Conference (ASYU)*, pages 1–6.

Marzieh Mozafari, Reza Farahbakhsh, and Noel Crespi. 2019. A BERT-based transfer learning approach for hate speech detection in online social media. In *International Conference on Complex Networks and Their Applications*, pages 928–940. Springer.

Marzieh Mozafari, Reza Farahbakhsh, and Noël Crespi. 2020. Hate speech detection and racial bias mitigation in social media based on BERT model. *PloS one*, 15(8):e0237861.

Chikashi Nobata, Joel Tetreault, Achint Thomas, Yashar Mehdad, and Yi Chang. 2016. Abusive language detection in online user content. In *Proceedings of the 25th international conference on world wide web*, pages 145–153.

Konstantinos Perifanos and Dionysis Goutsos. 2021. Multimodal hate speech detection in Greek social media. *Multimodal Technologies and Interaction*, 5(7):34.

Punyajoy Saha, Binny Mathew, Pawan Goyal, and Animesh Mukherjee. 2018. Hateminers: Detecting hate speech against women. *arXiv preprint arXiv:1812.06700*.

Maarten Sap, Saadia Gabriel, Lianhui Qin, Dan Jurafsky, Noah A. Smith, and Yejin Choi. 2020. Social bias frames: Reasoning about social and power implications of language. In *Proceedings of the 58th Annual Meeting of the Association for Computational Linguistics*, pages 5477–5490, Online. Association for Computational Linguistics.

Anna Schmidt and Michael Wiegand. 2019. A survey on hate speech detection using natural language processing. In *Proceedings of the Fifth International Workshop on Natural Language Processing for Social Media, April 3, 2017, Valencia, Spain*, pages 1–10. Association for Computational Linguistics.

Stefan Schweter. 2020. BERTurk - BERT models for Turkish.

Nitish Srivastava, Geoffrey Hinton, Alex Krizhevsky, Ilya Sutskever, and Ruslan Salakhutdinov. 2014. Dropout: a simple way to prevent neural networks from overfitting. *The journal of machine learning research*, 15(1):1929–1958.

Cagri Toraman, Furkan Şahinuç, and Eyup Yilmaz. 2022. Large-scale hate speech detection with cross-domain transfer. In *Proceedings of the Thirteenth Language Resources and Evaluation Conference*, pages 2215–2225, Marseille, France. European Language Resources Association.

William Warner and Julia Hirschberg. 2012. Detecting hate speech on the world wide web. In *Proceedings of the second workshop on language in social media*, pages 19–26.

Zeerak Waseem and Dirk Hovy. 2016. Hateful symbols or hateful people? predictive features for hate speech detection on twitter. *NAACL*.

Michael Wiegand, Josef Ruppenhofer, Anna Schmidt, and Clayton Greenberg. 2018. Inducing a lexicon of abusive words – a feature-based approach. In *Proceedings of the 2018 Conference of the North American Chapter of the Association for Computational Linguistics: Human Language Technologies, Volume 1 (Long Papers)*, pages 1046–1056, New Orleans, Louisiana. Association for Computational Linguistics.

Marcos Zampieri, Shervin Malmasi, Preslav Nakov, Sara Rosenthal, Noura Farra, and Ritesh Kumar. 2019. Predicting the type and target of offensive posts in social media. In *Proceedings of the 2019 Conference of the North American Chapter of the Association for Computational Linguistics: Human Language Technologies, Volume 1 (Long and Short Papers)*, pages 1415–1420, Minneapolis, Minnesota. Association for Computational Linguistics.

Team Curie at HSD-2Lang 2024: Hate Speech Detection in Turkish and Arabic Tweets using BERT-based models

Ehsan Barkhordar
Koç University
İstanbul, Turkey
ebarkhordar23@ku.edu.tr

Işık S. Topçu
Koç University
İstanbul, Turkey
itopcu21@ku.edu.tr

Ali Hürriyetoğlu
Wageningen
Food Safety Research (WFSR)
Wageningen, the Netherlands
ali.hurriyetoglu@wur.nl

Abstract

This study focuses on hate speech detection in Turkish and Arabic tweets using advanced BERT-based models. Performance metrics demonstrate the models' effectiveness, with the Turkish variant achieving a 71.8% F1 score and the Arabic model a 76.9% F1 score, ranking them fourth and third, respectively, in a competitive leaderboard. Performance enhancements were realized through targeted preprocessing, including emoji translation and user mention exclusion, and thoughtful data balancing approaches. Future directions include refining model accuracy and broadening language support. Our reproducible approach and detailed findings are accessible on GitHub[1].

1 Introduction

Social media platforms like Twitter, Facebook, and YouTube have become pivotal for expressing opinions and sharing information. However, hate speech—targeting ethnic, religious, gender, or other societal groups—poses a significant challenge to social harmony. The need for efficient detection mechanisms is amplified by the global reach of such content, yet languages like Turkish and Arabic present specific hurdles due to their intricate linguistic features and scarce annotated datasets (Beyhan et al., 2022).

The *Hate Speech Detection in Turkish and Arabic Tweets (HSD-2Lang)* shared task[2], part of CASE @ EACL 2024 Uludoğan et al. (2024), builds on the SIU2023-NST competition's groundwork in Turkish to include Arabic. This expansion highlights the need for language-specific solutions capable of accurately identifying hate speech in varied contexts.

Our contribution to Subtask A and Subtask B of this shared task underscores our commitment to advancing hate speech detection in Turkish and Arabic. Through our methodologies, we aim to contribute to the development of safer digital environments.

2 Related Work

The detection of hate speech, especially in linguistically complex languages like Turkish, has garnered significant attention in natural language processing research. Beyhan et al. (2022) presented a BERTurk-based approach at LREC 2022, highlighting the effectiveness of context-specific training with domain-specific datasets, achieving notable accuracies on the Istanbul Convention and Refugees datasets.

Toraman et al. (2022) advanced the field by creating large-scale, human-labeled tweet datasets, demonstrating the superiority of Transformer-based models over traditional methods. In the context of detecting homophobic and related hate comments in Turkish social media, Karayiğit et al. (2022) successfully employed a pre-trained Multilingual Bidirectional Encoder Representations from Transformers (M-BERT) model. Their approach yielded an impressive average F1-score of 90.15% on the Homophobic-Abusive Turkish Comments (HATC) dataset.

Hüsünbeyi et al. (2022) explored the integration of BERT models with linguistic features, showing their potential in surpassing traditional and CNN-based models in hate speech detection. Çam and Özgür (2023) examined the efficacy of ChatGPT and BERT variants in identifying Turkish hate speech, contributing to the evolving landscape of automated detection systems.

The SIU2023-NST Hate Speech Detection Contest, reported by Arın et al. (2023), emphasized the dominance of transformer-based and LightGBM models, with the leading entries achieving significant Macro F1 scores in both binary and multi-class hate speech detection tasks.

[1] https://github.com/politusanalytics/team-curie-case-2024-hsd-2lang

[2] https://github.com/boun-tabi/case-2024-hsd-2lang

Proceedings of the 7th Workshop on Challenges and Applications of Automated Extraction of Socio-political Events from Text (CASE 2024), pages 215–220
March 22, 2024

Epoch	Training Loss	Validation Loss	Validation Performance		
			F1 Score	Accuracy	Recall
1	0.5561	0.5600	0.7151	0.7250	0.7250
2	0.3997	0.5845	0.7486	0.7556	0.7556
3	0.3167	0.4701	0.8022	0.8028	0.8028

Table 1: Training and Validation Results for Subtask A over Epochs

3 System Architecture and Training

This section details the system architecture and training processes for each distinct subtask.

3.1 Subtask A: Turkish Hate Speech Detection

Our goal in Subtask A was to develop a model capable of accurately detecting hate speech in Turkish tweets, encompassing data handling, preprocessing, model tuning, and a strategic training approach.

3.1.1 Data Preparation and Preprocessing

Social media data is inherently noisy, containing informal language, slang, misspellings, and unique language usage. To address this, a thorough preprocessing pipeline is essential for cleaning and standardizing text data for model analysis. In our preprocessing for Subtask A, we employ the emoji library[3] to convert emojis into their English textual descriptions, preserving their semantic value. Newline characters are replaced with spaces, and extra spaces are trimmed to streamline the text. URLs, user mentions, and standalone '@' symbols are removed to reduce non-essential information. Hashtags are also removed; this step not only reduces the word count but also aids in better tokenization by eliminating characters that could disrupt the model's ability to understand the context. The entire text is then converted to lowercase to ensure consistency across the dataset.

3.1.2 Train-Test Split

The division of our dataset into training and testing subsets is crucial for the unbiased development and evaluation of our model. We employ a stratified sampling strategy to ensure a balanced representation of label-topic combinations across both subsets.

For the validation set, we use a specific configuration to determine the number of samples for each label-topic combination, as outlined in the Table 2. The allocation of more samples for certain topics,

Topic	Not Hateful	Hateful
Anti-Refugee	70	70
Israel-Palestine	60	60
Turkey-Greece	50	50

Table 2: Numbers of Validation Samples for Each Label-Topic Combination

such as Anti-Refugee, is informed by their proportion in the training data, ensuring a representative and balanced validation set.

This structured approach ensures that the validation set accurately reflects the diversity and distribution of the original dataset. The remaining data, after allocating the specified samples to the validation set, is used for training purposes.

3.1.3 Model Architecture

Our model architecture for detecting hate speech in Turkish tweets is based on the `dbmdz/bert-base-turkish-128k-uncased`[4] model, a pre-trained BERT variant optimized for Turkish text. We utilize the same tokenizer provided with this model to ensure consistency in text processing. The model is fine-tuned for binary classification, focusing on distinguishing between hateful and non-hateful content within various topics relevant to the subtask. Input sequences are processed with a maximum length of 128 tokens, aligning with the model's specifications.

3.1.4 Training Regime

The training regime for Subtask A is meticulously designed to balance representativeness and efficiency. We employ stratified sampling for the creation of training and validation sets and use the AdamW optimizer with a learning rate of 5×10^{-5} and a batch size of 128. The weight decay for the optimizer is set to 0.01 to prevent overfitting. The model is iterated over the dataset for 3 epochs,

[3] https://github.com/carpedm20/emoji/

[4] https://huggingface.co/dbmdz/bert-base-turkish-128k-cased

Epoch	Training Loss	Validation Loss	Validation Performance		
			F1 Score	Accuracy	Recall
1	0.3279	0.2201	0.8627	0.9070	0.9070
2	0.1957	0.1475	0.9207	0.9186	0.9186
3	0.1109	0.1573	0.9207	0.9186	0.9186
4	0.0569	0.1576	0.9070	0.9070	0.9070
5	0.0164	0.2253	0.9242	0.9186	0.9186

Table 3: Updated Training and Validation Results for Subtask B over Epochs

with careful monitoring of performance metrics to ensure optimal model tuning, as detailed in Table 1.

3.2 Subtask B: Hate Speech Detection with Limited Data in Arabic

This subsection outlines our strategy for detecting hate speech in Arabic tweets, a task challenged by the scarcity of comprehensive training data.

3.2.1 Data Preparation and Preprocessing

In addressing Subtask B—hate speech detection in Arabic tweets—we divided the dataset into training and validation sets. Initial preprocessing aimed to clean and standardize Arabic texts, typically involving noise reduction and format normalization for NLP tasks.

However, initial findings revealed that preprocessing diminished performance, suggesting that raw data, with its inherent linguistic nuances, might be more effective for this task. This led us to minimize preprocessing to preserve the original tweets' contextual and linguistic integrity, enhancing hate speech detection accuracy in Arabic.

3.2.2 Model Architecture

For Arabic hate speech detection, we utilized the `asafaya/bert-base-arabic`[5] model, a BERT variant optimized for Arabic (Safaya et al., 2020). This model was fine-tuned for binary classification to identify hateful versus non-hateful content. Data management was streamlined through a custom PyTorch `Dataset` class and `DataLoader` instances for efficient training and validation.

3.2.3 Training Regime

The training of the model for Subtask B was meticulously executed over the course of 5 epochs, employing a batch size of 128 for each iteration. We opted for the AdamW optimizer, configuring it with a learning rate set at 5×10^{-5} and incorporating a weight decay parameter of 0.01 to mitigate overfitting risks. Throughout the training process, we diligently monitored the model's loss metrics and subjected its performance to rigorous evaluation against the validation set upon the completion of each epoch. Please refer to Table 3 for more details.

4 Experimental Results

In this section, we summarize the performance of our models for each subtask. Our models were evaluated on a test dataset provided by the shared task organizers on Kaggle[6][7].

4.1 Performance Terminology Clarification

In this section, we clarify the terms used in Tables 4 and 6 to describe our model's performance and its comparison with other submissions within the competition.

Competition Best refers to the highest F1-score achieved by any team or participant in the official competition leaderboard. This score represents the best performance recorded during the competition period, under the contest's constraints and evaluation protocols.

Our Peak Performance denotes the highest F1-score our team achieved through late submissions, after the official competition period ended. These late submissions allowed us to further refine and test our models without the daily submission limits imposed during the competition. Thus, "Our Peak Performance" reflects our model's optimal performance obtained without the constraints of the competition's submission cap.

Official Submission represents the F1-score of our model that was officially submitted during the competition period, adhering to the contest's rules,

[5] `https://huggingface.co/asafaya/bert-base-arabic`

[6] `https://www.kaggle.com/competitions/hate-speech-detection-in-turkish/leaderboard?tab=public`

[7] `https://www.kaggle.com/competitions/hate-speech-detection-with-limited-data-in-arabic/leaderboard?tab=public`

including the limitation of three test evaluations per day. This score is what was officially recorded and considered in the competition's final rankings.

It is important to note that the methodologies and system architectures described in the sections for Subtask A and Subtask B were instrumental in achieving "Our Peak Performance". The results and insights derived from these sections are based on the models and approaches that contributed to our highest achieved scores, post-competition. This distinction is crucial for understanding the potential of our proposed solutions when not limited by the competition's constraints on model submissions and evaluations.

4.2 Subtask A: Hate Speech Detection in Turkish across Various Contexts

The performance of our model for Subtask A is summarized in Table 4. It is important to note that these results were obtained through a late submission, and as such, they might not appear on the official leaderboard. Despite this, our model's code is fully reproducible, allowing other researchers to verify our results and use them as a foundation for future work.

Metric	F1-Score	
	Public	Private
Competition Best	0.74876	0.69644
Our Peak Performance	0.71889	0.66129
Official Submission	0.71365	0.60790

Table 4: F1-Score Comparison in Subtask A

Furthermore, the confusion matrix depicted in Figure 1 offers valuable insights into the model's performance on the validation set.

4.3 Subtask B: Hate Speech Detection with Limited Data in Arabic

The performance of our model in Subtask B was rigorously evaluated over 5 training epochs, demonstrating the model's capability in accurately identifying hate speech within Arabic tweets, even with the constraints of limited data.

Metric	F1-Score	
	Public	Private
Competition Best	0.88888	0.68354
Our Peak Performance	0.76923	0.65853
Official Submission	0.76923	0.65853

Table 6: F1-Score Comparison in Subtask B

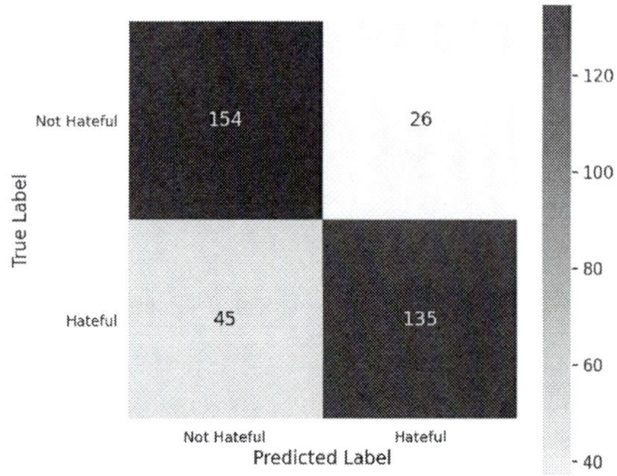

Figure 1: Confusion Matrix of the Model on the Validation Set for Subtask A

For a comparison of our model's F1-Score with the top scores in the task, see Table 6, which contrasts our results against the competition's best on both public and private leaderboards.

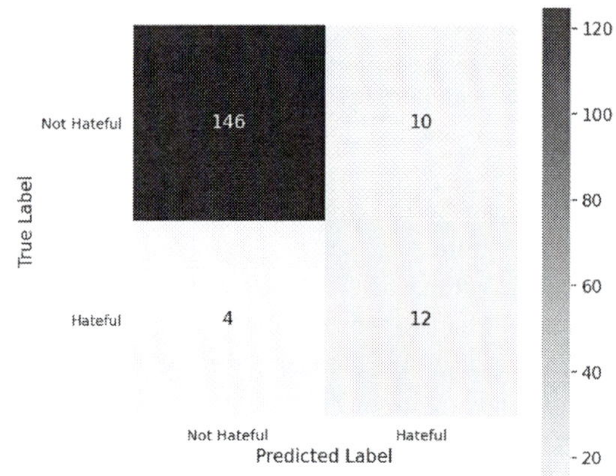

Figure 2: Confusion Matrix of the Model on the Validation Set for Subtask B

Additionally, the confusion matrix provided in Figure 2 further elucidates the model's classification prowess.

5 Ablation Study for Subtask A

In our ablation study for Subtask A, we systematically evaluated the impact of various preprocessing steps and data balancing techniques on the model's F1 score. This involved selectively omitting individual preprocessing steps—such as newline and extra space removal, URL removal, emoji conversion to text, mention and symbol removal, and hashtag processing—to assess their contribution to the model's overall performance. Additionally, we explored the effects of label and topic balancing, both

Experiment	Public F1 Score	Private F1 Score
Our Peak Performance	**0.71889**	**0.66129**
Preprocessing		
Without Newline/Extra Space Removal	0.71889	0.66129
Without URL Removal	0.71171	0.64947
Without Emoji Conversion	0.69868	0.64391
Without Mention/Symbol Removal	0.71544	0.63705
Without Hashtag Processing	0.67868	0.62391
Data Balancing		
With Label Balancing	0.70646	0.64332
With Topic Balancing	0.63917	0.60550
Data Balancing (1 Epoch Training)		
With Label Balancing	0.70769	0.64024
With Topic Balancing	0.64000	0.62585

Table 5: Effects of Preprocessing and Data Balancing on F1 Scores for Subtask A

with the standard training duration and a shortened training span of just one epoch.

Data Balancing Techniques: In our study, we employed two distinct data balancing strategies to mitigate class imbalance and enhance model performance:

- **Label Balancing:** We addressed class imbalance by equalizing the representation of labels in the training data. Specifically, we resampled the minority class (hateful content, labeled as '1') to match the quantity of the majority class (non-hateful content, labeled as '0'). This technique ensures that both classes contribute equally to the training process, preventing model bias toward the more prevalent class.
- **Topic Balancing:** Recognizing the importance of thematic representation, we also balanced the dataset based on topics. This involved resampling tweets within specific topics (e.g., Anti-Refugee, Israel-Palestine, Turkey-Greece) to ensure that hateful and non-hateful contents within each topic were equally represented. This approach acknowledges the contextual nuances of hate speech and aims for a model that is sensitive to topic-specific expressions of hate.

The findings from this study, as detailed in Table 5, are instrumental in elucidating the significance of each preprocessing step and data balancing strategy. For instance, the removal of hashtag processing exhibited a notable decrease in F1 scores, highlighting its critical role in the model's ability to accurately classify tweets. Similarly, the impact of data balancing techniques provides valuable insights into optimizing the training process for enhanced model performance.

Conclusion

Our participation in the HSD-2Lang 2024 contest underscored the effectiveness of BERT-based models in hate speech detection for Turkish and Arabic tweets. Leveraging innovative techniques and sophisticated architectures, we achieved notable F1 scores of 71.8% and 76.9% for Turkish and Arabic, respectively. These results highlight our system's proficiency in handling linguistic complexities and its contribution to improving online safety.

Acknowledgments

This work is supported by the European Research Council Politus Project (ID:101082050) and European Union's HORIZON projects EFRA (ID: 101093026) and ECO-Ready (ID: 101084201).

References

İnanç Arın, Zeynep Işık, Seçilay Kutal, Somaiyeh Deghan, Arzucan Özgür, and Berrin Yanikoğlu. 2023. Siu2023-nst - hate speech detection contest. In *2023 31st Signal Processing and Communications Applications Conference (SIU)*, pages 1–4.

Fatih Beyhan, Buse Çarık, İnanç Arın, Ayşecan Terzioğlu, Berrin Yanikoglu, and Reyyan Yeniterzi.

2022. A Turkish hate speech dataset and detection system. In *Proceedings of the Thirteenth Language Resources and Evaluation Conference*, pages 4177–4185, Marseille, France. European Language Resources Association.

Nur Bengisu Çam and Arzucan Özgür. 2023. Evaluation of chatgpt and bert-based models for turkish hate speech detection. In *2023 8th International Conference on Computer Science and Engineering (UBMK)*, pages 229–233. IEEE.

Zehra Melce Hüsünbeyi, Didar Akar, and Arzucan Özgür. 2022. Identifying hate speech using neural networks and discourse analysis techniques. In *Proceedings of the First Workshop on Language Technology and Resources for a Fair, Inclusive, and Safe Society within the 13th Language Resources and Evaluation Conference*, pages 32–41, Marseille, France. European Language Resources Association.

H. Karayiğit, A. Akdagli, and Ç. İ. Aci. 2022. Homophobic and hate speech detection using multilingualbert model on turkish social media. *Information Technology and Control*, 51(2):356–375.

Ali Safaya, Moutasem Abdullatif, and Deniz Yuret. 2020. KUISAIL at SemEval-2020 task 12: BERT-CNN for offensive speech identification in social media. In *Proceedings of the Fourteenth Workshop on Semantic Evaluation*, pages 2054–2059, Barcelona (online). International Committee for Computational Linguistics.

Cagri Toraman, Furkan Şahinuç, and Eyup Yilmaz. 2022. Large-scale hate speech detection with cross-domain transfer. In *Proceedings of the Thirteenth Language Resources and Evaluation Conference*, pages 2215–2225, Marseille, France. European Language Resources Association.

Gökçe Uludoğan, Somaiyeh Dehghan, İnanç Arın, Elif Erol, Berrin Yanikoglu, and Arzucan Özgür. 2024. Overview of the Hate Speech Detection in Turkish and Arabic tweets (HSD-2Lang) Shared Task at CASE 2024. In *"Proceedings of the 7th Workshop on Challenges and Applications of Automated Extraction of Socio-political Events from Text (CASE)"*, Malta. Association for Computational Linguistics.

Extended Multimodal Hate Speech Event Detection During Russia-Ukraine Crisis - Shared Task at CASE 2024

Surendrabikram Thapa[1], Kritesh Rauniyar[2], Farhan Ahmad Jafri[3], Hariram Veeramani[4], Raghav Jain[5], Sandesh Jain[1], Francielle Vargas[6], Ali Hürriyetoğlu[7], Usman Naseem[8]

[1]Virginia Tech, USA, [2]Delhi Technological University, India, [3]Jamia Millia Islamia, India, [4]UCLA, USA, [5]University of Manchester, UK, [6]University of São Paulo, Brazil, [7]Wageningen Food Safety Research, Netherlands, [8]Macquarie University, Australia

[1]surendrabikram@vt.edu, [2]rauniyark11@gmail.com, [6]francielleavargas@usp.br

Abstract

Addressing the need for effective hate speech moderation in contemporary digital discourse, the *Multimodal Hate Speech Event Detection* Shared Task made its debut at CASE 2023, co-located with RANLP 2023. Building upon its success, an extended version of the shared task was organized at the CASE workshop in EACL 2024. Similar to the earlier iteration, in this shared task, participants address hate speech detection through two subtasks. *Subtask A* is a binary classification problem, assessing whether text-embedded images contain hate speech. *Subtask B* goes further, demanding the identification of hate speech targets, such as individuals, communities, and organizations within text-embedded images. Performance is evaluated using the macro F1-score metric in both subtasks. With a total of 73 registered participants, the shared task witnessed remarkable achievements, with the best F1-scores in Subtask A and Subtask B reaching **87.27%** and **80.05%**, respectively, surpassing the leaderboard of the previous CASE 2023 shared task. This paper provides a comprehensive overview of the performance of seven teams that submitted results for Subtask A and five teams for Subtask B.

1 Introduction

The constant increase of radicalism and hate around the world has become an urgent global problem. Nowadays, social media has been explored by different radicalism groups to spread hate and terrorism using different data modalities (e.g. text, image, video). In this scenario, the investigation of Hate Speech Detection (HSD) technologies is undoubtedly important since the proposition of automated systems has implications for safe and unprejudiced societies (Vargas et al., 2023).

Nevertheless, there is a wide range of challenges to the detection of multimodal hate speech events on social media, including inaccurate definitions for offensiveness and hate speech, lack of contextual information, and scarce consideration of their social and stereotype bias.

Although there is no consensus related to the definition of hateful and offensive content, most relevant literature distinguishes offensive content and hate speech detection. Offensive content is defined as text, image, or video that disrespects, insults, or attacks the reader containing any form of untargeted profanity (Zampieri et al., 2019). On the other hand, hate speech is defined as a special form of offensive language that attacks or diminishes and incites violence or hate against groups, based on specific characteristics such as physical appearance, religion, or others, and it may occur with different linguistic styles, even in subtle forms as humor and sarcasm (Fortuna and Nunes, 2018). In addition, hate speech is also defined as a particular form of offensive language considering stereotypes to express an ideology of hate (Warner and Hirschberg, 2012).

Given the complex nature of hate speech, it is important to find novel technologies that can aid in the automated detection of hate speech (Parihar et al., 2021). Hate speech detection and moderation via automated techniques become even more complicated when multiple modalities are involved e.g. text and images. In order to bring in new ideas, the shared task on multimodal hate speech detection was organized in CASE 2023 (Thapa et al., 2023). Building on the interests shown by the research community, we have yet again conducted the shared task in CASE 2024.

In this paper, we present a comprehensive overview of the seven registered teams in our extended shared task at CASE 2024. In addition, we describe their proposed approaches, performances, and results, besides the discussion of future advances.The findings of this shared task are ex-

Proceedings of the 7th Workshop on Challenges and Applications of Automated Extraction of Socio-political Events from Text (CASE 2024), pages 221–228
March 22, 2024

pected to guide the research direction in finding appropriate research techniques for hate speech and target detection in multimodal settings like text-embedded images.

2 Related Works

Identifying hate speech on social media is an increasingly challenging task that demands the focus of researchers, policy-makers, and society (Jahan and Oussalah, 2023). The majority of studies have mostly concentrated on classifying individual tweets, disregarding the contextual aspects of the discourse (Meng et al., 2023). Various manifestations of hate speech, such as texts, images, and videos, should be identified and addressed swiftly to preserve the decorum of online platforms (Das, 2023). There have been limited attempts to identify text-embedded images for hate speech on social media (Bhandari et al., 2023; Gomez et al., 2020). Text-embedded images are visuals that include text as an integral part of their composition. Text-embedded images are frequently seen in several settings, including online social networks (OSNs) and video content (Das et al., 2023; Chhabra and Vishwakarma, 2023). The image functions as a means of establishing context, while the text that comes with it communicates the information contained throughout that context. Current research on hate speech classification has a main issue which is the lack of structured data creation and diverging annotation schema, resulting in weak adaptability of supervised-learning models to new datasets (Jin et al., 2023). To overcome this problem, Bhandari et al. (2023) proposed a dataset of text-embedded images related to the Russia-Ukraine crisis. Building on the dataset, this shared task aims to bring researchers and professionals to address the problem of hate speech and its target detection in text-embedded images.

3 Dataset

We utilized the same dataset as CASE 2023 (Thapa et al., 2023; Hürriyetoğlu et al., 2023) for our shared task. This dataset, known as CrisisHateMM, was introduced in work by Bhandari et al. (2023) and comprises a collection of 4,723 text-embedded images, all centered around the Russia-Ukraine Crisis (Thapa et al., 2022). Within this dataset, 2,058 images were found to be free from any instances of hate speech, whereas the remaining 2,665 images included elements of hate speech. Among the images containing hate speech, a subset of 2,428 text-embedded images displayed instances of targeted or directed hate speech. For our shared task, we exclusively considered text-embedded images that had directed hate speech, and those that did not have any hate speech. This selection resulted in the use of a total of 4,486 text-embedded images. To ensure a balanced and representative data set, we divide it into distinct training, evaluation, and test sets for Subtasks A and B. This division was carried out in a stratified manner, maintaining a consistent split ratio of approximately 80-10-10, mirroring the approach employed in CASE 2023 (Thapa et al., 2023). The details of the dataset can be found in Table 1.

Subtask	Classes	Train	Eval	Test
Subtask A	Hate	1942	243	243
	No Hate	1658	200	200
Subtask B	Individual	823	102	102
	Community	335	40	42
	Organization	784	102	98

Table 1: Statistics of the dataset at train, evaluation, and test phase of our shared task

4 Shared Task Description

According to Koushik et al. (2019), people from various cultural and educational backgrounds are sharing their thoughts on Twitter, Facebook, and Tumbler, thanks to the abrupt rise in popularity of microblogging services. Their ideas occasionally use language that is harsh, violent, or insulting and target a particular group of individuals who share something in common, such as a gender, an ethnic group, a belief system, or a geographic area. Because hate speech on social media has increased, it is exceedingly time-consuming and costly to manually detect hate speech on these platforms.

4.1 Subtask A: Hate Speech Detection

The objective of this task is to determine the presence of hate speech in text-embedded images. The dataset employed for this subtask comprises annotated images, categorizing them into two labels: 'Hate Speech' and 'No Hate Speech'. The dataset's focus is on images with embedded text, and the annotation process involves identifying whether the content falls into the hate speech category or not. The binary labels, 'Hate Speech' and 'No Hate Speech', precisely characterize the classification criteria for this task, providing a clear distinction between instances with offensive content and those without offensive content.

4.2 Subtask B: Targets of Hate Speech Detection

The objective of this specific task is to classify the specific targets of hate speech within text-embedded images. These images, containing hateful text, encompass a range of potential targets having diverse categories. However, our subtask specifically concentrates on identifying three predefined targets as specified in the dataset used for our shared task. The annotated targets in the dataset include 'community', 'individual', and 'organization'. As a result, our primary goal is to accurately pinpoint and categorize these particular targets within the text-embedded images that exhibit hate speech. This task involves understanding and classifying the hateful content, focusing on recognizing whether it is directed toward a community, an individual, or an organization. The aim is to enhance understanding and identification of hate speech by observing these predetermined target categories within the context of text-embedded images.

5 Evaluation and Competition

This section explains the nature of our competition, including the system for calculating rankings and other important details.

5.1 Evaluation Metrics

We employed accuracy, precision, recall, and macro F1-score to evaluate the performance of the participants' contributions. The macro F1-score sorting method was used to establish the participants' rank.

5.2 Competition Setup

We used the Codalab[1] to organize our competition. There were two stages to the competition: an evaluation stage where participants were introduced to the Codalab system, and a testing phase where the ultimate leaderboard ranking was established based on performance.

Registration: For our competition, 73 individuals registered in total. It was evident from the wide variety of email domains that were utilized that the competition was effective in drawing participants from different parts of the world. 7 teams out of the total number of registrants sent in their predicted outcomes.

Competition Timelines: On November 1, 2023, training and evaluation data were made available, marking the beginning of the competition. The first phase was the evaluation phase. Participant familiarization with Codalab was the primary goal of the evaluation phase, therefore participants were also given access to the evaluation data labels. Then, on November 30, 2023, test data without any ground truth labels were released, indicating the beginning of the test phase. The test period was extended until January 7, 2024, in response to requests from several participants, from its original end date of January 5, 2024. The system description paper submission deadline was ultimately decided upon as January 16, 2024.

6 Participants' Methods

In this section, we describe the various methods used by the participants who submitted the system description paper.

6.1 Overview

A total of 7 participants submitted scores for subtask A, while 5 participants submitted to subtask B. The leaderboards for subtask A and subtask B are presented in Table 2 and Table 3, respectively. In both subtasks, CLTL achieved the top performance, surpassing the other models by a significant margin. These models also outperformed the highest scores achieved by ARC-NLP in the same shared task, which was conducted during CASE 2023 at RANLP 2023. In the subsequent subsections, we provide detailed system descriptions for each participating team.

6.2 Methods

Below, we provide a summary of the system descriptions provided by the participating teams in the shared task. These summaries are derived from the approaches detailed by the participants in their system description papers.

6.2.1 Subtask A

CLTL (Wang and Markov, 2024) proposed a method that includes separate text and image processing modules coupled with a simple MLP and softmax, providing an optimal alternative to Large

[1]The competition page can be found here: https://codalab.lisn.upsaclay.fr/competitions/16203.

Rank	Team Name	Codalab Username	Accuracy	Precision	Recall	F1-score
1	CLTL (Wang and Markov, 2024)	Yestin	**87.36**	**87.20**	**87.37**	**87.27**
2	MasonPerplexity (Gangul et al., 2024)	Sadiya_Puspo	83.52	83.47	83.78	83.47
3	AAST-NLP (El-Sayed and Nasr, 2024)	AhmedElSayed	76.98	76.76	76.76	76.76
4	YYama (Yamagishi, 2024)	YYama	75.85	75.88	76.13	75.80
5	CUET_Binary_Hackers	Asrarul_Hoque_Eusha	68.62	68.61	68.79	68.55
6	-	kriti7	46.05	46.45	46.44	46.05
7	Team +1	pakapro	49.66	56.83	53.23	44.08

Table 2: Sub-task A (Hate Speech Classification) Leaderboard, Ranked by Macro F1-Score. All scores are presented as percentages (%). The highest score in each column is highlighted in bold. It is to be noted that this leaderboard contains the score till the test deadline and does not consider further runs done by participants as a part of the system description paper.

Vision Language Models (LVLMs). This method increases design flexibility and analytic capability. The presentation is distinguished by its cleanliness, straightforward but original ideas, and clarity. The results show that the implementation stands out as a competitive benchmark. It shows how multimodal models need not always be trained together for a specific task and a modular approach with simple MLP-based feature fusion could work at the same level if not better. This could also be easily noticed with some of the authors (Yamagishi, 2024) who used a pre-trained LVLM and achieved considerably lower scores than the one proposed in (Wang and Markov, 2024). This could also point toward the significance of fine-tuning in LVLM optimization. Overall, the approach exhibits a simple yet effective pipeline for hate speech detection in image-based data. Their approach achieved the first position with performances noted in Table 2.

MasonPerplexity (Gangul et al., 2024) experimented with various models like BERTweet-large (Ushio and Camacho-Collados, 2021; Ushio et al., 2022), BERT-base (Devlin et al., 2019), XLM-R (Conneau et al., 2020a), and GPT-3.5 [2] in their implementation. The test F1-score of the models were 75%, 81%, and 83% for BERT-base, BERTweet-large, and XLM-R respectively. GPT models also showed remarkable performance with a F1-score of 82% in the test dataset for fine tuned GPT 3.5.

AAST-NLP (El-Sayed and Nasr, 2024) initially fine-tuned the bert variants, RoBERTa (Liu et al., 2019), XLM-RoBERTa (Conneau et al., 2020b), and HateBERT (Caselli et al., 2021) on all of the datasets to attain the best results. They then proposed the **top-k** ensemble technique and various multimodal models, such as ViT Dosovitskiy et al. (2021) model and Swin Liu et al. (2021) as feature extractor to achieve higher macro F1-score. In order to get the highest F1-score, they utilized the 'Top-3' ensemble strategy, which combined several BERT versions. They have employed the most recent CLIP (Contrastive Language–Image Pre-training) Radford et al. (2021) model, which combines textual and visual data via cross-fusion and concatenation. 85.40% was the greatest recall on CLIP (Concat), and 85.50% and 85.44% were the highest precision and F1-score, respectively, on the **Top-3** ensemble technique. Out of 7 teams, they were able to secure the third position in this task.

YYama (Yamagishi, 2024) proposed an approach whose goal was to optimize user prompts for the LLaVa-1.5B LVLM architecture by applying simple prompt engineering approaches for hate-speech detection. Although there have been other LVLM-based techniques for image-based hate-speech recognition in recent years (Hermida and Santos, 2023; Van and Wu, 2023). Therefore the methodology is not fully novel; the author offers insightful information at the prompt level. The study indicates that simple prompts tend to perform better than complicated ones. This difference in performance is attributed to a narrower filter that is used to identify difficult instructions inside the prompts. The author makes strong arguments and highlights how the model uses a variety of implicit meanings for 'no hate speech' to effectively handle open-ended queries. On the other hand, adding more definitions causes the internal definition set to shrink, which might increase the number of false negatives. Overall, the paper presented us with an approachable method deploying existing LVLM models for specified tasks with open-ended and simpler prompts, which, contrary to popular methods such as chain-of-thoughts, presents us with a

[2] https://platform.openai.com/docs/models

lower barrier to generating appropriate responses. Their approach attained the fourth position with performances noted in Table 2.

6.2.2 Subtask B

CLTL (Wang and Markov, 2024) employ the same foundational model for subtask A, with only the output layer undergoing modification. Despite minimal customization, their approach surpasses all others and establishes a new benchmark. The key to their success lies in the embedded features captured and fused by the MLP. This layer effectively represents all essential features related to hate speech, simplifying the MLP's task in discerning whether the hate is directed towards an organization, individual, or community. This results in an impressive over 18% improvement over the baseline and a 2-5% lead over the previous state-of-the-art models. Furthermore, the paper underscores the importance and significance of fine-tuning in achieving these remarkable results. Lastly, the strategic use of RoBERTa, particularly in conjunction with Twitter's social interaction data, provides the authors with significant prior knowledge of the competition's domain, contributing significantly to their success. Their approach attained the first position in subtask B with performances noted in Table 3.

AAST-NLP (El-Sayed and Nasr, 2024) first optimized RoBERTa (Liu et al., 2019), XLM-RoBERTa (Conneau et al., 2020b), and HateBERT (Caselli et al., 2021) models of BERT (Devlin et al., 2019) variations on all datasets in order to get the greatest performance. To obtain a better score, they conducted experiments utilizing the **top-k** ensemble technique and the latest CLIP (Contrastive Language–Image Pre-training) model, which integrates textual and visual input through cross-fusion and concatenation. They used the 'Top-3' ensemble technique, combining multiple BERT variants, to obtain the greatest F1-score possible. Using the **Top-3** ensemble approach, they were able to achieve the maximum values of all three metrics: precision, recall, and F1-score, which were 74.99%, 82.73%, and 77.03%, respectively. In a challenge of five teams in this subtask, they took second place.

MasonPerplexity (Gangul et al., 2024) used the ensemble of BERTweet-large (Ushio and Camacho-Collados, 2021; Ushio et al., 2022), BERT-base (Devlin et al., 2019), and XLM-R (Conneau et al., 2020a) in order to achieve their best score. They also tested with various standalone models like BERTweet-large (Ushio and Camacho-Collados, 2021; Ushio et al., 2022), BERT-base (Devlin et al., 2019), XLM-R (Conneau et al., 2020a), and GPT 3.5. With the ensemble model, the F1-score was 67%. Similarly, the standalone models performed 61%, 64%, and 66% with BERT-base, XLM-R, and BERTweet-large respectively. Similarly, with various configurations of GPT, the authors achieved F1-scores of 53%, 57%, and 63% with zero shots, few shots, and fine-tuned settings, respectively.

7 Discussion

The results and methods presented in this shared task demonstrate diverse approaches to hate speech classification, shedding light on the complexity of addressing this pressing issue. CLTL's modular approach (Wang and Markov, 2024), separating text and image processing, exemplifies the adaptability of multimodal models. MasonPerplexity's exploration of various language models underscores the importance of thoughtful model selection (Gangul et al., 2024), while AAST-NLP's ensemble technique and CLIP utilization highlight the benefits of combining multiple models and modalities (El-Sayed and Nasr, 2024). YYama's focus on prompt optimization provides an accessible method for deploying existing models with straightforward prompts (Yamagishi, 2024). These approaches collectively contribute to the ongoing advancements in hate speech detection, emphasizing the significance of both model architecture and prompt design. The healthy competition and diversity of strategies among the participating teams contribute to the ongoing progress in the field of hate speech research.

8 Conclusion

In conclusion, the Multimodal Hate Speech Event Detection Shared Task, first introduced at CASE 2023 and extended to CASE 2024, provided a platform for exploring innovative approaches to combat hate speech in contemporary digital discourse. This shared task witnessed significant participation from a total of 73 registered participants, resulting in remarkable achievements in both Subtask A and Subtask B. The top-performing models in Subtask A achieved an impressive F1-score of 87.27%, while Subtask B saw a top F1-score of 80.05%, surpassing the previous CASE 2023 shared task

Rank	Team Name	Codalab Username	Accuracy	Precision	Recall	F1-score
1	CLTL (Wang and Markov, 2024)	Yestin	**82.64**	**81.48**	**79.07**	**80.05**
2	AAST-NLP (El-Sayed and Nasr, 2024)	AhmedElSayed	80.99	82.73	74.99	77.03
3	MasonPerplexity (Gangul et al., 2024)	Sadiya_Puspo	71.49	67.59	67.27	67.41
4	CUET_Binary_Hackers	Asrarul_Hoque_Eusha	51.24	34.50	41.35	37.48
5	Team +1	pakapro	28.10	28.12	30.31	24.78

Table 3: Sub-task B (Targets of Hate Speech Classification) Leaderboard, Ranked by Macro F1-score. All scores are presented as percentages (%). The highest score in each column is highlighted in bold. It is to be noted that this leaderboard contains the score till the test deadline and does not consider further runs done by participants as a part of the system description paper.

leaderboard. The diverse methods employed by the participating teams, including modular multimodal models, careful model selection, ensemble techniques, and prompt optimization, highlight the various approaches to tackle the complex problem of hate speech detection. These efforts collectively contribute to advancing the field and emphasize the importance of continuous research in addressing this critical issue in online discourse. The shared task fosters healthy competition and encourages future research in hate speech detection and multimodal analysis.

Acknowledgements

We would like to acknowledge Diego Alves, Samuel Guimarães, Isabelle Carvalho, and Siddhant Bikram Shah for helping us provide detailed reviews for the shared task. Their insights were instrumental in shaping the feedback provided to the participants. Moreover, this work is supported by the European Research Council Politus Project (ID:101082050) and European Union's HORIZON projects EFRA (ID: 101093026) and ECO-Ready (ID: 101084201).

Broader Impact

The Multimodal Hate Speech Event Detection Shared Task has the potential to profoundly impact society by advancing the development of more accurate and effective hate speech detection models. These advancements can create safer online spaces, reduce the spread of hate speech, and foster constructive digital discourse. However, ethical considerations are paramount, as the deployment of automated detection systems must balance the imperative to combat hate speech with concerns about potential biases and limitations that may inadvertently suppress free expression or disproportionately target specific groups. Additionally, from a technological perspective, this shared task drives innovation in multimodal AI research, benefiting fields beyond hate speech detection, such as content moderation, multimedia analysis, and human-computer interaction. Furthermore, in academia, it enriches the study of hate speech detection by providing benchmark datasets and promoting collaboration among researchers, leading to a deeper understanding of the challenges involved and the development of novel methodologies.

References

Aashish Bhandari, Siddhant B Shah, Surendrabikram Thapa, Usman Naseem, and Mehwish Nasim. 2023. Crisishatemm: Multimodal analysis of directed and undirected hate speech in text-embedded images from russia-ukraine conflict. In *Proceedings of the IEEE/CVF Conference on Computer Vision and Pattern Recognition*, pages 1993–2002.

Tommaso Caselli, Valerio Basile, Mitrovic Jelena, Granitzer Michael, et al. 2021. Hatebert: Retraining bert for abusive language detection in english. In *Proceedings of the 5th Workshop on Online Abuse and Harms (WOAH 2021)*, pages 17–25. Association for Computational Linguistics.

Anusha Chhabra and Dinesh Kumar Vishwakarma. 2023. A literature survey on multimodal and multilingual automatic hate speech identification. *Multimedia Systems*, pages 1–28.

Alexis Conneau, Kartikay Khandelwal, Naman Goyal, Vishrav Chaudhary, Guillaume Wenzek, Francisco Guzmán, Edouard Grave, Myle Ott, Luke Zettlemoyer, and Veselin Stoyanov. 2020a. Unsupervised cross-lingual representation learning at scale. In *Proceedings of the 58th Annual Meeting of the Association for Computational Linguistics*, pages 8440–8451, Online. Association for Computational Linguistics.

Alexis Conneau, Kartikay Khandelwal, Naman Goyal, Vishrav Chaudhary, Guillaume Wenzek, Francisco Guzmán, Edouard Grave, Myle Ott, Luke Zettlemoyer, and Veselin Stoyanov. 2020b. Unsupervised cross-lingual representation learning at scale.

Mithun Das. 2023. Classification of different participating entities in the rise of hateful content in social media. In *Proceedings of the Sixteenth ACM International Conference on Web Search and Data Mining*, pages 1212–1213.

Mithun Das, Rohit Raj, Punyajoy Saha, Binny Mathew, Manish Gupta, and Animesh Mukherjee. 2023. Hatemm: A multi-modal dataset for hate video classification. In *Proceedings of the International AAAI Conference on Web and Social Media*, volume 17, pages 1014–1023.

Jacob Devlin, Ming-Wei Chang, Kenton Lee, and Kristina Toutanova. 2019. BERT: Pre-training of deep bidirectional transformers for language understanding. In *Proceedings of the 2019 Conference of the North American Chapter of the Association for Computational Linguistics: Human Language Technologies, Volume 1 (Long and Short Papers)*, pages 4171–4186, Minneapolis, Minnesota. Association for Computational Linguistics.

Alexey Dosovitskiy, Lucas Beyer, Alexander Kolesnikov, Dirk Weissenborn, Xiaohua Zhai, Thomas Unterthiner, Mostafa Dehghani, Matthias Minderer, Georg Heigold, Sylvain Gelly, Jakob Uszkoreit, and Neil Houlsby. 2021. An image is worth 16x16 words: Transformers for image recognition at scale.

Ahmed El-Sayed and Omar Nasr. 2024. AAST-NLP at Multimodal Hate Speech Event Detection 2024 : A Multimodal Approach for Classification of Text-Embedded Images Based on CLIP and BERT-Based Models. In *Proceedings of the 7th Workshop on Challenges and Applications of Automated Extraction of Socio-political Events from Text (CASE)*, Malta. Association for Computational Linguistics.

Paula Fortuna and Sérgio Nunes. 2018. A survey on automatic detection of hate speech in text. *ACM Comput. Surv.*, 51(4).

Amrita Gangul, Al Nahian Bin Emran, Sadiya Sayara Chowdhury Puspo, Md Nishat Raihan, Dhiman Goswami, and Marcos Zampieri. 2024. Mason-Perplexity at Multimodal Hate Speech Event Detection 2024: Hate Speech and Target Detection Using Transformer Ensembles. In *Proceedings of the 7th Workshop on Challenges and Applications of Automated Extraction of Socio-political Events from Text (CASE)*, Malta. Association for Computational Linguistics.

Raul Gomez, Jaume Gibert, Lluis Gomez, and Dimosthenis Karatzas. 2020. Exploring hate speech detection in multimodal publications. In *Proceedings of the IEEE/CVF winter conference on applications of computer vision*, pages 1470–1478.

Paulo Cezar de Q Hermida and Eulanda M dos Santos. 2023. Detecting hate speech in memes: a review. *Artificial Intelligence Review*, pages 1–19.

Ali Hürriyetoğlu, Hristo Tanev, Osman Mutlu, Surendrabikram Thapa, Fiona Anting Tan, and Erdem Yörük. 2023. Challenges and applications of automated extraction of socio-political events from text (CASE 2023): Workshop and shared task report. In *Proceedings of the 6th Workshop on Challenges and Applications of Automated Extraction of Socio-political Events from Text*, pages 167–175, Varna, Bulgaria. INCOMA Ltd., Shoumen, Bulgaria.

Md Saroar Jahan and Mourad Oussalah. 2023. A systematic review of hate speech automatic detection using natural language processing. *Neurocomputing*, page 126232.

Yiping Jin, Leo Wanner, Vishakha Laxman Kadam, and Alexander Shvets. 2023. Towards weakly-supervised hate speech classification across datasets. *arXiv preprint arXiv:2305.02637*.

Garima Koushik, K. Rajeswari, and Suresh Kannan Muthusamy. 2019. Automated hate speech detection on twitter. In *2019 5th International Conference On Computing, Communication, Control And Automation (ICCUBEA)*, pages 1–4.

Yinhan Liu, Myle Ott, Naman Goyal, Jingfei Du, Mandar Joshi, Danqi Chen, Omer Levy, Mike Lewis, Luke Zettlemoyer, and Veselin Stoyanov. 2019. Roberta: A robustly optimized bert pretraining approach. *arXiv preprint arXiv:1907.11692*.

Ze Liu, Yutong Lin, Yue Cao, Han Hu, Yixuan Wei, Zheng Zhang, Stephen Lin, and Baining Guo. 2021. Swin transformer: Hierarchical vision transformer using shifted windows.

Qing Meng, Tharun Suresh, Roy Ka-Wei Lee, and Tanmoy Chakraborty. 2023. Predicting hate intensity of twitter conversation threads. *Knowledge-Based Systems*, page 110644.

Anil Singh Parihar, Surendrabikram Thapa, and Sushruti Mishra. 2021. Hate speech detection using natural language processing: Applications and challenges. In *2021 5th International Conference on Trends in Electronics and Informatics (ICOEI)*, pages 1302–1308. IEEE.

Alec Radford, Jong Wook Kim, Chris Hallacy, Aditya Ramesh, Gabriel Goh, Sandhini Agarwal, Girish Sastry, Amanda Askell, Pamela Mishkin, Jack Clark, Gretchen Krueger, and Ilya Sutskever. 2021. Learning transferable visual models from natural language supervision.

Surendrabikram Thapa, Farhan Jafri, Ali Hürriyetoğlu, Francielle Vargas, Roy Ka-Wei Lee, and Usman Naseem. 2023. Multimodal hate speech event detection-shared task 4, case 2023. In *Proceedings of the 6th Workshop on Challenges and Applications of Automated Extraction of Socio-political Events from Text*, pages 151–159.

Surendrabikram Thapa, Aditya Shah, Farhan Jafri, Usman Naseem, and Imran Razzak. 2022. A multimodal dataset for hate speech detection on social media: Case-study of russia-Ukraine conflict. In *Proceedings of the 5th Workshop on Challenges and Applications of Automated Extraction of Socio-political Events from Text (CASE)*, pages 1–6, Abu Dhabi, United Arab Emirates (Hybrid). Association for Computational Linguistics.

Asahi Ushio, Francesco Barbieri, Vitor Sousa, Leonardo Neves, and Jose Camacho-Collados. 2022. Named entity recognition in Twitter: A dataset and analysis on short-term temporal shifts. In *Proceedings of the 2nd Conference of the Asia-Pacific Chapter of the Association for Computational Linguistics and the 12th International Joint Conference on Natural Language Processing (Volume 1: Long Papers)*, pages 309–319, Online only. Association for Computational Linguistics.

Asahi Ushio and Jose Camacho-Collados. 2021. T-NER: An all-round python library for transformer-based named entity recognition. In *Proceedings of the 16th Conference of the European Chapter of the Association for Computational Linguistics: System Demonstrations*, pages 53–62, Online. Association for Computational Linguistics.

Minh-Hao Van and Xintao Wu. 2023. Detecting and correcting hate speech in multimodal memes with large visual language model. *arXiv preprint arXiv:2311.06737*.

Francielle Vargas, Isabelle Carvalho, Ali Hürriyetoğlu, Thiago Pardo, and Fabrício Benevenuto. 2023. Socially responsible hate speech detection: Can classifiers reflect social stereotypes? In *Proceedings of the 14th International Conference on Recent Advances in Natural Language Processing*, pages 1187–1196, Varna, Bulgaria.

Yeshan Wang and Ilia Markov. 2024. CLTL@Multimodal Hate Speech Event Detection 2024: The Winning Approach to Detecting Multimodal Hate Speech and Its Targets. In *Proceedings of the 7th Workshop on Challenges and Applications of Automated Extraction of Socio-political Events from Text (CASE)*, Malta. Association for Computational Linguistics.

William Warner and Julia Hirschberg. 2012. Detecting hate speech on the world wide web. In *Proceedings of the Second Workshop on Language in Social Media*, pages 19–26, Montréal, Canada. Association for Computational Linguistics.

Yosuke Yamagishi. 2024. YYama@Multimodal Hate Speech Event Detection 2024: Simpler Prompts, Better Results - Enhancing Zero-shot Detection with a Large Multimodal Model. In *Proceedings of the 7th Workshop on Challenges and Applications of Automated Extraction of Socio-political Events from Text (CASE)*, Malta. Association for Computational Linguistics.

Marcos Zampieri, Shervin Malmasi, Preslav Nakov, Sara Rosenthal, Noura Farra, and Ritesh Kumar. 2019. Predicting the type and target of offensive posts in social media. In *Proceedings of the 2019 Conference of the North American Chapter of the Association for Computational Linguistics: Human Language Technologies, Volume 1 (Long and Short Papers)*, pages 1415–1420, Minneapolis, Minnesota. Association for Computational Linguistics.

Overview of the Hate Speech Detection in Turkish and Arabic Tweets (HSD-2Lang) Shared Task at CASE 2024

Gökçe Uludoğan[1] and **Somaiyeh Dehghan**[2,3] and **İnanç Arın**[2,3]
Elif Erol[4] and **Berrin Yanikoglu**[2,3] and **Arzucan Özgür**[1]
[1] Department of Computer Engineering, Bogazici University, Turkey 34342
[2] Faculty of Engineering and Natural Sciences, Sabanci University, Istanbul, Turkey 34956
[3] Center of Excellence in Data Analytics (VERIM), Sabanci University, Istanbul, Turkey 34956
[4] Hrant Dink Foundation, Istanbul, Turkey 34373
{gokce.uludogan,arzucan.ozgur}@bogazici.edu.tr, eliferol@hrantdink.org
{somaiyeh.dehghan,inanc.arin,berrin}@sabanciuniv.edu

Abstract

This paper offers an overview of the Hate Speech Detection in Turkish and Arabic Tweets (HSD-2Lang) Shared Task at CASE workshop that was held jointly with EACL 2024. The task was divided into two subtasks: Subtask A, targeting hate speech detection in various Turkish contexts, and Subtask B, addressing hate speech detection in Arabic with limited data. The shared task attracted significant attention with 33 teams that registered and 10 teams that participated in at least one task. In this paper, we provide the details of the tasks and the approaches adopted by the participant along with an analysis of the results obtained from this shared task.

1 Introduction

Hate speech, which targets groups based on characteristics such as ethnicity, nationality, religion, colour, gender, and sexual orientation, is a significant problem on social media platforms. The automated detection of such content is crucial for efficient content moderation and the mitigation of societal harm. Moreover, it can also be instrumental in socio-political event analysis.

The effectiveness of current hate speech detection models is often hampered by issues such as limited data and lack of generalizability. Following the SIU2023-NST competition (Arın et al., 2023), which was organized to benchmark progress in Turkish hate speech detection and classification, we present a new shared task, Hate Speech Detection in Turkish and Arabic Tweets (HSD-2Lang) Shared Task, in conjunction with The 7th Workshop on Challenges and Applications of Automated Extraction of Socio-political Events from Text (CASE 2024). This shared task focuses on tackling the challenge of identifying hate speech in tweets in Turkish and Arabic languages.

2 Tasks

The shared task involves the development of models for hate speech detection in social media, with a specific focus on Turkish and Arabic languages. The task is divided into two distinct subtasks: a) Hate Speech Detection in Turkish across Various Contexts (Subtask A), b) Hate Speech Detection with Limited Data in Arabic (Subtask B).

Both subtasks are formulated as binary classification problems where the objective is to determine whether individual tweets are hateful or non-hateful.

Subtask A: Hate Speech Detection in Turkish across Various Contexts

The objective of this subtask is to develop a model capable of detecting hate speech in Turkish tweets.

Data. The dataset contains Turkish tweets on three topics, each annotated for the presence or absence of hate speech. The topics encompass tweets concerning refugees, the Israel-Palestine conflict, and Anti-Greek discourse. The training set contains a total of 9,140 tweets while the test set comprises 2,295 tweets. The distribution of data with respect to topics, labels, and splits is shown in Table 1.

Evaluation. The performance of the models is evaluated using the F1 metric on the combined test data from all three topics.

Table 1: Statistics for Subtask A data, with respect to topics, labels, and splits.

Topic	Train set		Test set	
	Hateful	Non-hateful	Hateful	Non-hateful
Anti-Refugee	1447	4477	361	1119
Isr-Pal conflict	880	1360	73	498
Anti-Greek	451	555	105	139
Total	2778	6392	539	1756

Proceedings of the 7th Workshop on Challenges and Applications of Automated Extraction of Socio-political Events from Text (CASE 2024), pages 229–233

Table 2: Statistics for Subtask B data splits.

Label	Train set	Test set
Hateful	82	52
Non-hateful	778	470
Total	860	522

Subtask B: Hate Speech Detection with Limited Data in Arabic

The goal in this subtask is to build a model for Arabic hate speech detection under data-constrained conditions.

Data. The dataset comprises Arabic tweets, particularly focusing on anti-refugee hate speech. This task is challenging with a smaller data set and high class imbalance. The data statistics are reported in Table 2.

Evaluation. The performance of the models is evaluated using the F1 metric on test data, which includes tweets related to anti-refugee hate speech.

3 System Descriptions

The HSD-2Lang shared task attracted participation from 33 teams associated with various universities and organizations. This task involved developing systems for specific subtasks, detailed in the following subsections.

3.1 Subtask A

A total of 33 teams registered for the subtask, with 10 eventually submitting their results. All systems were based on BERT (Devlin et al., 2019). However, teams employed diverse approaches, including different base models, data processing techniques, and training strategies. The base models varied from monolingual models such as BERTurk (Schweter, 2020) and TurkishBERTweet (Najafi and Varol, 2023), to the multilingual XLM-RoBERTa model (Conneau et al., 2019).

The winner in Subtask A, DetectiveReDASers (Qachfar et al., 2024), utilized the ConvBERTurk model[1] (Schweter, 2020), enhancing it with a novel pooling strategy, cross-lingual data augmentation, and a soft-voting ensemble approach. During preprocessing, they corrected encoding errors and translated emoji characters into corresponding text descriptions in Turkish. For cross-lingual data augmentation, the team translated Arabic tweets from Subtask B using Google Translate. Their pooling strategy combined the standard [CLS] token representation with mean and max pooling of token representations, further refined by additional linear and dropout layers. This approach aimed to improve sequence representation by integrating the [CLS] token with mean and max values from the last hidden layer. For ensembling, they utilized a soft-voting ensemble of five identical ConvBERTurk models, distinguished only by their initializations.

The second and third place teams, ReBERT (Yagci et al., 2024) and VRLLab (Najafi and Varol, 2024), both used TurkishBERTweet[2], which was specifically trained on a large corpus of Turkish tweets. While both utilized LoRA fine-tuning (Hu et al., 2021), they differed in their preprocessing, hyperparameters, and data filtering approaches. Both systems applied the TurkishBERTweet preprocessing pipeline, which transforms Twitter-specific entities into special tags and converts emojis' unicode characters into descriptive words. However, their configurations differed: ReBERT used a smaller batch size (32), a lower learning rate (5e-5), a longer training duration (100 epochs), and polynomial learning rate scheduling with a 10% warm-up steps in the AdamW optimizer (Loshchilov and Hutter, 2017). In contrast, VRLLab chose a batch size of 128, a learning rate of 3e-4, 20 epochs of training, and 6% warm-up steps.

3.2 Subtask B

Compared to Subtask A, this was a smaller dataset and also attracted fewer participants. Altogether, there were 15 teams who registered to the subtask, with 5 eventually submitting results. Among these submissions, all systems used BERT variants (Antoun et al., 2020; Safaya et al., 2020).

The winner of Subtask B, ReBERT (Yagci et al., 2024), finetuned AraBERTv0.2[3] (Antoun et al., 2020), which was pretrained on approximately 60 million Arabic tweets. This version of AraBERT includes emojis and previously omitted common words in its vocabulary, and was used without any preprocessing. Unlike their parameter-efficient approach in Subtask A, the team performed 4 epochs of full supervised fine-tuning using a batch size of

[1] https://huggingface.co/dbmdz/convbert-base-turkish-cased

[2] https://huggingface.co/VRLLab/TurkishBERTweet

[3] https://huggingface.co/aubmindlab/bert-base-arabertv02

Table 3: Scores of top three ranking teams in public and private leaderboards of Subtask A.

Rank	Team	Public			Private		
		Precision	Recall	F1 Score	Precision	Recall	F1 Score
1	DetectiveReDASers (Qachfar et al., 2024)	0.70588	0.76364	0.73362	0.68161	0.71194	**0.69645**
2	ReBERT (Yagci et al., 2024)	0.79167	0.69091	0.73786	0.75989	0.62998	0.68886
3	VRLLab (Najafi and Varol, 2024)	0.71296	0.70000	0.70642	0.66588	0.66276	0.66432

Table 4: Confusion matrices for the top three ranking systems in Subtask A.

Actual Label	**Predictions** (DetectiveReDASers)		**Prediction** (ReBERT)		**Prediction** (VRLLab)	
	Hateful	Non-Hateful	Hateful	Non-Hateful	Hateful	Non-Hateful
Hateful	388	149	345	192	360	177
Non-Hateful	177	1578	105	1650	173	1582

8, a learning rate of 5e-4 with a linear decay, and the AdamW optimizer.

The second place team, Team Curie (Barkhordar et al., 2024), employed a different Arabic BERT model[4] (Safaya et al., 2020), which was pretrained on around 8.2 billion words from the Arabic subset of OSCAR (Suárez et al., 2019) and Arabic Wikipedia. They fine-tuned this model on raw tweets, opting not to preprocess the data based on their findings that preprocessing could negatively impact performance. Their fine-tuning parameters included 5 training epochs, a batch size of 128, a learning rate of 5e-5 with a weight decay regularization parameter of 0.01, and they also used the AdamW optimizer.

In third place, Team Uriel also used the AraBERTv0.2 model trained on tweets, similar to the winning team. However, their approach differed by introducing an additional layer to map BERT representations to a lower dimension before output mapping. This process involved two fully connected layers with ReLU activation functions, distinguishing their method from the standard approach of direct mapping of BERT representations to outputs. The first layer reduced the dimensionality to 100, while the second served as a binary classification output layer.

4 Competition Results

For both tasks, the performance of models is evaluated using the test samples of the corresponding dataset. The test samples are randomly divided into public and private samples. Public samples make up 20% of the test samples and are used by participants for validation during the test phase. Private samples were used to evaluate the model's performance after the test phase has concluded and to generate the final leaderboard of the shared task. Table 3 and 5 display the precision, recall, and F1 scores achieved by the top three systems, officially ranked by F1 score, in the private leaderboard. The confusion matrices for these systems are presented in Table 4 and 6.

5 Results for Subtask A

DetectiveReDASers took first place on the private leaderboard and second on the public leaderboard, with F1 scores of 0.69645 and 0.73362, respectively. This system, leveraging a soft-ensemble of ConvBERTurk models, outperformed the competing systems in recall and F1 scores on both leaderboards. ReBERT and VRLLab, although employing a similar approach using TurkishBERTweet with LoRA fine-tuning, showed a noticeable difference in their F1 scores (ReBERT: 0.73786 public, 0.68886 private; VRLLab: 0.70642 public, 0.66432 private). Notably, ReBERT achieved significantly higher precision scores compared to VRLLab. This variation underscores the critical role of hyperparameter tuning in optimizing model performance.

6 Results for Subtask B

In Subtask B, ReBERT and Team Curie showed very similar performances in the public leaderboard, while their private leaderboard scores varied. ReBERT took the first-place with an F1 score of 0.683532, while Team Curie came second place with an F1 score of 0.65854.

Interestingly, despite using the same Arabic

[4] https://huggingface.co/asafaya/bert-base-arabic

Table 5: Scores of top three ranking teams in public and private leaderboards of Subtask B.

Rank	Team	Public			Private		
		Precision	Recall	F1 Score	Precision	Recall	F1 Score
1	ReBERT (Yagci et al., 2024)	0.76923	0.76923	0.76923	0.67500	0.69231	**0.68354**
2	Team Curie (Barkhordar et al., 2024)	0.76923	0.76923	0.76923	0.62791	0.69231	0.65854
3	Team Uriel	0.66667	0.61538	0.64000	0.57143	0.71795	0.63636

Table 6: Confusion matrices for the top three ranking systems in Subtask B.

Actual Label	**Prediction** (ReBERT)		**Prediction** (Team Curie)		**Prediction** (Team Uriel)	
	Hateful	Non-Hateful	Hateful	Non-Hateful	Hateful	Non-Hateful
Hateful	37	15	37	15	36	16
Non-Hateful	16	454	19	451	25	445

BERT model trained on tweets as the top-ranking system, Team Uriel lagged behind the second place system (Team Curie) that used an Arabic BERT model not specifically pre-trained on tweets. This result highlights the importance of hyperparameter tuning, especially in scenarios with limited data.

The winner of Subtask A, DetectiveReDASers (Qachfar et al., 2024), took 4th place in subtask B, with an F1 score of 0.6 on the private dataset. They reported that they did not use cross-lingual augmentation in this task (i.e. translating Turkish tweets into Arabic) as it degraded the performance, even though this strategy had worked well in Subtask A. This may be due to the relative numbers of the two datasets.

7 Conclusion

This paper presented an overview of the HSD-2Lang shared task that was organized to benchmark models for hate speech detection on social media platforms, in Turkish and Arabic languages. The task consisted of two distinct subtasks, each addressing unique challenges: Subtask A focused on hate speech detection in various contexts in Turkish, and Subtask B addressed the challenge of hate speech detection in Arabic under limited data conditions.

The results from these subtasks provided valuable insights into the efficacy of different models and strategies. All participating systems used BERT-based models, demonstrating their effectiveness. On the other hand, systems using the same model achieved noticeably different results due to hyperparameter choices.

In Subtask A, the top-performing system employed a soft-ensemble of ConvBERTurk models, achieving an F1 score of 0.69645 on the private test set. This shows the effectiveness of ensemble methods in tackling hate speech detection across various contexts. Moreover, the noticeable performance differences among systems using the same method, specifically TurkishBERTweet with LoRA fine-tuning, underscore the importance of hyperparameter tuning in improving model performance.

Subtask B yielded comparable results due to similar model implementations with minor variations. The top system achieved an F1 score of 0.68354 on the private test set. The small performance difference between the two tasks are interesting, considering that the Turkish dataset had three times more data compared to the Arabic set, showing the effectiveness of pretrained models. On the other hand, the difference between the performances of ReBERT and Team Uriel, even though they used the same Arabic BERT model, further highlights the importance of hyperparameter tuning, especially in scenarios with limited data availability.

Acknowledgements

This work was supported by the EU project "Utilizing Digital Technology for Social Cohesion, Positive Messaging and Peace by Boosting Collaboration, Exchange and Solidarity" (EuropeAid/170389/DD/ACT/Multi), carried out by the Hrant Dink Foundation.

References

Wissam Antoun, Fady Baly, and Hazem Hajj. 2020. AraBERT: Transformer-based model for Arabic language understanding. In *LREC 2020 Workshop Language Resources and Evaluation Conference 11–16 May 2020*, page 9.

İnanç Arın, Zeynep Işık, Seçilay Kutal, Somaiyeh Dehghan, Arzucan Özgür, and Berrin Yanikoğlu. 2023. SIU2023-NST- Hate speech detection contest. In *2023 31st Signal Processing and Communications Applications Conference (SIU)*, pages 1–4. IEEE.

Ehsan Barkhordar, Işık S. Topçu, and Ali Hürriyetoğlu. 2024. Team Curie at HSD-2Lang 2024: Hate speech detection in Turkish and Arabic tweets using BERT-based models. In *Proceedings of The Seventh Workshop on Challenges and Applications of Automated Extraction of Socio-political Events from Text (CASE)*, Malta. Association for Computational Linguistics.

Alexis Conneau, Kartikay Khandelwal, Naman Goyal, Vishrav Chaudhary, Guillaume Wenzek, Francisco Guzmán, Edouard Grave, Myle Ott, Luke Zettlemoyer, and Veselin Stoyanov. 2019. Unsupervised cross-lingual representation learning at scale. *CoRR*, abs/1911.02116.

Jacob Devlin, Ming-Wei Chang, Kenton Lee, and Kristina Toutanova. 2019. BERT: Pre-training of deep bidirectional transformers for language understanding. In *Proceedings of the 2019 Conference of the North American Chapter of the Association for Computational Linguistics: Human Language Technologies, Volume 1 (Long and Short Papers)*, pages 4171–4186, Minneapolis, Minnesota. Association for Computational Linguistics.

Edward J Hu, Yelong Shen, Phillip Wallis, Zeyuan Allen-Zhu, Yuanzhi Li, Shean Wang, Lu Wang, and Weizhu Chen. 2021. LoRA: Low-rank adaptation of large language models. *arXiv preprint arXiv:2106.09685*.

Ilya Loshchilov and Frank Hutter. 2017. Decoupled weight decay regularization. *arXiv preprint arXiv:1711.05101*.

Ali Najafi and Onur Varol. 2023. TurkishBERTweet: Fast and reliable large language model for social media analysis. *arXiv preprint arXiv:2311.18063*.

Ali Najafi and Onur Varol. 2024. VRLLab at HSD-2Lang 2024: Turkish hate speech detection online with TurkishBERTweet. In *Proceedings of The Seventh Workshop on Challenges and Applications of Automated Extraction of Socio-political Events from Text (CASE)*, Malta. Association for Computational Linguistics.

Fatima Zahra Qachfar, Bryan E. Tuck, and Rakesh M. Verma. 2024. DetectiveReDASers at HSD-2Lang 2024: A new pooling strategy with cross-lingual augmentation and ensembling for hate speech detection in low-resource languages. In *Proceedings of The Seventh Workshop on Challenges and Applications of Automated Extraction of Socio-political Events from Text (CASE)*, Malta. Association for Computational Linguistics.

Ali Safaya, Moutasem Abdullatif, and Deniz Yuret. 2020. KUISAIL at SemEval-2020 task 12: BERT-CNN for offensive speech identification in social media. In *Proceedings of the Fourteenth Workshop on Semantic Evaluation*, pages 2054–2059, Barcelona (online). International Committee for Computational Linguistics.

Stefan Schweter. 2020. BERTurk - BERT models for Turkish. `https://zenodo.org/records/3770924`.

Pedro Javier Ortiz Suárez, Benoît Sagot, and Laurent Romary. 2019. Asynchronous pipeline for processing huge corpora on medium to low resource infrastructures. In *7th Workshop on the Challenges in the Management of Large Corpora (CMLC-7)*. Leibniz-Institut für Deutsche Sprache.

Utku Ugur Yagci, Ahmet Emirhan Kolcak, and Egemen Iscan. 2024. ReBERT at HSD-2Lang 2024: Fine-tuning BERT with AdamW for hate speech detection in Arabic and Turkish. In *Proceedings of The Seventh Workshop on Challenges and Applications of Automated Extraction of Socio-political Events from Text (CASE)*, Malta. Association for Computational Linguistics.

Stance and Hate Event Detection in Tweets Related to Climate Activism - Shared Task at CASE 2024

Surendrabikram Thapa[1], **Kritesh Rauniyar**[2], **Farhan Ahmad Jafri**[3], **Shuvam Shiwakoti**[2], **Hariram Veeramani**[4], **Raghav Jain**[5], **Guneet Singh Kohli**[6], **Ali Hürriyetoğlu**[7], **Usman Naseem**[8]

[1]Virginia Tech, USA, [2]Delhi Technological University, India, [3]Jamia Millia Islamia, India, [4]UCLA, USA, [5]University of Manchester, UK, [6]Thapar University, India, [7]Wageningen Food Safety Research, Netherlands, [8]Macquarie University, Australia

[1]surendrabikram@vt.edu, [2]rauniyark11@gmail.com

Abstract

Social media plays a pivotal role in global discussions, including on climate change. The variety of opinions expressed range from supportive to oppositional, with some instances of hate speech. Recognizing the importance of understanding these varied perspectives, the 7th Workshop on Challenges and Applications of Automated Extraction of Socio-political Events from Text (CASE) at EACL 2024 hosted a shared task focused on detecting stances and hate speech in climate activism-related tweets. This task was divided into three subtasks: subtasks A and B concentrated on identifying hate speech and its targets, while subtask C focused on stance detection. Participants' performance was evaluated using the macro F1-score. With over 100 teams participating, the highest F1 scores achieved were **91.44%** in subtask C, **78.58%** in subtask B, and **74.83%** in subtask A. This paper details the methodologies of 24 teams that submitted their results to the competition's leaderboard.

1 Introduction

In an era dominated by digital communication, social media platforms serve as dynamic arenas where global conversations unfold in real-time. Twitter (now X)[1], in particular, with its diverse community, has emerged as a vital space for discussions on pressing global issues. Among these, the discourse surrounding climate change stands out as a critical topic that captivates the attention of users worldwide, with the masses expressing myriad opinions towards climate change (Fownes et al., 2018). As public awareness of climate change grows, and global movements like Friday For Future (FFF) (Wallis and Loy, 2021) that aim to draw policymakers' attention towards climate change house various social media platforms, the need for a nuanced understanding of the discourse around climate change in the digital realm becomes essential.

The escalating concern regarding climate change, coupled with the diverse range of discourse observed on Twitter, presents a distinctive amalgamation that encapsulates the intricate spectrum of emotions expressed by individuals toward this global issue. Within this spectrum lie various layers, including stance, which reflects individuals' inclinations toward specific viewpoints. As opinions are freely voiced, the prevalence of hate speech also emerges (Jafri et al., 2023; Thapa et al., 2023). Moreover, using humor in language is both an engaging and intricate mechanism for conveying ideas on pressing matters (Rauniyar et al., 2023). In order to unravel these complexities and enhance our understanding of online discussions concerning climate change, Shiwakoti et al. (2024) introduced a comprehensive multi-aspect dataset consisting of tweets related to climate change. This dataset includes five key aspects: the relevance of tweets to climate change, the stance conveyed in tweets, the presence of hate speech, the targets of such hate speech, and the presence of humor. Expanding upon this, we launched a shared task at the CASE 2024 workshop, held alongside EACL 2024, by utilizing this dataset. This shared task is subdivided into three subtasks: subtask A focuses on hate speech detection, subtask B revolves around identifying targets within hate speech, and subtask C delves into stance detection in tweets. Through this shared task, our objective is to foster active participation and cooperation in tackling the critical challenge of discerning stances on complex issues and identifying and curtailing hate speech within the digital sphere.

The subsequent sections of this paper are structured as follows: Section 2 presents an overview of the dataset used in our shared task. Section 3 out-

[1]In this paper, we have still used Twitter to refer X. The posts in X are referred to as tweets in our paper.

Proceedings of the 7th Workshop on Challenges and Applications of Automated Extraction of Socio-political Events from Text (CASE 2024), pages 234–247
March 22, 2024 ©2024 Association for Computational Linguistics

lines the specific subtasks of the shared task. Furthermore, Section 4 explains about methodologies used by the teams submitting system description papers. Section 5 discusses a brief analysis of these system descriptions, while Section 6 serves as the concluding segment of the paper.

2 Dataset

In our shared task, we utilized the ClimaConvo dataset introduced by Shiwakoti et al. (2024). This dataset includes a total of 15,309 tweets centered around the climate crisis issue. The dataset has 6 major tasks, viz. Relevance, Stance, Hate Speech, Hate Direction, Hate Targets, and Humor. Only 10,407 of the tweets in this data were relevant, while the remaining 4,902 were non-relevant. We only used three tasks in our shared task: hate speech detection, hate targets detection, and stance detection. A total of 10,407 tweets were used for both subtask A and subtask C, while 999 tweets were used for subtask B in the shared task. For each subtask, we divided the dataset into stages for training, evaluating, and testing in a stratified way, keeping a proportionate split ratio of approximately 70-15-15. Table 1 represents the dataset statistics for the shared task.

Subtask	Classes	Train	Eval	Test
Subtask A	Hate	899	190	188
	Non-Hate	6,385	1,371	1,374
Subtask B	Individual	563	120	121
	Organization	105	23	23
	Community	31	7	6
Subtask C	Support	4,328	897	921
	Oppose	700	153	141
	Neutral	2,256	511	500

Table 1: Dataset statistics for our shared task.

3 Shared Task Description

Hate speech refers to any form of communication that explicitly attacks an individual or a group based on their inherent characteristics, such as gender, religion, or race (Zhou et al., 2023). Stance describes the attitude or perspective expressed in a text towards a particular claim or topic (Hardalov et al., 2022; Rajaraman et al., 2023). Stance and hate detection can be used to analyze the structure of user interactions in conversational threads, providing valuable insights into the dynamics of online discussions.

3.1 Subtask A: Hate Speech Detection

This task involves determining whether a particular tweet exhibits hate speech. The dataset consists of tweets that have been annotated to indicate if the text includes hate speech or not. More precisely, the dataset is divided into two distinct classes: tweets that have been classified as ***Hate Speech*** and tweets that have been classified as ***No Hate Speech***.

3.2 Subtask B: Targets of Hate Speech Detection

This subtask aims to identify the target audience of hate speech within a specified set of hateful tweets. The subtask specifically focuses on classifying three specified targets outlined within the dataset, even though hate speech text may encompass different potential targets across multiple categories. The tweets in the dataset are labeled according to their targets, which can be classified as ***community***, ***individual***, or ***organization***. Therefore, we aim to identify these specific targets within tweets containing hate speech.

3.3 Subtask C: Stance Detection

The objective of the task is to identify various forms of stance within the specific tweet. This involves identifying three categories of stance in the dataset, labeled 'Support', 'Oppose', and 'Neutral'.

4 Participants' Methods

4.1 Overview

Out of the 100 participants who registered for the shared task, a total of 23 participants submitted scores for subtask A, 18 participants for subtask B, and 19 participants for subtask C. The leaderboards for these subtasks are provided in Table 2, Table 3, and Table 4. In subtask A, CUET_Binary_Hackers achieved the highest performance with an impressive F1-score of 91.44. Similarly, in subtask B, MasonPerplexity secured the top position with an F1-score of 78.58, while in subtask C, ARC-NLP emerged as the leader with the highest score of 74.83.

4.2 Methods

This section presents brief overviews of the system descriptions submitted by the participating teams in the shared task. These summaries are derived from the detailed approaches outlined in the participants' system description papers.

4.2.1 Subtask A

CUET_Binary_Hackers (Farsi et al., 2024) proposed multiple numbers of machine learning (ML), deep learning (DL), transformers, and hybrid (combination of ML, DL, and LLM) based models with and without oversampling. Additionally, they used various feature extraction techniques, including Word2Vec (Pennington et al., 2014) and TF-IDF (Ramos et al., 2003; Adhikari et al., 2021) for machine learning and FastText (Joulin et al., 2016) and GloVe (Mikolov et al., 2013) for DL models. After incorporating the oversampling technique, they achieved best macro F1-score of 88% on SVM (Support Vector Machine) (Evgeniou and Pontil, 2001) and 88% on RF (Random Forest) (Louppe, 2015) machine learning models. However, without the oversampling technique, they achieved the best F1-score of 86% on SVM and 89% on RF model with TF-IDF and Word2Vec vectorizer respectively. In deep learning models with oversampling and by using Glove and FastText as vectorizers, BiGRU Cho et al. (2014) and CNN+BiGRU (Gehring et al., 2017) attained 80% and 90% F1-score respectively, but without oversampling with the same set of vectorizers, CNN+BiGRU achieved 91% (with GloVe) and 90% (with FastText) respectively. In transformer models with oversampling, mBERT (Devlin et al., 2019) and ClimateBERT (Webersinke et al., 2022) both achieved 91% F1-score and without oversampling, mBERT attained 91% F1-score. With this F1-score, the stood first on the leaderboard.

AAST-NLP (El-Sayed and Nasr, 2024a) used the **top-k** ensemble technique to achieve higher F1-score. Initially, they finetuned the bert variants, RoBERTa Liu et al. (2019), XLM-RoBERTa (Conneau et al., 2020) and HateBERT Caselli et al. (2021) on all of the datasets to attain the best results. They employed the 'Top-3' and 'Top-5' ensemble types, each of which used a different approach to attain the greatest F1 score. They obtain the maximum recall of 96.11% on HateBERT, the highest precision of 86.88% on RoBERTa, and the highest F1-score of 89.14% on **Top-5** ensemble approach. Of the 23 teams who participated in subtask A, their 'Top-5' ensemble approach, combining various BERT-based models, obtained the second position.

ARC-NLP (Kaya et al., 2024) used a combination of generative and encoder models, focusing on tweet-specific elements like hashtags, URLs, and emojis and employing optimization techniques like Optuna (Akiba et al., 2019). The work explores implementing three primary methods: the Encoder model, the Generative model, and the Hybrid model. The hybrid approach utilized a combination of the encoder model, such as BERTweet (Nguyen et al., 2020), and the generative model, such as Llama2 (Touvron et al., 2023). In subtask A, the hybrid model (BERTweet + Llama2) outperformed with an F1-score of 89.01% and secured third position in the leaderboard.

HAMiSoN Baselines (Montesinos and Rodrigo, 2024) evaluated the performance of the RoBERTa (Liu et al., 2019) and DeBERTa (He et al., 2020) models in the classification-based subtask and further investigated their performance when supplemented with external data. They combine two additional datasets such as the Offensive Language Identification Dataset (OLID) (Zampieri et al., 2019b) proposed at SemEval-2019 and Stance Detection Dataset (Mohammad et al., 2016b) released at the SemEval-2016 Task 6. They adopt preprocessing techniques such as replacing identifiers with special tokens and further decomposing hashtags into individual words to positively reinforce the learning process. They then analyze the performance of Hate speech classification in subtask A with RoBERTa and DeBERTa with the presence and absence of external datasets and report that standalone RoBERTa performed the best in subtask A with an F1-score of 88.86%, taking the fourth position in the leaderboard.

MasonPerplexity (Emran et al., 2024) used a weighted ensemble model combining the XLM-Roberta-Large (Conneau et al., 2020), HateBert (Caselli et al., 2021), and fBert (Sarkar et al., 2021), which were selected as the best three models from a pool of models tested. To handle the class imbalance challenge, the submission involved the concept of 'Back Translation', where text is translated from one language to another and then back to the original. This approach was explicitly applied to labels with lower representation in the training data, translating them through chains of multiple languages like *Xhosa to Twi to English, Lao to Pashto to Yoruba to English, Yoruba to Somali to Kinyarwanda to English and Zulu to Oromo to Shona to Tsonga to English.* This multi-language translation process introduces nuanced variations in

Rank	Team Name	Codalab Username	Accuracy	Recall	Precision	F1-score
1	CUET_Binary_Hackers (Farsi et al., 2024)	Asrarul_Hoque_Eusha	**96.35**	**91.73**	**91.16**	**91.44**
2	AAST-NLP (El-Sayed and Nasr, 2024b)	AhmedElSayed	95.71	86.54	92.31	89.14
3	ARC-NLP (Kaya et al., 2024)	kagankaya1	95.26	89.73	88.33	89.01
4	HAMiSoN-baselines (Montesinos and Rodrigo, 2024)	julioremo	95.39	87.97	89.81	88.86
5	MasonPerplexity (Gangul et al., 2024)	Sadiya_Puspo	95.52	86.89	91.12	88.85
6	HAMiSoN-MTL (Rodriguez-Garcia and Centeno, 2024)	Raquel	95.33	86.55	90.53	88.40
7	Bryndza (Suppa et al., 2024)	mareksuppa	94.75	89.90	86.60	88.14
8	CUET_Binary_Hackers (Farsi et al., 2024)	SalmanFarsi	94.37	91.06	85.13	87.75
9	-	kojiro000	95.07	83.19	92.26	86.99
10	NLPDame (Christodoulou, 2024)	christiechris	94.62	84.32	89.09	86.49
11	CSI	RyszardStaurch	93.73	89.09	83.94	86.24
12	-	swatirajwal	94.43	84.21	88.33	86.11
13	-	refaat1731	94.94	79.68	96.07	85.56
14	-	d_rock	93.47	88.02	83.52	85.56
15	RACAI (Păiș, 2024)	pvf	94.37	82.79	89.07	85.55
16	Z-AGI Labs (Narayan and Biswal, 2024)	mrutyunjay_research	94.94	79.22	96.86	85.39
17	byteSizedLLM	mdp0999	94.17	80.16	90.44	84.29
18	JRC (Tanev, 2024)	htanev	94.05	77.79	92.46	83.10
19	-	Nikhil_7280	91.17	84.88	78.59	81.25
20	-	kriti7	88.92	91.18	75.66	80.26
21	Empty_heads	fayez94	87.96	50.00	43.98	46.80
21	pokemons	md_kashif_20	87.96	50.00	43.98	46.80
22	md_kashif_20	pakapro	50.38	52.28	50.97	42.42

Table 2: Sub-task A (Hate Speech Classification) Leaderboard, Ranked by Macro F1-score. All scores are presented as percentages (%). It is to be noted that this leaderboard contains the score till the test deadline and does not consider further runs done by participants as a part of the system description paper.

the dataset, effectively enriching and diversifying the training examples for these underrepresented classes. Their approach helped them achieve a 5th Rank out of 22 submissions in subtask A, with an F1 score of 89%. They also tested with an ensemble of BERTweet-large, XLM-Roberta-Large, and fBERT which, yielded an F1-score of 84%.

HAMiSoN-MTL (Rodriguez-Garcia and Centeno, 2024) took a Multi-task learning (MTL) approach with the help of multiple external datasets for classification problems across all 3 tasks. They took the hard parameter-sharing approach for MTL, using a different classification head for each task with a shared RoBERTa encoder. They performed extensive experimentation with multiple dataset combinations, and their best-performing model for hate speech detection (subtask A) achieved a F1-score of 88.40% and was ranked 6th among the 22 submissions. Although external datasets were used for experiments, their best performance was obtained using only the shared task dataset.

Bryndza (Suppa et al., 2024) investigates the utilization of GPT-4[2] (Brown et al., 2020), assessing its efficacy when used in both zero and few-shot learning (Hasan et al., 2023) and expanded through the incorporation of retrieval augmentation (Lewis et al., 2020) and re-ranking techniques (Mei et al., 2014). They discussed using the flashrank library (Damodaran, 2023) for re-ranking, aiming to enhance the model's performance in classification tasks. A suitable prompt was generated for subtask A by selecting a small sample of 30 Non-Hate and 30 Hate tweets and sending them to GPT-4. Chroma Vector Database[3] was utilized for retrieval augmentation to create an index of embeddings generated by pre-trained Sentence Transformer models[4], such as 'all-MiniLM-L6-v2' and 'all-mpnet-base-v2'. In subtask A, the model 'all-mpnet-base-v2' demonstrated notable effectiveness, yielding the ultimate submission with $k = 6$, k refers to the number of examples that can be chosen for retrieval augmentation, and the model achieved an F1-score of 88.14%.

NLPDame (Christodoulou, 2024) utilized parameter-efficient fine-tuning methodologies such as Low-Rank Adaptation (LoRA) (Hu et al., 2021) and prompt tuning with the recently proposed Mistral 7B (Jiang et al., 2023) models for the evaluation of subtask A. They preprocess emojis to convert them into their equivalent textual representations, UTF-8 apostrophe encoding and normalization of identifiers such as user, URL, and Email and then adopt weighted cross entropy as the loss function. Further, the work compares the Mistral LLM's performance against the models previously proposed such as BERT, DistilBERT, RoBERTa, and ClimateBERT. The Mistral prompt

[2] https://openai.com/gpt-4

[3] https://www.trychroma.com/

[4] https://www.sbert.net/docs/pretrained_models.html

tuning approach achieved the highest F1-score of 86.4% in subtask A.

RACAI (Păiș, 2024) implemented a BERT-based model fused with hand-crafted features to detect hate speech (subtask A). They performed extensive pre-processing with the data which is superior to the dataset paper and significantly contributed to improving the performance of the model. The features included several raw hashtags, remaining hashtags after pre-processing, hashtags that were split during pre-processing, user mentions, URLs, and TF-IDF prediction. The final architecture is completed with the help of a Decision Tree (DT), which combines the LLM predictions with the features. However, their best-performing model as per the competition's evaluation metric (F1-score) turned out to be the plain fine-tuned BERT implementation which gave a F1-score of 85.55% and ranked 15 among the 22 submissions.

Z-AGI Labs (Narayan and Biswal, 2024) presented using conventional ML methods combined with contemporary DL techniques. In their study, the architecture of the DL model included a framework based on Long Short-Term Memory (LSTM) (Hochreiter and Schmidhuber, 1997) with attention mechanisms (Vaswani et al., 2017). The Light Gradient Boosting Machine (LGBM) model (Ke et al., 2017), integrated with TF-IDF (Ramos et al., 2003) for feature extraction, yielded the most favorable results, achieving an F1-Score of 86.84%.

JRC (Tanev, 2024) participated in Sub-task A: 'Hate Speech Detection', where they employed a pure lexicon-based method (Gitari et al., 2015), avoiding statistical classifiers, and achieved moderate performance compared to other participants. Their model ranked 18 out of 22 participants, with an F1-score of 83.10%.

4.2.2 Subtask B

MasonPerplexity (Emran et al., 2024) in their approach for subtask B, they used a distinct set of individual models comprising XLM-R (Conneau et al., 2020), BERT-Base (Devlin et al., 2019), and BERTweet-Large (Nguyen et al., 2020). Among these, BERTweet-Large was particularly notable, achieving outstanding results with an accuracy of 91.33%, precision of 81.33%, and recall of 78.23%. This performance led to a test F1-score of 79%, securing the 1st rank among 18 submissions for the task. The research team also implemented the 'Back Translation' technique to address class imbalance in the dataset. This involved translating texts from underrepresented labels through various language sequences, such as *Xhosa to Twi to English, Lao to Pashto to Yoruba to English, Yoruba to Somali to Kinyarwanda to English, and Zulu to Oromo to Shona to Tsonga to English*, and then back to English. Introducing nuanced linguistic variations significantly enriched and diversified the training data, effectively improving the model's ability to handle underrepresented classes.

Bryndza (Suppa et al., 2024) presented the performance of different models with GPT-4 used for detecting the targets of hate speech in tweets. Within subtask B, the retrieval-augmentation approach utilizing hte 'all-MiniLM-L6-v2' model where $k = 6$, produced the most favorable outcomes, achieving an F1-score of 77.61% and second position in the leaderboard.

AAST-NLP (El-Sayed and Nasr, 2024a) presented the **top-k** ensemble strategy to reach higher F1-score. To get the best results, they first tweaked the BERT types on all datasets: RoBERTa, XLM-RoBERTa, and HateBERT. In this task, they also experimented with two named entity recognition (NER) modules: SpaCy [5] and BERT-based NER. While ORG and NoORG landmarks were extracted using SpaCy, names were extracted more effectively by the BERT-based NER. They employed the 'Top-3' and 'Top-5' ensemble styles, each taking a distinct method to get the highest F1-score. With the **Top-5** ensemble strategy, they achieve the maximum of all three metrics: F1-score of 76.65%, recall of 76.89%, and accuracy of 77.06%. Their 'Top-5' ensemble technique, which integrates multiple BERT-based models, secured a second place among the eighteen teams who took part in subtask B.

ARC-NLP (Kaya et al., 2024) focused on BERTweet, which is an encoder-based technique for classification, and achieved the highest F1-score of 76.38% among the other four models. Another model, BERTweet+NER (Nguyen et al., 2020; Ozcelik and Toraman, 2022), is a hybrid formed by combining encoder and generative models, and it also scored an F1-score of 75.00%.

CUET_Binary_Hackers (Farsi et al., 2024) presented various models and feature extraction tech-

[5] https://spacy.io/

Rank	Team Name	Codalab Username	Accuracy	Precision	Recall	F1-score
1	MasonPerplexity (Gangul et al., 2024)	Sadiya_Puspo	**91.33**	**81.33**	**78.23**	**78.58**
2	Bryndza (Suppa et al., 2024)	mareksuppa	92.67	78.13	77.61	77.61
3	AAST-NLP (El-Sayed and Nasr, 2024b)	AhmedElSayed	91.33	76.89	77.06	76.65
4	ARC-NLP (Kaya et al., 2024)	kagankaya1	91.33	77.28	75.88	76.38
5	-	kojiro000	91.33	73.23	77.06	74.88
6	CUET_Binary_Hackers (Farsi et al., 2024)	SalmanFarsi	90.00	74.31	75.33	74.33
7	-	amr8ta	90.00	71.29	78.26	73.65
8	HAMiSoN-MTL (Rodriguez-Garcia and Centeno, 2024)	Raquel	90.00	71.54	75.33	73.29
9	-	swatirajwal	89.33	67.39	69.78	68.48
10	HAMiSoN-baselines (Montesinos and Rodrigo, 2024)	julioremo	87.33	64.71	73.64	65.88
11	NLPDame (Christodoulou, 2024)	christiechris	84.00	61.51	72.85	61.06
12	byteSizedLLM	mdp0999	88.67	52.33	62.46	55.80
13	-	Nikhil_7280	88.00	51.66	61.01	54.96
14	EmptyMind	empty_box	87.33	52.39	56.04	54.07
15	Z-AGI Labs (Narayan and Biswal, 2024)	mrutyunjay_research	86.00	50.71	51.97	51.33
16	Team +1	pakapro	30.00	33.53	38.80	24.58
17	-	kriti7	7.33	13.95	4.91	7.18
18	pokemons	md_kashif_20	0.00	0.00	0.00	0.00

Table 3: Sub-task B (Targets of Hate Speech Detection) Leaderboard, Ranked by Macro F1-score. All scores are presented as percentages (%). It is to be noted that this leaderboard contains the score till the test deadline and does not consider further runs done by participants as a part of the system description paper.

niques similar to their approach in subtask A. The best F1-score of 74% were obtained with the oversampling technique with mBERT and DistillBERT models.

HAMiSoN-MTL (Rodriguez-Garcia and Centeno, 2024) leveraged MTL for all 3 tasks with the hard parameter-sharing approach, using a different classification head for each task and a shared RoBERTa encoder for all. They also performed extensive experimentation with external datasets, and their best-performing model for hate target detection achieved a F1-score of 73.29% and ranked 8th among 18 submissions. This score was obtained using the shared task dataset and the target identification task dataset from OLID (Zampieri et al., 2019a), which is an extensive offensive language detection dataset.

HAMiSoN Baselines (Montesinos and Rodrigo, 2024) Similar to subtask A, they analyze the performance of the RoBERTa and DeBERTa models in the three classification-based subtasks with external data augmentation using the two additional datasets such as Offensive Language Identification Dataset (OLID) (Zampieri et al., 2019b) proposed at SemEval-2019 and Stance Detection Dataset (Mohammad et al., 2016b) released at the SemEval-2016 Task 6. They continue to reuse the preprocessing techniques, such as replacing identifiers with special tokens and hashtag decomposition into simple words to improve the downstream model's prediction. Based on their performance report of Target Identification subtask B, they note that the standalone RoBERTa with external data performed the best in subtask B with an F1-score of 70.17%.

NLPDame (Christodoulou, 2024) Similar to their approach in subtask A, they adopted LoRA and prompt tuning methods based on Mistral for the target identification subtask B. They reuse the pre-processing techniques such as emoji conversion to their equivalent textual representations, apostrophe encoding in UTF-8 style, and normalization of identifiers of identifiers. They adopted weighted cross entropy as the loss function for the three-class classification task with inherent task imbalance. Finally, they discuss Mistral LLM's performance compared to transformer models like BERT, DistilBERT, RoBERTa, and ClimateBERT. The prompt tuning approach with Mistral yielded them the highest F1-score of 61.0% in subtask B.

Z-AGI Labs (Narayan and Biswal, 2024) worked on various ML and DL approaches where they used TF-IDF for the feature extraction. The CatBoost (Prokhorenkova et al., 2018) model exhibited superior performance, achieving an F1-score of 56.04%. In comparison, models such as Naive Bayes, LR, and RF closely followed with F1-scores of 54.82%, 55.77%, and 54.95%, respectively.

4.2.3 Subtask C

ARC-NLP (Kaya et al., 2024) used the optimized version of the BERTweet model. This model outperformed other encoder models in stance detection; it employed a short input tokenization length (96 tokens) and incorporated special tokens for tweet-specific elements. The highest macro F1-score was achieved by the BERTweet model,

Rank	Team Name	Codalab Username	Accuracy	Precision	Recall	F1-score
1	ARC-NLP (Kaya et al., 2024)	kagankaya1	**74.90**	**78.48**	**72.26**	**74.83**
2	HAMiSoN-Generative (Fraile-Hernandez and Peñas, 2024)	JesusFraile	74.78	78.27	72.23	74.79
3	IUST (Mahmoudi and Eetemadi, 2024)	gh_mhdi	73.11	78.63	71.45	74.47
4	HAMiSoN-MTL (Rodriguez-Garcia and Centeno, 2024)	Raquel	74.33	77.02	72.42	74.02
5	AAST-NLP (El-Sayed and Nasr, 2024b)	AhmedElSayed	74.39	79.31	70.78	73.98
6	MasonPerplexity (Gangul et al., 2024)	Sadiya_Puspo	73.69	77.80	70.90	73.73
7	-	kojiro000	73.43	77.44	70.89	73.58
8	-	refaat1731	72.22	77.49	70.06	73.15
9	HAMiSoN-baselines (Montesinos and Rodrigo, 2024)	julioremo	74.01	78.17	70.36	73.13
10	-	Nikhil_7280	71.90	76.62	68.13	70.81
11	-	swatirajwal	67.86	70.83	70.05	70.26
12	Bryndza (Suppa et al., 2024)	mareksuppa	71.19	68.72	71.23	69.33
13	NLPDame (Christodoulou, 2024)	christiechris	66.52	71.16	67.94	69.30
14	byteSizedLLM	mdp0999	65.24	72.55	66.85	69.10
15	CUET_Binary_Hackers (Farsi et al., 2024)	SalmanFarsi	66.13	69.08	66.91	67.94
16	Z-AGI Labs (Narayan and Biswal, 2024)	mrutyunjay_research	69.08	79.26	62.94	63.72
17	Team +1	pakapro	32.71	32.66	31.51	28.98
18	-	ankitha11	0.38	1.32	0.16	0.29
19	pokemons	md_kashif_20	0.00	0.00	0.00	0.00

Table 4: Sub-task C (Stance Detection) Leaderboard, Ranked by Macro F1-score. All scores are presented as percentages (%). It is to be noted that this leaderboard contains the score till the test deadline and does not consider further runs done by participants as a part of the system description paper.

which scored 74.83%. This score is slightly higher than the other models tested for the same subtask, with DeBERTa (He et al., 2021) coming close with an F1-score of 73.85%. The optimization of the BERTweet model, focusing on tweet-specific elements, was key to its top performance. For subtask C, BERTweet outperformed all the other models in the leaderboard securing the first position.

HAMiSoN-Generative (Fraile-Hernandez and Peñas, 2024) implemented variants/modifications of the Llama 2 7B generative LLM for stance prediction (subtask C). 3 of the 4 variants of the Llama 2 7B used are out-of-the-box chatbot models, but by using specific input formats, these models were adapted to be used in classification tasks. They also used an external data source (Mohammad et al., 2016a), which is related to the stance detection, to train and boost their models' performance. Despite the models used being chatbot models, they were able to achieve 2nd position in the stance detection sub-task among 19 submissions with an impressive F1-score of 74.79%.

IUST (Mahmoudi and Eetemadi, 2024) evaluated models such as BERT, RoBERTa, BERTWeet, XLM-RoBERTa, and DEBERTA for the three subtasks. Data augmentation strategies such as synonym substitution and Round-trip translation and German as the back translation language using nlpaug library[6] were adopted as part of the pipeline. The main focus of this work is to focus on optimal hyperparameter selection from the search space definition comprising of the optimizers, loss functions (Focal loss/Weighted cross-entropy loss), cleaning strategies, classification layer choices of a Fully Connected Layer/ Convolutional Neural Network (CNN) head architectures were investigated while demonstrating that CNN classifier heads performed across all their cleaning strategy/Embedding model based pipelines. The cleaning strategy of removing URL and username identifiers, in addition to stochastic gradient descent optimizer and CNN classifier head, was demonstrated to have achieved the highest F1-scores of 73.97%, 74.47% based on XLM-ROBERTa and BERTweet based systems on the Climate stance detection task.

HAMiSoN-MTL (Rodriguez-Garcia and Centeno, 2024) used a RoBERTa-based Multi-task learning approach for all 3 tasks by a RoBERTa shared encoder for all and a different classification head for each task. They used external datasets and performed multiple experiments with various dataset combinations. Combining the shared task dataset and the OLID (Zampieri et al., 2019a), they achieved their best performance with a F1-score of 74.02% and ranked 4th among 19 submissions in the stance detection task.

AAST-NLP (El-Sayed and Nasr, 2024a) leverage the **top-k** ensemble strategy to reach higher F1-score. To get the best results, they first tweaked the bert types on all datasets: RoBERTa, XLM-RoBERTa, and HateBERT. In this subtask, they only employed 'Top-5' ensemble styles, which made them get the highest F1-score. In this subtask, their RoBERTa model achieves the best precision value of 71.69% and with the use **Top-5** ensem-

[6]https://github.com/makcedward/nlpaug

ble strategy, they achieve the maximum recall and f1-score metrics value of 79.31% and 73.98% respectively. In subTask-C, they attained the fifth position on 18 participating teams by using the 'Top-5' ensemble technique.

MasonPerplexity (Emran et al., 2024) implemented a variety of models including BERTweet-large, BERT base, and BERTweet base. Of these, the BERTweet base model stood out, achieving the highest F1-score. Their system ranked 6th out of 19 submissions. The performance of the different models experimented with are as follows: GPT3.5 Zero Shot prompting had a Test F1-score of 63%, GPT-3.5 Few Shot prompting achieved a Test F1-score of 67%, BERT- BASE scored a Test F1-score of 69%, BERTweet-LARGE attained a Test F1-score of 70%, and BERTweet-Base led the group with a Test F1-score of 74%.

HAMiSoN Baselines (Montesinos and Rodrigo, 2024) Similar to subtask A and subtask B, they report the performance of the RoBERTa and DeBERTa models with external data augmentation using the two additional datasets such as OLID ((Zampieri et al., 2019b)) proposed at SemEval-2019 and Stance Detection Dataset ((Mohammad et al., 2016b)) released at the SemEval-2016 Task 6 reusing the similar pre-processing techniques they note that the standalone RoBERTa without external data performed the best in subtask C with a F1-score of 74.95%.

Bryndza (Suppa et al., 2024) made the use of 'all-mpnet-base-v2' model with GPT-4 API, which was highly effective, leading to its selection for the final submission. With $k = 8$, it achieved an F1-score of 69.33%, demonstrating its strong performance in classifying stance.

NLPDame (Christodoulou, 2024) Similar to their approach in subtask A and subtask B, they adopted LoRA and prompt tuning Parameter efficient fine-tuning methods based on Mistral and reused the pre-processing techniques such as emojis conversion to their equivalent textual representations, apostrophe encoding in UTF-8 style and normalization of identifiers of key identifiers part of the samples like user, URL, Email for the target identification subtask B. Following this approach, they conclude that superior performance of Mistral LLMs continues to emerge again in subtask C, similar to the previous subtasks as compared to the transformer models like BERT, DistilBERT, RoBERTa, and ClimateBERT fetching them the highest F1-score of 69.3% in subtask C.

CUET_Binary_Hackers (Farsi et al., 2024) presented various learning models with diverse feature engineering and oversampling techniques. The best results were obtained with oversampling techniques. DistillmBERT, ClimateBERT and BiGRU (with Glove embeddings) gave a same F1-score of 67%. F1-scores of 31% without oversampling and 62% with oversampling were obtained using their hybrid model. mBERT+BiLSTM+CNN (Mustavi Maheen et al., 2022).

Z-AGI Labs (Narayan and Biswal, 2024) focused on stance detection, the CatBoost model based on TF-IDF was the top performer. This model achieved the highest F1-score of 70.80%, indicating its effectiveness in accurately categorizing stances in the context of climate activism. The paper explores the strengths of the model and its proficiency in handling the complexities of stance detection, compared to other models like Logistic Regression (Indra et al., 2016) and XGBoost (Haumahu et al., 2021), which also showed close performance.

HAMiSoN-Ensemble (Rodriguez-Garcia et al., 2024) present an ensemble approach of Roberta, a generative LLM - Llama 2, and Multi-task learning for stance detection. For the Llama 2, they used the Llama-2 7B Chat model with necessary modifications to adapt it to classification tasks. As for Multi-task learning, they used a RoBERTa-based model. They also used external data to improve their model performance but do not seem to show an added advantage over just using the competition dataset. Although they performed a majority voting ensemble approach of the 3 models, their best-performing model was the fine-tuned Roberta model, which achieved a F1-score of 73.13%. However, as mentioned in their paper, on a post-competition analysis, through some modifications in their approach, their ensemble system achieved a F1-score of 75.29%, which surpasses their RoBERTa-based system.

5 Discussion

The results and methodologies presented by the teams participating in this shared task offer valuable insights into the current state-of-the-art in hate speech detection, target identification, and stance detection. These tasks are essential in understanding the dynamics of online discourse, particularly on social media platforms. A notable trend across all subtasks is the heavy reliance on transformer-based models, particularly BERT and its variants. These models have shown exceptional capability in understanding the intricacies of natural language, especially in informal and idiosyncratic texts commonly found on social media. Their success underlines the importance of advanced models in handling the complexities of language in these contexts. Ensemble and hybrid approaches have also been prevalent, adopted by teams like AAST-NLP (El-Sayed and Nasr, 2024a) and CUET_Binary_Hackers (Farsi et al., 2024). Another critical aspect highlighted by several teams is handling class imbalance in datasets. The use of external datasets to enrich training data, as seen in the approaches of HAMiSoN-MTL (Rodriguez-Garcia and Centeno, 2024) and HAMiSoN-Generative (Fraile-Hernandez and Peñas, 2024), indicates a growing recognition of the value of diverse and expansive data sources. This approach can lead to better generalization and robustness of the models. Preprocessing and feature engineering also play a crucial role, as demonstrated by teams like MasonPerplexity (Emran et al., 2024), and Bryndza (Suppa et al., 2024). The way data is prepared and presented to models can significantly impact their effectiveness, highlighting the importance of meticulous data handling. Incorporating the latest advancements in LLMs further enriches the discussion of shared tasks' outcomes and future directions. The use of LLMs, as demonstrated by teams like Bryndza (Suppa et al., 2024) and MasonPerplexity (Emran et al., 2024), marks a significant shift in the approach to understanding and processing natural language on social media platforms. Despite these advances, several challenges and potential future directions emerge. Ensuring that models perform well across different contexts remains a significant challenge, given the variability in expressions of hate speech and stances. Additionally, the subtlety and ambiguity in language use, especially in these domains, continue to pose significant hurdles.

6 Conclusion

The shared task at the CASE 2024 workshop has made significant strides in advancing our understanding of hate speech detection, target identification, and stance detection in social media contexts, focusing on Twitter conversations about climate change. The diversity of approaches employed by the participants, predominantly centered around sophisticated transformer-based models like BERT and its variants, demonstrates the complexity of analyzing online discourse. However, this field of study still faces significant challenges, including ensuring the adaptability of models across various contexts, refining language processing to capture subtle nuances, and navigating the ethical implications of automated content analysis. This task has provided a comprehensive benchmark for current methodologies and set the stage for future research in the rapidly evolving domain of NLP, emphasizing the need for continued innovation in understanding the complexities of digital communication.

Acknowledgements

We would like to acknowledge the support of numerous reviewers who helped to provide reviews for this shared task. We would also like to acknowledge the support of various researchers who helped us to advertise this shared task. Moreover, this work is supported by the European Research Council Politus Project (ID:101082050) and European Union's HORIZON projects EFRA (ID: 101093026) and ECO-Ready (ID: 101084201).

Broader Impact

The broader impact of the CASE 2024 workshop's shared task extends across various domains, significantly influencing social media moderation, public policy, academic research, ethical AI development, and more. This research aids in enhancing content moderation on social media platforms, helping to create safer and more inclusive online communities by effectively identifying and mitigating harmful content. In public policy and awareness, insights from stance detection, particularly on critical issues like climate change, are invaluable for policymakers and advocacy groups, aiding in developing resonant communication strategies and informed policies. The task fosters interdisciplinary collaboration, merging expertise from linguistics, computer science, sociology, and environmental studies, enriching academic research and encouraging innovative approaches in NLP and social media analysis. It also contributes to the broader discourse on ethical AI, emphasizing the need for transparent and accountable AI systems, especially in sensitive areas like hate speech analysis. The showcasing of advanced models like GPT-4 and BERT highlights the continual evolution of NLP technologies, opening doors for more sophisticated and context-aware AI tools. Given the global nature of social media, the advancements in NLP and AI have the potential to impact digital communication worldwide. This shared task contributes to possible scalable solutions that can be adapted across different languages and cultures.

References

Surabhi Adhikari, Surendrabikram Thapa, Priyanka Singh, Huan Huo, Gnana Bharathy, and Mukesh Prasad. 2021. A comparative study of machine learning and nlp techniques for uses of stop words by patients in diagnosis of alzheimer's disease. In *2021 International Joint Conference on Neural Networks (IJCNN)*, pages 1–8. IEEE.

Takuya Akiba, Shotaro Sano, Toshihiko Yanase, Takeru Ohta, and Masanori Koyama. 2019. Optuna: A next-generation hyperparameter optimization framework. In *Proceedings of the 25th ACM SIGKDD international conference on knowledge discovery & data mining*, pages 2623–2631.

Abeer ALDayel and Walid Magdy. 2021. Stance detection on social media: State of the art and trends. *Information Processing & Management*, 58(4):102597.

Tom Brown, Benjamin Mann, Nick Ryder, Melanie Subbiah, Jared D Kaplan, Prafulla Dhariwal, Arvind Neelakantan, Pranav Shyam, Girish Sastry, Amanda Askell, et al. 2020. Language models are few-shot learners. *Advances in neural information processing systems*, 33:1877–1901.

Tommaso Caselli, Valerio Basile, Jelena Mitrović, and Michael Granitzer. 2021. Hatebert: Retraining bert for abusive language detection in english.

Kyunghyun Cho, Bart van Merrienboer, Caglar Gulcehre, Dzmitry Bahdanau, Fethi Bougares, Holger Schwenk, and Yoshua Bengio. 2014. Learning phrase representations using rnn encoder-decoder for statistical machine translation.

Christina Christodoulou. 2024. NLPDame at ClimateActivism 2024: Mistral Sequence Classification with PEFT for Hate Speech, Targets and Stance Event Detection. In *Proceedings of the 7th Workshop on Challenges and Applications of Automated Extraction of Socio-political Events from Text (CASE)*, Malta. Association for Computational Linguistics.

Alexis Conneau, Kartikay Khandelwal, Naman Goyal, Vishrav Chaudhary, Guillaume Wenzek, Francisco Guzmán, Edouard Grave, Myle Ott, Luke Zettlemoyer, and Veselin Stoyanov. 2020. Unsupervised cross-lingual representation learning at scale.

Prithiviraj Damodaran. 2023. Flashrank, lightest and fastest 2nd stage reranker for search pipelines. https://doi.org/10.5281/zenodo.10426927.

Jacob Devlin, Ming-Wei Chang, Kenton Lee, and Kristina Toutanova. 2019. Bert: Pre-training of deep bidirectional transformers for language understanding.

Ahmed El-Sayed and Omar Nasr. 2024a. AAST-NLP at ClimateActivism 2024: Ensemble-Based Climate Activism Stance and Hate Speech Detection : Leveraging Pretrained Language Models. In *Proceedings of the 7th Workshop on Challenges and Applications of Automated Extraction of Socio-political Events from Text (CASE)*, Malta. Association for Computational Linguistics.

Ahmed El-Sayed and Omar Nasr. 2024b. AAST-NLP at Multimodal Hate Speech Event Detection 2024 : A Multimodal Approach for Classification of Text-Embedded Images Based on CLIP and BERT-Based Models. In *Proceedings of the 7th Workshop on Challenges and Applications of Automated Extraction of Socio-political Events from Text (CASE)*, Malta. Association for Computational Linguistics.

Al Nahian Bin Emran, Amrita Ganguly, Sadiya Sayara Chowdhury Puspo, Dhiman Goswami, and Md Nishat Raihan. 2024. MasonPerplexity at ClimateActivism 2024: Integrating Advanced Ensemble Techniques and Data Augmentation for Climate Activism Stance and Hate Event Identification. In *Proceedings of the 7th Workshop on Challenges and Applications of Automated Extraction of Socio-political Events from Text (CASE)*, Malta. Association for Computational Linguistics.

Theodoros Evgeniou and Massimiliano Pontil. 2001. Support vector machines: Theory and applications. volume 2049, pages 249–257.

Salman Farsi, Asrarul Hoque Eusha, and Mohammad Shamsul Arefin. 2024. CUET_Binary_Hackers at ClimateActivism 2024: A Comprehensive Evaluation and Superior Performance of Transformer Models in Hate Speech Detection and Stance Classification for Climate Activism. In *Proceedings of the 7th Workshop on Challenges and Applications of Automated Extraction of Socio-political Events from Text (CASE)*, Malta. Association for Computational Linguistics.

Jennifer R Fownes, Chao Yu, and Drew B Margolin. 2018. Twitter and climate change. *Sociology Compass*, 12(6):e12587.

Jesus M. Fraile-Hernandez and Anselmo Peñas. 2024. HAMiSoN-Generative at ClimateActivism 2024: Stance Detection using generative large language models. In *Proceedings of the 7th Workshop on Challenges and Applications of Automated Extraction of Socio-political Events from Text (CASE)*, Malta. Association for Computational Linguistics.

Amrita Gangul, Al Nahian Bin Emran, Sadiya Sayara Chowdhury Puspo, Md Nishat Raihan, Dhiman Goswami, and Marcos Zampieri. 2024. Mason-Perplexity at Multimodal Hate Speech Event Detection 2024: Hate Speech and Target Detection Using Transformer Ensembles. In *Proceedings of the 7th Workshop on Challenges and Applications of Automated Extraction of Socio-political Events from Text (CASE)*, Malta. Association for Computational Linguistics.

Akash Gautam, Puneet Mathur, Rakesh Gosangi, Debanjan Mahata, Ramit Sawhney, and Rajiv Ratn Shah. 2020. #metooma: Multi-aspect annotations of tweets related to the metoo movement. *Proceedings of the International AAAI Conference on Web and Social Media*, 14(1):209–216.

Jonas Gehring, Michael Auli, David Grangier, and Yann N. Dauphin. 2017. A convolutional encoder model for neural machine translation.

Njagi Dennis Gitari, Zhang Zuping, Hanyurwimfura Damien, and Jun Long. 2015. A lexicon-based approach for hate speech detection. *International Journal of Multimedia and Ubiquitous Engineering*, 10(4):215–230.

Momchil Hardalov, Arnav Arora, Preslav Nakov, and Isabelle Augenstein. 2022. A survey on stance detection for mis- and disinformation identification. In *Findings of the Association for Computational Linguistics: NAACL 2022*, pages 1259–1277, Seattle, United States. Association for Computational Linguistics.

Md Arid Hasan, Shudipta Das, Afiyat Anjum, Firoj Alam, Anika Anjum, Avijit Sarker, and Sheak Rashed Haider Noori. 2023. Zero-and few-shot prompting with llms: A comparative study with fine-tuned models for bangla sentiment analysis. *arXiv preprint arXiv:2308.10783*.

JP Haumahu, SDH Permana, and Y Yaddarabullah. 2021. Fake news classification for indonesian news using extreme gradient boosting (xgboost). In *IOP Conference Series: Materials Science and Engineering*, volume 1098, page 052081. IOP Publishing.

Pengcheng He, Jianfeng Gao, and Weizhu Chen. 2021. Debertav3: Improving deberta using electra-style pre-training with gradient-disentangled embedding sharing. *arXiv preprint arXiv:2111.09543*.

Pengcheng He, Xiaodong Liu, Jianfeng Gao, and Weizhu Chen. 2020. Deberta: Decoding-enhanced bert with disentangled attention. *arXiv preprint arXiv:2006.03654*.

Sepp Hochreiter and Jürgen Schmidhuber. 1997. Long short-term memory. *Neural computation*, 9(8):1735–1780.

Edward J Hu, Phillip Wallis, Zeyuan Allen-Zhu, Yuanzhi Li, Shean Wang, Lu Wang, Weizhu Chen, et al. 2021. Lora: Low-rank adaptation of large language models. In *International Conference on Learning Representations*.

ST Indra, Liza Wikarsa, and Rinaldo Turang. 2016. Using logistic regression method to classify tweets into the selected topics. In *2016 international conference on advanced computer science and information systems (icacsis)*, pages 385–390. IEEE.

Farhan Ahmad Jafri, Mohammad Aman Siddiqui, Surendrabikram Thapa, Kritesh Rauniyar, Usman Naseem, and Imran Razzak. 2023. Uncovering political hate speech during indian election campaign: A new low-resource dataset and baselines.

Albert Q Jiang, Alexandre Sablayrolles, Arthur Mensch, Chris Bamford, Devendra Singh Chaplot, Diego de las Casas, Florian Bressand, Gianna Lengyel, Guillaume Lample, Lucile Saulnier, et al. 2023. Mistral 7b. *arXiv preprint arXiv:2310.06825*.

Armand Joulin, Edouard Grave, Piotr Bojanowski, Matthijs Douze, Hérve Jégou, and Tomas Mikolov. 2016. Fasttext.zip: Compressing text classification models. *arXiv preprint arXiv:1612.03651*.

Ahmet Kaya, Oguzhan Ozcelik, and Cagri Toraman. 2024. ARC-NLP at ClimateActivism 2024: Stance and Hate Speech Detection by Generative and Encoder Models Optimized with Tweet-Specific Elements. In *Proceedings of the 7th Workshop on Challenges and Applications of Automated Extraction of Socio-political Events from Text (CASE)*, Malta. Association for Computational Linguistics.

Guolin Ke, Qi Meng, Thomas Finley, Taifeng Wang, Wei Chen, Weidong Ma, Qiwei Ye, and Tie-Yan Liu. 2017. Lightgbm: A highly efficient gradient boosting decision tree. *Advances in neural information processing systems*, 30.

Patrick Lewis, Ethan Perez, Aleksandra Piktus, Fabio Petroni, Vladimir Karpukhin, Naman Goyal, Heinrich Küttler, Mike Lewis, Wen-tau Yih, Tim Rocktäschel, et al. 2020. Retrieval-augmented generation for knowledge-intensive nlp tasks. *Advances in Neural Information Processing Systems*, 33:9459–9474.

Yinhan Liu, Myle Ott, Naman Goyal, Jingfei Du, Mandar Joshi, Danqi Chen, Omer Levy, Mike Lewis, Luke Zettlemoyer, and Veselin Stoyanov. 2019. Roberta: A robustly optimized bert pretraining approach. *arXiv preprint arXiv:1907.11692*.

Gilles Louppe. 2015. Understanding random forests: From theory to practice.

Ghazaleh Mahmoudi and Sauleh Eetemadi. 2024. IUST at ClimateActivism 2024: Towards Optimal Stance Detection: A Systematic Study of Architectural Choices and Data Cleaning Techniques. In *Proceedings of the 7th Workshop on Challenges and Applications of Automated Extraction of Socio-political Events from Text (CASE)*, Malta. Association for Computational Linguistics.

Tao Mei, Yong Rui, Shipeng Li, and Qi Tian. 2014. Multimedia search reranking: A literature survey. *ACM Computing Surveys (CSUR)*, 46(3):1–38.

Tomas Mikolov, Kai Chen, Greg Corrado, and Jeffrey Dean. 2013. Efficient estimation of word representations in vector space. *arXiv preprint arXiv:1301.3781*.

Saif Mohammad, Svetlana Kiritchenko, Parinaz Sobhani, Xiaodan Zhu, and Colin Cherry. 2016a. A dataset for detecting stance in tweets. In *Proceedings of the Tenth International Conference on Language Resources and Evaluation (LREC'16)*, pages 3945–3952.

Saif Mohammad, Svetlana Kiritchenko, Parinaz Sobhani, Xiaodan Zhu, and Colin Cherry. 2016b. Semeval-2016 task 6: Detecting stance in tweets. In *Proceedings of the 10th international workshop on semantic evaluation (SemEval-2016)*, pages 31–41.

Ioannis Mollas, Zoe Chrysopoulou, Stamatis Karlos, and Grigorios Tsoumakas. 2022. Ethos: a multi-label hate speech detection dataset. *Complex & Intelligent Systems*, 8(6):4663–4678.

Julio Reyes Montesinos and Alvaro Rodrigo. 2024. HAMiSoN-baselines at ClimateActivism 2024: A Study on the Use of External Data for Hate Speech and Stance Detection. In *Proceedings of the 7th Workshop on Challenges and Applications of Automated Extraction of Socio-political Events from Text (CASE)*, Malta. Association for Computational Linguistics.

Syed Mustavi Maheen, Moshiur Rahman Faisal, Md. Rafakat Rahman, and Md. Shahriar Karim. 2022. Alternative non-BERT model choices for the textual classification in low-resource languages and environments. In *Proceedings of the Third Workshop on Deep Learning for Low-Resource Natural Language Processing*, pages 192–202, Hybrid. Association for Computational Linguistics.

Nikhil Narayan and Mrutyunjay Biswal. 2024. Z-AGI Labs at ClimateActivism 2024: Stance and Hate Event Detection using Tf-Idf and LSTM. In *Proceedings of the 7th Workshop on Challenges and Applications of Automated Extraction of Socio-political Events from Text (CASE)*, Malta. Association for Computational Linguistics.

Dat Quoc Nguyen, Thanh Vu, and Anh Tuan Nguyen. 2020. Bertweet: A pre-trained language model for english tweets. In *Proceedings of the 2020 Conference on Empirical Methods in Natural Language Processing: System Demonstrations*, pages 9 14.

Oguzhan Ozcelik and Cagri Toraman. 2022. Named entity recognition in turkish: A comparative study with detailed error analysis. *Information Processing & Management*, 59(6):103065.

Jeffrey Pennington, Richard Socher, and Christopher D Manning. 2014. Glove: Global vectors for word representation. In *Proceedings of the 2014 conference on empirical methods in natural language processing (EMNLP)*, pages 1532–1543.

Liudmila Prokhorenkova, Gleb Gusev, Aleksandr Vorobev, Anna Veronika Dorogush, and Andrey Gulin. 2018. Catboost: unbiased boosting with categorical features. *Advances in neural information processing systems*, 31.

Vasile Păiș. 2024. RACAI at ClimateActivism 2024: Improving Detection of Hate Speech by Extending LLM Predictions with Handcrafted Features. In *Proceedings of the 7th Workshop on Challenges and Applications of Automated Extraction of Socio-political Events from Text (CASE)*, Malta. Association for Computational Linguistics.

Kanagasabai Rajaraman, Hariram Veeramani, Saravanan Rajamanickam, Adam Maciej Westerski, and Jung Jae Kim. 2023. Semantists at imagearg-2023: Exploring cross-modal contrastive and ensemble models for multimodal stance and persuasiveness classification. In *Proceedings of the 10th Workshop on Argument Mining*, pages 181–186.

Juan Ramos et al. 2003. Using tf-idf to determine word relevance in document queries. In *Proceedings of the first instructional conference on machine learning*, volume 242, pages 29–48. Citeseer.

Kritesh Rauniyar, Sweta Poudel, Shuvam Shiwakoti, Surendrabikram Thapa, Junaid Rashid, Jungeun Kim, Muhammad Imran, and Usman Naseem. 2023. Multi-aspect annotation and analysis of nepali tweets on anti-establishment election discourse. *IEEE Access*.

Raquel Rodriguez-Garcia and Roberto Centeno. 2024. HAMiSoN-MTL at ClimateActivism 2024: Detection of Hate Speech, Targets and Stance using Multitask Learning. In *Proceedings of the 7th Workshop on Challenges and Applications of Automated Extraction of Socio-political Events from Text (CASE)*, Malta. Association for Computational Linguistics.

Raquel Rodriguez-Garcia, Julio Reyes Montesinos, Jesus M. Fraile-Hernandez, and Anselmo Peñas. 2024. HAMiSoN-Ensemble at ClimateActivism 2024: Ensemble of RoBERTa, Llama 2 and Multitask for Stance Detection. In *Proceedings of the 7th Workshop on Challenges and Applications of Automated Extraction of Socio-political Events from Text (CASE)*, Malta. Association for Computational Linguistics.

Diptanu Sarkar, Marcos Zampieri, Tharindu Ranasinghe, and Alexander Ororbia. 2021. fBERT: A neural transformer for identifying offensive content. In *Findings of the Association for Computational Linguistics: EMNLP 2021*, pages 1792–1798, Punta Cana, Dominican Republic. Association for Computational Linguistics.

Shuvam Shiwakoti, Surendrabikram Thapa, Kritesh Rauniyar, Akshyat Shah, Aashish Bhandari, and Usman Naseem. 2024. Analyzing the dynamics of climate change discourse on twitter: A new annotated corpus and multi-aspect classification. *Preprint.*

Annika Stechemesser, Anders Levermann, and Leonie Wenz. 2022. Temperature impacts on hate speech online: evidence from 4 billion geolocated tweets from the usa. *The Lancet Planetary Health*, 6(9):e714–e725.

Marek Suppa, Daniel Skala, Daniela Jass, Samuel Sucik, and Andrej Svec. 2024. Bryndza at ClimateActivism 2024: Stance, Target and Hate Event Detection via Retrieval-Augmented GPT-4. In *Proceedings of the 7th Workshop on Challenges and Applications of Automated Extraction of Socio-political Events from Text (CASE)*, Malta. Association for Computational Linguistics.

Hristo Tanev. 2024. JRC at ClimateActivism 2024: Lexicon-based Detection of Hate Speech. In *Proceedings of the 7th Workshop on Challenges and Applications of Automated Extraction of Socio-political Events from Text (CASE)*, Malta. Association for Computational Linguistics.

Surendrabikram Thapa, Kritesh Rauniyar, Shuvam Shiwakoti, Sweta Poudel, Usman Naseem, and Mehwish Nasim. 2023. Nehate: Large-scale annotated data shedding light on hate speech in nepali local election discourse. In *ECAI 2023*, pages 2346–2353. IOS Press.

Hugo Touvron, Louis Martin, Kevin Stone, Peter Albert, Amjad Almahairi, Yasmine Babaei, Nikolay Bashlykov, Soumya Batra, Prajjwal Bhargava, Shruti Bhosale, et al. 2023. Llama 2: Open foundation and fine-tuned chat models. *arXiv preprint arXiv:2307.09288.*

Ashish Vaswani, Noam Shazeer, Niki Parmar, Jakob Uszkoreit, Llion Jones, Aidan N Gomez, Łukasz Kaiser, and Illia Polosukhin. 2017. Attention is all you need. *Advances in neural information processing systems*, 30.

Hannah Wallis and Laura S Loy. 2021. What drives pro-environmental activism of young people? a survey study on the fridays for future movement. *Journal of Environmental Psychology*, 74:101581.

Nicolas Webersinke, Mathias Kraus, Julia Anna Bingler, and Markus Leippold. 2022. Climatebert: A pretrained language model for climate-related text.

Marcos Zampieri, Shervin Malmasi, Preslav Nakov, Sara Rosenthal, Noura Farra, and Ritesh Kumar. 2019a. Predicting the type and target of offensive posts in social media. In *Proceedings of the 2019 Conference of the North American Chapter of the Association for Computational Linguistics: Human Language Technologies, Volume 1 (Long and Short Papers)*, pages 1415–1420, Minneapolis, Minnesota. Association for Computational Linguistics.

Marcos Zampieri, Shervin Malmasi, Preslav Nakov, Sara Rosenthal, Noura Farra, and Ritesh Kumar. 2019b. Semeval-2019 task 6: Identifying and categorizing offensive language in social media (offenseval). *arXiv preprint arXiv:1903.08983.*

Linda Zhou, Andrew Caines, Ildiko Pete, and Alice Hutchings. 2023. Automated hate speech detection and span extraction in underground hacking and extremist forums. *Natural Language Engineering*, 29(5):1247–1274.

A Related Works

In a range of social contexts, a link has been shown between weather and offline abuse. Concurrently, there is a significant number of online social issues as a result of almost every element of daily life becoming rapidly digitalized. Hate speech on the internet has become a major issue and has been demonstrated to exacerbate mental health issues, particularly in youth and marginalized communities (Stechemesser et al., 2022). ALDayel and Magdy (2021) explore the new trends and diverse uses of stance detection on social media. Stance detection on social media is a developing opinion-mining paradigm for various political as well as social purposes in which sentiment analysis may not be the best approach. Zampieri et al. (2019a) gathered the Offensive Language Identification Dataset (OLID), a new dataset containing tweets annotated for offensive content using a fine-grained three-layer annotation scheme, and compared the effectiveness of various machine learning models on OLID. They target a variety of different types of offensive content. Gautam et al. (2020) presented a dataset of 9,973 tweets on the MeToo movement that were manually annotated for five different language dimensions: dialogue acts, sarcasm, hate speech, relevance, and stance. The data was then examined in terms of keywords, label correlations, and geographical distribution. Mollas et al. (2022) provided access to 'ETHOS' (multi-labEl haTe speecH detectiOn dataSet), a textual dataset consisting of two variants: binary and multi-label, based on comments from Reddit and YouTube that were verified by the Figure-Eight crowdsourcing platform. Additionally, the annotation protocol—an active sampling process—that was utilized to create this dataset—was presented, in addition.

B Evaluation and Competition

This section describes the structure of our competition, along with the methodology used to determine ranks and other relevant data.

B.1 Evaluation Metrics

To evaluate the effectiveness of the participants' contributions, we used macro F1-score, accuracy, precision, and recall. The participants' ranks were determined using the macro F1-score sorting approach.

B.2 Competition Setup

We used the Codalab[7] to organize our competition. The competition consisted of two phases: an assessment phase where competitors got comfortable with the Codalab system and a testing phase where performance was used to determine the final ranking on the scoreboard.

Registration: A total of 100 participants registered for our competition, and the diverse array of email domains used indicated its success in attracting individuals from various parts of the world. Among the registrants, 23 teams submitted their predicted outcomes, reflecting active engagement and interest in the competition.

Competition Timelines: On November 1, 2023, training and evaluation data were made available, marking the commencement of the competition. The first half was evaluation-focused, with the main goal being to familiarize participants with Codalab. Participants were given access to the labels of the evaluation information in order to help with this process. The test phase then began on November 30, 2023, when test data was provided without any ground truth labels. The test session, which was originally scheduled to finish on January 5, 2024, was extended until January 7, 2024, in response to requests from many participants, displaying flexibility in meeting participant demands. In addition, it was finally determined that system description papers must be submitted by January 13, 2024. Participants were given a certain period to provide their system designs and approaches by this crucial deadline. The well-planned schedule made it possible for the competition to go through its phases thoroughly and organized, giving participants plenty of time to become involved, get familiar with one another, and submit their thoughtful submissions by the deadlines.

[7]The competition page can be found here: `https://codalab.lisn.upsaclay.fr/competitions/16206`.

A Concise Report of the 7th Workshop on Challenges and Applications of Automated Extraction of Socio-political Events from Text

Ali Hürriyetoğlu
Wageningen Food Safety Research, Netherlands
ali.hurriyetoglu@wur.nl

Surendrabikram Thapa
Virginia Tech
Blacksburg, USA
sbt@vt.edu

Gökçe Uludoğan
Bogazici University
Istanbul, Turkey
gokce.uludogan@bogazici.edu.tr

Somaiyeh Dehghan
Sabanci University
Istanbul, Turkey
somaiyeh.dehghan@sabanciuniv.edu

Hristo Tanev
European Commission, Joint Research Centre
Ispra, Italy
hristo.tanev@ec.europa.eu

Abstract

In this paper, we provide a brief overview of the 7th workshop on Challenges and Applications of Automated Extraction of Socio-political Events from Text (CASE) co-located with EACL 2024. This workshop consisted of regular papers, system description papers submitted by shared task participants, and overview papers of shared tasks held. This workshop series has been bringing together experts and enthusiasts from technical and social science fields, providing a platform for better understanding event information. This workshop not only advances text-based event extraction but also facilitates research in event extraction in multimodal settings.

1 Introduction

In today's digital era, the voluminous and readily available data on socio-political, economic, and environmental phenomena hold transformative potential for data-driven analysis in the social and human sciences (Hürriyetoğlu et al., 2021a; Chen et al., 2023). This wealth of data supports informed policymaking by providing comprehensive insights into complex issues ranging from political unrest and environmental disasters to global health and economic crises (Shu and Ye, 2023). The rising demand by governments, international organizations, and NGOs for high-quality, actionable information underscores the critical role of data in addressing challenges, aiding those impacted by crises, and enhancing citizen welfare in various domains (Hürriyetoğlu et al., 2021c).

Recent advancements underscore the importance of leveraging big data for social good, highlighting how data-driven approaches can revolutionize our understanding and intervention strategies in critical areas such as humanitarian aid, healthcare, and environmental protection. Evans et al. (2023) introduce a privacy-preserving data analysis system that offers both privacy guarantees for individuals and statistical validity for researchers, facilitating the use of sensitive data in social science research. Furthermore, crowd-sourced text analysis, as discussed by Benoit et al. (2016), represents a paradigm shift in how data is collected and analyzed, enabling rapid, flexible, and reproducible data production that matches expert-level accuracy.

The intersection of data science with policy analysis suggests a promising avenue for integrating data-driven insights into decision-making processes. Zhang et al. (2020) highlight the convergence of data science and policy analysis, indicating an emergent cross-disciplinary domain where data science accelerates and enriches policy research. This integration is crucial for developing effective policies that are informed by empirical data and grounded in a deep understanding of complex societal dynamics. Thus, it is evident that data science is instrumental in devising strategies to prevent or mitigate conflicts, deliver aid to affected populations, enhance the well-being of citizens, and safeguard them through a multitude of approaches. The public's resistance to COVID-19 measures during 2020-2022 (Prakash and Das, 2022; Fainstein et al., 2023) and the conflict between Russia and Ukraine (Bhandari et al., 2023; Thapa et al., 2022) serve as prime instances of the critical need to harness this data for real-world impact, highlighting the public's growing demand for

Proceedings of the 7th Workshop on Challenges and Applications of Automated Extraction of Socio-political Events from Text (CASE 2024), pages 248–255
March 22, 2024

timely information regarding mass gatherings and societal trends.

In this context, the workshop titled 'Challenges and Applications of Automated Extraction of Socio-political Events from Text' (CASE 2024) plays a pivotal role. Organized as part of EACL 2024, the seventh edition of this workshop marks the continuation of a workshop series that has been ongoing since its inception (Hürriyetoğlu et al., 2022, 2021b, 2020). This workshop aims to explore the advancements and hurdles in the automated extraction of socio-political events from textual data, offering a platform for discussing the latest research findings, innovative methodologies, and the future of automated text analysis in capturing and interpreting complex social phenomena. The workshop encompasses a range of activities, including presentations of accepted papers, shared tasks that challenge participants, and keynote speeches from leading experts in the field, providing valuable insights into the state of the art and fostering collaboration among researchers and practitioners. This paper is a brief overview giving insights into the wide range of activities at CASE 2024.

2 Accepted Papers

This year, seven papers were accepted out of twelve submissions. Below, we provide brief descriptions of accepted papers.

- Fellman et al. (2024) created a new dataset called FanConInfo of comic convention websites with cleaned HTML, rendered screenshots, and human annotations for event name, start date, end date, and location. The authors compared the performance of GPT-4 Vision, GPT-4 Text, and GPT-3.5 on the FanConInfo dataset. The findings revealed that the vision-based GPT-4 model outperformed the text-based versions, achieving an 85% accuracy in exact match, significantly higher than GPT-4 Text's 64% and GPT-3.5's 59%. This underscores the effectiveness of visual methods in extracting web data. The research highlighted the importance of integrating textual and visual data for improved web scraping and suggested multimodal comprehension as a key direction for future AI advancements.

- Loerakker et al. (2024) trained and evaluated several language models on Dutch tweets to analyze their ability to classify tweets that express discontent. They hypothesize that people expressing discontent are more likely to protest. The authors found that models specifically pretrained on Twitter data, like Bernice (DeLucia et al., 2022) and TwHIN-BERT (Zhang et al., 2022), substantially outperform other models in classifying discontent tweets. The results highlight the importance of selecting appropriate models trained on similar data to the task domain. Though discontent classification is nuanced, the authors show it can help filter relevant messages and identify possible protests if models optimized for low false positives are used.

- Bakker et al. (2024) proposed a novel pipeline to automatically extract timelines from decision letters of Dutch FOIA requests, using SpaCy[1] to extract dates and ChatGPT to extract and classify event phrases. The authors created a dataset of 100 manually annotated decision letters and showed that the pipeline achieved 94% date extraction accuracy. The key contribution is demonstrating how to leverage ChatGPT's few-shot learning capabilities to build an accurate timeline extractor for a low-resource domain using just a small annotated dataset, without needing extensive training. The proposed approach effectively extracts and classifies events into coherent timelines from decision letters.

- Tanev (2024) presented a new weakly supervised method for sentence-level event detection using linear prototype patterns and approximate pattern matching with BERT (Devlin et al., 2019) embeddings. The method involves creating a set of linear event detection patterns (e.g. 'disease outbreak', 'number people were infected') that serve as prototypes for events of interest. BERT's contextualized word representations are then utilized to find semantic similarities between these patterns and text fragments, allowing the identification of related event phrases with high lexical and syntactic variability. The approach was evaluated on detecting two event types – new disease cases and terrorist attacks– where it achieved promising F1 scores comparable to supervised systems. A key advantage of this BERT-based technique is that it combines

[1] spacy.io/

the interpretability of pattern-based methods with BERT's implicit semantic knowledge to effectively handle linguistic variations while avoiding extensive supervision.

- Olsen et al. (2024) presented a contrast of socio-political event datasets from political science and NLP fields, highlighting differences in abstraction, source accessibility, and temporal dynamics. The authors showed that political science datasets focus on abstract event representations, while NLP datasets offer precise textual annotations for event extraction. The discrepancies include the level of detail, availability of source texts, and dataset dynamism. Further, they showed that recent initiatives aim to integrate these approaches, enhancing the richness and applicability of event data, yet also caution against ethical and bias considerations in politically sensitive contexts.

- Dehghan and Yanikoglu (2024) evaluated ChatGPT's efficiency in identifying hate speech within Turkish tweets, contrasting its performance against BERTurk's (Schweter, 2020) supervised fine-tuning on the SIU2023-NST (Arın et al., 2023) dataset. Results demonstrate BERTurk's superior accuracy and lower mean squared error (MSE) in detecting hate speech and assessing its intensity over both zero-shot and few-shot learning approaches of ChatGPT. Despite ChatGPT's advanced capabilities, BERTurk's specificity for the task underlines the importance of model and prompt design, suggesting ChatGPT's potential as a supplementary tool for dataset annotation with careful prompt crafting.

- Uludoğan et al. (2024b) introduced TurkishHatePrintCorpus, a new dataset of over 6600 Turkish news articles annotated for hate speech against ethnic, national, or religious groups. They also developed a model called HateTargetBERT that combines BERT representations with linguistic features tailored to detecting hate speech against specific groups. Experiments demonstrate that HateTargetBERT performs comparably or better than BERT alone and substantially outperforms using just the linguistic features. The target-oriented linguistic features also enable explaining the model's predictions. By releasing the dataset, model code, and features, the authors provide an important new resource for studying hate speech and show that augmenting BERT with hate speech linguistic patterns for particular groups is an effective and interpretable approach to detecting such content in Turkish news.

3 Shared Tasks

This edition of the workshop featured two shared tasks. In addition to these two tasks, the workshop also welcomed submissions to previously organized shared tasks in earlier editions of CASE workshops.

3.1 Task 1: Climate Activism Stance and Hate Event Detection Shared Task

Realizing the important role of social media in global discussions on climate change, this shared task is built on the fact that there is a diversity of opinions, including different points of view and stances including instances of hate speech. By dissecting the varied perspectives on climate activism, the shared task aimed to advance capabilities of automated systems in processing and analyzing climate-related social media discourse, particularly on Twitter, now X. The task was divided into three subtasks: A) Hate Speech Detection, B) Targets of Hate Speech Detection, and C) Stance Detection, each addressing different facets of the discourse surrounding climate change activism on social media.

Subtask A (Hate Speech Detection) required participants to classify tweets as exhibiting hate speech or not. This subtask drew attention to the prevalence of aggressive and harmful language in online discussions on climate change, reflecting the intensity of emotions and opinions on the topic. Subtask B (Targets of Hate Speech Detection) delved deeper by identifying the hate speech targets within tweets, categorizing them into individuals, organizations, or communities. This nuanced approach aimed to understand the direction of hate and its potential impacts on targeted groups/individuals. Subtask C (Stance Detection) focused on detecting the stance expressed in tweets towards climate change, categorizing them as supportive, oppositional, or neutral. This subtask sheds light on the diverse viewpoints in the climate change debate, emphasizing the complexity of public opinion on this global issue.

Thapa et al. (2024a) provide an overview of the shared task along with brief detail on the methods used by participants. The shared task hosted on codalab[2] attracted over 100 teams, with 23 participants submitting results for Subtask A, 18 for Subtask B, and 19 for Subtask C, showcasing a wide range of methodologies and approaches. The participants' ranking was determined on the basis of the macro F1-score.

In Subtask A, the highest performance was achieved by the team CUET_Binary_Hackers (Farsi et al., 2024) with an impressive F1-score of 91.44%, indicating a high level of accuracy in detecting hate speech in tweets. Their approach, which included a variety of machine learning and deep learning models, emphasized the effectiveness of various advanced algorithms in processing and understanding the nuances of language used in social media discourse. The use of oversampling techniques and a range of feature extraction methods further highlighted the complexity of identifying hate speech and the need for advanced computational techniques in tackling this challenge.

Subtask B saw MasonPerplexity (Emran et al., 2024) securing the top position with an F1-score of 78.58%, demonstrating the challenge of accurately identifying the targets of hate speech in the context of climate activism tweets. Their approach involved the use of a weighted ensemble model, incorporating back translation techniques to address class imbalance. Their method highlighted the innovative strategies required to enhance model performance in the context of limited and imbalanced data. With BERTweet-Large (Nguyen et al., 2020), they were able to get the first position.

Finally, for Subtask C, ARC-NLP (Kaya et al., 2024) topped the leaderboard with the highest F1-score of 74.83%. They also used a modified version of BERTweet (Nguyen et al., 2020). Their method employed a short input tokenization length (96 tokens) and incorporated special tokens for tweet-specific elements. Overall, this subtask tried to aid a broader problem of stance detection which helps in understanding public opinion dynamics on pressing global issues like climate change.

The results and methodologies presented across all subtasks provide valuable insights into the state-of-the-art capabilities in processing and understanding social media discourse on climate change. The reliance on transformer-based models (Vaswani et al., 2017), Large-language models (Thapa et al., 2023b) and innovative data processing techniques across the subtasks reflects the advanced computational approaches required to tackle the complexities of natural language in social media. However, the subtasks also highlight ongoing challenges, such as dealing with data imbalance, understanding nuanced expressions of hate speech and stance, and the ethical considerations in automated content analysis.

3.2 Task 2: Hate Speech Detection in Turkish and Arabic Tweets

The HSD-2Lang Shared Task at CASE 2024 focused on detecting hate speech in Turkish and Arabic tweets, which is a significant problem on social media platforms. Divided into two subtasks, Subtask A aimed to identify hate speech in Turkish across various contexts, while Subtask B tackled hate speech detection in Arabic with limited data. Both subtasks were binary classification problems aimed at distinguishing hateful from non-hateful tweets. Uludoğan et al. (2024a) explain the overview of the shared task in detail.

Subtask A involved a dataset of Turkish tweets annotated for hate speech related to refugees, the Israel-Palestine conflict, and Anti-Greek discourse, with 9,140 tweets for training and 2,295 for testing. The objective was to develop a model capable of accurately identifying hate speech in these tweets, with performance evaluated using the F1 score across all topics. Subtask B presented a challenge in building hate speech models from a smaller and highly imbalanced dataset of Arabic tweets focusing on anti-refugee sentiment. The training set for Subtask B comprised 860 tweets, 82 of which were labeled as hateful, and the test set contained 522 tweets, 52 of them being hateful. Similarly to Subtask A, this subtask was also evaluated using the F1 score on the test data.

The shared task attracted 33 teams, with 10 submitting results for Subtask A and 5 for Subtask B. Participants employed various BERT-based models, highlighting the versatility and effectiveness of these models in processing and classifying social media content. The winning team in Subtask A, DetectiveReDASers (Qachfar et al., 2024), achieved an F1 score of 0.69645 using ConvBERTurk (Schweter, 2020) with a novel pooling strategy and cross-lingual data augmentation,

[2]The competition page can be found here: https://codalab.lisn.upsaclay.fr/competitions/16206.

demonstrating the impact of innovative approaches and ensemble methods on enhancing detection capabilities. The winning team of Subtask B, ReBERT (Yagci et al., 2024), achieved an F1 score of 0.68354 by fine-tuning AraBERTv0.2, originally developed by Antoun et al. (2020), which had been pretrained on around 60 million Arabic tweets. This updated AraBERT model incorporated emojis and common words previously excluded from its vocabulary and was applied directly without preprocessing. Notable performance differences were observed among systems using the same method, emphasizing the importance of hyperparameter tuning in improving model performance. The marginal performance gap between the two subtasks is intriguing, especially given that the Turkish dataset was three times larger than the Arabic set, highlighting the effectiveness of pretrained models. The findings of this shared task highlight the importance of model selection, tuning, and the impact of various preprocessing and hyper-parameter choices on detection capabilities, offering insights for future research in multilingual hate speech detection.

3.3 Extended Task: Multimodal Hate Speech Event Detection During Russia-Ukraine Crisis

This shared task was conducted for the first time in 2023 in CASE 2023 co-located at RANLP 2023. Following the massive interest in this task, this shared task saw an impressive number of impressions in 2024 as well. This task was structured into two subtasks aimed at detecting hate speech in text-embedded images and identifying the targets of such hate speech, with performance evaluated using the macro F1-score. The shared task, also hosted in codalab[3], attracted 73 registered participants and marked significant progress, achieving the best F1-scores of 87.27% and 80.05% in Subtask A and Subtask B, respectively. Thapa et al. (2024b) summarize the findings of different teams in this extended shared task.

In Subtask A, participants demonstrated remarkable achievements with CLTL (Wang and Markov, 2024) leading the pack by attaining an F1-score of 87.27%, setting a new benchmark for detecting hate speech in text-embedded images. This score beats the top-score by ARC-NLP (Sahin et al., 2023) from the same shared task in CASE 2023 (Thapa et al., 2023a; Hürriyetoğlu et al., 2023). CLTL (Wang and Markov, 2024) proposed a method for the Multimodal Hate Speech Event Detection Shared Task that combines separate text and image processing modules with a simple MLP and softmax layer, offering a flexible and efficient alternative to complex Large Vision Language Models (LVLMs). Their modular, MLP-based feature fusion approach not only set a competitive benchmark by achieving the first position but also demonstrated the importance of model simplicity and the potential for significant performance gains through fine-tuning.

Similarly, subtask B saw CLTL (Wang and Markov, 2024) once again achieving the top performance with an F1-score of 80.05%, showcasing the feasibility and effectiveness of their approach in identifying hate speech targets in a multimodal setting. Their approach yet again beats the highest leaderboard score from CASE 2023. The diverse methodologies and significant accomplishments reported in this shared task reflect the ongoing efforts to advance hate speech detection technologies. The results from both subtasks indicate a growing capability to not only detect hate speech in multimodal content but also understand its targets, contributing to safer digital environments.

4 Conclusion

In conclusion, the diverse range of papers and shared tasks presented at the workshop, from multimodal data analysis to fine-tuning language models for detecting hate speech and extracting event timelines, underscores the potential of automated text analysis in understanding complex socio-political phenomena. The workshop's emphasis on addressing real-world issues, such as understanding discourse related to climate change, online hate speech, and misinformation, through state-of-the-art computational techniques, not only sets new benchmarks for future research but also highlights the growing commitment within the community to leverage natural language processing for social good. In the coming years, the workshop will continue to advance the intersection of natural language processing and social good, promoting cutting-edge research and interdisciplinary collaboration to tackle complex socio-political challenges through automated text analysis.

[3]The competition page can be found here: https://codalab.lisn.upsaclay.fr/competitions/16203.

Acknowledgements

This work is supported by the European Research Council Politus Project (ID:101082050) and European Union's HORIZON projects EFRA (ID: 101093026) and ECO-Ready (ID: 101084201).

References

Wissam Antoun, Fady Baly, and Hazem Hajj. 2020. Arabert: Transformer-based model for arabic language understanding. In *Proceedings of the 4th Workshop on Open-Source Arabic Corpora and Processing Tools, with a Shared Task on Offensive Language Detection*, pages 9–15.

İnanç Arın, Zeynep Işık, Seçilay Kutal, Somaiyeh Dehghan, Arzucan Özgür, and Berrin Yanikoğlu. 2023. Siu2023-nst-hate speech detection contest. In *2023 31st Signal Processing and Communications Applications Conference (SIU)*, pages 1–4. IEEE.

Femke Bakker, Ruben van Heusden, and Maarten Marx. 2024. Timeline extraction from decision letters using chatgpt. In *Proceedings of The Seventh Workshop on Challenges and Applications of Automated Extraction of Socio-political Events from Text (CASE)*, Malta. Association for Computational Linguistics.

Kenneth Benoit, Drew Conway, Benjamin E Lauderdale, Michael Laver, and Slava Mikhaylov. 2016. Crowd-sourced text analysis: Reproducible and agile production of political data. *American Political Science Review*, 110(2):278–295.

Aashish Bhandari, Siddhant B Shah, Surendrabikram Thapa, Usman Naseem, and Mehwish Nasim. 2023. Crisishatemm: Multimodal analysis of directed and undirected hate speech in text-embedded images from russia-ukraine conflict. In *Proceedings of the IEEE/CVF Conference on Computer Vision and Pattern Recognition*, pages 1993–2002.

Yan Chen, Kate Sherren, Michael Smit, and Kyung Young Lee. 2023. Using social media images as data in social science research. *New Media & Society*, 25(4):849–871.

Somaiyeh Dehghan and Berrin Yanikoglu. 2024. Evaluating chatgpt's ability to detect hate speech in turkish tweets. In *Proceedings of The Seventh Workshop on Challenges and Applications of Automated Extraction of Socio-political Events from Text (CASE)*, Malta. Association for Computational Linguistics.

Alexandra DeLucia, Shijie Wu, Aaron Mueller, Carlos Aguirre, Philip Resnik, and Mark Dredze. 2022. Bernice: a multilingual pre-trained encoder for twitter. In *Proceedings of the 2022 conference on empirical methods in natural language processing*, pages 6191–6205.

Jacob Devlin, Ming-Wei Chang, Kenton Lee, and Kristina Toutanova. 2019. BERT: Pre-training of deep bidirectional transformers for language understanding. In *Proceedings of the 2019 Conference of the North American Chapter of the Association for Computational Linguistics: Human Language Technologies, Volume 1 (Long and Short Papers)*, pages 4171–4186, Minneapolis, Minnesota. Association for Computational Linguistics.

Al Nahian Bin Emran, Amrita Ganguly, Sadiya Sayara Chowdhury Puspo, Dhiman Goswami, and Md Nishat Raihan. 2024. MasonPerplexity at ClimateActivism 2024: Integrating Advanced Ensemble Techniques and Data Augmentation for Climate Activism Stance and Hate Event Identification. In *Proceedings of the 7th Workshop on Challenges and Applications of Automated Extraction of Socio-political Events from Text (CASE)*, Malta. Association for Computational Linguistics.

Georgina Evans, Gary King, Margaret Schwenzfeier, and Abhradeep Thakurta. 2023. Statistically valid inferences from privacy-protected data. *American Political Science Review*, 117(4):1275–1290.

Susan S Fainstein, John Forester, Kevin Lujan Lee, Tiara Na'puti, Julian Agyeman, Nicholas J Stewart, Johannes Novy, Aysin Dedekorkut Howes, Paul Burton, Stefan Norgaard, et al. 2023. Resistance and response in planning: Edited by susan s. fainstein and john forester. *Planning Theory & Practice*, pages 1–39.

Salman Farsi, Asrarul Hoque Eusha, and Mohammad Shamsul Arefin. 2024. CUET_Binary_Hackers at ClimateActivism 2024: A Comprehensive Evaluation and Superior Performance of Transformer Models in Hate Speech Detection and Stance Classification for Climate Activism. In *Proceedings of the 7th Workshop on Challenges and Applications of Automated Extraction of Socio-political Events from Text (CASE)*, Malta. Association for Computational Linguistics.

Evan Fellman, Jacob Tyo, and Zachary Lipton. 2024. The future of web data mining: Insights from multimodal and code-based extraction methods. In *Proceedings of The Seventh Workshop on Challenges and Applications of Automated Extraction of Socio-political Events from Text (CASE)*, Malta. Association for Computational Linguistics.

Ali Hürriyetoğlu, Osman Mutlu, Erdem Yörük, Farhana Ferdousi Liza, Ritesh Kumar, and Shyam Ratan. 2021a. Multilingual protest news detection - shared task 1, CASE 2021. In *Proceedings of the 4th Workshop on Challenges and Applications of Automated Extraction of Socio-political Events from Text (CASE 2021)*, pages 79–91, Online. Association for Computational Linguistics.

Ali Hürriyetoğlu, Hristo Tanev, Osman Mutlu, Surendrabikram Thapa, Fiona Anting Tan, and Erdem Yörük.

2023. Challenges and applications of automated extraction of socio-political events from text (CASE 2023): Workshop and shared task report. In *Proceedings of the 6th Workshop on Challenges and Applications of Automated Extraction of Socio-political Events from Text*, pages 167–175, Varna, Bulgaria. INCOMA Ltd., Shoumen, Bulgaria.

Ali Hürriyetoğlu, Hristo Tanev, Vanni Zavarella, Jakub Piskorski, Reyyan Yeniterzi, Osman Mutlu, Deniz Yuret, and Aline Villavicencio. 2021b. Challenges and applications of automated extraction of socio-political events from text (CASE 2021): Workshop and shared task report. In *Proceedings of the 4th Workshop on Challenges and Applications of Automated Extraction of Socio-political Events from Text (CASE 2021)*, pages 1–9, Online. Association for Computational Linguistics.

Ali Hürriyetoğlu, Hristo Tanev, Vanni Zavarella, Reyyan Yeniterzi, Osman Mutlu, and Erdem Yörük. 2022. Challenges and applications of automated extraction of socio-political events from text (CASE 2022): Workshop and shared task report. In *Proceedings of the 5th Workshop on Challenges and Applications of Automated Extraction of Socio-political Events from Text (CASE)*, pages 217–222, Abu Dhabi, United Arab Emirates (Hybrid). Association for Computational Linguistics.

Ali Hürriyetoğlu, Erdem Yörük, Osman Mutlu, Fırat Duruşan, Çağrı Yoltar, Deniz Yüret, and Burak Gürel. 2021c. Cross-context news corpus for protest event-related knowledge base construction. *Data Intelligence*, 3(2):308–335.

Ali Hürriyetoğlu, Vanni Zavarella, Hristo Tanev, Erdem Yörük, Ali Safaya, and Osman Mutlu. 2020. Automated extraction of socio-political events from news (AESPEN): Workshop and shared task report. In *Proceedings of the Workshop on Automated Extraction of Socio-political Events from News 2020*, pages 1–6, Marseille, France. European Language Resources Association (ELRA).

Ahmet Kaya, Oguzhan Ozcelik, and Cagri Toraman. 2024. ARC-NLP at ClimateActivism 2024: Stance and Hate Speech Detection by Generative and Encoder Models Optimized with Tweet-Specific Elements. In *Proceedings of the 7th Workshop on Challenges and Applications of Automated Extraction of Socio-political Events from Text (CASE)*, Malta. Association for Computational Linguistics.

Meagan Loerakker, Laurens Müter, and Marijn Schraagen. 2024. Fine-tuning language models on dutch protest event tweets. In *Proceedings of The Seventh Workshop on Challenges and Applications of Automated Extraction of Socio-political Events from Text (CASE)*, Malta. Association for Computational Linguistics.

Dat Quoc Nguyen, Thanh Vu, and Anh Tuan Nguyen. 2020. BERTweet: A pre-trained language model for English tweets. In *Proceedings of the 2020 Conference on Empirical Methods in Natural Language Processing: System Demonstrations*, pages 9–14, Online. Association for Computational Linguistics.

Helene Bøsei Olsen, Étienne Simon, Erik Velldal, and Lilja Øvrelid. 2024. Socio-political events of conflict and unrest: A survey of available datasets. In *Proceedings of The Seventh Workshop on Challenges and Applications of Automated Extraction of Socio-political Events from Text (CASE)*, Malta. Association for Computational Linguistics.

Ashish Viswanath Prakash and Saini Das. 2022. Explaining citizens' resistance to use digital contact tracing apps: A mixed-methods study. *International Journal of Information Management*, 63:102468.

Fatima Zahra Qachfar, Bryan E. Tuck, and Rakesh M. Verma. 2024. DetectiveReDASers at HSD-2Lang 2024: A new pooling strategy with cross-lingual augmentation and ensembling for hate speech detection in low-resource languages. In *Proceedings of The Seventh Workshop on Challenges and Applications of Automated Extraction of Socio-political Events from Text (CASE)*, Malta. Association for Computational Linguistics.

Umitcan Sahin, Izzet Emre Kucukkaya, Oguzhan Ozcelik, and Cagri Toraman. 2023. Arc-nlp at multimodal hate speech event detection 2023: Multimodal methods boosted by ensemble learning, syntactical and entity features. In *Proceedings of the 6th Workshop on Challenges and Applications of Automated Extraction of Socio-political Events from Text*, pages 71–78.

Stefan Schweter. 2020. BERTurk - BERT models for Turkish. https://zenodo.org/records/3770924.

Xiaoling Shu and Yiwan Ye. 2023. Knowledge discovery: Methods from data mining and machine learning. *Social Science Research*, 110:102817.

Hristo Tanev. 2024. Leveraging approximate pattern matching with bert for event detection. In *Proceedings of The Seventh Workshop on Challenges and Applications of Automated Extraction of Socio-political Events from Text (CASE)*, Malta. Association for Computational Linguistics.

Surendrabikram Thapa, Farhan Jafri, Ali Hürriyetoğlu, Francielle Vargas, Roy Ka-Wei Lee, and Usman Naseem. 2023a. Multimodal hate speech event detection-shared task 4, case 2023. In *Proceedings of the 6th Workshop on Challenges and Applications of Automated Extraction of Socio-political Events from Text*, pages 151–159.

Surendrabikram Thapa, Usman Naseem, and Mehwish Nasim. 2023b. From humans to machines: can chatgpt-like llms effectively replace human annotators in nlp tasks. In *Workshop Proceedings of the 17th International AAAI Conference on Web and Social Media*.

Surendrabikram Thapa, Kritesh Rauniyar, Farhan Ahmad Jafri, Shuvam Shiwakoti, Hariram Veeramani, Raghav Jain, Guneet Singh Kohli, Ali Hürriyetoğlu, and Usman Naseem. 2024a. Stance and hate event detection in tweets related to climate activism - shared task at case 2024. In *Proceedings of the 7th Workshop on Challenges and Applications of Automated Extraction of Socio-political Events from Text (CASE)*.

Surendrabikram Thapa, Kritesh Rauniyar, Farhan Ahmad Jafri, Hariram Veeramani, Raghav Jain, Sandesh Jain, Francielle Vargas, Ali Hürriyetoğlu, and Usman Naseem. 2024b. Extended multimodal hate speech event detection during russia-ukraine crisis - shared task at case 2024. In *Proceedings of the 7th Workshop on Challenges and Applications of Automated Extraction of Socio-political Events from Text (CASE)*.

Surendrabikram Thapa, Aditya Shah, Farhan Ahmad Jafri, Usman Naseem, and Imran Razzak. 2022. A multi-modal dataset for hate speech detection on social media: Case-study of russia-ukraine conflict. In *CASE 2022-5th Workshop on Challenges and Applications of Automated Extraction of Socio-Political Events from Text, Proceedings of the Workshop*. Association for Computational Linguistics.

Gökçe Uludoğan, Somaiyeh Dehghan, İnanç Arın, Elif Erol, Berrin Yanikoglu, and Arzucan Özgür. 2024a. Overview of the Hate Speech Detection in Turkish and Arabic Tweets (HSD-2Lang) Shared Task at CASE 2024. In *Proceedings of The Seventh Workshop on Challenges and Applications of Automated Extraction of Socio-political Events from Text (CASE)*, Malta. Association for Computational Linguistics.

Gökçe Uludoğan, Atıf Emre Yüksel, Ümit Can Tunçer, Burak İşık, Yasemin Korkmaz, Didar Akar, and Arzucan Özgür. 2024b. Detecting Hate Speech in Turkish Print Media: A corpus and a hybrid approach with target-oriented linguistic knowledge. In *Proceedings of The Seventh Workshop on Challenges and Applications of Automated Extraction of Socio-political Events from Text (CASE)*, Malta. Association for Computational Linguistics.

Ashish Vaswani, Noam Shazeer, Niki Parmar, Jakob Uszkoreit, Llion Jones, Aidan N Gomez, Łukasz Kaiser, and Illia Polosukhin. 2017. Attention is all you need. *Advances in neural information processing systems*, 30.

Yeshan Wang and Ilia Markov. 2024. CLTL@Multimodal Hate Speech Event Detection 2024. The Winning Approach to Detecting Multimodal Hate Speech and Its Targets. In *Proceedings of the 7th Workshop on Challenges and Applications of Automated Extraction of Socio-political Events from Text (CASE)*, Malta. Association for Computational Linguistics.

Utku Ugur Yagci, Ahmet Emirhan Kolcak, and Egemen Iscan. 2024. Rebert at HSD-2Lang 2024: Finetuning BERT with AdamW for hate speech detection in Arabic and Turkish. In *Proceedings of The Seventh Workshop on Challenges and Applications of Automated Extraction of Socio-political Events from Text (CASE)*, Malta. Association for Computational Linguistics.

Xinyang Zhang, Yury Malkov, Omar Florez, Serim Park, Brian McWilliams, Jiawei Han, and Ahmed El-Kishky. 2022. Twhin-bert: a socially-enriched pre-trained language model for multilingual tweet representations. *arXiv preprint arXiv:2209.07562*.

Yi Zhang, Alan L Porter, Scott Cunningham, Denise Chiavetta, and Nils Newman. 2020. Parallel or intersecting lines? intelligent bibliometrics for investigating the involvement of data science in policy analysis. *IEEE Transactions on Engineering Management*, 68(5):1259–1271.

Author Index

Association for Computational Linguistics
209 N. Eighth Street
Stroudsburg, Pennsylvania 18360

ISBN 978-1-7138-9449-0

CURRAN ASSOCIATES INC.
proceedings.com